# The Official Guide to the HiSET® Exam

## Educational Testing Service (ETS)

### McGraw-Hill Education Editors

Mc
Graw
Hill
Education

New York | Chicago | San Francisco | Athens | London | Madrid
Mexico City | Milan | New Delhi | Singapore | Sydney | Toronto

2 3 4 5 6 7 8 9 10    QVS/QVS    1 2 1 0 9 8 7 6 5

ISBN  978-0-07-184584-7
MHID  0-07-184584-4

e-ISBN  978-0-07-184585-4
e-MHID  0-07-184585-2

McGraw-Hill Education products are available at special quantity discounts to use as premiums and sales promotions or for use in corporate training programs. To contact a representative, please visit the Contact Us pages at: www.mhprofessional.com.

# Contents

## I  Introduction

# II  Diagnostic Test: *HiSET*® Exam Questions from ETS

# III  Language Arts—Writing

# IV Social Studies

# V  Science

# VI Language Arts—Reading

# VII  Mathematics

# VIII  Practice Tests

# Part I
# Introduction

# 1 About the *HiSET*® Exam

## What Is the *HiSET*® Exam?

The *HiSET*® (High School Equivalency Test) Exam is a new high school equivalency testing program that will help you take the next step toward a college degree or a rewarding career. Educational Testing Service (ETS) and the Iowa Testing Programs recently created the HiSET program to provide you with a more affordable, more accessible alternative to other high school equivalency tests. It is another way for you to get the credentials you need to continue your education or to succeed in the workplace. HiSET Exam scores will identify those candidates who have performed at a level consistent with high school equivalency. Information from the HiSET program also will help identify areas in which candidates are career- and college-ready, as well as areas in which additional preparation may be needed.

- **More flexible.** The HiSET program is available in English or Spanish and in paper-based and computer-based format; the computer-based exams feature a test-taker-friendly design. The program also provides a number of accommodations for test takers with disabilities and health-related needs. Please check with your local test center for availability.
- **More accessible.** You can take the HiSET Exam at any of your state's existing test centers, so you can choose the one that is most convenient for you. The staff at your test center can help you devise the best testing plan to fit your needs.
- **More affordable.** Not only does the HiSET Exam cost less than other tests, but you get more for your money—including free practice tests to help you prepare as well as two free retests within a 12-month period of your original purchase when you buy the full battery of HiSET tests in one purchase. The full battery refers to the purchase of all five subtests at one time for a discounted price.

## What Is Tested?

The HiSET Exam lets you demonstrate that you have attained the knowledge equivalent to a high school graduate. It consists of five subtests that measure your knowledge in five core areas:

**Language Arts—Reading:** contains 40 multiple-choice questions and measures your ability to understand, comprehend, interpret, and analyze a variety of reading material.

**Language Arts—Writing:** contains two sections of 51 multiple-choice and one essay question, and measures a test taker's ability to edit and revise written text, and to generate and organize ideas in writing.

**Mathematics:** contains 50 multiple-choice questions and assesses your ability to solve quantitative problems using fundamental concepts and reasoning skills.

**Science:** contains 50 multiple-choice questions and measures your ability to use science content knowledge, apply principles of scientific inquiry, and interpret and evaluate scientific information.

**Social Studies:** contains 50 multiple-choice questions and measures your ability to analyze and evaluate various kinds of social studies information.

## Language Arts—Reading

### Test at a Glance

| | |
|---|---|
| Test Name | Language Arts—Reading |
| Time | 65 minutes |
| Number of Questions | 40 |
| Format | Multiple-choice questions |

**Content Categories**

Application of concepts, analysis, synthesis, and evaluation involving:

   I.  Literary Texts
   II. Informational Texts

**Process Categories**

   A.  Comprehension
   B.  Inference and Interpretation
   C.  Analysis
   D.  Synthesis and Generalization

### About This Test

The Language Arts—Reading test provides evidence of a candidate's ability to understand, comprehend, interpret, and analyze a variety of reading material. The item pool from which the HiSET test forms will be assembled is 60 percent literary content and 40 percent informational content, as defined by CCSS. We note that this is a closer representation of CCSS than the current high school equivalency test. In the ETS HiSET program, candidates will be required to read a broad range of high-quality, increasingly challenging literary and informational texts. The selections are presented in multiple genres on subject matter that varies in purpose and style. The selections may take the form of memoirs, essays, biographical sketches, editorials, or poetry. The texts generally range in length from approximately 400 to 600 words.

The following sections provide an outline of the content and process categories for each subject area.

## Reading Process Categories

In addition to the variety of reading texts, candidates also will answer questions that may involve one or more of the processes described below.

### Comprehension

Understand restatements of information
Determine the meaning of words and phrases as they are used in the text
Analyze the impact of specific word choices on meaning and tone
I 60% II 40%

### Inference and Interpretation

Make inferences from the text
Draw conclusions or deduce meanings not explicitly present in the text
Infer the traits, feelings, and motives of characters or individuals
Apply information
Interpret nonliteral language

### Analysis

Analyze multiple interpretations of a text
Determine the main idea, topic, or theme of a text
Identify the author's or speaker's purpose or viewpoint
Distinguish among opinions, facts, assumptions, observations, and conclusions
Recognize aspects of an author's style, structure, mood, or tone
Recognize literary or argumentative techniques

### Synthesis and Generalization

Draw conclusions and make generalizations
Make predictions
Compare and contrast
Synthesize information across multiple sources

## Language Arts—Writing

### Test at a Glance

| Test Name | Language Arts—Writing |
|---|---|
| Time | Part 1: 75 minutes |
| | Part 2: 45 minutes |
| Number of Questions | 51 |
| Format | Multiple-choice questions |
| | Essay question |

**Content Categories—Part 1**

   I. Organization of Ideas

  II. Language Facility

 III. Writing Conventions

5

---

**Content Categories—Part 2**

    A.  Development of Ideas

    B.  Organization of Ideas

    C.  Language Facility

    D.  Writing Conventions

---

## About This Test

The Language Arts—Writing test provides information about a candidate's skill in recognizing and producing effective standard American written English. Part 1 of the test measures a candidate's ability to edit and revise written text. Part 2 of the test measures a candidate's ability to generate and organize ideas in writing.

Part 1 requires candidates to make revision choices concerning organization, diction and clarity, sentence structure, usage, and mechanics. The test questions are embedded in complete texts in the form of letters, essays, newspaper articles, personal accounts, and reports.

The texts are presented as drafts in which parts have been underlined to indicate a possible need for revision. Questions present alternatives that may correct or improve the underlined portions. Aspects of written language that are tested may include appropriate style, logical transitions, discourse structure and organization, conciseness and clarity, or usage and mechanics.

Part 2 of the test measures proficiency in the generation and organization of ideas through a direct assessment of writing. Candidates are evaluated on development, organization, language facility, and writing conventions.

## Content Descriptions

The following are descriptions of the topics covered in the basic content categories of Part 1. Because the assessments were designed to measure the ability to analyze and evaluate writing, answering any question may involve aspects of more than one category.

### Organization of Ideas

    Select logical or effective opening, transitional, and closing sentences

    Evaluate relevance of content

    Analyze and evaluate paragraph structure

    Recognize logical transitions and related words and phrases

### Language Facility

    Recognize appropriate subordination and coordination, parallelism, and modifier placement

    Maintain consistent verb tense

    Recognize effective sentence combining

### Writing Conventions

    Recognize verb, pronoun, and modifier forms

    Maintain grammatical agreement

    Recognize idiomatic usage

    Recognize correct capitalization, punctuation, and spelling

Part 2 of the Language Arts—Writing test requires that candidates create written responses that are evaluated for development of ideas, organization of ideas, language facility, and conventions.

### Development of Ideas
Focus on central idea, supporting ideas
Explanation of supporting ideas

### Organization of Ideas
Introduction and conclusion
Sequencing of ideas
Paragraphing
Transitions

### Language Facility
Word choice
Sentence structure
Expression and voice

### Writing Conventions
Grammar
Usage
Mechanics

## Mathematics

### Test at a Glance

| Test Name | Mathematics |
|---|---|
| Time | 90 minutes |
| Number of Questions | 50 |
| Format | Multiple-choice questions |

**Content Categories**

| |
|---|
| I. Numbers and Operations on Numbers |
| II. Measurement/Geometry |
| III. Data Analysis/Probability/Statistics |
| IV. Algebraic Concepts |

**Process Categories**

| |
|---|
| A. Understand Mathematical Concepts and Procedures |
| B. Analyze and Interpret Information |
| C. Synthesize Data and Solve Problems |

### About This Test

The Mathematics test assesses mathematical knowledge and competencies. The test measures a candidate's ability to solve quantitative problems using fundamental concepts and reasoning skills. The questions present practical problems that require numerical operations, measurement, estimation, data interpretation, and logical thinking. Problems are based on realistic situations and may test abstract concepts such as algebraic patterns, precision in measurement, and probability. The use of calculators is an option for candidates.

## Content Descriptions

The following are descriptions of the topics covered in the basic content categories. Because the assessments were designed to measure the ability to integrate knowledge of mathematics, answering any question may involve content from more than one category.

**Numbers and Operations on Numbers** may include the following topics: properties of operations, vectors, and matrices; real and complex numbers; absolute values; and computation and estimation with real numbers, exponents, radicals, ratios, proportions, and percents.

**Measurement and Geometry** may include the following topics: measurable attributes of objects and the appropriate techniques, tools, and formulas to determine measurement and achieve specified degrees of precision. Key ideas in geometry include: properties of geometric figures; theorems of lines and triangles; and the perimeter, surface area, volume, lengths, and angles for geometric shapes.

**Data Analysis, Probability, and Statistics** may include the basic concepts of probability, linear relationships, and measures of central tendency and variability to solve problems. Concepts and processes may include understanding relations among events, data collection, counting principles, and the aspects of distributions.

**Algebraic Concepts** may include the concepts of analyzing mathematical situations and structures using algebraic symbols. Candidates should understand patterns, relations, and functions. Topics may include linear functions and inequalities as well as nonlinear functional relations. Candidates may be required to analyze and interpret algebraically, numerically, and graphically; represent, generalize, and solve problem situations; simplify algebraic expressions; analyze and interpret functions of one variable by investigating rates of change and intercepts; and understand the meaning of equivalent forms of expressions, equations, inequalities, and relations.

## Mathematics Process Categories

In addition to knowing and understanding the mathematics content explicitly described in the Content Descriptions section, candidates also will answer questions that may involve one or more of the processes described below. Any of the processes may be applied to any of the content areas of the mathematics test.

### Understand Mathematical Concepts and Procedures
Select appropriate procedures
Identify examples and counter-examples of concepts

### Analyze and Interpret Information
Make inferences or predictions based on data or information
Interpret data from a variety of sources

**Synthesize Data and Solve Problems**
Reason quantitatively
Evaluate the reasonableness of solutions

# Science

## Test at a Glance

| Test Name | Science |
|---|---|
| Time | 80 minutes |
| Number of Questions | 50 |
| Format | Multiple-choice questions |
| **Content Categories** | |
| I. Life Science | |
| II. Physical Science | |
| III. Earth Science | |
| **Process Categories** | |
| A. Interpret and Apply | |
| B. Analyze | |
| C. Evaluate and Generalize | |

## About This Test

The Science test provides evidence of a candidate's ability to use science content knowledge, apply principles of scientific inquiry, and interpret and evaluate scientific information. Most of the questions in the test are associated with stimulus materials that provide descriptions of scientific investigations and their results. Scientific information is based on reports that might be found in scientific journals. Graphs, tables, and charts are used to present information and results.

The science situations use material from a variety of content areas such as: physics, chemistry, botany, health, and astronomy. The questions may ask candidates to identify the research question of interest, select the best design for a specific research question, and recognize conclusions that can be drawn from results. Candidates also may be asked to evaluate the adequacy of procedures and distinguish among hypotheses, assumptions, and observations.

## Content Descriptions

The following are descriptions of the topics covered in the basic content categories. Because the assessments were designed to measure the ability to analyze and evaluate scientific information, answering any question may involve content from more than one category.

**Life Science** topics may include fundamental biological concepts, including organisms, their environments, and their life cycles; the interdependence of organisms; and the relationships between structure and function in living systems.

**Physical Science** topics may include observable properties such as size, weight, shape, color, and temperature; concepts relating to the position and motion of objects; and the principles of light, heat, electricity, and magnetism.

**Earth Science** topics may include properties of earth materials, geologic structures and time, and Earth's movements in the solar system.

### Science Process Categories

In addition to knowing and understanding the science content explicitly described in the Content Descriptions section, candidates also will answer questions on this assessment that may involve one or more of the processes described below. Any of the processes may be applied to any of the content topics.

**Interpret and Apply**
> Interpret observed data or information
> Apply scientific principles

**Analyze**
> Discern an appropriate research question suggested by the information presented
> Identify reasons for a procedure and analyze limitations
> Select the best procedure

**Evaluate and Generalize**
> Distinguish among hypotheses, assumptions, data, and conclusions
> Judge the basis of information for a given conclusion
> Determine relevance for answering a question
> Judge the reliability of sources

## Social Studies

### Test at a Glance

| Test Name | Social Studies |
| --- | --- |
| Time | 70 minutes |
| Number of Questions | 50 |
| Format | Multiple-choice questions |

**Content Categories**

> I. History
>
> II. Civics/Government
>
> III. Economics
>
> IV. Geography

**Process Categories**

> A. Interpret and Apply
>
> B. Analyze
>
> C. Evaluate and Generalize

## About This Test

The Social Studies test provides evidence of a candidate's ability to analyze and evaluate various kinds of social studies information. The test uses materials from a variety of content areas, including history, political science, psychology, sociology, anthropology, geography, and economics. Primary documents, posters, cartoons, timelines, maps, graphs, tables, charts, and reading passages may be used to present information. The questions may ask candidates to distinguish statements of fact from opinion; recognize the limitations of procedures and methods; and make judgments about the reliability of sources, the validity of inferences and conclusions, and the adequacy of information for drawing conclusions.

## Content Descriptions

The following are descriptions of the topics covered in the basic content categories. Because the assessments were designed to measure the ability to analyze and evaluate various kinds of social studies information, answering any question may involve content from more than one category.

**History** may include historical sources and perspectives; the interconnections among the past, present, and future; and specific eras in U.S. and world history, including the people who have shaped them and the political, economic, and cultural characteristics of those eras.

**Civics/Government** may include the civic ideals and practices of citizenship in a democratic society; the role of the informed citizen and the meaning of citizenship; the concepts of power and authority; the purposes and characteristics of various governance systems, with particular emphasis on the U.S. government; and the relationship between individual rights and responsibilities, and the concepts of a just society.

**Economics** may include the principles of supply and demand; the difference between needs and wants; the impact of technology on economics; the interdependent nature of economies; and how the economy can be affected by governments, and how that effect varies over time.

**Geography** may include concepts and terminology of physical and human geography; geographic concepts to analyze spatial phenomena and discuss economic, political, and social factors; and interpretation of maps and other visual and technological tools, and the analysis of case studies.

## Social Studies Process Categories

In addition to knowing and understanding the social studies content described in the Content Descriptions section, candidates also will answer questions that may involve one or more of the processes described below. Any of the processes may be applied to any of the content topics.

**Interpret and Apply**
Make inferences or predictions based on data or other information
Infer unstated relationships
Extend conclusions to related phenomena

**Analyze**
Distinguish among facts, opinions, and values
Recognize the author's purpose, assumptions, and arguments

**Evaluate and Generalize**
Determine the adequacy of information for reaching conclusions
Judge the validity of conclusions
Compare and contrast the reliability of sources

# How Can I Prepare for the HiSET Exam?

## Practice, Practice, Practice!

This book offers a review of the content and hundreds of practice questions. There is a half-length practice test in Chapter 3, plus two full-length practice tests at the end of the book. In addition, the HiSET program offers free and low-cost options to familiarize candidates with the exam questions and the computer-based testing experience. The HiSET website offers free sample questions, practice tests, and tips to help candidates get ready for the HiSET Exam. In addition, test centers and adult education centers may offer test preparation. To learn more about how to prepare for the exam, contact a test center or visit www.hiset.ets.org.

## What Should I Study?

Preparation for the test will depend on the amount of time you have available and your personal preferences for how to prepare. At a minimum, before you take the HiSET Exam you should know the:

- types of questions and directions
- approximate number of questions
- amount of time for each section

Here are some tips and strategies to help you do your best on the HiSET Exam, whether you take it on a computer or on paper.

1. **Learn what the test covers.**

   You can find test specifications in this chapter. The Test at a Glance outlines the content categories that are measured by each subtest.

2. **Assess how well you know the content.**

   Research has shown that test takers tend to overestimate their preparedness—this is why some test takers assume they did well and then find out they did not pass.
   The longer you have been away from the content, the more preparation you will most likely need. If it has been longer than a few months since you have studied your content area, you will want to make a concerted effort to prepare.

3. **Plan and organize your time.**

Allow yourself plenty of time to review so you can avoid "cramming" new material at the end. Here are a few tips:

- Choose a test date far enough in the future to leave you plenty of preparation time.
- Work backward from that date to figure out how much time you will need for review.
- Set a realistic schedule and stick to it.

4. **Understand how questions will be scored.**

Each of the five subtests in the HiSET Exam is scored on a scale of 1-20. In order to pass, you must do all three of the following:

- Achieve a score of at least 8 on each of the five individual subtests
- Score at least 2 out of 6 on the essay portion of the writing test
- Have a total combined score on all five tests of at least 45

Score requirements may vary depending on the state where you are taking the HiSET Exam. Some states may set passing scores that are higher, but under no circumstances can you pass with a total score lower than 45 on the full battery of tests.

5. **Develop a study plan.**

A study plan provides a road map to prepare for the HiSET Exam. It can help you understand what skills and knowledge are covered on the test and where to focus your attention. Use the study plan template in this chapter to help you get started.

6. **Become comfortable with the types of questions you will find on the HiSET Exam.**

The HiSET Exam includes two types of questions: multiple-choice (for which you select your answers from a list of choices) and essay (for which you write a response of your own).

## How to Approach Multiple-Choice Questions

All of the subtests contain multiple-choice questions. Answer choices are provided to help you focus your thinking about the question. Make sure when answering a question that you understand what response is required.

**NOTE:** When taking the computer-based exam, you can skip questions that you might have difficulty answering. The testing software has a "mark and review" feature that allows you to mark questions you want to come back to during the time you are working on that section. The testing software also:

- lets you view a complete list of all the questions in the section on which you are working
- indicates whether you have answered each question
- identifies the questions you have marked for review

Additionally, you can review questions you have already answered and change your answers as long as you still have time remaining to work on that section.

**Watch out for multiple-choice questions containing "NOT," "LEAST," and "EXCEPT."** This type of question asks you to select the choice that does not fit. You must be very careful because it is easy to forget that you are selecting the negative. This question type is used in situations in which there are several good solutions or ways to approach something, but also a clearly wrong way.

## How to Approach Essay Questions

Only the Language Arts—Writing subtest contains an essay question. While working on your essay, remember to budget your time. You need to allow sufficient time to think about the question, plan a response, and write your essay. Although the raters scoring the essays understand the time constraints you are writing under and consider that when scoring your response, you still want to produce the best possible example of your writing. Keep these things in mind when writing your response:

1. **Answer the question accurately.** Analyze what each part of the question is asking you to do. If the question asks you to describe or discuss, you should provide more than just a list.

2. **Answer the question completely.** If a question asks you to do three distinct things in your response, you should cover all three things for the best score. Otherwise, no matter how well you write, you will not be awarded full credit.

3. **Answer the question that is asked.** Do not change the question or challenge the basis of the question. You will receive no credit or a low score if you answer another question or if you state, for example, that there is no possible answer.

4. **Give a thorough and detailed response.** You must demonstrate that you have a thorough understanding of the subject matter. However, your response should be straightforward and not filled with unnecessary information.

5. **Reread your response.** Check that you have written what you thought you wrote. Be sure not to leave sentences unfinished or omit clarifying information. Save a few minutes at the end of the essay portion of your exam to check for obvious errors. Although an occasional typographical, spelling, or grammatical error will not affect your score, severe and persistent errors will detract from the overall effectiveness of your writing and lower your score.

## How to Approach Questions about Graphs, Tables, or Reading Passages

When answering questions about graphs, tables, or reading passages, provide only the information that the questions ask for. You might want to read the questions first, and then look at the map, graph, or reading passage. You can note places you think are important on your scratch paper, and then answer the questions. Again, the most important thing is to be sure you answer the questions as they refer to the material presented. Read the questions carefully.

# Testing Tips

First and foremost, you should get ready for test day so that you will be calm and confident. Plan to end your review a day or two before the actual test date so you avoid cramming. Take a dry run to the test center so you are sure of the route, traffic conditions, and parking. Most of all, you want to eliminate any unexpected factors that could distract you from your ultimate goal—passing the HiSET Exam. On the day of the test, you should:

- be well rested
- wear comfortable clothes and dress in layers
- eat before you take the test and bring food with you to eat during break to keep your energy level up
- bring your state's required identification for entrance to the exam. Bring test center payment and fees, if applicable. Check your state's HiSET website or contact your test center.
- bring a supply of well-sharpened No. 2 pencils (at least three)
- be prepared to stand in line to check in or to wait while other test takers check in

You cannot control the testing situation, but you can control yourself. Stay calm. The supervisors are well trained and make every effort to provide uniform testing conditions, but do not let it bother you if the test does not start exactly on time. You will have the necessary amount of time once it does start. You can think of preparing for this test as training for an athletic event. Once you have trained, prepared, and rested, give it everything you have.

## Complete the Following Checklist to Determine Whether You Are Ready

- Do you know the testing requirements for the state where you plan to take the test?
- Have you followed all of the test registration procedures?
- Do you know the topics that will be covered in each test you plan to take?
- Have you reviewed any textbooks, class notes, and course readings that relate to the topics covered?
- Do you know how long the test will take and the number of questions it contains?
- Have you considered how you will pace your work?
- Are you familiar with the types of questions for your test?
- Are you familiar with the recommended test-taking strategies?
- Have you practiced by working through the practice questions in this study companion or in a study guide or practice test?
- If you are repeating a HiSET Exam, have you analyzed your previous score report to determine areas where additional study and test preparation could be useful?

If you answered "yes" to the questions above, your preparation has paid off. Now take the HiSET Exam, do your best, pass it—and move forward in your career and/or college education!

### During the Test

1. **For a paper-delivered test, put your answers in the right bubbles.** It seems obvious, but be sure that you fill in the answer bubble that corresponds to the question you are answering. A significant number of test takers fill in a bubble without checking to see that the number matches the question they are answering.

2. **Skip the questions you find extremely difficult.** Rather than trying to answer these on your first pass through the test, leave them blank and mark them in your test booklet. Pay attention to the time as you answer the rest of the questions on the test, and try to finish with 10 or 15 minutes remaining so that you can go back over the questions you left blank. Even if you do not know the answer the second time you read the question, see if you can narrow down the possible answers, and then guess.

3. **Keep track of the time.** Bring a watch to the test, just in case the clock in the test room is difficult for you to see. Keep the watch as simple as possible—alarms and other functions may distract others or may violate test security. If the test center supervisor suspects there could be an issue with your watch, he or she will ask you to remove it, so simpler is better! You will probably have plenty of time to answer all of the questions, but if you find yourself becoming bogged down in one section, you might decide to move on and come back to that section later.

4. **Read all of the possible answers before selecting one.** Then reread the question to be sure the answer you have selected really answers the question. Remember, a question that contains a phrase such as "Which of the following does NOT…" is asking for the one answer that is NOT a correct statement or conclusion.

5. **Check your answers.** If you have extra time left over at the end of the test, look over each question and make sure that you have answered it as you intended.

6. **Do not worry about your score while you are taking the test.** No one is expected to answer all of the questions correctly. If you meet the minimum passing score on each of the HiSET subtests, and you meet the HiSET cumulative score requirement as well as any state requirements, the state will issue your high school equivalency certification or diploma.

## Develop Your Study Plan

Following is a template you can use to design your own personalized study plan.

## My Study Plan

**Use this worksheet to:**

1. **Define Content Areas:** List the most important content areas for your test as defined in the Test at a Glance and Topics Covered sections.

2. **Determine Strengths and Weaknesses:** Identify your strengths and weaknesses in each content area.

3. **Identify Resources:** Identify the books, courses, and other resources you plan to use for each content area.

4. **Study:** Create and commit to a schedule that provides for regular study periods.

**HiSET Test Name:** _____

**Test Date:** _____

| Content covered | Description of content | How well do I know the content? (scale 1–5) | What resources do I have/need for the content? | Where can I find the resources I need? | Dates I will study the content | Date completed |
|---|---|---|---|---|---|---|
|  |  |  |  |  |  |  |
|  |  |  |  |  |  |  |
|  |  |  |  |  |  |  |
|  |  |  |  |  |  |  |
|  |  |  |  |  |  |  |
|  |  |  |  |  |  |  |
|  |  |  |  |  |  |  |
|  |  |  |  |  |  |  |
|  |  |  |  |  |  |  |
|  |  |  |  |  |  |  |
|  |  |  |  |  |  |  |
|  |  |  |  |  |  |  |
|  |  |  |  |  |  |  |

# Frequently Asked Questions

### Should I guess?

Yes. Your score is based on the number of questions you answer correctly, with no penalty or subtraction for an incorrect answer. When you do not know the answer to a question, try to eliminate any obviously wrong answers and then guess at the correct one. Try to pace yourself so that you have enough time to carefully consider every question.

### Can I answer the questions in any order?

Yes. You can go through the questions from beginning to end, as many test takers do, or you can create your own path. Perhaps you will want to answer questions in your strongest area of knowledge first and then move from your strengths to your weaker areas. On computer-delivered tests, you can use the "Skip" function to skip a question and come back to it later. There is no right or wrong way. Use the approach that works best for you.

### Are there trick questions on the test?

No. There are no hidden meanings or trick wording. All of the questions on the test ask subject matter knowledge in a straightforward manner.

### Are there answer patterns on the test?

No. You might have heard this myth: the answers on multiple-choice tests follow patterns. Another myth is that there will never be more than two questions with the same lettered answer following each other. Neither myth is true. Select the answer you think is correct based on your knowledge of the subject.

### Will the test be paper-based, computer-based, or both?

The HiSET exams will be available in paper- and computer-based formats. However, not every state or test center will offer both formats, so be sure to check online at HiSET.ets.org before you register.

### Can I write in the test booklet?

No. You may not write in the HiSET Exam test booklet. However, you can use your scratch paper to work out problems, make notes to yourself, or note questions you want to review later. But be sure to mark your answers on the answer sheet or enter them on the computer.

### What is different about computer-based testing?

The computer-based tests offer a clear and simple design, with useful tools to enhance your test experience including:

- An onscreen calculator on the math test
- Word-processing software with insert, delete, cut, paste, and undo features on the essay test
- A special toolbar with Spanish-language characters on the essay test
- A help button and a timer so you can budget your time during the test
- A mark and skip feature that lets you bypass a question and return to it later
- A review tool that tells you which questions you still need to answer

### Are the questions the same on paper-based as on computer-based tests?

Yes. Both tests ask the same questions.

### What should I do before test day?

Before test day, there are some important things you should do to get ready.

- Verify your test location by logging into your My HiSET account or contacting your test center.
- *Find out what you need to bring on test day. Review the ID and payment requirements for your state at http://hiset.ets.org/requirements/ or contact your test center for more information.*
- Check with the test center to see what time you need to be there on the day of your test. It may vary depending on whether you are taking the computer test or the paper test.
- Create a study plan to help identify your strengths and weaknesses in each of the content areas using Test at a Glance.
- Review the test material and take the practice exams provided in this book.

# 2 About This Book

## How This Book Can Help

The most effective way to study is to learn about the test and find out what information will be on it. The better prepared you are, the more likely you will be to do well.

This book was designed to help you prepare for the *HiSET*® Exam in several ways:

- First, it will help you review the concepts that are assessed on the test.
- Second, it will familiarize you with the format of the test and the question types.
- Third, it will help you identify your areas of strength and weakness so that you can focus on the test-taking skills you most need to improve.
- Fourth, it will give you opportunities to take HiSET Exam practice tests.

## What Is in This Book

The book begins with a diagnostic test to assess your strengths and weaknesses and allow you to focus your study on the areas in which you need the most preparation. The HiSET Exam includes separate tests that assess your knowledge in five different content areas: Language Arts—Reading, Language Arts—Writing, Mathematics, Science, and Social Studies. In this book, each of these subject area exams is broken down into specific skills. Each of these skills is reviewed in a separate chapter dedicated solely to helping you master that concept. For example, the HiSET Exam Science test measures your knowledge of life science, earth and space science, chemistry, and physics; therefore, this book includes a separate chapter on each of these areas. Take a look at the chapter topics related to each of the HiSET Exam tests:

### Language Arts—Writing

- Basic English Usage
- Mechanics
- Sentence Structure
- Organization of Ideas
- The HiSET Exam Essay

**Social Studies**

- World History
- U.S. History
- Civics and Government
- Economics
- Geography

**Science**

- Life Science
- Earth and Space Science
- Physical Science: Chemistry
- Physical Science: Physics

**Language Arts—Reading**

- Interpreting Prose Fiction
- Interpreting Poetry
- Interpreting Informational Texts

**Mathematics**

- Whole Numbers
- Number Sense
- Decimals
- Fractions
- Percents
- Number Relationships
- Measurements
- Geometry
- Statistics
- Probability
- Data Analysis
- Algebra
- Mathematical Formulas

## In Each Subject Section

Since there are five subject tests on the HiSET Exam, there are five sections following the introductory chapters of this book, one for each subject area test. Each section begins with a chapter introducing you to that subject test. It will include information about the number of questions on that particular subject test and the time limit for completing the test. As you will see, the number of questions varies from one test to the next, and the time limits vary as well. This information will be important as you prepare for the tests.

### Subject Preparation

At the beginning of each subject section of the book, you will find a box titled "Question Steps." This section gives you six steps to use when answering questions on that subject test. For example, the following box shows the steps for answering questions on the Mathematics subject test.

*Mathematics Question Steps*

**Step 1:** Read the Problem

**Step 2:** Determine What Is Being Asked

**Step 3:** Identify Pertinent Information

**Step 4:** Choose Which Operation(s) or Steps to Use

**Step 5:** Solve the Problem

**Step 6:** Check Your Work

Following the list is a brief explanation of how to apply each step and why it is necessary and important.

The question steps suggested in each of the individual math chapters are the same, those suggested in each of the social studies chapters are the same, and so on. There are two reasons for this. First, the steps you will use to answer any math problem, for example, are basically the same regardless of whether you are dealing with fractions, decimals, or geometry. Likewise, the steps you will use to answer any social studies question are the same, regardless of whether the topic is geography, civics, or history. There is no reason to follow a different set of steps for each topic. Second, since all topics within a subject area follow the same steps, you will only need to learn a single set of steps for each test. That is much simpler and more practical than learning a different set of steps for each individual topic.

## Chapters in Each Section

After the introductory chapter in each section, you will find several chapters that each discuss a specific topic found on that HiSET Exam subject area test. Here is what you will find in these chapters:

### Review of Information

Each chapter reviews information you will need to know for the subject area tests and offers examples and advice for how to apply the information. For example, in the chapter that explains fractions and operations, you will find definitions and explanations of different types of fractions, examples of fractions, a review of how to perform various operations involving fractions, and step-by-step instructions for how to complete the operations. Since you probably already are familiar with the majority of the information on the HiSET Exam, the chapters provide an overview of each topic to refresh your memory and your skills.

### Sample Items

Following the review of information are two or three sample questions that are similar to those on the HiSET Exam. The first example will show you how to use the steps for that subject to answer the question. This gives you the opportunity to think through the steps as you work and to practice using the process. Where appropriate, there will be additional sample questions to help you familiarize yourself with other question formats.

### Independent Practice Items

After the sample questions is a set of practice questions related to the specific topic of the chapter. On the HiSET Exam, all of the questions related to the subject area of the test will be mixed together rather than separated by topic. For example, on the HiSET Exam Science test, the life science questions will be mixed in with the earth and space science, chemistry, and physics questions. However, all the questions in each chapter address only the information from that chapter; the life science chapter includes only life science questions and so on. You will be able to practice doing mixed question topics on the full-length practice tests.

## The Final Section

After reviewing and practicing with the types of information found on the HiSET Exam, the final section of this book offers two practice tests. They are similar in length and structure to the actual test and give you the chance to practice taking the tests and to become more familiar and comfortable with the HiSET Exam.

### Types of Questions in This Book

The HiSET Exam assesses more than simply your ability to comprehend reading passages or compute sets of numbers. It also assesses your abilities at increasingly higher cognitive levels. The HiSET Exam will evaluate your ability to:

- Apply information
- Assess data
- Compare
- Contrast
- Distinguish facts from opinions or hypotheses
- Draw conclusions
- Evaluate information
- Identify cause-and-effect relationships
- Identify implications
- Make inferences
- Recognize unstated assumptions
- Restate information
- Summarize
- Synthesize information

The sample items and questions in each chapter, as well as the questions on the practice tests at the end of the book, allow you to develop and hone these skills. Hopefully, by the time you read the chapters and answer all of the practice questions, you will be confident in your knowledge of the subject matter and comfortable with the format of the test.

# How to Use This Book

## Diagnose Your Test-Taking Strengths and Weaknesses

The next chapter in this book includes a diagnostic exam with *HiSET*® Exam practice questions created by ETS, the makers of the HiSET Exam. This diagnostic exam will allow you to become familiar with the HiSET Exam and identify your strengths and weaknesses. Answers and explanations follow the exam.

## Review the Content

As mentioned in the previous chapter, this book breaks each of the HiSET Exam subject areas into specific skills or content areas. For example, the Language Arts—Reading test assesses your ability to interpret and comprehend prose, poetry, and informational, or nonfiction, works, so each of these literary forms is discussed in a separate chapter. Each chapter reviews the skills and information that relate to the topic. Since the majority of the information on the HiSET Exam is likely to be familiar to you already, the reviews in this book are not in-depth; they are meant to serve as a refresher.

Use this book to go over the ideas, skills, and information that will be important when you take the HiSET Exam. As you read through each chapter, take notes or highlight the skills you would like to go over again. If you find a concept that is unfamiliar or with which you are not completely comfortable, research it further. For concepts with which you are more familiar, a simple review and some practice questions may be sufficient.

You will notice that the social studies and science chapters are a bit different from the math and language arts chapters. Many social studies and science topics are ideas that you spend months or even years studying in school, such as World War I or the periodic table of elements. It would be impossible to include all of the information related to World War I in the World History chapter, so you will instead find a list of topics with which you should be familiar. Read through the lists in these chapters, be sure you know the major points and important themes, and spend a little time reading about or studying those you do not know well.

The required skills in the language arts and mathematics chapters are explained briefly and often illustrated by examples. Read each of the explanations, work through the examples, and determine how well you know the information. Keep in mind that although you may recognize some of the concepts, you must be able to apply them as well. Use these chapters to find out what you know and what you need to review in more depth.

## Learn the Steps

Each section includes a list of six question steps that will help you solve the problems or answer the questions. The steps in each of the social studies chapters are the same, as are those in each of the science chapters, math chapters, and so on. Here is how to use these steps:

1. Read through all the steps.

2. Notice how the steps are used to answer the sample questions. Sometimes seeing how they are applied can be helpful in understanding how they are used.

3. Practice using the steps. Follow the steps as you answer the practice questions. See how each step works. You will find that they are sequential and often build off of one another.

4. Memorize the steps. Since you will not be able to take this book or any other notes with you to the HiSET Exam, you need to know any pertinent information by heart. That includes the steps used to answer the questions. Remember, you will need to memorize only one set of steps for each of the five tests.

## Practice Taking the Tests

The final section in this book includes two full-length practice tests that are similar to the actual HiSET Exam. Use these practice tests to:

- Become familiar with the test format
- Continue to identify your strengths and weaknesses
- Practice your test-taking skills
- Plan your pace for test day

When you practice, pretend you are taking the actual HiSET Exam. Turn off your phone, put a Do Not Disturb sign on the door, set a timer for the correct number of minutes, and start working. Consider writing your answers on a separate sheet of paper rather than in the book so you can take the tests again in a few weeks or months if you wish.

Now that you have learned *how* to take the practice tests, here are the reasons *why* you should take them.

## Become Familiar with the Format

Taking the practice tests at the end of this book will help you become familiar with the format of the HiSET Exam. You may already know that, with the exception of the language arts essay, all of the questions on the test are multiple choice; however, you will learn that the tests have a few other key features with which you should be familiar. For example, some of the questions on the Language Arts—Writing test will present a set of sentences and then ask you to select the most effective way to combine them. The sentences in each passage on this test will be numbered, and some questions will ask you to identify the best way to correct an error in a given sentence. Knowing these things ahead of time and getting used to seeing passages and questions presented in this manner will help you be more comfortable with the format of the test.

## Analyze Your Performance

After answering all of the questions on the practice tests, go back and find out which questions you answered correctly and which you did not. Do not be discouraged if you made a few mistakes. See this as a learning opportunity. Now you know which skills to focus on as you study and prepare for the HiSET Exam.

Look for patterns in your correct and incorrect answers. Did you answer all of the algebra questions correctly but struggle with those pertaining to data analysis? Did you excel at interpreting plays but not at understanding poetry? Analyzing this information can be very useful. The more you know about your own strengths and weaknesses, the more effectively you can use your study time. Take this opportunity to improve the skills you will need to do well on the HiSET Exam. Then, when test day arrives, you will be able to approach all of the questions with confidence.

**Keep in Mind**

> Keep in mind that these strategies can be used when answering the practice questions at the end of each chapter as well. If you missed any of the questions, go back through the chapter and review the corresponding information again before moving on to the next skill.

## Practice Your Test-Taking Skills

Using certain test-taking skills can help you to do your best. Apply these skills on the practice tests at the end of the book so that they become routine and you no longer need to remind yourself to use them on the real HiSET Exam.

- **Try to answer the questions before looking at the answers.** Read the passage or information and read the question, but do not look at the answer choices at first. Decide what the correct answer should be before you look at the choices. If your answer is there, you can feel more confident about choosing it. If the answer you are looking for is listed, reread the question to be sure you understood it and consider all the choices.
- **Read every choice.** The first answer choice may look tempting, but do not mark anything until you have read all the options. Several may appear to be at least partially correct, but only one is completely right. Make sure you read them all to find the one best answer. Even if the first choice seems to match the answer you came up with before looking at the choices, read every choice to be sure it is the best option.
- **Answer everything.** There is no penalty for guessing on the HiSET Exam. This means that if you leave a question blank, it is the same as marking the wrong answer. You should mark an answer to every question to get the best score you possibly can. Do not use too much time on any one question and run out of time on the test. If you do not know an answer, take your best guess and move on. You can always go back to a difficult question if you have time left over at the end of the test.
- **Make educated guesses.** You need to mark an answer for every single question. There may be times when a question leaves you completely baffled, and guessing is necessary. You should, however, make educated guesses. First, eliminate as many of the incorrect answer choices as possible. Often, an answer choice that is extremely different from the rest can be eliminated. Also, answer choices that include absolutes such as *always*, *every*, and *never* may be incorrect. Math answer choices that are far off your estimate may be incorrect. Once you have eliminated as many incorrect options as possible, guess among those that remain. Keep in mind that randomly selecting between five answer choices gives you a one in five chance of getting the answer correct. That is only 20 percent. However, eliminating three of the incorrect choices improves your chances to one in two, giving you a 50 percent chance of selecting the right answer.
- **Keep up.** If you are taking the paper-based HiSET Exam, you will mark your answers to the multiple-choice questions on a separate answer sheet. Make sure the answer to each question is correctly marked in the corresponding place on the answer sheet. In other words, be careful to mark the answer to question 10

in the correct space for answer 10. If you are taking the computer-based HiSET Exam, you will choose an answer on the screen, so this is less of a concern. On either format of the test you have the ability to go back to a question so that you can change an answer if you wish.

- **Mark only one answer.** If you decide to change an answer, be sure to erase the original answer completely. Only one answer can be marked for each item.

## Plan Your Pace for Test Day

As you work through the questions, notice how much time it takes you to complete the practice test. Remember, each of the HiSET Exam tests has a time limit. Figure out if you will need to work more quickly or if you can spend a little longer on each question and still finish before time is called. It is a good idea to try to leave a few minutes at the end of the test to check your work. That way, you also have a cushion of time at the end if a few of the questions take longer than anticipated.

This book will tell you how many questions are on each test and how long you will have to complete them. To determine the pace at which you need to work, divide the number of minutes by the number of questions on the test. Be sure to save some of the minutes for reviewing your answers. For example, the Mathematics test is comprised of 50 questions, and you will have 90 minutes to answer them all. If you want to leave 15 minutes to check your work, you will have approximately one and a half minutes for each question. Here are a few ideas for how to stick to the pace you have set for yourself:

- **Keep an eye on the clock.** Focus on the test, but be aware of how much time has passed and how much time you have left. Check your pace every now and then. For example, to complete the 50 math questions before time is up, you will need to have eight or nine questions done by the time the first 15 minutes have passed. If you notice that you are running behind, try to work a little faster, without moving so quickly that you begin to make mistakes. If you are running ahead of time, keep moving along with the confidence that you will have a couple of minutes to spare at the end of the section.
- **Do not spend too long on any one question.** It is important not to let one question significantly slow you down. If you cannot figure out the answer to a question, take your best guess and move on. You can always come back to it at the end of the test if time allows. It would be a shame to waste precious minutes on one question and not have enough time to answer a later question on something you know well.
- **Complete all the questions before time runs out.** When you are down to only a minute or so, start marking answers for any questions you have not yet completed. Even if you are making random guesses, you still might get a question right by chance. Remember, any items left blank will be marked wrong. At least by marking something, you have a chance of picking up a few extra points.

Now that you know how to use this book to review the HiSET Exam content, learn the steps to answer questions, and practice taking the tests, it is time to get to work.

# Part II
# Diagnostic Test: *HiSET*® Exam Questions from ETS

# 3 HiSET® Exam Diagnostic Test

The following diagnostic test contains questions written by ETS, the makers of the HiSET Exam. These questions will allow you to evaluate your strengths and weaknesses on the HiSET Exam so that you can focus your studies appropriately. The diagnostic exam has the same five subject tests as the real HiSET:

- Language Arts—Writing (Parts I and II)
- Social Studies
- Science
- Language Arts—Reading
- Math

This test is half the length of the actual HiSET because its purpose is to quickly allow you to identify your strengths and weaknesses before you begin your studies. When you take this test, pretend you are taking the actual HiSET Exam. Turn off your phone, put a Do Not Disturb sign on the door, set a timer for the correct number of minutes, and start working.

Answer Sheets are provided for each test section. However, you may want to consider writing your answers on a separate sheet of paper rather than in the book so you can take the test again in a few weeks or months if you wish.

# *HiSET*® Exam Diagnostic Test
## Answer Sheet
## Language Arts—Writing, Part 1

C   D

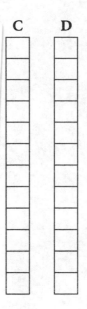

# LANGUAGE ARTS—WRITING, PART 1

## 25 Questions
## 38 Minutes

## Directions

This is a test of some of the skills involved in revising written materials. There are selections similar to the reports, letters, and articles high-school students often need to write. Each selection is presented twice, first in a box in a conventional format and then in a spread-out format with certain parts underlined and numbered. Read quickly through the boxed text to get an idea of its purpose and style. Then go on to the spread-out format.

For each underlined part there are alternatives listed in the right-hand column. Choose the alternative that

- makes the statement grammatically correct
- expresses the idea in the clearest or most appropriate way
- is worded most consistently with the style and purpose of the writing
- organizes the ideas in the most effective way

In some cases, there may be more than one problem to correct or improve.

When you have decided which alternative is best, mark your choice on the answer sheet. If you think the original underlined version is best, choose "*No change*." In questions about organization, you will probably find it helpful to look at the boxed text. In the questions about spelling, you are to indicate which of three underlined words is misspelled, if any. If there are no errors in any of the words, mark "*None.*"

Work as quickly as you can without becoming careless. Don't spend too much time on any question that is difficult for you to answer. Instead, skip it and return to it later if you have time. Try to answer every question even if you have to guess.

Mark all your answers on the answer sheet. Give only one answer to each question and make every mark heavy and dark. If you decide to change one of your answers, be sure to erase the first mark completely. Be sure that the number of the question you are answering matches the number of the row of answer choices you are marking on your answer sheet.

**GO ON TO THE NEXT PAGE ➡**

**Read this welcome letter to new employees at an electronics company. Then go to the spread-out version and consider the suggestions for revision.**

---

### Bridgewater Electronics
#### Expanding the Future—One Byte at a Time

1. Hello, and welcome to your future at Bridgewater Electronics.

2. When founder and engineer Markus Whiley brought Bridgewater Electronics into existence in 1973, he had ambitious ideas and planned to employ the most creative, forward-thinking professionals to assist in his mission to create innovative electronics in every form. As a leader of the fast-paced electronics industry, Bridgewater Electronics upholds its mission by employing a diverse group of visionaries and providing them with the tools they needed to foster their ideas. With your knowledge and expertise, Bridgewater Electronics plans to continue to impress its customers and lead the industry for generations to come.

**Support**

3. The in-house trainings, professional development opportunities, and mentoring program will be helpful in further developing your skills and learning about the company. As a new employee, you are encouraged to take advantage of our monthly networking lunches. Attending these lunches will allow you to meet with staff at all levels, helps you get to know your coworkers, and gaining more insight into the work we do.

4. You will be paired with a seasoned staff member to mentor and support you as you learn your role within the company. You and your mentor will meet weekly to discuss work flow, assignments, and processes. Your mentor will also be able to help you determine which trainings will be of value to you and help you identify external professional development opportunities for which the company will pay.

**Next Steps**

5. Your mentor will also introduce you to your supervisor and other staff in your department. He or she will give you a tour of the building and show you where the Employee Services Office is located. Your mentor will help you become acquainted on the first day. You can expect to be photographed for your identification badge, and you will need to request a parking sticker. Remember to smile, make eye contact, and give a firm handshake to everyone you meet. Before the end of the day, you and your mentor will have an opportunity to brainstorm based on what you will have observed.

6. You will get an Employee Welcome Package through interoffice mail within two days. It will consist of information about your benefits as well as detailed information about company policies, including the probationary period, employee expectations, dress code, and work schedules. Carefully review and sign all pertinent documents, and return them to the Employee Services Office by the end of your first week of employment. Any questions or concerns should be directed to Jamie Washington, Director of Employee Services, Monday through Friday, 8 A.M. to 5 P.M.

7. I welcome and applaud your future contributions to Bridgewater Electronics. I hope you find your employment with the company to be a great learning experience and an opportunity to accomplish exceptional feats.

Sincerely,

Mike Fowler
President

## Bridgewater Electronics
### Expanding the Future—One Byte at a Time

1. Hello, and welcome to your future at Bridgewater Electronics.

2. When founder and engineer Markus Whiley brought Bridgewater Electronics into existence in 1973, he had ambitious ideas and planned to employ the most creative, forward-thinking professionals to assist in <u>his</u>
1
mission to create innovative electronics in every form. As a leader of the fast-paced electronics industry, Bridgewater Electronics upholds its mission by <u>employing a</u>
2
<u>diverse group of visionaries and</u>
2
<u>providing them with the tools they</u>
2
<u>needed to foster</u> their ideas. With
2
your knowledge and expertise, Bridgewater Electronics plans to continue to impress its customers and lead the industry for generations to come.

**Support**

3. The in-house trainings, professional development opportunities, and mentoring program will be helpful in further developing your skills and learning about the company. As a new employee, you are encouraged to

**1**
A  (*No change*)
B  your
C  our
D  their

**2**
A  (*No change*)
B  employing a diverse group of visionaries and providing them with the tools they need to foster
C  employing a diverse group of visionaries and provided them with the tools they needed to foster
D  employed a diverse group of visionaries and provided them with the tools they needed to foster

GO ON TO THE NEXT PAGE ➡

37

take advantage of our monthly networking lunches. Attending these lunches will allow you to <u>meet with staff at all levels, helps</u><sub>3</sub> <u>you get to know your coworkers,</u><sub>3</sub> <u>and gaining</u><sub>3</sub> more insight into the work we do.

4. You will be paired with a seasoned staff member to mentor and support you as you learn your role within the company. You and your mentor will meet weekly to discuss work flow, assignments, and processes. Your mentor will also be able to help you determine which trainings will be of value to you and help you identify external professional development opportunities for which the company will pay.

**Next Steps**

5. Your mentor will also introduce you to your supervisor and other staff in your department. He or she will give you a tour of the building and show you where the Employee Services Office is located. Your mentor will help you become acquainted on the first day. You can expect to be photographed for your identification badge, and you will need to request a parking sticker.

**3**

A (*No change*)

B meet with staff at all levels, help you get to know your coworkers, and give you

C meet with staff at all levels, which will help you get to know your coworkers, and having given you

D have meetings with staff at all levels, while helping you get to know your coworkers, and to be able to gain

**4** **Which sentence best introduces the information in the section titled "Support"?**

A Although you are a novice employee at Bridgewater Electronics, you should not be afraid to ask questions.

B Starting a new job can be overwhelming, but the multiple resources available to Bridgewater Electronics employees will help you settle into your new position quickly.

C As a growing company with a history of hiring talented professionals, Bridgewater Electronics offers its employees several opportunities for advancement across the company.

D With the creation of several new positions at Bridgewater Electronics, we are committed to cross-training employees to find where their true talents lie.

**5** **Read this sentence from paragraph 4.**

*You will be paired with a seasoned staff member to mentor and support you as you learn your role within the company.*

Remember to smile, make eye contact, and give a firm handshake to everyone you meet. Before the end of the day, you and your mentor will have an opportunity to brainstorm based on what you will have observed.

6. You will <u>get</u> an Employee Welcome
   <sub>7</sub> Package through interoffice mail within two days. It will consist of information about your benefits as well as detailed information about company policies, including the probationary period, employee expectations, dress code, and work schedules. Carefully review and sign all pertinent documents, and return them to the Employee Services Office by the end of your

**Which phrase is the best transition to begin the sentence?**

A  At any rate,

B  On the other hand,

C  When you have the time,

D  During your first six months,

**6  Read these sentences from paragraph 5.**

*[1] Your mentor will also introduce you to your supervisor and other staff in your department. [2] He or she will give you a tour of the building and show you where the Employee Services Office is located. [3] Your mentor will help you become acquainted on the first day. [4] You can expect to be photographed for your identification badge, and you will need to request a parking sticker.*

**Which sequence provides the most logical order of the sentences?**

A  1, 4, 3, 2

B  1, 2, 4, 3

C  3, 2, 4, 1

D  3, 4, 1, 2

**7**

A  (*No change*)

B  collect

C  locate

D  receive

**GO ON TO THE NEXT PAGE ➡**

first week of employment. Any questions or concerns should be directed to Jamie Washington, Director of Employee Services, Monday through Friday, 8 A.M. to 5 P.M.

7. I welcome and applaud your future contributions to Bridgewater Electronics. I hope you find your employment with the company to be a great learning experience and an opportunity to accomplish exceptional feats.

Sincerely,

Mike Fowler
President

**8 Which sentence from the letter is irrelevant and should be deleted?**

A *As a new employee, you are encouraged to take advantage of our monthly networking lunches.*

B *You and your mentor will meet weekly to discuss work flow, assignments, and processes.*

C *Remember to smile, make eye contact, and give a firm handshake to everyone you meet.*

D *I welcome and applaud your future contributions to Bridgewater Electronics.*

**Read this draft about creating a budget. Then answer question 9–17 that follow.**

## Make a Plan

1. A budget is simply a plan showing how much money a person will generate and spend within a given time frame. Some people think making a budget is like taking a tool such as a sledgehammer and knocking all the fun out of life. In reality, though, following a budget is more like using a shovel to move resources in the best possible way.

2. The optimal way to begin a budget is to record your income and expendatures. If you work a set number of hours each week, your typical income should remain fairly stable. Calculate your regular income, and then identify your expenses. To identify your expenses, make a list of everything you spend money on each month. The list will most likely include rent, utilities, buying groceries, transportation, phone service, getting new clothing, entertainment, etc. Note every expense. This list will give you a clear idea of where your money goes each month.

3. Once you identified your spending habits, set some realistic financial goals for the future. Do you want to save for a new car or a home? Do you want to put money away for a special vacation? It is important to make a plan to help you reach your savings goals. It is also wise to build a cash reserve for large unpredictable expenses such as car repairs, health care, or pet care.

4. With spending habits and financial goals identified, you should begin tracking your expenses. First, at the beginning of each month, record your income and expenses. Then you will need to prioritize the remainder of the items on which you spend money. Make sure all of your living expenses, such as rent, utilities, and groceries, are paid first. Sometimes deciding what is most important can be a balancing act. For example, you may want to go to a movie, but it is not budgeted for this week. Can you delete something else—those new shoes you want, for instance? Another item on the budget should be nonnegotiable. This includes saving for future goals and emergencies. You do not need a large income to save money. Setting aside even a few dollars each week into a special account can add up to big savings over time.

5. Fortunately online, there is a variety of resources for creating a budget. What is important is to select what works for you and begin to budget right now. Like with any learned behavior, once you do it over and over, they become a habit. This habit just happens to be good for you and your future. The experience of living within your means allows for stress-free spending and the security of knowing your savings are growing.

GO ON TO THE NEXT PAGE ➡

# Make a Plan

1. A budget is simply a plan showing how much money a person will generate and spend within a given time frame. Some people think making a budget is like taking a tool such as a sledgehammer and knocking all the fun out of life. In reality, though, following a budget is more like using a shovel to <u>move</u><sub>9</sub> resources in the best possible way.

2. The optimal way to begin a budget is to record your income and <u>expendatures</u><sub>10</sub>. If you work a set number of hours each week, your <u>typical</u><sub>10</sub> income should remain fairly stable. <u>Calculate</u><sub>10</sub> your regular income, and then identify your expenses. To identify your expenses, make a list of everything you spend money on each month. The list will most likely include <u>rent, utilities, buying groceries,</u><sub>11</sub> <u>transportation, phone service,</u><sub>11</sub> <u>getting new clothing,</u><sub>11</sub> <u>entertainment, etc</u><sub>11</sub>. Note every expense. This list will give you a clear idea of where your money goes each month.

**9** Which word is the most precise replacement for the underlined word in the sentence?

A release

B administer

C distribute

D assign

**10** Which word in these sentences is misspelled?

A None of them

B *expendatures*

C *typical*

D *calculate*

**11**

A (*No change*)

B rent, utilities, buying groceries, transportation, paying for phone service, clothing, entertainment, etc.

C rent, utilities, groceries, transportation, phone service, clothing, entertainment, etc.

D rent and utilities, buying groceries and clothes, paying for clothes, transportation and phone service, entertainment, etc.

3. Once you <u>identified</u> your spending
   <sub>12</sub>
   habits, set some realistic financial
   goals for the future. Do you want to
   save for a new car or a home? Do
   you want to put money away for a
   special vacation? It is important to
   make a plan to help you reach your
   savings goals. It is also wise to build

<u>a cash reserve for large</u>
   <sub>14</sub>
<u>unpredictable expenses</u> such as car
   <sub>14</sub>
repairs, health care, or pet care.

4. With spending habits and financial
   goals identified, you should begin
   tracking your expenses. First, at the
   beginning of each month, record
   your income and expenses. Then
   you will need to prioritize the
   remainder of the items on which you
   spend money. Make sure all of your
   living expenses, such as rent,
   utilities, and groceries, are paid first.
   Sometimes deciding what is most
   important can be a balancing act.
   For example, you may want to go to
   a movie, but it is not budgeted for
   this week. Can you delete something

**12**

A (*No change*)

B will identify

C identifies

D have identified

**13 Read this sentence from
paragraph 3.**

*Do you want to save for a new car or a
home?*

**Which word or phrase provides the
best transition to introduce this
sentence?**

A Moreover

B For example

C Chiefly

D In other words

**14**

A (*No change*)

B a cash reserve, for large
   unpredictable expenses

C a cash reserve for large,
   unpredictable expenses

D a cash, reserve for large
   unpredictable expenses,

**15 Read these sentences from
paragraph 4.**

*Another item on the budget should be
nonnegotiable. This includes saving for
future goals and emergencies.*

**GO ON TO THE NEXT PAGE ➡**

else—those new shoes you want, for instance? Another item on the budget should be nonnegotiable. This includes saving for future goals and emergencies. You do not need a large income to save money. Setting aside even a few dollars each week into a special account can add up to big savings over time.

5. <u>Fortunately online, there is a variety of resources for creating a budget.</u>
   16
   
   16
   
   What is important is to select what works for you and begin to budget right now. Like with any learned behavior, once you do it over and

   over, <u>they become</u> a habit. This
   17
   habit just happens to be good for you and your future. The experience of living within your means allows for stress-free spending and the security of knowing your savings are growing.

**What is the best way to combine the sentences?**

A  Saving for future goals and emergencies is an item on the budget that should be nonnegotiable.

B  Future goals and emergencies should be considered as nonnegotiable and still be on the budget.

C  Other budget items like savings and emergencies, they should be nonnegotiable.

D  Saving for future goals and emergencies is an item on the budget, and it should be nonnegotiable.

**16**

A  (*No change*)

B  Fortunately, there is a variety of resources for creating an online budget.

C  Fortunately, there is a variety of online resources for creating a budget.

D  Fortunately, there is an online variety of resources for creating a budget.

**17**

A  (*No change*)

B  it became

C  they are becoming

D  it becomes

**Read this draft of a student's letter about school censorship. Then answer questions 18–25 that follow.**

Dear Teachers, Administrators, and Students:

1. It has come to my attention that our school board recently banned a classic novel from our high school library. The library at our school is one of the best in the county and has won many awards for excellence. While I understand the concern of some parents, teachers, and administrators who want to protect students, I disagree with the school board's actions in the matter and strongly oppose censorship in schools. Rather than ban books altogether, it seems as if schools should reconsider the approach taken with potentially controversial books.

2. The novel that has been banned from our library is William Faulkner's *As I Lay Dying*. From what I understand, the controversy arose when a concerned parent claims that the book contains profanity. In this particular case, the teacher simply may have been trying to expose her students to a sample of Southern literature. Her only mistake, in my opinion, was that she avoids the issue of Faulkner's use of profanity and missed an opportunity to explain the regional and historical context of the work to her students.

3. I understand the concerns and agree that parents have the right to question the appropriateness of any book. I do not think books should be banned altogether or that one parent should be able to make decisions for all others. In my opinion, censorship is a clear violation of our right to freedom of speech. It is also a violation of a teacher's right to choose which texts he or she will use in the classroom. Ironically, teachers who encounter problems with censorship are often teachers who merely seek to connect their curriculum with real-life experiences and who do not cave in when faced with a potentially controversial topic.

4. I hope that in the future, school administrators and teachers can address parentel issues by discussing them openly and coming to a mutually agreeable compromise. Some schools for example handle the challenge of presenting potentially controversial texts by asking teachers to explain how the selected reading fulfills the curriculum requirements. Teachers are also asked to describe the educational merit of chosen reading materials. Other schools offer alternative reading assignments if they feel that a text might upset students or parents. Both solutions seem to be more viabel alternatives to banning classic novels altogether.

5. Unfortunately, the trend toward censorship will continue until people can agree on how to present controversial texts to students. Students must learn to evaluate controversial topics and issues. This way we become informed and active participants in our society. Our country was founded on the belief that every person has a right to his or her own opinion, and I believe that this principle should be reflected in our educational decisions and practices at our school.

Sincerely,

Mary Lewis
Student Council President

GO ON TO THE NEXT PAGE ➡

Dear Teachers, Administrators, and Students:

1. It has come to my attention that our school board recently banned a classic novel from our high school library. The library at our school is one of the best in the county and has won many awards for excellence. While I understand the concern of some parents, teachers, and administrators who want to protect students, I disagree with the school board's actions in the matter and strongly oppose censorship in schools. Rather than ban books altogether, it seems as if schools should reconsider the approach taken with potentially controversial books.

2. The novel that has been banned from our library is William Faulkner's *As I Lay Dying*. From what I understand, the controversy arose when a concerned parent <u>claims</u> that the book contains profanity. In this particular case, the teacher simply may have been trying to expose her students to a sample of Southern literature. Her only mistake, in my opinion, was that she

**18** **Which sentence from paragraph 1 is irrelevant and should be deleted from the letter?**

A *It has come to my attention that our school board recently banned a classic novel from our high school library.*

B *The library at our school is one of the best in the county and has won many awards for excellence.*

C *While I understand the concern of some parents, teachers, and administrators who want to protect students, I disagree with the school board's actions in the matter and strongly oppose censorship in schools.*

D *Rather than ban books altogether, it seems as if schools should reconsider the approach taken with potentially controversial books.*

**19**

A (*No change*)

B is claiming

C claimed

D has claimed

46

avoids the issue of Faulkner's use of [20] profanity and missed an opportunity [20] to explain [20] the regional and historical context of the work to her students.

3. I understand the concerns and agree that parents have the right to question the appropriateness of any book. I do not think books should be banned altogether or that one parent should be able to make decisions for all others. In my opinion, censorship is a clear violation of our right to freedom of speech. It is also a violation of a teacher's right to choose which texts he or she will use in the classroom. Ironically, teachers who encounter problems with censorship are often teachers who merely seek to connect their curriculum with real-life experiences and who do not cave in when faced with [22] a potentially controversial topic.

4. I hope that in the future, school administrators and teachers can address parentel [23] issues by discussing them openly and coming to a mutually [23] agreeable compromise. [23]

**20**

A (*No change*)

B avoid the issue of Faulkner's use of profanity and misses an opportunity to explain

C is avoiding the issue of Faulkner's use of profanity and was missing an opportunity to explain

D avoided the issue of Faulkner's use of profanity and missed an opportunity to explain

**21 Read these sentences from paragraph 3.**

*I understand the concerns and agree that parents have the right to question the appropriateness of any book. _____, I do not think books should be banned altogether or that one parent should be able to make decisions for all others.*

**Which is the best transition between these two sentences?**

A However

B Otherwise

C Consequently

D In addition

**22 How should the underlined text be written to maintain the tone of the letter?**

A (*No change*)

B who carry on when faced with

C who persist despite being faced with

D who do not give up while being faced with

**23 Which, if any, of the underlined words is misspelled?**

A None of them

B parentel

C mutually

D compromise

Some schools for example handle the challenge of presenting potentially controversial texts by asking teachers to explain how the selected reading fulfills the curriculum requirements. Teachers are also asked to describe the educational merit of chosen reading materials. Other schools offer alternative reading assignments if they feel that a text might upset students or parents. Both solutions seem to be more viable alternatives to banning classic novels altogether.

5. Unfortunately, the trend toward censorship will continue until people can agree on how to present controversial texts to students. Students must learn to evaluate controversial topics and issues. This way we become informed and active participants in our society. Our country was founded on the belief that every person has a right to his or her own opinion, and I believe that this principle should be reflected in our educational decisions and practices at our school.

Sincerely,

Mary Lewis
Student Council President

**24**

A (*No change*)

B Some schools, for example, handle the challenge of presenting potentially controversial texts by asking teachers to explain how the selected reading fulfills the curriculum requirements.

C Some schools for example, handle the challenge of presenting potentially controversial texts, by asking teachers to explain how the selected reading fulfills the curriculum requirements.

D Some schools for example, handle the challenge of presenting potentially controversial texts by asking teachers to explain how, the selected reading, fulfills the curriculum requirements.

**25 Read these sentences from paragraph 5.**

*Students must learn to evaluate controversial topics and issues. This way we become informed and active participants in our society.*

**Which of these shows the best way to combine the two sentences?**

A We students must learn to evaluate controversial topics and issues so that we may become informed and active participants in our society.

B We students must learn to evaluate controversial topics and issues; and this way we may become informed and active participants in our society.

C We students must learn to evaluate controversial topics and issues because this is the way we may become informed and active participants in our society.

D We students must learn to evaluate controversial topics and issues, and then this way we become informed and active participants in our society.

# ANSWERS AND EXPLANATIONS— LANGUAGE ARTS—WRITING, PART 1

| Question Number | Correct Answer | Content Category | Rationale |
|---|---|---|---|
| 1 | A | Writing Conventions | "His" refers to Markus Whiley's mission. |
| 2 | B | Organization of Ideas | The sentence has an inappropriate verb shift: of the four verbs in it, three are in the present tense and one is in the past. |
| 3 | B | Language Facility | All the verbs are parallel by being aligned into simple present tense. |
| 4 | B | Organization of Ideas | The introductory sentence for paragraph 3, like option B, is a broad statement about available services to help get acquainted, which is expanded upon in the next sentence. |
| 5 | D | Organization of Ideas | The transition works to add the factor of time into the sentence about expectations. |
| 6 | C | Language Facility | The sentences should be placed into a chronological order with prepositional phrases and pronoun markers distinguishing correct sentence order. |
| 7 | D | Language Facility | "Get" — "receive" as it is used in the sentence. |
| 8 | C | Organization of Ideas | This is the only sentence that describes recommendations for employee behavior in the paragraph about the first day's activities. |
| 9 | C | Language Facility | "Move" = "distribute" as it is used in the sentence, describing how a shovel can take from one big place and transport parts of the contents around a large area. |
| 10 | B | Writing Conventions | "Expenditures" is misspelled in the passage. |
| 11 | C | Language Facility | The correct sentence demonstrates parallel use of predicate nouns. |
| 12 | D | Writing Conventions | Correct present tense that fits all of the choices uses present participle; other choice that could work is wrong form. |
| 13 | B | Organization of Ideas | Using the previous sentence, the transition should bridge the instruction with a list of models or examples, which option B does. |

*(Continued)*

| Question Number | Correct Answer | Content Category | Rationale |
|---|---|---|---|
| 14 | C | Writing Conventions | Appropriate use of commas for prepositional phrase and pair of adjectives before a noun. |
| 15 | A | Language Facility | Option A is a coherent and logical sentence that is not awkward and wordy like the others. |
| 16 | C | Writing Conventions | The modifier "online" correctly describes "resources" and not "fortunately," "the variety," or "the budget." |
| 17 | D | Writing Conventions | The pronoun and corresponding verb match the antecedent—"any learned behavior"—correctly. |
| 18 | B | Organization of Ideas | The second sentence in the paragraph presents a detail, the quality of the school library, that is not relevant to the purpose of the letter. |
| 19 | C | Language Facility | "Claims" should be changed to "claimed" to be consistent with the verb, "arose." |
| 20 | D | Writing Conventions | The student is describing something that has happened in the past, so "avoids" should be changed to "avoided" to make the sentence correct. |
| 21 | A | Organization of Ideas | Because the second sentence provides an alternate viewpoint, "however" is the logical transition. |
| 22 | C | Writing Conventions | Use of "persist despite" is the only option that maintains the serious tone of the letter. |
| 23 | B | Writing Conventions | "Parentel" is a misspelling of "parental." |
| 24 | B | Writing Conventions | Option B is the only option that uses correct comma placement for a transition and dependent clause. |
| 25 | A | Language Facility | Option A most succinctly and correctly combines the two sentences without awkward wordiness and punctuation. |

# *HiSET*® Exam Diagnostic Test
# Answer Sheet
# Language Arts—Writing, Part 2

# LANGUAGE ARTS—WRITING, PART 2

## Essay Directions and Topic

In the box below is your assigned topic and the letter of that topic.

You must write on the assigned topic ONLY.

You will have 45 minutes to write on your assigned essay topic. The essay is evaluated based on the following features:

- Well-focused main points
- Clear organization
- Specific development of your ideas
- Control of sentence structure, punctuation, grammar, word choice, and spelling

REMEMBER, YOU MUST COMPLETE BOTH THE MULTIPLE-CHOICE QUESTIONS (PART 1) AND THE ESSAY (PART 2) TO RECEIVE A SCORE ON THE LANGUAGE ARTS—WRITING TEST. To avoid having to repeat both parts of the test, be sure to do the following:

- Do not leave the pages blank.
- Write legibly so that the evaluators will be able to read your writing.
- Write on the assigned topic. If you write on a topic other than the one assigned, you will not receive a score for the Language Arts—Writing Test.

---

### TOPIC A

There are many ways for people to stay informed about current events. Some people watch news on the television or listen to news programs on the radio. Other people rely on the Internet to get their news. Still other people prefer to read newspapers or news magazines.

Write an essay that explains which method of obtaining news about current events you feel is best and why. Think carefully about what reasons will help others understand your perspective, as well as what examples and details you can use to support your view.

---

# ANSWERS: LANGUAGE ARTS—WRITING, PART 2

All essays will be scored according to the HiSET Exam essay rubric.

| Score Code | Description |
| --- | --- |
| 6 | **Proficient** |

Essays at this score point show proficient skill in responding to the task. The response demonstrates proficient skill in developing ideas. It maintains focus on a clear central idea throughout the response. The response provides several ideas with effective and thorough explanation, offering relevant and fully elaborated reasons, examples, and/or details to support ideas. The response demonstrates strong critical thinking and insight by discussing complications of the issue and/or successfully addressing counterarguments. The response demonstrates proficient skill in organization. It has an effective, well-developed introduction and conclusion, with an engaging introduction that clearly sets up the rest of the response. Clear and appropriate paragraphing is used, creating a coherent whole. Logical sequencing of ideas is demonstrated throughout the response. Effective transitions are used throughout the response to support coherence. The response demonstrates proficient skill in language. Word choice is precise, varied, and engaging. The response effectively varies sentence length and complexity. Voice is appropriate for audience and purpose, and enhances the effectiveness of the response. No errors or only a few superficial errors appear, and the response demonstrates sophisticated use of grammar, usage, and mechanics.

| 5 | **Competent** |

Essays at this score point show competent skill in responding to the task. The response demonstrates competent skill in developing ideas. It maintains focus on a clear central idea throughout the response. The response provides several ideas with complete explanation, offering specific, relevant, and somewhat elaborated reasons, examples, and/or details to support ideas. The response demonstrates some critical thinking by introducing and addressing complications of the issue and/or addressing counterarguments. The response demonstrates competent skill in organization. The introduction and conclusion are clear and generally well-developed, and the introduction clearly sets up the rest of the response. Clear and appropriate paragraphing is used, with logical sequencing of ideas through most of the response. Varied transitions are used between and within paragraphs to support coherence. The response demonstrates competent skill in language. Word choice is usually precise and varied. The response uses well-controlled sentences that are varied in length and complexity. Voice is appropriate for audience and purpose. There are few grammar, usage, or mechanics errors and most are superficial.

| 4 | **Adequate** |

Essays at this score point show adequate skill in responding to the task. The response demonstrates adequate skill in developing ideas. It maintains focus on a central idea, though there may be a few minor lapses. The response provides several ideas with adequate explanation, offering some specific and relevant examples and/or details to support ideas. The response demonstrates adequate skill in organization, with a clear introduction and conclusion that are somewhat developed. The response uses appropriate paragraphing and demonstrates some evidence of logical sequencing of ideas. Transitions are consistently used between and/or within paragraphs, though the transitions may be simple. Adequate skill in language use is demonstrated. Mostly specific and somewhat varied word choice is used. The response demonstrates control of sentences with some variety in length and structure. Voice is usually appropriate for audience and purpose. Some errors in sentence construction, pronoun use, verb forms, and/or spelling are present but do not interfere with understanding.

**3      Limited**

Essays at this score point show limited skill in responding to the task. The response demonstrates limited skill in developing ideas. It maintains focus on a central idea through some of the response. The response provides several ideas with limited or uneven explanation, offering few or only general examples and/or details to support ideas. Organization demonstrates some developing skill. The response has an introduction and conclusion, though one or both of these may be over- or underdeveloped. Ideas are grouped together in paragraphs, though the relationship among ideas may at times be unclear. The response uses a few transitions between and/or within paragraphs to support coherence. Some developing skill in language is demonstrated. Word choice is general and the response demonstrates a little variety in sentence structure, although a few long, uncontrolled sentences may be used. Errors in sentence construction, pronoun use, verb forms, and/or spelling are present and may occasionally interfere with understanding.

**2      Minimal**

Essays at this score point show minimal skill in responding to the task. The response demonstrates minimal development. It provides a few ideas but explanation is minimal or superficial and parts of the explanation may be repetitious or lack relevance. Organization is weak. There is minimal evidence of an introduction and/or conclusion. Some related ideas are grouped together, though paragraphing may not be used. If transitions appear, their use is not controlled. Beginning skill in language is demonstrated. Word choice is awkward and/or repetitive. The response has repetitive sentence structure and/or long, uncontrolled sentences. Numerous errors in sentence construction, pronoun use, verb forms, and/or spelling interrupt the flow of communication and some errors may interfere with understanding.

**1      Deficient**

Essays at this score point show little or no skill in responding to the task. The response has little or no development. It may provide a few ideas but lacks explanation of ideas, only repeats ideas, or the ideas lack relevance. Organization is minimal. The response lacks an introduction and conclusion and does not demonstrate any understanding of paragraphing. If transitions appear, their use is not controlled. Language control is minimal. Word choice and sentence structure are simple. Errors in sentence construction, pronoun use, verb forms, and/or spelling are frequent and may interfere with understanding.

# *HiSET*® Exam Diagnostic Test
# Answer Sheet
# Social Studies

|     | A | B | C | D |
|-----|---|---|---|---|
| 1   | ☐ | ☐ | ☐ | ☐ |
| 2   | ☐ | ☐ | ☐ | ☐ |
| 3   | ☐ | ☐ | ☐ | ☐ |
| 4   | ☐ | ☐ | ☐ | ☐ |
| 5   | ☐ | ☐ | ☐ | ☐ |
| 6   | ☐ | ☐ | ☐ | ☐ |
| 7   | ☐ | ☐ | ☐ | ☐ |
| 8   | ☐ | ☐ | ☐ | ☐ |
| 9   | ☐ | ☐ | ☐ | ☐ |
| 10  | ☐ | ☐ | ☐ | ☐ |
| 11  | ☐ | ☐ | ☐ | ☐ |
| 12  | ☐ | ☐ | ☐ | ☐ |
| 13  | ☐ | ☐ | ☐ | ☐ |

|     | A | B | C | D |
|-----|---|---|---|---|
| 14  | ☐ | ☐ | ☐ | ☐ |
| 15  | ☐ | ☐ | ☐ | ☐ |
| 16  | ☐ | ☐ | ☐ | ☐ |
| 17  | ☐ | ☐ | ☐ | ☐ |
| 18  | ☐ | ☐ | ☐ | ☐ |
| 19  | ☐ | ☐ | ☐ | ☐ |
| 20  | ☐ | ☐ | ☐ | ☐ |
| 21  | ☐ | ☐ | ☐ | ☐ |
| 22  | ☐ | ☐ | ☐ | ☐ |
| 23  | ☐ | ☐ | ☐ | ☐ |
| 24  | ☐ | ☐ | ☐ | ☐ |
| 25  | ☐ | ☐ | ☐ | ☐ |

# SOCIAL STUDIES

## 25 Questions

## 35 Minutes

## Directions

This is a test of your skills in analyzing social studies information. Read each question and decide which of the four alternatives best answers the question. Then mark your choice on your answer sheet. Sometimes several questions are based on the same material. You should carefully read this material, then answer the questions.

Work as quickly as you can without becoming careless. Don't spend too much time on any question that is difficult for you to answer. Instead, skip it and return to it later if you have time. Try to answer every question even if you have to guess.

Mark all your answers on the answer sheet. Give only one answer to each question and make every mark heavy and dark. If you decide to change one of your answers, be sure to erase the first mark completely. Be sure that the number of the question you are answering matches the number of the row of answer choices you are marking on your answer sheet.

1. **Which role do political parties play in the election process?**
   A   Protecting citizens from voter discrimination
   B   Petitioning the government for campaign funding
   C   Donating money to special interest groups
   D   Nominating candidates to run for office

2. **Which of the following directly influences the climate of a region?**
   A   Tectonic plates
   B   Latitude
   C   Ocean tides
   D   Longitude

**GO ON TO THE NEXT PAGE ➡**

3. **Consider the graph.**

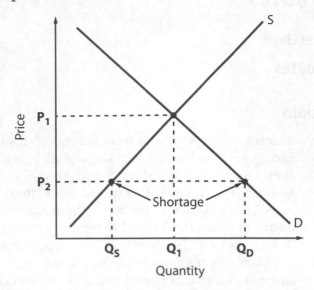

**How would a company most likely respond to the situation illustrated by this graph?**

A   By raising the price of the product until market equilibrium is established

B   By increasing production of new products in order to increase demand

C   By decreasing the quantity produced until market equilibrium is established

D   By reducing the costs of production in order to meet the demand

4. **What was the result of the Allied victory in Europe in World War II?**

A   The United States introduced capitalism and free enterprise to Europe.

B   The British Empire expanded by acquiring new territory in Europe.

C   The Soviet Union was prevented from spreading communism in Europe.

D   Europe was liberated and Nazi rule was ended in Germany.

5. **Which of the following describes a primary economic activity?**

A   Converting raw materials into products such as cloth and steel

B   Designing new products based on research and application of scientific principles

C   Obtaining raw materials from the land through farming and mining

D   Supplying services such as transporting goods and providing medical care

> Equality of rights under the law shall not be denied or abridged by the United States or by any state on account of sex.
>
> —Equal Rights Amendment, 1972

6. **Which phrase best describes the goal of this proposed amendment?**

A   To encourage more women to participate in elections

B   To eliminate discrimination against women

C   To require affirmative action programs for women

D   To enable more women to enter the workforce

**These programs were established to help address the problems of the Great Depression in the United States.**

| New Deal Programs | Year Enacted | Description |
|---|---|---|
| Agricultural Adjustment Administration (AAA) | 1933 | Farm-relief measure designed to stabilize prices of agricultural goods by paying farmers to reduce production |
| Civilian Conservation Corps (CCC) | 1933 | Unemployment-relief measure that sent young men to work on national park and conservation projects |
| Federal Deposit Insurance Corporation (FDIC) | 1933 | Federal agency created to insure bank deposits and help prevent bank failures |
| Federal Emergency Relief Administration (FERA) | 1933 | Agency established to provide millions of dollars in cash aid to the impoverished |
| Social Security | 1935 | Social insurance program that established old-age pensions, unemployment insurance, and funds to aid dependent children and the disabled |
| Works Progress Administration (WPA) | 1935 | Organization that provided jobs in construction, as well as work in art, music, theater, and writers' projects |

7. **Which of these programs focused on creating jobs?**

   A   Agricultural Adjustment Administration

   B   Civilian Conservation Corps

   C   Federal Deposit Insurance Corporation

   D   Federal Emergency Relief Administration

8. **How did Social Security help address the problems of the Great Depression?**

   A   By providing incomes to retired persons

   B   By funding programs for the arts

   C   By stabilizing the cost of living

   D   By providing more home mortgages

9. **The Agricultural Adjustment Administration helped farmers by**

   A   improving the quality of crops to increase production levels.

   B   increasing land values to enable farmers to borrow more money.

   C   decreasing the production of crops in order to improve prices.

   D   requiring farmers to accept lower wages in order to cut costs.

10. **Which information would be most useful in determining the effectiveness of the Works Progress Administration as a relief measure?**

   A   Number of states involved

   B   Total annual cost

   C   Types of jobs created

   D   Number of people employed

**GO ON TO THE NEXT PAGE ➡**

11. **Which of these programs has become a permanent part of the government?**

    A   Agricultural Adjustment Administration

    B   Civilian Conservation Corps

    C   Federal Emergency Relief Administration

    D   Social Security

**Questions 12 to 17 refer to the information below.**

**These two accounts offer summaries of a local public hearing about development over the recharge zone[1] of an aquifer.**

### Account 1

The Water Quality Board and Planning Commission met yesterday to listen to citizens' concerns about allowing new construction over the recharge zone of the aquifer.

    Citizens expressed grave concerns about the danger this construction poses to the local water supply. James Weatherford, a local resident of forty years, recalled a similar discussion that took place before the local outlet mall was developed. "We were concerned that unless sufficient precautions were taken, we would be endangering our water supply. The aquifer is the only water source we have. Parking lots and pollutants will cause water quality issues."

    Developers attempted to reassure residents that the same care will be taken to collect and purify runoff from parking lots. The developers emphasized that "the future of this area depends on whether or not companies will move to this location. This is the economic reality."

    Residents were not satisfied with the developers' answers. The board will meet on Thursday to make its final decision.

*Line 5*

*Line 10*

### Account 2

The Water Quality Board and Planning Commission met yesterday to hear citizens' input about issuing building permits for development over the recharge zone of the aquifer.

    Developers of the multimillion-dollar residential and commercial project spoke at the hearing. Thomas Allen of Terex Development stated, "This is the single most important development project in the area in fifteen years. It will bring jobs and prosperity to residents. We look forward to a long and productive future for the new properties."

    Citizens, including longtime resident James Weatherford, asked about water quality. They received assurances from Terex that studies have been completed and precautions are in place to preserve water quality, including enforcing restrictions on pesticides used on golf courses in the area.

    The developers would like to break ground in May and host a large celebration. The board will meet on Thursday to make its final decision.

*Line 5*

*Line 10*

12. **What is one way the authors of these accounts attempt to influence the reader?**

    A   The authors present arguments that favor one side of the issue.

    B   The authors refer to the opposing argument as uninformed.

    C   The authors report scientific research about the proposed project.

    D   The authors fail to mention the final outcome of the project.

[1]**recharge zone:** an area where water enters and recharges an aquifer

13. **Which phrase from Account 1 reveals the author's bias?**

A "grave concerns"

B "water quality"

C "purify runoff"

D "economic reality"

14. **Which statement summarizes the point of view expressed in Account 2?**

A The board should carefully consider the opinions of residents.

B Development over the recharge zone of the aquifer will benefit the community.

C Residents have the right to express opinions to the board.

D Construction over the recharge zone of the aquifer will affect water quality.

15. **Which question should a board member consider when deciding how to vote on this issue?**

A Which streets will be used during construction?

B How many voters live near the aquifer?

C Which school district will be affected by construction?

D How much water runoff will be generated by the development?

16. **What is one benefit of public hearings like the one held before the Water Quality Board and Planning Commission?**

A They allow citizens to make changes to existing laws.

B They offer citizens the chance to vote on an issue.

C They provide citizens with a chance to express opinions.

D They ask citizens for financial support for a project.

17. **Which action would be an effective way for citizens to influence the final vote of the board?**

A Sign a petition to prevent construction

B Refuse to participate in future local elections

C Boycott businesses participating in the new development

D Join an organization dedicated to water conservation

**Questions 18 to 20 refer to the information below.**

Monetary policy refers to what the Federal Reserve does to regulate the supply of money and credit in the U.S. economy. The tools of monetary policy are intended to influence the willingness of people and businesses to spend money on goods and services.

| Tool | Definition | Expansionary Policy | Contractionary Policy |
|---|---|---|---|
| Discount rate | Interest rate charged by the Federal Reserve on short-term loans to financial institutions | Lower discount rate | Raise discount rate |
| Reserve requirements | Percentage of deposits that banks must maintain either in their vaults or on deposit at a Federal Reserve Bank | Decrease reserve requirements | Increase reserve requirements |
| Open market operations | Buying and selling of government debt | Buy government bonds | Sell government bonds |

18. **Which action by the Federal Reserve would most likely raise employment levels?**

    A   Decreasing the money supply

    B   Increasing the reserve requirements

    C   Lowering the discount rate

    D   Selling government bonds

19. **Why would the Federal Reserve pursue a contractionary monetary policy?**

    A   To fight inflation

    B   To discourage tax increases

    C   To improve benefits for workers

    D   To promote growth of industry

20. **Why is decreasing the reserve requirements an expansionary policy?**

    A   Banks will have more money available to contribute to charities.

    B   Banks will have more funds available to make loans.

    C   Corporations will have fewer funds available for investment.

    D   Corporations will have less money available for lobbying the government.

**Questions 21 to 25 refer to the information below.**

**These lines are excerpted from the *Declaration of Independence*, signed in 1776.**

We hold these truths to be self-evident, that all men are created equal, that they are endowed by their Creator with certain unalienable Rights, that among these are Life, Liberty and the pursuit of Happiness.—That to secure these rights, Governments are instituted among Men, deriving their just powers from the consent of the governed,—

*Line*

5    That whenever any Form of Government becomes destructive of these ends, it is the Right of the People to alter or to abolish it, and to institute new Government. . . .

The history of the present King of Great Britain is a history of repeated injuries . . . all having in direct object the establishment of an absolute Tyranny over these States. . . .

He has [given] his Assent to . . . Acts of pretended legislation:

10    1) For Quartering large bodies of armed troops among us: . . .

2) For cutting off our Trade with all parts of the world:

3) For imposing Taxes on us without our Consent:

4) For depriving us in many cases, of the benefits of Trial by Jury . . .

We, therefore, the Representatives of the united States of America . . . do, in the

15    Name, and by Authority of the good People of these Colonies, solemnly publish and declare, That these United Colonies are, and of Right ought to be Free and Independent States. . . .

21. **Based on this information, which individual right is the king accused of violating?**

   A    Freedom of religion

   B    Right to free speech

   C    Right to due process

   D    Freedom of the press

---

The Stamp Act of 1765 affected every type of printed paper created in the colonies, including newspapers, playing cards, and legal documents.

---

22. **Which numbered grievance from the passage indicates the colonists' objections to this type of act?**

   A    1

   B    2

   C    3

   D    4

23. **Based on the information, which justification did the colonists use as a basis for declaring independence?**

    A  Religious leaders have the power to create government.

    B  Governments should defend the right of equality.

    C  A monarchy is a better form of government than a democracy.

    D  The purpose of government is to protect the rights of the people.

> It shall and may be lawful for the governor . . . to order and direct such . . . uninhabited houses, out-houses, barns, or other buildings, as he shall think necessary to be taken . . . and make fit for the reception of . . . officers and soldiers. . . .
>
> —Act of Parliament, 1774

24. **Which numbered grievance from the passage is an objection to this act?**

    A  1

    B  2

    C  3

    D  4

25. **Which conclusion is best supported by this information?**

    A  The king had the right to abolish government in the colonies.

    B  Violating the rights of colonists was a form of tyranny.

    C  The colonists wanted to create a government without taxation.

    D  Limiting the right to vote to male colonists created inequality.

# ANSWERS AND EXPLANATIONS—SOCIAL STUDIES

| Question Number | Correct Answer | Content Category | Rationale |
| --- | --- | --- | --- |
| 1 | D | Civics/Government | Political parties nominate candidates to run for office. |
| 2 | B | Geography | The climate of a region is directly influenced by latitude, or distance of a region from the poles and equator. |
| 3 | A | Economics | An increase in price will increase the quantity supplied while decreasing the quantity demanded to reach equilibrium and remedy the shortage. |
| 4 | D | History | Allied victory in World War II liberated Europe from occupation by Axis powers and ended Nazi rule in Germany. |
| 5 | C | Geography | Primary activities, such as farming and mining, obtain goods directly from the earth. |
| 6 | B | Civics/Government | The goal of the ERA is to end discrimination based on sex. |
| 7 | B | History | The CCC was a relief measure designed to create jobs for young men. |
| 8 | A | History | Social Security addressed the problems of the Great Depression by providing incomes to retired persons. |
| 9 | C | History | The Agricultural Adjustment Act helped farmers by paying them to reduce production. |
| 10 | D | History | The most useful information in determining the effectives of the WPA would be the number of people employed by the program. |
| 11 | D | History | Of the programs listed, only Social Security has become a permanent part of the government. |
| 12 | A | Civics/Government | The authors attempt to influence the reader by presenting only one side of the issue. |
| 13 | A | Civics/Government | The phrase "grave concerns" reveals the author's bias against the development. |
| 14 | B | Civics/Government | Account 2 is in favor of development over the aquifer. |

(Continued)

| Question Number | Correct Answer | Content Category | Rationale |
| --- | --- | --- | --- |
| 15 | D | Civics/Government | Knowing how much runoff the proposed development would generate would help a board member decide how to vote. |
| 16 | C | Civics/Government | Public hearings give citizens a chance to express opinions to public officials. |
| 17 | A | Civics/Government | Citizens could influence the final vote of the board by showing support for or against the project through a petition drive. |
| 18 | C | Economics | Lowering the discount rate is an expansionary policy, which would be most likely to raise employment levels. |
| 19 | A | Economics | A contractionary policy is intended to fight inflation. |
| 20 | B | Economics | Decreasing reserve requirements allows banks to make more loans, which would expand the money supply. |
| 21 | C | History | By imposing taxes without consent and denying trial by jury, the king is violating the individual right to due process. |
| 22 | C | History | The Stamp Act is an example of Parliament imposing taxes without the consent of colonists. |
| 23 | D | History | The colonists accused the British government of violating their unalienable rights, and therefore, the colonists had the right to form a new government. |
| 24 | A | History | This act of Parliament is about housing soldiers, which is referred to in line 1 of the passage. |
| 25 | B | History | Violating individual rights is a form of tyranny, and the colonists accused the king of establishing an absolute tyranny over them. |

# *HiSET*® Exam Diagnostic Test
# Answer Sheet
# Science

|   | A | B | C | D |   |   | A | B | C | D |
|---|---|---|---|---|---|---|---|---|---|---|
| 1 | ☐ | ☐ | ☐ | ☐ |   | 14 | ☐ | ☐ | ☐ | ☐ |
| 2 | ☐ | ☐ | ☐ | ☐ |   | 15 | ☐ | ☐ | ☐ | ☐ |
| 3 | ☐ | ☐ | ☐ | ☐ |   | 16 | ☐ | ☐ | ☐ | ☐ |
| 4 | ☐ | ☐ | ☐ | ☐ |   | 17 | ☐ | ☐ | ☐ | ☐ |
| 5 | ☐ | ☐ | ☐ | ☐ |   | 18 | ☐ | ☐ | ☐ | ☐ |
| 6 | ☐ | ☐ | ☐ | ☐ |   | 19 | ☐ | ☐ | ☐ | ☐ |
| 7 | ☐ | ☐ | ☐ | ☐ |   | 20 | ☐ | ☐ | ☐ | ☐ |
| 8 | ☐ | ☐ | ☐ | ☐ |   | 21 | ☐ | ☐ | ☐ | ☐ |
| 9 | ☐ | ☐ | ☐ | ☐ |   | 22 | ☐ | ☐ | ☐ | ☐ |
| 10 | ☐ | ☐ | ☐ | ☐ |   | 23 | ☐ | ☐ | ☐ | ☐ |
| 11 | ☐ | ☐ | ☐ | ☐ |   | 24 | ☐ | ☐ | ☐ | ☐ |
| 12 | ☐ | ☐ | ☐ | ☐ |   | 25 | ☐ | ☐ | ☐ | ☐ |
| 13 | ☐ | ☐ | ☐ | ☐ |   |   |   |   |   |   |

# SCIENCE

## 25 Questions
## 40 Minutes

## Directions

This is a test of your skills in analyzing science information. Read each question and decide which of the four alternatives best answers the question. Then mark your choice on your answer sheet. Sometimes several questions are based on the same material. You should carefully read this material, then answer the questions.

Work as quickly as you can without becoming careless. Don't spend too much time on any question that is difficult for you to answer. Instead, skip it and return to it later if you have time. Try to answer every question even if you have to guess.

Mark all your answers on the answer sheet. Give only one answer to each question and make every mark heavy and dark. If you decide to change one of your answers, be sure to erase the first mark completely. Be sure that the number of the question you are answering matches the number of the row of answer choices you are marking on your answer sheet.

### Questions 1–3 are based on the following information.

### Emerald Sea Slug

*Elysia chlorotica* is a sea slug found in saltwater habitats along the eastern United States coastline. This sea slug, shown in the illustration, feeds by sucking specific organelles out from plantlike organisms called algae. The organelles contain DNA and a pigment that causes the green color of the sea slug. The sea slugs can store these organelles for months in clear digestive glands.

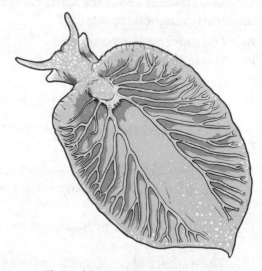

*Elysia chlorotica* (Emerald Sea Slug)

**GO ON TO THE NEXT PAGE ➡**

Scientists did research to determine if the sea slugs used the organelles taken from the algae to become solar powered. In experiments, sea slugs exposed to light absorbed carbon dioxide and went months without food. Another group of scientists hypothesized that these results were because the sea slugs saved some of the organelles for use later as food. Both groups agreed that if young sea slugs are never exposed to algae, the young sea slugs stop growing and are unable to survive.

1. **Scientists want to investigate whether the organelles the emerald sea slugs take from algae are controlled by a negative feedback mechanism. Which variable should the scientists manipulate?**

   A   The type of algae

   B   The species of sea slug

   C   The level of oxygen emitted

   D   The amount of exposure to light

2. **Scientists think that mitosis in young sea slugs is being impaired, preventing growth from occurring in sea slugs that lack algal exposure. Scientists want to build a model of mitosis in emerald sea slugs for further study. Which structures should the scientists include in their model?**

   A   Duplicated chromosomes

   B   Large central vacuoles

   C   Four haploid cells

   D   Cell walls

3. **Researching which question would help scientists determine how emerald sea slugs are able to control the function of the organelles?**

   A   Will emerald sea slugs eat other organelles that are found in the algae?

   B   Can emerald sea slugs ingest organelles from other types of organisms?

   C   Do emerald sea slugs integrate algal genes into chromosomes?

   D   How do emerald sea slugs locate a resource when in the wild?

4. **Which statement about the universe is supported by evidence of a red shift in the electromagnetic spectrum?**

   A   The universe is expanding.

   B   The universe is contracting.

   C   New galaxies are forming in the universe.

   D   New black holes are forming in the universe.

5. **Which characteristic of a star CANNOT be observed by examining its spectral lines?**

   A   The mass of the star by looking at the thickness of the spectral lines

   B   The speed at which the star rotates by looking at the blurring of the spectral lines

   C   The age of the star by looking at the number of hydrogen and helium spectral lines

   D   The number of planets orbiting the star by looking at the number of spectral lines

The diagram shows part of the periodic table of the elements.

PART OF THE PERIODIC TABLE OF THE ELEMENTS

| H | | | | | | | | | | | | | | | | | He |
|---|---|---|---|---|---|---|---|---|---|---|---|---|---|---|---|---|---|
| Li | Be | | | | | | | | | | | B | C | N | O | F | Ne |
| Na | Mg | | | | | | | | | | | Al | Si | P | S | Cl | Ar |
| K | Ca | Sc | Ti | V | Cr | Mn | Fe | Co | Ni | Cu | Zn | Ga | Ge | As | Se | Br | Kr |
| Rb | Sr | Y | Zr | Nb | Mo | Tc | Ru | Rh | Pd | Ag | Cd | In | Sn | Sb | Te | I | Xe |
| Cs | Ba | * | Hf | Ta | W | Re | Os | Ir | Pt | Au | Hg | Tl | Pb | Bi | Po | At | Rn |
| Fr | Ra | ** | Rf | Db | Sg | Bh | Hs | Mt | | | | | | | | | |

| *La | Ce | Pr | Nd | Pm | Sm | Eu | Gd | Tb | Dy | Ho | Er | Tm | Yb | Lu |
|---|---|---|---|---|---|---|---|---|---|---|---|---|---|---|
| **Ac | Th | Pa | U | Np | Pu | Am | Cm | Bk | Cf | Es | Fm | Md | No | Lr |

6. Which group of elements has valence electrons in the same energy level?

   A   B, Si, As, Te

   B   Ga, As, Se, Kr

   C   H, Li, Na, K

   D   La, Pt, Os, Hg

7. Plants can maintain homeostasis by controlling the opening and closing of their stomata. Which investigation would best determine the resources maintained by the stomata?

   A   Measuring the surface area of each leaf on a plant

   B   Measuring the rate of transpiration from a plant

   C   Measuring the height of a plant after a certain amount of time

   D   Measuring the quantity of nutrients a plant absorbs from the soil

8. Every year, an estimated 20,000 zebras migrate across the Kalahari Desert to find suitable grazing land. Which of the following best describes why zebras migrate in large herds instead of individually?

   A   Increased defense against predators

   B   Decreased resistance to biting flies

   C   Increased competition for food

   D   Decreased chance of mating

GO ON TO THE NEXT PAGE ➡

**Questions 9–11 are based on the following information.**

A group of students study various types of chemical reactions. The group observes the reaction of sodium hydroxide (NaOH) and sulfuric acid ($H_2SO_4$). The equation shows the chemical reaction.

$$H_2SO_4(aq) + 2NaOH(aq) \rightarrow 2H_2O(l) + Na_2SO_4(s)$$

The diagram shows a part of the periodic table of the elements.

PARTIAL PERIODIC TABLE OF THE ELEMENTS

| 1 | | | | | | | | | | | | 13 | 14 | 15 | 16 | 17 | 18 |
|---|---|---|---|---|---|---|---|---|---|---|---|---|---|---|---|---|---|
| **H** 1.01 | **2** | | | | | | | | | | | | | | | | **He** 4.00 |
| **Li** 6.94 | **Be** 9.01 | | | | | | | | | | | **B** 10.81 | **C** 12.01 | **N** 14.00 | **O** 16.00 | **F** 19.00 | **Ne** 20.18 |
| **Na** 22.99 | **Mg** 24.31 | **3** | **4** | **5** | **6** | **7** | **8** | **9** | **10** | **11** | **12** | **Al** 26.98 | **Si** 28.09 | **P** 30.97 | **S** 32.07 | **Cl** 35.45 | **Ar** 39.95 |
| **K** 39.10 | **Ca** 40.08 | **Sc** 44.96 | **Ti** 47.88 | **V** 50.94 | **Cr** 52.00 | **Mn** 54.94 | **Fe** 55.85 | **Co** 58.93 | **Ni** 58.69 | **Cu** 63.55 | **Zn** 65.39 | **Ga** 69.73 | **Ge** 72.64 | **As** 74.92 | **Se** 78.96 | **Br** 79.90 | **Kr** 83.80 |

9.  Which statement best describes the type of chemical reaction observed by the group of students?

    **A**   A decomposition reaction

    **B**   A neutralization reaction

    **C**   A combustion reaction

    **D**   A synthesis reaction

10.  How many moles of NaOH are used to yield 2.4 moles of $Na_2SO_4$?

    **A**   0.4 mole

    **B**   1.2 moles

    **C**   4.4 moles

    **D**   4.8 moles

11.  What approximate mass of NaOH will react completely to form 36 g of $H_2O$?

    **A**   40 g NaOH

    **B**   80 g NaOH

    **C**   120 g NaOH

    **D**   160 g NaOH

**Questions 12–16 are based on the following information.**

**Background Information**

The Comal Springs ecosystem is located in Central Texas. This unique aquatic ecosystem provides a habitat for a wide range of plants and animals, some of which can be found nowhere else in the world. The ecosystem consists of the Comal River, the springs from an aquifer that flow into the river, and a dammed portion of the river known as Landa Lake.

Some human activities can threaten the Comal Springs ecosystem. Recreational use of the river can damage aquatic vegetation. Construction in the area can introduce pollution. In addition, pumping water from the aquifer that feeds the springs can reduce the amount of water in the ecosystem. Invasive species can also threaten the ecosystem. One such species is the giant ramshorn snail. These aquatic snails are common in home aquariums. Some individual giant ramshorn snails were released into the ecosystem in the 1980s. Since then, the snail population has significantly increased. The snail feeds on submerged plants, which has caused reduced plant mass in the ecosystem. Some fish, including the endangered fountain darter, depend on these plants for food and shelter.

Researchers have conducted studies to understand the biological impact of the snail on the ecosystem. In one field study, researchers monitored the daily vertical movements of snails on submerged plants. This movement pattern is known as vertical migration. The researchers followed these field study procedures:

### Field Study Procedures

I. Survey the river and lake to identify three sampling sites, each about 1.0 meter deep.
II. Capture 100 snails from each site.
III. Mark the shell of each snail using a nontoxic waterproof marker.
IV. Release each snail back into the site from which it was collected.
V. Wait 3 hours.
VI. Monitor snail movement within 4 square meters of each site. Measure and record the distance of each marked snail above the substrate (mud).
VII. Repeat step VI every 2 hours for 24 hours.
VIII. Calculate the average distance between all marked snails and the substrate.

### Results

The graph shows the field study data.

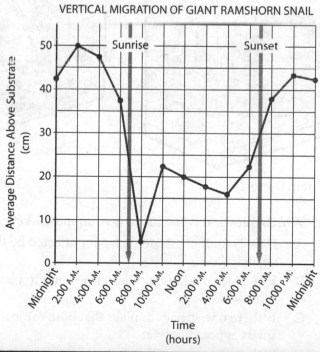

VERTICAL MIGRATION OF GIANT RAMSHORN SNAIL

12. **The giant ramshorn snail population increased significantly following its initial introduction into the Comal Springs ecosystem. This indicates that, compared to native organisms, the snails most likely**

    A  have more predators.

    B  produce fewer offspring.

    C  compete more successfully for resources.

    D  are less tolerant of environmental changes.

13. **Water that flows out of Comal Springs comes from the Edwards Aquifer. Water for human use is pumped from the aquifer through wells throughout the region. During periods of drought, overpumping of aquifer water can decrease the amount of water that flows out of Comal Springs. Which strategy would most likely reduce the pumping demand on the aquifer?**

    A  Constructing additional dams across the Comal River

    B  Limiting recreational activities in the Comal River

    C  Monitoring water quality of the spring water

    D  Following restrictions for residential water usage

Researchers want to collect data on the fountain darter and the giant ramshorn snail. The researchers design an investigation by modeling the ecosystem in a laboratory. They set up identical fish tanks, each with the same three types of plants that grow in the Comal Springs ecosystem. The researchers put fountain darters in one tank and giant ramshorn snails in the other tank. The diagram shows the investigational setup.

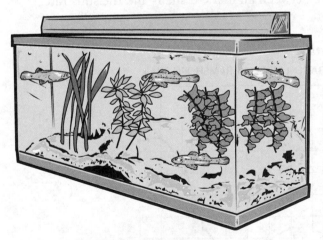

Fountain Darters

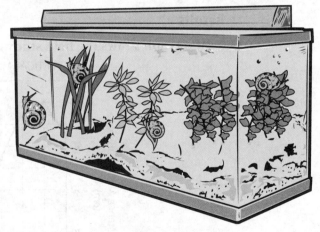

Giant Ramshorn Snails

14. **Which question is the investigation most likely designed to answer?**

    A  How is fountain darter behavior affected by the presence of giant ramshorn snails?

    B  How does the fountain darter respond to plant loss caused by giant ramshorn snails?

    C  Is there one species of plant that both fountain darters and giant ramshorn snails appear to prefer?

    D  Is there one type of substrate that aids in reproduction of both fountain darters and giant ramshorn snails?

Researchers collected population data for fountain darters in the Comal Springs ecosystem. Each spring and fall between 2002 and 2011, they netted, counted, and then released fountain darters. The density graph shows how the fountain darter population changed over time and between seasons.

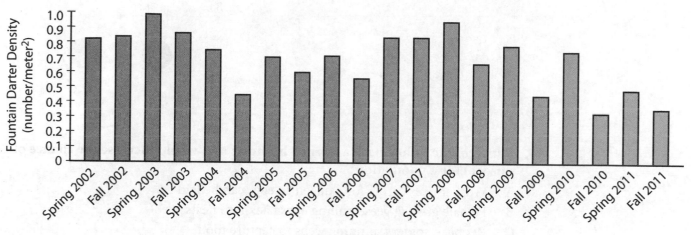

FOUNTAIN DARTER DENSITY VS. SEASON OF THE YEAR

15. **Which statement is best supported by these data?**

   A   The fountain darter population steadily decreased during the study period.

   B   The fountain darter population increased as water temperatures decreased.

   C   The fountain darter population was generally larger in the spring than in the fall.

   D   The fountain darter population was directly related to the availability of plant material.

16. **Which of these actions would most likely help increase the fountain darter population in Landa Lake?**

   A   Removing giant ramshorn snails from plants in the lake

   B   Eliminating the aquatic plants on which giant ramshorn snails feed

   C   Introducing another fish that consumes the same plants as the giant ramshorn snail

   D   Lowering the lake's water level to keep giant ramshorn snails from feeding on submerged plants

GO ON TO THE NEXT PAGE ➡

17. **Which model best illustrates a process occurring in the Sun that emits energy to Earth as radiation?**

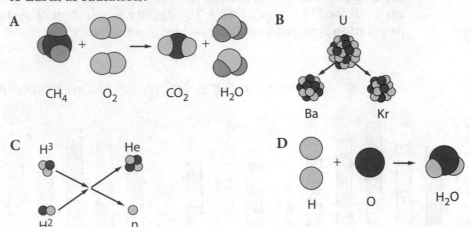

18. **Which of the following is a learned behavior that would increase the chance of survival for a population?**

    A   Worker bees caring for a queen so eggs can be laid
    B   Female greylag geese pulling eggs back into nests
    C   Redback spiders spinning webs to capture food
    D   Young prairie dogs running into burrows when they hear a warning call

**A group of students use Newton's law of universal gravitation to determine the force of attraction between various objects. The table shows the objects the students use in their investigation.**

LIST OF OBJECTS

| Object | Mass (kg) |
| --- | --- |
| Baseball | 0.145 |
| Basketball | 0.620 |
| Golf Ball | 0.046 |
| Soccer Ball | 0.450 |

**The equation represents Newton's law of universal gravitation.**

$$F = \frac{Gm_1 m_2}{r^2}$$

*G* **is the universal gravitational constant,** $6.67 \times 10^{-11}\,\mathrm{N} \cdot \dfrac{\mathrm{m}^2}{\mathrm{kg}^2}$**,** $m_1$ **is the mass of the first object,** $m_2$ **is the mass of the second object, and** *r* **is the distance between them.**

19. **Which pair of objects would have the least attraction at a distance of 0.5 m?**

    A   Basketball and golf ball

    B   Soccer ball and basketball

    C   Baseball and soccer ball

    D   Golf ball and baseball

20. **Under which condition would animal cells undergo anaerobic respiration?**

    A   When cells are in need of additional ATP after all stored oxygen has been used

    B   When cells release the chemical energy stored in food in the presence of oxygen

    C   When cells need to remove lactic acid from the body due to an oxygen deficit

    D   When cells begin to grow too large and need to divide in the absence of oxygen

**A group of students studied thermal energy transfer within a closed system. The graph shows the results of their investigation.**

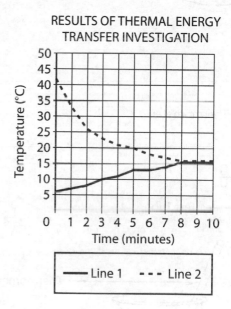

RESULTS OF THERMAL ENERGY
TRANSFER INVESTIGATION

**21.** Which investigational setup did the students most likely use to obtain the data?

A

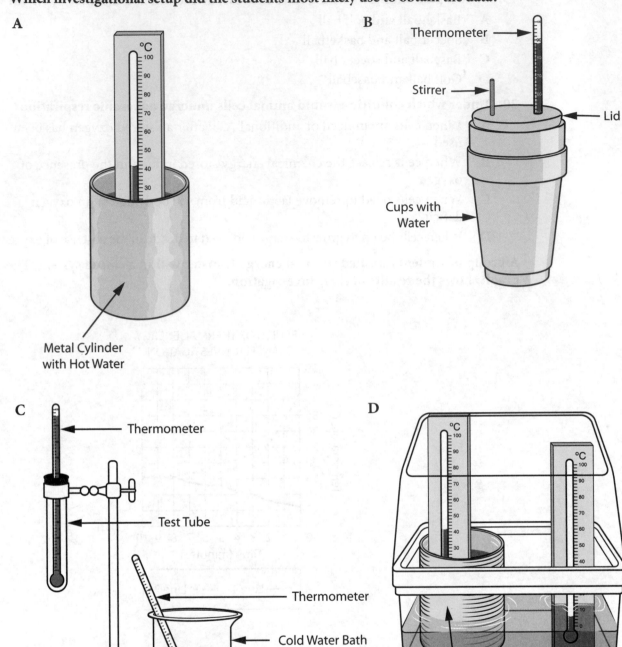

°C
100
90
80
70
60
50
40
30

Metal Cylinder
with Hot Water

B

Thermometer

Stirrer

Lid

Cups with
Water

C

Thermometer

Test Tube

Thermometer

Cold Water Bath

Ring Stand

D

°C
100
90
80
70
60
50
40
30

°C
100
90
80
70
60
50
40

Hot Water
(inside can)

Cold Water

22. **What can be determined from the embryonic development of the organisms shown in the diagram?**

Fish    Salamander    Tortoise    Chicken    Pig    Cow    Rabbit

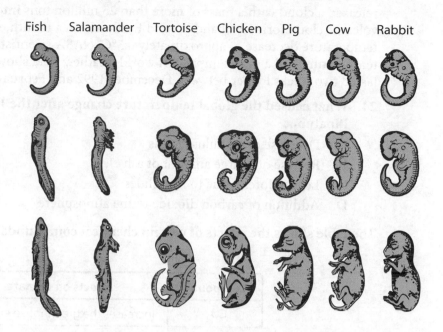

A    The organisms all evolved from a common ancestor.

B    The organisms all formed analogous structures.

C    The organisms all occupied different niches.

D    The organisms all shared the same habitat.

23. **Which method is best used to determine the absolute age of Earth?**

A    Examining rocks from recent volcanic eruptions

B    Applying radiation measurements to geologic rocks

C    Using the principle of superposition for rock layers

D    Dating rocks based on estimates from the fossil record

**GO ON TO THE NEXT PAGE ➡**

**Questions 24–25 are based on the following information.**

Mount Pinatubo is a volcano in the Philippines that erupted in 1991. The volcano released a cloud with a mass of more than 25 million tons into the stratosphere. The volcanic cloud formed a band around Earth within a month, resulting in a global temperature decrease of approximately 0.5°C. NASA scientists said the drop in global temperature had a major impact on world weather. Data showed that winter conditions lasted two weeks longer between December 1992 and February 1993.

24. **What caused the global temperature change after the 1991 eruption of Mount Pinatubo?**

    A   Decrease of cumulus clouds

    B   Release of a large amount of ash

    C   Loss of forests due to mudslides

    D   Addition of carbon dioxide to the atmosphere

The table shows the effects of certain chemical compounds on the climate.

| Compound | Effects on Climate |
|----------|--------------------|
| $CO_2$ | Increases the greenhouse effect |
| $H_2O$ | Traps thermal energy from Earth |
| $SO_2$ | Reflects the sun's radiation |
| HCl | Depletes the ozone layer |

25. **Based on the table, which compound most likely caused the cooling of Earth's atmosphere after the eruption of Mount Pinatubo?**

    A   $CO_2$

    B   $H_2O$

    C   $SO_2$

    D   HCl

# ANSWERS AND EXPLANATIONS—SCIENCE

| Question Number | Correct Answer | Content Category | Rationale |
|---|---|---|---|
| 1 | D | Life Science | This variable is part of the feedback mechanism for the organelles taken by the sea of slugs. |
| 2 | A | Life Science | This occurs in the mitosis process. |
| 3 | C | Life Science | Studying this question will help scientists determine if sea slugs control the function of the organelles taken from algae. |
| 4 | A | Earth and Space Science | A red shift in the spectrum supports the universe is expanding thus providing evidence for the Big Bang Theory |
| 5 | D | Earth and Space Science | Spectral lines provide identification for specific elements, not number of planets. |
| 6 | B | Physical Sciences | These elements have valence electrons in the same energy level. |
| 7 | B | Life Science | Transpiration is a feedback mechanism controlled by the stomata. |
| 8 | A | Life Science | Evidence of zebra herd behavior is evaluated for benefits of survival. |
| 9 | B | Physical Sciences | The reaction produces salt and water which identifies a neutralization reaction. |
| 10 | D | Physical Sciences | $2.4 \times 2 = 4.8$ |
| 11 | B | Physical Sciences | $(36 \text{ g } H_2O \times 1 \text{ mol } H_2O \times 2 \text{ mol } NaOH \times 40 \text{ g } NaOH)/(18 \text{ g } H_2O \times 2 \text{ mol } H_2O \times 1 \text{ mol } NaOH)$ |
| 12 | C | Life Science | Students evaluate the impact of the release of an invasive species in an aquatic environment. |
| 13 | D | Life Science | Students evaluate the impact of over pumping in an aquatic environment. |
| 14 | C | Life Science | Students evaluate a simulation to study the impact of a human released invasive species on another species. |
| 15 | C | Life Science | Students determine changes to the population based on seasonal changes, which could contribute to the expansion or decline of the species. |

*(Continued)*

| Question Number | Correct Answer | Content Category | Rationale |
|---|---|---|---|
| 16 | A | Life Science | Students determine a solution to the simulation regarding the fountain darter population. |
| 17 | C | Earth and Space Science | This model shows a nuclear fusion which provides the Sun's radiation to Earth. |
| 18 | D | Life Science | This behavior provides evidence for the role of group behavior for survival. |
| 19 | D | Physical Sciences | $F = (6.67 \times 10^{-11})(0.046)(0.145)/(0.5)^2$ $= 1.8 \times 10^{-12}$ N |
| 20 | A | Life Science | Provides evidence for the flow of energy in anaerobic conditions. |
| 21 | D | Physical Sciences | This investigation measures the change in temperature of water at two different initial temperatures until the final temperature for both is the same. |
| 22 | A | Life Science | The similar embryonic sequence supports common ancestry. |
| 23 | B | Earth and Space Science | Applying this process to Earth materials provides information/evidence for determining the absolute age of Earth. |
| 24 | B | Earth and Space Science | The Mt. Pinatubo eruption released enough ash into the stratosphere to impact and cool the climate. |
| 25 | C | Earth and Space Science | This compound would have reflected the sun's radiation and caused a decrease in temperature. |

# HiSET® Exam Diagnostic Test
# Answer Sheet
# Language Arts—Reading

| | A | B | C | D |
|---|---|---|---|---|
| 1 | | | | |
| 2 | | | | |
| 3 | | | | |
| 4 | | | | |
| 5 | | | | |
| 6 | | | | |
| 7 | | | | |
| 8 | | | | |
| 9 | | | | |
| 10 | | | | |

| | A | B | C | D |
|---|---|---|---|---|
| 11 | | | | |
| 12 | | | | |
| 13 | | | | |
| 14 | | | | |
| 15 | | | | |
| 16 | | | | |
| 17 | | | | |
| 18 | | | | |
| 19 | | | | |
| 20 | | | | |

# LANGUAGE ARTS—READING

**20 Questions**

**25 Minutes**

## Directions

This is a test of some of the skills involved in understanding what you read. The passages in this test come from a variety of published works, both literary and informational. Each passage is followed by a number of questions. The passages begin with an introduction presenting information that may be helpful as you read the selection. After you have read a passage, go on to the questions that follow. For each question, choose the best answer, and mark your choice on the answer sheet. You may refer to a passage as often as necessary.

Work as quickly as you can without becoming careless. Don't spend too much time on any question that is difficult for you to answer. Instead, skip it and return to it later if you have time. Try to answer every question even if you have to guess.

Mark all your answers on the answer sheet. Give only one answer to each question and make every mark heavy and dark. If you decide to change one of your answers, be sure to erase the first mark completely. Be sure that the number of the question you are answering matches the number of the row of answer choices you are marking on your answer sheet.

### Questions 1 to 11 refer to the passage below.

**In the excerpt below by Saki, a young lady entertains a guest while he waits to be introduced to her aunt.**

#### The Open Window

"My aunt will be down presently, Mr. Nuttel," said a very self-possessed young lady of fifteen; "in the meantime you must try and put up with me."

Framton Nuttel endeavoured to say the correct something which should duly flatter
Line the niece . . . without unduly discounting the aunt that was to come. Privately he
5 doubted more than ever whether these formal visits on a succession of total strangers would do much towards helping the nerve cure which he was supposed to be undergoing.

"I know how it will be," his sister had said when he was preparing to migrate to this rural retreat; "you will bury yourself down there and not speak to a living soul, and
10 your nerves will be worse than ever from moping. I shall just give you letters of introduction to all the people I know there. Some of them, as far as I can remember, were quite nice."

Framton wondered whether Mrs. Sappleton, the lady to whom he was presenting one of the letters of introduction, came into the nice division.

15 "Do you know many of the people round here?" asked the niece, when she judged that they had had sufficient silent communion.

"Hardly a soul," said Framton. "My sister was staying here, . . . some four years ago, and she gave me letters of introduction to some of the people here."

**GO ON TO THE NEXT PAGE ➡**

87

. . . "Then you know practically nothing about my aunt?" pursued the self-possessed
young lady.

"Only her name and address," admitted the caller. . . .

"Her great tragedy happened just three years ago," said the child; "that would be
since your sister's time."

"Her tragedy?" asked Framton; somehow in this restful country spot tragedies
seemed out of place.

"You may wonder why we keep that window wide open on an October afternoon,"
said the niece, indicating a large French window that opened on to a lawn.

"It is quite warm for the time of the year," said Framton; "but has that window got
anything to do with the tragedy?"

"Out through that window, three years ago to a day, her husband and her two young
brothers went off for their day's shooting. They never came back. In crossing the moor
to their favourite snipe-shooting ground they were all three engulfed in a treacherous
piece of bog. . . . Their bodies were never recovered." . . . Here the child's voice lost its
self-possessed note and became falteringly human. "Poor aunt always thinks that they
will come back some day, they and the little brown spaniel that was lost with them, and
walk in at that window just as they used to do. That is why the window is kept open
every evening till it is quite dusk. Poor dear aunt, she has often told me how they went
out, her husband with his white waterproof coat over his arm, and Ronnie, her
youngest brother, singing 'Bertie, why do you bound?' as he always did to tease her,
because she said it got on her nerves. Do you know, sometimes on still, quiet evenings
like this, I almost get a creepy feeling that they will all walk in through that window—"

She broke off with a little shudder. It was a relief to Framton when the aunt bustled
into the room with a whirl of apologies for being late in making her appearance.

"I hope Vera has been amusing you?" she said.

"She has been very interesting," said Framton.

"I hope you don't mind the open window," said Mrs. Sappleton briskly; "my husband
and brothers will be home directly from shooting, and they always come in this way.
They've been out for snipe in the marshes today, so they'll make a fine mess over my
poor carpets."

She rattled on cheerfully about . . . the scarcity of birds and the prospects for duck in
the winter. To Framton it was all purely horrible. He made a desperate but only
partially successful effort to turn the talk on to a less ghastly topic; he was conscious
that his hostess was giving him only a fragment of her attention, and her eyes were
constantly straying past him to the open window and the lawn beyond. It was certainly
an unfortunate coincidence that he should have paid his visit on this tragic
anniversary.

"The doctors agree in ordering me complete rest, an absence of mental excitement,
and avoidance of anything in the nature of violent physical exercise," announced
Framton, who laboured under the tolerably widespread delusion that total strangers
and chance acquaintances are hungry for the least detail of one's ailments and
infirmities, their cause and cure. "On the matter of diet they are not so much in
agreement," he continued.

"No?" said Mrs. Sappleton, in a voice which only replaced a yawn at the last
moment. Then she suddenly brightened into alert attention—but not to what
Framton was saying.

"Here they are at last!" she cried. "Just in time for tea, and don't they look as if they
were muddy up to the eyes!"

88

Framton shivered slightly and turned towards the niece with a look intended to
convey sympathetic comprehension. The child was staring out through the open
70 window with dazed horror in her eyes. In a chill shock of nameless fear, Framton
swung round in his seat and looked in the same direction.

In the deepening twilight, three figures were walking across the lawn towards the
window; they all carried guns under their arms, and one of them was additionally
burdened with a white coat hung over his shoulders. A tired brown spaniel kept close
75 at their heels. Noiselessly they neared the house, and then a hoarse young voice
chanted out of the dusk: "I said, Bertie, why do you bound?"

Framton grabbed wildly at his stick and hat; the hall-door, the gravel-drive, and the
front gate were dimly-noted stages in his headlong retreat. A cyclist coming along the
road had to run into the hedge to avoid an imminent collision.

80 "Here we are, my dear," said the bearer of the white mackintosh,[1] coming in through
the window; "fairly muddy, but most of it's dry. Who was that who bolted out as we
came up?"

"A most extraordinary man, a Mr. Nuttel," said Mrs. Sappleton; "could only talk
about his illnesses, and dashed off without a word of good-bye or apology when you
85 arrived. One would think he had seen a ghost."

"I expect it was the spaniel," said the niece calmly; "he told me he had a horror of
dogs. He was once hunted into a cemetery somewhere on the banks of the Ganges by a
pack of . . . dogs, and had to spend the night in a newly dug grave with the creatures
snarling . . . just above him. Enough to make anyone lose their nerve."

90 Romance at short notice was her speciality.

1. **Read this sentence from lines 78–79.**

*A cyclist coming along the road had to run into the hedge to avoid an __imminent__ collision.*

**What is the meaning of __imminent__ as it is used in this sentence?**
   A   ambiguous
   B   dangerous
   C   looming
   D   surprising

2. **What can the reader infer about Framton's sister?**
   A   She often interferes in her brother's life.
   B   She focuses solely on her brother's health.
   C   Her concerns about her brother's condition are unfounded.
   D   Her involvement in her brother's relationships is unwanted.

3. **What is the underlying purpose of Mr. Framton's visit?**
   A   He wants to learn more about Mrs. Sappleton and her niece.
   B   He hopes to address his medical issues.
   C   He plans to meet Mrs. Sappleton using his letter of introduction.
   D   He intends to meet with all of the local residents.

---

[1]**mackintosh:** a rainproof coat

4. **Read this excerpt from lines 15–20.**

*"Do you know many of the people round here?" asked the niece, when she judged that they had had sufficient silent communion.*

*"Hardly a soul," said Framton. "My sister was staying here, . . . some four years ago, and she gave me letters of introduction to some of the people here."*

*. . . "Then you know practically nothing about my aunt?" pursued the self-possessed young lady.*

**The niece's primary motive for asking these questions is to**

    **A**   learn additional details about Framton's past.

    **B**   see if she and Framton have friends in common.

    **C**   find out how Framton knows her aunt.

    **D**   determine if she can trick Framton.

5. **In lines 30–40, the author provides a detailed description of the hunters in order to**

    **A**   foreshadow an event.

    **B**   create a nostalgic mood.

    **C**   develop a universal theme.

    **D**   establish a hopeless tone.

6. **Read this sentence from lines 42–43.**

*It was a relief to Framton when the aunt* <u>bustled into the room with a whirl of apologies</u> *for being late in making her appearance.*

**The author uses the underlined text to show that**

    **A**   Framton is impatient.

    **B**   Framton is annoyed.

    **C**   the aunt is irresponsible.

    **D**   the aunt is distracted.

7. **Which excerpt from the passage best supports the idea that Framton is awkward around other people?**

    **A**   "I know how it will be," his sister had said when he was preparing to migrate to this rural retreat; "you will bury yourself down there and not speak to a living soul, . . ."

    **B**   ". . . your nerves will be worse than ever from moping."

    **C**   Framton wondered whether Mrs. Sappleton, the lady to whom he was presenting one of the letters of introduction, came into the nice division.

    **D**   "Her tragedy?" asked Framton; somehow in this restful country spot tragedies seemed out of place.

**8.** Read these sentences from lines 69–71.

*The child was staring out through the open window with dazed horror in her eyes. In a chill shock of nameless fear, Framton swung round in his seat and looked in the same direction.*

**The author's word choice in these sentences affects the tone of the passage by creating a sense of**

    **A** dismay.

    **B** confusion.

    **C** dread.

    **D** urgency.

**9.** **One way Framton differs from the niece is**

    **A** Framton is confident while the niece is timid.

    **B** Framton is gullible while the niece is cunning.

    **C** Framton is uncaring while the niece is concerned.

    **D** Framton is calm while the niece is nervous.

**10.** **Which statement best describes a theme of the passage?**

    **A** New friendships often lead to betrayal.

    **B** Courage is needed to cope with conflict.

    **C** Discovering inner peace requires solitude.

    **D** Perception and reality do not always align.

**11.** **What have the aunt and uncle most likely learned about their niece?**

    **A** Their niece does not enjoy entertaining guests in their home.

    **B** Their niece delights in making others uncomfortable.

    **C** Their niece does not take pleasure in typical pastimes.

    **D** Their niece acts much younger than her age.

**Questions 12 to 20 refer to the passage below.**

David H. Onkst wrote this online article about the first woman in the United States to earn a pilot's license.

### Harriet Quimby

Harriet Quimby, a journalist by training, was the first major female pilot in the United States, and one of the world's best women aviators. In 1911, she became the first licensed female pilot in the United States, and less than a year later, became the first
*Line* woman to fly across the English Channel. Although Quimby lived only to age 37, she
*5* had a major impact on women's roles in aviation; she was a true pioneer and helped break down stereotypes about women's abilities during the first decade of flight. Quimby was also very beautiful and stylish. At a time when other pilots, most of whom were male, flew in undistinguished gear, she designed her own trademark flight suit, a purple satin outfit with a hood, which she wore whenever she flew.
*10*     Quimby was born to a family of farmers on May 11, 1875, near Coldwater, Michigan. Because none of her early records still exist, scholars have been unable to piece together much about her early life. Her story consequently picks up when her

GO ON TO THE NEXT PAGE ➡

family moved to San Francisco in the early 1900s. At that time, Quimby was an aspiring actress, but despite her beauty and apparent theatrical flair, she chose to become a journalist and drama critic.

In 1903, Quimby moved to New York City and quickly acquired a job as a regular contributor and photographer for the well-known periodical *Leslie's Illustrated Weekly*. During her career with *Leslie's*—which would span nine years—Quimby contributed more than 250 articles. She wrote about housekeeping and also published several drama reviews. But Quimby wanted more exhilarating assignments, and she got her wish. In 1906, she told readers what it was like to zip along in an open-air automobile at speeds in excess of 100 miles per hour. The article revealed her strong interest in machines and speed, some of the qualities that would attract her to aviation.

Quimby became interested in aviation in late October 1910, when she attended the Belmont Park International Aviation Tournament on Long Island. There she met John Moisant, a well-known American aviator, and his sister Matilde. John and his brother Alfred operated a flight school on Long Island. Quimby, who had become enamored with flight while watching the meet, suddenly wanted to learn to fly and asked Alfred to instruct her and Matilde. Alfred agreed.

Quimby had originally intended to keep her flight lessons a secret, but eventually the press discovered that women were learning to fly, and she and Matilde became a big story (although it is uncertain whether the press "discovered" the story or whether Harriet led them to it). Whatever the case, Harriet took matters into her own hands and capitalized on the situation by beginning a series of articles for *Leslie's* about her aviation experiences. On August 1, 1911, Quimby took her pilot's test and became the first U.S. woman to earn a pilot's license.

Quimby sailed for England in March 1912 to pursue her main aviation goal: to become the first woman to fly across the English Channel. Although Louis Blériot had flown the Channel in July 1909, no woman had ever accomplished the feat. Blériot, intrigued by Quimby's goal, shipped her one of his Blériot monoplanes—a 50-horsepower, single-seat aircraft—for her flight. Except for Blériot and a few others, no one knew of Quimby's plan. She wanted to keep it secret because she feared that another woman might try to make the flight before she did. She also feared that people might try to stop her because of the dangers involved, especially the Channel's unpredictable weather.

On April 16, 1912, Quimby took off from Dover, England, en route to Calais, France. Flying at altitudes between 1,000 and 2,000 feet, Quimby fought her way through the fog-choked sky and made the flight in 59 minutes, having drifted somewhat off target and landing about 25 miles from Calais on a beach in Hardelot, France. She had become the first woman to fly the English Channel. Very few people learned of her accomplishment, though, because of the poor press coverage it received. The *Titanic* had sunk only two days before and was still the major news of the day. Quimby's story was relegated to the last page.

After crossing the Channel, Quimby returned to New York and resumed exhibition flying. But her career ended prematurely in tragedy. On July 1, 1912, flying in the Third Annual Boston Aviation Meet at Squantum, Massachusetts, with William Willard, the event's organizer aboard, her brand-new 70-horsepower, two-seat, Blériot monoplane unexpectedly pitched forward, ejecting both Willard and Quimby. The two plunged to their deaths in front of some 5,000 horrified spectators.

There has been considerable debate about the cause of the accident. As aviation writers Patricia Browne and Giacinta Bradley Koontz noted, there are several theories about the tragedy. Both the *Boston Globe* and the well-known aviator Glenn Martin

claimed within days of the accident that the tragedy would not have happened if Quimby and Willard had been wearing seat belts. Earle Ovington, one of the meet's
65 officials, argued that some of the plane's cables had gotten tangled in the steering mechanisms, causing Quimby to lose control. Whatever the cause, the result was still the same. Quimby, one of aviation's early pioneers, had lost her life only 11 months after she had learned to fly.

Although Quimby was not a suffragette,[2] she did champion many women's issues.
70 During her journalism career, she wrote articles about child welfare and political corruption and vice in New York City. She also pressed for an expanded role for women aviators. As she noted in an exclusive article for *Good Housekeeping*, which was published posthumously, "There is no reason why the aeroplane [the spelling of the day] should not open up a fruitful occupation for women. I see no reason why they
75 cannot realize handsome incomes by carrying passengers between adjacent towns, why they cannot derive incomes from parcel delivery, from taking photographs from above, or from conducting schools for flying. Any of these things it is now possible to do."

One woman whom Quimby inspired was Amelia Earhart. As Earhart would say about her personal hero: "To cross the Channel in 1912 required more bravery and
80 skill than to cross the Atlantic today . . . we must remember that, in thinking of America's first great woman flier's accomplishment." For Earhart and other women, Quimby was a pioneer who helped overturn stereotypes about women's roles in society, and who made it possible for them to achieve their dreams.

**12.** **In line 8, "undistinguished" means**

   **A**  plain.

   **B**  inferior.

   **C**  seasonal.

   **D**  customary.

**13.** **Which generalization can be made based on information in lines 30–35?**

   **A**  The pilot test Quimby took was difficult compared to today's tests.

   **B**  The articles Quimby wrote about flying were more popular than her previous work.

   **C**  It is likely that Quimby gave the story of her learning to fly to the press.

   **D**  Both Quimby and Alfred strived to keep her flying lessons a secret.

**14.** **The author included information in lines 37–45 most likely to show that Quimby**

   **A**  needed to keep her plans private so that she could write an exclusive story about the event.

   **B**  appreciated Louis Blériot for offering her use of his monoplane.

   **C**  wanted recognition for being the first woman to fly over the Channel.

   **D**  recognized that uncertain weather conditions might impede her flight over the Channel.

---

[2]**suffragette:** a woman who advocates voting rights for women

GO ON TO THE NEXT PAGE ➡

15. **Read the quotation by Jacqueline Cochran, a United States aviator who held several speed records and headed the Women Airforce Service Pilots (WASP) in World War II.**

> I can't give up. If I concede this [flying in the Bendix Race], women will be barred from racing for years, maybe even forever.
>
> —*Jacqueline Cochran, 1935*

**Based on information in the passage about Quimby and the quotation from Cochran, both female aviators would most likely agree that women**

   **A**   should have modified rules for flying.

   **B**   must be diligent about their right to fly.

   **C**   can aspire to setting records in aviation.

   **D**   have aviation skills superior to those of men.

16. **Which sentence from the passage expresses an opinion?**

   **A**   Because none of her early records still exist, scholars have been unable to piece together much about her early life.

   **B**   Quimby became interested in aviation in late October 1910, when she attended the Belmont Park International Aviation Tournament on Long Island.

   **C**   After crossing the Channel, Quimby returned to New York and resumed exhibition flying.

   **D**   Earle Ovington, one of the meet's officials, argued that some of the plane's cables had gotten tangled in the steering mechanisms, causing Quimby to lose control.

17. **What can the reader predict would have happened if Quimby had not perished at such a young age?**

   **A**   Aviation safety would have become a focus of Quimby's career.

   **B**   Quimby would have fulfilled her ambition of becoming an actress.

   **C**   A biography would have been written about Quimby's other accomplishments.

   **D**   Quimby would have continued to support issues that helped women succeed.

18. **Which accomplishment was most likely Quimby's proudest moment?**

   **A**   Becoming a drama critic

   **B**   Writing for the popular journal *Leslie's*

   **C**   Earning a license to fly

   **D**   Inspiring a pilot like Amelia Earhart

19. **Which words from the passage best support the significance of Quimby's accomplishments?**

   **A**   Pilot, trademark, aviation

   **B**   Major, exhilarating, champion

   **C**   Stereotypes, decade, achieve

   **D**   Abilities, contributor, instruct

**20.** **Which sentence best states the main idea of lines 69–77?**

   **A**   Quimby advocated for progress for women, especially in aviation as a career.

   **B**   Quimby wanted women to become involved in government to control corruption.

   **C**   Quimby was a suffragette because she supported women's rights.

   **D**   Quimby used journalism to draw attention to social issues, including welfare programs for children.

# ANSWERS AND EXPLANATIONS—READING

| Question Number | Correct Answer | Content Category | Rationale |
| --- | --- | --- | --- |
| 1 | C | Comprehension | In lines 78–79, "imminent" is used to explain that a collision with Framton was "looming" had the cyclist not swerved into the hedge. |
| 2 | A | Inference and interpretation | The reader can infer that Framton's sister often interferes in his life since she insists that he use her introductory letters to meet people during his stay in the country. |
| 3 | B | Comprehension | Lines 57–62 support the idea that the underlying purpose of Framton's visit is to address his medical issue of a nervous condition. |
| 4 | D | Inference and interpretation | Based on the niece's subsequent actions, the reader can infer that she is trying to determine if and how she can deceive the visitor. |
| 5 | A | Analysis | The author foreshadows the hunters' return in order to set up the ensuing climax. |
| 6 | D | Inference and interpretation | Bustling into a room with a "whirl of apologies" for keeping her visitor waiting indicates that the aunt is distracted by other concerns. |
| 7 | A | Inference and interpretation | The fact that Framton's sister suspects he will not socialize with others indicates that he is likely awkward around other people. |
| 8 | C | Comprehension | The words "dazed horror," "chill shock," and "nameless fear" create a sense of dread. |
| 9 | B | Analysis | Framton is gullible and readily believes the story the niece tells him. The niece is cunning since she plays a trick on Framton. |
| 10 | D | Analysis | Framton's, and the reader's, perceptions turn out to be quite different from what is actually real. |
| 11 | B | Synthesis and Generalization | The reader can conclude that the aunt and uncle realize that the niece is quite dramatic and enjoys making up stories that make others feel uneasy. |

| Question Number | Correct Answer | Content Category | Rationale |
| --- | --- | --- | --- |
| 12 | A | Comprehension | In line 8, "undistinguished" refers to the "plain" attire worn by male pilots compared to the colorful and stylish flight suit worn by Quimby. |
| 13 | C | Synthesis and Generalization | The information in the parentheses (lines 32–33) intimates that Quimby likely released the story to the press. |
| 14 | C | Analysis | Quimby wanted recognition for being the first woman to fly over the channel, which is why she kept her plan a secret. She did not want another woman to make the flight before she did. |
| 15 | B | Synthesis and Generalization | Quimby was adamant about women having the opportunity to fly, "There is no reason why the aeroplane should not open up a fruitful occupation for women." By "never giving up," Cochran also showed her support for women in aviation. |
| 16 | D | Analysis | All of the options are facts except for option D, which describes Ovington's opinion about why Quimby lost control of her plane. |
| 17 | D | Synthesis and Generalization | Had Quimby lived beyond the age of 37, she would most likely have continued to support women's issues so that they could succeed (lines 69–77). |
| 18 | C | Inference and interpretation | Because Quimby was the first woman to earn a pilot's license, this is most likely her proudest moment. |
| 19 | B | Comprehension | Major, exhilarating, and champion best describe the significance of Quimby's accomplishments. The other options offer descriptors that do not necessarily describe her accomplishments. |
| 20 | A | Analysis | The quotation in lines 73–77 supports the idea that Quimby advocated women's rights and their involvement in aviation as a career; they could carry passengers, deliver parcels, take photographs from above, or teach others how to fly. |

# *HiSET*® Exam Diagnostic Test
# Answer Sheet
# Math

|    | A | B | C | D | E |    | A | B | C | D | E |
|----|---|---|---|---|---|----|---|---|---|---|---|
| 1  |   |   |   |   |   | 14 |   |   |   |   |   |
| 2  |   |   |   |   |   | 15 |   |   |   |   |   |
| 3  |   |   |   |   |   | 16 |   |   |   |   |   |
| 4  |   |   |   |   |   | 17 |   |   |   |   |   |
| 5  |   |   |   |   |   | 18 |   |   |   |   |   |
| 6  |   |   |   |   |   | 19 |   |   |   |   |   |
| 7  |   |   |   |   |   | 20 |   |   |   |   |   |
| 8  |   |   |   |   |   | 21 |   |   |   |   |   |
| 9  |   |   |   |   |   | 22 |   |   |   |   |   |
| 10 |   |   |   |   |   | 23 |   |   |   |   |   |
| 11 |   |   |   |   |   | 24 |   |   |   |   |   |
| 12 |   |   |   |   |   | 25 |   |   |   |   |   |
| 13 |   |   |   |   |   |    |   |   |   |   |   |

# MATH (4-function calculators allowed)

### 25 Questions

### 45 Minutes

## Directions

This is a test of your skills in applying mathematical concepts and solving mathematical problems. Read each question carefully and decide which of the five alternatives best answers the question. Then mark your choice on your answer sheet. There are relatively easy problems scattered throughout the test. Thus, do not waste time on problems that are too difficult; go on, and return to them if you have time.

Work as quickly as you can without becoming careless. Don't spend too much time on any question that is difficult for you to answer. Instead, skip it and return to it later if you have time. Try to answer every question even if you have to guess.

Mark all your answers on the answer sheet. Give only one answer to each question and make every mark heavy and dark. If you decide to change one of your answers, be sure to erase the first mark completely. Be sure that the number of the question you are answering matches the number of the row of answer choices you are marking on your answer sheet.

1. **Which fraction is equivalent to $0.\overline{2}$?**

    A $\dfrac{2}{9}$

    B $\dfrac{2}{10}$

    C $\dfrac{2}{99}$

    D $\dfrac{2}{100}$

    E $\dfrac{20}{99}$

**GO ON TO THE NEXT PAGE** ➡

2.  The box-and-whisker plots summarize the numbers of leaves collected by students in Group A and Group B.

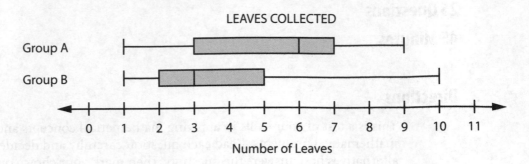

LEAVES COLLECTED

Number of Leaves

What percentage of the number of students in Group A collected more leaves than the median number of leaves collected by students in Group B?

    A   10%

    B   25%

    C   50%

    D   75%

    E   90%

3.  This set of ordered pairs represents some input and output values for a function.

$$\{(1, 7), (-3, 0), (5, 6), (9, 4), (2, 2)\}$$

Which set of ordered pairs could also belong to this function?

    A   $\{(4, 7), (3, -6), (-1, 5), (0, -3), (-8, 4)\}$

    B   $\{(3, 1), (-4, -6), (8, 5), (2, -9), (-7, 2)\}$

    C   $\{(3, 7), (0, -2), (9, 8), (-1, -1), (-6, 5)\}$

    D   $\{(-8, -2), (4, 9), (6, -7), (3, 0), (2, 5)\}$

    E   $\{(-6, 2), (5, 1), (-7, -4), (8, -5), (3, 9)\}$

4. **Rhombus *PQRS* is shown on the coordinate grid.**

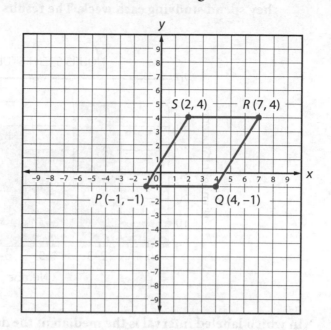

Rhombus *PQRS* is reflected across the *x*-axis to create rhombus *P′Q′R′S′*. Which statements are true?

    I.  The slope of $\overline{PS}$ is equal to the slope of *P′S′*

   II.  $\angle QRS \cong \angle Q′R′S′$

  III.  The coordinates of *P′* are $(-1, 1)$.

  IV.  $\angle PSR \cong \angle S′P′Q′$

  **A**  I and II only

  **B**  II and III only

  **C**  III and IV only

  **D**  I and III only

  **E**  II and IV only

5. **Which polynomial is equivalent to the expression shown?**

$$(2x - 3)(x^2 + x - 5)$$

  **A**  $2x^3 - x^2 + 7x - 15$

  **B**  $2x^3 - x^2 - 13x + 15$

  **C**  $2x^3 - x^2 - 13x - 15$

  **D**  $2x^3 + 5x^2 - 7x - 15$

  **E**  $2x^3 + 5x^2 + 13x + 15$

GO ON TO THE NEXT PAGE ➡

6.  Students at Johnson Middle School took a survey about the number of hours they spend studying each week. The results are shown in the histogram.

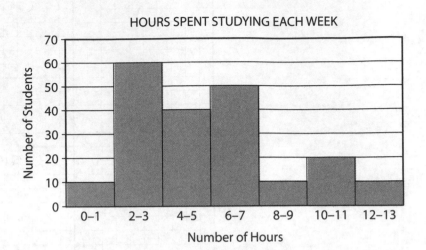

HOURS SPENT STUDYING EACH WEEK

In which labeled interval is the median of the data located?

A   0–1

B   2–3

C   4–5

D   6–7

E   12–13

7.  Which number is irrational?

A   $\pi$

B   $-\dfrac{5}{6}$

C   $\sqrt{81}$

D   $-0.\overline{4}$

E   $1.34 \times 10^4$

8. The graph of $y = \sqrt{16 - x^2 - 6x + 2}$ is shown.

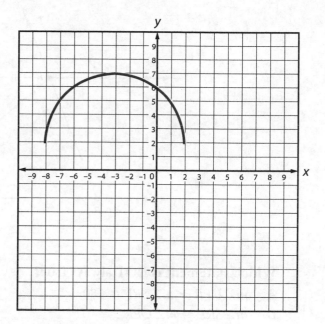

What appears to be the domain of the function?

A $2 \leq x \leq 7$

B $2 \leq y \leq 7$

C $-8 \leq x \leq 2$

D $-8 \leq y \leq 2$

E $-10 \leq x \leq 10$

9. A national service organization has proposed to change their logo.

- Four hundred randomly selected members of the organization were surveyed.
- Of those surveyed, 51% did not support changing the logo.
- The margin of error for the survey is 3%.

Based on this information, which conclusion is the most valid?

A The results of the survey are not valid because the margin of error is large.

B The results of the survey are not valid because only 400 members were surveyed.

C The margin of error is not necessary when interpreting the data because the sample was random.

D The percentage of the members who support changing the logo may be more than 50% given the margin of error.

E The organization can be confident that there is less than 50% of the members who support changing the logo because the sample was random.

GO ON TO THE NEXT PAGE ➡

10. In the figure shown, $\overline{RS} \mid \overline{PQ}$ and points $P$, $R$, and $T$ are collinear.

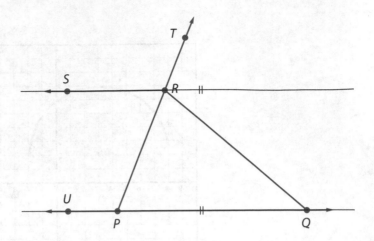

Which statement is NOT always true?

A   $m\angle UPR + m\angle SRP = 180$

B   $m\angle SRP = m\angle QPR$

C   $m\angle SRT = m\angle RPQ + m\angle RQP$

D   $m\angle RPU = m\angle PRQ + m\angle RQP$

E   $m\angle PRQ + m\angle RQP + m\angle QPR = m\angle SRP + m\angle SRT$

11. The average distance from Earth to the Sun is approximately $9 \times 10^7$ miles. The average distance from Saturn to the Sun is approximately $9 \times 10^8$ miles. Based on these values, the average distance from Saturn to the Sun is how many times the average distance from Earth to the Sun?

A   $\dfrac{1}{90}$

B   $\dfrac{1}{10}$

C   1

D   10

E   90

12. **The graph of a function is shown.**

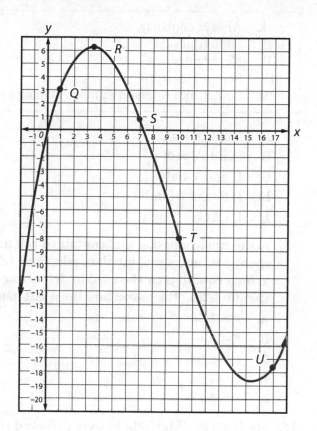

**Which point on the graph of the function is located where the function appears to be negative and increasing?**

  A   Point *Q*
  B   Point *R*
  C   Point *S*
  D   Point *T*
  E   Point *U*

13. **The masses, in grams, of 11 apples are listed.**

70, 72, 75, 77, 82, 83, 83, 90, 92, 94, 95

**An additional apple with a mass of 143 grams was added to the list. Which two statistical measures had the greatest combined increase when the mass of the twelfth apple was added?**

  A   The mean and the range
  B   The median and the range
  C   The mean and the interquartile range
  D   The interquartile range and the range
  E   The median and the interquartile range

GO ON TO THE NEXT PAGE ➡

14. **Which descriptions about parallel lines are true?**

> I.   Always coplanar
> II.  Sometimes collinear
> III. Never intersect
> IV.  Sometimes skew
> V.   Sometimes intersect at more than one point

   **A**  I and III only

   **B**  I and IV only

   **C**  II and V only

   **D**  I, II, and III only

   **E**  I, IV, and V only

15. **Justin made a basket that contained gift bags for visitors to the health fair. He spent 5 minutes making the basket and 1.5 minutes assembling each gift bag. Which equation can be used to determine $t$, the total number of minutes Justin spent making the basket and the $n$ gift bags it contained?**

   **A**  $t = 1.5n$

   **B**  $t = 5n$

   **C**  $t = 6.5n$

   **D**  $t = 1.5n + 5$

   **E**  $t = 5n + 1.5$

16. **Students at a high school were surveyed regarding their favorite subject from the four listed in the table. The results of the survey are shown.**

STUDENT SURVEY

|  | Freshman | Sophomore | Junior | Senior | Total |
|---|---|---|---|---|---|
| **English** | 225 | 240 | 115 | 90 | 670 |
| **Math** | 225 | 150 | 110 | 162 | 647 |
| **Science** | 150 | 120 | 175 | 162 | 607 |
| **Social Studies** | 150 | 90 | 100 | 36 | 376 |
| **Total** | 750 | 600 | 500 | 450 | 2,300 |

**Based on the data in the table, approximately what percentage of Juniors and Seniors chose English as their favorite subject?**

   **A**  9%

   **B**  12%

   **C**  17%

   **D**  22%

   **E**  31%

17. Bobby and Sally each released one helium balloon at the same time. The equation represents $h_1$, the height of Bobby's balloon in feet, $t$ seconds after Bobby released his balloon.

$$h_1 = 3t + 5$$

The table shows $h_2$, the height of Sally's balloon in feet, $t$ seconds after Sally released her balloon.

SALLY'S BALLOON

| Time, $t$ (seconds) | Height, $h_2$ (feet) |
|---|---|
| 1 | 8 |
| 3 | 15 |
| 8 | 32.5 |

The equation and the table both represent linear functions. Which statements are true?

    I.   Bobby's balloon was released at a greater height than Sally's balloon.
    II.  Sally's balloon was released at a greater height than Bobby's balloon.
    III. Bobby's balloon rose faster than Sally's balloon.
    IV.  Sally's balloon rose faster than Bobby's balloon.
    V.   Bobby's balloon was at a greater height than Sally's balloon at $t = 8$ seconds.

   A   I and III only
   B   I and IV only
   C   II and V only
   D   II and IV only
   E   III and V only

18. The radii of a cone and of a sphere are each 9 inches. The volume of the cone is equal to the volume of the sphere. What is the height of the cone in inches?

   A   6
   B   9
   C   12
   D   36
   E   108

GO ON TO THE NEXT PAGE ➡

19. The manager at Rusty's Rent-A-Bike uses the equation shown to determine the total cost, $c$, of renting a bike for $h$ hours.

$$c = 5h + 15$$

Which statement best interprets the slope and $y$-intercept of the equation?

A  There is an initial deposit of $5 and a charge of $15 per hour.

B  There is an initial deposit of $15 and a charge of $5 per hour.

C  There is an initial deposit of $20 and a charge of $5 per hour.

D  There is an initial deposit of $20 and a charge of $15 per hour.

E  There is an initial deposit of $15 and a charge of $20 per hour.

20. Which expression is equivalent to $(3g)^{\frac{1}{3}}$?

A  $\sqrt[3]{g}$

B  $\sqrt[3]{g^3}$

C  $\sqrt[3]{3g}$

D  $\sqrt{3g^3}$

E  $\sqrt{(3g)^3}$

21. Square $PQRS$ is used to prove the Pythagorean theorem.

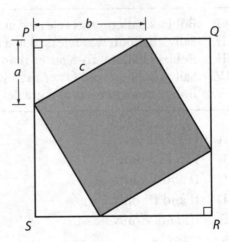

Which statement is NOT valid or necessary to prove the Pythagorean theorem?

A  $PQ = a + b$

B  The area of $PQRS$ is $a^2 + b^2$.

C  The area of the shaded square is $c^2$.

D  The area of each triangle is $\frac{1}{2}ab$.

E  The area of $PQRS$ is equal to the sum of the areas of the 4 triangles and the shaded square.

22. Which expression is equivalent to $\sqrt[4]{(4t)^5}$?

    A  $t^{\frac{4}{5}}$

    B  $t^{\frac{5}{4}}$

    C  $4t^{\frac{5}{4}}$

    D  $(4t)^{\frac{4}{5}}$

    E  $(4t)^{\frac{5}{4}}$

23. Solve for $r$.

$$\frac{3}{5}(15r + 2) + r = \frac{5}{3}(3 + 6r) - \frac{19}{5}$$

    A  $-\dfrac{1}{2}$

    B  $-\dfrac{2}{5}$

    C  0

    D  No solution

    E  Infinitely many solutions

24. Rectangle *PQRS* on a coordinate plane has vertices located at $P(-5, 8)$, $Q(5, 8)$, $R(5, -8)$, and $S(-5, -8)$. Which transformation does NOT map *PQRS* onto itself?

    A  A reflection across the $x$-axis

    B  A reflection across the $y$-axis

    C  A 90° clockwise rotation about the origin

    D  A 180° clockwise rotation about the origin

    E  A 360° clockwise rotation about the origin

25. Which expression is equivalent To $5^3 \cdot 5^{-6}$?

    A  $5^{18}$

    B  $5^{-18}$

    C  $25^3$

    D  $5^3$

    E  $5^{-3}$

# ANSWERS AND EXPLANATIONS—MATH

| Question Number | Correct Answer | Content Category | Rationale |
| --- | --- | --- | --- |
| 1 | A | Numbers and Operations on Numbers | $= 0.\overline{2}$ |
| 2 | D | Data Analysis, Probability, Statistics | Each division $= 25\%$; 3 divisions of A have values greater than the median of B, therefore 75%. |
| 3 | A | Algebraic Concepts | The ordered pairs have no $x$-coordinate repeats with the function. |
| 4 | B | Measurement and Geometry | A reflection across the $x$-axis preserves angle measure and segment length, and changes the sign of all $y$-coordinates, making II and III true and making I and IV false. |
| 5 | B | Algebraic Concepts | $(2x - 3)(x^2 + x - 5) = 2x^3 - x^2 - 13x + 15$ |
| 6 | C | Data Analysis, Probability, Statistics | The median is where the 100th person goes, #100 is between 4 and 5 |
| 7 | A | Numbers and Operations on Numbers | $\pi$ is irrational. |
| 8 | C | Algebraic Concepts | The domain is all the possible $x$ values and the $x$ values run from $-8$ to 2. |
| 9 | D | Data Analysis, Probability, Statistics | 49% support the change. A 3% error could make the percentage that supports the change rise to 52%. |
| 10 | C | Measurement and Geometry | $m\angle SRT = m\angle RPQ + m\angle RQP$ only when $180 = 2m\angle RPQ + m\angle RQP$ |
| 11 | D | Numbers and Operations on Numbers | $(9 \times 10^8) \div (9 \times 10^7) = 10$ |
| 12 | E | Algebraic Concepts | The function is negative and increasing at point U. |
| 13 | A | Data Analysis, Probability, Statistics | An outlier affects the mean and the range the most. |
| 14 | A | Measurement and Geometry | If two lines are collinear, then they are the same line and have an infinite number of points of intersection. Two lines that are skew are defined as two lines that do not lie in one plane. Parallel lines are defined as two coplanar lines that never intersect. Thus only I and III are correct. |

| Question Number | Correct Answer | Content Category | Rationale |
|---|---|---|---|
| 15 | D | Algebraic Concepts | $t = 1.5n + 5$ correctly calculates the total minutes |
| 16 | D | Data Analysis, Probability, Statistics | $205/950 = 0.21578$ |
| 17 | B | Algebraic Concepts | Bobby's balloon was released from a height of 5 feet and Sally's from a height of 4.5 feet. Bobby's rose at a rate of 3 ft/s and Sally's at a rate of 3.5 ft/s. |
| 18 | D | Measurement and Geometry | Setting $(1/3)\pi r^2 h = (4/3)\pi r^3$ with $r = 9$ yields $h = 36$ |
| 19 | B | Data Analysis, Probability, Statistics | The slope is 5 and the $y$-intercept is 15. |
| 20 | C | Numbers and Operations on Numbers | $(3g) = \sqrt[3]{3g}$ |
| 21 | B | Measurement and Geometry | The area of $PQRS$ is $(a + b)^2 = a^2 + 2ab + b^2$ |
| 22 | E | Numbers and Operations on Numbers | $\sqrt[4]{(4t)^5} = (4t)^{\frac{5}{4}}$ |
| 23 | E | Algebraic Concepts | The equation reduces to $0 = 0$. |
| 24 | C | Measurement and Geometry | A 90° clockwise rotation switches the values for $x$ and $y$ |
| 25 | E | Numbers and Operations on Numbers | $5^3 \cdot 5^{-6} = 5^{3-6} = 5^{-3}$ |

# Part III
# Language Arts—Writing

# The Language Arts—Writing Test

4

The *HiSET®* Exam Language Arts—Writing test is comprised of two parts. Part 1 tests your knowledge of writing conventions, language facility, and organization of ideas. You will have 75 minutes to answer 50 multiple-choice questions on these topics. This part of the test measures your ability to revise and edit sentences. Part 2 consists of a written essay that tests your ability to develop and organize your ideas using standard American English. You will have 45 minutes to write your essay for Part 2.

Chapters 5 through 8 will cover Part 1 of the Language Arts—Writing test. Chapters 5 and 6 will include writing conventions skills, Chapter 7 will cover language facility, and Chapter 8 will discuss organization of ideas.

Chapter 9 is devoted to Part 2 of the Language Arts—Writing test. This chapter will discuss the essay and help you plan how best to approach it.

## Question Steps

Part 1 contains all multiple-choice questions, including ones about the organization of the ideas in the passage. These may ask you to identify transitions and conclusions, evaluate the relevance of information, and analyze the overall structure of a paragraph or passage. For questions on Part 1 that deal with writing conventions and language facility, you should follow these six steps:

*Language Arts—Writing Question Steps*

**Step 1:** Read the Sentence

**Step 2:** Check for Agreement

**Step 3:** Check for Errors in Mechanics

**Step 4:** Review the Sentence Structure

**Step 5:** Evaluate Word Choice

**Step 6:** Read Each Answer Choice

## Step 1: Read the Sentence

On Part 1 of the HiSET Exam Language Arts—Writing Test, you will be selecting the answer choice that corrects an error in the passage. Read the sentence alone as well as in the context of the paragraph so you can spot any corrections that need to be made.

This step may seem basic, but many people do not read carefully. Some errors may be obvious to you, while others are better disguised and may appear to be correct if you are reading too quickly and are not focused.

## Step 2: Check for Agreement

You should check each sentence for subject-verb agreement, pronoun agreement, and verb tense consistency.

### Subject-Verb Agreement

Every complete sentence must have a subject and verb. To identify the subject, ask yourself who or what the sentence is about. To identify the verb, ask yourself what the subject or subjects did. Remember that a sentence may have more than one subject or verb. Be sure to identify all of them. The subject or subjects are often found at the beginning of a sentence, but they can be anywhere. While the verb often follows the subject, it can also come first. Make sure that each verb agrees with its subject.

As you know, a singular subject requires a singular verb, and a plural subject requires a plural verb. Groups and gerunds are considered singular when it comes to subject-verb agreement. A simple subject is the one word (without any modifiers) that is the subject of the verb. One way to determine whether the subject and verb agree is to just read the simple subject with the simple verb and ignore the rest of the sentence. For example, read the following sentence:

*On Tuesday, Isabella, who lives in the same neighborhood as I do, was caught in a terrible rainstorm.*

With so many other words in the sentence, it can be easy to lose sight of the subject and verb and to overlook errors in agreement. Isolate the simple subject and the verb.

*Isabella was*

This has a singular subject and a singular verb, so they are in agreement.

What happens if the subject and verb do not agree? Determine what changes could be made to the sentence to correct the error. Do not look at the answer choices just yet. Think about what revisions you would make to the sentence to best correct the disagreement. Then, when you do look at the answer choices, you can see if your answer is among them.

### Pronoun Agreement

The sentence may or may not contain a pronoun. If there is a pronoun, determine what noun or nouns it replaces in the sentence. You may need to look back to the previous sentence in the passage or possibly earlier in the paragraph to determine the antecedent. Make sure that the pronoun agrees with the antecedent.

To determine whether the pronoun is correct, you must first identify the antecedent. These have to match in regard to gender and number. Also, if the pronoun is the subject of the sentence, it must be a subject pronoun. For example, read the following sentence:

*Noah liked to put each of his ties in their own box.*

The pronoun *his* replaces the antecedent *Noah* and is correct. The pronoun *their* replaces the antecedent *each*, which is singular, so this is an error.

If there is an error with a pronoun, decide what pronoun would be correct. When you read the answer choices, look for your response. For the sentence above, you would look for an answer choice that uses *its own box* with *each of his ties.*

### Verb Tense

In general, the paragraph from which the sentence is selected should have consistent verb tense. To know whether the verb tense is correct, you will have to determine whether the events being discussed are taking place in the past, present, or future. In order to do this, you may have to look beyond the indicated sentence. The verb or verbs in the sentence should match the tense of the entire paragraph. As you read the paragraph, look for clues about when the events occurred. Words and phrases such as *yesterday, tomorrow, right now, last week, currently, someday, as of now,* or *at this time* suggest time frame and can let you know what verb tense should be used.

If you determine that the verb tense is wrong, figure out what changes are needed to correct it. When you look at the answer choices, see if your correction is on the list.

## Step 3: Check for Errors in Mechanics

Chapter 6 will explain all the major rules for mechanics, which include capitalization, punctuation, and spelling. Check the sentence to be sure any proper nouns or titles are capitalized. For punctuation, check the use of any commas, semicolons, colons, apostrophes, and quotations marks. Finally, look for any misspelled words, especially homonyms such as *two*, *too*, and *to*.

If you determine that there is an error in mechanics, decide what changes are needed to correct it. When you look at the answer choices, see if your correction is on the list.

## Step 4: Review the Sentence Structure

After you have checked for errors in agreement and mechanics, which will often be easier to notice, review the elements of good sentence structure. Check to be sure the sentence is complete. Sentence fragments and run-on sentences are considered incorrect usage. Be sure that the sentence uses parallel construction for any lists or comparisons. Check the placement of any modifying words or phrases. Identify any transitions and be sure they are appropriate; identify the lack of a transition if one is needed.

If you find a problem with the structure of the sentence, decide how you would correct it. Then read the answer choices to see which option is the best correction.

## Step 5: Evaluate Word Choice

Even a single word can make the difference between correct usage and incorrect usage. To evaluate the word choice in a sentence, you will need to look at transitions, redundancy, adjective and adverb use, comparative and superlative forms, and idiomatic expressions. Transitions are words and phrases that improve the organization of a sentence or show relationships between ideas. A few examples of transitions include: *for example, therefore, on the other hand,* and *especially.* Redundancy is saying the same thing twice, such as *the towering man was tall.* You probably know what adjectives and adverbs are, but be sure the sentence does not confuse the two. Adjectives modify nouns, adverbs, and other adjectives. Adverbs modify verbs. Comparatives are the "er" form of an adjective, such as *bigger.* Superlatives are the "est" form, such as *biggest.* Watch out for sentences that confuse the two. Comparatives are for comparing two items, while superlatives compare three or more. Idiomatic expressions are simply the way something is phrased in standard American English. For example, you should say *different from* instead of *different than.* A list of common idioms is in Chapter 5 for you to review. If you find a problem with an idiomatic expression, look for the correct idiom among the answer choices.

## Step 6: Read Each Answer Choice

Read every answer choice carefully. See if the correction you had in mind is among the choices. If it is, you can be fairly confident in your choice. Remember, even if your correction is shown as the first answer choice, you still need to read all of the choices diligently. The difference of one little letter or comma can cause a very tempting answer choice to be incorrect. As with any test, there is only one best answer. Make sure you find it.

After choosing the answer, substitute it in the original sentence, and read the corrected sentence. Does it sound correct now? If not, go back to Step 1 and see what you have missed. Then select the best correction for the sentence.

# Examples

Here is a sample question that is similar to the ones you will find on the actual Language Arts—Writing test, Part 1. Keep in mind that you will be reading entire paragraphs. For practice purposes, only isolated sentences will be used in the following two examples.

**<u>After arriving at the test center, the student will sharpen their pencil</u> and then find a seat.**

1. **Which correction should be made to the underlined part of the sentence?**
   A   (*No change*)
   B   After arriving at the test center, the student will sharpen his or her pencil
   C   After arriving at the test center, the student has sharpened their pencil
   D   After arrives at the test center, the student will sharpen their pencil

**Apply the six question steps:**

**Step 1:** Read the sentence

**Step 2:** Check for agreement

The simple subject is *student* and the verb is *will sharpen*. The subject and the verb agree. The pronoun *student* is singular, but the pronoun *their* is plural, so this is a mistake. Check the answer choices and eliminate ones that use an incorrect pronoun. The correct pronoun should be *his or her* since the sentence does not indicate whether the student is male or female. Choice B makes the correct replacement, while none of the others correct the mistake. Since all other choices have been eliminated, you can skip to Step 6. Read your choice in the sentence to be sure it is correct and then choose B.

For this example, you only needed to go to Step 2 in order to answer the question. This, of course, will not always be the case. Try the next example.

**At last Friday's club meeting, <u>president Bumguardner chose between Marisa, Kalee, Lori, and Amee to head up the decorating committee.</u>**

2.  **Which correction should be made to the sentence?**

    **A**   (*No change*)

    **B**   At last Friday's club meeting, President Bumguardner chose between Marisa, Kalee, Lori, and Amee to head up the decorating committee.

    **C**   At last Friday's club meeting, president Bumguardner chose among Marisa, Kalee, Lori, and Amee to head up the decorating committee.

    **D**   At last Friday's club meeting, President Bumguardner chose among Marisa, Kalee, Lori, and Amee to head up the decorating committee.

**Step 1:** Read the sentence

**Step 2:** Check for agreement

The simple subject is *president* and *chose* is the verb. Those agree. There are no pronouns in the sentence. Check the verb tense. A meeting last Friday is in the past, so the past tense *chose* is appropriate.

**Step 3:** Check for errors in mechanics

Check punctuation. This sentence has a number of commas. There is an introductory phrase, which is correctly set off by a comma, and a list, which correctly separates each element with a comma. No other punctuation is used except for the period at the end. Check capitalization. In this sentence there are several proper nouns. Names of people are always capitalized, as they are here. Titles should also be capitalized, so the lower-case *president* is incorrect. Eliminate any answer choices that have this error. Choices B and D both fix the capitalization problem, so there must be more going on with this sentence. Continue checking for errors in mechanics. No spelling errors are present, so move on to Step 4.

**Step 4:** Review the sentence structure

This is a complete sentence with an introductory phrase appropriately set off by a comma. The ideas in the sentence are expressed clearly.

**Step 5:** Evaluate word choice

Most of the underlined portion is names, and you already corrected the error in capitalization. There is one adjective, *decorating*, that correctly modifies *committee*. There are no transitions, no comparatives or superlatives, and no redundancy. There are hundreds of idioms in English, so the easiest way to identify one may be to compare the answer choices you are given. Since Choices A and C were eliminated in Step 3, compare choices B and D. The only difference is the substitution of *among* for the original *between*. When more than two items are involved, the correct construction is to choose *among* them.

**Step 6:** Read each answer choice. **The best answer is D**.

# 5 Writing Conventions: Basic English Usage

## What Is Tested?

Basic English usage questions on the *HiSET*® Exam assess your knowledge of subject-verb agreement, verb tense, pronoun usage, and idiomatic expressions. These are skills you use every day, probably without even thinking about them. The questions that test your knowledge of writing conventions and basic English usage will make up 55 percent of the Language Arts—Writing Test, Part 1. To answer them, you will read a passage and then be expected to recognize errors related to verbs and pronouns in a particular sentence from the passage. You will then select the answer choice that shows the best way to correct the error.

Even though many of the skills needed on this part of the exam are probably familiar to you, some of the grammar rules can be tricky at times. The correct answer may not always be obvious. Remember to read every answer choice to be sure you are choosing the best one.

## Usage Rules

You should begin by reviewing the basic grammar rules related to verbs and pronouns. Keep in mind that this is just a quick review of a few of the basics and is by no means an all-inclusive list of everything there is to know about English usage. If you have trouble with any of these topics, you should do further review.

### Subject-Verb Agreement

Every sentence has a subject. This is who or what the sentence is about. Every sentence also has a verb, or action word. The subject and the verb must agree, or fit together.

*Correct:* <u>Kim</u> <u>was</u> the first to arrive.

*Incorrect:* <u>Kim</u> <u>were</u> the first to arrive.

Notice that the subject, Kim, is singular, so the sentence requires a singular verb. When the subject is plural, a plural verb is needed.

*Correct:* <u>Kim and Ryan</u> <u>were</u> seated at the same table.

## Groups

Some groups of people, such as teams, businesses, and institutions, are considered singular and require a singular verb.

<u>The debate club</u> <u>was</u> planning to meet on Thursday before school.

---

**Keep in Mind**

Keep in mind that determining whether a group of people or items is singular or plural may take a little thought on your part. Some collective nouns refer to a set of items or people as a group, such as a dozen eggs. In this case, *dozen* is singular.

A dozen eggs is enough to bake several cakes.

However, if the collective nouns are seen as separate individuals, the nouns are plural, such as a dozen goldfish.

A dozen goldfish share the tank in the dentist's office.

It is important to pay attention to the context in which words are used. It may be tempting to focus only on the subject of the sentence to decide whether it requires a singular or plural verb, but to make an accurate decision, you must consider the sentence and its message.

---

## Gerunds

*Gerunds* are verbs that end with *-ing* and serve as nouns. When a gerund is the subject of a sentence, it is considered singular.

<u>Running</u> late on the first day of a new job <u>is</u> not wise.

## Either / or and Neither / nor

This is one of the more complicated rules of usage. If two singular subjects are connected by *or* or *nor*, the verb should also be singular.

*<u>Erlene</u> or <u>Bob</u> <u>is</u> planning to come to the party.*

*Neither <u>Carolyn</u> nor <u>Preston</u> <u>is</u> planning to come to the party.*

If one subject is plural, then the plural subject is placed closest to the verb, which must also be plural.

If the subjects are of different persons (first, second, or third person), then the verb must agree with the subject closest to the verb.

*Either Kathy or <u>you</u> <u>have</u> to bring chips to the party.*

*Either you or <u>Kathy</u> <u>has</u> to bring chips to the party.*

## Verb Tense

Verb tense indicates the time of an action and tells whether the sentence is happening in the past, present, or future.

You are probably comfortable with using the simple past, present, and future tenses, but there are several other tenses that will be tested as well.

### Simple Present Tense

Simple present tense refers to an action that is currently taking place or an action that happens on a regular basis.

> *Jim lives on the third floor of his apartment building.*

> *Vicki attends acting classes three afternoons each week.*

### Present Perfect Tense

Present perfect tense refers to an action that started in the past and continues in the present. Alternatively, the action began in the past but continues to have an effect on the present. Perfect tense verbs use the words *have* or *has* along with the past participle form of the verb (the *–ed* form of the verb).

> *Bruce has walked to school every day since kindergarten.*

### Simple Past Tense

Use of the simple past tells you that an action has already happened.

> *Randy learned to ride a bike fifteen years ago.*

### Past Perfect Tense

A verb in the past perfect tense shows an action in the past that was completed before something else took place. The action that was completed in the past uses the word *had* along with the past participle form of the verb. The action that occurred second uses the simple past tense.

> *Cassie had worked at a law office before she became a police officer.*

### Simple Future Tense

This tense shows an action that will take place in the future.

> *Our family will go to the airport to pick up Grandmother next week.*

### Future Perfect Tense

An action in future perfect tense has not yet occurred but will take place by a specific time in the future. The tense is constructed by using *will* or *shall*, plus *have*, plus the past participle form of the verb.

> *Roger will have finished painting the entire house by Friday.*

## Pronoun Usage

Pronouns take the place of nouns. A pronoun must agree with the noun it replaces, called the antecedent.

*Aaron plans to study biology in college because he has always loved science.*

In this sentence, *he* is the pronoun and *Aaron* is the antecedent.

### Number

Singular pronouns must replace singular antecedents, and plural pronouns must replace plural antecedents.

*Students attending the pep rally must return to their classes afterward.*

### Gender

Pronouns must be the same gender as the antecedent in order to agree.

*Vivian was promoted to supervisor because she is a dedicated employee.*

Since Vivian is a female, the pronoun must also be feminine.

### Pronoun Case

Pronouns must also agree in case. A subject pronoun must replace the subject of a sentence, an object pronoun must replace an object, and a possessive pronoun must be used to replace a possessive noun. Subject pronouns can be the subject of a sentence and include: *I, you, he, she, it, we, they,* and *who*. Object pronouns receive action and do not function as the subject of a sentence. These include: *me, you, her, him, it, us, them,* and *whom*. Possessive pronouns include: *my, your, his, hers, its, our, their,* and *whose*.

Subject pronoun: *Britt was surprised because he had no idea about the party.*

Object pronoun: *When Zane returned, I gave the book to him.*

Possessive pronoun: *The Meinharts gave their car to charity.*

### Indefinite Pronouns

Most pronouns replace specific nouns. When the pronoun does not refer to a specific noun, it is indefinite. Indefinite pronouns can be singular (*each, anyone, everyone, nobody, something,* etc.) or plural (*few, many, both,* and *several*). Some indefinite pronouns can be either singular or plural if they are followed by a prepositional phrase (*some, any, all, none, either, more, most*). In this case, the pronoun will agree with the object of the preposition.

*Anyone who wants to join the study group is welcome to do so.*

*Both of the teachers are in the gym.*

*Some of the teachers are in the gym.*

*Some of the work is finished.*

### Pronoun Person

Pronouns in a passage must remain in the same person. For example, if a sentence begins by using a first person pronoun, all pronouns must be in the first person. Changing from one point of view to another is called a *pronoun shift*, which is inconsistent.

Incorrect: *The professor told us you could work together on the project.*

*Us* is a first person pronoun; *you* is third person.

Correct: *The professor told us we could work together on the project.*

## Idiomatic Expressions

An idiom is simply the way something is said in standard written English. Many of the idioms tested on the Language Arts—Writing test are **phrasal verbs**. These are verbs that are always paired with the same adverb or preposition. However, not all idioms involve verbs. Unfortunately, there are no rules for idioms. What you should do is make note of any idioms you come across that are not natural to you. For example, if you would naturally say *different than*, you should make note that the correct phrasing is *different from*. Following is a list of common idioms that many people say incorrectly.

| | |
|---|---|
| responsibility to | either ___ or ___ |
| responsible for | neither ___ nor ___ |
| result of | depend on |
| as great/good/bad as | forbid ___ to ___ |
| as much/little as | forbidden from ___ |
| agree with | in contrast to |
| debate over | not only ___ but also ___ |
| both ___ and ___ | not so much ___ as ___ |
| attribute to | prohibit from |
| based on | regard as |
| concerned with | so (adjective) that |
| defined as | so ___ as to be ___ |
| distinguish from | such as |
| between ___ and ___ | contrast ___ with ___ |

# Examples

Here are two sample questions that are similar to the ones you will find on the actual test. Keep in mind that you will be reading passages that contain several paragraphs. For practice purposes, there is only one paragraph for this example.

**Para 1. Our dental office <u>is expanding</u> operations and will be hiring several new**
<sub>1</sub>
**employees. Currently, <u>the owner is accepting applications of the receptionist and**
<sub>2</sub>
**office clerk positions</u>, which will be filled by the end of the month.**
<sub>2</sub>

1. **Which correction should be made to sentence 1?**

   A  (*No change*)

   B  expands

   C  expanding

   D  was expanding

### Explanation

First, read the sentence. In this sentence, the only part underlined is the verb, so that narrows down the list of things to check. Next, check for agreement. Since there are no pronouns in the sentence, you only need to check for subject-verb agreement and verb tense. The singular subject *office* does agree with the singular verb *is*. Since the sentence says *currently*, you know that the tense should be present tense, so the tense used in the sentence is also correct. There are no mechanics issues in the underlined portion, so move on to Step 4 and check the sentence structure. The verb directly follows the subject, no modifiers are underlined, and *expanding* is parallel to *hiring*, so everything looks good with the structure. Word choice here is quite simple to evaluate, since only two words are underlined and they both make up the verb. Go to Step 6 and read each answer choice. The original version of the sentence did not have an error, but the other choices each create a verb error. **The best answer is A.**

2. **Which correction should be made to sentence 2?**

   A  (*No change*)

   B  the owner accepted applications of the receptionist and office clerk positions

   C  the owner is accepting applications for the receptionist and office clerk positions

   D  the owner accepted applications for the receptionist and office clerk positions

### Explanation

First, read the sentence. Unlike the first example, this example has most of the sentence underlined. Check for agreement. Since there are no pronouns in the sentence, you only need to check for subject-verb agreement and verb tense. The singular subject *owner* does agree with the singular verb *is*. Since Sentence 1 says *currently*, you know that the tense should be present tense, so *is accepting* is correct. Check for errors in mechanics. There is no need for any capitalization and there is no need for any punctuation within the underlined portion. Check the sentence structure. All the modifiers directly follow the nouns and adjectives they modify and there do not appear to be any problems with the structure. Word choice is next, and if nothing seems off to you, it may be easier to check the word choice by comparing the answer choices. Go to Step 6 and read each answer choice. Two choices, including the original version, say *applications **of** the receptionist and office clerk positions,* and two say *applications **for** the receptionist and office clerk positions.* This is a difference in idiom and the correct idiom is *applications **for***. Eliminate choices A and B. Choice D changes the correct verb tense (present) to an incorrect tense (past), so eliminate it. **The best answer is C.**

# BASIC ENGLISH USAGE DRILLS

For each of the following, choose the best answer.

**Questions 1–15 refer to the following passage.**

1. Harbor View Accounting Services

    3719 West Lakeside Lane

    Chicago, IL 60610

    April 2, 2012

    Dear Ms. Lopart,

2. We have reviewed your recent employment application and would like to further discuss opportunities within our company. We believe you are well qualified for the customer service representative position, <u>which was currently available</u>.
    <sub>1</sub>

    **1**
    A  (*No change*)
    B  currently available
    C  that was currently available
    D  which is currently available

    <u>Everyone in this position work</u> full
    <sub>2</sub>
    time. Mr. Wong is the supervisor in this department.

    **2**
    A  (*No change*)
    B  Anyone in this position work
    C  Everyone in this position works
    D  Everyone in their position work

**GO ON TO THE NEXT PAGE** ➡

The <u>employees and him have built</u> a
<u>　　　　　　3</u>
strong working relationship.

**3**

A　(*No change*)

B　employees and they have built

C　employees and he have built

D　employees and he has built

<u>Seldom does the representatives</u>
<u>　　　　　4</u>
<u>have problems</u> in this department.
<u>　4</u>

**4**

A　(*No change*)

B　Seldom do the representatives have problems

C　Often do the representatives have problems

D　Seldom does the representative have problems

The <u>employees and Mr. Wong</u>
<u>　　　　　　5</u>
<u>demonstrates positive attitudes,</u>
<u>　　　　5</u>
<u>which create</u> an enjoyable work
<u>　5</u>
environment.

**5**

A　(*No change*)

B　employees and him demonstrates positive attitudes, which create

C　employees and Mr. Wong demonstrate a positive attitude, which creates

D　employees and Mr. Wong demonstrate positive attitudes, which create

3. <u>Harbor View Accounting Services</u>
<u>　　　　　　　6</u>
<u>are pleased</u>
<u>　6</u>

**6**

A　(*No change*)

B　Harbor View Accounting Services were pleased

C　Harbor View Accounting Services is pleased

D　Harbor View Accounting Services was pleased

<u>to offer a comprehensive benefits</u>
<u>　　　　　7</u>
<u>package to their employees</u>. Health
<u>　　　7</u>
insurance, dental insurance, and

**7**

A　(*No change*)

B　to offer a comprehensive benefits packages to its employees.

C　to offering a comprehensive benefits packages to their employees.

D　to offer a comprehensive benefits packages to your employees.

optical benefits are provided <u>to each</u>

<u>employee and his or her family</u>.
8

Both short- and long-term

disability coverage <u>are also available</u>

<u>and will be popular options since</u>
9

<u>they were added</u> to our benefits
9

menu.

Either of these <u>begin</u> immediately
10

upon being hired. Choosing which

benefits your

family <u>needs is</u> important.
11

A representative from the human

resources department is available to

further explain the insurance

benefits available.

4. Customer service representatives at

Harbor View <u>works five days each</u>
12

<u>week</u>, with weekends off. We expect
12

<u>their employees</u> to arrive promptly
13

by 8:00 A.M. and to work until

5:00 P.M., with a one hour

lunch break during the day.

**8**

A  (*No change*)

B  for each employee and their family

C  to each employee and their family

D  to employees and his or her family

**9**

A  (*No change*)

B  are also available and are popular options since they were added

C  is also available and was popular options since they were added

D  are also available and have been popular options since they were added

**10**

A  (*No change*)

B  begins

C  began

D  beginning

**11**

A  (*No change*)

B  needs are

C  need is

D  need are

**12**

A  (*No change*)

B  work five days each week

C  worked five days each week

D  work five days a week

**13**

A  (*No change*)

B  their employee

C  our employees

D  your employees

**GO ON TO THE NEXT PAGE** ➡

Anyone needing to adjust these
<sub>14</sub>
hours due to appointments or
emergencies are able to do so
occasionally.

5.  We look forward to further
    discussing the customer service
    representative position with you.
    Sincerely,
    Ms. Wilma Harrington

**14**

A  (*No change*)

B  Anyone needs

C  Anyone need

D  Employees needing

**15  If a line were to be added before
the signature, what would be the
best choice for that line?**

A  Thank you for your interest in
working with our company.

B  We offer two weeks of vacation
time per year.

C  See you soon!

D  Mr. Wong will be out of the office
on Thursday.

**Answers are on page 717.**

# 6 Writing Conventions: Mechanics

## What Is Tested?

The mechanics of English include capitalization, punctuation, and spelling. On Part 1 of the *HiSET®* Exam Language Arts—Writing Test, you will use what you know about mechanics to revise and edit sentences. In Part 2, you will have to use mechanics correctly when writing your essay. This chapter will review the rules about when to use a capital letter, show you how to correctly use various forms of punctuation, and point out common spelling mistakes people make.

## Capitalization

You probably know that a person's name begins with a capital letter and that every sentence should start with a capital letter; however, there are many more rules to capitalization. While some of them are fairly simple and are rules that you apply every day without even thinking, a few might confuse even the best English language users at times.

### Proper Nouns

Proper nouns name specific people, places, or things. While you would not need to capitalize a common noun, such as *dog*, you would capitalize the proper noun that names a specific dog, such as *Fido*.

> *The newest woman in our department, Elena, will be in the corner office.*

> *We have lived in several states, including Illinois, Pennsylvania, and Georgia.*

> *While attending Webster High School in Washington, D.C., we visited the Lincoln Memorial, as well as several other monuments, while on a school field trip.*

Notice that common nouns such as *woman, states, monuments*, and *school* are not capitalized, but proper nouns naming specific people, places, and things are.

### Titles of People

Titles are capitalized when they refer to a specific person.

> *The students' talking stopped when Professor Hanks entered the room.*

> *I always call Mom and send flowers on her birthday.*

On the other hand, when titles simply refer to an occupation or relationship, they are not capitalized.

*Have you heard who the professor will be for Biology 101 this semester?*

*My mom goes to yoga class every day after work.*

> **Keep in Mind**
>
> Keep in mind that when *Mom* is used as a name, it is capitalized. However, when you are referring to a relationship, *mom* is lowercase. Confusing? Think of it this way: you would capitalize your sister's name (Valerie) but would not capitalize her relationship to you (sister).
>
> *In my opinion, Valerie is the most amazing sister in the world!*
>
> The same is true of other relationship names, such as dad, grandmother, and uncle. Sometimes, the word *my* can be a clue. If *my* is before the title, such as *my grandpa*, the name is not capitalized.

### Titles of Written Works

Since titles are actually the names of books, plays, songs, shows, or magazines, they should also be capitalized. The exceptions are short prepositions and articles; these should not be capitalized unless they are the first word of the title.

*My nephew sings "The Farmer in the Dell" over and over.*

### Groups

As you know, specific names are capitalized. This is true for the names of groups, teams, organizations, and clubs.

*Chris had season tickets to the Red Sox games last year, because this is his favorite team.*

*The purpose of the fund-raising event was to raise money for charities, including the American Cancer Society.*

### Locations

Cardinal directions are not capitalized when they are used as directions but do begin with a capital letter when naming a specific location.

*The Voelkle family saved for years to take a trip to the West.*

*Drive west on Maple Avenue; then turn north on Market Street.*

### Special Days and Events

As you can see on any calendar, the names of days, months, and holidays are capitalized. Seasons, however, are not, unless they are part of a title.

*The school's Spring Fling carnival will be held on Friday, April 8, which is only a few days after Easter.*

The names of historic events are also capitalized. Notice that both words begin with a capital letter, since both are part of the name of the event.

*Matthew's grandfather is a veteran of World War II.*

## Punctuation

Punctuation can do much more than simply end a sentence. When used correctly, it can help to clarify meaning. Take a look at a few of the types of punctuation you will need to understand to do well on the HiSET Exam.

### Commas

A comma is used to separate things. Use a comma to separate items in a list, in dates, in locations, and in coordinate adjectives. Commas set off introductory phrases, parenthetical elements, and quotations. When used with a coordinating conjunction, a comma can separate independent clauses to prevent run-on sentences. The biggest problem most people have with commas is their overuse. Learn the reasons to use a comma and only use one when it is actually needed.

#### Commas in Dates

A comma should be placed between the day and the year when writing a date. A comma should also follow the year when a complete date, including month, day, and year, is given within a sentence. A comma is not necessary when only the month and year are given.

*The first semester will begin August 18, 2012, and run through the middle of December. January 2013 will bring the new semester.*

#### Commas in Locations

A comma should be used to set off addresses (except between the street number and name) and geographical locations (city, state, country, etc.).

*New London, Connecticut, gets its name from London, England.*

*The White House is at 1600 Pennsylvania Avenue, Washington, DC.*

#### Commas in a Series

Commas are used to separate a list of more than two items.

*At the market, please buy a dozen eggs, a loaf of whole-wheat bread, and a quart of orange juice.*

Sometimes, a list of adjectives is used to describe a noun. If each of these adjectives can stand alone to describe the item, the adjectives are separated by commas.

*Jim flashed a bright, cheerful smile upon hearing the election results.*

### Commas and Quotations

Commas are also used to introduce quotations, including dialogue and information being quoted from a source, such as an encyclopedia or a website.

When the source of the quotation appears before the quote, the comma appears after the source name and before the first set of quotation marks.

*According to a recent article in the* New York Times, *"students have shown academic gains that exceed any reported over the past decade."*

When the source of the quote is named in the middle of the quote, a comma goes inside the quotation marks to interrupt the quote and then another comma is used after the interruption before the quote is continued.

*"My greatest accomplishment during this term," the mayor explained, "was improving the educational programs in our community."*

Notice that in both the previous examples, the end punctuation (period) goes inside the quotation marks.

When the source is given after the quote, the comma goes inside the closing quotation marks.

*"Take your shoes off before you come inside," said Mrs. Eichenberg.*

The exception to these rules comes into play when the quotation ends with a question mark or exclamation point. A comma cannot replace a question mark or exclamation point, since these are essential to the message.

*"What are you planning to do about that?" asked Hayleigh.*

*"Look out!" Raegan shouted.*

### Commas and Phrases

A phrase that appears at the beginning of a sentence is an introductory phrase. Such phrases should be followed by a comma.

*As you know, it is important to prepare for the HiSET Exam.*

Other phrases may appear in the middle of a sentence and interrupt the idea being expressed by adding in a piece of information that may be interesting but is not vital. In other words, the phrase could be removed without changing the meaning of the sentence. In such cases, a comma is placed both before and after the interrupting phrase.

*Ali, who has a degree in marketing, was just promoted to head of the human relations department.*

Words or modifying phrases that explain, define, or identify the noun or pronoun preceding them are called appositives. When the appositive is crucial to understanding the meaning of the noun, commas are not used. If the noun can be understood without the appositive, use commas before and after it.

*The woman who answered the phone is the owner of the company.*

*The owner of the company, who answered the phone, is a friend of our family.*

### Commas and Compound Sentences

A compound sentence is created when two independent clauses are joined by a coordinating conjunction. The coordinating conjunctions include: *for, and, nor, but, or, yet,* and *so.* An easy acronym to help you remember these is FANBOYS. A comma must precede the coordinating conjunction in a compound sentence.

*The Cape Hatteras Lighthouse is the tallest in the United States, and its light can be seen for more than twenty miles across the Atlantic Ocean.*

### Commas and Conjunctive Adverbs

Conjunctive adverbs show relationships between clauses such as comparing or contrasting, showing cause or effect, indicating sequence, etc. For example, the conjunctive adverbs *accordingly, on the other hand,* and *for example* can be used to join two independent clauses. After the first independent clause, a semicolon is used, followed by the conjunctive adjective, followed by a comma, and then the second independent clause is used.

*Jason did not return a signed permission slip; consequently, he will not be going on the class trip to the fine arts museum.*

You can also begin a sentence with a conjunctive adjective as an introductory phrase. In that case, there is no semicolon used, but the conjunctive adverb introducing the independent clause is still followed by a comma.

*Furthermore, he will have to attend study hall on the day of the field trip.*

When a conjunctive adverb joins an independent clause and a dependent clause, it is preceded and followed by commas (not a semicolon and comma).

*He is, however, planning to visit the museum this weekend.*

### Commas and Dependent Clauses

When a sentence begins with a dependent clause, it is followed by a comma.

*Even though they are both cities in Florida, Pensacola and Tallahassee are located in different time zones.*

When the dependent clause follows the independent clause, a comma is not used.

*Pensacola and Tallahassee are located in different time zones even though they are both cities in Florida.*

## Semicolons

### Semicolons in a Series

Generally, commas are used to separate a list of items or phrases. However, when the phrases in the list already include commas, the components of the list are separated by semicolons.

*The Smiths' three children were born on February 9, 2002; April 2, 2004; and March 24, 2007.*

### Semicolons and Clauses

Two related independent clauses can be combined with a comma and coordinating conjunction. They can also be joined using a semicolon and no conjunction.

*Andy entered his physics project in the school science fair; he won first place.*

As mentioned earlier, a semicolon can also be used to join two independent clauses with a conjunctive adverb.

*This weekend's weather is expected to include thunderstorms; therefore, the class picnic will be postponed until further notice.*

## Apostrophes

### Apostrophes and Singular Possessive Nouns

A possessive noun shows ownership. In a singular possessive noun, the apostrophe is placed before the *s*. This holds true even if the singular noun ends with an *s*.

*Delaware's state flower is the peach blossom.*

*Arkansas's state flower is the apple blossom.*

---

**Keep in Mind**

Keep in mind that some proper names, such as *Tess* or *Lucas*, end in the letter *s*. To show ownership, an apostrophe and another *s* are added to the end, as they would be with any other name.

*We went to Tess's graduation party on Saturday.*

---

### Apostrophes and Plural Possessive Nouns

If a plural noun already ends with *s*, the apostrophe follows the *s*.

*The teachers' lounge is located beside the office.*

If a plural noun does not end with *s*, an apostrophe and *s* are added to the end of the word.

*Women's shoes can be expensive and uncomfortable.*

### Apostrophes and Compound Possessive Nouns

For a singular compound noun, use the apostrophe before the *s*.

*My mother-in-law's hat was so ugly that I laughed when I saw it.*

For a plural compound noun, form the plural first and then use the apostrophe after it.

*We should not joke about our mothers-in-law's hats.*

Note: The plural of *mother-in-law* is *mothers-in-law*, not *mother-in-laws*. For two or more people sharing possession, use *'s* only on the last noun.

*Elba and Jack's honeymoon was in Vietnam.*

### Apostrophes and Possessive Pronouns

Possessive pronouns, such as *hers, his, its, ours,* and *theirs,* show ownership without including an apostrophe and *s.* A common mistake is to use apostrophes with any type of possession, but they should not be used with possessive pronouns.

*Mohammed said his shirt needs to be ironed.*

*The sign on the front of the building has lost one of its letters.*

### Apostrophes and Plurals of Letters and Numbers

Apostrophes are not generally used to indicate plurals of letters and numbers, unless forming the plural with simply an *s* would create confusion. For example, the plural of the letter *a* would be *as,* which looks exactly the same as the word *as.* In this case, you should form the plural of the letter *a* by using an apostrophe before the *s.*

*Carrie earned all A's on her report card.*

Note: A common mistake is to use an apostrophe with the numerals for decades or centuries, such as *in the 1970's.* This is incorrect. You should simply write, *in the 1970s.*

### Apostrophes and Contractions

A contraction is created when two words are combined to make a single, shorter word, such as when *can* and *not* are used to create *can't.* An apostrophe takes the place of the missing letter or letters in the new word.

*The student body president doesn't plan to run for reelection next year because she'll be involved in other activities.*

## Quotation Marks

### Quotation Marks and Quotes

Quotation marks indicate the beginning and end of a direct quote and are placed around the exact words that were spoken or copied from a source.

*"We are going to the football game," Sergio explained, "but we may not get there until halftime."*

*According to the* Atlanta Business Journal, *"Sales have risen by 23% over the past quarter."*

### Quotation Marks and Titles

Titles of short works, such as poems, chapters, songs, short stories, television shows, and articles, are enclosed in quotation marks.

*Our homework tonight is to read "The Roosevelt Era," which is chapter four in the history book.*

## Spelling

Spelling questions on the HiSET Exam are not like the spelling tests you took in third grade. Instead, you will have to recognize whether homonyms, contractions, and possessives are used and spelled correctly in a sentence.

### Homonyms

When you read the words *sale* and *sail*, or *blue* and *blew*, they sound identical. But, as you know, their definitions are nothing alike. Words that sound the same but have different meanings and spellings are called homonyms.

*John learned to write with his right hand.*

*The pitcher accidentally threw the ball through the windshield of the car.*

*We were not sure whether the weather would be warm or cool this morning.*

On the HiSET Exam, you will find sentences that include the wrong homonym. You will need to identify the incorrect word and recognize the correct spelling. When writing your essay, you will need to use the correct spelling of any homonyms that you include.

Incorrect: *While on our for-day vacation, we saw the White House and the Capital building, witch are located in Washington, D.C.*

Correct: *While on our <u>four</u>-day vacation, we saw the White House and the <u>Capitol</u> building, <u>which</u> are located in Washington, D.C.*

### Contractions

As mentioned earlier, contractions such as *I'm* and *don't* are formed by combining two words. The apostrophe in a contraction replaces the letter or letters that are left out when the words are combined. In many cases, omitting the apostrophe creates a different word. Without the apostrophe, contractions are not spelled correctly.

*Adam hasn't left for school yet because he's not finished eating breakfast.*

*It's 7:00 now; we'll be at the party within an hour.*

### Possessives

As already discussed, possessives show ownership. An apostrophe and *s* are added to the end of singular nouns. An apostrophe is added to the end of plural nouns that already end in *s*. An apostrophe and *s* are added to the end of plural nouns that do not already end in *s*.

*David's house is two blocks south of the children's museum.*

*Girls' clothing is located upstairs in that department store.*

### Possessive Pronouns

Possessive pronouns, such as *yours, theirs,* and *his,* also show ownership. However, they do so without the use of an apostrophe and *s.*

> *Rhonda said that the yellow coat is hers.*

> *The basket on the table is ours; their basket is on the floor.*

---

**Keep in Mind**

Keep in mind that it can be easy to confuse the spelling of certain possessive pronouns and contractions. For example *its* and *it's* are homonyms. *Its* shows ownership, whereas *it's* is a contraction for *it is.* Make sure you know when to use each spelling of words such as these.

---

# Examples

Read the paragraph below and then work through the two sample questions using the six question steps.

**Para 1. Many students would <u>rather cram for a test then plan ahead</u>, study early,**
<u> </u>
<sub>1</sub>
**and be prepared. We read <u>Emily Dickinson's poem, the Bee</u>, in class. Most students**
<sub>2</sub>
**did not look at it again until Thursday night, when the test was on Friday morning.**

1. Which correction should be made to sentence 1?

   A  (*No change*)
   B  rather cram four a test then plan ahead
   C  rather cram for a test than plan ahead
   D  rather cram four a test than plan ahead

### Explanation

First, read the sentence. Check for agreement. Since there are no pronouns in the sentence, you only need to check for subject-verb agreement and verb tense. The plural subject *students* does agree with the verb. Since Sentence 1 is describing a general belief, present tense is appropriate for *cram.* Check for errors in mechanics. There is no need for any capitalization and there is no need for any punctuation within the underlined portion. There is a problem with spelling, however. The homonym *then* is used when the writer should use *than.* If you did not notice this when you read the sentence, do not be worried. You would probably pick up on the error in Step 6 when you read the answer choices. Eliminate choices A and B. Move on to Step 4 and check the sentence structure. This sentence contains a comparison and a list of actions, so check for parallelism. *Cram, plan, study,* and *be* are all parallel. Word choice is next, and if nothing seems off to you, it may be easier to check the word choice by comparing the answer choices. Go to Step 6 and read each answer choice. Two choices (including B, which you already eliminated) create spelling errors by using the homonym *four* instead of *for.* Eliminate choice D. Choice C corrects the original error and does not create any new ones. **The best answer is C.**

2. **Which correction should be made to sentence 2?**

   **A**  (*No change*)
   **B**  Emily Dickinson's poem, the Bee
   **C**  Emily Dickinson's poem, "The Bee,"
   **D**  Emily Dickinson's poem "The Bee"

## Explanation

First, read the sentence. Check for agreement. The pronoun *we* is not underlined and is not relevant to the underlined portion. The subject *we* agrees with the verb *read* and past tense is appropriate since the action is in the past. Check for errors in mechanics. There is a need for capitalization since a person's name and the title of a poem are both present. *Emily Dickenson* is properly capitalized, but the full title of the poem should be capitalized as well. Articles are capitalized when they begin the title, so it should be *The Bee*. Eliminate choices A and B. In addition, poem titles should be in quotation marks, which is done correctly in the original sentence. Check the punctuation. Commas should not be used here since the title of the poem is important information necessary to the meaning of the sentence. Eliminate choice C. Choice D is the only one left, so check that everything is done correctly in that choice and then choose it. **The best answer is D.**

# MECHANICS DRILLS

For each of the following, choose the best answer.

| Questions 1–15 refer to the following passage. |

<u>Over time</u>, many new words
1

**1**

**A**  (*No change*)
**B**  In time
**C**  Over time;
**D**  Over time

<u>have been added to our Language</u>.
2

**2**

**A**  (*No change*)
**B**  have been added to your language.
**C**  were added to our language.
**D**  have been added to our language.

<u>Not to many years ago</u>, no one had
3
even heard of a cell phone.

**3**

**A**  (*No change*)
**B**  Not too many years ago,
**C**  Not too many years ago;
**D**  Not two many years ago,

A laptop <u>was where you sat with your</u>
<sub>4</sub>
<u>Grandmother</u> on her front porch
<sub>4</sub>
swing to enjoy the sunset.

<u>And, a cloud only referred to</u>
<sub>5</sub>
<u>something seen in the sky indicating</u>
<sub>5</sub>
<u>possible rain showers.</u>
<sub>5</sub>

<u>Today, *telecommute* is</u> a word that
<sub>6</sub>
is familiar

<u>to many, yet, was unheard of</u> only a
<sub>7</sub>
few decades in the past.

*Telecommute* means <u>to work from</u>
<sub>8</sub>
<u>home rather than in an office via</u>
<sub>8</sub>
<u>computer.</u>
<sub>8</sub>

**4**

**A** (*No change*)

**B** was where you sat with you're
Grandmother

**C** was where you sat with your
grandmother

**D** was where you sit with your
Grandmother

**5**

**A** (*No change*)

**B** And, a cloud only referred to
something scene in the sky
indicating possible rain showers.

**C** A cloud only referred to something
seen in the sky indicating possible
rain showers.

**D** A cloud only referred to something
seen, in the sky, indicating possible
rain showers.

**6**

**A** (*No change*)

**B** Today, *telecommute,* will be

**C** Today *telecommute* is

**D** Today *telecommute* will be

**7**

**A** (*No change*)

**B** too many, yet was unheard of

**C** to many yet was unheard of

**D** to many, yet was unheard of

**8**

**A** (*No change*)

**B** to work from home, rather than in
an office, via computer.

**C** to work from home, rather than in
an office via computer.

**D** to work from home rather than in
an office on a computer.

**GO ON TO THE NEXT PAGE** ➡

Thanks to today's technology many
<u>9</u>
people around the world enjoy this
employment option.

**9**

A  (*No change*)

B  Thanks to today's technology,

C  Thank's to today's technology,

D  Thanks to todays' technology

<u>While its not convenient or possible</u>
**10**
<u>for everyone</u> telecommuting does
**10**
offer advantages. These employees
save money

**10**

A  (*No change*)

B  While it's not convenient or
   possible for everyone

C  While its not convenient or
   possible for everyone,

D  While it's not convenient or
   possible for everyone,

<u>on clothes, gasoline, and lunch, may</u>
**11**
<u>be able to set flexible hours, and save</u>
**11**
<u>time</u> commuting.
**11**

**11**

A  (*No change*)

B  on clothes, gasoline and lunch; may
   be able to set flexible hours, and
   save time

C  on clothes, gasoline, and lunch;
   may be able to set flexible hours;
   and save time

D  on clothes, gasoline, and lunch,
   may be able to set flexible hours,
   and save time

<u>Companies' reap benefits from this</u>
**12**
<u>arrangement</u> as well. Fewer sick days
**12**
are taken,

**12**

A  (*No change*)

B  Company's reap benefits from this
   arrangement

C  Company reaps benefits from this
   arrangement

D  Companies reap benefits from this
   arrangement

<u>medical and Doctor expenses</u>
**13**
<u>decrease, and less office space</u> is
**13**
needed.

**13**

A  (*No change*)

B  medical and Doctor expense
   decreases, and less office space

C  medical and doctor expenses
   decreases, and less office space

D  medical and doctor expenses
   decrease, and less office space

As more and more people become
14
comfortable with this less traditional
14
work environment, we can expect its
14
popularity to increase.
14

**14**

A (*No change*)

B As more and more people become comfortable with this less, traditional work environment, we can expect its popularity

C As more and more people become comfortable with this less traditional work environment we can expect its popularity

D As more and more people become comfortable with this less traditional work environment, we can expect it's popularity

In the future, half the population may
15
telecommute. This will benefit both
15
employees and employers.
15

**15** **Which of the following is the best way to combine these two sentences?**

A In the future, half the population may telecommute, but this will benefit both employees and employers.

B In the future, half the population may telecommute, and this will benefit both employees and employers.

C In the future, half the population may telecommute, this will benefit both employees and employers.

D In the future, half the population may telecommute, and, this will benefit both employees and employers.

**Answers are on page 717.**

# 7 Language Facility: Sentence Structure

## What Is Tested?

Recognizing mistakes in how sentences are structured accounts for 25 percent of the questions on the *HiSET*® Exam Language Arts—Writing Test, Part 1. You will not only need to recognize sentence fragments, run-ons, comma splices, and lack of parallel structure, but you will also need to know what changes to make to correct these sentence structure problems.

When you get to Part 2 of the test, you will need to demonstrate proper sentence structure in writing your own essay, so think of this chapter as instruction for the essay as well. By understanding what does and does not make a proper sentence, you will be preparing for both sections of the test.

### The Basics of Sentence Structure

As you know, a sentence expresses a complete thought and has to have a subject and a verb. The subject is the *who* or the *what* that is completing an action. The verb is the action that tells what the subject is or what the subject does.

*Shannon walked her dog.*

*Shannon* is the subject, because she is the *who* that is completing the action. *Walked* is the verb because it tells what Shannon, the subject, did.

### Dependent and Independent Clauses

A **clause** is a group of words that contains a subject and a verb. A **dependent clause** cannot stand alone, because it does not express a complete thought, despite the fact that it has a subject and a verb. It depends on another clause to be able to create a complete sentence.

*After Gayle heard the doorbell*

An **independent clause** can stand alone. It has a subject and a verb and expresses a complete thought. It is a complete sentence.

*She rushed to the peephole to look outside.*

### Compound Subjects

A sentence may have more than one subject.

*Adi and I walked the dog.*

### Compound Verbs

A sentence may also have more than one verb.

*Ning walked the dog and gave him a bath.*

### Compound Sentences

Compound sentences are two or more independent clauses that are joined together to create a single sentence. The independent clauses may be joined by a coordinating conjunction, such as *and, but, for, nor, or, so, or yet*, or by a semicolon.

*Luis did not study for the final exam, yet he still managed to ace the class.*

*Luis did not study for the final exam; he still managed to ace the class.*

Notice that each of the clauses is independent and expresses a complete thought. Also notice that the end of the first clause is followed by either a semicolon or by a comma and then the coordinating conjunction.

### *Coordination*

Combining two independent clauses with a coordinating conjunction is called **coordination**. Coordination gives equal weight to both clauses. This combining of ideas not only allows for varied sentence structure, but it also helps the ideas flow more smoothly. Sometimes, words may need to be removed to avoid repetition.

Two sentences: *Sophia will stay for cheerleading practice. She will not stay for the game.*

Single sentence with coordination: *Sophia will stay for cheerleading practice, but she will not stay for the game.*

### Complex Sentences

A complex sentence is formed by joining an independent clause to a dependent clause with a subordinating conjunction, such as *although, because, unless,* or *while*. The conjunction appears at the beginning of the dependent clause and highlights the unequal relationship between the two clauses.

*Ruby got to work on time, even though her alarm did not go off this morning.*

The order of the clauses does not matter; either can come first. When the sentence begins with the dependent clause, a comma separates the clauses.

*Even though her alarm did not go off this morning, Ruby got to work on time.*

## Keep in Mind

Keep in mind that a subordinating conjunction should point out how the clauses relate to one another. Here a few examples of conjunctions to show certain relationships:

- **Cause and effect:** because, now that, so that, in order that, since
- **Condition:** as long as, if, provided that, unless, in case
- **Contrast:** although, even though, whereas, while
- **Time:** after, before, during, once, since, as soon as, still, until, when, while

### Subordination

**Subordination** combines independent clauses by adding a subordinating conjunction. This creates a complex sentence structure and causes one of the clauses to become dependent on the other.

Two sentences: *Emma is planning to buy a new dress. She wants to look professional for a job interview on Friday.*

Single sentence with subordination: *Since she wants to look professional for a job interview on Friday, Emma is planning to buy a new dress.*

## Keep in Mind

Keep in mind that by making one of the clauses dependent on the other, you are establishing that clause as less important. Make sure you combine the clauses in such a way that the most important idea remains an independent clause and the less important idea becomes subordinate to that.

### Compound-Complex Sentences

A compound-complex sentence is formed by joining two or more independent clauses with one or more dependent clauses.

*Before breakfast each morning, Calvin fed the cattle, and Walter gathered eggs.*

This sentence begins with a dependent introductory phrase and then has two independent clauses joined by a comma and coordinating conjunction.

## Common Errors in Sentence Structure

### Run-On Sentences

Like compound and compound-complex sentences, **run-on sentences** also include two independent clauses. The difference is, the clauses in a run-on sentence are not joined properly. The clauses run into one another.

Incorrect: *Olivia is a terrific dancer she has taken ballet classes since she was young.*

There are four ways to correct a run-on sentence:

1. Break the run-on into two separate sentences. Simply add a period to the end of the first clause.

   *Olivia is a terrific dancer. She has taken ballet classes since she was young.*

2. Create a compound sentence by inserting a semicolon at the end of the first clause to separate the two ideas. You can only do this if the two clauses are closely related.

   *Olivia is a terrific dancer; she has taken ballet classes since she was young.*

3. Create a compound sentence by inserting a comma and coordinating conjunction at the end of the first clause.

   *Olivia is a terrific dancer, for she has taken ballet classes since she was young.*

4. Subordinate one clause to the other by adding a subordinating conjunction.

   *Olivia is a terrific dancer because she has taken ballet classes since she was young.*

## Comma Splice

Like a run-on sentence, a **comma splice** also includes two independent clauses. In this case, a comma has been placed between the clauses, which does not join them properly.

Incorrect: *Alfredo is renting a house near campus, it is much larger than a dorm room.*

As you can see, the only difference between that sentence and a run-on is the comma. To fix a comma splice, you can use the same four options as you would to fix a run-on sentence.

*Alfredo is renting a house near campus. It is much larger than a dorm room.*

*Alfredo is renting a house near campus; it is much larger than a dorm room.*

*Alfredo is renting a house near campus, and it is much larger than a dorm room.*

*Alfredo is renting a house near campus since it is much larger than a dorm room.*

## Sentence Fragments

A sentence fragment is a group of words that may look like a sentence but is not. The fragment might be missing the subject or the verb. It may be a dependent clause, which fails to express a complete thought.

No subject: *Fixed eggs and bacon for breakfast.*

No verb: *The majority of the employees in that department.*

Dependent clause (not a complete thought): *Even though the stock market rose significantly yesterday.*

Once you have identified what causes a group of words to be a sentence fragment, the error is easy to fix. Simply add whatever is missing—a subject, a verb, or an independent clause.

> _Wendy_ fixed eggs and bacon for breakfast.

> The majority of the employees in that department _work hard_.

> Even though the stock market rose significantly yesterday, _I have no plans to invest right now_.

## Rules for Modifiers

**Modifiers**, including adverbs and adjectives, are words or phrases that offer details to clarify and add information to a sentence.

> Adjectives modify nouns.

> I wore a **blue** shirt.

> The adjective _blue_ modifies the noun _shirt_.

> Adverbs modify verbs, adjectives, and other adverbs.

> I yawned **loudly**.

> The adverb _loudly_ modifies the verb _yawned_.

> The **pink** spotted umbrella is mine.

> The adverb _pink_ modifies the adjective _spotted_ (which modifies the noun _umbrella_).

> I ran **very** quickly.

> The adverb _very_ modifies the adverb _quickly_.

The important thing to remember about modifiers is that what they are intended to modify must be crystal clear. In general, a modifier must be right next to the word it modifies.

## Misplaced Modifiers

**Misplaced modifiers** can lead to confusion. While you might be able to guess which object is being modified, the intended message of the sentence is vague because the modifier is not next to what it modifies.

> _Incorrect:_ Having been tossed three feet in the air, the chef caught the pizza dough.

What was tossed three feet in the air? Probably the pizza dough, but the sentence makes it sound as if the chef was tossed. To clarify the meaning here, you could do one of several things. You could change the modifying phrase to a dependent clause. You could also rearrange the words so that the modifier is beside the word it is supposed to describe.

> _After the pizza dough was tossed three feet in the air, the chef caught it._

> _After the chef tossed the pizza dough three feet in the air, he caught it._

> _Incorrect:_ The shoes were too tight in the closet.

This sentence seems more confusing. Are the shoes only too tight when they are in the closet? Move the modifying phrase *in the closet* closer to what it modifies, *the shoes*.

*The shoes in the closet were too tight.*

### Dangling Modifiers

A **dangling modifier** is a word or phrase that modifies something not clearly stated in the sentence; in other words, it modifies nothing.

Incorrect: *Without knowing her name, it was hard to find her.*

Who did not know her name? Fix the problem by naming the person who did not know her name.

*Since Bradley did not know her name, it was hard to find her.*

Incorrect: *After reading the book, the movie seemed shallow.*

Correct: *After I read the book, the movie seemed shallow.*

# Parallelism

When a list of ideas or a comparison is included in a sentence, it should be written using a parallel, or similar, grammatical form. **Parallelism** not only helps the writing flow more smoothly, it also helps to express the ideas clearly.

Incorrect: *Nicholle bought her train ticket, will find a seat, and is reading the paper before the train left the station.*

This sentence includes past, future, and present tense verbs. To create parallelism, the verbs should all be in the same tense.

*Nicholle bought her train ticket, found a seat, and read the paper before the train left the station.*

Incorrect: *Laura spent her vacation on a cruise, at the beach, and went to New York.*

This sentence includes a list of places Laura went. Two of the places begin with a preposition, but the third does not. The key to parallelism is consistency.

*Laura spent her vacation on a cruise, at the beach, and in New York.*

Incorrect: *Audree likes broccoli more than me.*

This sentence contains a comparison. The meaning is unclear because of a lack of parallel structure. According to the way this sentence is structured, it means that Audree likes broccoli more than she likes the writer. Since that is probably not what the writer meant to say, you should be clear about what is being compared.

*Audree likes broccoli more than I do.*

# Examples

Here are two sample questions that are similar to the ones you will find on the actual test. Keep in mind that you will be reading passages that contain several paragraphs. For practice purposes, there is only one paragraph for this example.

**Para 1. Colleen spends every Saturday <u>cleaning her house and then makes dinner</u>**
1

**for her family and guests. <u>Today, Colleen is planning to make chicken stew for</u>**
2

**<u>Omar when he comes to dinner. Omar does not eat beef.</u>**
2

1. **Which correction should be made to sentence 1?**

   A   (*No change*)

   B   cleaning her house and then making dinner

   C   to clean her house and then make dinner

   D   cleaning her house and then made dinner

## *Explanation*

First, read the sentence. Check for agreement. In this sentence, the main subject and verb are not underlined, but there are two verb forms underlined: *cleaning* and *makes*, so pay careful attention to verb issues. Both uses of the pronoun *her* agree with *Colleen*, so there are no pronoun problems. The verb tense should be present since the sentence says *every Saturday*, so the tense used in the sentence is also correct. There are no mechanics issues in the underlined portion, so move on to Step 4 and check the sentence structure. There are two actions being performed, so they need to be in parallel structure. To correct the problem, you could say *cleans* and *makes* or *cleaning and making*; either way is fine as long as the terms are parallel. Eliminate choices A and D. Choice C says *clean* and *make,* but has changed the verb form into the infinitive *to clean,* which does not make sense with the rest of the sentence. Eliminate C. Since Choice B is the only one left, read it and make sure it fixes the issue without creating any new problems. **The best answer is B.**

2. **What would be the most effective combination of these sentences?**

   A   Today, Colleen is planning to make chicken stew for Omar when he comes to dinner, Omar does not eat beef.

   B   Today, Colleen is planning to make chicken stew for Omar when he comes to dinner so that Omar does not eat beef.

   C   Today, Colleen is planning to make chicken stew for Omar when he comes to dinner because Omar does not eat beef.

   D   Today Omar does not eat beef, and Colleen is planning to make chicken stew for him when he comes to dinner.

## *Explanation*

Your task here is to combine two sentences into one. This means that there are no grammar mistakes in the sentences that you need to correct. Instead, you will have to watch out for creating grammar mistakes in the combined version. First, read the two sentences. Colleen is making chicken stew for Omar and Omar does not eat beef. How would you combine these ideas? A logical way to connect them would be to say that

Colleen is making chicken stew for Omar *because* he does not eat beef. There are different ways to phrase that idea, but now at least you know what to look for. Go to Step 6 and read each answer choice. Choice A combines incorrectly with only a comma, creating a comma splice. Eliminate A. Choice B uses *so that*, which does not have the same meaning as *because*. Choice B makes it sound if Colleen is trying to make Omar avoid beef, rather than being polite and honoring his preferences. Eliminate B. Choice C correctly subordinates the second sentence to the first with the meaning you intended. Choice D completely changes the meaning of the sentence by connecting the modifier *today* with *Omar does not eat beef*. Eliminate D. **The best answer is C.**

# SENTENCE STRUCTURE DRILLS

For each of the following, choose the best answer.

**Questions 1–15 refer to the following passage.**

1. At some point, <u>most people will</u>
   <sub>1</sub>
   <u>need to fill out a job application.</u>
   <sub>1</sub>

   **1**
   A (*No change*)
   B most people needs to fill out a job application.
   C most people will need to fill out a job application?
   D most people need to fill out a job application.

   This can cause <u>feelings of excitement,</u>
   <sub>2</sub>
   <u>fear, and being worried.</u> You
   <sub>2</sub>

   **2**
   A (*No change*)
   B feelings of being excited, fear, and being worried
   C feelings of excitement, fearful, and being worried
   D feelings of excitement, fear, and worry

   <u>may be nervous, since being</u> well
   <sub>3</sub>
   prepared can help this to be a
   positive experience.

   **3**
   A (*No change*)
   B may be nervous, and since being
   C may be nervous, but being
   D may be nervous since being

**2.** <u>If you will be completing the</u>
<sub>4</sub>
<u>application at the job site.</u>
<sub>4</sub>

It is a good idea to bring <u>your own</u>
<sub>5</sub>
<u>pen never fill out</u> an application
<sub>5</sub>
in pencil.

<u>Blue or black ink.</u> By having
<sub>6</sub>

your <u>own pen. You will look</u> better
<sub>7</sub>
prepared than if you had to ask to

borrow one. Most applications will

**4**

**A** (*No change*)

**B** If you will be completing the application at the job site, be sure to bring everything you might need.

**C** If you will be completing the application at the job site, during regular business hours.

**D** If you will be completing the application at the job site; it is important to be prepared for this process.

**5**

**A** (*No change*)

**B** your own pen, never fill out

**C** your own pen; never fill out

**D** your own pen, or never fill out

**6**

**A** (*No change*)

**B** Blue or black ink;

**C** Blue or black ink will look most professional.

**D** Blue or black ink, which are dark colors.

**7** **Which is the best way to write the underlined portions of these sentences?**

**A** own pen, you will look,

**B** own pen, you will look

**C** own pen; you will look

**D** own pen you will look

GO ON TO THE NEXT PAGE ➡

require certain <u>personal information, have your social security number and previous addresses</u>[8] handy. If you have had

other jobs <u>in the past, you will need to provide</u>[9] information regarding your work history. You may need to

submit <u>the names of your supervisors, the addresses of the companies, and when you worked</u>[10] with each.

3. Many potential employers also require a list of at least three people to be <u>personal references. Write down people</u>[11] you can use.

**8**

A  (*No change*)

B  personal information, have your social security number, and previous addresses

C  personal information, and have your social security number and previous addresses

D  personal information; have your social security number and previous addresses

**9**

A  (*No change*)

B  in the past; you will need to provide

C  in the past you will need to provide

D  in the past. You will need to provide

**10**

A  (*No change*)

B  the name of your supervisors, the addresses of the companies, and when you worked

C  the names of your supervisors, the addresses of the companies, and the dates you worked

D  the names of your supervisors, the addresses of their companies, and when you have worked

**11  Which is the best way to write the underlined portion of these sentences?**

A  personal references so write down people

B  personal references, so write down who

C  personal references; before write down people

D  personal references, and write down who

Include <u>teachers, previous</u>
<u>_12_</u>
<u>employers, reputable friends, or not</u>
<u>_12_</u>
<u>members of your family.</u> Make sure
<u>_12_</u>
beforehand that the people

<u>are willing to give you a positive</u>
<u>_13_</u>
<u>reference on the list.</u>
<u>_13_</u>

4. <u>After completing it in neat</u>
<u>_14_</u>
<u>handwriting, the supervisor should</u>
<u>_14_</u>
<u>be given the application.</u> Leaving it
<u>_14_</u>
on a service counter, table, or desk

does not ensure that <u>the application</u>
<u>_15_</u>
<u>will get into the proper hands to be</u>
<u>_15_</u>
<u>reviewed.</u>
<u>_15_</u>

**12**

**A** (*No change*)

**B** teachers, and previous employers, reputable friends, or not members of your family.

**C** teachers, previous employers, reputable friends, and not members of your family.

**D** teachers, previous employers, reputable friends, but not members of your family.

**13**

**A** (*No change*)

**B** are willing on the list to give you a positive reference.

**C** on the list are willing to give you a positive reference.

**D** are willing to give you a positive reference, who are on the list.

**14**

**A** (*No change*)

**B** After you complete it in neat handwriting, the application should be given to the supervisor.

**C** After he completes it in neat handwriting, the supervisor should be given the application.

**D** After you complete it in neat handwriting, the supervisor should be given the application.

**15**

**A** (*No change*)

**B** the application, however, will get into the proper hands for review

**C** the application will get into the proper hands, to be reviewed

**D** the proper hands will review the application

**Answers are on pages 717-718.**

# 8 Organization of Ideas

## What Is Tested?

The way writing is organized helps readers to understand the meaning of the text. Think back to when you were a child. You knew that the words *once upon a time* meant that a story was beginning. You knew that every story had a beginning, a middle, and an end and that the words *the end* signaled that the story was over. At this point, the materials you read are a little more complicated than that; however, you can still expect to find certain things when you read that will enhance your comprehension.

In this chapter, you will review and practice the proper way to organize writing in order to maximize comprehension. On Part 1 of the *HiSET*® Exam Language Arts—Writing test, you will be expected to recognize well-organized writing and to make corrections to organization that would make the writing more effective. On Part 2 of the test, you will need to apply this knowledge to your own writing.

## Effective Organization

Just as a good story contains a beginning, a middle, and an end, good nonfiction writing contains an introduction, a body, and a conclusion. The introduction is exactly what it sounds like; it introduces the topic or idea. The body explains the idea using facts and examples. The conclusion sums up the idea, often by restating the main point introduced at the beginning of the essay.

Generally, paragraphs are the building blocks of these sections of an essay. In order to understand the organization of an entire passage, you should first learn what makes a good paragraph.

### Strong Paragraphs

Suppose you wanted to write an effective paragraph about e-book readers, those handheld electronic devices that let you read nearly any book in the library on a screen the size of a small book page. Here is what might be included in the paragraph.

#### Main Idea

The sentences in a paragraph should focus on the same idea. The **main idea** of a paragraph is the main message that the writer wants to convey. Each paragraph should have a single main idea; the rest of the sentences should help readers clearly understand this key concept. This might be the main idea for a paragraph on e-book readers: *E-book readers are a popular means of accessing information.*

### Topic Sentence

The **topic sentence** states the main idea of the paragraph. Usually, this is the first or last sentence; however, it can be anywhere in the paragraph. The purpose of the topic sentence is to give readers an idea of what the paragraph will be about. It is not intended to give all of the important information about the main idea. For your essay in Part 2 of the Language Arts—Writing Test, put the topic sentence for each paragraph as the first sentence of the paragraph. This allows the reader to quickly get your main idea. Here is a sample topic sentence for the e-book reader paragraph: *Over the past few years, many companies have introduced their versions of e-book readers, which have become a popular means of accessing information.*

### Supporting Details

While the purpose of the topic sentence is to introduce the main idea of a paragraph, the purpose of the remaining sentences is to provide **supporting details**. These are data, details, definitions, or examples that help to explain or prove the main idea. The details paint a picture for readers so they are able to understand the main point that the writer is trying to make. Here are two supporting details for your paragraph.

*E-book readers are smaller and lighter than traditional bound books, and they are being used by some school districts to replace traditional textbooks.*

*A single e-book reader is able to access countless books, offering the opportunity to begin reading a fiction or nonfiction selection within a matter of minutes.*

### Summary Statement

After providing the supporting details, your paragraph should tie the information back to the main idea of the essay. This is best done with a **summary statement** at the end of the paragraph. This sentence is basically a restatement of the topic sentence, emphasizing the relevance to your overall thesis. Here is a sample summary statement for your paragraph.

*Due to these advantages, the use of e-book readers is growing at a rapid rate.*

## Organizational Patterns

There are a number of ways authors may choose to organize information. The organizational pattern depends on the type of information included and the purpose of the writing. Using the proper organizational pattern helps readers better understand the ideas included in the paragraphs.

### Chronological Order

Chronological order tells events in the order in which they occurred. This is most effective when the actual sequence in which the actions took place—or the sequence of steps in a process—is important for the reader to understand. Depending on the message of the passage, the events may be told in reverse chronological order, beginning with what took place most recently and moving backward in time.

## Order of Importance

When a passage uses this organizational structure, the information may be arranged in one of two ways. First, the most important idea may be discussed at the beginning, followed by the second most important idea, and so on. The passage ends with the idea that the author believes is least important. The advantage of this type of organization is that the most important information catches the reader's attention at the very beginning.

Second, the least important idea may be discussed first, and the following ideas build in importance until the passage concludes with the most important one. The advantage of this type of organization is that the reader is left to ponder the most important idea, which is fresh in his or her mind.

## Compare and Contrast

This organizational structure highlights the similarities and differences between people, ideas, or objects. This may be done by describing the first item completely and then describing the second completely. For example, an essay comparing and contrasting Hawaii and Bermuda might fully discuss one island and then the other.

Another way to organize a compare-and-contrast structure is to discuss how a particular attribute relates to each of the objects, then discuss each of the items in reference to a second attribute, and so on. In this case, one paragraph might discuss the locations of Hawaii and Bermuda, the next paragraph might talk about each location's climate, and the following paragraph might describe sightseeing on both islands.

## Cause and Effect

A cause-and-effect organizational structure points out how one idea or event impacts another. Words such as *consequently, as a result,* and *if . . . then* often signal a cause-and-effect relationship between concepts.

### Keep in Mind

Keep in mind that a single event may be the cause of several other events. Likewise, several causes may lead to the same result. For example, the single event of forgetting to set your alarm clock may cause you to skip breakfast, miss the carpool, and be late for school or work. This one cause could lead to all three effects. On the other hand, studying hard, completing the practice questions, and carefully reading each of the chapters in this book could lead to your success on the HiSET Exam. In this case, three causes could bring about one positive effect.

### Problem and Solution

In this organizational structure, a problem is stated and then one, or several, possible solutions are discussed. If only one solution is proposed, the body paragraphs will typically focus on the benefits of that solution.

### Question and Answer

In this organizational structure, a question is posed, followed by an answer. An essay may include several sets of questions and answers. This essay structure is generally easy to recognize.

## Transitions

**Transitions** are words or phrases that help to organize effective writing by pointing out the correct order of ideas or by highlighting how ideas are related. Different transitions serve different purposes. On the HiSET Exam, you will be asked to select the transition that could improve a given passage. Here are a few transitions that signal different types of relationships in writing.

**Cause and effect**: *accordingly, as a result, because, consequently, hence, since*
**Comparison**: *as well as, both, in common, likewise, similarly*
**Contrast**: *although, however, on the other hand, nevertheless, rather, unlike, yet*
**Introducing examples**: *for example, in fact, specifically*
**Showing addition**: *also, furthermore, in addition*
**Time or sequence**: *first, finally, initially, meanwhile, next, preceding, then, until*

# Question Steps

For questions involving effective organization of a passage, the six steps are a bit different. Instead of focusing on grammar, mechanics, and other details, you will focus on the big picture. Here are the six steps that will help you.

---

*Steps in Identifying Effective Organization*

**Step 1:** Read the Passage

**Step 2:** Read the Question

**Step 3:** Identify the Main Idea and Supporting Details

**Step 4:** Identify the Organizational Pattern

**Step 5:** Look for Transitions

**Step 6:** Select the Best Revision

---

## Step 1: Read the Passage

You should already be in the habit of reading the passage, so this is not a difficult step to remember. Read the entire passage carefully.

## Step 2: Read the Question

After reading the paragraph, you may already have a few ideas about revisions that should be made to improve the writing, but read the question without looking at the answer choices. Find out exactly which part of the passage the question addresses. Then reread not only the sentence or section in the question but the surrounding sentences in the passage as well. This will help you to see the sentence or paragraph in the context of the passage as a whole. Organization generally deals with a paragraph or large section of text. Do not try to answer the questions by focusing solely on a single word or sentence. It will be easier to make the correct revision when you view the information in context.

## Step 3: Identify the Main Idea and Supporting Details

As you read, look for the main idea and supporting details. Pay attention to the order in which the ideas are presented. Keep in mind that what you are reading is not a perfect passage. In fact, it was purposely written to include errors, since the whole point of the test is for you to find the errors and fix them. As you go, think about which sentences belong and which ones do not. Think about which ones seem to be in the correct order and which do not. Think about which paragraphs have a clear main idea and which do not.

Depending on the content of the question, you may need to identify the main idea of the entire passage or of a specific paragraph. Read carefully, find the main point the author intended to convey, and look for details and information that support this key concept.

## Step 4: Identify the Organizational Pattern

As you read the imperfect passage, try to figure out what organizational pattern the author used—or attempted to use. Once you have figured this out, you will know what information you should be looking for. For example, if the passage uses a cause-and-effect organizational pattern, you will need to identify the cause and then look for what happened as a result of this action or event. If the effects are not clear, you may have just found one revision that needs to be made when you answer the questions about the passage.

## Step 5: Look for Transitions

There are several reasons you will be looking for transitions at this point. First, identifying transitions can help you connect the information in the passage. This, in turn, can help to clarify the information. Second, transitions can offer a clue about the type of organizational pattern being used. Third, if you do not find enough transitions to clearly understand the information or the organizational pattern, you may have determined one way to improve the passage. In this case, decide what transition would be helpful, as you may need to answer a question related to this issue.

## Step 6: Select the Best Revision

Finally, read all of the answer choices. Do not stop reading once you find an answer choice that sounds good; it might not be the best choice or most effective revision. The only way to know for sure that any answer choice is the best one is to know what all of them say.

Once you have read every answer choice, select the best revision. Read the section of the passage as you have revised it to be sure that you have selected the best revision.

# Examples

Here are two sample questions that deal with organization. Remember to use the big picture steps for organization questions.

> Over the past few years, the popularity of virtual schools has increased. More and
> through online learning. Virtual schools have as many supporters as opponents, and there
> are definitely advantages and disadvantages to these nontraditional teaching forums.
>
> Line
> 5
> What is often viewed as one of the greatest benefits of virtual schools is the flexibility
> they offer. Many programs allow students to learn at their own pace and set their own
> schedules. This allows schoolwork to be completed around work or sports schedules.  This
> flexibility also offers students the opportunity to study at the times of the day when they
> are most ready to learn. Many students pursuing professional sports careers find this to be
> a great advantage.
>
> 10
> <u>Virtual schools do not offer the same type of socialization that students are exposed to
> in traditional classrooms.</u> While students do interact with each other and with teachers
> via the computer, they do not have the face-to-face contact that traditional students
> experience. Many educators agree that cooperative learning is essential in preparing
> children to enter the world, specifically the workforce. The types of interactions offered
> 15
> through virtual learning are different than the types of interactions students will
> experience when dealing with other people in the world around them.
>
> While it is unlikely that virtual schools will ever completely replace traditional
> classrooms, some school districts are beginning to require students to take at least a few
> online classes prior to graduation. There are undoubtedly some disadvantages to taking
> 20
> such classes. However, there are some benefits to consider as well.

1. **Which of the following would be the best improvement for the second paragraph?**
   A   Delete the last sentence.
   B   Move the final sentence to directly follow the first sentence.
   C   Move the first sentence to the end of the paragraph.
   D   Move the last sentence to follow the third sentence.

## Explanation

First, read the passage. Read the question. Since the question focuses on the second paragraph, reread this paragraph. Look for the main idea and supporting details of this paragraph. The main idea is that virtual schools offer flexibility. The supporting details are that students learn at their own pace, set their own schedules, and learn at the time of day when they are most ready to learn. Identify the organizational pattern. The entire passage compares and contrasts the advantages and disadvantages of virtual schools. This paragraph lists details in order of importance. Look for transitions. In this paragraph, you will find the transition *also*. Select the best revision. The last sentence discusses the flexibility of virtual schools in relation to sports. It would make more sense for this to follow the third sentence, which introduces the idea of a sports schedule. **The best answer is D.**

**Sentence 9:** Virtual schools do not offer the same type of socialization that students are exposed to in traditional classrooms.

2. **Which of the following would be the best improvement for the underlined sentence?**
   A   Add *On the other hand* to the beginning of the sentence.
   B   Add *In addition* to the beginning of the sentence.
   C   Move the sentence to the end of paragraph 2.
   D   Move the sentence to the end of paragraph 3.

## Explanation

You read the passage already, so read the question. Since the question focuses on the first sentence of the third paragraph, review paragraph 2 and reread paragraph 3. Look for the main idea and supporting details of the third paragraph. The main idea is that virtual schools do not offer the same social benefits as traditional schools. The supporting details are that students do not have face-to-face contact, that educators think cooperative learning is essential, and that virtual learning has different interactions from those students will have in the real world. Identify the organizational pattern. The entire passage compares and contrasts the advantages and disadvantages of virtual schools. This paragraph focuses on the disadvantages. Look for transitions. In this paragraph, you will find the transition *while*. Select the best revision. The underlined sentence is the first one in the paragraph and paragraph 3 shifts from the advantages in paragraph 2 to disadvantages. You need a transition that signals a change in direction to make this shift. Choices A and B add transitions, but Choice B is a same-direction transition. **The best answer is A.**

# ORGANIZATION OF IDEAS DRILLS

**Questions 1–9 refer to the following passage.**

*(1) Although many children can state what they want to be when they grow up, selecting a career path is a major decision. (2) Often people waver between several options before settling on the job that is just right. (3) Before making such a major decision, there are a number of factors that should be seriously considered.*

*(4) Everyone has certain things they like to do better than other things. (5) Someone who enjoys working with animals might consider a career in veterinary medicine, while someone who is allergic to dogs should think of other options. (6) Most dogs have to go to the vet for regular checkups. (7) A career as a coach or P.E. teacher might be a good choice for a person who enjoys being outside and staying active, whereas this would not be a good choice for someone who tries to avoid being in the sun.*

*(8) Next, the education required for a career should be considered. (9) Some careers require a high school diploma, while others require a college education. (10) This is important to think about, since someone who is not a strong student would likely be frustrated by the amount of schooling required by some careers.*

*(11) On the other hand, attending four years of college and then going on to law school to become an attorney might be an exciting adventure for students who like to study. (12) In addition to the amount of schooling needed to pursue a career, the types of classes required should also be considered. (13) A career in accounting would require taking a number of math classes in college. (14) While this might sound like a lot of fun for some people, others might cringe at the thought of studying numbers for four years.*

*(15) Then, lifestyle goals should be thought about as well. (16) While some of these goals may be financial, others may relate to leisure and family time. (17) Obviously, some careers will offer more substantial paychecks than others. (18) However, these same careers may also require more work hours, less flexible schedules, and more demands on personal time. (19) It is important to determine an acceptable balance between salary and self. (20) Some people are happy to work nights, weekends, and holidays in order to earn a larger paycheck, while other people choose to work more traditional business hours for a more modest paycheck in order to have time with their families. (21) There is no single job choice that is right for everyone. (22) Choosing a career path to follow is a very personal decision. (23) If you choose a career that requires a college education, be sure to apply to schools early. (24) The most important thing is to carefully consider each and every factor to ensure that the best option is chosen.*

1. **Which sentence below would be most effective at the beginning of the second paragraph?**

   A Second, it is important to think about what types of things one would enjoy.

   B First, interests, talents, and hobbies should be taken into consideration.

   C People should think about what types of jobs would interest them.

   D Furthermore, different careers would be best for different people.

2. **Which revision would improve the effectiveness of the second paragraph?**

   A remove sentence 6

   B remove sentence 7

   C reverse sentences 5 and 6

   D move sentence 4 to the end of the paragraph

3. **Which transition would best be added to the beginning of sentence 13?**

   A   nevertheless

   B   in addition

   C   as a result

   D   for example

4. **In order to improve the effectiveness of this passage, a new paragraph could begin with**

   A   sentence 21

   B   sentence 7

   C   sentence 10

   D   sentence 13

5. **Which revision should be made to sentence 15?**

   A   replace *Then* with *Similarly*

   B   replace *Then* with *Finally*

   C   replace *as well* with *in addition*

   D   replace *as well* with *however*

6. **Which revision would improve the effectiveness of this passage?**

   A   remove sentence 16

   B   remove sentence 17

   C   move sentence 1 to the end of the first paragraph

   D   move sentence 11 to the end of the fourth paragraph

7. **Which sentence could be removed to improve the effectiveness of the final paragraph?**

   A   sentence 18

   B   sentence 20

   C   sentence 23

   D   sentence 24

8. **Which of the following sentences could best be added to the second paragraph?**

   A   While dogs are one of the most popular pets, many people choose to have cats.

   B   Someone who enjoys exercise might also enjoy working as a personal trainer.

   C   These people should be sure to wear sunscreen any time they are outside.

   D   Some veterinarians are on call for emergencies over the weekend.

9.  **To which paragraph would the following sentence best be added?**

    **Someone planning a career in medicine should expect to take quite a few science courses, such as biology, chemistry, and anatomy.**

    A   the first paragraph

    B   the second paragraph

    C   the fourth paragraph

    D   the fifth paragraph

---

**Questions 10–15 refer to the following passage.**

*(1) There are three main components of the life of an academic: research and writing, teaching, and service. (2) Each of these three are important, but of the three, research (and publishing) is by far the most important. (3) For a new academic, life centers around one thing: securing tenure. (4) Academics are left with little time for a social life.*

*(5) The adage "publish or perish" seems to be the rule at most colleges and universities. (6) Excellence in teaching and service, while admirable, will not assure tenure. (7) A new faculty member has six years before tenure review and must spend that time wisely. (8) Research and writing takes time and getting published may take even more time. (9) Scholars seeking tenure should work on smaller pieces, rather than a large project that may take years to complete. (10) Scholars may read papers at conferences, do reviews for journals, and write articles for magazines and newspapers, but nothing looks as good at tenure time as having numerous publications in well-respected journals.*

*(11) Faculty members are expected to serve on departmental and faculty-wide committees. (12) Committee membership involves attending meetings and events, listening to the ideas of others with respect, and contributing ideas when appropriate. (13) The third component of the academic life is service. (14) A scholar seeking tenure should never miss a meeting, cultural event, or social event sponsored by her department and if asked to serve on a faculty-wide committee.*

*(15) Teaching is another important component in the life of an academic. (16) Student and faculty evaluations affect tenure decisions, so this component cannot be neglected. (17) First, an instructor's primary job is to motivate and engage her students. (18) Second, she must be organized. (19) She must use concrete examples and be able to adapt her explanations to the different learning styles of her students. (20) Finally, she must be able to offer overviews of the topic, not just details. (21) She must show how the information is synthesized and affects the whole of the topic.*

*(22) These three components make up the professional life of an academic, both before and after tenure. (23) After achieving tenure, the pressure may be off, but the job does not change. (24) An experienced instructor may become better at teaching and more students may seek her as an advisor. (25) She may be asked to serve on more important committees. (26) As she increases her knowledge of her field, she should be able to publish more erudite works and, with the pressure of achieving tenure off, she can devote more time to a single work.*

10.  **Which revision would improve the effectiveness of the first paragraph?**

    A   remove sentence 2

    B   reverse sentences 2 and 3

    C   remove sentence 4

    D   move sentence 5 to the end of the first paragraph

11. **Which of the following sentences would best be added to the end of the second paragraph?**

   A  "Publish or perish" is an unfair standard for universities to impose on their faculty.

   B  They must do all this while teaching and serving.
   C  An academic must make the time for research by sacrificing class preparation.
   D  Service is not as important as research and publication, but it must be done.

12. **Which transition would best be added to the beginning of sentence 19?**
   A  For example,
   B  Therefore,
   C  As a result,
   D  Third,

13. **Which revision would improve the effectiveness of the third paragraph?**
   A  move sentence 13 to the beginning of the paragraph
   B  reverse sentences 12 and 13
   C  remove sentence 14
   D  move sentence 14 to the beginning of the paragraph

14. **Which revision would improve the effectiveness of this passage?**
   A  Switch the order of paragraphs 2 and 3
   B  Switch the order of paragraphs 3 and 4
   C  Switch the order of paragraphs 2 and 4
   D  Combine paragraphs 3 and 4

15. **Which of the following sentences would best be added to the end of the final paragraph?**

   A  Details may change, but an academic life remains one of research, teaching, and service.

   B  Teaching should be the most important role, but sadly, it is not.
   C  Without publications, tenure will be impossible to achieve.
   D  Since an academic's main goal is to achieve tenure, research should be the primary focus.

**Answers are on page 718.**

# 9 Preparing for the *HiSET*® Exam Essay

Part 2 of the HiSET Exam Language Arts—Writing test will involve writing an expository essay on a familiar topic. You will be given a prompt and have 45 minutes to plan, write, and revise your writing. The essay is not intended to be a research paper. The topic will be something of general interest and will likely ask you to state your opinion on a subject and use examples from your own knowledge and experience to support your opinion. Your score will not be based on whether or not you have the "right" answer. It will be based on how well you develop your essay and support your opinion.

## What Is Tested?

The essay will be scored using a six-point rubric, meaning you will be able to earn up to six points for a response that demonstrates the following writing characteristics. The better each of these traits is addressed, the higher your score will be.

- **Response to the prompt.** To earn the highest possible score, your essay needs to include a clearly focused main idea that addresses the prompt, or topic, given.
- **Organization of ideas.** Your essay should clearly demonstrate a logical organizational pattern, including an introduction and conclusion, logical paragraphs, and effective transition.
- **Development and details.** An essay that scores six points is well developed and includes relevant supporting details and examples to support the main idea of the text.
- **Written conventions.** You need to consistently and accurately apply the rules of sentence structure, grammar, capitalization, punctuation, and spelling to your essay.
- **Language facility.** Your essay should include precise words and varied sentence structure to express your ideas clearly.

## The Parts of an Essay

As you learned in the previous chapter on organization, an expository essay should include an introduction, a body, and a conclusion.

## Introduction

The introduction is the first paragraph of the essay. The purpose of this paragraph is to catch the reader's attention, introduce the topic, and state the main idea of the entire passage. In an essay, the main idea is given in a sentence called the **thesis statement**, which is usually found at the end of the introduction. It states the point that the essay is going to make.

### Keep in Mind

Keep in mind that you will be scored on how well your essay addresses the prompt. Make sure your thesis statement clearly refers to the ideas you're asked to discuss. If possible, word your thesis statement in such a way that it repeats some of the wording of the prompt. By doing this and supporting your thesis statement in the body of the text, you should be able to stay on topic and clearly respond to the prompt given.

## Body

The body of the essay is where all of the supporting details are found. If an essay were a sandwich, the introduction and conclusion would be the bread, and the body of the essay would be the meat. All of the facts, examples, definitions, and explanations that support the thesis statement are found in the body of the essay.

There is no magic number of paragraphs that the body of an essay should include. Forty-five minutes is not a lot of time, so the essay you write on the HiSET Exam may be somewhat limited in length. The prompt will be direct enough that you should be able to address it completely within this time.

With that in mind, your essay will most likely include about five paragraphs; one will be the introduction, three will be the body, and one will be the conclusion. Of course, you may find that you need more than three paragraphs to fully develop the information in the body of your essay, which is fine. For most topics, five paragraphs will generally be sufficient.

Each paragraph in the body will have a main idea that supports your thesis statement. The remaining sentences in each paragraph will support the main idea of the paragraph. Start each body paragraph with a topic sentence that states the main idea of that paragraph.

### Keep in Mind

Keep in mind that part of your score on this part of the test will be based on how well you develop your ideas. The body of the essay is where these points will be earned. Make sure that the main idea of each paragraph is a reason, fact, or example that helps to explain your thesis statement. Then make sure that each paragraph includes enough information to prove the main idea. Answer any appropriate question words about the main idea: *who, what, where, when, why,* and *how.*

## Conclusion

The last paragraph of the essay is the conclusion. This paragraph should restate the main idea given in your thesis statement, reminding the reader of your answer to the prompt. The conclusion should also provide a sense of closure; readers should feel that the essay is complete. This final paragraph should let readers know this is the end, without actually saying *the end*.

# Steps for Writing the Essay

Here are six steps for writing an effective passage.

### Steps for Writing an Essay

**Step 1:** Read the Prompt

**Step 2:** Determine Your Main Idea

**Step 3:** Select Your Supporting Details

**Step 4:** Write the Draft

**Step 5:** Revise the Draft

**Step 6:** Edit the Essay

## Step 1: Read the Prompt

The prompt for the essay is not stated in the form of a simple question, such as *What is your favorite color?* It will most likely include several sentences, along with a directive regarding what you should write. Read it carefully, and know exactly what information you are being asked to give. If you realize halfway through the essay that you misunderstood the prompt, you probably will not have time to go back and start over, so read it carefully. (Read it twice if you need to.) Do whatever is necessary to make sure you understand exactly what you are being asked to write about.

Look for key words in the prompt. This can help you to focus on what and how you should write. Look for verbs such as *explain* or *describe*. Also look for words that state specifics that should be included, such as *one special person* or *three reasons*. A prompt that asks you to tell about *three important events in your life* is asking for something completely different than one that asks you to give *three reasons why one event was important*.

To help you learn the steps for writing an essay, here is a sample prompt:

*What does it take to be a good student?*

*In your essay, describe the characteristics of a good student. Use specific details to explain your opinion. Use your personal knowledge, experience, and observations.*

It may be helpful to restate the prompt in your own words. This can help you to focus on exactly what you need to write. You might restate this prompt as: What are the characteristics of a good student?

## Step 2: Determine Your Main Idea

Before you begin writing, you must think about what information you want to include and plan how to organize it most effectively. The first step in planning will be to determine the main idea of your essay.

The main idea should be directly related to the requirements of the prompt. To make sure you are addressing the topic directly, try restating a few words from the prompt in the main idea. This can help you stay on track. Remember, there is no single correct way to write the thesis statement for any essay. If ten people were to write effective essays on the same prompt, they might have ten different thesis statements. The most important thing is to be sure that your thesis statement addresses the prompt and is something you can adequately support.

Sample thesis statement: *Good students share a number of positive characteristics.*

## Step 3: Select Your Supporting Details

The details you choose must provide strong support for the idea or opinion given in your thesis statement. These facts, examples, and opinions must clearly explain the main idea of the essay and convince readers that your thesis statement is true.

Before you start writing, decide which supporting details will be most effective in your essay. Begin by brainstorming a list of possibilities; then select about three to include. These supporting details will each become the main idea of one body paragraph. Make sure you select ideas that you will be able to write several sentences about. Also, select the three that best explain your thesis statement.

Sample supporting details: *Good students are well prepared for class; good students are often well organized; good students always complete their homework; good students always do the required reading; good students take responsibility for their own learning.*

If you have more than three ideas for supporting details, as shown above, find the three that will best explain your thesis statement to readers. Then look at the remaining ideas on the list to see if some of these are closely related to the top three. If so, you may be able to use them as support in one of the paragraphs. For example, suppose one of your strongest supporting details is *good students are well prepared for class*. Other ideas on your list, such as *good students always complete their homework* and *good students always do the required reading*, could fit into the paragraph about being well prepared.

Once you have selected the supporting details, determine how to organize them most effectively. Would they work best if arranged in a compare-and-contrast format? Would they be conveyed most effectively using a cause-and-effect organizational pattern? In the case of the sample prompt, you might organize the supporting details in order of least to most important.

## Keep in Mind

Keep in mind that any planning and prewriting should be completed on scrap paper. Only the actual essay will be turned in. The good news here is that you do not have to work neatly as you complete Steps 2 and 3; you can cross things off, draw graphic organizers, or mark arrows to move information around. The bad news is that you will need to work quickly to get all of these ideas onto the actual page of the essay. You may have written great ideas on your planning page, but they will only be scored if they make it into your final essay.

## Step 4: Write the Draft

Here is where the actual writing begins. Begin by writing an introduction that is interesting enough to make readers want to hear what you have to say. Include your thesis statement in this first paragraph.

### Sample Introduction

*In any class, whether in elementary school, high school, or college, some students are stronger and more academically successful than others. What makes some students more likely to do well in school than others? While all of these successful learners are individuals, a number of positive characteristics are often seen in good students.*

Then begin writing the body. Each of the supporting statements selected in Step 3 is now the main idea of its own body paragraph. Include enough examples, facts, details, and explanations about each main idea to justify clearly why you felt this statement was important enough to include. Remember to arrange the paragraphs according to the organizational structure that is most effective for the type of essay you are writing. Include appropriate transitions to move from topic to topic.

### Sample Body Paragraph

*One characteristic commonly demonstrated by good students is that they are well prepared for class. These students have completed their homework assignments and done any required reading before the beginning of class. They also have their textbooks, calculators, pencils, and class notes with them each day. So when the teacher or professor arrives, these students are ready to learn.*

Finally, write the conclusion. Remember to revisit your thesis statement and to wrap up the essay in a way that leaves readers feeling that you have completely covered the topic.

### Sample Conclusion

*Being a good student often goes hand in hand with being well prepared, organized, and responsible. These characteristics of good students often make a significant difference in the level of academic success achieved in school.*

## Step 5: Revise the Draft

Once the draft is completed, take a few minutes to read your essay carefully. Ask yourself questions such as, *Does that make sense? Would more details help to explain this idea better? Does every sentence support the main idea?*

As you read, look for places where more information or additional details would make the piece more effective. Add words, clarify ideas, and rearrange information to improve the essay. Remove any information that does not fit or is not relevant.

## Step 6: Edit the Essay

Editing is not the same as revising. Revising is about clarity and organization, the big picture. Editing is about the details. Editing is where you apply all of those rules you learned about grammar, capitalization, punctuation, and spelling. Carefully check your writing to make sure that you have applied these conventions correctly. Make any necessary changes. Remember, errors in mechanics and conventions can impact the overall quality of writing, as well as the reader's ability to clearly comprehend your ideas, both of which can affect your score.

### Keep in Mind

Keep in mind that you will have 45 minutes to complete this portion of the test. That means you have a total of 45 minutes to plan, draft, revise, and edit your essay. While that may sound like a lot of time, you will need to budget these minutes wisely to ensure that you have time to complete all six of the steps. The following is a basic guideline for how you may want to allot the time given to complete the essay.

- **Step 1:** Read the prompt—2 minutes
- **Step 2:** Determine the main idea—3 minutes
- **Step 3:** Select supporting details—5 minutes
- **Step 4:** Write the draft—25 minutes
- **Step 5:** Revise the draft—5 minutes
- **Step 6:** Edit the essay—5 minutes

Time yourself as you work through the sample prompts in this book. At first, try to follow this guideline for budgeting the time. Then customize the plan to fit your specific needs. If you find that you need a little bit longer to plan your writing, for example, take a couple of extra minutes to plan and shave a few minutes from the amount of time used for writing the draft. However you decide to allot the 45 minutes, make sure that you have plenty of time to complete the writing and leave time at the end to double-check your work.

# Example

Following is an example of a student essay that would receive a high score on the HiSET Exam. As you read it, notice how it addresses the prompt, how it is organized, and how it follows the conventions for good writing.

**How have "smart phones" transformed society? Use your personal observations, experience, and knowledge to support your essay.**

### Smart Phones

"Ding ding" has become a commonly heard noise from smart phones. Today's generation revolves completely around the use of smart phones. Smart phones have completely transformed our society and are now seen as a need in everyday life. Even though some people claim that smart phones have "dumbed down" users, no one can deny that smart phones have made this world easier to live in. Smart phones make communication easier, provide information, and entertain their users.

Communicating with people has become so much easier and faster because it only takes a few seconds to communicate through a smart phone. Whether it is to call a loved one that lives in another state or send a quick note through text messaging, smart phones make it simple. Text messaging has become one of the easiest ways to communicate because it is literally right at the fingertips. The traditional function, making a phone call, allows the user to easily keep in touch with family or have a long conversation with an old friend. This is much quicker than writing a letter that might take a few days to reach its destination. Another way to communicate with your family and friends is through social media such as Facebook and Twitter. Communication through text messaging, calling, and social media on a smart phone has made it so much easier to interact with friends and family.

Smart phones also provide instant information. Website and application technology have improved dramatically over the years. Live news feeds keep users updated on what is happening anywhere in the world. Keeping up with a favorite band, company, political party, or sports team is easy with a web browser on a smart phone. Applications let users use GPS, do instant banking, schedule appointments, and find out answers to nearly any question possible. In fact, the iPhone has a search engine called Siri, which can be talked to and asked questions. Siri will talk back to the user! It is like having a virtual assistant. Smart phones allow all this information to be in the palm of a hand.

In addition to providing instant access to information and easing communication, smart phones are portable entertainment devices. Games, videos, and music are all examples of entertainment smart phone users have access to. When waiting in a long line or in a lobby, a game on a smart phone can be at hand. There are many varieties of games, whether the game is just for fun or to help brain skills. The game "Words with Friends" is like the game of Scrabble, in which players try to make words to earn more points than their opponents. "Angry Birds" is a game that involves flinging birds at structures to knock them down. Smart phones also play music and videos. Users can listen to radio stations or download music that they want to keep. Movies can be rented or purchased, and some video content is free. *YouTube* is an internet website that allows users to upload videos and watch others' videos for free. Searching for any video is possible whether it be funny, serious, or informational. Netflix and Amazon offer on-demand videos for a fee. The smart phone has many options for entertainment that fit everybody.

40    There are many things smart phones can help with these days; without them, things would not be so simple. Communication with the touch of a finger would not be possible. Getting in touch with distant family members and friends would not be so easy and it would take much longer to talk. News would not be able to be travel the world as quickly. People would have to work much harder to get information. Smart

45    phones can also provide hours of entertainment in various forms. The technology that has been put into the smart phone has made the smart phone very popular. Without the smart phone today, life would be more difficult for many people.

# ESSAY WRITING DRILLS

Now it is your turn to put all of this information into practice. Read the following prompt, and follow the six steps for writing an effective HiSET Exam essay. Get a timer and set it for 45 minutes. When you are ready to begin, start the timer and begin with Step 1 by reading the prompt. If you finish before the timer stops, go back and check your work. If the timer rings before you are finished with your essay, stop and take a look at how far you have gotten. Then go ahead and finish the essay. Make sure to work through all six steps for practice, regardless of the time.

**What one place that you have never been would you like to visit someday?**

**In your essay, name one place you would like to visit someday, and explain why you would like to go there. Use your personal observations, experience, and knowledge to support your essay.**

_____

_____

_____

_____

_____

_____

_____

_____

_____

_____

_____

_____

_____

_____

_____

_____

_____

_____

_____

_____

_____

_____

_____

Writing a sample essay such as this can be very informative. You may have learned that the 45-minute time limit should be adjusted a bit to fit your needs. You may have found that you are completely comfortable selecting a main idea and supporting details. If you found any areas in which you need a little extra practice or review, go back over these sections of the book. For example, if you were unsure of exactly where to place commas in your essay, glance back at the section that discusses punctuation.

Now take another look at the prompt and reread your essay. Be critical. Did you stay on topic? Does every part of the essay explain why you would like to visit a single place? Are there enough reasons included to show why visiting this location is important to you? If not, go back and make any revisions that will improve your essay.

Here is a second practice topic. This time refine your timing and your process to improve your performance.

Choosing a college is an important decision. Write an essay to explain what factors should be taken into consideration when selecting which college to attend. Use your personal observations, experience, and knowledge to support your essay.

_____

_____

_____

_____

_____

_____

_____

_____

_____

_____

_____

_____

_____

_____

_____

_____

_____

_____

_____

_____

_____

# Part IV
# Social Studies

# 10 The Social Studies Test

The *HiSET*® Exam Social Studies test is a one-part multiple-choice test. You will be given 70 minutes to answer a total of 50 questions in the areas of world and U.S. history, civics and government, economics, and geography. Some of the questions will be based on reading passages containing 250 words or less. Others will be based on graphics such as maps, tables, illustrations, diagrams, political cartoons, or graphs. Some questions will combine a reading passage with a visual.

To answer these questions, you will need to demonstrate the ability to comprehend, restate, summarize, and draw inferences based on the information in the passage, document, quotation, or illustration. The good news is that you will not have to recall everything you have ever learned about social studies. However, you will need to rely on what you already know about important social studies concepts and events and combine this information with the facts and data given in each question.

Chapters 11 through 15 each cover one area of the Social Studies test: World History, U.S. History, Civics and Government, Economics, and Geography.

## Question Steps

As with each test on the HiSET Exam, there are some steps you can follow to help you approach the questions. For the Social Studies test, here are the six steps you will use to find the correct answer:

> ### Social Studies Steps
>
> **Step 1:** Read All the Information
>
> **Step 2:** Identify the Question
>
> **Step 3:** Underline Key Words and Phrases
>
> **Step 4:** Determine Meanings
>
> **Step 5:** Think About What You Already Know
>
> **Step 6:** Select the Best Answer

## Step 1: Read All the Information

The first step to correctly answer any question is to read all of the information carefully. Since so many of the questions on this test involve graphics, reading may include titles, captions, keys, graphs, charts, and labels, in addition to the reading passages and the questions themselves. Be sure to pay attention to what is included in illustrations, drawings, photos, and cartoons as well.

### Keep in Mind

Keep in mind that certain types of social studies questions are more likely to depend on visual aids than others. For example, you can expect to find more graphs that relate to economics and civics questions than to other areas of social studies and more maps that relate to geography questions than to other types of questions.

## Step 2: Identify the Question

After reading everything you can find, make sure you understand exactly what the question is asking. For example, you may need to identify what occurred during a given historical event, what led up to the event, or what took place afterward. Carefully read the question and determine what information you are being asked to explain. It may be helpful to restate the question in your own words to be sure you understand it.

## Step 3: Key Words and Phrases

Now that you know what the question is asking, go back through the passage or graphics and look for any pertinent key words, dates, phrases, or facts. For example, if the question refers to artifacts from an ancient Egyptian civilization, note the word *artifacts* as well as any examples mentioned. If the question asks about who discovered the artifacts or when they were found, look for relevant names and dates as well. During the test, you will be reading a lot of facts in a relatively short time. It would be easy to confuse information from one passage to the next. Take a few seconds to search for important information to ensure that you are focusing on the correct facts.

## Step 4: Determine Meanings

As you know, there are times when words or phrases in a reading passage are unfamiliar. It is important on a timed test that you not let that frustrate you. First, take a look at the word or words you are unsure of and then use contextual clues to try to figure out their meanings. Think about what would make sense in the context of the sentence or passage. Look for hints in the sentence and the surrounding sentences that can offer clues about what the word or phrase means. You might find a definition or example that can help you out.

If that does not work, break the word apart and see if the root word, prefix, or suffix looks familiar. Do you know another word with a similar root? If so, see if that gives you an idea of what the new word might mean. Think back to all of the reading tricks you learned in elementary and middle school and put them to use now. Also, take a look at Part V of this book that deals with reading comprehension. It reviews several helpful reading skills that could come in handy when you are faced with unfamiliar words.

## Step 5: Think About What You Already Know

After reading everything you can find, figuring out what the question is asking, and determining the meanings of key words, consider what you already know about the topic. Remember that many of the questions will require some thinking on your part. In other words, the answers may not be directly stated in the passage. Try to make connections between your own prior knowledge and the facts presented on the test.

## Step 6: Select the Best Answer

The key word in this final step is *best*. More than one answer may appear to be at least partially correct, so be sure you read every choice. Your job is to select the single *best* answer choice.

# Examples

To show you how the steps work, here is a sample question dealing with U.S. history:

*Anne Hutchinson was tried, convicted, and banished from the Massachusetts Bay colony in 1637 for heresy. During the trial, Governor Winthrop and the other judges accused her of seducing others to her religious opinions, of vanity, of not knowing her*

Line

*place as a woman in Puritan society. Afterwards, Winthrop intensified his vilification of*

5

*Hutchinson, calling her "an instrument of Satan" and comparing her to the "Whore of Babylon." Seen through the eyes of these men, Hutchinson seems practically demonic. Yet she had many followers, both men and women. She formed close personal bonds with her family, fellow worshippers, and the women she aided in childbirth. The only surviving words of hers are in the trial transcripts, recorded by men. In the transcripts, she proves to*

10

*be a worthy legal adversary, verbally sparring with her judges. She demands specifics of what laws she broke, proof of her alleged words, and formal oaths from the ministers. She focuses on the difference between public and private discourse and defends her right to speak. Her skill forced Winthrop to alter the charges against her several times, but the verdict was most likely assured before the trial even began. The male authorities needed*

15

*to remove the threat she posed to their doctrine of works as well as to their control over the speech of the colony.*

1.  **Which of the following can be most properly inferred from the passage?**
    A   Some people in the Massachusetts Bay Colony supported Anne Hutchinson.
    B   Anne Hutchinson was imprisoned after her conviction in 1637.
    C   Governor Winthrop had a personal grudge against Hutchinson.
    D   Hutchinson was the first woman put on trial in the American colonies.

### Explanation

**Step 1:** Read All the Information

**Step 2:** Identify the Question

The question asks you to *infer* something from the passage. This means that you will be reading the answer choices and determining which of them is supported by the passage. It does not mean that three of the choices are false. You might also see choices that are irrelevant or beyond the scope of the passage. Be sure that the one you choose is true, based on what you read in the passage.

**Step 3:** Key Words and Phrases

You need to determine which answer choice contains accurate information. Since names and a date are mentioned, look for them in the answer choices. You might also take note of *supported, imprisoned, personal grudge*, and *first woman*. You can look for these terms (or similar ones) in the passage.

**Step 4:** Determine Meanings

The words *vilification, sparring*, and *discourse* may be unfamiliar, so use information in the surrounding text to figure out what they mean. Take a look at the sections of the passage in which those terms appear.

>   *Winthrop intensified his <u>vilification</u> of Hutchinson, calling her "an instrument of Satan"*

This shows Winthrop was saying bad things about Hutchinson. Vilification probably means something similar to insulting.

>   *She proves to be a worthy legal adversary, verbally <u>sparring</u> with her judges. She demands specifics of what laws she broke, proof of her alleged words, and formal oaths from the ministers.*

What was Hutchinson doing at her trial? She was fighting back against the judges, arguing with them and questioning them. *Sparring* most likely means fighting.

>   *She focuses on the difference between public and private <u>discourse</u> and defends her right to speak.*

Since Hutchinson is defending her right to speak, she must be talking about speaking here. She is saying that there is a difference between speaking in public and speaking in private. *Discourse* probably means something similar to speaking.

**Step 5:** Think About What You Already Know

Even if you do not remember anything about Anne Hutchinson, you probably know something about Puritan society in colonial America. Consider what you have learned, heard, or read about the Puritans in the past. Use this information, along with the information in the text, to complete Step 6.

**Step 6:** Select the Best Answer

According to the passage, answer choice A is the best answer. The passage does not say that Hutchinson was imprisoned but does say she was banished from the colony after her trial, so answer choice B can be eliminated. The passage also does not claim that she was the first woman put on trial, so choice D can be eliminated. Choice C may seem tempting since the passage makes it sound like Winthrop did not like Hutchinson, but the passage does not say that this was because of a personal reason. You do not even know if he had any prior contact with her before the trial itself. The passage says that Hutchinson had many followers and formed close personal bonds, so certainly some people supported her. **Choice A is the best answer**.

Try using the steps with a question involving a graphic.

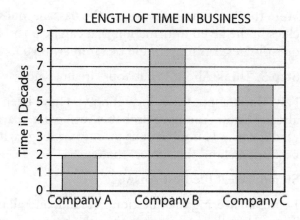

2.  **How much longer than Company A has Company C been in business?**
    A   4 years
    B   30 years
    C   40 years
    D   60 years

## Explanation

**Step 1:** Read All the Information

Make sure you read any and all information associated with each question. That includes not only the passage but also the visual aids. If an illustration includes a caption, read it. If a cartoon includes dialogue, read it. It may be tempting to assume that you know what type of information is included in a graph and skip over titles, labels, and keys to save time, but if you spend the few extra seconds it takes to read this information it can make a tremendous difference in your understanding of the data. For example, without reading the vertical axis of this graph, how would you know the increments by which the data are shown?

By reading the labels on this graph, you know that Company A has been in business for two decades, or 20 years, and Company C has been in business for six decades, or 60 years. Knowing all the material makes a big difference. Make sure you take time to read as much information as you can find before trying to answer any questions on the HiSET Exam Social Studies test.

**Step 2:** Identify the Question

Once you have read every bit of information related to each question, including the question itself, determine exactly what is being asked. Try restating the question to be sure you clearly understand the task. This question is basically a subtraction problem. How many more years than A has C been in business is like asking what is C minus A.

**Step 3:** Key Words and Phrases

What are the most important facts or details? What information will you need to answer the question? Search for these words and phrases in the passage or graphic so you can locate them quickly and easily when selecting the best answer.

**Step 4:** Determine Meanings

Were there unfamiliar words in the passage, question, or answer choices? If so, look for clues in the given information that can help you figure out the meaning. For this question, everything should be familiar to you.

**Step 5:** Think About What You Already Know

Now think about the information you have been given, and figure out what you already know. You have probably seen a bar chart before and you may know how to read it easily. Combine your prior knowledge with the ideas included on the test to best understand the subject matter.

**Step 6:** Select the Best Answer

Before answering the question, reread it and all of the answer choices one more time. Then select the answer that gives the best and most complete response to the question. If Company C has been in business for 60 years and A has been in business for 20 years, that is a difference of 40 years. **Choice C is the best answer.**

# 11 World History

This chapter will review the types of questions you may find on the *HiSET*® Exam that relate to world history. Keep in mind that many questions will cover more than one area of social studies. For example, a question asking about the Declaration of Independence deals not only with an important event in the history of our country but with our government as well.

It may seem impossible to prepare for a test that could ask questions about any event since the beginning of time. However, you have been learning about world history since you were a small child. You will need to refresh your memory of some events and learn about ones with which you are unfamiliar. You do not need to read history books from cover to cover to study for the test, but there are some important events and themes that are likely to be tested.

## What Is Tested?

Forty-five percent of the questions on the HiSET Exam Social Studies test will deal with U.S. and world history going as far back as beginning and early civilizations. That is a long time to be familiar with, but remember that you will not have to recall facts about these events; you will simply need to read or review the information given on the test and consider it as it relates to what you know about history.

As you go through textbooks, library materials, and news magazines, pay close attention to the topics on the following lists. Keep in mind that this is not a comprehensive list of everything that could be on the test. It simply suggests a few topics that some of the questions may tackle. Also, the topics are listed alphabetically, not by historical importance or by chronology. As you study, add any other topics you want to learn more about to the lists.

### Civilizations and Countries

- Ancient Egyptian Civilizations
- Chinese Dynasties
- The Discovery of America
- The French Revolution
- Greek and Roman Empires
- New Democracies of Africa, Asia, and South America

### Religions

- Catholicism
- Christianity
- The Crusades
- Judaism
- The Reformation

### Eras, Ages, and Historical Periods

- The Dark Ages
- The Enlightenment
- The First Global Age
- The Industrial Revolution
- The Middle Ages
- The Renaissance
- The Stone Age
- Urbanization

### Leaders, Explorers, and Significant Historical Figures

- John Cabot
- Julius Caesar
- Christopher Columbus
- Ponce de Leon
- Leif Eriksson
- Gandhi
- Martin Luther
- Karl Marx
- Napoleon
- Peter the Great
- Amerigo Vespucci

### Wars and Revolutions

- The Cold War
- The Hundred Years' War
- The Korean Conflict
- The League of Nations
- The Russian Revolution and the Rise of Communism
- The United Nations
- World War I
- World War II

### Documents and Treaties

- The Magna Carta
- The Treaty of Versailles

# Examples

Here are two sample questions dealing with world history. Both are based on the following passage.

*Julius Caesar is known as one of history's greatest military leaders, at one time even declaring that he would be dictator for life. In the early sixties B.C., he became a leading ruler in Rome, alongside Pompey the Great and Crassus, with the three men becoming the first triumvirate. Together, they controlled the region for several years, until Crassus died, and the remaining two men began a civil war against one another. After several battles, Caesar defeated his former partner the following year. By 45 B.C., he had enjoyed widespread victories across the Mediterranean, although his joy was short-lived. Caesar was assassinated in 44 B.C. by political rivals.*

1.  **According to the passage, which of the following is true?**
    A   Caesar ruled Rome as a lone dictator during the sixties B.C.
    B   Caesar and Pompey the Great ruled Rome as equal partners.
    C   Caesar ruled the entire Mediterranean as a dictator for several decades.
    D   Caesar, Pompey the Great, and Crassus formed a committee of three equal rulers.

## Explanation

First, read all the information. Identify the question. The question asks you to read the answer choices and determine which of them is supported by the passage. Look for key words and phrases. Notice the men's names, dates, and locations in the passage. Determine the meanings of any unfamiliar words. The word *triumvirate* may be unfamiliar, so use information in the surrounding text to figure out what it means. Take a look at this section of the passage:

*. . . he became a leading ruler in Rome, alongside Pompey the Great and Crassus, with the three men becoming the first triumvirate. Together, they controlled the region for several years.*

This shows that Caesar ruled alongside two other men. Together they controlled the region. Also, you may know that the prefix tri- means "three." A *triumvirate* probably is a group of three rulers who work together to lead a region. Think about what you already know; consider what you have learned, heard, or read about Julius Caesar in the past. Use this information, along with the information in the text, to complete Step 6. Evaluate the answer choices based on information in the passage. Although Caesar did rule Rome during the sixties B.C., he did this with two other men, which eliminates answer choice A. Also, since the three rulers were equal partners, answer choice B is not the best answer since it only mentions two of the rulers. Although Caesar did conquer much of the Mediterranean, he was assassinated within a short time afterward, making answer choice C incorrect. Choice D correctly states that Caesar, along with Pompey the Great and Crassus, formed a committee of three equal rulers. **The best answer is D.**

2.  **Which conclusion can be drawn based on the information in the passage?**
    A   Caesar and Pompey the Great did not agree on the best way to rule Rome.
    B   Caesar battled Pompey the Great to be the sole ruler of Rome.
    C   Crassus was the most experienced and most popular of the Roman leaders.
    D   The death of Crassus caused conflict among the leaders of Rome at the time.

### Explanation

You read all the information in the passage for the first question, so just be sure to read and identify what this question is asking. The question asks you to draw a conclusion based on the passage. This is similar to the previous question in that you need to read the answer choices and determine which of them is supported by the passage. Since you are asked to draw a conclusion, the best answer choice may not be stated directly in the passage, but it is something that the passage supports. You have already made note of key words and phrases and determined the meanings of any unfamiliar words. Use what you have learned, heard, or read about Julius Caesar, along with the information in the text, to complete Step 6. Evaluate the answer choices based on information in the passage. The passage does not discuss either Caesar or Pompey's views on ruling Rome, but you may think they must have disagreed if they fought a civil war after Crassus's death. Keep choice A, but evaluate the other choices to see if there is a better one. Choice B is directly supported by the passage. You know that Caesar and Pompey fought a civil war, so this is a better choice than A. Eliminate A. The passage does not give any information about Crassus, except that he was part of the triumvirate and that he died. There is no support for choice C. Choice D may seem tempting, but the passage does not say that Crassus's death *caused* the civil war. Eliminate choice D. **The best answer is B**.

# WORLD HISTORY DRILLS

**Use the following information to answer questions 1–3.**

*Apartheid was a system of racial segregation in South Africa enforced by the National Party government from 1948 until 1994. People were classified into four racial groups: black, white, colored, and Indian. Under this system, whites had the highest standard of living in Africa, comparable to that of a European country. Blacks had a much lower standard of living by any metric: income, education, housing, life expectancy, etc. (infant mortality was 40% in rural areas, while for whites it was 2.7%). The government developed "Homelands" as a way to separate the 9 million blacks from the whites based on tribal classification (which was decided by the white government). This resulted in the forced removal of blacks to their "homelands." Over time, 3.5 million non-whites were forced to leave their homes for these segregated areas. People in the homelands only had political rights within their homeland and non-whites were not allowed to act as political representatives. Non-whites were even stripped of their South African citizenship and issued passports to enter South Africa. Whites owned almost all the industrial, agricultural, and good quality residential land. People of different races were legally prohibited from sexual relations and marriage. Opposition to apartheid abroad included boycotts, economic sanctions, and divestment. Opposition to apartheid within South Africa took the form of strikes, marches, protests, and sabotage. This opposition was met with harsh suppression by the government. Finally, in 1990, President de Klerk began attempts to end apartheid, which culminated in the 1994 democratic election of Nelson Mandela and the African National Congress.*

*Line*
*5*
*10*
*15*
*20*

1. **Which of the following was an advantage given to whites, but not to non-whites, by apartheid?**

   A  free land for development

   B  the ability to marry anyone of any race

   C  medical care provided by the government

   D  the right to travel within South Africa

2. **Which of the following can be inferred from the passage?**

   A  no whites relocated after the "homelands" were created

   B  many blacks did not want to relocate to the "homelands"

   C  anyone who did not relocate to his or her "homeland" was imprisoned

   D  more non-whites were relocated than were allowed to stay where they were

3. **Based on the information in the passage, which of the following is most likely a way in which a foreign government or body showed its opposition to apartheid in South Africa?**

   A  The United Nations passed an embargo on arms sales to South Africa.

   B  Nigeria sent soldiers to Johannesburg to fight the South African army.

   C  Diplomats from the United States were withdrawn from South Africa.

   D  South African government officials were denied entry into other African nations.

**Use the following information to answer questions 4–6.**

*The Reformation, a primarily religious revolt during the sixteenth century, is one of the greatest revolutions of all time and caused changes that extended far beyond the reaches of the church. In fact, it is considered to be a turning point in history. This major and oftentimes brutal conflict divided the Christians in Western Europe into two separate groups: Protestants and Catholics. Prior to this, Roman Catholicism was the only religion in Western Europe. The Catholic Church had been quite powerful, even insisting that no one else had the authority to interpret the Bible.*

*Martin Luther, a Saxon monk, had been influenced by the work of a fourteenth-century priest, John Wycliffe, who believed that people should have the opportunity to interpret the Bible for themselves. Like Wycliffe, Luther also developed ideas that contradicted those of the church and became a leader of the Reformation in Germany. Other scholars assisted him in spreading his ideas, some by encouraging the study of Hebrew and Greek languages, others by adding new ideas to those preached by Luther. The Reformation was supported in other countries by those with similar views, and soon new churches appeared. For example, John Calvin's work supported the Presbyterian and Reformed churches' foundation in Geneva, which became the world center for these religions.*

*Religion, however, was not the sole cause of the Reformation, although many believed political and social problems were spurred by the support of religious leaders. As a result of the loss of religious unity experienced up to this point, people began to consider their own religious interests for the first time, and the Modern Age began.*

4.  **Following the Reformation, new political, social, and economic problems began to arise. In what way did the religious conflict spur issues outside the church?**

    A   The church encouraged people to revolt in social and political arenas in addition to taking a stand against their religion.

    B   All of the political leaders prior to the Reformation had been members of the church, so it was difficult to determine which religion new leaders should support.

    C   People's diverse religious interests began to impact other areas of their thinking, causing new social and political beliefs as well.

    D   Since the church had been so powerful prior to the Reformation, the lack of support caused economic and financial problems.

5.  **In what way would learning a new language encourage religious change?**

    A   All of the religious leaders preached only in languages other than German.

    B   Only German religious leaders were able to study the Bible up to this time.

    C   Knowledge of Greek and Hebrew allowed people to study the Bible in its original language.

    D   Learning Greek and Hebrew allowed people to talk with religious leaders who spoke only those languages.

6.  **Which of the following inferences can be made based on the passage?**

    A   Religious leaders were the only people who were satisfied with the strong role of the church prior to the Reformation.

    B   People throughout Western Europe were becoming unhappy with the church prior to the Reformation.

    C   Without the influence of Martin Luther, the Reformation never would have taken place.

    D   The Reformation came on suddenly, as the result of the actions of a few people.

---

**Use the following information to answer questions 7–9.**

*In the early part of the twentieth century, Germany's leader believed it was best to side with the majority in any conflict among the five European powers and to remain on peaceful terms with Russia. However, when a new leader took the reins of Germany, he* Line *refused to maintain the country's relationship with Russia, leaving his country with only* 5 *one European ally, Austria-Hungary, the weakest of the five.*

*In 1914, Austria declared war against Serbia following the assassination of the heir to the Austro-Hungarian throne by a Serbian supporter. As an ally of Serbia, Russia was pulled into the conflict. Likewise, as an ally of Austria, Germany was now involved in a war against Russia. France and Britain were bound by an alliance with Russia, which* 10 *brought them into the conflict as well. The result was that nearly the entire continent was at war. Russia, France, and Great Britain, through the Treaty of London, agreed not to make peace individually with the Central Powers, and from this point, the three countries and those supporting them were known as the Allies.*

15 *Although this war was fought primarily in Europe, it is called World War I. In time, 27 countries became involved. Although the United States remained neutral at the beginning of the war, it did produce a significant amount of food and weapons for Great Britain and France. In fact, U.S. exports to these countries quadrupled during the first two years of the war. Germany used submarines to prevent these supplies from being exported by the United States and later encouraged Mexico to become involved in a war with the United*

20 *States. Consequently, the U.S. Congress declared war on Germany in 1917, and the United States officially entered the Great War.*

**7. In what ways can you infer that the United States benefitted from World War I?**

A   Exports to all European countries increased.

B   Relations with Germany were strengthened.

C   An agricultural economy was replaced by an industrial economy.

D   Industry prospered as a result of producing supplies for the Allies.

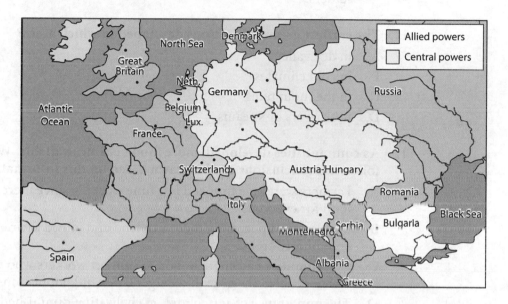

**8. Based on the passage and the map, which conclusion can be drawn?**

A   Switzerland remained neutral throughout the war.

B   Denmark and Russia supported the same war efforts.

C   The same number of troops came from Serbia and Greece.

D   Spain was not involved in the war because it is located so far from Russia.

**9. Why was World War I known as "The Great War"?**

A   because the war lasted for so many years

B   because so many countries were involved

C   because every country in the world played a part

D   because the war was fought by sea as well as by land

*From the beginning of civilization, agriculture has played a key role in the rise of permanent settlements. The development of farming practices allowed people to remain in an area without having to move their families, belongings, and herds in search of*
Line
5 *food. Communities began to develop in areas where the water supply could be used for irrigation.*

**10.** **Which best explains the role of agriculture in the development of settlements?**

    **A** Being able to grow their own food allowed people to settle in an area.

    **B** Having a common interest provided people with a sense of community.

    **C** People were able to use the available timber to build permanent homes.

    **D** The development of farming provided jobs and a source of income for settlers.

**11.** **The earliest great civilizations developed in which areas?**

    **A** in dry valleys

    **B** in cold climates

    **C** in the mountains

    **D** near rivers or streams

**12.** **As communities developed, more food became available. Which of the following conclusions can be drawn based on this information?**

    **A** Farmers were able to spend less time working since there was plenty of food for everyone.

    **B** People gave up farming their own land and joined their efforts to develop community crops.

    **C** Communities had enough food to support workers who were not farmers, which enabled the growth of larger cities and populations.

    **D** The importance of agriculture on civilization diminished, and people began to focus on learning a different trade.

*In 1835 Thomas McCauley produced his "Minute upon Indian Education" for the British Council of India, in which he argues that Indian subjects should be educated in English for two basic reasons: imperialist racism and political expediency. First, he*
Line
5 *declares the worthlessness of native languages, that they are "so poor and rude that, until they are enriched from some other quarter, it will not be easy to translate any valuable work into them." This statement presupposes that there are not any existing valuable works in native languages and that the languages are not sophisticated enough to express works that are valuable. He says that since it is not possible to educate the natives in their own languages, the British government must choose a foreign language*
10 *in which to educate them. Since English is superior to all other languages, he urges that it be used.*

The second basis for McCauley's proposition is for the practical application of imperialism. Since the native ruling class in India already learns English, it will be easier to proceed in that direction. He proposes the creation of an educated class of interpreters, "a class of persons, Indian in blood and colour, but English in taste, in opinions, in morals, and in intellect." These interpreters can intercede with the masses on behalf of the British. By separating these compradors from the rest of the population through language and economic advancement, Britain hoped to fulfill the practical purpose of communicating the ideology of British superiority and keep the mass population compliant and obedient.

13. **Which of the following can be most properly inferred from the passage?**
   A   Prior to 1835, the dominant language in India was English.
   B   Prior to 1835, only the upper ruling class in India could read and write.
   C   Prior to 1835, no books were published in a native Indian language.
   D   Prior to 1835, there were multiple languages spoken in India.

14. **The word *comprador* most likely means**
   A   a person who serves as an intermediary between peoples of different cultures
   B   a person who speaks multiple languages
   C   someone who has emigrated from his or her homeland
   D   someone who has abandoned his or her own culture in favor of another

15. **What is one argument that McCauley made for education in India being conducted in English?**
   A   the majority of the people in India already spoke English
   B   upper class Indian people had already studied English
   C   it was easier to find teachers who spoke English
   D   all the existing materials were published in English

**Answers are on page 718.**

# 12 U.S. History

Forty-five percent of the questions on the *HiSET®* Exam Social Studies test will deal with U.S. and world history. As you know, you will not be required to recall facts about the history of our country; however, you will need to relate what you already know to passages and graphics provided on the test.

### Keep in Mind

Keep in mind that U.S. history questions may also relate to other areas of social studies found on the test: world history, civics and government, economics, or geography. As long as you are familiar with the information, the area in which any topic is categorized is irrelevant.

## What Is Tested?

Although it is impossible to know exactly what questions will appear on the test, there will most likely be at least one question related to the *Declaration of Independence*, the *Federalist Papers*, the *U.S. Constitution*, or an important Supreme Court landmark case. As you study, make sure to review each of these areas.

As you study textbooks, library materials, news magazines, and the Internet to prepare for this test, pay close attention to the topics that follow. Remember, this list does not include everything that could possibly be on the test. It simply suggests a number of people, events, and documents with which you should be familiar. As you study, add any other topics you want to learn more about to the lists.

### Historical Periods and Events

- The Boston Tea Party
- The Civil War
- Colonization
- The Confederate States of America
- The Contemporary United States
- The Emergence of Modern America
- The Expansion
- The French and Indian War
- The Great Depression
- The Industrial Revolution

- The Louisiana Purchase
- The New Nation
- Pearl Harbor
- Reconstruction
- The Revolution
- The Roaring Twenties
- The Secession
- Settlement
- The Spanish American War
- Urbanization
- The Vietnam War
- The War of 1812
- Watergate
- World Wars I and II

### Leaders, Explorers, and Significant Historical Figures

- Abolitionists
- Christopher Columbus
- The Continental Congress
- Hernando de Soto
- Robert E. Lee
- Lewis and Clark
- Loyalists
- Native Americans
- Thomas Paine
- Pilgrims
- Presidents, past and present
- Paul Revere
- Dred Scott

### Documents

- The Articles of Confederation
- *Common Sense*
- The Declaration of Independence
- The Emancipation Proclamation
- The Federalist Papers
- The Gettysburg Address
- The Intolerable Acts
- The Monroe Doctrine
- The SALT Agreement
- The Stamp Act
- Supreme Court landmark cases
- The Townshend Acts
- The Treaty of Ghent
- The U.S. Constitution

### Concepts and Beliefs

- Federalism
- Isolationism
- Manifest Destiny

- The Peace Corps
- Popular Sovereignty
- Progressivism
- Suffrage
- Tariffs

# Examples

Here are two sample questions dealing with U.S. history. Both are based on the passage below.

> In 1773 and 1774, the British Parliament enacted several measures over the United States colonies. The first of these was the Boston Port Bill, which closed the harbor until restitution was made for the tea destroyed during the Boston Tea Party. Following this, the
> *Line*  Massachusetts Government Act was imposed, which ended the agreements included in the
> *5*  colony's existing charter and required approval for any town meetings. The Administration of Justice Act protected British officials who were charged with serious criminal offenses while enforcing the law by allowing them to stand trial either in England or in a different colony. The fourth of these measures was the Coercive Act, which offered new arrangements allowing British troops to stay in occupied American houses.

1. **Which conclusion can be drawn based on the passage?**
   A  The British desired to maintain control over the U.S. colonies.
   B  The British worked to help the colonies establish their own laws.
   C  The U.S. colonies wanted assistance from the British to pass new laws.
   D  Parliament immediately recognized the colonies as an independent country.

### Explanation

First, read all the information. Identify the question. *Which statement does the passage support?* You must figure out which statement is most likely true, based on the information in the passage. Underline key words and phrases. Since the passage is about the measures enacted by Parliament, you should underline each of them. Clearly understanding these will help you determine which answer choice is the best conclusion. Determine meanings of unfamiliar words. If the word Parliament is unfamiliar, use the information in the passage to determine what this word means.

*In 1773 and 1774, the British <u>Parliament</u> enacted several measures over the United States colonies.*

Since Parliament was able to make rules for the colonies, it must be a legislative group. Now think about what you already know. You probably already know that the colonies were established by people who wanted to form their own country and come out from under British control. Read the answer choices and see which choice is best supported. According to the passage, Choice A is the best answer. All of the acts were ways for Parliament to maintain some sort of control over what happened in the colonies. **The best answer is A.**

2.  **When were these acts put into place?**

    A   before the colonies were formed

    B   before the Pilgrims arrived in America

    C   after the development of the U.S. Constitution

    D   prior to the signing of the Declaration of Independence

### Explanation

You have already read the passage, so now identify the question: *When were these acts put into place?* You must figure out when the acts of Parliament were passed, which may seem easy since the passage directly says: *In 1773 and 1774, the British Parliament enacted several measures over the United States colonies.* However, if you glance at the answer choices, you can see that the question is not asking for a year, but a time frame in relation to other events. For this, you will need to find clues in the passage and use what you already know. Underline key words and phrases. Since the passage is about when the measures were enacted by Parliament, you should underline any events mentioned. You can see that the first act was a response to the Boston Tea Party, so you know the laws were after that. The passage discusses British troops and colonists, so this is before the American Revolution, during the colonial period. This eliminates choices A and B. Now think about what you already know. You probably already know that the Constitution was written after the Revolution, so eliminate C. Signing the Declaration of Independence began the Revolution, so these acts of Parliament were passed before that. **The best answer is D.**

# U.S. HISTORY DRILLS

For each of the following questions, choose the best answer.

1.  **Tisquantum, or Squanto, is known for**

    A   helping the colonists battle the British during the American Revolution

    B   fighting General Custer at the Battle of Little Big Horn

    C   assisting the pilgrims through their first winter in North America

    D   forming the Five Nations of the Iroquois

---

**Use the following information to answer questions 2–4.**

*For hundreds of years, European nations set their sights on beginning settlements in America as a means of increasing their wealth and expanding their influence around the world. Spain was the first European nation to successfully found a settlement in what we now know as the United States. Shortly thereafter, England's attempts to settle this new land met with success. Many of those who arrived had chosen to leave their homeland in order to gain religious freedom. English settlers in both Massachusetts and Virginia received help from Native Americans who taught them how to grow grains as a source of food and tobacco as a form of income.*

*Line*
*5*

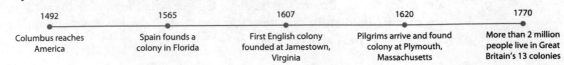

| 1492 | 1565 | 1607 | 1620 | 1770 |
|------|------|------|------|------|
| Columbus reaches America | Spain founds a colony in Florida | First English colony founded at Jamestown, Virginia | Pilgrims arrive and found colony at Plymouth, Massachusetts | More than 2 million people live in Great Britain's 13 colonies |

2. **Which of the following colonies was founded first?**

A   the Spanish colony of La Florida

B   the British colony of Jamestown

C   the British colony of Plymouth

D   the Spanish colony of Hispaniola

3. **Which of the following can best be inferred from the passage?**

A   Columbus reached America before the Native Americans arrived.

B   The Pilgrims founded the first successful British colony in America.

C   Virginia was home to the first successful European settlement in North America.

D   Native Americans lived in the new land prior to the arrival of the Europeans.

## The 13 British Colonies

4.  **Based on the details shown in the map, what can be said about the colonies?**

    A   The first colonies settled were in the north, with later settlements moving toward the south.

    B   Many of the first settlements were established near the coastline of the new land.

    C   Each colony occupied an equal amount of land area.

    D   Most major settlements were located in the southern colonies.

5.  **Which of the following was *not* a reason that European countries wanted to establish settlements in the New Land?**

    A   to expand wealth

    B   to increase their power

    C   to spread organized religion

    D   to strengthen global influence

**Use the following excerpt from the *Declaration of Independence* to answer questions 6–8.**

*We hold these truths to be self-evident, that all men are created equal, that they are endowed by their Creator with certain unalienable Rights, that among these are Life, Liberty and the pursuit of Happiness.—That to secure these rights, Governments are*
Line *instituted among Men, deriving their just powers from the consent of the governed,—*
5 *That whenever any Form of Government becomes destructive of these ends, it is the Right of the People to alter or to abolish it, and to institute new Government, laying its foundation on such principles and organizing its powers in such form, as to them shall seem most likely to effect their Safety and Happiness. Prudence, indeed, will dictate that Governments long established should not be changed for light and transient causes; and*
10 *accordingly all experience hath shewn, that mankind are more disposed to suffer, while evils are sufferable, than to right themselves by abolishing the forms to which they are accustomed. But when a long train of abuses and usurpations, pursuing invariably the same Object evinces a design to reduce them under absolute Despotism, it is their right, it is their duty, to throw off such Government, and to provide new Guards for their future*
15 *security.—Such has been the patient sufferance of these Colonies; and such is now the necessity which constrains them to alter their former Systems of Government. The history of the present King of Great Britain is a history of repeated injuries and usurpations, all having in direct object the establishment of an absolute Tyranny over these States.*

6.  **The *Declaration of Independence* was signed in 1776. According to the document, which of the following practices of the time contradicted the beliefs of the United States?**

    A   women voting

    B   owning slaves

    C   religious freedom

    D   free public education

7. **Which supports the main idea of the *Declaration of Independence*?**

   A   Citizens have the right to have their voices heard in government.

   B   Only certain people have the right to pursue freedom and happiness.

   C   People have a responsibility to be loyal to the leaders of their country.

   D   Leaders should have the ability to establish and enforce laws as they see fit.

8. **According to the document, from where does a government derive its power?**

   A   from the strength of its military

   B   from the divine right of the king

   C   from the people it governs agreeing to be governed

   D   from the wisdom of its leaders

**Use the following information to answer questions 9–11.**

*During the Civil War, President Lincoln issued the Emancipation Proclamation, a presidential order that declared that all slaves being held in the states that were in rebellion against the Union would be free within the following 100 days. Since these states were not under the control of the Union at the time, the proclamation essentially did not free anyone. However, as these states were recaptured, those enslaved in that region gained their freedom.*

Line

5

*By proclaiming the anticipated end of slavery, the Emancipation Proclamation also turned the goal of the war into a battle against slavery. Although the president was strongly against slavery, he had been careful from the beginning of the war to frame its purpose as being to restore the Union rather than for abolition. This history-making order also announced that black men could serve in the Union army and navy. Following the issuing of the proclamation, about 180,000 African Americans joined the Union army, and an additional 18,000 joined the navy.*

10

9. **Which is an opinion, rather than a fact, about the Civil War?**

   A   Freeing the slaves changed the goal of the war.

   B   African Americans should have been able to fight from the beginning of the war.

   C   Many African Americans were anxious to support the efforts of the war.

   D   The Union expected to regain control of the states that had seceded.

10. **Which inference can be made based on the passage?**

   A   Everyone in the northern states shared Lincoln's beliefs about slavery.

   B   The Emancipation Proclamation was a presidential order rather than a law since slavery was already unconstitutional.

   C   Lincoln wanted African Americans to remain in slavery for several more months.

   D   Lincoln originally had concerns that citizens would not support a war with the aim of freeing the slaves.

11. **At the time of the Civil War, Britain was against slavery. Which of the following was *not* an effect of the Emancipation Proclamation?**

    **A**  Britain's opinion of the Confederate states was negatively impacted.

    **B**  The Confederacy's attempt to separate would no longer be viewed by Britain as an attempt to gain freedom but rather as a desire to support slavery.

    **C**  Political tensions deepened between the Union and many European countries.

    **D**  The Confederate states were viewed as a slave nation and were no longer able to receive foreign aid.

12. **The Great Depression followed the stock market crash of 1929, causing a decrease in consumer spending, investing, and industry. Unemployment increased, leading to as many as 15 million Americans being jobless. Nearly half of the banks in the United States failed. Which of the following events helped to turn the American economy around?**

    **A**  World War II

    **B**  Pearl Harbor

    **C**  the Vietnam War

    **D**  World War I

### Questions 13–15 are based on the following passage.

*The Puritan mindset encouraged hard work for reward. Unlike John Smith's writing, which portrayed America as a land of plenty where anyone could work a little and earn a lot, Edward Winslow's writing does not gloss over hardship. He acknowledges that*
Line  *America is a fertile land, but he does not make success sound easy. He details many*
5  *hardships that the pilgrims faced both with the weather and with acquiring food. They were "weak" and "raw" at the start, but through hard work and their trading relationship with the Indians, they are able to build a society. He cautions Englishmen considering emigration to be aware of the challenges. The characteristics of a successful colonist have become integral parts of the American identity. Winslow paints a picture of*
10  *what has become known as "the American Dream." If you work hard, you can succeed. You must be able to get along with others and be willing to live lean at first, but through your efforts (and God's providence), America can be a land of plenty.*

13. **Which of the following became a part of the "American identity"?**

    **A**  moving to a new place to find easy wealth

    **B**  relying on other people for survival

    **C**  taking from others to benefit yourself

    **D**  hard work leading to prosperity

14. **Which of the following can be inferred from the passage?**

    **A**  Winslow and Smith both advertised the easy life in the New World

    **B**  Winslow's picture of life in the colonies conflicted with that of Smith in some ways

    **C**  Smith's writing ignored all the difficulties of life in the colonies

    **D**  Winslow and Smith were the only people reporting on life in the New World

15. **To whom was Edward Winslow most likely writing?**
     A   Englishmen considering a move to the colonies
     B   his wife and children back in England
     C   the Pilgrims in the other colonies
     D   native tribes in the New World

**Answers are on page 719.**

# 13 Civics and Government

Questions related to civics and government will comprise about 30 percent of the questions on the *HiSET*® Exam Social Studies test. They will address politics, government, the founding of our political system, our country's relationship with other nations, and the important role U.S. citizens play in our democracy. As we mentioned in the previous chapter, at least one question on the test will come from the *U.S. Constitution*, the *Bill of Rights*, a Supreme Court landmark case, the *Declaration of Independence*, or the *Federalist Papers*. These questions could be considered history questions, or they could be considered civics and government questions. Either way, it will be important to be familiar with these documents. You will also be asked questions based on practical documents, such as tax forms, voter's guides, a public notice, or political speeches. Keep in mind that you will need to demonstrate the ability not only to understand the information provided on the test, but also to apply, analyze, and evaluate this information.

## What Is Tested?

As you study for the HiSET Exam Social Studies test, be sure to review information related to the topics listed in this chapter. As you know, the lists provided in this book are not comprehensive; they suggest topics with which you should be familiar before test day. Any subject regarding civics and government could pop up on the test, regardless of whether or not it is on these lists. Consider the lists a starting point. Remember, you will need to combine your prior knowledge of civics and government with the information provided to answer the test questions completely.

You can review your old textbooks, take a trip to the library, surf the Web, watch the news, and browse a few good newspapers or news magazines. Become familiar with topics related to civics and government. As you study, look for information related to the following topics, and be sure to add any other topics that strike you as interesting or important.

**Concepts and Terms**

- Branches of U.S. Government
- The Census
- The Chief Justice
- Citizenship
- Congress
- Council-Manager Form of Government

- Democracy
- Dictatorship
- Divine Right
- The Electoral Process and Voting
- Federalism
- The House of Representatives
- Immigration and Naturalization
- Interest Groups
- Judicial Restraint
- Judicial Review
- Lobbying
- Mayor-Council Form of Municipal Government
- Monarchy
- Oligarchy
- Political Continuum
- Political Parties
- Popular Vote
- The Senate
- The Supreme Court
- System of Checks and Balances
- Veto

## Legislation and Landmark Supreme Court Cases

- *Brown v. Board of Education*
- Civil Rights Act of 1957
- *Cooper v. Aaron*
- *Dred Scott v. Sandford*
- *Gibbons v. Ogden*
- *Gideon v. Wainwright*
- *Hazelwood v. Kuhlmeier*
- *Korematsu v. United States*
- *Mapp v. Ohio*
- *Marbury v. Madison*
- *McCulloch v. Maryland*
- *Miranda v. Arizona*
- *New Jersey v. T.L.O.*
- *Plessy v. Ferguson*
- *Regents of the University of California v. Bakke*
- *Roe v. Wade*
- *Terry v. Ohio*
- *Texas v. Johnson*
- *Tinker v. Des Moines*
- *United States v. Nixon*

## Documents

- The Bill of Rights
- The Declaration of Independence
- The Federalist Papers
- Political Speeches
- The U.S. Constitution and Amendments

**Practical Documents**

- Driver's License Manual
- Tax Forms
- Voter's Guide or Handbook
- Voter's Registration Form

# Examples

Here are two civics and government sample questions.

1. **In 1954, the Supreme Court ruled on *Brown v. Board of Education*, which challenged a ruling established by the 1896 case *Plessy v. Ferguson*. The 1954 case was brought against the school system of Topeka, Kansas, by the NAACP. Which best summarizes the outcome of this case?**

    A   Separate schools are inherently unequal.

    B   Schools segregated by race are separate but equal.

    C   The First Amendment does support obscene speech in schools.

    D   School-initiated prayer in public schools is protected by the First Amendment.

### Explanation

First, read all the information. Identify the question: *What was the outcome of* Brown v. Board of Education? In other words, what was the result of this case? Look for key words and phrases. To answer this question, it is important to note the date as well as who was involved in the ruling. Key information to underline includes *1954; school system of Topeka, Kansas;* and *NAACP.* Determine the meanings of any unfamiliar words. The words *inherently* and *segregated* in the answer choices may be unfamiliar. *Inherently* is used as an adjective that modifies *unequal.* The word means "basically;" however, omitting an adjective from a sentence does not necessarily change the meaning. If you were unable to determine the meaning, you would still be able to understand answer choice A: Separate schools are unequal. In answer choice B, the words *race* and *separate* are clues to the meaning of *segregated.* You probably know that in 1954, students were separated by race, so you can infer that segregated means "separated." Now think about what you already know. You probably already know that an issue in 1954 was that students were assigned to schools based on the color of their skin. You probably also know that the NAACP is the National Association for the Advancement of Colored People, and its goal was equality for all citizens, regardless of race. Select the best answer. In 1954, the NAACP challenged the constitutionality of schools being segregated. Today, as a result of this Supreme Court ruling, students are no longer separated by race. Answer choice A best summarizes the outcome. **The best answer is A.**

Form **1040** Department of the Treasury—Internal Revenue Service (99)

**U.S. Individual Income Tax Return** **2011** OMB No. 1545-0074 IRS Use Only—Do not write or staple in this space.

For the year Jan. 1–Dec. 31, 2011, or other tax year beginning , 2011, ending , 20 **See separate instructions.**

| Your first name and initial | Last name | | Your social security number |
| If a joint return, spouse's first name and initial | Last name | | Spouse's social security number |

Home address (number and street). If you have a P.O. box, see instructions. | Apt. no. | ▲ Make sure the SSN(s) above and on line 6c are correct.

City, town or post office, state, and ZIP code. If you have a foreign address, also complete spaces below (see instructions).

**Presidential Election Campaign**
Check here if you, or your spouse if filing jointly, want $3 to go to this fund. Checking a box below will not change your tax or refund. ☐ You ☐ Spouse

| Foreign country name | Foreign province/county | Foreign postal code |

**Filing Status**

Check only one box.

1 ☐ Single
2 ☐ Married filing jointly (even if only one had income)
3 ☐ Married filing separately. Enter spouse's SSN above and full name here. ▶
4 ☐ Head of household (with qualifying person). (See instructions.) If the qualifying person is a child but not your dependent, enter this child's name here. ▶
5 ☐ Qualifying widow(er) with dependent child

**Exemptions**

6a ☐ **Yourself.** If someone can claim you as a dependent, **do not** check box 6a . . . . .
b ☐ **Spouse** . . . . . . . . . . . . . . . . . . . . . . . .

} Boxes checked on 6a and 6b ____

c **Dependents:**

| (1) First name  Last name | (2) Dependent's social security number | (3) Dependent's relationship to you | (4) ✓ if child under age 17 qualifying for child tax credit (see instructions) |
|---|---|---|---|
| | | | ☐ |
| | | | ☐ |
| | | | ☐ |
| | | | ☐ |

If more than four dependents, see instructions and check here ▶ ☐

No. of children on 6c who:
• lived with you ____
• did not live with you due to divorce or separation (see instructions) ____

Dependents on 6c not entered above ____

d Total number of exemptions claimed . . . . . . . . . . . . . . . .

Add numbers on lines above ▶ ____

**Income**

**Attach Form(s) W-2 here. Also attach Forms W-2G and 1099-R if tax was withheld.**

If you did not get a W-2, see instructions.

Enclose, but do not attach, any payment. Also, please use **Form 1040-V.**

| | | | |
|---|---|---|---|
| 7 | Wages, salaries, tips, etc. Attach Form(s) W-2 . . . . . . . . . . | 7 | |
| 8a | **Taxable** interest. Attach Schedule B if required . . . . . . . . | 8a | |
| b | **Tax-exempt** interest. **Do not** include on line 8a . . . | 8b | | |
| 9a | Ordinary dividends. Attach Schedule B if required . . . . . . . . | 9a | |
| b | Qualified dividends . . . . . . . . . . | 9b | | |
| 10 | Taxable refunds, credits, or offsets of state and local income taxes | 10 | |
| 11 | Alimony received . . . . . . . . . . . . . . . . . | 11 | |
| 12 | Business income or (loss). Attach Schedule C or C-EZ . . . . . | 12 | |
| 13 | Capital gain or (loss). Attach Schedule D if required. If not required, check here ▶ ☐ | 13 | |
| 14 | Other gains or (losses). Attach Form 4797 . . . . . . . . . . | 14 | |
| 15a | IRA distributions . | 15a | | b Taxable amount . . . | 15b | |
| 16a | Pensions and annuities | 16a | | b Taxable amount . . . | 16b | |
| 17 | Rental real estate, royalties, partnerships, S corporations, trusts, etc. Attach Schedule E | 17 | |
| 18 | Farm income or (loss). Attach Schedule F . . . . . . . . . . | 18 | |
| 19 | Unemployment compensation . . . . . . . . . . . . . | 19 | |
| 20a | Social security benefits | 20a | | b Taxable amount . . . | 20b | |
| 21 | Other income. List type and amount _____ | 21 | |
| 22 | Combine the amounts in the far right column for lines 7 through 21. This is your **total income** ▶ | 22 | |

**Adjusted Gross Income**

| | | | |
|---|---|---|---|
| 23 | Educator expenses . . . . . . . . . . | 23 | |
| 24 | Certain business expenses of reservists, performing artists, and fee-basis government officials. Attach Form 2106 or 2106-EZ | 24 | |
| 25 | Health savings account deduction. Attach Form 8889 . | 25 | |
| 26 | Moving expenses. Attach Form 3903 . . . . . . | 26 | |
| 27 | Deductible part of self-employment tax. Attach Schedule SE . | 27 | |
| 28 | Self-employed SEP, SIMPLE, and qualified plans . . | 28 | |
| 29 | Self-employed health insurance deduction . . . | 29 | |
| 30 | Penalty on early withdrawal of savings . . . . . | 30 | |
| 31a | Alimony paid b Recipient's SSN ▶ _____ | 31a | |
| 32 | IRA deduction . . . . . . . . . . . . | 32 | |
| 33 | Student loan interest deduction . . . . . . . | 33 | |
| 34 | Tuition and fees. Attach Form 8917 . . . . . . | 34 | |
| 35 | Domestic production activities deduction. Attach Form 8903 | 35 | |
| 36 | Add lines 23 through 35 . . . . . . . . . . . . . . . . ▶ | 36 | |
| 37 | Subtract line 36 from line 22. This is your **adjusted gross income** . . . . . . ▶ | 37 | |

**For Disclosure, Privacy Act, and Paperwork Reduction Act Notice, see separate instructions.** Cat. No. 11320B Form **1040** (2011)

The next example refers to the IRS income tax form shown.

2. **Which of the following is NOT true?**

   A   Income tax must be paid on interest earned on investments.

   B   Unemployed citizens are not required to pay any income taxes.

   C   School teachers are permitted to deduct some of the costs of classroom supplies.

   D   A waitress is required to pay income tax on both her hourly wage and any tips she earns.

### Explanation

First, read all the information. Identify the question: *Which of the following is NOT true?* Here you will look for an answer choice that is false. Underline key words and phrases. Since you are determining which choices are true and which is false, underline key phrases in the answer choices such as *interest earned on investments, unemployed, school teachers,* and *tips.* Look for those phrases on the tax form. Determine the meanings of any unfamiliar words. There are probably not any in these choices. Now think about what you already know about paying taxes. You probably already know that people pay taxes on what they earn, but you may question whether an unemployed person would pay taxes. Check the form for information on that. You will see that unemployment compensation is listed on the form and taxes would be paid on those earnings, so choice B is false. **The best answer is B.**

# CIVICS AND GOVERNMENT DRILLS

For each of the following questions, choose the best answer.

1. **Which of the following is NOT a branch of the U.S. government?**

   A   legislative

   B   judicial

   C   corporate

   D   executive

## New Jersey
## Voter Registration Application

**76**

*Please print clearly in ink. All information is required unless marked optional.*

**1** Check boxes that apply:
- ☐ New Registration
- ☐ Name Change
- ☐ Address Change
- ☐ Signature Update
- ☐ Political Party Affiliation or Non-affiliation Change

**FOR OFFICIAL USE ONLY**

**2** Are you a U.S. Citizen? ☐ Yes ☐ No
*(If No, DO NOT complete this form)*

Will you be 18 years of age by the next election? Yes No
*(If No, DO NOT complete this form)*

Clerk

| **3** Last Name | First Name | Middle Name or Initial | Suffix *(Jr., Sr., III)* |
|---|---|---|---|

Registration #

**4** Date of Birth

Office Time Stamp

**5** NJ Driver's License Number or MVC Non-driver ID Number

If you DO NOT have a NJ Driver's License or MVC Non-Driver ID, provide the last 4 digits of your Social Security Number. __ __ __ __

☐ "I swear or affirm that I DO NOT have a NJ Driver's License, MVC Non-driver ID or a Social Security Number."

| **6** Home Address *(DO NOT use PO Box)* | Apt. | Municipality | County | State | Zip Code |
|---|---|---|---|---|---|

| **7** Mailing Address if different from above | Apt. | Municipality | County | State | Zip Code |
|---|---|---|---|---|---|

| **8** Last Address Registered to Vote *(DO NOT use PO Box)* | Apt. | Municipality | County | State | Zip Code | ☐ by mail ☐ in person |
|---|---|---|---|---|---|---|

**9** Former Name if Making Name Change

a. Day Phone Number *(Optional)*

b. E-Mail Address *(Optional)*

**10** Do you wish to declare a political party affiliation? *(Optional)*
- ☐ Yes, the party name is ___
- ☐ No, I do not wish to be affiliated with any political party.

**11** Gender
- ☐ Female
- ☐ Male

**Declaration - I swear or affirm that:**
- I am a U.S. Citizen
- I live at the above address
- I will be at least 18 years old on or before the next election
- I will have resided in the State and county at least 30 days before the next election
- I am not on parole, probation or serving a sentence due to a conviction for an indictable offense under any federal or state laws
- I understand that any false or fraudulent registration may subject me to a fine of up to $15,000, imprisonment up to 5 years, or both pursuant to R.S. 19:34-1

Signature: Sign or mark and date on lines below

If applicant is unable to complete this form, print the name and address of individual who completed this form.

Name ___
Date ___
Address ___

X ___ Date ___

## Important Instructions for sections 5, 6 and 10

5) Registrants who are submitting this form by mail and are registering to vote for the first time: If you do not have any of the information required by section 5, or the information you provide cannot be verified, you will be asked to provide a COPY of a current and valid photo ID, or a document with your name and current address on it to avoid having to provide identification at the polling place.

   **Note:** *ID Numbers are Confidential and will not be released by any governmental agency. Any person who uses such numbers illegally shall be subject to criminal penalties.*

6) If you are homeless, you may complete section 6 by providing a contact point or the location where you spend most of your time.

10) You may declare a political affiliation or you may declare to be unaffiliated, regardless of any prior party affiliation. Completing section 10 is OPTIONAL and will not affect the acceptance of your voter registration application.

**Need More Information?** Check boxes below if you would like to receive more information about:

- ☐ voting by mail
- ☐ becoming a poll worker
- ☐ polling place accessibility
- ☐ voting if you have a disability, including visual impairment
- ☐ available election materials in this alternative language: ___

For further information visit **Elections.NJ.gov** or call toll-free **1-877-NJVOTER** (1-877-658-6837)

NJ Division of Elections - 6/22/12

Use the Voter Registration Application shown to answer questions 2–4.

2.  **According to the form, which is true?**
    A   Only U.S. citizens are eligible to vote.
    B   Only residents born in the U.S. may vote.
    C   Residents of New Jersey must have a driver's license in order to vote.
    D   New Jersey residents must be 18 years old before registering to vote.

3.  **Which group of people may NOT register to vote?**
    A   those with disabilities
    B   those who are homeless
    C   those who are on parole
    D   those who do not speak English

4.  **What is the best way to get reliable information about voting in New Jersey?**
    A   ask a friend or neighbor
    B   call 1-800-CANVOTE
    C   go to the polling location on election day
    D   visit the Elections.NJ.gov website

**The *U.S. Constitution* was written in 1787. Since that time, portions of the document have been amended or superseded. Read the excerpt of the original document and answer questions 5–7 that follow.**

*The House of Representatives shall be composed of Members chosen every second Year by the People of the several States, and the Electors in each State shall have the Qualifications requisite for Electors of the most numerous Branch of the State Legislature.*

*Line*

*5*    *No Person shall be a Representative who shall not have attained to the Age of twenty five Years, and been seven Years a Citizen of the United States, and who shall not, when elected, be an Inhabitant of that State in which he shall be chosen.*

*Representatives and direct Taxes shall be apportioned among the several States which may be included within this Union, according to their respective Numbers, which shall be determined by adding to the whole Number of free Persons, including those*

*10*   *bound to Service for a Term of Years, and excluding Indians not taxed, three fifths of all other Persons. The actual Enumeration shall be made within three Years after the first Meeting of the Congress of the United States, and within every subsequent Term of ten Years, in such Manner as they shall by Law direct. The Number of Representatives shall not exceed one for every thirty Thousand, but each State shall have at Least one*

*15*   *Representative; and until such enumeration shall be made, the State of New Hampshire shall be entitled to chuse three, Massachusetts eight, Rhode-Island and Providence Plantations one, Connecticut five, New-York six, New Jersey four, Pennsylvania eight, Delaware one, Maryland six, Virginia ten, North Carolina five, South Carolina five, and Georgia three.*

5. **Which state had the greatest population at the time the U.S. Constitution was written?**

   A  Virginia

   B  New Hampshire

   C  New York

   D  Pennsylvania

6. **According to the document, which statement is true?**

   A  Men could join the House of Representatives as soon as they arrived from England.

   B  Slaves counted as three-fifths of a person.

   C  Residents had to be 25 years old to be able to vote.

   D  Each state was responsible for an equal amount of taxes.

7. **Which of the following is NOT a requirement to be a representative?**

   A  Representatives must live in the state they represent at the time of election.

   B  Representatives must be at least 25 years old.

   C  Representatives must have lived in the United States for at least seven years.

   D  Representatives must be male.

**Use the following table to answer questions 8–9.**

| | Bill of Rights |
|---|---|
| **Amendment** | **Summary** |
| I | Grants freedoms of religion, speech, and the press and to assemble and petition the government to remedy grievances. |
| II | Gives the right to bear arms. |
| III | Establishes that private citizens cannot be forced to house soldiers during times of peace. |
| IV | Guarantees protection against search and seizure without a warrant. |
| V | States the rights of citizens who are accused of crimes. |
| VI | Outlines the rights of citizens in regard to trials and juries. |
| VII | Gives the right to a trial by jury in a federal civil court case. |
| VIII | Offers protection against "cruel and unusual" punishments and extremely large fines for criminals. |
| IX | States that rights not specifically listed in the Constitution may still be respected. |
| X | Explains that powers that have not been granted to the federal government are granted to either the states or the people. |

8.  After being charged with a felony, Clarence Earl Gideon asked the judge to provide him with an attorney at no cost, based on the fact that he was unable to afford representation. The judge denied the request, so Gideon turned to the Supreme Court. Which amendment did the Court uphold in *Gideon v. Wainwright* (1963) when it ruled that indigent defendants must be provided legal representation without being charged?

    A   the Fourth Amendment

    B   the Fifth Amendment

    C   the Sixth Amendment

    D   the Seventh Amendment

9.  The Supreme Court case of *Tinker v. Des Moines* (1969) ruled in favor of Mary Beth Tinker and her brother, who wore black armbands to school in protest of the Vietnam War. The administrators of their school worried that the armbands would cause a disruption and prohibited students from expressing their opposition in this manner. The Court ruled that the Tinkers' actions were protected by which amendment?

    A   the First Amendment

    B   the Second Amendment

    C   the Third Amendment

    D   the Ninth Amendment

10. In our country, the president is selected by the electoral college. Which type of political system is this?

    A   anarchy

    B   democracy

    C   dictatorship

    D   monarchy

11. Queen Elizabeth II began ruling England at age 25, following the death of her father, King George VI. Which type of political system is practiced in her country?

    A   oligarchy

    B   democracy

    C   dictatorship

    D   monarchy

### MINORS' PERMIT RESTRICTIONS

Your permit is not valid until you begin driver training; your instructor will sign the permit to validate it. You must practice with a licensed California driver: parent, guardian, driving instructor, spouse, or an adult 25 years of age or older. The person must sit close enough to you to take control of the vehicle at any time. A provisional permit does not allow you to drive alone – not even to a DMV office to take a driving test.

### MINORS' DRIVER LICENSE REQUIREMENTS

You must:

- Be at least 16 years old.
- Prove that you have finished both driver education and driver training.
- Have had a California instruction permit or an instruction permit from another state for at least six months.
- Provide parent(s) or guardian(s) signature(s) on your instruction permit stating that you have completed 50 hours of supervised driving practice (10 hours must be night driving) as outlined in the *California Parent-Teen Training Guide* (DL 603). Visit the Teen website at **www.dmv.ca.gov/teenweb/** or call 1-800-777-0133 to request this booklet.
- Pass the behind-the-wheel driving test. You have three chances to pass the driving test while your permit is valid. If you fail the behind-the-wheel driving test, you must pay a retest fee for a second or subsequent test and wait two weeks before you are retested.

Once you have your provisional driver license, you may drive **alone**, as long as you do not have any collisions or traffic violations.

When you become 18 years old, the "provisional" part of your driver license ends. You may keep your provisional photo license or pay a fee for a duplicate driver license without the word "provisional."

During the first 12 months after you are licensed, you cannot drive between 11 p.m. and 5 a.m. **and** you cannot transport passengers under 20 years of age, unless you are accompanied by a licensed parent or guardian, a licensed driver 25 years of age or older, or a licensed or certified driving instructor.

### EXCEPTIONS - MINORS' DRIVER LICENSE RESTRICTIONS

The law allows the following exceptions when reasonable transportation is not available and it is necessary for you to drive. A signed note explaining the necessity to drive and the date when this driving necessity will end must be kept in your possession for the following exceptions (emancipated minors are excluded from this requirement):

- Medical necessity to drive when reasonable transportation alternatives are inadequate. The note must be signed by a physician.

---

**Use this page from the *2012 California Driver Handbook* to answer questions 12–13.**

12. **Which assumption can be made based on this information?**

    A  Drivers must be at least 25 years old to legally operate a car alone.

    B  After obtaining a California driver license, minors have the same driving privileges as adults.

    C  A driver education class is required for anyone under the age of 18 wishing to obtain a California driver license.

    D  High school students may carpool to campus, as long as the driver is at least 16 years old and has his or her license.

13. **Which of the following would qualify for an exception to the rules for minor drivers?**

    A  the driver is an agricultural worker performing job duties

    B  the driver is on the way to obtain his or her permanent adult license

    C  the driver is rushing to the hospital to visit a sick family member

    D  the driver has a note from a doctor stating the medical necessity of driving

**Martin Luther King Jr. delivered his "I Have a Dream" speech on August 28, 1963 at the Lincoln Memorial in Washington D.C. Read the excerpt of the speech that follows to answer questions 14 and 15.**

*As we walk, we must make the pledge that we shall always march ahead. We cannot turn back. There are those who are asking the devotees of civil rights, "When will you be satisfied?" We can never be satisfied as long as the Negro is the victim of the unspeakable horrors of police brutality. We can never be satisfied, as long as our bodies, heavy with the*
Line 5 *fatigue of travel, cannot gain lodging in the motels of the highways and the hotels of the cities. We cannot be satisfied as long as the Negro's basic mobility is from a smaller ghetto to a larger one. We can never be satisfied as long as our children are stripped of their selfhood and robbed of their dignity by signs stating "For Whites Only." We cannot be satisfied as long as a Negro in Mississippi cannot vote and a Negro in New York believes*
10 *he has nothing for which to vote. No, no, we are not satisfied, and we will not be satisfied until justice rolls down like waters and righteousness like a mighty stream.*

14. **Which of the following does King NOT cite as a racial injustice?**
    A   children choosing to play only with children of their same race
    B   blacks being denied rooms at hotels that serve whites
    C   being or simply feeling politically disenfranchised
    D   blacks being subject to excessive violence from authorities

15. **For whom does King seek justice and equality?**
    A   future generations
    B   all people regardless of race
    C   blacks living in the segregated South
    D   people who have been unjustly imprisoned

**Answers are on page 719.**

# 14 Economics

One definition of *economics* is "the study of goods and services." Another is "the financial aspect of something." Basically, economics involves money matters. Fifteen percent of the questions on the *HiSET*® Exam Social Studies test will address this area of learning.

Believe it or not, you work with economics every day. For example, grabbing the last pair of jeans off the department store shelf during a sale, while a handful of other customers stomp away empty-handed, is an example of supply and demand. This is part of the study of goods and services. When you decide that the amount of money in your wallet is not quite enough to purchase the jeans and a new belt too, that is an example of the financial aspect of something. Economics is everywhere.

As you know, you will need to combine your own knowledge and experiences of economics with the information and graphics provided to answer the questions on the HiSET Exam Social Studies test. Remember, you will be demonstrating your ability not only to comprehend the information, but also to analyze, restate, summarize, and draw inferences based on the data.

In this chapter, you will practice with a few of the types of economics questions you might encounter on the test. To prepare effectively, make sure to go over any information related to economics in your textbooks. The newspaper is also a great source of material on the topic. The Internet, news magazines, and television can also be valuable sources of information.

## What Is Tested?

Economics questions on the test may cover quite a range of subject matter. Be comfortable with your understanding of economic reasoning, different types of economic systems, how businesses operate in a free enterprise system, financial institutions, the role of the government in economics, labor, production, consumers, global markets, and foreign trade. The following lists suggest a few topics to review; however, pretty much anything related to economics could be fair game. Start by reviewing the ideas on the lists. As you study, add any other important or interesting economic concepts you come across.

Keep in mind that practical documents such as tax forms, bank statements, workplace benefits forms, and contracts may be included on the test. Make sure you are comfortable working with these everyday papers.

### Types of Economic Systems

- Capitalism
- Communism
- Mixed Economy
- Socialism

### Economics and the Government

- Child Labor Laws
- The Economic Opportunity Act
- Minimum Wage Laws
- The Sherman Anti-Trust Act

### Economic Terms Related to Goods and Services

- Capital
- Consumers
- Demand
- E-commerce
- Equilibrium
- Free Enterprise
- Labor
- Natural Resources
- Production
- Shortage
- Surplus

### Economic Terms Related to Finance

- Balanced Budget
- Budget Surplus
- Consumer Price Index
- Deficit Spending
- Deflation
- Discount Rate
- Econometrics
- The Federal Reserve Board
- Fiscal Policy
- Fixed Expense
- Flexible Expense
- Gross Domestic Product (GDP)
- Gross National Product (GNP)
- Inflation
- Inflationary Spiral
- Luxury Expense
- Money
- Reserve Ratio

# Examples

Here are two sample economics questions.

1. **Supply and demand work together to determine the market price for goods. The graph shows the supply and demand for a product.**

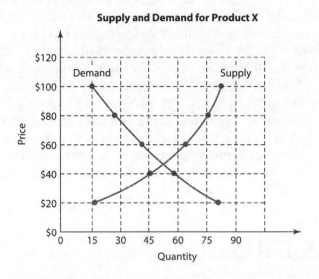

**Supply and Demand for Product X**

According to the chart, what is the market price for the item?

A  $20

B  $45

C  $50

D  $100

## Explanation

First, read all the information, including everything on the chart. Identify the question: *At what price does supply equal demand?* You will be looking for the number on the curves that is the same for both the supply and the demand of the product. Look for key words and phrases. The information needed to solve this problem is on the graph. Underline the axis labels *Price* and *Quantity* and the *Supply* and *Demand* labels on each line. Determine the meanings of any unfamiliar terms. Suppose the phrase *market price* is unfamiliar. The information states that supply and demand work together to determine market price. Take a look at the graph to see how supply and demand work together, and notice that the lines meet where the quantity and price are balanced, so *market price* is the point at which quantity and price balance. Think about what you already know. What have you learned, heard, or read about supply and demand and market price in the past? Use this information, along with the information in the statement and the graph, to complete Step 6. Select the best answer. Supply and demand are balanced at approximately $45. **The best answer is B.**

The following question is based on the same supply and demand graph.

2. **Based on the graph, which is true?**
   A   Less of the product would sell if it were priced below $40.
   B   When the price is lower, the demand is lower as well.
   C   When the supply is greatest, the price is also greatest.
   D   When the price is increased, the demand is decreased.

### Explanation

First, read all the information, including everything on the chart. Identify the question: *Based on the graph, which is true?* You will be looking at the answer choices here and determining whether they are true or false (or unknown). You will choose the one that is true. You have already underlined key words and phrases and there are probably no unfamiliar terms in this question. Think about what you already know. What have you learned, heard, or read about supply and demand and market price in the past? Use this information, along with the information in the statement and the graph, to complete Step 6. Select the best answer. All four choices relate to changes in price and three of the choices are about the demand, so start by following the demand curve and see what happens when the price is lowered. The demand increases. Eliminate choices A and B. When the price is raised, the demand decreases. Choice D correctly states this. **The best answer is D.**

# ECONOMICS DRILLS

For each of the following questions, choose the best answer.

*"The very same bourgeois mentality which extols the manufacturing division of labour, the life-long annexation of the worker to a partial operation, and the unconditional subordination of the detail worker to capital, extols them as an organisation of labour which increases productivity - denounces just as loudly every kind of deliberate social control and regulation of the social process of production, denounces it as an invasion of the inviolable property rights, liberty and self-determining genius of the individual capitalist. It is characteristic that the inspired apologists of the factory system can find nothing worse to say of any proposal for the general organisation of social labour, than that it would transform the whole of society into a factory."* Karl Marx, *Das Kapital*

*Line*
*5*

1. **According to Marx, capitalists believe that**
   A   Division of labor in factories increases efficiency and output.
   B   Workers are an unimportant part of the factory system.
   C   Factories are the best way to manufacture all types of products.
   D   Menial labor subverts people's right to liberty.

2. **Following a successful advertising campaign, the demand for a certain product increases. Which of the following can most likely be expected?**

   A   decrease in product sales

   B   increase in supply

   C   decrease in market price

   D   increase in market price

---

**Use the following information to answer questions 3–5.**

*In 1964, President Johnson passed the Economic Opportunity Act, which established the Office of Economic Opportunity to help combat poverty. The Economic Opportunity Act stated, "It is the policy of the United States to eliminate the paradox of poverty in the midst of plenty in this nation by opening, to everyone, the opportunity for education and training, the opportunity to work, and the opportunity to live in decency and dignity." And so, the act became known as "the war on poverty."*

*This act was the first of several antipoverty steps taken by the U.S. government during the 1960s. Through this first step, a range of programs were established that could be used by communities to access federal funds and professional help to deal with causes of poverty. Although health care and loans were offered, educational programs were at the center of the act. One such program, HEAD START, enrolled more than half a million preschool-aged students during the first summer it was in operation, providing children from economically and culturally deprived families with health care, welfare, and academic training. The act also supported the National Youth Corps, the Job Corps, and Upward Bound, which were each related to education and offered job training to help tackle high unemployment rates among teens from low-income families.*

*The following year, the act was amended to include the creation of offices at the state level to support economic opportunity and encourage state governments to help fight the war on poverty.*

3. **Which can be inferred from the passage?**

   A   Adolescents were not looking for jobs.

   B   President Johnson saw education as key to ending poverty.

   C   Undereducated children were one cause of poverty in the nation.

   D   President Johnson believed local government should take full responsibility for ending poverty.

4. Upon signing the Economic Opportunity Act, President Johnson stated, "This is not in any sense a cynical proposal to exploit the poor with a promise of a handout or a dole. We know—we learned long ago—that answer is no answer. The measure before me this morning for signature offers the answer that its title implies—the answer of opportunity. For the purpose of the Economic Opportunity Act of 1964 is to offer opportunity, not an opiate." Which of the following inferences can be made?

   A   People from low-income families were given plenty of opportunities but were not taking advantage of them.

   B   This was the first time the government had done anything to help those faced with poverty.

   C   President Johnson believed that past programs had not done enough to solve the underlying problems that caused poverty.

   D   President Johnson believed programs that offered financial assistance to low-income families were sufficient.

5. Which of the following did the Economic Opportunity Act do?

   A   provided education and job training to adolescents
   B   offered jobs to unemployed citizens
   C   eliminated poverty in the United States
   D   supplied homes and food for those facing poverty

**Use the following information to answer questions 6–8.**

The Waak family bought a new home. They obtained a 30-year mortgage for $100,000 at 6 percent interest. The amortization schedule shows the amount of principal and interest they will pay each month for the life of the loan.

| Payments | Yearly Total | Principal Paid | Interest Paid | Balance |
|---|---|---|---|---|
| Year 1 (1–12) | $57,194.61 | $1,228.00 | $5,967.00 | $98,771.99 |
| Year 2 (13–24) | $57,194.61 | $1,304.00 | $5,891.00 | $97,468.24 |
| Year 3 (25–36) | $57,194.61 | $1,384.00 | $5,810.00 | $96,034.07 |
| Year 4 (37–48) | $57,194.61 | $1,470.00 | $5,725.00 | $94,614.53 |
| Year 5 (49.00) | $57,194.61 | $1,560.00 | $5,634.00 | $93,054.36 |
| Year 6 (61–72) | $57,194.61 | $1,656.00 | $5,538.00 | $91,397.95 |
| Year 7 (73–84) | $57,194.61 | $1,759.00 | $5,436.00 | $89,639.39 |
| Year 8 (85–96) | $57,194.61 | $1,867.00 | $5,328.00 | $87,772.35 |
| Year 9 (97–108) | $57,194.61 | $1,982.00 | $5,212.00 | $85,790.17 |
| Year 10 (109–120) | $57,194.61 | $2,104.00 | $5,090.00 | $83,685.72 |
| Year 11 (121–132) | $57,194.61 | $2,234.00 | $4,960.00 | $81,451.48 |
| Year 12 (133–144) | $57,194.61 | $2,372.00 | $4,823.00 | $79,079.44 |
| Year 13 (145–156) | $57,194.61 | $2,518.00 | $4,676.00 | $76,561.09 |
| Year 14 (157–168) | $57,194.61 | $2,674.00 | $4,521.00 | $73,887.42 |

*(Continued)*

| Payments | Yearly Total | Principal Paid | Interest Paid | Balance |
|---|---|---|---|---|
| Year 15 (169–180) | $57,194.61 | $2,839.00 | $4,356.00 | $71,048.84 |
| Year 16 (181–192) | $57,194.61 | $3,014.00 | $4,181.00 | $68,035.19 |
| Year 17 (193–204) | $57,194.61 | $3,200.00 | $3,995.00 | $64,835.66 |
| Year 18 (205–216) | $57,194.61 | $3,397.00 | $3,798.00 | $61,438.79 |
| Year 19 (217–228) | $57,194.61 | $3,606.00 | $3,588.00 | $57,832.40 |
| Year 20 (229–240) | $57,194.61 | $3,829.00 | $3,366.00 | $54,003.59 |
| Year 21 (241–252) | $57,194.61 | $4,065.00 | $3,130.00 | $49,938.62 |
| Year 22 (253–264) | $57,194.61 | $4,316.00 | $2,879.00 | $45,622.93 |
| Year 23 (265–276) | $57,194.61 | $4,582.00 | $2,613.00 | $41,041.06 |
| Year 24 (277–288) | $57,194.61 | $4,864.00 | $2,330.00 | $36,176.59 |
| Year 25 (289–300) | $57,194.61 | $5,165.00 | $2,030.00 | $31,012.09 |
| Year 26 (301–312) | $57,194.61 | $5,483.00 | $1,712.00 | $25,529.05 |
| Year 27 (313–324) | $57,194.61 | $5,821.00 | $1,373.00 | $19,707.84 |
| Year 28 (325–336) | $57,194.61 | $6,180.00 | $1,014.00 | $13,527.58 |
| Year 29 (337–348) | $57,194.61 | $6,561.00 | $633.00 | $6,966.14 |
| Year 30 (349–360) | $57,194.61 | $6,966.00 | $228.00 | $50.00 |
| Totals | $215,838.19 | $100,000.00 | $115,838.19 | |

6. **How much principal will the family have paid on the loan by the end of the fifth year?**

   A   $1,560.00

   B   $5,385.47

   C   $5,634.00

   D   $6,945.64

7. **How much interest will the family pay over the life of the loan?**

   A   $6,000.00

   B   $15,838.19

   C   $100,000.00

   D   $115,838.19

8. **Which is true based on the table?**

   A   During the first 10 years, the amount of interest paid each month is approximately twice the amount of principal.

   B   Approximately one-fourth of the principal will be repaid during the final four years of the loan.

   C   The amount of interest paid over the life of the loan will be 6 percent of the total amount of principal paid.

   D   After the first 15 years of payments, approximately half of the total loan amount will have been repaid.

9.  *Capitalism* refers to a type of economic system that includes private ownership and operation of all, or most, means of production that are motivated by profit. Which of the following is associated with capitalism?

    A   fascism

    B   state ownership

    C   free enterprise

    D   social equality

10. The Federal Reserve System was established, in 1913 by the Federal Reserve Act, as the central banking system of the United States, partially as a result of several serious financial panics in our country. The purpose for the act was to maximize employment, to provide stability in prices, to moderate long-term interest rates, and to give the United States a safer and more stable financial system. However, these goals have since been expanded to include a number of other objectives, including influencing financial and credit conditions, protecting consumers' credit rights, and providing financial services not only to banks but also to our government. Based on this information, as well as your own knowledge, which of the following is true?

    A   The idea of a central banking system is unique to the United States.

    B   Widespread financial problems afflicted our country during the late nineteenth and early twentieth centuries.

    C   The establishment of the Federal Reserve has eliminated financial crisis in our country.

    D   The banking system in the United States was stable and secure from the time the country gained independence.

**Use the following information to answer question 11.**

## United States Gross Domestic Product (GDP) Graph

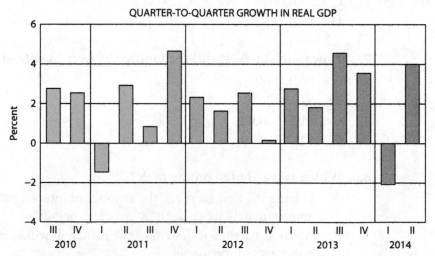

QUARTER-TO-QUARTER GROWTH IN REAL GDP

*Real GDP growth is measured at seasonally adjusted annual rates.*

11. **Which is true based on the table?**

    A   During the first quarter of 2014, GDP fell further than it ever had previously.

    B   GDP rises and falls in a regular pattern.

    C   During the first two quarters of 2014, GDP both rose and fell.

    D   GDP remained the same during 2013.

12. **Microeconomics is concerned with**

    A   economic aggregates

    B   industry behavior

    C   national economic policy

    D   the behavior of individual consumers

13. **The study of inflation is a part of**

    A   macroeconomics

    B   microeconomics

    C   normative economics

    D   descriptive economics

14. **Which of the following is NOT one of the four types of economic systems?**

    A   traditional economy

    B   micro economy

    C   market economy

    D   command economy

15. **Which of the following describes an opportunity cost?**

    A   something given up when one makes a choice

    B   a cost that cannot be avoided

    C   the cost incurred by delaying a decision

    D   a per-item discount received when one buys multiple units

Answers are on pages 719–720.

# 15 Geography

For many people, the word *geography* brings to mind spinning globes and pull-down world maps in the front of a classroom. These items would definitely be studied in a geography class, but this branch of social studies is much more than simply learning about maps. Geography also includes learning about the physical features of our planet, including bodies of water, mountains, climate, and the impact these have on our lives.

Ten percent of the questions on the *HiSET®* Exam Social Studies test will address your understanding of geography. You will be asked questions about places and regions, physical systems, the environment and society, and the uses of geography.

## What Is Tested?

Geography questions may cover a wide range of topics. While you probably will not have to identify the capital of Tajikistan, you will need to be comfortable using a variety of types of maps and be able to understand the characteristics of each. It will also be important for you to understand how geographic features impact other factors, such as weather, population, and international relations. The following lists cover a few topics to review. Keep in mind that these lists include suggestions and are by no means exhaustive. Review the information in your geography textbook. Pay attention to geographic concepts mentioned in the news. Think about how geography has affected historical events in the past and how it affects events today. As you study, add any important or interesting concepts to the lists.

### Maps and Publications

- Almanac
- Atlas
- Climate Map
- Conic Map
- Economic or Resource Map
- Gnomic Map
- Mercator Map
- Physical Map
- Political Map
- Thematic Map
- Topographical Map

## Geography Vocabulary

- Contour Lines
- Equator
- Hemispheres
- Key
- Latitude
- Legend
- Longitude
- Prime Meridian
- Time Zones

## Geographic Features

- Climate
- Hills
- Mountains
- Plains
- Plateaus
- Sea Level

### Keep in Mind

Keep in mind that geography questions are likely to involve maps. Make sure you are comfortable using many kinds of maps. Look through books, magazines, and newspapers, and pay attention to the different maps. Notice the features of each. Pay close attention to the key and what type of information is being displayed.

# Examples

Here are two sample geography questions.

1.  **Julio is traveling on business. The current location of his airplane is approximately 9.5° N latitude and 43° E longitude. Over which location is the airplane currently located?**

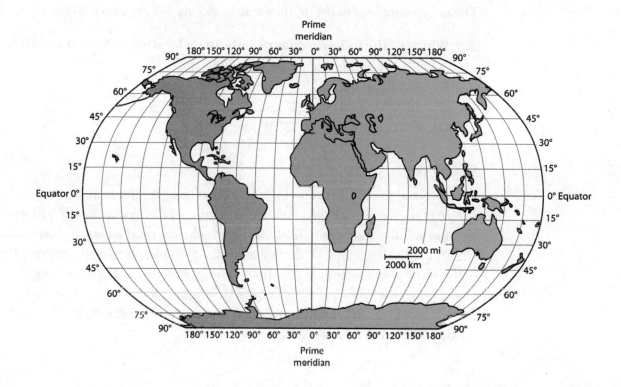

    A   Africa
    B   the Atlantic Ocean
    C   Europe
    D   the Pacific Ocean

## Explanation

First, read all the information, including everything on the map. Identify the question: *Which location is found at 9.5° N latitude and 43° E longitude?* You will need to plot the latitude and longitude on the map and see where the point lies. Look for key words and phrases. The information you need to solve this problem are the latitude and longitude, *9.5° N latitude* and *43° E longitude*. Determine the meanings of any unfamiliar terms. Suppose you cannot remember the directions in which latitude and longitude run. The letter N in 9.5° N latitude can be used as a clue that latitude is north of the equator. The letter E in 43° E longitude can be used as a clue that longitude is east of the prime meridian. Think about what you already know. In the past, you may have learned some type of trick to remind you the direction in which lines of latitude and/or longitude run. For example, you may have been taught that <u>longitude</u> lines are long, as a way to remember that these lines are vertical. You may have learned that the *t*'s in latitude must be crossed, so these lines run across, or horizontal. You also probably already know the names of the oceans and continents, which will be important since the map does not label any landmasses or bodies of water. Anything you already know about the topic could be helpful in answering the question. Select the best answer. The point given is approximately 10 degrees north of the equator and about 45 degrees east of the prime meridian, so the location is in Africa. **The best answer is A.**

The next example is based on the same world map as the previous question.

2.  **Which of the following points indicates a location in the United States?**
    A   17° N latitude and 88° W longitude
    B   34° S latitude and 92° W longitude
    C   40° N latitude and 72° E longitude
    D   67° N latitude and 153° W longitude

### Explanation

First, read all the information, including everything on the map. Identify the question: *Which of the following points indicates a location in the United States?* You will need to plot the latitude and longitude of the answer choices on the map and see which one lies within the United States. Underline the key words and phrases, in this case the coordinates in the answer choices. You should know the terms latitude and longitude and have already reviewed your previous knowledge of how those work. Select the best answer. Plot each of the points and you will find that the location for choice D lies somewhere in Alaska. **The best answer is D.**

# GEOGRAPHY DRILLS

For each of the following questions, choose the best answer.

1.  **Which of the following climate types CANNOT be found in the continental United States?**
    A   temperate areas with cold, wet winters and warm, dry summers
    B   dry regions with very limited precipitation
    C   polar regions with temperatures rarely above freezing
    D   continental areas with cold winters and warm, dry summers

2. Many countries around the world export oil. Saudi Arabia and Russia export the most, with Saudi Arabia exporting nearly eight million barrels per day and Russia exporting more than six million barrels per day. Which inference can be made based on the map shown below?

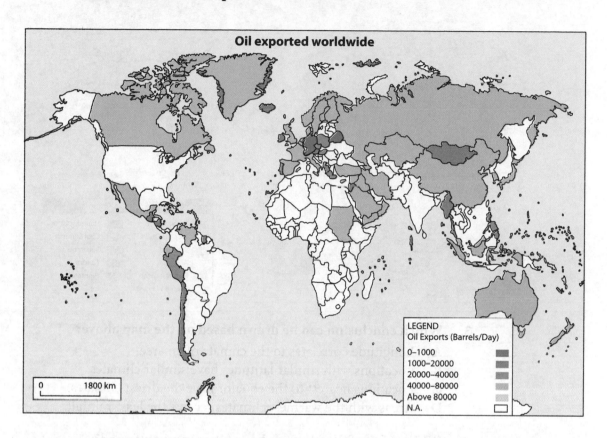

**Oil exported worldwide**

LEGEND
Oil Exports (Barrels/Day)

0–1000
1000–20000
20000–40000
40000–80000
Above 80000
N.A.

0        1800 km

A   Less oil is exported from Iceland each day than from Australia.
B   There is very little oil in South America.
C   Africa's economy is dependent on exporting oil.
D   The majority of the world's oil comes from Europe.

**World climates**

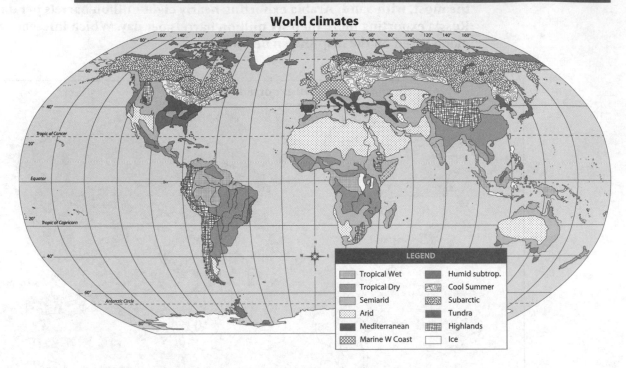

LEGEND

Tropical Wet    Humid subtrop.
Tropical Dry    Cool Summer
Semiarid    Subarctic
Arid    Tundra
Mediterranean    Highlands
Marine W Coast    Ice

3. **Which conclusion can be drawn based on the map above?**

   **A**   Longitude correlates to the climate of an area.

   **B**   Locations with similar latitudes have similar climates.

   **C**   Locations nearest to the equator have the driest climates.

   **D**   Areas with the warmest climates receive the least rainfall.

4. **Which of the following can be most properly inferred?**

   **A**   Arid climates are found only near the equator.

   **B**   All islands experience tropical, wet climates.

   **C**   A range of climates can be found in both hemispheres.

   **D**   Areas bordering an ocean experience wet climates.

*As altitude increases, temperature decreases. For this reason, mountains have colder climates than surrounding flatlands. They also receive more rainfall. This is due to the fact that as moist air rises to move above the mountain, it cools, allowing it to carry less moisture, resulting in precipitation. In fact, some mountaintops are covered with snow year-round due to weather conditions associated with the altitude rather than the climate of the surrounding areas.*

5. **Based on this information, which conclusion can be drawn?**

   **A**   Plains located in mountainous regions have cold climates.

   **B**   Flatlands surrounding a mountain range generally have dry, arid climates.

   **C**   Deserts are not found in the same geographic regions as mountain ranges.

   **D**   The land on one side of a mountain range may be rainy, while the other side may experience drought conditions.

6.  **Which best describes the characteristics of plant life found on or near mountains?**

    **A**   Mountain peaks often have sparse grasses or bare rocks.

    **B**   Broad, lush forests are located near a mountain's highest points.

    **C**   Thin, sparse trees are generally found near the foothills of a mountain.

    **D**   Mountains are mostly covered with rock, making plant life uncommon.

---

**Use the following information to answer questions 7–10.**

*The largest tropical rain forest in the world is located in the Amazon Basin. This area receives a measurable amount of rainfall nearly 200 days each year, with yearly totals of approximately 100 inches. The Amazon River, as well as more than 1,000 tributaries, runs through this area as well.*

7.  **Which conclusion can be drawn about this region?**

    A   The lowest lying areas in South America are located near the Pacific coastline.

    B   The amount of rainfall is comparable in all areas of the continent.

    C   The majority of the coastal regions of South America are at sea level.

    D   The Andes Mountains are the source of most rivers in South America.

8.  **Which is true about the Atacama Desert?**

    A   It is located in Uruguay.

    B   It is located in the Andes Mountains.

    C   It is found on the equator and has a warm climate.

    D   It is part of the Amazon Basin and has a damp climate.

9.  **About how many miles in length are the Andes Mountains?**

    A   600 miles

    B   1000 miles

    C   2,000 miles

    D   4,500 miles

10. **Based on the physical features of South America, where are the most highly populated cities located?**

    A   along the southwest coast

    B   along the east coast

    C   in the Amazon Basin

    D   along the northwest coast

11.  In 2007, approximately 10–20 percent of the residents of the United States were under the age of fifteen years old. The map below shows these data worldwide. Which inference can be made based on this information?

**Percent of Population Under 15 Years of Age (2007)**

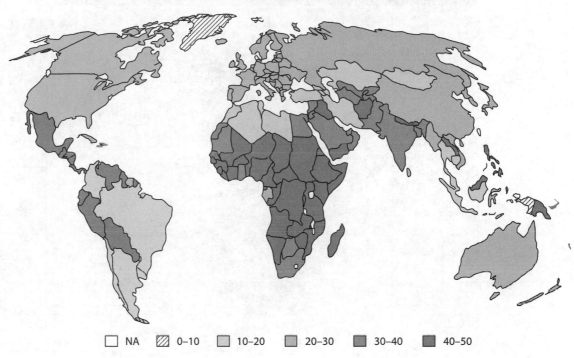

NA     0–10    10–20    20–30    30–40    40–50

A  The life expectancy in many African countries is less than that of most other places in the world.

B  The annual birth rate in much of Europe is greater than the mortality rate in the region.

C  There are more teen-aged residents than elderly residents in most of Central America.

D  The average number of children per family is greater in the United States than in South America.

12. Craig's flight from Anchorage, Alaska, leaves at 3:00 P.M., local time and arrives in Dallas approximately six hours later. Approximately what time will it be in Dallas when the flight lands?

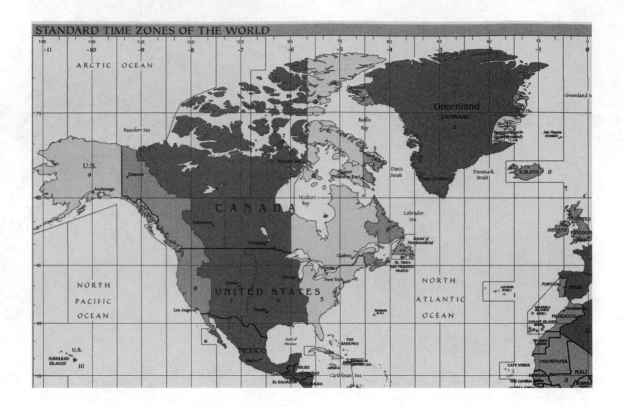

STANDARD TIME ZONES OF THE WORLD

A  9:00 A.M.

B  11:00 A.M.

C  5:00 P.M.

D  7:00 P.M.

13. The Beringia theory states that there was once a land bridge connecting North America and Asia across what is now the Bering Strait. Which of the following serves as evidence for this theory?

A  The first human migration from Asia into the Americas took place between 14,000 and 20,000 years ago.

B  Certain genetic markers in Native Americans are found only in the modern inhabitants of southern Siberia.

C  No fossils of human remains have been found in the area thought to have been the land bridge.

D  Sediment cores from the Bering Strait dated to between 15,000 to 30,000 years ago contained the spores of shrubs that are not currently found in that region.

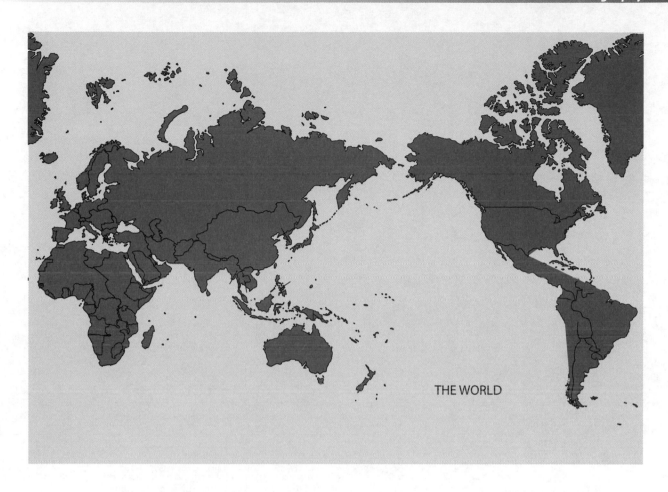

THE WORLD

14. The map shown above is an example of a
    A   resource map
    B   conic map
    C   Mercator map
    D   topographical map

15. Which of the following is the term for the formation that results when a river meets an inlet of the sea?
    A   delta
    B   estuary
    C   outwash plain
    D   berm

Answers are on page 720.

# Part V
# Science

# 16 The Science Test

The next few chapters will discuss information related to the *HiSET*® Exam Science test. This test will include 50 questions covering basic science concepts relating to life science and biology, earth and space science, chemistry, and physics. You will be given 1 hour and 20 minutes to complete the test. Many of the questions will include some type of visual aid, such as a graph, table, chart, or diagram. Some of the questions will simply require that you comprehend the information given in the passage or graphic. To answer other questions, you will need to restate or summarize data, evaluate the information, identify assumptions related to the material, and make judgments or hypotheses based on the facts. You may also need to relate the information to your prior knowledge of the topic.

## Question Steps

Here are the six steps you will use to find the best answer for each question on the HiSET Exam Science test.

> ### Science Question Steps
>
> **Step 1:** Read All the Information
>
> **Step 2:** Identify the Question
>
> **Step 3:** Underline Key Words and Phrases
>
> **Step 4:** Determine Meanings
>
> **Step 5:** Think About What You Already Know
>
> **Step 6:** Select the Best Answer

## Step 1: Read All the Information

The first step in correctly answering any test question is to carefully and completely read all of the information. This includes anything included in passages, graphs, tables, and captions, as well as the question and all of the answer choices.

Some people find it helpful to read the question before reading the passage. This alerts you to what information you will need to use to answer the question and gives you the chance to look for it as you read. The important thing is to make sure that you read all the information carefully, regardless of what you choose to read first.

## Step 2: Identify the Question

Once you have read everything, the next step is to determine exactly what the question is asking. Try restating the question in your own words. This can be helpful in determining how well you understand what it is asking.

## Step 3: Key Words and Phrases

Now identify what facts and information will be needed to answer the question. Go back through the passage and graphics and look for key words, pertinent facts, and other ideas that will help you select the correct answer. This draws your attention to the most important ideas and allows you to identify them quickly when it comes time to choose your answer.

## Step 4: Determine Meanings

There may be times when a word in the passage is unfamiliar. Take a look at the surrounding information, which may offer a definition, explanation, or example that can help you determine the word's meaning. Such context clues can be great hints.

If you are still unsure of the meaning of the new word, try breaking it into parts, such as the root, prefix, and suffix. Do you know another word with a similar root? If so, this can be helpful in figuring out the meaning of the word in the passage.

## Step 5: Think About What You Already Know

You have been learning science since kindergarten—or maybe even before. When you read information on the HiSET Exam Science test, think about how it relates to what you already know. Combining the new information with your prior knowledge can help you fully understand the topic.

## Step 6: Select the Best Answer

Before choosing the one best answer, reread the question, and carefully read every answer choice. Several of the choices may look good. The key is to select the single answer that gives the best and most complete response to the question.

# Examples

Here are two examples of science questions to show you how the steps work.

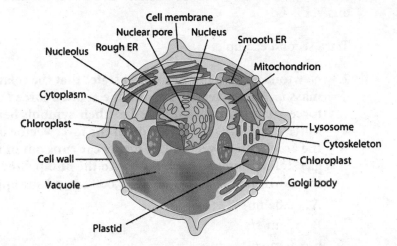

Use the diagram of a plant cell shown above to answer the question.

1.  **What is the function of the cell wall?**
    A   to build proteins
    B   to convert solar energy into chemical energy
    C   to protect and provide support for the cell
    D   to take in carbon dioxide

## Explanation

**Step 1: Read All the Information.**

This includes everything on the diagram as well as in the question.

**Step 2: Identify the Question**

Here, you will need to know what the cell wall does.

**Step 3: Look for Key Words and Phrases**

On the diagram, find the label for the cell wall and see what structure the label refers to.

**Step 4: Determine Meanings**

Determine the meanings of any unfamiliar terms. While there may be terms labeled on the diagram that you do not know, the only ones relevant to this question are *cell wall* and you probably know those words.

**Step 5: Think About What You Already Know**

Think about what you already know about plant cells and their structure. You may know what a cell wall does.

### Step 6: Select the Best Answer

Even if you do not have previous knowledge of the function of the cell wall, you can look at the diagram and see that it completely surrounds the outside of the cell, like a shell. A *wall* is usually for protection, and that is the case with a cell wall too. **The best answer is C.**

Try a second example.

2. **Newton's second law of motion states that the relationship between an object's mass *m*, its acceleration *a*, and the applied force *F* is *F* = *ma*. Acceleration and force are vectors (as indicated by their symbols being displayed in slant bold font); in this law the direction of the force vector is the same as the direction of the acceleration vector. If Helena's car runs out of gas near the entrance to the gas station and she must push it to the pump, how fast will she be able to push the car if the car has a mass of 1,000 kg and she applies a force of 50N?**

   A   0.05 m/s/s
   B   .5 m/s/s
   C   5 m/s/s
   D   20 m/s/s

### *Explanation*

### Step 1: Read All the Information

Here, all the information is within the question, so you can do Steps 1 and 2 at the same time.

### Step 2: Identify the Question

Here, you will calculate the speed using Newton's formula.

### Step 3: Look for Key Words and Phrases

You are given the formula, the mass, and the force, so look for those items.

### Step 4: Determine Meanings

While there may be terms here that you do not know, all you really need to do is plug the values given into the formula. For that you will need to know what each variable represents, and the question tells you that *F* is force, *m* is mass, and *a* is acceleration.

### Step 5: Think About What You Already Know

You may have worked with this physics formula before, but if not, you have probably worked algebra problems, and this one is no different.

### Step 6: Select the Best Answer

Substitute the values given into the formula. 50N = 1000kg × *a*. Divide 50 by 1000 to solve for *a*. Select the best answer choice. The acceleration is .05 m/s/s. **The best answer is A.**

# 17 Life Science

Fifty percent of the questions on the *HiSET*® Exam Science test will relate to life science, or biology. Basically, you will be asked about living things, including humans, plants, and animals. It will be important to understand the cell, heredity, the interdependence of organisms, and the behavior of organisms. This chapter will discuss some of the concepts you can expect to find on the test.

## What Is Tested?

Life science questions may cover a large range of subject matter. The following are lists of suggested topics to understand before the test. Keep in mind that these lists are by no means exhaustive; however, understanding these ideas will put you on the right track.

In addition to topics related to life science, the lists also include subjects about scientific inquiry. You probably learned this process when completing science experiments in school or a science fair project at home, so the concepts will most likely be familiar. Questions about scientific inquiry may address any area of science, not just life science.

To prepare for the test, watch television shows that discuss science and health-related topics. Read newspaper and magazine articles related to life science. Take a look at the list of ingredients on the grocery items in your kitchen. Think about how everyday life is affected by disease and improvements in medical technology; be aware of current events. Add any applicable topics you find interesting or important as you research and study.

### Scientific Inquiry (the Scientific Method)

- Control Group
- Dependent Variable
- Experiment
- Hypothesis
- Independent Variable
- Result
- Trial

## Cells

- Active Transport
- Anaphase
- Animal Cells
- Cell
- Cell Membrane
- Cell Wall
- Chromosome
- Cytoplasm
- Diffusion
- Diploid Cell
- Endoplasmic Reticulum
- Gametes
- Golgi Apparatus
- Haploid Cell
- Meiosis
- Metaphase
- Mitochondrion
- Mitosis
- Nucleus
- Nucleolus
- Organelles
- Osmosis
- Plant Cells
- Prophase
- Telophase

## Human Body

- Alveoli
- Aorta
- Artery
- Axons
- Ball-and-Socket Joints
- Blood
- Brain
- Bronchial Tubes
- Capillaries
- Cardiac Muscles
- Cerebellum
- Cerebrum
- Circulatory System
- Dendrites
- Diaphragm
- Digestive System
- Endocrine System
- Enzymes
- Epiglottis
- Esophagus
- Excretory System
- Fixed Joints
- Gallbladder
- Glands
- Gliding Joints
- Heart
- Hinge Joints
- Hormones
- Intestines
- Involuntary Muscles
- Ligaments
- Liver
- Marrow
- Muscular System
- Nervous System
- Occipital Lobe
- Pancreas
- Pivot Joints
- Plasma
- Platelets
- Red Blood Cells
- Reproductive System
- Respiratory System
- Senses
- Sensory nerves
- Skeletal System
- Smooth Muscles
- Spinal Cord
- Synapses
- Temporal Lobe
- Tendons
- Trachea
- Valve
- Veins
- Ventricle
- Voluntary Muscles
- White Blood Cells

## Animals

- Amphibian
- Arthropods
- Bird
- Cold-blooded
- Exoskeleton
- Fish
- Invertebrate
- Jellyfish
- Mammal
- Mollusks
- Reptile
- Sponges
- Vertebrate
- Warm-blooded
- Worms

### Keep in Mind

Keep in mind that some of the vocabulary in these lists relates to more than one topic. For example, *mammal* is listed under the "Animals" heading. However, since humans are mammals, the word relates to humans as well. Likewise, *heart* and *brain* are listed under "Human Body," but animals have hearts and brains too. The important thing is not so much where the words are located on the lists but that you understand each of them.

## Plants

- Amino Acids
- Carotene
- Cellular Respiration
- Chlorophyll
- Chloroplasts
- Fern
- Fertilization
- Flowers
- Fungi
- Gametophyte
- Germination
- Glucose
- Leaf
- Moss
- Nitrates
- Nitrogen
- Nitrogenase
- Nitrogen Cycle
- Nodules
- Nonvascular Plants
- Phloem
- Photosynthesis
- Pistil
- Pollen
- Roots
- Spores
- Stamen
- Stem
- Vascular Plants
- Xanthophylls
- Xylem

## Organisms

- Class
- Eukaryotes
- Family
- Genus
- Kingdom
- Multicellular Organisms
- Order
- Phylum
- Prokaryotes
- Simple Organisms
- Species
- Unicellular Organisms

### Heredity

- Chromosomes
- Cloning
- DNA
- Dominant Gene
- Fraternal Twins
- Genes
- Genetic Disorder
- Genetics

- Heredity
- Identical Twins
- Mitosis
- Mutation
- Recessive Gene
- RNA
- Species

### Ecosystems and Nutrients

- Calories
- Carbohydrates
- Carbon Cycle
- Carbon Dioxide
- Consumers
- Decay
- Decomposers
- Ecosystem
- Fats
- Food Chain
- Food Web
- Glucagon
- Habitat

- Insulin
- Minerals
- Nutrients
- Oxygen
- Population
- Primary Consumers
- Producers
- Proteins
- Respiration
- Secondary Consumers
- Tertiary Consumers
- Vitamins

### Behaviors

- Instinct
- Learned Behavior

- Reflex
- Self-Preservation

### Health

- Acquired Immunity
- Age-related Diseases
- Assimilation
- Digestion
- Environmental Diseases
- Hereditary Issues
- Immune System
- Immunization

- Immunodeficiency
- Infection
- Inflammation
- Life Cycle
- Medical Defenses
- Non-infectious Diseases
- Public Health
- Regulation

### General Vocabulary

- Adaptation
- Creationist Theory
- Darwinism
- Diversity

- Energy
- Interdependence
- Natural Selection
- Theory of Evolution

# Examples

Here are two examples of life science questions.

1. **For the school science fair, Audree wanted to determine the optimal amount of water for marigold plants. She planted the same number of marigold seeds in each of 30 pots. She divided the pots into three groups, with 10 in each group, and labeled the groups A, B, and C. She watered the plants in group A daily, group B twice a week, and group C once a week. The plants received an equal amount of water each time. She predicted that the plants watered daily would be the tallest at the end of one month. Which would NOT be necessary for the experiment to be valid?**

   A   using the same size pots

   B   including a control group

   C   planting all of the seeds in the same type of soil

   D   making sure the plants received an equal amount of sunlight

## Explanation

First, read all the information and identify the question. Here you will choose the answer choice that was not necessary for the experiment. Underline key words and phrases. In this question, it would be important to underline the word <u>NOT</u> in the question. Overlooking this word would completely change what is being asked. Determine the meanings of unfamiliar words. Suppose the word *optimal* is unfamiliar. What words have a similar root? *Optimistic* means "hopeful;" *optimum* means "best." Using these and considering what makes sense in the context of the sentence, you can figure out that *optimal* probably means "best" or "most favorable." Think about what you already know. What do you know about scientific inquiry? To test one variable, everything else must be the same, so answer choices A, C, and D would be necessary. Select the best answer. Since three different watering schedules are being tested, a control group is not necessary. **The best answer is B.**

The next example is based on the previously mentioned experiment. Use the information, as well as your own prior knowledge, to answer the question.

2. **The watering schedule Audree used in the experiment is the**

   A   dependent variable

   B   hypothesis

   C   independent variable

   D   result

## Explanation

First, read all the information and identify the question. Here you will choose the answer choice that describes the role of the watering schedule in the experiment. Look for key words and phrases, in this case *watering schedule*. Determine the meanings of unfamiliar words. If you do not know what a *hypothesis* is, think about the root *thesis*. You know that a thesis for an essay is the main idea, so a hypothesis may be similar to a main idea, or what Audree is trying to show. Think about what you already know. What do you know about scientific inquiry? An experiment attempts to answer a question. Variables are things that change. Audree is changing the watering schedule, so it is a variable. A dependent variable is the output or effect of the experiment and an independent variable is the input or cause. Audree is changing the input by varying the watering schedule to see what the effects would be. Select the best answer. Choice C describes a changing input. **The best answer is C.**

# LIFE SCIENCE DRILLS

## Use the following information to answer questions 1–5.

*The CDC recommends that children in the United States receive certain vaccinations at given ages. Several of these vaccinations are repeated at specific intervals between birth and age six. Many of the diseases for which children are routinely vaccinated today used to pose serious health concerns in the past; however, since vaccinations began, some of these diseases have declined by 100 percent. For example, in the years just prior to the introduction of the measles vaccine, more than 503,000 cases were reported annually. In 2007, there were only 43 cases of the disease. (See chart.)*

### Recommended Immunization Schedule for Persons Aged 0 Through 6 Years—United States • 2011
For those who fall behind or start late, see the catch-up schedule

| Vaccine ▼ Age ► | Birth | 1 month | 2 months | 4 months | 6 months | 12 months | 15 months | 18 months | 19–23 months | 2–3 years | 4–6 years | |
|---|---|---|---|---|---|---|---|---|---|---|---|---|
| Hepatitis B[1] | HepB | HepB | | | HepB | | | | | | | |
| Rotavirus[2] | | | RV | RV | RV[2] | | | | | | | Range of recommended ages for all children |
| Diphtheria, Tetanus, Pertussis[3] | | | DTaP | DTaP | DTaP | see footnote[3] | DTaP | | | | DTaP | |
| *Haemophilus influenzae* type b[4] | | | Hib | Hib | Hib[4] | Hib | | | | | | |
| Pneumococcal[5] | | | PCV | PCV | PCV | PCV | | | | PPSV | | |
| Inactivated Poliovirus[6] | | | IPV | IPV | | IPV | | | | | IPV | |
| Influenza[7] | | | | | | Influenza (Yearly) | | | | | | Range of recommended ages for certain high-risk groups |
| Measles, Mumps, Rubella[8] | | | | | | MMR | | see footnote[8] | | | MMR | |
| Varicella[9] | | | | | | Varicella | | see footnote[9] | | | Varicella | |
| Hepatitis A[10] | | | | | | HepA (2 doses) | | | | HepA Series | | |
| Meningococcal[11] | | | | | | | | | | MCV4 | | |

1. **According to the information given, which of the following can be most properly inferred?**

   A  Children receive the varicella vaccine on the same schedule at which they receive the measles, mumps, and rubella vaccine.

   B  Children receive the rotavirus vaccine on the same schedule at which they receive the pneumococcal vaccine.

   C  All children receive the meningococcal vaccine between the ages of 2 and 6.

   D  The influenza vaccine is not given to children in high-risk groups.

2. **According to the information given, which is a true statement?**
   A   Children receive the rotavirus vaccine one time between ages 2 months and 6 months.
   B   All children should receive the meningococcal vaccine between the ages of 2 and 6 years old.
   C   Children are vaccinated against diphtheria, tetanus, and pertussis four times before their second birthday.
   D   The hepatitis B vaccine must be repeated at ages 6 months, 12 months, 15 months, and 18 months.

3. **A patient receives the same vaccination each winter. According to the chart, which disease is this vaccination preventing?**
   A   hepatitis A
   B   influenza
   C   pneumococcus
   D   varicella

*Diphtheria, a disease caused by bacteria found in the mouth and throat, causes patients to suffer from a sore throat, as well as fever and chills. Untreated, it can lead to complications including heart failure and paralysis. It can be fatal in approximately 10 percent of those who contract the disease and used to be a major cause of death in children. As recently as the 1920s, about 15,000 people died from diphtheria each year.*

4. **Which assumption can be made regarding this disease?**
   A   More people die from diphtheria today than 100 years ago.
   B   The diphtheria vaccine has eliminated sore throats among young children.
   C   Diphtheria was the most serious health concern facing people in the 1920s.
   D   Widespread use of the diphtheria vaccine has significantly reduced its threat.

*Pertussis, also known as whooping cough, looks like the common cold; however, after a few weeks, it causes patients to suffer violent coughing spells and may lead to pneumonia, seizures, and brain infections. In some cases, it can be fatal. It is spread through the air from one person to the next but can be prevented through vaccination.*

5. **Which type of disease is pertussis?**
   A   age-related
   B   environmental
   C   hereditary
   D   infectious

**Use the information that follows to answer questions 6–7.**

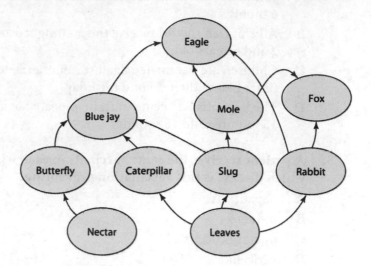

6.   **What is the role of the mole in the food web shown?**
   A   secondary consumer
   B   decomposer
   C   tertiary consumer
   D   primary consumer

7.   **During which link in the food web is the most energy transferred?**
   A   caterpillar–blue jay
   B   nectar–butterfly
   C   rabbit–eagle
   D   mole–eagle

*Behavior is the way in which organisms interact with other organisms and their environment. In both people and animals, behavior occurs in response to an external stimulus, an internal stimulus, or both. Some behaviors are innate, or built in. These innate behaviors include reflexes and instincts. Other behaviors are learned as a result of experiences.*

8.   **Which is an example of a reflex?**
   A   a person blinking when something is thrown toward him or her
   B   a baby crawling on the floor before it begins to walk
   C   a bird gathering material to build its nest
   D   a dog barking when it hears a doorbell

9.   **The anther and filament comprise which part of the flower?**

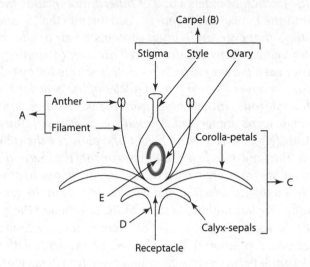

A   ovule

B   pedicel

C   stamen

D   pistil

*The brain controls nearly everything our bodies do, whether we are awake or asleep. There are five main parts of the brain. The cerebrum is the largest part and accounts for approximately 85 percent of the brain's weight. It is responsible for our thinking, short- and long-term memory, reasoning, and voluntary muscles. It is divided into two halves, with the right half controlling the left side of the body and the left half controlling the right side of the body.*

*The cerebellum is at the back of the brain and is located below the cerebrum. It is approximately one-eighth the size of the cerebrum. This part of the brain controls balance, movement, and coordination. Beneath the cerebrum and in front of the cerebellum is the brain stem, which connects the brain to the spinal cord. It is responsible for functions such as breathing; digestion; circulation; and involuntary muscle control, including the heart and stomach.*

*The pituitary gland is about the size of a pea and is responsible for releasing hormones into the body, which are responsible for many things, including growth and metabolism. The hypothalamus is the part of the brain that regulates the body's temperature. Reactions such as sweating and shivering are attempts to control temperature and help it to return to normal.*

10.  **Which part of the brain would control the activities needed for riding a bicycle?**

A   pituitary gland

B   cerebellum

C   cerebrum

D   hypothalamus

*In genetics, Mendel's Laws of Inheritance include the Law of Segregation (the "First Law") and the Law of Independent Assortment (the "Second Law"). The Law of Segregation states that every individual contains a pair of alleles for each particular trait which segregate or separate during cell division (assuming diploidy) for any particular trait and that each parent passes a randomly selected copy (allele) to its offspring. The offspring then receives its own pair of alleles of the gene for that trait by inheriting sets of homologous chromosomes from the parent organisms. Interactions between alleles at a single locus are termed dominance, and these influence how the offspring expresses that trait (e.g., the color and height of a plant, or the color of an animal's fur).*

*The Law of Independent Assortment (the "Second Law") states that separate genes for separate traits are passed independently of one another from parents to offspring. That is, the biological selection of a particular gene in the gene pair for one trait to be passed to the offspring has nothing to do with the selection of the gene for any other trait. More precisely, the law states that alleles of different genes assort independently of one another during gamete formation. While Mendel's experiments with mixing one trait always resulted in a 3:1 ratio between dominant and recessive phenotypes, his experiments with mixing two traits (dihybrid cross) showed 9:3:3:1 ratios. But each of the two genes is independently inherited with a 3:1 phenotypic ratio. Mendel concluded that different traits are inherited independently of each other, so that there is no relation, for example, between a cat's color and tail length. This is actually only true for genes that are not linked to each other.*

11. **An organism's expressed physical trait, such as hair color or nose shape, is called its**

   A  genotype

   B  phenotype

   C  cytosol

   D  gamete

12. **If the allele for green pod color (G) is dominant over the allele for yellow pod color (g), which of the following genotypes would a plant with yellow pods have?**

   A  GG

   B  Gg

   C  gg

   D  gG

13. **In a dihybrid cross, the expected ratio in the F2 generation is**

   A  4:1

   B  3:1

   C  9:3:3:1

   D  1:3

*Mitosis, or somatic cell division, has four stages: prophase, metaphase, anaphase, and telophase. During interphase the chromosomes are dispersed in the nucleus and appear as a network of long, thin threads or filaments, called the chromatin. The chromosomes replicate themselves to form pairs of identical sister chromosomes, or chromatids; the DNA of the chromosomes is synthesized only during interphase. During prophase the two chromatids remain attached to one another at a region called the centromere, but each contracts into a compact tightly coiled body. The nucleolus and, in most cases, the nuclear envelope break down and disappear and the spindle begins to form. In animal cells the centrioles separate and move apart, and radiating bundles of fibers, called asters, appear around them. In plant cells the spindle forms without centrioles. During metaphase the chromosomes congregate at a plane midway between the two ends to which the spindle tapers. This is called the equatorial plane and marks the point where the whole cell will divide when nuclear division is completed. The ends of the spindle are the poles to which the chromatids will migrate and the chromatids are attached to the spindle fibers at the centromeres. During anaphase the two chromatids of each chromosome separate and move to opposite poles. During telophase new nuclear envelopes form around the two groups of daughter chromosomes, the new nucleoli begin to appear, and eventually the spindle fibers disappear. Cytokinesis, which may begin before or after mitosis is completed, finally separates the daughter nuclei into two new individual daughter cells.*

14. **During which phase of mitosis do spindle fibers form?**
   A   metaphase
   B   anaphase
   C   prophase
   D   telophase

15. **Which phase of mitosis is shown in the diagram below?**

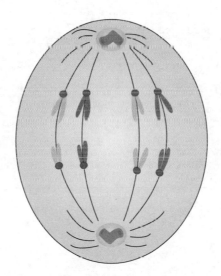

   A   prophase
   B   anaphase
   C   telophase
   D   metaphase

**Answers are on page 720.**

# 18 Earth and Space Science

**Q**uestions related to earth and space science will account for 25 percent of the *HiSET*® Exam Science test. You may find information connected to geology, meteorology, oceanography, paleontology, geochemistry, ecology, and environmental science. By combining your own prior knowledge with the ideas presented in the passages and visual aids on the test, you will be ready to demonstrate your ability to comprehend, analyze, summarize, and apply earth and space science concepts.

## What Is Tested?

Earth and space science questions can cover a wide range of material. The following lists include suggested topics to study. Keep in mind that these lists are not all-inclusive; any ideas related to our planet and space may appear on the test. That's literally a whole world of possible topics. To prepare for the test, familiarize yourself with the ideas given here. As you watch science- and health-related television shows, read newspaper and magazine articles, and look through science textbooks, add any other important or interesting ideas to the lists.

### Earth

- Atmosphere
- Axis
- Continental Drift
- Core
- Crust
- Exosphere
- Fault Lines
- Geologic Time
- Glaciers
- Global Warming
- Greenhouse Effect
- Hydrosphere
- Igneous Rocks
- Ionosphere
- Magma
- Mantle
- Mesosphere
- Metamorphic Rocks
- Minerals
- Ozone
- Pangaea
- Plate Tectonics
- Revolution
- Rotation
- Sedimentary Rocks
- Stratosphere
- Subduction
- Thermosphere
- Trench
- Troposphere
- Volcanoes
- Water Cycle

**Weather and Natural Disasters**

- Air Pressure
- Barometric Pressure
- Cirrus Clouds
- Cold Front
- Condensation
- Coriolis Effect
- Cumulonimbus Clouds
- Cumulus Clouds
- Earthquake
- Evaporation
- Flooding
- Front
- Gulf Stream
- Humidity
- Hurricane
- Landslides
- Precipitation
- Relative Humidity
- Richter Scale
- Runoff
- Seasons
- Seismic Waves
- Stationary Front
- Stratus Clouds
- Temperature
- Tsunami
- Warm Front
- Weather
- Wind

**The Environment**

- Air Pollution
- Conservation
- Hazardous Waste
- Nonrenewable Natural Resources
- Prevention of Extinction
- Protection of Biodiversity
- Recycling
- Renewable Natural Resources
- Soil Pollution
- Solid Waste Disposal
- Water Pollution

**Changes in the Earth**

- Abrasion
- Chemical Weathering
- Creep
- Deposition
- Erosion
- Exfoliation
- Fossils
- Gravity Erosion
- Leaching
- Physical Weathering
- Water Erosion
- Weathering
- Wind Erosion

**Space**

- Asteroids
- Astronomy
- Black Dwarf Star
- Black Hole
- Blue Star
- Comets
- Copernican Theory
- Elliptical Galaxy
- Galaxies
- Gas Clouds
- Giant Star
- Globular Clusters
- Gravity
- Inner Planets
- Irregular Galaxy
- Meteor
- Milky Way Galaxy
- Light-years
- NASA
- Nebulae
- Neutron Star
- Nova
- Open Clusters
- Orbiters
- Outer Planets
- Planets
- Pulsar
- Quasars
- Red Giant Star
- Satellite

- Solar Nebula
- Solar System
- Spiral Galaxy
- Star

- Sun
- Supernova
- White Dwarf Star

### The Moon

- Lunar Eclipse
- Neap Tides
- Orbit
- Phases

- Solar Eclipse
- Spring Tides
- Tides

### Theories

- Big Bang Theory
- Closed Universe Theory

- Flat Universe Theory
- Open Universe Theory

# Examples

Here are two examples of earth and space science questions.

*The physical structure of the Earth includes three basic layers. At the center of the planet is a solid, very dense inner core surrounded by a liquid outer core. The outer core, which contains iron, spins as the planet rotates, generating a magnetic field as it flows. Together, the inner and outer cores are approximately 2,200 miles thick and make up about one-third of the Earth's mass.*

*The core is covered by a layer called the mantle. It is semisolid, and although it is not the hottest layer of the planet, it is still so hot that some of the rock in this layer is molten. This rock flows slowly, similar to hot asphalt.*

*The mantle is covered by a rigid outside layer, or crust. This layer is about 25 miles thick beneath the continents and four miles thick beneath the oceans, which is relatively thin compared to the other two layers. The uppermost part of the mantle is cooler than the deeper parts and combines with the planet's thin crust to form the lithosphere. This layer has broken into pieces known as tectonic plates, which are constantly moving as they float on a layer of melted rock.*

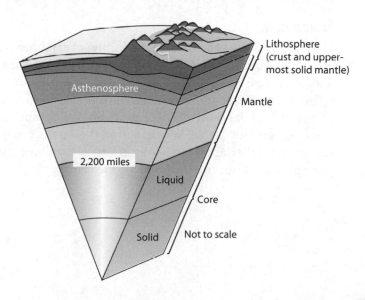

1.  **Which layer of the Earth is responsible for a compass pointing toward north?**
    A   crust
    B   outer core
    C   lithosphere
    D   mantle

## Explanation

First, read all the information, including everything on the diagram. Identify the question, which can be translated as *Which layer affects a compass?* Look for key words and phrases. To answer the question, it is important to understand each of the layers, so taking note of these would be helpful. Since a compass points toward magnetic north, noting any information about magnetism is also beneficial. Determine the meanings of any unfamiliar words. The word *lithosphere* may be unfamiliar. Clues in the sentence, as well as the following sentence, provide a definition of the word. Take another look:

> *The <u>uppermost part of the mantle</u> is cooler than the deeper parts and <u>combines with the planet's thin crust to form the lithosphere.</u> <u>This layer has broken into pieces</u> known as tectonic plates, <u>which are constantly moving</u> as they float on a layer of melted rock.*

The lithosphere is the upper mantle and crust. Think about what you already know. What do you already know about how a compass works? Most likely, you recognize the fact that a compass relies on magnetism to indicate direction. Select the best answer. Since you know that a compass relies on the Earth's magnetic field, and the passage states that the outer core generates a magnetic field, you can conclude that answer choice D is correct. **The best answer is D**.

Select the best answer to the following question, using the same information about the layers of the Earth.

2.  **Beneath which location is the Earth's crust the thickest?**
    A   Mount Everest
    B   Atlantic Ocean
    C   Grand Canyon
    D   Mojave Desert

## Explanation

First, read all the information, including everything on the diagram. Identify the question, which can be translated as *Where is the crust the thickest?* Look for key words and phrases. This question is about only the crust, or lithosphere, so note those terms where they appear, along with anything relating to thickness. Determine the meanings of any unfamiliar words. There probably are no unfamiliar words here. Think about what you already know. Where would the earth's crust be thickest? Most likely, you will realize that taller areas have thicker crust. Combine this knowledge with what the passage says about the thickness of the crust:

*The mantle is covered by a rigid outside layer, or crust. This layer is about 25 miles thick beneath the continents and four miles thick beneath the oceans, which is relatively thin compared to the other two layers.*

The crust is thinnest under the ocean and would be thickest under tall mountains. You can also see this shown on the diagram. Select the best answer. The only choice that contains mountains is choice A. **The best answer is A.**

# EARTH AND SPACE SCIENCE DRILLS

1. **The Grand Canyon is the result of which type of erosion?**
   A  gravity erosion
   B  physical weathering
   C  water erosion
   D  wind erosion

**Use the following information to answer questions 2 and 3.**

*Between the years of 1980 and 2010, the United States experienced 99 weather-related disasters with damages in excess of $1 billion each. The total cost for these events was more than $725 billion.*

*In March 2010, flooding occurred in several states in the Northeast. Over the following two months, several states in the Mid-South faced severe weather, tornadoes, and flooding. That fall, Arizona dealt with unusually severe weather. In 2005, Hurricanes Dennis, Katrina, Rita, and Wilma pounded several states, while the Midwest faced a spring and summer drought. The year 2004 also brought a number of hurricanes, including Charley, Frances, Ivan, and Jeanne. Prior to this, only one $1 billion hurricane hit our country in 2003, one in 2001, and one in 1999.*

*Northwestern Texas experienced severe weather disasters during six of the years between 1999 and 2010; however, it did not report any between the years 1980 and 1999. Likewise, Illinois reported eight flooding disasters between 1999 and 2009 and none during the nearly 20 years prior to this period.*

## Billion-Dollar Weather Disasters, 1980–2010

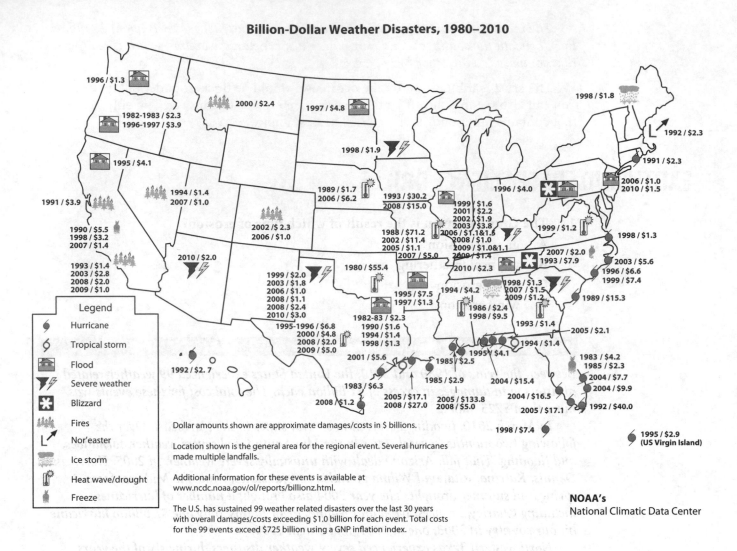

Dollar amounts shown are approximate damages/costs in $ billions.

Location shown is the general area for the regional event. Several hurricanes made multiple landfalls.

Additional information for these events is available at www.ncdc.noaa.gov/ol/reports/billionz.html.

The U.S. has sustained 99 weather related disasters over the last 30 years with overall damages/costs exceeding $1.0 billion for each event. Total costs for the 99 events exceed $725 billion using a GNP inflation index.

**NOAA's**
National Climatic Data Center

**2. Which generalization can be made based on these data?**

A   Flooding usually occurs in coastal regions.

B   Damage from blizzards is most severe in northern states.

C   Northern states are most likely to suffer high-cost damage from a freeze.

D   Severe hurricanes are most likely along the Gulf and Atlantic coastlines.

**3. Which statement can NOT be supported by the information?**

A   Patterns of severe weather are consistent from one year to the next in any given region.

B   Blizzards and snowstorms are less likely to cause high-cost damage than most other weather disasters.

C   Tropical storms, while not as severe as hurricanes, have the potential to generate higher costs in damages.

D   Most regions of the United States were affected by at least one major weather disaster during the reported period.

**Use the following information to answer questions 4–6.**

*For centuries, people have been fascinated by our moon. The moon, Earth's only natural satellite, orbits our planet one time every 29½ days. It does not have any light of its own but rather reflects the light of the sun from its surface. As it circles around the Earth, the moon changes position with respect to the sun, causing it to go through a series of phases during which different amounts of the satellite are visible from Earth. A new moon cannot be seen from Earth, since the lighted side is pointed away from our planet. We can, however, view the other phases: new crescent, first quarter, waxing gibbous, full moon, waning gibbous, last quarter, and old crescent. Following the new moon, each phase allows a larger portion of the moon to be visible until reaching the full moon phase, during which the entire moon is visible during the entire night. From that point, each phase shows a decreasing amount of the moon until it reaches the new moon phase again.*

*Occasionally, the moon enters the shadow of our planet and is dimmed almost completely. Such a lunar eclipse can be partial or total and can last from less than half an hour to as long as several hours. An eclipse can occur only during the full moon phase and only if the moon passes through at least part of the shadow of the Earth. When the moon passes between the sun and our planet, this causes a different type of eclipse, known as a solar eclipse. Unlike a lunar eclipse, this is only possible during the new moon phase. When this takes place, the shadow of the moon is cast on the Earth, and we are unable to see a portion of the sun.*

*The gravitational interaction between the moon and the Earth is responsible for the tides in large bodies of water on our planet. The gravitational pull of the moon is stronger on the side of the Earth that is nearest to the moon. This causes the water in our oceans to bulge out toward the moon. The Earth, itself being pulled toward the moon, also causes a bulge on the opposite side of the planet.*

*Different circumstances cause different types of tides. Spring tides occur when the Earth, sun, and moon are in line. These are especially strong since the moon and the sun both have gravitational forces that act upon the tide. These occur during full moon and new moon phases. Proxigean spring tides are unusually high and occur when the moon is especially close to our planet during the new moon phase. This rare occurrence takes place only about every year and a half. Neap tides are the weakest type and take place when the moon, sun, and Earth form a right angle, with the Earth at the vertex. These take place during the quarter moon phase.*

4.  **Look at the following diagram. Which does the diagram show?**

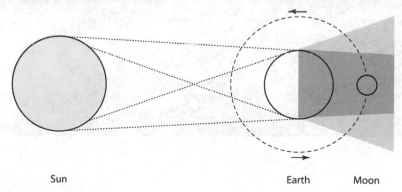

Sun                              Earth        Moon

   **A**   first quarter
   **B**   lunar eclipse
   **C**   new moon
   **D**   solar eclipse

5. **Which conclusion can be drawn?**

   A   Tides occur at the same time each day.

   B   Spring tides only take place during the spring season.

   C   The moon's gravitational force only impacts water in the ocean.

   D   Differences occur in the extent of the tides experienced in different locations.

6. **Which represents an opinion rather than a fact?**

   A   The length of time an eclipse is visible can vary.

   B   The phases of the moon occur in a repeated cycle.

   C   Certain types of tides are associated with the moon's phases.

   D   A lunar eclipse is more interesting to view than a solar eclipse.

**Use the following information to answer questions 7–9.**

7. **Which best summarizes the information in the diagram below?**

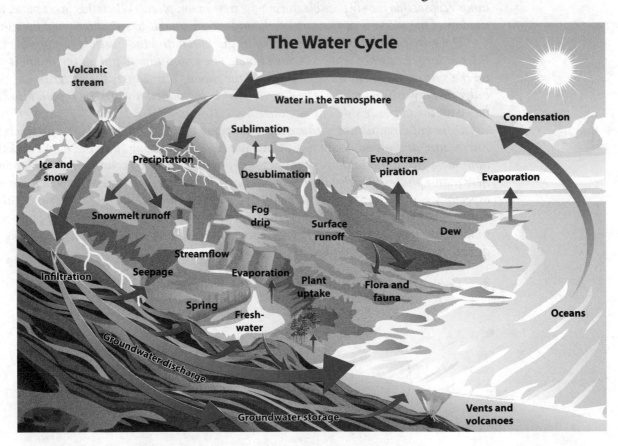

A  The sun heats water on Earth, causing some of it to turn to vapor in the air. Rising air currents carry the vapor into the atmosphere, where cooler temperatures cause the vapor to condense and form clouds. Air currents carry the clouds, which return the water to Earth as rain, ice, or snow.

B  Water in the Earth's oceans and streams is heated by the sun. The warm water then evaporates, becoming water vapor in the air. As the water meets the warmer temperatures in the atmosphere, the vapor forms clouds. The clouds then precipitate and return the water to the Earth as condensation.

C  The sun's energy causes the water to condense. It then evaporates and forms water vapor in the atmosphere. Cooler temperatures cause the vapor to become condensation, which then collects as clouds. The clouds are carried around the Earth, and they return the water to Earth as precipitation.

D  Energy from the sun warms water on the surface of the oceans. This causes some of the water to become vapor, which is carried into the atmosphere by rising air currents. The vapor meets cooler air in the atmosphere and precipitates to form clouds and fog. Wind carries the clouds. As the precipitation warms, it forms condensation.

8.  **Which of the following is NOT a type of precipitation?**
   A  ice
   B  snow
   C  flora
   D  rain

9.  **During condensation**
   A  liquid turns to solid
   B  water vapor turns to liquid
   C  liquid turns to water vapor
   D  liquid falls to Earth as rain or snow

**Use the following information to answer questions 10–13.**

*Relative humidity indicates how much moisture is in the air compared to how much moisture the air can hold at that temperature. Generally, the amount of moisture in the air is less than the amount needed to saturate the air. When the air is saturated, the relative humidity will be near 100 percent.*

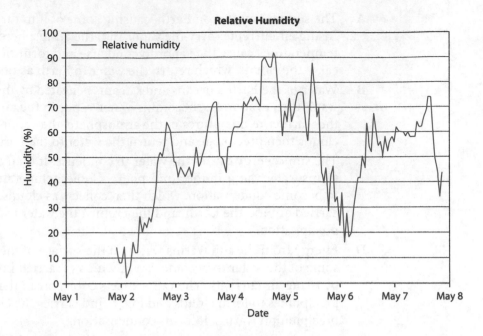

10. **On which day is precipitation most likely to occur?**
    A   May 2
    B   May 3
    C   May 4
    D   May 5

11. **Suppose the temperature was 15 degrees higher on May 8 than originally reported. Which would occur?**
    A   The relative humidity would decrease.
    B   The relative humidity would increase.
    C   The relative humidity would not change.
    D   The relative humidity would be 100 percent.

12. **Which statement is true?**
    A   Snow is indicated by 100 percent relative humidity.
    B   A dry climate generally has 100 percent relative humidity.
    C   Fog and rain are indicated by 100 percent relative humidity.
    D   Relative humidity remains constant throughout the day.

13. **Which day experienced the greatest change in relative humidity?**
    A   May 2
    B   May 3
    C   May 4
    D   May 5

14. Subduction zones are sites of convective downwelling of Earth's lithosphere (the crust plus the top non-convecting portion of the upper mantle). Subduction zones exist at convergent plate boundaries where one plate of oceanic lithosphere converges with another plate. The descending slab—the subducting plate—is over-ridden by the leading edge of the other plate. The oceanic Pacific Plate subducts under the North American Plate (composed of both continental and oceanic sections). Which of the following features might be found in this subduction zone?

    **A**   the East African Rift Valley

    **B**   the Aleutian Trench

    **C**   the Mid-Atlantic Ridge

    **D**   New Zealand's Alpine Fault

15. **What caused the formation of the Himalayan Mountains?**

    **A**   the collision of the Indo-Australian plate and the Eurasian plate

    **B**   the subduction of the Indo-Australian plate underneath the Eurasian plate

    **C**   the subduction of the Eurasian plate underneath the Indo-Australian plate

    **D**   the Eurasian plate grinding past the Indian plate

Answers are on page 721.

# 19 Physical Science: Chemistry

As you know, there are a total of 50 questions on the *HiSET*® Exam Science test. Twenty-five percent of the questions will be related to physical science. Of that 25 percent, some of the physical science questions will focus on chemistry, and some will focus on physics. This chapter will review the types of information you should know to answer questions dealing with chemistry.

## What Is Tested?

To answer the chemistry questions on the HiSET Exam Science test, you will need to rely on your knowledge of atoms, the structure and properties of matter, and chemical reactions. Quite a few concepts fall under these topics. The following lists suggest some ideas for you to brush up on before the test. Being able to combine your own knowledge of the subject matter with the information given on the test will help you fully comprehend the material and select the best answer to each question.

You will not need to memorize the periodic table of elements, but you should familiarize yourself with it well enough to know how to use it. The same holds true for other information related to chemistry. You will not be asked to recall facts, but you will need to be able to apply the concepts in order to analyze information, solve problems, and make judgments.

As you study your textbooks, science-related periodicals, and the Internet, add any other information that sounds interesting or important to the lists.

### The Structure of Atoms

- Allotrope
- Atom
- Atomic Mass
- Atomic Number
- Atomic Theory
- Chemical Bonding
- Chemical Formula
- Compound
- Covalent Bond
- Electric Force
- Electron
- Element

- Ion
- Ionic Bond
- Isobar
- Isotope
- Metalloids
- Metals
- Nonmetals
- Molecule
- Nuclear Fission
- Nuclear Force
- Nucleus
- Neutron

- Periodic Law
- Periodic Table of Elements
- Proton

- Radioactive
- Symbol

**Chemistry and Living Things**

- Carbon
- Hydrocarbons
- Organic

- Organic Chemistry
- Polymer

**Matter**

- Acids
- Aerate
- Alkaline
- Alloy
- Amalgam
- Bases
- Boil
- Chemical Change
- Chlorinate
- Compounds
- Condense
- Distilled
- Filtered

- Freeze
- Gas
- Liquid
- Matter
- Melt
- Mixture
- Oxidize
- Physical Change
- Plasma
- Solid
- Solute
- Solution
- Sublimation

**Changes**

- Activation Energy
- Bond
- Carnot Process
- Catalyst
- Chemical Change
- Chemical Equation
- Chemical Reaction
- Chemical Reaction Rate
- Combination Reaction

- Covalent Bond
- Decomposition Reaction
- Law of Conservation of Matter
- Nuclear Change
- Physical Change
- Plastics
- Polymers
- Products
- Reactants

**Keep in Mind**

Keep in mind that questions relating to scientific inquiry can pop up in reference to any science topic. Make sure you are comfortable with this process.

# Examples

Here are two examples of chemistry questions.

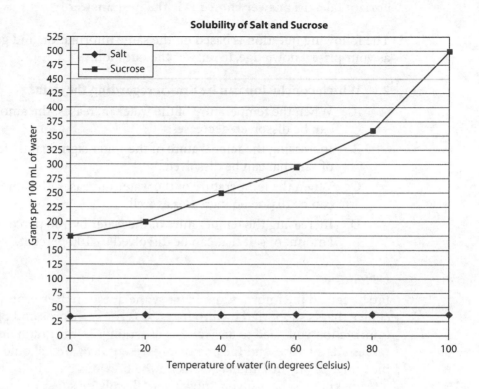

Solubility of Salt and Sucrose

1. **Both sucrose, or sugar, and salt will dissolve in water. The temperature of the water determines the amount of each solute that can be dissolved. Once a certain amount of the solute is dissolved in the water, the water becomes saturated, meaning no more of the salt or sugar will dissolve in the solution. Approximately how many grams of sugar will saturate 100 mL of water at 40°C?**

   A   45 g

   B   100 g

   C   175 g

   D   250 g

## *Explanation*

First, read all the information. Identify the question, which can be stated as: *How many grams of sucrose will dissolve in the water at 40°C?* Underline key words and phrases. The information you need to answer this question is in the graph. Identify the line that represents sucrose, and underline the value that corresponds to 40°C. Determine the meanings of any unfamiliar words. Suppose the word *solute* is unfamiliar. The sentence that introduces this word explains that the solute can be dissolved. The previous sentence says that sucrose and salt will dissolve in water. These are examples of solutes. Using these hints, you can determine that a solute is something that is being dissolved. Think about what you already know. What do you know about dissolving sugar in water? What do you already know about reading a line graph? Use this information to help you determine the best answer to the question. Select the best answer. Since 250 g is marked directly above 40°C on the horizontal axis, **answer choice D is the best answer**.

The following question is based on the same information and graph. Use them, as well as your prior knowledge, to answer the question.

2. **Which conclusion can be drawn regarding the data?**

   **A**   When the temperature of the water increases, the amount of sucrose that can be dissolved decreases.

   **B**   Increasing the temperature of the water significantly increases the amount of salt that can be dissolved.

   **C**   When the temperature of the water increases, the amount of sucrose that can be dissolved increases as well.

   **D**   Increasing the temperature of the water by 100 percent also increases the amount of salt that can be dissolved by 100 percent.

## Explanation

First, read all the information. Identify the question. Here you will look for an answer choice that is supported by the chart. Look for key words and phrases. The information you need to answer this question is in the graph. Identify the line that represents sucrose, and the line that represents salt. You should have determined the meanings of any unfamiliar words for the previous question. Think about what you already know. What do you know about dissolving sugar or salt in water? If you use sugar in your coffee or hot tea, you will know that sugar dissolves faster in warmer water. What do you already know about reading a line graph? Use this information to help you determine the best answer to the question. Choice C is supported by the data in the chart, while choices A, B, and D are not. **The best answer is C.**

# CHEMISTRY DRILLS

1. **Organic compounds, such as lipids, carbohydrates, proteins, and nucleic acids, are examples of molecular compounds. They consist of non-metals bonded to each other. Which of the following is NOT an organic compound?**

   **A**   $H_2O$ (water)

   **B**   HCl (hydrogen chloride)

   **C**   MgO (magnesium oxide)

   **D**   $CH_4$ (methane)

*Both sucrose, or sugar, and salt will dissolve in water. The temperature of the water determines the amount of each solute that can be dissolved. Once a certain amount of the solute is dissolved in the water, the water becomes saturated, meaning no more of the salt or sugar will dissolve in the solution.*

2.  **Based on the information above, which statement is true?**

    A   At any temperature, the amount of sucrose that will dissolve in 100 mL of water is nearly 10 times greater than the amount of salt that will dissolve.

    B   All solutes have an equal saturation rate when the temperature of the water reaches a certain point.

    C   The amount of sucrose that will dissolve in boiling water is approximately 10 times greater than the amount of salt that will dissolve.

    D   The amount of sucrose that will dissolve in cold water is approximately the same as the amount of salt that will dissolve in the same water.

**Use the following diagram to answer questions 3–5.**

**Sugar (Sucrose) Molecule**

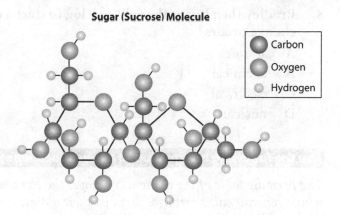

Carbon
Oxygen
Hydrogen

3.  **The diagram shows one molecule of sucrose, or sugar. Which shows the chemical formula of the molecule?**

    A   $C_6H_{11}O_5$

    B   $C_{12}H_{22}O_{11}$

    C   $Ca_6H_{11}O_5$

    D   $Ca_{12}H_{22}O_{11}$

4.  **Which of the following is true?**

    A   There are more oxygen atoms than carbon atoms.

    B   There are twice as many hydrogen atoms as carbon atoms.

    C   If the number of carbon, oxygen, and hydrogen atoms were each decreased by one, this would still be a sucrose molecule.

    D   There are more carbon atoms than oxygen atoms.

5.  **Which best describes sucrose?**

    A   atom

    B   compound

    C   element

    D   mixture

6. The smallest unit of magnesium that maintains all of its properties is a(n)

   A   atom

   B   electron

   C   ion

   D   proton

7. Bradley uses an axe to split an oak log. Which type of change occurs?

   A   atomic

   B   chemical

   C   physical

   D   electrical

8. Bradley then burns the split oak log to start a campfire. Which type of change occurs?

   A   atomic

   B   chemical

   C   electrical

   D   nuclear

**Use the following information to answer questions 9–13.**

*The periodic table of the elements arranges the elements in order of their atomic number, which generally also arranges them by their atomic mass. The rows of elements displayed in the table are known as periods. The number of electrons in each period increases as we move down the table. The columns of the table are known as groups. The elements in group 8A are known as noble gases because they are odorless, colorless, monatomic gases with very low chemical reactivity.*

*Each element is defined by the number of protons in the atom. This is known as the atomic number. Hydrogen (H) has an atomic number of 1, indicating that a single atom of this element contains one proton. The standard atomic weight for each element is the average mass of the element. The atomic number and the atomic weight appear in the table along with the element's symbol. As the table shows, the atomic weight of hydrogen is 1.008. The average number of neutrons can be determined by calculating the difference between the atomic number and the atomic weight.*

# Periodic Table of the Elements

| 1A | | | | | | | | | | | | | | | | | 8A |
|---|---|---|---|---|---|---|---|---|---|---|---|---|---|---|---|---|---|
| 1<br>hydrogen<br>**H**<br>1.008 | 2A | | | | | | | | | | | 3A | 4A | 5A | 6A | 7A | 2<br>helium<br>**He**<br>4.003 |
| 3<br>lithium<br>**Li**<br>6.941 | 4<br>beryllium<br>**Be**<br>9.012 | | | | | | | | | | | 5<br>boron<br>**B**<br>10.81 | 6<br>carbon<br>**C**<br>12.01 | 7<br>nitrogen<br>**N**<br>14.01 | 8<br>oxygen<br>**O**<br>16.00 | 9<br>fluorine<br>**F**<br>19.00 | 10<br>neon<br>**Ne**<br>20.18 |
| 11<br>sodium<br>**Na**<br>22.99 | 12<br>magnesium<br>**Mg**<br>24.31 | 3B | 4B | 5B | 6B | 7B | ——— | 8B | ——— | 11B | 12B | 13<br>aluminum<br>**Al**<br>26.98 | 14<br>silicon<br>**Si**<br>28.09 | 15<br>phosphorus<br>**P**<br>30.97 | 16<br>sulfur<br>**S**<br>32.07 | 17<br>chlorine<br>**Cl**<br>35.45 | 18<br>argon<br>**Ar**<br>39.95 |
| 19<br>potassium<br>**K**<br>39.10 | 20<br>calcium<br>**Ca**<br>40.08 | 21<br>scandium<br>**Sc**<br>44.96 | 22<br>titanium<br>**Ti**<br>47.88 | 23<br>vanadium<br>**V**<br>50.94 | 24<br>chromium<br>**Cr**<br>52.00 | 25<br>manganese<br>**Mn**<br>54.94 | 26<br>iron<br>**Fe**<br>55.85 | 27<br>cobalt<br>**Co**<br>58.93 | 28<br>nickel<br>**Ni**<br>58.69 | 29<br>copper<br>**Cu**<br>63.55 | 30<br>zinc<br>**Zn**<br>65.39 | 31<br>gallium<br>**Ga**<br>69.72 | 32<br>germanium<br>**Ge**<br>72.64 | 33<br>arsenic<br>**As**<br>74.92 | 34<br>selenium<br>**Se**<br>78.96 | 35<br>bromine<br>**Br**<br>79.90 | 36<br>krypton<br>**Kr**<br>83.79 |
| 37<br>rubidium<br>**Rb**<br>85.47 | 38<br>strontium<br>**Sr**<br>87.62 | 39<br>yttrium<br>**Y**<br>88.91 | 40<br>zirconium<br>**Zr**<br>91.22 | 41<br>niobium<br>**Nb**<br>92.91 | 42<br>molybdenum<br>**Mo**<br>95.94 | 43<br>technetium<br>**Tc**<br>98 | 44<br>ruthenium<br>**Ru**<br>101.1 | 45<br>rhodium<br>**Rh**<br>102.9 | 46<br>palladium<br>**Pd**<br>106.4 | 47<br>silver<br>**Ag**<br>107.9 | 48<br>cadmium<br>**Cd**<br>112.4 | 49<br>indium<br>**In**<br>114.8 | 50<br>tin<br>**Sn**<br>118.7 | 51<br>antimony<br>**Sb**<br>121.8 | 52<br>tellurium<br>**Te**<br>127.6 | 53<br>iodine<br>**I**<br>126.9 | 54<br>xenon<br>**Xe**<br>131.3 |
| 55<br>cesium<br>**Cs**<br>132.9 | 56<br>barium<br>**Ba**<br>137.3 | * | 72<br>hafnium<br>**Hf**<br>178.5 | 73<br>tantalum<br>**Ta**<br>180.9 | 74<br>tungsten<br>**W**<br>183.9 | 75<br>rhenium<br>**Re**<br>186.2 | 76<br>osmium<br>**Os**<br>190.2 | 77<br>iridium<br>**Ir**<br>192.2 | 78<br>platinum<br>**Pt**<br>195.1 | 79<br>gold<br>**Au**<br>197.0 | 80<br>mercury<br>**Hg**<br>200.5 | 81<br>thallium<br>**Tl**<br>204.4 | 82<br>lead<br>**Pb**<br>207.2 | 83<br>bismuth<br>**Bi**<br>209.0 | 84<br>polonium<br>**Po**<br>209 | 85<br>astatine<br>**At**<br>210 | 86<br>radon<br>**Rn**<br>222 |
| 87<br>francium<br>**Fr**<br>223 | 88<br>radium<br>**Ra**<br>226 | ** | 104<br>rutherfordium<br>**Rf**<br>261 | 105<br>dubnium<br>**Db**<br>262 | 106<br>seaborgium<br>**Sg**<br>266 | 107<br>bohrium<br>**Bh**<br>264 | 108<br>hassium<br>**Hs**<br>277 | 109<br>meitnerium<br>**Mt**<br>268 | 110<br>darmstadtium<br>**Ds**<br>271 | 111<br>roentgenium<br>**Rg**<br>272 | 112<br>copernicium<br>**Cn**<br>285 | 113<br>**Uut**<br>286 | 114<br>**Uuq**<br>289 | 115<br>**Uup**<br>289 | 116<br>**Uuh**<br>291 | 117<br>**Uus**<br>294 | 118<br>**Uuo**<br>294 |

| Lanthanide series* | 57<br>lanthanum<br>**La**<br>138.9 | 58<br>cerium<br>**Ce**<br>140.1 | 59<br>praseodymium<br>**Pr**<br>140.9 | 60<br>neodymium<br>**Nd**<br>144.2 | 61<br>promethium<br>**Pm**<br>145 | 62<br>samarium<br>**Sm**<br>150.4 | 63<br>europium<br>**Eu**<br>152.0 | 64<br>gadolinium<br>**Gd**<br>157.25 | 65<br>terbium<br>**Tb**<br>158.9 | 66<br>dysprosium<br>**Dy**<br>162.5 | 67<br>holmium<br>**Ho**<br>164.93 | 68<br>erbium<br>**Er**<br>167.3 | 69<br>thulium<br>**Tm**<br>168.9 | 70<br>ytterbium<br>**Yb**<br>173.0 | 71<br>lutetium<br>**Lu**<br>175.0 |
|---|---|---|---|---|---|---|---|---|---|---|---|---|---|---|---|
| Actinide series** | 89<br>actinium<br>**Ac**<br>227 | 90<br>thorium<br>**Th**<br>232.0 | 91<br>protactinium<br>**Pa**<br>231 | 92<br>uranium<br>**U**<br>238 | 93<br>neptunium<br>**Np**<br>237 | 94<br>plutonium<br>**Pu**<br>244 | 95<br>americium<br>**Am**<br>243 | 96<br>curium<br>**Cm**<br>247 | 97<br>berkelium<br>**Bk**<br>247 | 98<br>californium<br>**Cf**<br>251 | 99<br>einsteinium<br>**Es**<br>252 | 100<br>fermium<br>**Fm**<br>257 | 101<br>mendelevium<br>**Md**<br>258 | 102<br>nobelium<br>**No**<br>259 | 103<br>lawrencium<br>**Lr**<br>262 |

9. Which element has an atomic weight of approximately 7?

   A  beryllium

   B  boron

   C  fluorine

   D  lithium

10. Approximately how many neutrons does the average atom of iron contain?

   A  26

   B  29.85

   C  55.85

   D  77

11. The chemical formula for table salt is NaCl. Which elements does table salt contain?

    A  sodium and carbon

    B  sodium and chlorine

    C  nitrogen and chloride

    D  nitrogen, actinium, and lithium

12. Which of the following can be inferred from the table?

    A  an atom of sodium has a greater mass than an atom of carbon

    B  an atom of sodium has more electrons than an atom of calcium

    C  an atom of nitrogen has more electrons than an atom of xenon

    D  an atom of nitrogen has a greater mass than an atom of xenon

13. Which of the following elements is NOT a noble gas?

    A  krypton

    B  argon

    C  chlorine

    D  helium

14. Cinnamon and sugar are combined for a recipe. What is produced by combining these ingredients?

    A  atom

    B  compound

    C  chemical

    D  mixture

15. The law of conservation of matter explains that during an ordinary chemical change, the quantity of matter does not increase or decrease. Which best explains this law?

    A  Different atoms combine to create new molecules.

    B  A portion of matter is destroyed when it changes form.

    C  Atoms are not created or destroyed in a chemical reaction.

    D  The atomic mass is greater in atoms with greater atomic numbers.

**Answers are on page 721.**

# 20 Physical Science: Physics

Twenty-five percent of the *HiSET*® Exam Science questions will relate to physical science. Some of them will address chemistry, and the rest will deal with physics. This chapter will review the types of physics information you should know in order to do well on the test.

Physics is the study of matter, energy, force, and motion. On the HiSET Exam Science test, you can expect to find questions about the different forms of energy, motion and forces, the conservation of energy, and how energy and matter interact with one another. Remember, you will need to add your own knowledge of physics to the information given on the test to best answer the questions.

## What Is Tested?

A number of concepts relate to matter, energy, force, and motion. The following lists suggest some ideas with which to familiarize yourself before the test. The good news is that you will probably recognize many of these ideas, even if you did not take an actual physics class. For example, you have probably heard of Sir Isaac Newton, even if physics is not your best subject. You probably remember learning about solids, liquids, and gasses back in elementary school. You may find that you know more about physics than you realize.

To refresh your memory on some of the other information in the lists, flip through some of your science textbooks, read about these ideas in the newspaper and good-quality news magazines, look up related articles online, and keep your ears open for physics-related information on television. As you review, add any other pertinent ideas or information you come across to the lists.

### Energy

- Alternating Current
- British Thermal Unit
- Calorie
- Celsius (Centigrade) Scale
- Conservation of Energy
- Convection
- Diffraction
- Direct Current
- Doppler Effect
- Electricity

- Electromagnetic Energy
- Energy
- Entropy
- Fahrenheit Scale
- Frequency
- Gamma Rays
- Geothermal Energy
- Heat Energy
- Hydroelectric Power
- Infrared Rays

- Interaction of Energy and Matter
- Interference
- Kinetic Energy
- Light Energy
- Longitudinal Wave
- Magnetic Energy
- Magnetic Fields
- Magnetism
- Mechanical Energy
- Nuclear Energy
- Nuclear Power
- Polarization
- Poles
- Potential Energy
- Radiation
- Radio Waves
- Reflection
- Refraction
- Rotational Energy
- Solar Energy
- Sound
- Static Electricity
- Steam Energy
- Transfer of Energy
- Trough
- Transverse Wave
- Ultrasonic Wave
- Ultraviolet Rays
- Wave
- Wavelength
- Wind Energy

**Matter**

- Conductor
- Ductility
- Electrical Conductivity
- Electric Current
- Electromagnet
- Gas
- Half-life
- Heat Conductivity
- Liquid
- Luster
- Malleability
- Mass
- Plasma
- Solid
- Temperature
- Viscosity
- Weight

**Physics Laws and Theories**

- Kinetic Theory of Matter
- Law of Acceleration
- Law of Action and Reaction
- Law of Applied Force
- Law of Inertia
- Law of Interaction
- Law of Universal Gravitation
- Particle Theory of Light
- Wave Theory of Light

**Keep in Mind**

Keep in mind that you will not have to recite physics laws or give definitions, but you will need to be able to apply the concepts. With that in mind, do not spend a lot of time memorizing things such as the law of conservation of energy. Just make sure you understand it and are able to use the principles behind it.

**Force, Work, and Machines**

- Centripetal Force
- Electrical Force
- Force
- Fulcrum
- Gravitational Force
- Lever
- Magnetic Force
- Nuclear Force

- Power
- Pulley
- Synergy

- Wheel and Axle
- Work

## Motion

- Acceleration
- Action
- Displacement
- Distance
- Momentum
- Position and Motion of Objects

- Pressure
- Properties of Objects and Materials
- Reaction
- Resistance
- Speed

## Friction

- Fluid Friction
- Rolling Friction

- Sliding Friction
- Static Friction

# Examples

Here are two sample physics questions.

1. **Levers, inclined planes, and pulleys are all examples of simple machines. A lever pivots around a point and is used to move or lift an object by applying force to the opposite end. Which of the following is NOT an example of a lever?**
   A   crowbar
   B   fork
   C   scissors
   D   screw

## *Explanation*

First, read all the information and identify the question. Basically, three of the items in the answer choices are levers. Which is not? Look for key words and phrases. The definition of *lever* is important to understanding the information. The word *not* is also important. Determine the meanings of unfamiliar words. Suppose that on the day of the test, you cannot remember what a *lever* is. The second sentence in the passage offers a definition of the word. What if that definition were not included? What could you do then? Think about the answer choices. Three are levers, and one is not. You can figure out which is not a lever by determining which of these things is not like the others. Think about what you already know. What is the first thing that comes to mind when you think of a lever? You may be picturing a playground teeter-totter or a crowbar prying open a door. In both cases, a weight on one end of the bar lifts a weight on the opposite end. Use this example to help you determine which of the answer choices works in a similar way and which do not. Select the best answer. A crowbar, fork, and scissors all move by applying force to one end. A screw does not. **The best answer is D.**

Answer the following question about a simple machine, using the information on levers provided before question 1 along with the drawing below.

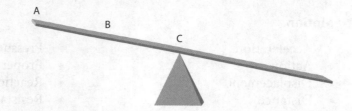

2. **Which statement is true regarding levers?**
   A   The force in the diagram is applied to point B.
   B   The fulcrum in the diagram is located at point A.
   C   The fulcrum in the diagram is located at point C.
   D   The force in the diagram is applied to point A.

### Explanation

First, read all the information and identify the question. Which of the answer choices is a true statement? Underline key words and phrases. The definition of *lever* is important to understanding the information. Note the labeled points in the drawing. Determine the meanings of unfamiliar words. If *fulcrum* is unfamiliar, use the context to help you figure out the definition. The bar has two ends and a point at which it meets the triangular base. Most likely, a fulcrum is that single center point. Think about what you already know. The picture looks like a playground teeter-totter. The lighter person would be sitting at point A and the heavy person would be on the opposite end. The pivot point, or fulcrum, is point C. Use the drawing to help you determine which of the answer choices is true. Select the best answer. The fulcrum is located at point C. **The best answer is C.**

### Keep in Mind

Keep in mind that the purpose of the practice questions in this book is to familiarize you with the type of questions that will be on the HiSET Exam, to help you figure out what topics you know well, and to alert you to concepts you should spend a little more time studying. If you select an incorrect answer while working on the sample questions, use the experience as a learning opportunity. Take the time to go back and study the topic further.

# PHYSICS DRILLS

1. **If a bar magnet is broken into two pieces, each of the resulting pieces**

   A   is no longer magnetic

   B   has a single magnetic pole

   C   has two magnetic poles

   D   has a net electric charge

2. **A pulley is used to lift the 1,000-pound weight in the diagram. Which statement is true?**

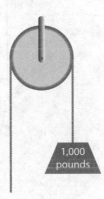

   A   The weight can be lifted using 500 pounds of force.

   B   The weight can be lifted using 100 pounds of force.

   C   Adding a second pulley would allow the weight to be lifted using 500 pounds of force.

   D   Adding a second pulley would allow the weight to be lifted using 100 pounds of force.

**Use the following information to answer questions 3–5.**

*The United States uses a combination of fossil fuels, renewable sources, nuclear, and electricity net imports for energy. The chart shows the percentages of energy used from each source in 2008, as reported by the US Energy Information Agency.*

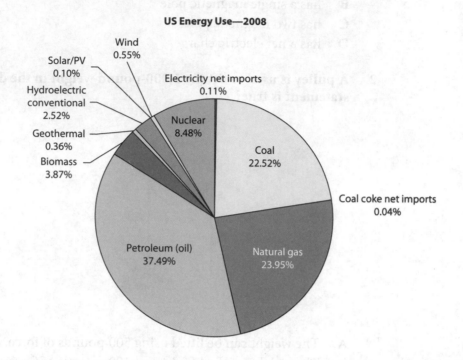

US Energy Use—2008

3. Fossil fuels include coal, coal coke net imports, natural gas, and petroleum. Approximately what percentage of the total US energy came from fossil fuels?

   A   24%

   B   37%

   C   47%

   D   84%

4. According to the graph, approximately what percentage of the total US energy came from renewable sources?

   A   4%

   B   7%

   C   10%

   D   19%

5. In 2008, 39.9 percent of Maine's energy came from renewable sources. Based on the data, which inference can be made?

   A   Maine relied more heavily on renewable energy sources than most other states.

   B   Maine's use of renewable energy was the highest in the nation.

   C   Fossil fuels were less readily available in Maine than in other states.

   D   A greater amount of renewable sources than fossil fuels was used in Maine.

*Sir Isaac Newton is widely known for his observations of apples falling from a tree and his resulting universal law of gravitation. It explains that any two objects exert a gravitational force of attraction on each other. The direction of this force is along the line that joins the centers of the objects, and the magnitude of the force is directly proportional to the product of the objects' masses and inversely proportional to the square of the distance between the objects. This explanation of gravity is but one of the scientist's contributions to our understanding of the world around us.*

*Newton also stated several other laws that are central to the study of physics. He presented his three laws of motion in 1686. His first law of motion, often called the law of inertia, states that every object in a state of rest or uniform motion remains in that state unless an external force is applied to it. His second law of motion explains that the rate of change of the momentum of an object is directly proportional to the resultant force acting on it. The relationship is shown by the equation F = ma, where F represents force, m represents mass, and a represents acceleration. Newton's third law of motion states that for every action, there is an equal and opposite reaction.*

*In addition to his work with gravitation and movement, Newton is also noted for his law of cooling, which states that the rate of change of an object's temperature is proportional to the difference between its own temperature and the temperature of its surroundings. In other words, the rate at which a hot object cools depends on its temperature and the temperature around it.*

6. **Which of Newton's laws is demonstrated by the diagram of the rocket?**

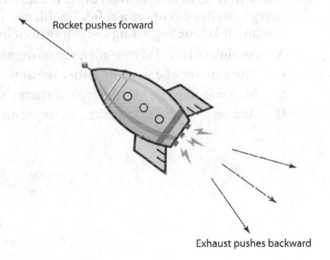

Rocket pushes forward

Exhaust pushes backward

    **A**    universal law of gravitation

    **B**    first law of motion

    **C**    second law of motion

    **D**    third law of motion

7. The amount of force required to lift an airplane is different from the amount of force required to launch a rocket. Which of Newton's laws is this an example of?

    A   universal law of gravitation
    B   first law of motion
    C   second law of motion
    D   third law of motion

8. A dish of enchiladas is removed from a hot oven and placed on the counter to cool. Which of the following affects the rate at which the enchiladas cool?

    A   the amount of time the enchiladas spent in the oven
    B   what type of pot holder was used to remove the dish from the oven
    C   the temperature of the countertop the enchiladas were placed on
    D   whether the oven was electric or gas

9. Many daily tasks involve the changing of energy from one type to another. What type of energy change occurs when using an iron to press clothes before work or school?

    A   mechanical energy to heat energy
    B   heat energy to electrical energy
    C   electrical energy to heat energy
    D   chemical energy to heat energy

10. The universe, as well as everything it contains, is composed of matter and energy. Matter occurs as a solid, liquid, gas, or occasionally plasma. Which statement is true regarding the interaction between matter and energy?

    A   As energy is added to matter, the movement of the molecules increases.
    B   The amount of energy in matter remains in a constant state.
    C   Matter is impacted by the type of energy added, not the amount of energy.
    D   As energy is added to matter, the movement of the molecules decreases.

*Friction is a force acting along the surfaces of objects that opposes motion. There are several types of friction. Static friction opposes the movement of a stationary object along a surface. Sliding friction is created when two surfaces slide over one another and is affected by the weight of the moving objects, the type and texture of the surfaces, and any temporary bonding between the two. Rolling friction is created when an object rolls over a surface and opposes less motion than sliding friction. Fluid friction is created when an object is moving through a fluid, such as a gas or liquid.*

11. **A deer runs out into the road, causing a driver to slam on his brakes. Which type of friction is demonstrated when the car skids to a stop?**
    A   fluid friction
    B   static friction
    C   rolling friction
    D   sliding friction

12. **Which type of friction is used when a bird flies through the air or fish swim in schools?**
    A   fluid friction
    B   static friction
    C   rolling friction
    D   sliding friction

13. **The source of the Earth's magnetic field is most likely**
    A   a large region of magnetized iron near Antarctica
    B   the magnetic iron at the center of the core of the planet
    C   the motion of charged particle in the outer layers of the molten core of the planet
    D   the alignment of the planet in relation to the sun

14. **If an object is electrically polarized, then the**
    A   object is magnetic
    B   object has a net electrical charge
    C   charges on the object have been rearranged
    D   object is a partial conductor

15. **A wave in which the individual particles of a medium vibrate back and forth perpendicular to the direction that the wave travels is called a**
    A   longitudinal wave
    B   transverse wave
    C   particle wave
    D   harmonic wave

**Answers are on pages 721–722.**

# Part VI
# Language Arts—Reading

# 21 The Language Arts—Reading Test

The next few chapters will discuss information related to the *HiSET*® Exam Language Arts—Reading test.

On the HiSET Exam Language Arts—Reading test, you will read passages and then answer questions based on the information in the text. Sixty percent of these passages will be literary texts. Some of them will be prose, while others will be poetry. *Prose* is just a fancy word that means the writing is not poetry. Basically, prose passages are written in regular, everyday paragraph style. Some of the passages will be fiction, and some will be nonfiction.

The reading comprehension questions you will encounter on the HiSET Exam go beyond simply recalling information that is directly stated in the text. You will have to apply, analyze, and synthesize ideas to show that you truly understand what you have read.

## Keep in Mind

Keep in mind that the comprehension strategies reviewed for the Language Arts—Reading questions do not apply to a single style of writing. What you read in the poetry chapter may also be helpful in answering questions about prose nonfiction. Likewise, what you learn in the chapter about nonfiction prose may be helpful in answering prose fiction questions as well. The strategies are simply organized according to the type of passage in which they are most likely to be applied.

## Question Steps

Here are the six steps you will use to answer questions on the HiSET Exam Language Arts—Reading test.

> **Reading Test Question Steps**
>
> **Step 1:** Read All of the Questions
>
> **Step 2:** Read the Passage
>
> **Step 3:** Reread the Question You Are Preparing to Answer
>
> **Step 4:** Answer the Question in Your Own Words
>
> **Step 5:** Read Each Answer Choice Carefully
>
> **Step 6:** Select the Best Answer Choice

## Step 1: Read All of the Questions

Read all of the questions before you read the passage. Doing so will help you to locate important information in the text as you read.

## Step 2: Read the Passage

Read the passage carefully. Your understanding of the material is crucial to answering the questions correctly and earning the best possible score on the test. Take your time. Read every word. Remember to use what you know about roots and affixes, contextual clues, and multiple meanings to figure out unfamiliar words in the passage. If you come to the end of a sentence or paragraph and realize that you did not quite understand it, go back and read it again.

## Step 3: Reread the Question You are Preparing to Answer

Even though you may have already read every question before reading the passage, read the questions again, one at a time, as you are ready to answer them. Read each question carefully to be sure you understand exactly what it is asking. Do not look at the answer choices for that question yet.

## Step 4: Answer the Question in Your Own Words

Figure out what the correct answer to the question is without looking at the answer choices given. Think about what you read; then go back and find the answer in the passage. You may have to synthesize information from several parts of the passage to answer the question completely. Just make sure that your answer is based on the material.

Once you have found the necessary information in the passage, state your answer to the question. Make sure your response answers the entire question.

## Step 5: Read Each Answer Choice Carefully

Now that you know the correct answer to the question, go ahead and read the answer choices. Several answers may include correct information or be partially correct, so be sure to read them all closely and identify differences between them.

## Step 6: Select the Best Answer Choice

Select the answer choice that most closely matches the answer you stated in Step 5. You may think that more than one of the choices could be correct, but you should select the one that best and most completely answers the question.

# Examples

Here are two examples of Language Arts—Reading questions to show you how the steps work.

*The following passage was written as a journal response to the question: What is the best writing assignment you ever had?*

*The best writing assignment I ever had was a semester-long assignment in my high school senior English class. Our teacher, Mrs. Schulte, asked us to keep a writer's journal throughout the whole semester. We had fifteen minutes set aside at the beginning of each class to write in it, sometimes on a topic she assigned and sometimes on anything we wanted. Her topics were always fun. I remember one about imagining that you were a fork in the dishwasher and describing what was happening. Sometimes she brought in a cartoon without a caption and we wrote the scene. She also let us bring in prompts of our own from newspapers and magazines and sometimes she would use one of them as a prompt. From the very beginning, she explained that the purpose of this journal was simply to give us a place for ideas to grow. We wouldn't be graded on their quality or quantity, so there was no pressure to be brilliant or to write polished pieces. We were to have fun and be creative and when it was time to write our semester papers, maybe we could find something in our writer's journals that we wanted to further develop. Without the pressure of grades, I felt free to be silly, to write anything that came into my head, and some of it did turn out really well. I did end up doing my semester papers on ideas I had generated through the journal and I felt like that gave me a leg up on my papers. When I turned the journal in near the end of the semester, I felt no worries at all about my grade. I had done each of the prompts, so that was all I needed. When Mrs. Schulte returned my journal, I was surprised to see how many comments she had made. I thought she would have just looked to see that we did the work, but she put a lot more into it. She wrote nice comments about things that she thought could be developed into essays or poems. That assignment was so good and generated so many cool ideas in the grade-free environment that I went back to it several times over my college years to mine it for ideas!*

1. **How might the author's feelings about this assignment have been different if the journal had been graded?**
   A    Nothing would have changed.
   B    She would have felt pressure to write more and use proper language conventions.
   C    She would have been more creative.
   D    She would have copied work from her classmates in order to get a high grade.

## Explanation

### Step 1: Read All of the Questions

There are two questions for this passage, so read them both to help you know what to look for when you read the passage.

### Step 2: Read the Passage

Read the introductory sentence and then read the entire passage carefully.

### Step 3: Reread the Question You are Preparing to Answer

Reread the first question: what would be different if the assignment had been graded?

### Step 4: Answer the Question in Your Own Words

The writer mentions feeling free and feeling no pressure to be brilliant or polished. If the journal had been graded, she might have felt constrained and pressured to do well and write properly.

### Step 5: Read Each Answer Choice Carefully

Of the four choices, choice B best expresses the answer developed in Step 4.

### Step 6: Select the Best Answer Choice

The best answer is B.

Try one more example from the same passage.

**Reread the last sentence of the passage:** *That assignment was so good and generated so many cool ideas in the grade-free environment that I went back to it several times over my college years to mine it for ideas!*

2. **What does the word *mine* in this context most likely mean?**
   A   belonging to the writer
   B   to dig under the ground
   C   to use as a natural resource
   D   to draw useful information from

## Explanation

### Step 1: Read All of the Questions

You should have already done this step for the first question, so there is no need to do it again.

### Step 2: Read the Passage

Again, you should have already done this for the first question, so move on to Step 3.

### Step 3: Reread the Question You are Preparing to Answer

Reread the question: what does the word *mine* mean here?

**Step 4: Answer the Question in Your Own Words**

The writer talks about using ideas from her journal to develop her semester paper and says that it generated many ideas. She returned to it in college to *get more ideas*. In this context, *mine* means *to get ideas from*.

**Step 5: Read Each Answer Choice Carefully**

Be sure that you do not get distracted by other definitions of the word *mine*. Focus on what you are looking for.

**Step 6: Select the Best Answer Choice**

**The best answer is D.**

# 22 Interpreting Prose Fiction

## What Is Tested?

**S**ixty percent of the passages on the *HiSET®* Exam Language Arts—Reading test will be literary texts. The prose passages are fictional accounts, written in regular paragraph style. You will need to show that you not only understand what you have read, but that you can also apply, analyze, and synthesize the ideas.

The prose fiction passages will be between 400 and 600 words and will represent a broad range of topics in multiple genres that vary in purpose and style. Following each passage, you will find between four and eight multiple-choice comprehension questions. You will select the one best answer for each question based solely on the information in the passage.

## Comprehension Strategies

When you read a newspaper or magazine, you are doing so to learn about a topic or an event. When you read a novel, you are doing so to find out what happens next in the story. When you read a passage on the HiSET Exam, you are doing so to answer questions correctly. The entire purpose of reading is to gain information. Here are a few strategies that can help you to make the most of what you read and fully understand the material.

### Discovering the Author's Purpose

Knowing why a passage was written can be helpful in understanding the text. An author usually writes a selection to entertain, inform, or persuade. The purpose of most prose fiction passages is to entertain, although some are written to persuade. The purpose of nonfiction is generally to inform, although some of these are also written to persuade. The author's word choice, as well as the facts and opinions he or she includes, can offer clues about the purpose of the writing.

*To entertain:* The light of the silvery moon sparkled on the lake's surface.

*To inform:* The average distance of the moon from the Earth is 385,000 km.

*To persuade:* Spacecraft should not be sent to the moon again because the danger outweighs any potential benefits.

## Making Predictions Based on Text

By considering information in the text, and thinking about what is likely to happen next, readers are able to increase their comprehension of a passage. Such predictions may be based on the events that have already taken place in the selection; titles and headings; and graphics such as illustrations, charts, or diagrams.

## Understanding Theme

The theme of a story is the underlying message the author is trying to convey. Usually, rather than being stated directly, the theme is implied by the beliefs and attitudes in the passage that lead you to a particular idea or conclusion.

Many themes are ideas related to society or human nature. By considering the words and actions of the characters, ideas that are repeated throughout the story, and suggested opinions, you can figure out what "life lesson" the author wants you to take away from the passage. Here are some common themes.

*True beauty is on the inside.*

*Do not give up when facing difficult situations.*

*It is important to accept people and their differences.*

## Synthesizing Information

To synthesize means to gather and combine information from more than one source or from more than one location within a single source. Putting ideas together in this way leads to a deeper comprehension of the topic.

One type of question on the HiSET Exam Language Arts—Reading test is an extended synthesis question. In this question type, an additional piece of information will be given in the question. You will need to consider this new information, along with what you read in the passage, to select the best answer to the question.

## Determining Point of View

The type of information given in a passage depends on the point of view from which the story is told. A story written in the **first person** point of view is being told by one of the characters. Therefore, readers experience the events through the eyes of this character. In other words, readers only know the thoughts and feelings of this character. They are only aware of events involving the character telling the story. First person pronouns such as *I, we,* and *us* indicate this point of view.

*When we arrived at the museum, I headed directly to the large sculpture in the garden.*

A story written in the **third person** is told by a narrator. Since the narrator is outside of the story, rather than being a character involved in the action, he or she is aware of the thoughts, feelings, and actions of everyone involved. Third person pronouns such as *they, he,* and *she* indicate this point of view.

*When Cheri arrived at the museum with her family, she headed directly to the large sculpture in the garden.*

# Determining Word Meanings

Every reading passage you will be given on the HiSET Exam will be written at an adult reading level. There may be some words with which you are unfamiliar. Your understanding of a passage depends on your ability to understand the words that make up the passage, so you will need skills that help you figure out the meanings of unfamiliar words.

## Contextual Clues

Other words or phrases in a passage can offer hints about the meaning of an unfamiliar word. Look for synonyms, antonyms, examples, and definitions. These may be found within the same sentence as the word you would like to define, or they may appear in surrounding sentences.

*After only listening to the first few seconds of her <u>fabricated</u> account of what happened, we knew that the entire story was <u>made up</u>. On the other hand, Philip's story was completely <u>true</u>.*

The definition of *fabricated* can be found later in the same sentence. The opposite of *fabricated* is offered in the following sentence.

*Ms. Furse was unsure which of her <u>culinary</u> masterpieces to enter in the contest. Her friends had given rave reviews to both her pineapple-coconut <u>cake</u> and her veal <u>stew</u>.*

In this sentence, examples of *culinary* items suggest that the word is related to cooking.

## Multiple-Meaning Words

Many words in our language have more than one meaning. To determine which meaning an author has in mind for a particular sentence, pay close attention to how the word is used in the passage.

*Mrs. Riggs's testimony was <u>instrumental</u> in the lawsuit.*

*The <u>instrumental</u> piece on the CD is the most beautiful of all the songs.*

## Roots and Affixes

The **root** is the part of the word that contains the meaning. Often, the meaning of an unfamiliar word can be determined by thinking of another word that contains a similar root.

Words such as *recur* and *occurrence* have the same root as *occur*. Recognizing this fact can be helpful in determining the meanings of these words.

A **prefix** may be added to the beginning of a word to change its meaning; a **suffix** may be added to the end of a word to change its meaning.

re + occur + ing = reoccurring

Recognizing roots and affixes—and knowing their meanings—can be helpful in determining the meaning of an unfamiliar word in a passage. A few affixes and their meanings are listed here. This list is by no means comprehensive; a number of prefixes and suffixes can be added to words. These are simply a few examples to show how their addition to a root word can change its meaning.

| Prefixes | Suffixes |
|----------|----------|
| *ex-*: out of, previous | *-able, -ible*: able to, can be accomplished |
| *inter-*: among, between | *-ive*: likely to |
| *mis-*: badly, wrongly | *-ly*: in a particular way |
| *post-*: after | *-ous*: full of |
| *trans-*: not | *-tion*: an act or process |

# Examples

Here are two sample questions to show you how the six steps can be used on a prose fiction passage.

**Will They Find the Perfect Piece?**

*Ding-ding.*

*The tiny, tarnished bell rang as we opened the door and entered the store. It somehow seemed fitting that the old-fashioned bell that was tied to the door frame had not been replaced by a more modern electronic chime to signal the entry of guests into the antique shop. Our hunt for pieces to furnish the historic farmhouse had led us to this destination. Upon entering, it appeared that we might have found the right place.*

*The walls of the crowded shop were lined with heavy chests, dressers, and armoires, standing side by side like heavy, wooden soldiers. The sizes of the large pieces of furniture seemed disproportionate in the tiny room. Slowly, we walked past each of the furnishings, rubbing our hands across the aged woods, sliding drawers open, examining discolored knobs and hinges. Then we came to a dark cherrywood china hutch and froze. A few seconds passed before I realized I was holding my breath. The hutch was the exact color of Grandmother's dining table. The decorative carving around the edges was identical to the carving on the backs of the dining chairs. Slowly, we walked toward the amazing piece, which would be the ideal complement to the furnishings already in the home. It was perfect. Despite its age, there was not a single scratch anywhere on the amazing cabinet.*

1. **Read this sentence from the third paragraph:**

   *The sizes of the large pieces of furniture seemed <u>disproportionate</u> in the tiny room.*

   **What is the meaning of *disproportionate*?**

   A  comparable

   B  petite

   C  size

   D  unequal

## Explanation

First, read all the questions for this passage. There are two: the first asks for the meaning of *disproportionate* and the second asks what will happen after the ending. Keep these questions in mind as you move to Step 2. Read the passage carefully. Reread the question you will be answering: What does *disproportionate* mean? Answer the question in your own words. If the room is tiny and the furniture is large, then the furniture seems out of place or unbalanced in the small room. In addition, the root of *disproportionate* is *proportion*, which means "balanced in size." The prefix *dis-* means "not." So *disproportionate* means "not balanced in size." Does that make sense in the context of the passage? Yes, because the large furniture was not balanced in size with the tiny room. Read each answer choice carefully and then choose the best one. Answer choice D means about the same as "not balanced." **The best answer is D.**

2.   **What will MOST LIKELY happen next?**
   A   They will purchase the china hutch.
   B   They will return to the store on another day.
   C   They will replace the dining table and chairs.
   D   They will continue shopping in another store.

### Explanation

You have already read both questions and the passage, so move to Step 3. Reread the question you will be answering: What will happen next? Answer the question in your own words. If the hutch is so perfect, they will probably buy it. Read each answer choice carefully and then choose the best one. Answer choice A makes the most sense given the excited reaction the narrators had to seeing the hutch. **The best answer is A.**

# PROSE FICTION READING COMPREHENSION DRILLS

**Questions 1–9 are based on the following passage.**

*As was the case most days at this time, students wandered into the quad to cram for the afternoon's test, eat lunch, meet up with friends, or simply relax in the shade of the lush oak trees. For as many students as were present, the noise level remained surprisingly low. Laughter and chatter could be heard, but the sound was nowhere near what would be considered disruptive.*

*A young man with a guitar began to play quietly on one side of the lawn. Two friends beside him continued reading their textbooks as his music quietly floated through the air around them. Within a couple of minutes, another young man with a guitar began playing as well and slowly walked toward the first man. The two smiled at each other, and without a word being spoken, the solo became a duet. Around them, students began to look up from their laptops and notebooks. A couple of students slowly walked closer to the source of the melody in order to hear it better.*

*A few notes later, a young woman with a flute wandered over, smiled at the men, and lifted her instrument to her lips. The duet became a trio, and more students gathered. Without a word, the trio was soon joined by a clarinet, a bongo drum, and a harmonica. The impromptu concert began to draw a crowd, which was as spontaneous as the music itself. The harmonies of the instruments eclipsed the students' plans to study, as nearly everyone on the lawn was drawn to gather near the musicians.*

*The single song grew into a medley, combining a number of familiar tunes, one after the other. A professor, on his way to his office, noticed the crowd and went to investigate. Upon hearing the music, he stopped. A glazed look came over his eyes as he allowed his head to nod to the rhythm of the music, and his foot precisely tapped the beat.*

*A few minutes later, the music quieted, and the students clapped loudly. The musicians smiled and shook hands with each other, as the members of the crowd slowly returned to their routines. The professor anxiously approached the players and introduced himself. The group of six students, who had never before met one another, stood in a circle and listened to the man whose words would impact them for years to come.*

1. **What would be the best title for this piece?**

   A    Birth of the Band

   B    When the Music Dies

   C    Studying Can Wait

   D    Guitars on the Quad

2. **What is the meaning of the word *cram* in the first sentence?**

   A    to study intensely

   B    to eat food greedily

   C    to force into a small space

   D    the state of being packed tightly

3. **Which was MOST LIKELY the author's purpose for writing the selection?**

   A    to tell a true story about real events

   B    to entertain by telling a story that did not actually happen

   C    to persuade readers to take music lessons

   D    to inform readers about musical instruments

4. **Reread this sentence from the third paragraph:**

   *The <u>impromptu</u> concert began to draw a crowd, which was as spontaneous as the music itself.*

   **What does *impromptu* mean?**

   A    eclipsed

   B    harmonies

   C    instrument

   D    spontaneous

5. **Reread this sentence from the third paragraph:**

   *The harmonies of the instruments <u>eclipsed</u> the students' plans to study, as nearly everyone on the lawn was drawn to gather near the musicians.*

   **Which meaning of the word *eclipsed* is used in this sentence?**

   A    to cast a shadow by blocking the light on an object

   B    a decline in status or power

   C    the partial or total hiding of the sun or moon

   D    to become more important than something else

6. **Reread these sentences from the fourth paragraph:**

   *The single song grew into a <u>medley</u>, combining a number of familiar tunes, one after the other. A professor, on his way to his office, noticed the crowd and went to investigate.*

   **What is the meaning of *medley*?**

   A  assembly

   B  mixture

   C  recognizable

   D  tune

7. **What is the meaning of the word *glazed* in the fourth paragraph?**

   A  fixed and staring

   B  having a shiny outside layer

   C  protected by a finish

   D  covered in a sweet coating

8. **The professor is the director of the school's band and is also head of the performing arts department. What is the most likely reason he is speaking to the students?**

   A  to ask them not to disrupt the other students' study time

   B  to suggest the names of vocalists who might want to sing with them

   C  to encourage them to become involved in the school's music program

   D  to find out if they will let him join them the next time they play together

9. **What will MOST LIKELY happen next?**

   A  The musicians will plan to play their instruments together again in the future.

   B  The students will ask them to play music during their lunch break the next day.

   C  The group will decide that the concert was a one-time event and not perform again.

   D  The crowd will not gather on the lawn again the next time the musicians play their instruments.

---

**Questions 10–15 are based on the following excerpt from *Utopia* by Sir Thomas More.**

*Agriculture is that which is so universally understood among them that no person, either man or woman, is ignorant of it; they are instructed in it from their childhood, partly by what they learn at school and partly by practice; they being led out often into the fields, about the town, where they not only see others at work, but are likewise exercised in it themselves. Besides agriculture, which is so common to them all, every man has some peculiar trade to which he applies himself, such as the manufacture of wool, or flax, masonry, smith's work, or carpenter's work; for there is no sort of trade that is not in great esteem among them. . . . The same trade generally passes down from father to son, inclinations often following descent; but if any man's genius lies another way, he is by adoption translated into a family that deals in the trade to which he is inclined: and when that is to be done, care is taken not only by his father, but by the magistrate, that he may be put to a discreet and good man. And if after a person has learned one trade, he desires to acquire another, that is also allowed, and is managed in the same manner as the former. When he has learned both, he follows that which he likes best, unless the public has more occasion for the other. . . . They dividing the day and night into twenty-four hours, appoint six of these for work; three of which are before dinner, and three after. They then sup, and at eight o'clock, counting from noon, go to bed and sleep eight hours. The rest of their time besides that taken up in work, eating and sleeping, is left to every man's discretion; yet they are not to abuse that interval to luxury and idleness, but must employ it in some proper exercise according to their various inclinations, which is for the most part reading. It is ordinary to have public lectures every morning before daybreak; at which none are obliged to appear but those who are marked out for literature; yet a great many, both men and women of all ranks, go to hear lectures of one sort of other, according to their inclinations. But if others, that are not made for contemplation, choose rather to employ themselves at that time in their trades, as many of them do, they are not hindered, but are rather commended, as men that take care to serve their country. After supper, they spend an hour in some diversion, in summer in their gardens, and in winter in the halls where they eat; where they entertain each other, either with music or discourse. They do not so much as know dice, or any such foolish and mischievous games. . . . The magistrates never engage the people in unnecessary labor, since the chief end of the constitution is to regulate labor by the necessities of the public, and to allow all the people as much time as is necessary for the improvement of their minds, in which they think the happiness of life consists.*

10. **What job is common to all people in Utopia?**
    A   weaving cloth
    B   cooking
    C   tending livestock
    D   farming

11. **What game is described as foolish?**
    A   dice
    B   chess
    C   tag
    D   play fighting

12. **If a man works as a carpenter, what will most likely be his son's profession?**
    A   magistrate
    B   carpenter
    C   farmer
    D   whatever the son chooses

13. **Which of the following activities would a Utopian think is the greatest joy in life?**

    A  having and raising a child

    B  working in the fields, growing his own food

    C  learning about an unfamiliar subject to improve her knowledge

    D  reading a work of fiction about a distant land

14. **Reread this portion of the passage:**

    *but if any man's genius lies another way, he is by adoption <u>translated</u> into a family that deals in the trade to which he is inclined*

    **The word *translated* most nearly means**

    A  to turn one language into another

    B  to change from one form into another form

    C  to move from one place to another

    D  to retransmit or forward

15. **Which of the following would a citizen of Utopia NOT be doing during the hour after supper?**

    A  playing music

    B  gambling

    C  gardening

    D  listening to music

**Answers are on page 722.**

# 23 Interpreting Literary Texts: Poetry

**S**ixty percent of the questions in the reading section of the *HiSET*® Exam Language Arts—Reading test will be based on fiction writing. At least one of the selections you will read and answer questions about will be poetry. This chapter will review several reading comprehension skills that will help you to understand any poetry you may encounter. Keep in mind that some of the comprehension strategies reviewed in this chapter may also be useful in understanding other forms of literature as well.

## What Is Tested?

There are several differences between poetry and prose. A poem is usually arranged in short lines or phrases that are grouped into stanzas. Each line of a poem may or may not express a complete thought; often a single thought is spread over several lines. Prose, on the other hand, includes sentences that are grouped together in paragraphs. Each sentence, by definition, expresses a complete thought. Figurative language, a pattern of syllables, rhyming words, and rhythm are common characteristics of poetry that may be tested.

## Comprehension Strategies

You may think that poems are shorter than prose passages, but that is not actually the case. Some poems can be as long as a novel. For example, Shakespeare's famous play *Romeo and Juliet*, which you may have spent weeks studying in high school, is also a poem. *The Mahabharata*, an Indian scripture, is actually the longest poem in the world, with a length of more than 1.8 million words.

Not only does poetry look and sound different from prose, interpreting poetry is different from interpreting other forms of literature. To help you, here are some features of poetry that you should note in order to analyze a poem and comprehend its structure and meaning.

## Stanzas

Poems are written in short lines or phrases that are arranged into groups called **stanzas**. Each stanza is set apart from the rest by a space. Poems may contain any number of stanzas.

### Keep in Mind

Keep in mind that unlike sentences, which end in a period, the lines of a poem do not necessarily express a complete thought. In other words, you should not stop reading at the end of a line and assume you have gotten the whole idea. Each line may begin with a capital letter, but that does not mean it is the beginning of a new sentence or idea. Read a line and then continue until you come to ending punctuation or the end of a stanza to make sure you have read the entire thought.

## Rhythm

The **rhythm** of a poem is the musical pattern, or beat, that is created by the syllables. A poem's rhythm influences the feeling associated with the piece. Faster rhythms tend to suggest a lively, upbeat feeling, while slower rhythms suggest a calmer, possibly even somber, feeling.

## Rhyme

Poems may or may not contain rhyming words at the ends of the lines. When a poem does include **rhyme**, these similar sounding words are arranged in a pattern. For example, the words ending alternating lines may rhyme, or the words on every third line may rhyme. The pattern of rhyming words is the **rhyme scheme**.

Take a look at the rhyme scheme in this stanza from Elizabeth Barrett Browning's "The Poet's Vow." The letter A is given to the first line of the poem; any line that rhymes with this would also be given the letter A. The next line, since it does not rhyme with line A, is assigned the letter B, as is any line that rhymes with it, and so on.

*Eve is a twofold mystery;* (A)

*The stillness Earth doth keep,* (B)

*The motion wherewith human hears* (C)

*Do each to either leap* (B)

*As if all souls between the poles* (D)

*Felt "Parting comes in sleep."* (B)

The rhyme scheme for this stanza is ABCBDB. It shows that lines 2, 4, and 6, which are all labeled B, rhyme with each other.

## Mood and Tone

The **mood** of a poem is the feeling or emotion it suggests and is created by the words and details the writer selects. Notice the two descriptions of the same situation that follow. The first suggests a happy, cheerful, or excited mood. The second suggests an ominous, uncomfortable, or nervous mood.

*After being introduced, Malcolm bounced across the stage to the podium, soaking in the cheers and applause of his supporters.*

*After being introduced, Malcolm trudged across the stage to the podium, cringing at the commotion created by the audience.*

The **tone** is also created by the words and details a writer uses; it refers to his or her attitude about the topic.

*The contagious excitement of the crowd continued long after the speaker had made his victorious march across the stage to deliver yet another inspiring message.*

*The raucous noise of the crowd would not end soon enough, despite the fact that the speaker had already approached the podium to deliver a message that would not be unlike the sound of fingernails on a chalkboard.*

### Keep in Mind

Keep in mind that **mood** refers to the emotions the *reader* gets from a passage. The mood might be mysterious, romantic, serious, lighthearted, gloomy, or a hundred other feelings you may experience.

**Tone** refers to the attitude of the *writer*. The tone might be sarcastic, humorous, outraged, somber, or any other attitude you can think of.

## Figurative Language

**Figurative language** helps literature be more descriptive by using words in a way that gives them meanings that are different from their ordinary meanings. This strategy helps to paint a clear picture in your mind and increases comprehension of the text. Here are several common types of figurative language.

### Hyperbole

An overexaggeration, which may be used with humor, is a **hyperbole**. Such language is used for emphasis or effect rather than for giving a literal explanation.

*Adrienne made her famous mile-high chocolate fudge cake for dessert.*

*The car stereo was so loud that the people in the next town could hear it.*

### Idioms

An **idiom** is an expression that has a different meaning from that which the words indicate literally.

*She was <u>up a creek</u> when her dad found out she had not gone to the library to study.*

The literal meaning of the phrase *up a creek* would mean that she was sitting in a narrow body of water, but this was not actually the case. The figurative meaning of *up a creek* indicates that she was in trouble.

### Metaphors

**Metaphors** compare two unlike things by stating that one is actually the other.

*Trevor's eyes were stars when he saw her enter the coffee shop.*

Trevor's eyes did not actually become stars. This is simply a more interesting and descriptive way to say, "Trevor was happy to see her."

### Simile

A **simile** is a comparison using the words *like* or *as*.

*When the election results were posted, Madison was as happy as a clam.*

*Marcella sings like a canary, so she was given the starring role in the musical.*

### Personification

Sometimes, human characteristics are attributed to nonhuman things to provide a clear description. This type of figurative language is called **personification**.

*The waves danced across the surface of the lake.*

## Alliteration

**Alliteration** is one way writers emphasize and connect words by repeating similar sounds. The repeated sounds are often found at the beginning of words or at the beginning of stressed syllables. The two types of alliteration are assonance and consonance.

**Assonance** is the repetition of vowel sounds.

*The <u>kite</u> <u>flies</u> <u>beside</u> the billowy cloud.*

**Consonance** is the repetition of consonant sounds. Notice in the example that it is the repetition of the sound, not the letter, that creates alliteration.

*He <u>gently</u> <u>juggled</u> the delicate items to ensure their safe arrival.*

## Style

The type of language a writer uses determines the style of the poem or passage. The appropriate style is determined by the purpose of the writing, the intended audience, and the feeling that the writer wants to achieve.

A **formal writing style** is often used for workplace documents and school assignments, as well as for passages or poems that deal with serious or somber topics. Complicated words and technical jargon may be included.

*During the current semester, students enrolled in Ancient Greek Literature for Modern Times will be required to research the history of poetry and present poems that serve as examples of iambic pentameter and dactylic hexameter.*

An **informal style** uses words and information that are intended for pretty much anyone to be able to understand.

*Emily Dickinson is a famous poet who was born in 1830 in Massachusetts. She wrote nearly 2,000 poems. Only about a dozen of these poems were published while she was living.*

A **conversational style** uses words and phrases that someone might use when talking with a friend. In fact, the writing sounds like a conversation.

*I read the most amazing poem today! It was hanging in this new store in the mall— you know, the one by the food court. The poem was written on kind of old-looking paper and was in the coolest frame. The dude at the store said they're having a sweet sale next week. I'll definitely check that out!*

## Word Usage

One factor that helps to set the style of a poem or passage is the words the writer selects to set the tone and express his or her ideas. **Word usage** can alter the impression you take away from the text. Take a look at how word usage affects the following examples.

*Kirk requested an extra-credit assignment to improve his final grade.*

*Kirk begged for an extra-credit assignment to recover his final grade.*

# Examples

Here are two sample questions about poetry. Read the following poem by William Butler Yeats to answer them.

### "These Are the Clouds"

These are the clouds about the fallen sun,
The majesty that shuts his burning eye;
The weak lay hand on what the strong has done,
Till that be tumbled that was lifted high
5 And discord follow upon unison,
And all things at one common level lie.
And therefore, friend, if your great race were run
And these things came, so much the more thereby
Have you made greatness your companion,
10 Although it be for children that you sigh:
These are the clouds about the fallen sun,
The majesty that shuts his burning eye.

1. **Which example of personification is found in the poem?**
   A   The clouds fall
   B   The sun shuts his eye
   C   The weak lay hands
   D   Children sigh

## Explanation

First, read all the questions about this poem. Reading all of the questions ahead of time can alert you to what information you should keep an eye out for as you read the poem. Will you need to look for examples of alliteration? Will you be expected to identify the tone or mood? Again, take advantage of any resource you have. Use these questions to focus your attention on which information and techniques will be most important.

Then read the poem carefully, keeping those questions in mind. Remember not to read a poem line by line; rather, read it from the beginning of a thought to the end of the thought. A single idea may be expressed over several lines. To best understand the message of the poem, focus on identifying complete thoughts as you read. Pay attention to punctuation. As with prose writing, punctuation can be helpful in separating ideas and keeping thoughts from running together. Pause where there are commas or semicolons. Stop where there are periods. Be careful not to pause or stop where there is no punctuation, regardless of whether you have come to the end of a line. Also pay attention to the rhythm. The rhythm works to set the mood of the poem. You may find it helpful to read poetry aloud to hear the beats; however, you will have to listen to yourself read aloud in your head during the actual test. Practice doing this in the weeks and months beforehand. Notice any figurative language, and read it carefully enough to be able to create the image in your mind that the poet intended. This will help you to understand exactly what he or she is describing.

Reread the first question about the poem and answer it in your own words. Always look back at the poem to double-check your answer. Explain to yourself why your answer is correct, and make sure that it answers the question completely.

1. **Which example of personification is found in the poem?**

*The sun is the majesty that shuts his eye.* Shutting eyes is a human trait and is attributed to the sun, a nonhuman object.

Finally, read the answer choices and see which one best matches your answer. Remember that the incorrect answer choices are based on test takers' common mistakes and misconceptions. Look at each option and explain to yourself why it is not the best answer. Then make sure the answer you chose is definitely the best choice.

Answer choice B is the same as your answer. **The best answer is B.**

2. **What is the rhyme scheme in the poem?**
   A   AABB
   B   ABCD
   C   ABAB
   D   ABCB

### *Explanation*

Since you have already read the questions and the poem, start by making sure you understand the question. In order to find the rhyme scheme, assign the letter A to the word at the end of the first line. Since *sun* is the last word of the first line, it gets an A. The next line ends with *eye*, which does not rhyme with *sun*, so that line gets a B. The next line returns to the A rhyme, and the fourth line is the B rhyme. This makes the rhyme scheme ABAB. **The best answer is C.**

# POETRY READING COMPREHENSION DRILLS

For each of the following questions, choose the best answer.

**Questions 1–6 are based on the excerpt below from a poem by Henry Wadsworth Longfellow.**

#### "Voices of the Night"

Pleasant it was, when woods were green,
And winds were soft and low,
To lie amid some sylvan scene.
Line   Where, the long drooping boughs between,
5   Shadows dark and sunlight sheen
Alternate come and go;

Or where the denser grove receives
No sunlight from above,
But the dark foliage interweaves
10   In one unbroken roof of leaves,
Underneath whose sloping eaves
The shadows hardly move.

Beneath some patriarchal tree
I lay upon the ground;
15   His hoary arms uplifted he,
And all the broad leaves over me
Clapped their little hands in glee,
With one continuous sound;—

A slumberous sound, a sound that brings
20   The feelings of a dream,
As of innumerable wings,
As, when a bell no longer swings,
Faint the hollow murmur rings
O'er meadow, lake, and stream.

1.  **What is the rhyme scheme of the poem?**
    A   ABAAAB
    B   ABABAB
    C   ABAABA
    D   ABBABB

2.  **Which word best expresses the mood of the poem?**
    A   anxious
    B   content
    C   frightening
    D   gloomy

3.  **Which line contains an example of figurative language?**
    A   1
    B   5
    C   12
    D   17

4.  **Which line contains an example of consonance?**
    A   *Alternate come and go*
    B   *No sunlight from above*
    C   *A slumberous sound, a sound that brings*
    D   *And all the broad leaves over me*

5.  **Which line contains an example of assonance?**
    A   *The feelings of a dream*
    B   *His hoary arms uplifted he*
    C   *The shadows hardly move*
    D   *Where, the long drooping boughs between*

6.  **How does the poet feel about the sound of the leaves?**
    A   He feels that the sound is eerie.
    B   He thinks it sounds like a stream.
    C   The sound makes him feel peaceful.
    D   He believes the sound is too quiet.

**Questions 7–10 are based on the following excerpt from the same poem.**

Line 25  And dreams of that which cannot die,
Bright visions, came to me,
As lapped in thought I used to lie,
And gaze into the summer sky,
Where the sailing clouds went by,
30  Like ships upon the sea;

Dreams that the soul of youth engage

Ere Fancy has been quelled;
Old legends of the monkish page,
*Line* Traditions of the saint and sage,
35 Tales that have the rime of age,
And chronicles of Eld.

And, loving still these quaint old themes,
Even in the city's throng
I feel the freshness of the streams,
40 That, crossed by shades and sunny gleams,
Water the green land of dreams,
The holy land of song.

Therefore, at Pentecost, which brings
The Spring, clothed like a bride,
45 When nestling buds unfold their wings,
And bishop's-caps have golden rings,
Musing upon many things,
I sought the woodlands wide.

7. **Which use of figurative language is found in the poem?**
   A   A simile compares clouds to ships.
   B   A simile compares dreams and visions.
   C   A metaphor compares legends and monks.
   D   A metaphor compares the city and streams.

8. **Which shows the rhyme scheme of the final stanza?**
   A   AABBCC
   B   ABCABC
   C   ABAAAB
   D   ABABAB

9. **Which of the following is included in a simile?**
   A   buds
   B   Pentecost
   C   sea
   D   Spring

10. **Which best expresses the tone of the poem?**
   A   angry
   B   amused
   C   humorous
   D   reminiscent

### "Edward Hopper's *Nighthawks*, 1942"

The three men are fully clothed, long sleeves,
even hats, though it's indoors, and brightly lit,
and there's a woman.  The woman is wearing

*Line*    a short-sleeved red dress cut to expose her arms,

5    a curve of her creamy chest; she's contemplating
a cigarette in her right hand, thinking that
her companion has finally left his wife but
can she trust him?  Her heavy-lidded eyes,
pouty lipsticked mouth, she has the redhead's

10   true pallor like skim milk, damned good-looking
and she guesses she knows it but what exactly
has it gotten her so far, and where?—he'll start
to feel guilty in a few days, she knows
the signs, and actual smell, sweaty, rancid, like

15   dirty socks; he'll slip away to make telephone calls
and she swears she isn't going to go through that
again, isn't going to break down crying or begging
nor is she going to scream at him, she's finished
with all that.  And he's silent beside her,

20   not the kind to talk much but he's thinking
thank God he made the right move at last,
he's a little dazed like a man in a dream—
*is* this a dream?—so much that's wide, still,
mute, horizontal, and the counterman in white,

25   stooped as he is and unmoving except to sip
his coffee; but he's feeling pretty good,
it's primarily relief, this time he's sure
as hell going to make it work, he owes it to her
and to himself, Christ's sake. And she's thinking

30   the light in this place is too bright, probably
not very flattering, she hates it when her lipstick
wears off and her makeup gets caked, she'd like
to use a ladies' room but there isn't one here
and Jesus how long before a gas station opens?—

11. **What literary device is used in the line "she has the redhead's true pallor, like skim milk"?**

    A  alliteration

    B  allusion

    C  simile

    D  metaphor

12. **What type of narration is used in the poem?**

    A  third person omniscient

    B  third person limited

    C  second person

    D  first person

13. **Which of the following phrases contains assonance?**

    A  *the light in this place is too bright*

    B  *so much that's wide, still, mute, horizontal,*

    C  *a little dazed like a man in a dream*

    D  *actual smell, sweaty, rancid*

14. **Which of the following phrases contains consonance?**

    A  *her companion has finally left his wife*

    B  *a curve of her creamy chest*

    C  *she hates it when her lipstick wears off*

    D  *Her heavy-lidded eyes, pouty lipsticked mouth*

15. **What is the mood of the poem?**

    A  exciting

    B  satisfied

    C  sad

    D  tense

**Answers are on page 722.**

# 24 Interpreting Informational Texts

## What Is Tested?

As you know, 60 percent of the reading selections you will find on the *HiSET*®  Exam Language Arts—Reading test will be fiction. That means the remaining 40 percent will be informational texts. These are nonfiction, or factual, passages. The selections may take the form of memoirs, essays, biographical sketches, or editorials. You may also have to read legal documents, manuals, or other types of employee communications.

After reading, you will answer questions that require you to show how well you understood the material. This may call for making inferences, summarizing the information, identifying relationships between ideas, and interpreting the text. In this chapter, you will learn a few comprehension strategies to help you do your best on this section.

Nonfiction writing is different from fiction writing in several ways. For example, since the purpose of nonfiction is generally to share information, you will not usually see the story elements that are common to fiction passages. A true story about an actual person may include characters and a plot; however, a literature review, employee handbook, or company mission statement will not.

With that in mind, recognizing other characteristics of nonfiction can improve your comprehension of the material. Here are some of the skills that will prove helpful.

### Identifying the Main Idea and Supporting Details

You already know that the main idea and supporting details are important to writing. Recognizing them in a nonfiction reading passage can help you organize the information and gain a better understanding of the text.

The **main idea** is the most important point the author wants to make. It is the central message of the text, the single most important idea the author wants you to gain from the passage. In reality, sharing the main idea is the author's reason for writing a nonfiction piece.

The **supporting details** are the facts, examples, and definitions the author uses to explain the main idea so that you clearly understand the most important piece of information.

To identify the main idea, you must first recognize the topic of the passage. The **topic** is what the passage is about and can generally be identified in one word, or possibly a couple of words. For example, *dress code* might be a topic.

Once you recognize the topic, ask yourself what idea about the topic was so important to the author that he or she wrote a passage about it. The main idea is a complete sentence and tells what the author wants to share about the topic.

*Employees will be required to follow new dress code guidelines.*

After identifying the main idea, look for details that support it.

*All employees must wear closed-toe shoes. Jeans will not be permitted. Male employees must wear collared shirts.*

Each paragraph of a nonfiction passage contains its own main idea, which is generally one of the supporting details of the overall paragraph. For example, take a look at the following paragraph. One of the supporting details about the new employee dress code is the main idea of this paragraph, which supports the main idea of the overall passage.

*Male employees must wear collared shirts. These shirts may either be polo-style or button ups, and they can have either long or short sleeves. Men may wear a necktie with these shirts; however, neckwear is not required.*

## Distinguishing Facts and Opinions

**Facts** are true statements that can be proven or verified. Informational texts will contain mostly facts.

*All employees in the company are at least 18 years of age.*

**Opinions** are personal views that cannot be verified.

*Everyone should have some work experience by the time they reach 16 years of age.*

Being able to differentiate between facts and opinions can help readers evaluate the importance of statements. In a nonfiction text, facts provide the information about the topic; opinions tell how the writer feels about it.

## Summarizing Information

Being able to restate the most important information from a passage in your own words shows how well you understood what you read. When summarizing information, be sure to include the main idea and key details, since these are the most pertinent facts. A summary of the dress code example might look like the following:

*The dress code requires male employees to wear collared shirts; both males and females must have closed-toe shoes and must not wear jeans.*

## Making Inferences

**Making inferences** is similar to drawing conclusions. Authors will suggest information without stating it directly. Readers then consider the information in the text, as well as their own knowledge and experiences, and read between the lines to fully understand the selection. The key to making inferences is to focus on ideas that are implied and steer away from guessing.

# Recognizing the Organizational Structure

As discussed in Chapter 8, a text can be organized in various ways, depending on the type of information being shared and the purpose of the passage. Recognizing the **organizational structure**, or the way the writer chose to arrange the information, can help you identify what type of information will likely be found in the text and lets you know what information to look for as you read. The way information is organized tells you how the ideas are related.

## Cause and Effect

When a **cause-and-effect** structure is used, the author focuses on how ideas or events are related. An event that makes something else happen is a **cause**; the resulting event or events are **effects**. When a cause is discussed in a passage, you know to look for effects. If you recognize effects, read to find out why they happened.

## Classification

Some writers elect to group related ideas together in a **classification** structure. The information is arranged so that it is categorized according to similarities. When you recognize this structure in a passage, watch for several ideas that have something in common and then look for another set of ideas that have something in common.

## Compare and Contrast

A **compare-and-contrast** organizational structure focuses on similarities and differences between the topics being discussed. When you recognize that the author is using this structure, you know to look for ways in which the topics are alike and ways in which they are different.

Authors may use this structure in one of two ways. They may completely describe the first topic and then completely describe the second. This is known as **whole-to-whole comparison**. On the other hand, authors may use **part-to-part comparisons**, in which both topics are discussed in light of one aspect, and then both are discussed in light of another, and so on.

## Description

A **description** is exactly what it sounds like; a topic is introduced and its characteristics are described. Recognizing this structure is a red flag that you should expect to find facts and details that explain and clarify the topic.

## Problem and Solution

When a **problem-and-solution** structure is used, a problem is introduced; then one or more possible ways of solving it are discussed. When you encounter this type of organization, keep an eye out for the problem and then search for solutions.

## Sequence

**Sequence** is the order in which events and ideas are presented in a passage. **Time order** means that the sequence of events is chronological. **Order of importance** means exactly what it says; the events and ideas are presented according to which ones are most important. Some passages are arranged to present ideas in order from most to least important; others go from least to most important.

### Keep in Mind

Keep in mind that reading for pleasure is different from reading for information. When reading for information, your purpose is to learn something or to locate facts. To do this, focus on the details as you read. Monitor your comprehension of the selection by stopping periodically to think about how well you understand the passage. If you are unsure about any of the information or do not completely understand the text, go back and reread the section that is unclear. Continuing to read when you are not 100 percent sure of the previous information can prevent you from fully comprehending the remainder of the passage as well.

# Examples

Here are two sample questions using a nonfiction passage. Practice using the six steps to answer each question.

### How Does One Species Protect Another?

The Anatolian shepherd is a breed of guard dog originally from areas of Turkey and Asia Minor. These large canines are known for their terrific eyesight and keen sense of hearing, as well as for being very dedicated to their herd. These qualities have allowed them to become protectors of an endangered species that is generally their enemy, the cheetah.

The number of cheetahs has declined by nearly 90 percent since 1900, leaving only between 10,000 and 12,000 worldwide. One of the reasons for the decrease of the fastest land animal is the fact that these cats feed on livestock in areas where their natural prey is not plentiful. As a result, farmers have killed the cheetahs in order to protect their herds.

Anatolian shepherds have been used to guard livestock for hundreds of years. In 1994, the Cheetah Conservation Fund's Anatolian Shepherd Livestock Guarding Dog program in Namibia introduced the dogs as a way to protect farmers' herds in Africa without harming the cheetah predators. Young Anatolian shepherds were raised with the livestock. When cheetahs or other animals threaten their herd, the dogs bark to frighten the intruders, who then run away.

Now the cheetahs are not being killed for attacking the livestock. And the livestock is no longer being preyed upon by the cheetahs. By protecting its herd, the Anatolian shepherd is also protecting the cheetah.

1. **Which most likely states the opinion of the author?**

   A  Predators that attack livestock should be stopped by any means necessary.

   B  Cheetahs are the most dangerous predator attacking the farmers' herds.

   C  Anatolian shepherds are protective of the herds with which they are raised.

   D  Purchasing an Anatolian shepherd would be a wise investment for farmers.

## Explanation

First, read all of the questions for this passage (there are two). Then read the passage carefully, looking for the main idea and supporting details. Reread the question you are about to answer: Which most likely states the opinion of the author? This is asking you to infer which statement is an opinion with which the author would probably agree. The correct answer will not be a fact, even if the statement is true. State the answer in your own words. The author seems to think that the dogs are a good way to protect the herds. He or she also seems to believe that the dogs are beneficial to the cheetahs and to the farmers. Read the answer choices and select the best one. Answer choice D reflects the ideas you are looking for. **The best answer is D.**

2. **Which does *not* correctly state a cause-and-effect relationship discussed in the passage?**

   A  There are more of the dogs in Africa as a result of the cheetahs increasing in number.

   B  The cheetahs' food supply was insufficient; therefore, they began to approach the farmers' herds.

   C  The number of cheetahs is increasing because the dogs do not kill them when they approach the herds.

   D  Cheetah populations are no longer declining because the cats are retreating from potentially deadly situations.

## Explanation

You should have already read all of the questions for this passage and the passage itself. Reread the question you are about to answer: Which does NOT correctly state a cause-and-effect relationship in the passage? This is asking you to find the one answer choice that does not show a cause-and-effect relationship from the passage. State the answer in your own words. To do this, review the cause-and-effect relationships that were mentioned in the passage. You will eliminate answer choices that describe those relationships. Read the answer choices and select the best one. Answer choices B, C, and D all correctly state reasons why the cheetah population is no longer declining. Choice A is not a correct relationship; the number of dogs is increasing because of the conservation program. **The best answer is A.**

# INFORMATIONAL TEXTS READING COMPREHENSION DRILLS

### How Will These Changes Affect the Employees?

*To: All Employees*

*From: Dwayne Callahan, Director of Human Resources*

*As you are aware, our company has recently come under new management. Many changes will be taking place as a result of this restructuring. Many of these changes will affect our product lines. There will also be several changes that will affect you, our valued employees.*

*First, a new evaluation system will be put in place as of the first of next month. Under this new system, employee performance will be reviewed each quarter. Each employee will complete a self-evaluation checklist prior to his or her individual conference with a group of three management representatives. During the conference, the team will discuss the checklist, as well as the employee's progress toward performance goals and the observations of the direct supervisor. Employee performance will then be rated on a five-point scale, with five being the highest score. Employees receiving an exemplary review will receive an increase in hourly wages.*

*Another change will be the implementation of a bonus system based on customer satisfaction surveys. Each quarter, the department earning the highest scores on these surveys will be rewarded. Each employee in the department will earn a bonus based on the number of hours worked during that time period. This is a fair means of determining the size of each employee's bonus.*

*The final change that we are pleased to share with you is the addition of three more paid vacation days each year. Current guidelines for requesting vacation time will remain in place. These days are available immediately.*

*We appreciate your dedication during the recent change of management. We look forward to implementing these changes for our employees and believe that they will have a positive impact on our staff.*

1. **What organizational structure is used for the overall passage?**
   A   sequence
   B   classification
   C   cause and effect
   D   order of importance

2. **What organizational structure is demonstrated in the second paragraph?**
   A   description
   B   classification
   C   problem and solution
   D   question and answer

3. **Which is the main idea of the passage?**

   A Additional paid vacation time will be offered.

   B The company has recently come under new management.

   C Employees will be subjected to a new system of evaluations.

   D Upcoming changes in the company will affect the employees.

4. **Which statement can be inferred by reading the section?**

   A Customer satisfaction surveys are only used in some of the departments.

   B Employees with lower evaluation scores will not receive an increase in salary.

   C Employees with less than adequate scores on their reviews will be terminated.

   D Those working in larger departments have a greater likelihood of earning bonuses.

5. **Which of the following statements from the passage is an opinion?**

   A As you are aware, our company has recently come under new management.

   B There will also be several changes that will affect you, our valued employees.

   C Each employee will complete a self-evaluation checklist prior to his or her individual conference with a group of three management representatives.

   D This is a fair means of determining the size of each employee's bonus.

6. **Which best summarizes the passage?**

   A Three additional paid vacation days are available to all employees, effective immediately.

   B Employees have the opportunity to earn bonuses if their department receives the highest scores on customer satisfaction surveys.

   C Many of these changes will affect our product lines; however, there will also be several changes that will affect our valued employees.

   D Upcoming changes that will affect the employees include a new evaluation system, a bonus opportunity, and an increase in the amount of vacation time.

7. **Which of the following statements is a fact that can be inferred from information in the passage?**

   A The new system of evaluations will be an improvement over the current plan.

   B The changes being put in place have the potential to benefit the employees.

   C All of the employees will earn a bonus for positive customer survey results.

   D Employees will be able to take time off anytime they would like.

**Questions 8–15 are based on the following.**

*Molière is considered one of the greatest writers of comedy in Western literature. Comedy began in the Greek theater and is essentially a conflict between two opposing societies. Comedy typically features elements of surprise, incongruity, dramatic irony, repetitiveness, and the effects of opposing expectations. Molière's works fuse all these elements in biting satire. He essentially invented a new style of comedy that was based on a double vision of normal and abnormal. He juxtaposed opposing ideas for humorous purposes. Moliere's political satires also have their root the Greek theater and he is considered a master satirist. His plays* Le Misanthrope, Tartuffe, Dom Juan, *and* Le Malade imaginaire *remain some of the most frequently performed plays in the modern theater.*

*Molière was born Jean-Baptiste Poquelin in 1673 to a wealthy family in Paris. He studied law at the Collège de Clermont, but abandoned that career path and worked for thirteen years as an actor. He began writing plays while he performed. Molière's early plays combined the traditional French comedy of his contemporaries with Italian Commedia dell'Arte elements. His patron, Philippe I, Duke of Orléans, the brother of Louis XIV, secured for him a command performance of one of his plays for the King at the Louvre. The King enjoyed* Le Docteur amoureux *and gave Molière a theater space. Here, he became successful performing his works for the Parisian society. He was given a royal pension and became the official playwright of the court.*

*Molière did not, however, find success with critics and the Roman Catholic Church.* Tartuffe *was condemned by the Church for its attack on religious hypocrisy. Both it and* Dom Juan *were banned from performance. Molière was careful in his satires never to mock the monarchy and he continued to receive the support of the King. In 1666 he wrote* Le Misanthrope, *which had little success at the time, but is now considered his most refined masterpiece. Molière suffered from pulmonary tuberculosis and collapsed during a production of* Le Malade imaginaire *in 1673. He finished the performance, but died later that night of a hemorrhage.*

8. **Reread this sentence from the passage:**

   *He juxtaposed opposing ideas for humorous purposes.*

   **What does the word juxtaposed mean?**

   A   used

   B   brought to life

   C   placed together

   D   ridiculed

9. **What was Molière doing when he died?**

   A   attending a play

   B   sleeping in his bed

   C   acting in one of his own plays

   D   riding in a carriage

10. **Which is the main idea of the passage?**

   A   Molière was a great comedic playwright.

   B   Molière was treated unfairly by the Catholic Church.

   C   Without the support of the king, a playwright could not succeed.

   D   Molière was appreciated more after his death than during his life.

11. **Reread the section of the passage below**

    *His plays* Le Misanthrope, Tartuffe, Dom Juan, *and* Le Malade imaginaire *remain some of the most frequently performed plays in the modern theater.*
      *Molière was born Jean-Baptiste Poquelin in 1673 to a wealthy family in Paris.*

    **Which statement can be inferred by reading the section?**

    A  Molière wrote only four famous plays.

    B  Molière wrote his plays in French.

    C  Molière did not have to work because he was wealthy.

    D  Molière's works were not popular until modern times.

12. **Which of the following people did NOT enjoy Molière's plays?**

    A  theater critics

    B  the Duke of Orléans

    C  King Louis XIV

    D  Parisian society

13. **Molière's early works blended French comedy with which of the following?**

    A  Greek comedic theater

    B  political satire

    C  Italian Commedia dell'Arte

    D  Roman farce

14. **Which of the following statements can be inferred from information in the passage?**

    A  Molière failed his classes at the Collège de Clermont.

    B  Molière wanted to be an actor because his father was an actor.

    C  Molière tried to anger the church leaders.

    D  Molière did not want to be a lawyer.

15. **Which of the following groups did Molière never satirize in his plays?**

    A  ministers of the government

    B  clergy

    C  royalty

    D  high members of society

**Answers are on page 723.**

# Part VII
# Mathematics

# 25 The Mathematics Test

The *HiSET®* Exam Mathematics test is comprised of 50 multiple choice questions that you will answer in 90 minutes. You are allowed to use a calculator for the test and if a formula is required to solve a problem, it is included in the question itself.

**Numbers and Operations on Numbers**—this includes the properties of operations, vectors, matrices, real and complex numbers, absolute value, computation and estimation with real numbers, exponents, radicals, rations, proportions, and percents.

**Measurement and Geometry**—this includes the measurable attributes of objects, the appropriate tools and techniques of measurement, the properties of geometric figures, theorems of lines and triangles, perimeter, surface area, volume, lengths, and angles.

**Data Analysis**—this includes probability, linear relationships, measures of central tendency and variability, understanding relationships among events, data collection, counting principles, and the aspects of distribution.

**Algebraic Concepts**—this includes analyzing mathematical situations and structures using algebraic symbols, understanding patterns, functions, inequalities, problem solving, rates of change, and intercepts.

You will need to be able to understand mathematical concepts and procedures, analyze and interpret information, synthesize data, and solve problems.

## Question Steps

Here are the six steps you can use to help you solve questions on the HiSET Exam Mathematics test.

### Mathematics Steps

**Step 1:** Read the Problem

**Step 2:** Determine What Is Being Asked

**Step 3:** Identify Pertinent Information

**Step 4:** Choose Which Operation(s) to Use

**Step 5:** Solve the Problem

**Step 6:** Check Your Work and Select the Answer

## Step 1: Read the Problem

Most of the questions on the HiSET Exam Mathematics test are word problems. Just like any other question involving words, read everything very carefully. Look for words such as *not* or *except*, which can completely change the question.

## Step 2: Determine What Is Being Asked

After reading the problem, make sure you understand what the question is asking you to find. For instance, a question may mention that an item is on sale. You could be asked to determine the sale price, the original price, the amount of sales tax charged, the total price including tax, the amount of the discount, or the total cost for purchasing several of the same item. Make sure you know exactly what the question is asking.

## Step 3: Identify Pertinent Information

Some math problems may include more information than is needed to solve the problem. To correctly solve the problem, you must determine which pieces of information are important and which are not. When a problem includes the word *sum*, it may be tempting to add all of the numbers you can find. However, extra numbers may have been written into the problem. Including these would result in an incorrect answer.

Once you have figured out what the question is asking, you should be able to determine what information will be necessary to solve the problem. Reread the question, underlining or circling the numbers or information that you will need to find the correct answer. Cross out any information that you will not need to use.

## Step 4: Choose Which Operation(s) to Use

Look for key words in the question that offer hints about which operation, or operations, will be required to solve the problem. Not every problem will be straightforward. Think about what is being asked and then decide what operations you need to use.

## Step 5: Solve the Problem

Use the order of operations to solve the problem. Be sure to show each step as you work. Not only will this help you focus on using the correct process, but it can also save you time if you determine that you have made a mistake. Rather than having to start over from scratch, you can see where the error occurred and rework the problem from that point.

## Step 6: Check Your Work and Select the Answer

Once you have solved the math question, go back and check your work. Look over the steps you used, make sure you correctly applied the order of operations, and double-check that you carried out each operation accurately. It is easy to make careless mistakes when you are working quickly. Leaving out a negative sign, not regrouping an addition or subtraction problem correctly, or reversing the base and the exponent can make a huge difference in your answer.

Next, think about the problem and determine whether or not your answer is reasonable. For example, if the question asks for the cost of an item including tax, a reasonable answer would be slightly higher than the original cost. If your answer is *less* than the original cost, your answer is not reasonable. Likewise, if your answer is *double* the original cost, it is not reasonable.

### Keep in Mind

> Keep in mind that just because your answer is among the answer choices, it is not necessarily correct. The incorrect choices are based on common errors and misconceptions. They reflect incorrect answers that test takers are likely to come up with. Even if your answer is among the choices, it is still important to double-check your work

# Examples

Here are two sample questions to help you learn how to apply the question steps.

1. A bookstore is having a three-day sale that offers customers a 20 percent discount on all items. Alex finds several books by his favorite author on sale for $14.75 each. What is the final price of four books, including 6 percent sales tax?

   A   $46.91
   B   $50.03
   C   $59.00
   D   $60.77
   E   $62.54

### Explanation

**Step 1: Read the Problem**

**Step 2: Determine What Is Being Asked**

Find the final cost of four books, plus tax.

**Step 3: Identify Pertinent Information**

You need to know that the books are $14.75 each, he wants four books, and tax is 6 percent. You do not need to know that it is a three-day sale or that the items are 20 percent off, since the sale price is already given. Here is what the problem might look like if you underlined important information and crossed off unnecessary ideas: Alex finds several books by his favorite author <u>on sale for $14.75 each</u>. What is the <u>final price of four books, including 6 percent sales tax</u>?

**Step 4: Choose Which Operation(s) to Use**

You will multiply $14.75 by 4 to find the price of the books and then multiply the result by 1.06 to find the price including tax.

**Step 5: Solve the Problem**

$14.75 \times 4 = $59.00$

$59.00 \times 1.06 = $62.54$

**Step 6: Check Your Work and Select the Answer**

The answer is E.

Here is another example.

2.  **A box contains only 4 white marbles and 6 black marbles. If Lynda selects one marble at random from the box, what is the probability that the marble she selects will be black?**
    A   2/5
    B   3/5
    C   2/3
    D   4/5
    E   3/2

*Explanation*

**Step 1: Read the Problem**

**Step 2: Determine What Is Being Asked**

The probability of getting a black marble.

**Step 3: Identify Pertinent Information**

You need to know that there are 6 black marbles and 4 white marbles, for a total of 10 marbles.

**Step 4: Choose Which Operation(s) to Use**

To find the probability of drawing a black marble, you will to divide the number of black marbles by the total number of marbles.

**Step 5: Solve the Problem**

$$6 \div 10 = \frac{6}{10} = \frac{3}{5}$$

**Step 6: Check Your Work and Select the Answer**

The answer is B.

# 26 Numbers and Operations on Numbers: Whole Numbers

Questions relating to numbers and operations on numbers will make up 25 percent of the test items on the *HiSET*® Exam Mathematics test. Chapters 26–31 will cover information related to numbers and operations on numbers. This chapter will review whole numbers, operations, exponents, and roots.

**Whole numbers** are not fractions or decimals. **Operations** include: *addition, subtraction, multiplication,* and *division.* This chapter will review adding, subtracting, multiplying, and dividing numbers that are not fractions or decimals.

## What Is Tested?

### Words Related to Whole Numbers

**Even numbers** are those that are divisible by 2: 0, 2, 4, 6, 8, 10, 12, 14 . . .
**Odd numbers** are not evenly divisible by 2: 1, 3, 5, 7, 9, 11, 13, 15 . . .
**Consecutive numbers** follow one another in counting order: 5, 6, 7, 8 . . .

A **prime number** only has two distinct factors: 1 and itself. For example, 3 is a prime number because its only factors are 1 and itself (3). More examples of prime numbers include 5, 7, 11, 13, 17 . . . Note that the number 1 is not prime because it does not have two *distinct* factors.

A **composite number** has more than two distinct factors. For example, 4 is a composite number because it is evenly divisible by 1, 2, and 4; 12 is a composite number because it is evenly divisible by 1, 2, 3, 4, 6, and 12.

**Factors** are numbers by which another number is evenly divisible. For example, the factors of 10 are 1, 2, 5, and 10, because 10 can be divided evenly by these numbers.

### Operations

The four basic operations used in math are addition, subtraction, multiplication, and division.

### Addition

The numbers being added together in addition are the **addends**; the total is the **sum**.

$$3 + 2 = 5$$

In this example, 3 and 2 are the addends, and 5 is the sum.

Clue words such as *in all, altogether, increase*, and *total* often suggest that a problem calls for addition.

### Subtraction

The answer to a subtraction problem is the **difference**. Two other words you might encounter when dealing with subtractions are **subtrahend** and **minuend**. In a subtraction problem, the minuend is the amount you start off with and the subtrahend is the amount you take away from it.

$$7 - 4 = 3$$

In this example, 3 is the difference.

Clue words such as *decrease, have left*, and *less* than often indicate that subtraction is needed.

### Multiplication

The numbers being multiplied are the **factors**; the answer is the **product**.

$$5 \times 6 = 30$$

In this example, 5 and 6 are the factors, and 30 is the product.

Clue words such as *by, times*, and *twice* often suggest that multiplication should be used to solve a problem.

### Division

The number being divided is the **dividend**; the number that is divided into the dividend is the **divisor**; and the answer is the **quotient**.

$$24 \div 3 = 8$$

In this example, 24 is the dividend, 3 is the divisor, and 8 is the quotient.

Clue words such as *average, equal parts*, and *per* may indicate that division is required to find the correct answer.

## Exponents and Roots

An **exponent** is a small number positioned slightly higher and to the right of another number; it indicates repeated multiplication. For example, $4^3$ is read as "four to the third power." Here, 4 is the **base**, and 3 is the exponent. The exponent tells how many times the base should be multiplied by itself: $4^3 = 4 \times 4 \times 4 = 64$.

When an exponent is 2, you say that the number is *squared*. For example, $7^2$ is read as "seven squared." **Square numbers** are those that result from multiplying a number by itself. Square numbers are the product of two identical factors.

$$2^2 = 2 \times 2 = 4$$
$$3^2 = 3 \times 3 = 9$$
$$4^2 = 4 \times 4 = 16$$
$$5^2 = 5 \times 5 = 25$$

and so on. Numbers such as 4, 9, 16, and 25 are squares.

The opposite of exponents are **roots**. The **square root** is the number that can be multiplied by itself to equal a given number: $36 = 6^2$. Since $6 \times 6 = 36$, 6 is the square root of 36. The symbol $\sqrt{\ }$ indicates square root: $\sqrt{36} - 6$.

On the calculator you will be given during the test, use the $\sqrt{\ }$ key to find roots.

## Order of Operations

Some math problems require using more than one operation. In this case, it is necessary to solve the operations according to a certain sequence. The **order of operations** is a set of rules stating the order in which operations must be performed.

- Parentheses
- Exponents
- Multiplication, from left to right
- Division, from left to right
- Addition, from left to right
- Subtraction, from left to right

### Keep in Mind

Keep in mind that solving arithmetic problems from left to right, or in any other sequence that does not follow the order of operations, may result in the wrong answer. To remember the correct sequence, take a look at the first letter of *each* of the steps: P, E, M, D, A, and S. The saying *Please excuse my dear Aunt Sally* is often used as a reminder of the order of operations, since each word in the phrase begins with the same letters as the steps.

# Examples

Here are two sample questions involving whole numbers and operations.

1.  **The art museum has a special exhibit on display for the weekend. Tickets are $15 each. On Saturday, 462 people attended the exhibit, and on Sunday, 513 people attended. Which shows the total dollar amount of the tickets sold for both days?**

    A   $15 + 462 + 513$

    B   $15 \times 462 + 513$

    C   $15(462 + 513)$

    D   $462 + 513 \times 15$

    E   $(462 \times 15) + 513$

### Explanation

First, read the problem. Determine the relevant information. You need to know the price of the tickets and the numbers of people who attended. Decide which operations to use. Here, you will need to multiply the ticket price by the total number of tickets sold. Since the answer choices for this question do not show the total dollar amount, but rather the operations performed to find it, it is not necessary to perform the operation. You merely have to plan it out. 15 (462 + 513) = total dollars. **The answer is C.**

2. **The square root of 2,975 is between which pair of numbers?**

   A  50 and 60
   B  60 and 70
   C  70 and 80
   D  80 and 90
   E  90 and 100

### Explanation

First, read the problem. Determine the relevant information: square root and 2,975. Decide which operations to use: square root. Solve the problem. Since you are asked to estimate the square root, you can do this in one of two ways. (1) Enter 2,975 into your calculator and press the square root button. This will give you 54.54. (2) Estimate the root. $50^2 = 2,500$ and $60^2 = 3,600$, so the root of 2,975 must be between 50 and 60. Either way, **the answer is A.**

# WHOLE NUMBER AND OPERATIONS DRILLS

1. **This week Laura worked 40 hours regular time and 3 hours overtime. If she earns $12.00 per hour regularly and gets 1½ times that for overtime, how much did Laura earn last week?**

   A  $480
   B  $516
   C  $534
   D  $552
   E  $774

2. **Which of the following problems has an answer called a *product*?**

   A  12(8)
   B  25 − 17
   C  $\sqrt{64}$
   D  81/9
   E  15 + 13

3. Which of the following is equal to $144 \div (9 - 3)$?

    A  $6 \times 2 + 1$

    B  $4 + 5 \times 4$

    C  $36 \div 2 - 2$

    D  $2 \times (12 + 4)$

    E  $36 \div (5 - 2)$

4. Fay is buying a new washing machine, which is on sale for $1,479. She can either pay the entire amount at the time of purchase or make a down payment of $250 and make monthly payments of $125 for one year. How much more will it cost her to choose the payment plan than to pay the full sale price?

    A  $21

    B  $102

    C  $229

    D  $271

    E  $3,021

5. Evaluate the expression: $7 + 8(15 - 9)^2$

    A  8,100

    B  2,311

    C  540

    D  295

    E  70

6. Charlie bought a new computer desk that was on clearance for $485 and a chair for $199. The desk was originally $350 more than the price he paid for it. What was the original price of the desk?

    A  $835

    B  $684

    C  $450

    D  $334

    E  $135

**Questions 7 and 8 are based on the following information.**

*The owners of an apartment complex took out a loan for $35,000 to remodel some of the units. They put new carpeting in 12 of the units for $975 each and bought new appliances for 8 of the units for $1,350 each. They also repainted the interior of 15 of the units.*

7. How much of the loan money do they have left after purchasing the carpeting and appliances?

    A  $22,500

    B  $16,400

    C  $12,500

    D  $11,700

    E  $10,800

8. The owners paid a total of $2,460 for paint. If the same amount of paint was used for each of the apartments, what was the cost of paint per unit?

   A   $70.29

   B   $123

   C   $164

   D   $205

   E   $307.50

9. On Friday, Saturday, and Sunday, a theater sold 665 tickets each day for a newly released movie. The theater sold 220 fewer tickets per day from Monday through Thursday. Which shows how to find the total number of tickets sold during the seven-day period?

   A   $3 \times 665 + 4 \times 665 - 220$

   B   $3 \times 665 + 4(665 - 220)$

   C   $3 \times 665 + 4 \times 220$

   D   $7 \times (665 - 220)$

   E   $7 \times 665 - 220$

10. A chef purchased 26 pounds of beef, 38 pounds of chicken, and 16 pounds of pork. He prepared an equal amount of meat for each of four dinner parties. Which explains how to find the number of pounds of meat he served at each party?

   A   add 26, 38, and 16; then divide the total by 4

   B   add 26 and 38; then add 16 divided by 4

   C   add 26, 38, and 16; then subtract 4

   D   divide 26 and 38 by 4; then add 16

   E   multiply 26, 38, and 16 by 4

**Answers are on page 723.**

# 27 Numbers and Operations on Numbers: Number Sense

## What Is Tested?

This chapter will review a few things about how numbers work. As you know, where a digit appears in a number affects its value. As you also know, there are times when an estimate is good enough, and an exact answer is not necessary. Understanding skills such as these and being comfortable applying them is important to doing your best on the *HiSET*® Exam Mathematics Test.

### Classifying Numbers

#### Natural Numbers

**Natural numbers** are those you use when you count, beginning with 1: 1, 2, 3, 4, 5 . . .

#### Whole Numbers

**Whole numbers** include all of the natural numbers, as well as 0: 0, 1, 2, 3, 4, 5 . . .

#### Integers

The whole numbers, as well as the negatives of the natural numbers, are **integers**: . . . −5, −4, −3, −2, −1, 0, 1, 2, 3, 4, 5 . . .

#### Rational Numbers

Integers and the fractions formed by dividing one integer by another are **rational numbers**. Rational numbers can be written as a fraction or a ratio, and they include decimals, repeating decimals, and terminating decimals. Take a look at a few examples of rational numbers: 7/8, 3¼, 0.721, 0.592592592 . . ., 8.3.

### Irrational Numbers

Rational numbers can be written as fractions. **Irrational numbers**, on the other hand, cannot be written as fractions. Square roots of numbers that are not perfect squares are irrational. Decimals that are nonterminating or nonrepeating are also irrational. Here are a few examples of irrational numbers: $\sqrt{5}$, $0.325487\ldots$, $\pi$.

### Real Numbers

**Real numbers** are any that can name a position on a number line, and they include all rational and irrational numbers: $-17.5$, $0.26$, $0.59204\ldots$, $5/6$, $\sqrt{23}$.

## Place Value

The position of each digit in a number determines its value. Look at the digit 4 in each of the following numbers.

2<u>4</u>

<u>4</u>7

<u>4</u>91

In 24, the 4 is in the ones place, giving it the value of 4 ones, which is 4. In 47, it is in the tens place, giving it the value of 4 tens, which is 40. In 491, it is in the hundreds place, giving it the value of 4 hundreds, or 400.

From right to left, here is the place value of the digits in a number:

Ones
Tens
Hundreds
Thousands
Ten thousands
Hundred thousands
Millions
Ten millions
Hundred millions
Billions

That means that the value of the 4 in 5,348,912 is 4 ten thousands, or 40,000.

## Rounding Numbers

When a number is rounded, it ends with a zero. To round a number to the nearest ten, for example, find the ten to which the number is closest (10, 20, 30, 40, 50, and so on). Each place value to the right of the tens will be a zero. For example, 58 rounded to the nearest ten is 60, because 60 is the ten that is closest to 58 on a number line.

To round to the nearest hundred, find the hundred to which the number is closest (0, 100, 200, 300, and so on). Each place value to the right of the hundreds place will be a zero, so there will be a zero in the tens and ones places. For example, 732 rounded to the nearest hundred is 700, because 732 is closer to 700 than 800 on a number line.

To round a number, underline the digit in the place to which it is being rounded. For example, when rounding to the nearest ten, underline the digit in the tens place.

When rounding to the nearest hundred, underline the digit in the hundreds place. Then look at the digit immediately to the right of the underlined digit. If the number is less than 5, do not change the underlined digit. If the number to the right is 5 or greater, round up by increasing the underlined digit by 1. Change all digits to the right of the underlined number to zero.

Round 82,764 to the nearest thousand.

Underline the place value to which you are rounding.

8<u>2</u>,764

Look at the digit to the right, which in this example is 7. Since 7 is greater than 5, you will change the underlined digit by adding 1 to it. Then change the hundreds, tens, and ones places to zeros.

8<u>3</u>,000

## Estimating

Suppose you went to a concert in a venue that accommodates 3,000 people. The concert was nearly sold out. You might make an educated guess and say that about 2,800 people were there. This is not an exact amount; you did not actually count every single person in the audience. This amount is an **estimate**, or an approximate value. Sometimes, an estimate is good enough and you do not need to know an exact answer.

One way to estimate is **front-end estimation**, in which you round a number to the greatest place value. For example, the greatest place value in 26,983 is the ten thousands place. Front-end estimation would round this number to the nearest ten thousand, or 30,000.

### Keep in Mind

Keep in mind that estimation can be great for determining the reasonableness of a computed answer. After performing the operations to find an exact answer, you can estimate approximately what the answer should be and then make sure the answer you came up with is about right.

## Properties of Numbers

You probably learned about the properties of numbers way back in elementary school, but by now you have had plenty of time to forget all about them. The good news is that whether you realize it or not, you most likely use these mathematical rules without even thinking.

### Commutative Property of Addition

Basically, this rule states that the order of the addends does not matter.

$$a + b = b + a$$
$$3 + 5 = 5 + 3$$

Both sides equal 8, so the order of the addends did not make any difference. The same holds true even when a whole list of numbers is added together.

### Commutative Property of Multiplication

Like the commutative property of addition, this rule states that the order of the factors will not affect the product. In other words, when you multiply, the numbers can be in any order.

$$a \times b = b \times a$$
$$2 \times 6 = 6 \times 2$$

Both sides equal 12, so it does not matter which factor is listed first. Again, this is true if you are multiplying three, four, five, or even more numbers.

### Associative Property of Addition

This rule refers to the fact that addends can be grouped, or associated, in any way without changing the sum.

$$(a + b) + c = a + (b + c)$$
$$(5 + 2) + 8 = 5 + (2 + 8)$$

The way the addends are grouped on the left side, $(5 + 2) + 8$, results in $7 + 8$. Suppose you want to group addends together to form a set of 10. By grouping the 2 and 8 together, as on the right side, you can add $5 + 10$.

### Associative Property of Multiplication

Just like the associative property of addition, this multiplication rule states that factors can be grouped in any way. This can come in handy when you find it easier to multiply certain factors together first.

$$(a \times b) \times c = a \times (b \times c)$$
$$(17 \times 25) \times 4$$

Multiplying $17 \times 25$ would probably require you to write down the factors and work out the problem the long way. Using the associative property of multiplication, you can re-group the numbers:

$$17 \times (25 \times 4)$$

You already know that $25 \times 4 = 100$. So by grouping these factors together, you can now multiply them first and then multiply $17 \times 100$.

$$17 \times (25 \times 4) = 17 \times 100 = 1,700$$

Grouping the factors differently turned a long multiplication problem into one you could do in your head.

### Distributive Property of Addition

This addition rule actually involves both addition and multiplication. Basically, it means that multiplication is distributed over addition.

$$a(b + c) = ab + ac$$

As you can see on the left side of the equation, $a$ is being multiplied by the sum of $b + c$. On the right side, $a$ is multiplied by $b$ and then multiplied by $c$, and the products are added together.

$$5(7 + 4) = 5 \times 7 + 5 \times 4$$
$$5(11) = 35 + 20$$
$$55 = 55$$

### Distributive Property of Subtraction

This property is essentially the same as the previous one, except that it includes multiplication and subtraction rather than multiplication and addition.

$$a(b - c) = ab - ac$$
$$8(6 - 4) = 8 \times 6 - 8 \times 4$$
$$8(2) = 48 - 32$$
$$16 = 16$$

Using this property, you can either subtract first and then multiply the difference by 8, or you can multiply both numbers by 8 and then find the difference between the products.

### Number Sequences

A **number sequence** is a list of numbers that follows a particular pattern or order. In the following sequence, for example, each number is three more than the number to its left: 2, 5, 8, 11, 14.

To determine what number comes next in a number sequence, or number series, you must determine the pattern that is being followed. Make sure the pattern holds true for the entire sequence.

# Examples

Here are two examples of questions dealing with number sense.

1. **Which is the next number in the sequence? 1, 4, 9, 16, 25, ___**

   A   28

   B   30

   C   34

   D   36

   E   49

### Explanation

Read the problem and determine what is being asked. Here you must find the next number in the pattern. Identify pertinent information and key words. The word *sequence* is important, and the number pattern itself is important. Choose which operations to use. You need to determine what pattern is used to get from one number to the next. Each of the numbers is a perfect square; 1 is the square of 1, 4 is the square of 2, 9 is the square of 3, and so on. Since 25 is the square of 5, you need to find the square of 6. Solve the problem. $6^2 = 36$. Check your work and select the correct answer. **The answer is D**.

2. **In the number 5,972,341, which digit is in the hundred thousands place?**

   A  2

   B  3

   C  5

   D  7

   E  9

### Explanation

Read the problem and determine what is being asked. Here you must identify the number in the hundred thousands place. Identify pertinent information and key words. The words *hundred thousands place* are important, and the number itself is important. Choose which operations to use. You need to determine the place value of the digits. Solve the problem. 1 is in the ones place, 4 is in the tens place, 3 is in the hundreds place, 2 is in the thousands place, 7 is in the ten thousands place, and 9 is in the hundred thousands place. Check your work and select the correct answer. **The answer is E**.

# NUMBER SENSE DRILLS

For each question, choose the best answer.

1. **Which is the best estimate of the sum of 2,402 + 101,873 + 75,601?**

   A  170,000

   B  182,000

   C  193,000

   D  200,000

   E  202,000

**The following information will be used to answer questions 2 and 3.**

*The Earth's orbit around the sun is a distance of 92,956,050 miles.*

2. **What is the value of the underlined digit?**

   9<u>2</u>,956,050

   A  two

   B  two hundred

   C  two thousand

   D  two million

   E  two hundred million

3.  What is the distance of the Earth's orbit around the sun, rounded to the nearest hundred thousand?

    A   90,000,000

    B   92,000,000

    C   93,000,000

    D   95,000,000

    E   1,000,000,000

---

**The following information will be used to answer questions 4 and 5.**

*The following table shows the number of employees a company had each year between 2006 and 2010.*

| Year | Employees |
|------|-----------|
| 2006 | 13 |
| 2007 | 39 |
| 2008 | 117 |
| 2009 | 351 |
| 2010 | 1,053 |

4.  If the pattern continues, how many employees will the company have in 2011?

    A   1,404

    B   1,755

    C   2,106

    D   3,159

    E   9,477

5.  Which is the best estimate of how many employees the company will have in 2013 if the pattern continues?

    A   10,000

    B   30,000

    C   50,000

    D   70,000

    E   90,000

6.  Which of the following is an example of a rational number that is an integer and a whole number?

    A   47

    B   0

    C   3/8

    D   0.25

    E   −19

7. **Which is equal to 15(24 − 18)?**
   A   $15 \times 24 - 15 \times 18$
   B   $18 \times 15 - 24 \times 15$
   C   $15 \times 24 - 18$
   D   $18(24 - 15)$
   E   $15(18 - 24)$

8. **The answer to (43,987 + 12,302) − 27,546 is between which of the following pairs of numbers?**
   A   80,000 and 85,000
   B   55,000 and 60,000
   C   25,000 and 30,000
   D   15,000 and 20,000
   E   0 and 5,000

9. **Which accurately describe $\sqrt{95}$?**
   A   real and rational
   B   real and irrational
   C   rational and whole
   D   integer and rational
   E   natural and irrational

10. **Which is equal to (23 + 17) + 31?**
    A   $(23 + 31) + (17 + 31)$
    B   $23 + 17 + 31 + 17$
    C   $(23 + 17) \times 31$
    D   $23 + (31 + 17)$
    E   $31 + 17 \times 23$

**Answers are on page 723.**

# 28

# Numbers and Operations on Numbers: Decimals

A s you know, whole numbers represent whole amounts. **Decimal numbers**, on the other hand, represent parts of a whole. Whether you realize it or not, you probably use decimals every day. A soda from the snack machine might cost $1.25, or you might get 14.6 gallons of gasoline. Those amounts are decimals.

This chapter will review the skills you need to do well on the *HiSET*® Exam Mathematics test questions related to decimal numbers. Remember, you will be able to use a calculator to answer questions on the test; you may also use pencil and paper or mental math to answer questions.

## What Is Tested?

A decimal number may include both a whole number and a decimal, as you probably noticed in the preceding example that referred to 14.6 gallons of gasoline. The whole number is separated from the decimal, or the partial number, by a decimal point. The digits to the left of the decimal point are the whole number part. The digits to the right of the decimal point are the decimal places.

In 14.6 gallons of gas, there are 14 whole gallons of gas; since the 6 is to the right of the decimal point, it represents part of a gallon of gas. One thing you might be tested on is decimal place value.

### Decimal Place Value

Just like the digits in whole numbers each represent a specific place value, the values of the digits in decimal numbers also depend on their positions. Look at the 5 in each of the following decimal numbers.

1.5

3.85

0.475

In 1.5, the 5 is in the tenths place, giving it a value of five-tenths, or 0.5. In 3.05, the 5 is in the hundredths place, giving it a value of five-hundredths, or 0.05. In 0.475, the 5 is in the thousandths place, giving it a value of five-thousandths, or 0.005.

Here, from left to right, is the place value of the digits to the right of the decimal point in a number. Notice that the value of each decimal place ends with the letters -*ths*.

Tenths
Hundredths
Thousandths
Ten-thousandths
Hundred-thousandths

The value of each place follows the same pattern as the values of the digits in whole numbers.

## Reading and Writing Decimal Numbers

When reading decimal numbers, pay attention to the place value position of the final digit.

0.54 is fifty-four hundredths

0.927 is nine hundred twenty-seven thousandths

If both a whole number and a decimal are included, read the whole number first, say *and* for the decimal point, and then read the decimal according to its place value.

273.9 is two hundred seventy three and nine-tenths

1,804.0236 is one thousand, eight hundred four, and two hundred thirty-six ten-thousandths

Noticing the place value is key to writing decimal numbers as well. Write the final digit in the number in the corresponding place value position, and use zeros as place holders when necessary.
Write four hundred twenty and seventeen thousandths in standard form.
You already know how to write the whole number part, so look at the decimal. *And* indicates the position of the decimal point. The 7 in *seventeen* is the final digit and must be in the thousandths place value position, which is three places to the right of the decimal point.

420.017

## Rounding Decimals

Rounding decimals is basically the same as rounding whole numbers. Underline the digit that is in the place value to which you are rounding. Then take a look at the digit to the right of the underlined digit. If the number to the right is less than 5, leave the underlined digit as it is. If the number to the right is 5 or greater, add 1 to the underlined digit.
The difference between rounding whole numbers and decimals is that when rounding whole numbers, all digits to the right of the underlined digit become zeros and when rounding decimals, all digits to the right of the underlined digits are dropped.

Round 2,361 to the nearest hundred.
2,361 rounded to the nearest hundred is 2,400.

Round 0.2361 to the nearest hundredth.
0.2361 rounded to the nearest hundredth is 0.24.

## Operations with Decimals

Adding, subtracting, multiplying, and dividing decimals are quite similar to performing these operations with whole numbers. There are just a few important differences to remember.

### Adding and Subtracting Decimals

When adding and subtracting decimal numbers, make sure to align the decimal points in each addend and the sum, and in the subtrahend, minuend, and difference. In other words, make sure the decimal points line up. Then add and subtract as usual.

$$
\begin{array}{r}
24.901 \\
5.76 \\
+\,308.7236 \\
\hline
339.386
\end{array}
\qquad
\begin{array}{r}
65.13 \\
-7.926 \\
\hline
57.204
\end{array}
$$

### Multiplying Decimals

Decimal numbers are multiplied in the same way as whole numbers. The difference comes in placing the decimal point in the product.

After multiplying the factors, count the number of digits to the right of the decimal point in each of the factors. Then place the decimal point so that there are the same number of digits to the right of the decimal point in the product. Take a look at the following example. There are three digits to the right of the decimal point in the first factor and two digits to the right of the decimal point in the second factor. Since $3 + 2 = 5$, there must be five digits to the right of the decimal point in the product.

$$
\begin{array}{r}
4.697 \\
\times\,1.18 \\
\hline
5.54246
\end{array}
$$

### Dividing Decimals

As with multiplying decimal numbers, dividing decimal numbers is similar to dividing whole numbers, with the exception of placing the decimal point. First, if the divisor has a decimal point, move it to the right to make the divisor a whole number. Then move the decimal point in the dividend the same number of places to the right. If the dividend does not have enough digits to move the decimal point the necessary number of places, add zeros to the end of the number.

Once the decimal points have been moved, divide as always. Make sure to place the decimal point in the quotient directly above its position in the dividend.

Take a look at the following example. Notice that the decimal point in the divisor, 4.36, must be moved two places to the right to make the divisor a whole number, 436. That means the decimal point in the dividend must also be moved two places. After the decimal point is moved, the dividend becomes 19,707.2.

$$
4.36\overline{)197.072}
$$

Move the decimal point two places in divisor and dividend; then solve.

$$436\overline{)19707.2}^{\phantom{1}45.2}$$

### Keep in Mind

Keep in mind that the divisor must be a whole number; however, the dividend does not. The dividend and the quotient can contain a decimal point. Only the divisor cannot have a decimal point.

## Decimals and Scientific Notation

**Scientific notation** is a means of writing extremely large or extremely small numbers using a decimal number and a power of 10.

### Using Scientific Notation for Large Numbers

In scientific notation, the decimal number must be between 1 and 10, so the first step in writing a large number in this form is to move the decimal point to the left until the number is greater than 1 but less than 10. Count the number of places the decimal point was moved, and use this number as the exponent beside the number 10.

Write 496,000,000,000 in scientific notation.

First, move the decimal point to create a whole number between 1 and 10. Count the number of places the decimal point is moved.

4.<u>96000000000</u>

The decimal was moved 11 places, so the exponent beside the power of ten will be 11.

$4.96 \times 10^{11}$

### Using Scientific Notation for Small Numbers

There are only two differences between writing large numbers and writing small numbers in scientific notation. First, when writing small numbers, move the decimal point to the right rather than to the left to create a number between 1 and 10. Second, after counting the number of places the decimal point is moved, write this number as a negative, rather than a positive, exponent.

Write 0.0000032 in scientific notation.

Move the decimal point to the right and count the number of places it is moved.

<u>000003</u>.2

The decimal point was moved six places, so the exponent beside the power of ten will be −6.

$3.2 \times 10^{-6}$

# Examples

Here are two sample questions involving decimal numbers.

1. **When Izzy received her credit card statement this month, she owed a balance of $385.92. She made a payment of $127.13 and then charged a pair of shoes for $64.76 and a jacket for $84.79. What is the new balance on the card?**

   A   $258.79

   B   $323.58

   C   $385.92

   D   $408.34

   E   $450.68

## Explanation

First, read the problem and determine what is being asked. What is the balance on Izzy's card after making one payment and two purchases? Identify the pertinent information. The beginning balance was $385.92, her payment was $127.13, and the two purchases were $64.76 and $84.79. Choose which operations to use. There are no key words to suggest which operations to use; however, you know that making a payment lowers a credit card balance. Making purchases increases the balance. Subtract the payment from the beginning balance and then add the price of the purchases. Solve the problem:

$$\$385.92 - \$127.13 = \$258.79$$

$$\$258.79 + \$64.76 + \$84.79 = \$408.34$$

Check your work and select the correct answer. **The answer is D**

2. **The owner of a taxi cab company purchased a total of 189.48 gallons of gasoline. If he put an equal amount into each of his 12 cars, how many gallons of gas did he use for each car, rounded to the nearest tenth?**

   A   15.7

   B   15.79

   C   15.8

   D   22.7

   E   22.73

## Explanation

First, read the problem and determine what is being asked. How many gallons of gas were used for each car, rounded to the nearest tenth? Identify the pertinent information. The total number of gallons was 189.48 and there were 12 cars. Also, underline *to the nearest tenth* so you do not forget that important detail. Choose which operations to use. You will need to divide the total number of gallons by 12 and then round off the answer to the nearest tenth. Solve the problem:

$$189.48 \div 12 = 15.79$$

15.79 rounded to the nearest tenth is 15.8. Check your work and select the correct answer. **The answer is C.**

# DECIMAL DRILLS

1.  If 20 pieces of gum cost $5.00, then at the same rate, what is the greatest number of pieces of gum Harrison can buy with $7.40?

    A   28
    B   29
    C   30
    D   32
    E   40

2.  What is the value of the 7 in the number 25.3479?

    A   seven tenths
    B   seven hundredths
    C   seven thousandths
    D   seven ten-thousandths
    E   seven hundred-thousandths

3.  Kai's living room is 4.76 meters long. He bought a piece of carpeting that is 5.2 meters long. How many meters of carpeting will he have to cut off in order for the length to fit exactly into the room?

    A   0.24
    B   0.26
    C   0.44
    D   1.74
    E   4.24

4.  The speed of light is 300,000,000 meters per second. What is this number written in scientific notation?

    A   $0.3 \times 10^9$
    B   $0.3 \times 10^{-7}$
    C   $3.0 \times 10^7$
    D   $3 \times 10^8$
    E   $3 \times 10^{-8}$

5.  What is four hundred sixteen thousand, seven hundred ten, and eighty-two thousandths in decimal form?

    A   416,710.0082
    B   416,710.082
    C   416,710.82
    D   416,782
    E   482,000

6. Last week, three packages arrived weighing 6.09 kg, 10.8 kg, and 0.72 kg. This week, two packages arrived, each weighing 3.147 kg. What is the total weight of the packages, rounded to the nearest hundredth?

   A   24.7

   B   23.91

   C   23.9

   D   20.76

   E   20.75

7. On a four-day trip, Bella drove a total of 677.6 miles and used 30.25 gallons of gasoline. How many miles per gallon was she able to drive?

   A   51.24

   B   22.4

   C   16.9

   D   8.96

   E   2.24

8. A pet supply store buys a 20-pound bag of dog food for $3.78 and sells it for $9.49. How much profit does the store make on 35 bags of food?

   A   $199.85

   B   $189.80

   C   $142.35

   D   $132.30

   E   $114.20

9. A restaurant uses 0.47 pound of ground beef in each burger and 0.53 pound in each serving of meatloaf. How many pounds of beef are needed to make 180 burgers?

   A   8.46

   B   9.54

   C   77.4

   D   84.6

   E   95.4

10. Which shows nine hundred thirty-five ten-thousandths?

   A   0.00935

   B   0.0935

   C   0.90035

   D   0.9035

   E   0.935

Answers are on page 724.

# 29 Numbers and Operations on Numbers: Fractions

## What Is Tested?

Fractions are a part of your daily life. You put one-fourth of a cup of butter in a chocolate-chip cookie recipe. You watch a favorite television show for half an hour. You walk five-eighths of a mile to the market. Fractions are parts of a whole number. On the *HiSET®* Exam Mathematics test, some of the questions will involve working with fractions. This chapter will review the processes for adding, subtracting, multiplying, and dividing fractions, and will discuss how to change fractions to decimals.

Like decimals, **fractions** also describe parts of a whole. The **denominator** is the bottom number in a fraction, and it tells how many equal parts make up the whole. The **numerator** is the top number, and it tells how many parts of the whole the fraction names. For example, the fraction $\frac{1}{4}$ names one out of a total of four parts. If your friend eats three slices of a pizza with a total of eight slices, then your friend ate $\frac{3}{8}$ of the pizza.

## Proper Fractions

**Proper fractions** have a numerator that is less than the denominator. These fractions name a portion of a single whole: $\frac{1}{3}, \frac{7}{8}, \frac{5}{12}$.

## Improper Fractions

**Improper fractions** have a numerator that is greater than or equal to the denominator. When the numerator is greater than the denominator, the fraction names more than the whole. In other words, improper fractions refer to at least one whole and part of another: $\frac{10}{3}, \frac{7}{5}, \frac{13}{9}$.

When the numerator is equal to the denominator, the improper fraction is equal to 1. For example, suppose you have $\frac{4}{4}$ of a dollar in your pocket. The denominator says that the dollar is divided into four equal parts, such as four quarters. The numerator says that you have four of those equal parts, or four quarters. If you have all four of the four equal parts, you have the whole thing. Any time the numerator and denominator are equal, the fraction is equal to 1: $\frac{8}{8} = 1$; $\frac{12}{12} = 1$.

## Mixed Numbers

A **mixed number** contains a whole number and a fraction. It names one or more wholes, as well as a portion of another, such as $1\frac{1}{2}, 3\frac{4}{5}, 5\frac{1}{3}$.

## Equivalent Forms of Fractions

Fractions that name equal amounts are called **equivalent fractions**. Here are several strategies for finding equivalent fractions.

## Converting Mixed Numbers to Improper Fractions

There are times when mixed numbers need to be changed to improper fractions. Often, it is easier to add or subtract improper fractions than it is mixed numbers. Also, mixed numbers must be changed to improper fractions before multiplying or dividing. To change a mixed number to an improper fraction, multiply the denominator by the whole number and then add the product to the numerator.

Convert $4\frac{3}{8}$ to an improper fraction.

Multiply the denominator by the whole number; then add the product to the numerator.

$$4 \times 8 = 32$$
$$32 + 3 = 35$$
$$\frac{35}{8} = 4\frac{3}{8}$$

## Converting Improper Fractions to Mixed Numbers

To change an improper fraction to a mixed number, divide the numerator by the denominator. The result becomes the whole number part of the mixed number.

The remainder becomes the numerator of the fraction part. The denominator stays the same.

Change $\dfrac{26}{7}$ to a mixed number.

Divide the numerator by the denominator.

$26 \div 7 = 3$, remainder 5

The quotient, 3, becomes the whole number part of the mixed number. The remainder, 5, becomes the numerator.

$$\dfrac{26}{7} = 3\dfrac{5}{7}$$

## Reducing Fractions

**Reducing fractions** simply means using smaller numbers to express the same amount. Since the reduced fraction is the same amount as the original, the two fractions are equal. Take a look at the following squares. The first shows $\dfrac{2}{4}$ shaded. The second shows $\dfrac{1}{2}$ shaded. Notice that the shaded portions of the squares are equal. This shows that $\dfrac{2}{4} = \dfrac{1}{2}$.

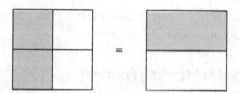

To reduce a fraction, divide both the numerator and the denominator by a common factor. In other words, divide the numerator and denominator by a number that goes into both evenly.

Reduce $\dfrac{16}{24}$.

Since 8 is a factor of both 16 and 24, divide both numbers by 8.

$$\dfrac{16}{24} = \dfrac{16 \div 8}{24 \div 8} = \dfrac{2}{3}$$

So $\dfrac{16}{24}$ is equivalent to $\dfrac{2}{3}$.

## Finding Common Denominators

Before adding or subtracting, fractions must have common denominators, which means the bottom number of the fractions must be the same. To do this, you must find the smallest number that is divisible by both of the denominators. Start by checking the largest denominator. Will the other denominators go into it evenly? If not, mentally list the multiples of the largest denominator and see if the other denominators are also factors of the number. For example, look at the denominators of $\frac{2}{3}$ and $\frac{4}{5}$. The largest denominator is 5, but 3 is not a factor of 5. List the multiples of 5. Ten is a multiple of 5, but 3 is not a factor of 10. The next multiple of 5 is 15. Since 3 is a factor of 15, use this as the common denominator for both fractions.

Once the common denominator is found, multiply the numerator and denominator of each fraction by the number that will create the common denominator. Take a look at the examples. Keep in mind that the common denominator will be 15.

Find the lowest common denominator for $\frac{2}{3}$ and $\frac{4}{5}$.

$$\frac{2}{3} \times \frac{5}{5} = \frac{10}{15}$$

$$\frac{4}{5} \times \frac{3}{3} = \frac{12}{15}$$

## Operations with Fractions

On the HiSET Exam Mathematics test, you will need to be able to add, subtract, multiply, and divide fractions.

### Adding and Subtracting Fractions

To add or subtract fractions, they must have the same denominator. The first step is to find a common denominator and then add or subtract the numerators. The common denominator will also be the denominator in the sum or difference.

$$\frac{3}{8} + \frac{5}{6} =$$

$$\left(\frac{3}{8} \times \frac{3}{3}\right) + \left(\frac{5}{6} \times \frac{4}{4}\right) =$$

$$\frac{9}{24} + \frac{20}{24} = \frac{29}{24}$$

$$\frac{29}{24} = 1\frac{5}{24}$$

Notice that the addends in this example have denominators of 8 and 6. The lowest number that is divisible by both 8 and 6 is 24, so 24 will be the common denominator.

To change $\frac{3}{8}$ to an equivalent fraction with a denominator of 24, multiply both the numerator and denominator by 3, since 3 multiplied by the denominator (8) equals 24. Because $\frac{3}{3}$ is equal to 1, multiplying the fraction by $\frac{3}{3}$ does not change its value.

Multiply the second addend, $\frac{5}{6}$, by $\frac{4}{4}$ to create a fraction with a denominator of 24.

After finding common denominators, the addends $\frac{3}{8}$ and $\frac{5}{6}$ become $\frac{9}{24}$ and $\frac{20}{24}$.

Add the numerators, $9 + 20$. The numerator of the sum is 29, and the denominator remains 24. So the sum is $\frac{29}{24}$. This is an improper fraction and is equivalent to $1\frac{5}{24}$.

$$\frac{2}{3} - \frac{5}{18} =$$

$$\left(\frac{2}{3} \times \frac{6}{6}\right) - \frac{5}{18} =$$

$$\frac{12}{18} - \frac{5}{18} = \frac{7}{18}$$

**Keep in Mind**

Keep in mind that if you do not find your answer among the choices, it may need to be put it in the simplest terms. Improper fractions may need to be written as mixed numbers, and proper fractions may need to be simplified, or reduced.

When adding or subtracting mixed numbers, convert them to improper fractions first and then find a common denominator. After that, add or subtract the numerators.

## Multiplying Fractions

The steps to multiply fractions are actually much simpler than the steps for adding or subtracting. First, multiply the numerators and then multiply the denominators. No need to worry about finding common denominators. Remember that it may be necessary to convert the product to its simplest terms. In other words, reduce the fraction after finding the answer.

$$\frac{2}{5} \times \frac{3}{8} =$$

$$\frac{2}{5} \times \frac{3}{8} = \frac{6}{40}$$

$$\frac{6}{40} = \frac{3}{20}$$

As with other operations involving fractions, convert mixed numbers to improper fractions before multiplying. Simplify the product.

$$2\frac{7}{9} \times 4\frac{1}{2} =$$

$$2\frac{7}{9} \times 4\frac{1}{2} = \frac{25}{9} \times \frac{9}{2} = \frac{225}{18} = \frac{25}{2} = 12\frac{1}{2}$$

## Dividing Fractions

Dividing fractions is also pretty straightforward. Simply invert one of the fractions; then multiply.

$$\frac{7}{12} \div \frac{3}{4} =$$

$$\frac{12}{7} \times \frac{3}{4} = \frac{36}{28} = \frac{9}{7} = 1\frac{2}{7}$$

## Operations with Fractions and Whole Numbers

Sometimes, it will be necessary to add, subtract, multiply, or divide a fraction and a whole number. To do that, you need to turn the whole number into a fraction.

To convert a whole number to a fraction, simply create a fraction with the whole number as the numerator, and the number 1 as the denominator.

For example, 25 becomes $\frac{25}{1}$. Then perform the operation as usual with the fractions.

$$36 \div 2\frac{1}{4} =$$

$$36 \div 2\frac{1}{4} = \frac{36}{1} \div \frac{9}{4} = \frac{36}{1} \times \frac{4}{9} = \frac{144}{9} = 16$$

## Fractions and Decimals

As you know, both fractions and decimals name parts of a whole. Sometimes, it is necessary to change a fraction to a decimal or vice versa.

### Changing Fractions to Decimals

The fraction bar, that little line between the numbers in a fraction, means to divide. To change a fraction to a decimal, divide the numerator by the denominator.

Write $\frac{1}{4}$ as a decimal.

$$1 \div 4 = 0.25$$

### Changing Decimals to Fractions

To change a decimal to a fraction, you have to remember the place value of the decimal. First, write the digits in the decimal places as the numerator. Leave out the decimal point and write them as a whole number. Then take a look at how many digits are to the right of the decimal point and determine which place value is represented. Write this number as the denominator. For example, two digits to the right of the decimal point indicate hundredths, so the denominator of the fraction will be 100.

Write 0.247 as a fraction.

$$0.247 = \frac{247}{1,000}$$

Look at the preceding example. The digits 247 are included in the decimal number, so these become the numerator of the fraction. There are three digits to the right of the decimal point, which is the thousandths place. The denominator of the fraction is therefore 1,000.

If digits are included to the left of the decimal point, the decimal becomes a mixed number. The digits to the left of the decimal point become the whole number, and those to the right become the fraction.

Write 9.7 as a fraction.

$$9.7 = 9\frac{7}{10}$$

# Examples

Here are two examples of fraction questions.

1. **Each serving of hot spiced tea that Katie gives her dinner guests calls for $\frac{1}{8}$ teaspoon of cinnamon and $1\frac{1}{2}$ teaspoons of sugar. How much more sugar than cinnamon will she use to make 6 servings of tea?**

   A   $8\frac{1}{4}$ tsp

   B   $8\frac{7}{8}$ tsp

   C   9 tsp

   D   $9\frac{3}{4}$ tsp

   E   10 tsp

## Explanation

Read the problem and determine what is being asked. How much more sugar than cinnamon is needed for 6 servings of tea? Identify the pertinent information. Each serving of tea uses $\frac{1}{8}$ teaspoon of cinnamon and $1\frac{1}{2}$ teaspoons of sugar. Choose which operations to use. First, to find out how much cinnamon and sugar are used, multiply each amount by the number of servings. The words *how much more* tell you that you will need to subtract these amounts. Solve the problem:

$$\frac{1}{8} \times 6 = \frac{1}{8} \times \frac{6}{1} = \frac{6}{8} \text{ tsp of cinnamon}$$

$$1\frac{1}{2} \times 6 = \frac{3}{2} \times \frac{6}{1} = \frac{18}{2} = 9 \text{ tsp of sugar}$$

$$9 - \frac{6}{8} = \left(\frac{9}{1} \times \frac{8}{8}\right) - \frac{6}{8} = \frac{72}{8} - \frac{6}{8} = \frac{66}{8} = 8\frac{2}{8} = 8\frac{1}{4}$$

Check your work and select the correct answer. **The answer is A.**

2. At the market, Nanny bought $4\frac{1}{2}$ pounds of peaches, $2\frac{1}{8}$ pounds of plums, and $\frac{1}{2}$ gallon of milk. Which shows how many pounds of fruit she bought?

A   $6\frac{3}{8}$

B   $7\frac{1}{8}$

C   $7\frac{5}{8}$

D   $\frac{50}{8}$

E   $\frac{53}{8}$

### Explanation

Read the problem and determine what is being asked. How many pounds of fruit did she buy? Identify the pertinent information. She bought peaches and plums. Do not include the milk, since it is not a fruit. Choose which operations to use. You will need to add the amounts for peaches and plums. To do this you will need to convert the mixed fractions to improper fractions and find a common denominator. Solve the problem:

$$4\frac{1}{2} = \frac{9}{2} \text{ pounds of peaches}$$

$$2\frac{1}{8} = \frac{17}{8} \text{ pounds of plums}$$

Use a common denominator of 8. $\frac{9}{2} \times \frac{4}{4} = \frac{36}{8}$ pounds of peaches.

$$\frac{36}{8} + \frac{17}{8} = \frac{53}{8} \text{ total pounds of fruit.}$$

Check your work and select the correct answer. **The answer is E.**

# FRACTIONS DRILLS

1. If a hydrochloric acid solution is made of $\frac{2}{3}$ water, how much water will be needed to make 36 ounces of hydrochloric acid?

   A  24
   B  26
   C  28
   D  30
   E  32

2. Which of the following is greater than 2?

   A  $\frac{3}{4} + 1\frac{1}{8}$

   B  $\frac{8}{6} + \frac{9}{12}$

   C  $\frac{13}{20} + \frac{11}{12}$

   D  $\frac{15}{16} + \frac{3}{7}$

   E  $\frac{2}{9} + 1\frac{1}{6}$

3. Ashley made five deliveries for her employer.
   Delivery A = 0.7 mile
   Delivery B = $\frac{5}{8}$ mile
   Delivery C = 0.45 mile
   Delivery D = $\frac{6}{10}$ mile
   Delivery E = $\frac{3}{4}$ mile

   Which shows the delivery distances in order from shortest to longest?

   A  A, D, B, C, E
   B  C, A, D, B, E
   C  C, D, B, A, E
   D  E, A, B, D, C
   E  E, C, B, D, A

4. Devin made $4\frac{1}{2}$ pounds of fudge, which he wants to divide evenly among six friends. Assuming he gives away all of the fudge, how many pounds will each friend receive?

A $\frac{1}{6}$

B $\frac{2}{3}$

C $\frac{3}{4}$

D $\frac{5}{6}$

E $\frac{7}{12}$

5. On Monday morning, $\frac{1}{12}$ of the total number of employees in an office called in sick. Throughout the day, $\frac{4}{15}$ of the employees went home early. What fraction of the total workforce remained in the office by the end of the day?

A $\frac{2}{3}$

B $\frac{7}{12}$

C $\frac{7}{20}$

D $\frac{13}{20}$

E $\frac{33}{40}$

6. Two hundred people were surveyed about which of the four seasons is their favorite. Of those surveyed, $\frac{1}{8}$ selected spring, $\frac{2}{5}$ selected summer, and $\frac{3}{10}$ selected autumn. The remainder of the participants selected winter. How many people surveyed selected winter as their favorite season?

   A   25

   B   35

   C   60

   D   70

   E   80

7. Which of the following is equal to $\frac{-34}{-85}$?

   A   $-0.4$

   B   $\frac{-2}{5}$

   C   $0.04$

   D   $\frac{2}{5}$

   E   $\frac{5}{2}$

**Keep in Mind**

Keep in mind that the fraction bar is a division sign. The same rules for dividing negative and positive numbers apply to fractions as to whole numbers.

8. A baker uses $\frac{42}{3}$ cups of flour in a cookie recipe. He has 36 cups of flour. What is the greatest number of times he can make the recipe?

   A   2

   B   3

   C   4

   D   5

   E   6

9. Helena used $5\frac{1}{8}$ pounds of coffee beans to make coffee for people attending a business seminar hosted by her company. She paid $7.84 per pound for the beans. What is the cost of the coffee she served?

   A   $39.20

   B   $39.98

   C   $40.18

   D   $40.61

   E   $45.47

10. Evaluate $\left(\dfrac{3}{5}\right)^3$.

   A   $\dfrac{9}{25}$

   B   $\dfrac{27}{125}$

   C   $\dfrac{81}{125}$

   D   $1\dfrac{4}{5}$

   E   $5\dfrac{2}{5}$

**Answers are on page 724.**

# 30 Numbers and Operations on Numbers: Percents

Percents, as do fractions and decimals, describe parts of a whole. The difference is that percents always refer to parts of 100. This chapter will review how to solve problems involving percents, as well as how to relate percents to fractions and decimals. You will also become familiar with how percents are tested on the *HiSET*® Exam Mathematics test.

## What Is Tested?

**Percent** means "per 100." In other words, 64% means 64 out of 100. If a model shows 100 squares, and 64 of the 100 squares are shaded, that means that 64% of the squares are shaded.

Suppose 100% of students are planning to go on the senior class trip. That means 100 out of every 100 students will be packing their bags. Everyone, the whole class, is going. 100% is equal to one whole.

$$72 \text{ out of } 100 = 72\%$$
$$100 \text{ out of } 100 = 100\%$$

Percents can be greater than 100. If you were to be given a raise at work, for example, your salary might be 115% of what it was the year before. That means, you made 100% of what you made the previous year, plus an extra 15%.

Likewise, percents may be less than 1. For example, a survey might show that only 0.3% of employees feel that they earn too much money. That is less than 1% of the employees surveyed. The decimal indicates a number that is less than 1.

### Decimals and Percents

Decimals and percents can easily be converted from one form to the other. To convert a decimal to a percent, simply move the decimal point two places to the right and add a percent sign.

Convert 0.23 to a percent.
$$0.23 = 23\%$$

Make sure that you move the decimal two places to the right and do not simply drop it. While the decimal point is no longer needed if the original number includes only two digits to the right of the decimal, it is still needed when more digits are present.

Convert 0.547 to a percent.
0.547 = 54.7%

Also, be careful when there is only one digit to the right of the decimal point in the original number. Since percents are part of 100, the decimal must be moved to follow the digit in the hundredths place. When only one digit is to the right of the decimal point, add a zero in the hundredths place and move the decimal.

Convert 0.7 to a percent.
0.7 = 0.70 = 70%

Converting percents to decimals simply involves dropping the percent sign and moving the decimal point two places to the left.

Convert 91% to a decimal.
91% = 0.91

Convert 120% to a decimal.
120% = 1.20 = 1.2

Remember, the decimal point must be moved two places to the left, so you may need to add a zero.

Convert 3% to a decimal.
3% = 0.03

Convert 0.8% to a decimal.
0.8% = 0.008

## Fractions and Percents

Since fractions and percents both name parts of a whole, fractions can be converted to percents and vice versa. To change a percent to a fraction, drop the percent sign. Then write the number as the numerator of a fraction that has a denominator of 100. Finally, reduce the fraction.

Convert 85% to a fraction.

$$85\% = \frac{85}{100}$$

$$\frac{85}{100} = \frac{17}{20}$$

To change a fraction to a percent, follow the same process you would to change a fraction to a decimal: divide the numerator by the denominator. Then write a percent sign rather than a decimal point.

$$\text{Convert } \frac{3}{4} \text{ to a percent.}$$

$$\frac{3}{4} = 3 \div 4$$

$$3 \div 4 = 0.75 = 75\%$$

Again, be careful when the quotient only includes one digit. One digit to the right of the decimal point is tenths, not hundredths. Percents are always out of 100, so when you convert fractions to decimals and then to percents, there must be two digits to the right of the decimal point.

$$\text{Convert } \frac{7}{10} \text{ to a percent.}$$

$$\frac{7}{10} = 0.7 = 0.70 = 70\%$$

## Word Problems Involving Percents

Most of the questions on the HiSET Exam Mathematics test are word problems. Here are some of the skills you will need to solve word problems involving percents.

### Finding the Percent of a Number

When a word problem on the HiSET Exam Mathematics test asks you to find the percent of a number, you will need to change the percent to a decimal and multiply.

There were 400 people at the ballet performance. Of those, 72% were women. How many women attended the performance?

$$\text{Find } 72\% \text{ of } 400.$$
$$72\% = 0.72$$
$$0.72 \times 400 = 288$$

### Finding What Percent One Number Is of Another Number

Some questions may require you to find what percent one number is of another.

In a box of 500 circuits, 25 of the circuits did not work. What percent of the circuits were faulty?

To do this, make a fraction with the part over the whole. In this example, 25 is the part, and 500 is the whole.

$$\frac{25}{500}$$

Then reduce the fraction and convert it to a percent.

$$\frac{25}{500} = \frac{1}{20}$$

$$\frac{1}{20} = 0.05$$

$$0.05 = 5\%$$

### Finding a Number When Given the Percent

Some questions may tell you a percent and ask you to find the original number. Sixty-three percent of the books checked out from the public library yesterday were fiction. If the number of fiction books chosen was 315, what was the total number of books checked out?

To solve this problem, first change the percent to a decimal or a fraction.

$$63\% = 0.63$$

Then divide the number by the decimal or fraction.

$$315 \div 0.63 = 500$$

The total number of books checked out was 500.

### Finding the Rate of Change

The rate of change compares a new amount to an original amount.

According to a recent census, the population of Kingwood is 18,000. The previous census 10 years ago showed the population as 15,000. By what percentage did the population increase?

To solve rate of change problems, first determine how much change occurred.

$$18,000 - 15,000 = 3,000$$

Next, divide the amount of change by the original amount. Write the quotient as a percent.

$$3,000 \div 15,000 = 0.2 = 20\%$$

### Finding Interest

You probably know that *interest* is the payment made by a bank for the use of money, such as the amount you earn on a savings account. It is also the charge paid for borrowing money, such as the monthly fee on a car loan or credit card. Interest is a percentage of the money in the savings account or a percentage of the amount of the loan.

The following formula is used to figure interest.

$$\text{Interest} = \text{Principal} \times \text{Rate} \times \text{Time}$$

*Principal* is the amount of money that is in an account or the amount of money that is borrowed for a loan. The *rate* is the percentage of interest. *Time* is the length of time the principal is saved or borrowed, and it is usually reported in years. For example, you might borrow the money for a car for a period of five years. In other words, you will pay the money back over this length of time.

> **Keep in Mind**
>
> Keep in mind that if a formula is needed to solve a problem on the HiSET Exam Mathematics test, the formula is included in the question itself. There is no need to memorize a formula; however, you will need to be familiar with how to use it.

Use the interest formula to solve a percent problem involving interest.

To buy a new car, Kimberly took out a loan of $16,500, which she will pay back over five years. Her annual interest rate is 7.2%. What is the total amount of interest she will pay for the car?

To solve the problem, plug each of the amounts into the formula. Be sure to convert the interest rate to a decimal.

$$\text{Interest} = \text{Principal} \times \text{Rate} \times \text{Time}$$
$$\text{Interest} = 16{,}500 \times 0.072 \times 5 = 5{,}940$$

Kimberly will pay $5,940 in interest on the loan over a period of five years.

# Examples

Here are two examples of percent questions.

1. **Abby bought living room furniture costing $4,250. She made a down payment of 10% and financed the balance over three years at 9.5% interest. How much interest will Abby pay per month, rounded to the nearest penny?**

   A  $30.28
   B  $31.88
   C  $33.65
   D  $90.84
   E  $100.94

### Explanation

Read the problem and determine what is being asked. What is the amount of interest for one month? Identify the pertinent information. The original cost of $4,250, the down payment of 10%, 9.5% interest, and per month are important to know. Choose which operations to use. Use the formula for interest, which is Principal × Rate × Time. To find the principal, find 10% of $4,250 and subtract this from the original price.

Convert the interest rate to a decimal. The time will be $\frac{1}{12}$, since you need to know the interest for one month rather than for the entire length of the loan. Solve the problem:

$$\$4{,}250 \times 10\% = \$4{,}250 \times 0.1 = \$425 \text{ down payment}$$
$$\$4{,}250 - \$425 = \$3{,}825 \text{ principal}$$

$$\text{Interest} = \$3{,}825 \times 0.095 \times \frac{1}{12} = \$30.28$$

Check your work and select the correct answer. **The answer is A.**

2. There are approximately 12,500 students at a local university. According to school records, 2,200 students are history majors. What percentage of the student population is majoring in history?

   A   4.7%

   B   5.7%

   C   14.9%

   D   15.7%

   E   17.6%

### Explanation

Read the problem and determine what is being asked. What percent of the students are majoring in history? Identify the pertinent information. The total number of students and the number of history majors. Choose which operations to use. You will need to find the percent of the total. Solve the problem:

$$\frac{2200}{12500} = \frac{22}{125} = .176$$
$$.176 = 17.6\%$$

Check your work and select the correct answer. **The answer is E.**

# PERCENT DRILLS

1. A clock is usually sold for $30. It was discounted 30%. What is the new price of the clock?

   A   $9

   B   $21

   C   $24

   D   $27

   E   $29

2. Which of the following fractions is equal to 16%?

   A   $\dfrac{1}{6}$

   B   $\dfrac{1}{16}$

   C   $\dfrac{4}{25}$

   D   $\dfrac{16}{25}$

   E   $\dfrac{12}{50}$

---

**Questions 3 and 4 are based on the information below.**

*Aiden opens a savings account with a deposit of $4,500. The account pays 3% simple interest.*

3.  If Aiden does not make any more deposits or withdrawals, how much will he have in the account at the end of two years?

    A   $4,527
    B   $4,635
    C   $4,680
    D   $4,774
    E   $4,905

4.  At the end of the second year, Aiden makes a deposit of $300. How much will be in the account at the end of the third year?

    A   $4,652.10
    B   $4,770
    C   $4,922.10
    D   $5,070
    E   $5,226.27

5.  Ginger earned a score of 82% on her final math exam. She answered 123 questions correctly. How many questions were on the exam?

    A   101
    B   150
    C   189
    D   205
    E   223

6.  A car dealership sold 4,120 automobiles during the past year. Approximately 58% of the vehicles sold were preowned, and the rest were new. About how many new cars did the dealership sell?

    A   174
    B   238
    C   1,730
    D   2,390
    E   3,882

7.  Over the past four years, 5,620 students have graduated from Lakeville High School. Following graduation, 70% of these students attended college. How many of the graduates attended college?

    A   393
    B   802
    C   3,934
    D   4,375
    E   5,227

8.  A pair of boots that normally sells for $65.00 is on sale for 20% off. What is the final price of the boots, including 6% sales tax?

    A   $47.70

    B   $48.10

    C   $52.00

    D   $55.12

    E   $55.90

9.  Debbie finished her first marathon in approximately 5.2 hours. She was able to complete her most recent marathon in about 3.9 hours. By what percent did her time decrease?

    A   25%

    B   30%

    C   33%

    D   40%

    E   75%

10. A survey showed that $\frac{3}{8}$ of the customers in a bookstore prefer to read hardcover selections, and 21.6% of customers prefer reading paperbacks. The remaining customers have no preference. What percent of the customers have no preference between paperbacks and hardcovers?

    A   37.5%

    B   40.9%

    C   48.2%

    D   51.8%

    E   59.1%

**Answers are on page 724.**

# 31 Numbers and Operations on Numbers: Number Relationships

**N**umber relationships span just about every area of math and are part of your everyday life as well. When you drive, you pay close attention to how many miles per hour you are driving. This number on your speedometer represents a number relationship. When you answer 8 out of 10 questions correctly on a quiz, you are dealing with another number relationship. This chapter will review a few number relationship skills that you will need when answering questions on the *HiSET*® Exam Mathematics test.

## What Is Tested?

### Ratios

**Ratios** compare two numbers using words, numbers, or a fraction. Suppose you have 6 apples and 8 bananas in a fruit bowl. The ratio of apples to bananas is 6 to 8. Since the word *apples* was listed first in the statement, the number of apples is listed first in the ratio. Since the word *bananas* appeared second, the number of bananas is also second in the ratio.

### Writing Ratios

Ratios can also be written using a colon. The ratio of apples to bananas is 6 to 8, or 6:8. Notice that the numbers stay in the same order as their labels appear in the statement.

Another way to write a ratio is as a fraction. The ratio of apples to bananas can be written as $\frac{6}{8}$. Notice that this is different than a fraction in the sense that the total number of fruits in the bowl is not written as the denominator. The denominator in the ratio of apples to bananas is the number of bananas.

There are 3 employees and 12 customers in a store. What is the ratio of employees to customers?

The ratio of employees to customers is 3 to 12.

This answer can also be written in one of the other forms.

$$3:12$$

$$\frac{3}{12}$$

Suppose this example had asked for the ratio of employees to the total number of people in the store. In this case, the denominator would be the total, since that is what the ratio reports. To solve this ratio, find the sum of the employees and customers to show the total number of people.

The ratio of employees to the total number of people in the store is $\frac{3}{15}$.

Like fractions, ratios can be simplified.

The ratio of employees to customers is $\frac{3}{12}$, or $\frac{1}{4}$.

The ratio of employees to customers is 3:12, or 1:4.

### Solving Problems with Ratios

Take a look at the following problem involving ratios.

In a video store, the ratio of DVDs to Blu-rays sold is 3:7. If the store sells 90 movies, how many of the movies were DVDs?

The ratio explains that for every 3 DVDs sold, the store sells 7 Blu-rays. That means that if 10 movies are sold, 3 are DVDs and 7 are Blu-rays. The fraction $\frac{3}{10}$ shows that out of 3 of 10 movies sold are DVDs. This fraction can be used to find how many DVDs were sold out of a total of 90 movies.

$$\frac{3}{10} \times 90 = \frac{270}{10} = 27$$

This tells you that of the 90 movies sold, 27 were DVDs. That means the remaining 63 movies sold were Blu-rays. Double-check the ratio again.

The ratio of DVDs to Blu-rays sold was 27:63.

$$27:63 = 3:7$$

## Proportions

A **proportion** is an equation that states that two ratios are equivalent—for example, $\frac{3}{4} = \frac{6}{8}$. In the example, $\frac{3}{4}$ and $\frac{6}{8}$ are the **terms**, or **elements**, of the proportion. One way to verify that the terms of a proportion are equal is to cross multiply. To cross multiply the terms in the example, $\frac{3}{4}$ and $\frac{6}{8}$, first multiply 3 × 8, then multiply 4 × 6. Since these products are equal, the ratios are equal. So the proportion is true.

### Solving Problems with Proportions

At times, one value in a ratio may be unknown. Solving a proportion reveals the missing value.

$$\frac{x}{15} = \frac{1}{5}$$

To find the missing value, cross multiply the terms.

$$x \times 5 = 15 \times 1$$
$$5x = 15$$

You know that $5 \times 3 = 15$, so the missing value is 3. Write the proportion using this value and make sure the ratios are equal.

$$\frac{3}{15} = \frac{1}{5}$$

These ratios are equal, so they form a proportion.

## Comparing Numbers

One way to compare numbers is to determine if one is **greater than, less than**, or **equal to** another. As you know, 10 is greater than 4. You can compare these numbers using a symbol for *greater than*.

10 is greater than 4

$$10 > 4$$

As you also know, 15 is less than 25. This can also be represented using the symbol for *less than*.

15 is less than 25

$$15 < 25$$

When two numbers are equal, use the equal sign to represent their relationship.

$$(3 + 2) = 5$$

### Keep in Mind

Keep in mind that the greater than and less than symbols open toward the larger number. Think back to when you were in elementary school, and the teacher explained that the symbol looks like an open alligator mouth eating the biggest number.

## Prime and Composite Numbers

Numbers can be classified based on how many factors they have. Numbers greater than 1 with only two distinct factors (1 and the number itself) are **prime numbers**. For example, since the only numbers that can be multiplied together to equal 5 are 1 and 5, 5 is a prime number. Take a look at the following list of prime numbers. The list could go on, but these are the prime numbers between 0 and 100. The number 1 is not included, since it is not greater than 1 and does not have two distinct factors.

**Prime Numbers Between 0 and 100**

2, 3, 5, 7, 11, 13, 17, 19, 23, 29, 31, 37, 41, 43, 47, 53, 59, 61, 67, 71, 73, 79, 83, 89, 97

Notice that the only even prime number is 2. 2 has only 1 and 2 as its factors, but all other even numbers also have 2 as a factor, so they are not prime. Numbers that are not prime are called composite numbers.

**Composite numbers** have more than two factors. For example, the factors of 10 are 1, 2, 5, and 10. So 10 is a composite number. To determine whether a number is prime or composite, determine whether it is divisible by another number. Remember, all even numbers are divisible by 2. All numbers with a 5 in the ones place are divisible by 5. And all numbers with a 0 in the ones place are divisible by 10. Another trick is that all numbers whose digits have a sum that is a multiple of 3 are divisible by 3. Likewise, all numbers whose digits have a sum that is a multiple of 9 are divisible by 9. These tricks will not help you determine whether every single number is prime or composite, but they will at least give you a starting point.

3,574 is even, so it is divisible by 2.

495 has a 5 in the ones place, so it is divisible by 5.

29,470 has a 0 in the ones place, so it is divisible by 10.

474 is divisible by 3 because the sum of its digits (4 + 7 + 4) is 15, which is a multiple of 3.

657 is divisible by 9 because the sum of its digits (6 + 5 + 7) is 18, which is a multiple of 9.

## Greatest Common Factor

The largest number that is a factor of two or more given numbers is known as the **greatest common factor** (GCF). To find the GCF, list all the prime numbers that are factors of each number. Then identify which factors are common to both numbers and multiply these factors.

What is the greatest common factor of 30 and 75?

First, list the prime factors of each:

Prime factors of 30: $2 \times 3 \times 5$
Prime factors of 75: $3 \times 5 \times 5$

Second, identify the factors they have in common:

Prime factors of 30: $2 \times \underline{3} \times \underline{5}$
Prime factors of 75: $\underline{3} \times \underline{5} \times 5$

Third, multiply the factors they have in common:

$$3 \times 5 = 15$$

The greatest common factor of 30 and 75 is 15. In other words, the largest number that is a factor of both 30 and 75 is 15.

## Lowest Common Multiple

**Multiples** are numbers that can be evenly divided by a particular number. For example, 5, 10, 15, 20, and 25 are all multiples of 5 because they can be evenly divided by 5.

What numbers are multiples of 7?
7, 14, 21, 28, 35, 42 . . .

A **common multiple** is a multiple that two or more numbers have in common. For example, 36 is a common multiple of both 4 and 6, since it is evenly divisible by both of these numbers.

The **lowest common multiple**, also known as the least common multiple (LCM), is the lowest number that is a common multiple of two or more numbers. To find the lowest common multiple, list the multiples of each number. Then find the lowest number that appears on both lists.

What is the lowest common multiple of 8 and 12?
Multiples of 8: 8, 16, <u>24</u>, 32, 40, 48, 64, 72, 80, 88, 96 . . .
Multiples of 12: 12, <u>24</u>, 36, 48, 60, 72, 84, 96, 108, 120 . . .

Since 24 is the lowest number that is common to both sets of multiples, it is the LCM of 8 and 12.

---

**Keep in Mind**

Keep in mind that two numbers may have several common multiples. For example, 48 and 96 are also common multiples of 8 and 12. However, the LCM is the lowest number that is a common multiple of both.

---

# Examples

Here are two sample questions dealing with number relationships.

1. **On his third math quiz of the semester, Cooper answered 28 questions correctly and got 7 answers wrong. What is the ratio of the number of questions he got right on the quiz to the total number of questions?**

   A   1:4
   B   1:5
   C   4:1
   D   4:5
   E   5:4

### Explanation

Read the problem and determine what is being asked. What is the ratio of correct answers to the number of questions on the quiz? Identify pertinent information. The phrases *answered 28 questions correctly, 7 answers wrong,* and *ratio of the number of questions he got right . . . to the total number of questions* are important. Choose which operations to use. First, find the total number of correct answers and then find the total number of questions. Write these numbers as a ratio and simplify the ratio. Solve the problem.

> Number of correct answers: 28
> Total number of questions: $28 + 7 = 35$
> $28:35 = 4:5$

Check your work and select the correct answer. **The answer is D**.

2.  **What is the lowest common multiple of 16 and 40?**
    A   640
    B   160
    C   80
    D   8
    E   4

### Explanation

Read the problem and determine what is being asked. What is the lowest common multiple of 16 and 40? Identify pertinent information. The phrase *lowest common multiple* and the numbers 16 and 40 are important. Choose which operations to use. First, write out the first few multiples of 16 and then write out the first few multiples of 40. Keep going until you find one they have in common. Solve the problem.

> Multiples of 16: 16, 32, 48, 64, 80 . . .
> Multiples of 40: 40, 80 . . .
> Least common multiple = 80

Check your work and select the correct answer. **The answer is C**.

# NUMBER RELATIONSHIP DRILLS

1.  **If 3 pens cost $.80, what do 12 pens cost?**
    A   $3.20
    B   $4.80
    C   $6.40
    D   $8.00
    E   $9.60

2. The Espinol family paid a handyman $930 for 60 hours of work on their rental property. At this rate, what would they pay him for 24 hours of work on their home?

    A   $154
    B   $155
    C   $362.50
    D   $372
    E   $387.50

3. What is the greatest common factor of 56 and 84?

    A   7
    B   14
    C   28
    D   168
    E   336

4. A movie theater sold 112 student tickets and 144 adult tickets to a matinee showing of a newly released film. Which of the following is equal to the ratio of student to adult tickets sold?

    A   7:9
    B   7:16
    C   9:7
    D   9:16
    E   16:9

5. The ratio of men to women at a business conference was 3:7. How many women attended the seminar if there were a total of 420 men in attendance?

    A   840
    B   980
    C   1,260
    D   2,520
    E   2,940

6. What is the lowest common multiple of 18 and 45?

    A   3
    B   9
    C   90
    D   180
    E   810

7. Which correctly compares the greatest prime number less than 50 and the greatest composite number less than 50?

   A   47 < 48

   B   47 < 49

   C   47 > 49

   D   48 < 49

   E   48 > 49

8. The art museum will earn $6.75 for every $10 raised during a fund-raising auction. Which shows the ratio of the proceeds the museum will keep to the total amount raised?

   A   13:27

   B   13:40

   C   27:40

   D   27:67

   E   40:67

9. What is the sum of the greatest prime factor of 60 and the least prime factor of 18?

   A   7

   B   6

   C   5

   D   4

   E   3

10. If a paint mixture is 3 parts blue, 1 part white, and 2 parts green, how much green paint will be needed to make 18 gallons of the mixture?

   A   1

   B   2

   C   3

   D   5

   E   6

Answers are on pages 724–725.

# 32 Measurement/ Geometry: Measurements

**T**hink about the numbers you use every day. The half-gallon of milk in the fridge, the 10-pound dumbbells you lifted in the gym, and the three miles you drove to work. All of these involve measurement. Some of the questions on the *HiSET*® Exam Mathematics test will involve measurement too.

This chapter will review both standard and metric units of measure, as well as conversions within each system, and will review measurements used for length, weight, capacity, and time.

## What Is Tested?

### Standard Units

In the United States, the measurements we use most commonly are known as **standard units**, which may also be referred to as **customary units**. These include inches, feet, ounces, cups, pounds, and gallons. You should learn the standard units of measure and understand how they relate to one another.

#### Length

To measure length or distance with standard units, use **inches**, **feet**, **yards**, and **miles**.

> 12 inches = 1 foot
> 3 feet = 1 yard
> 1,760 yards = 1 mile
> 5,280 feet = 1 mile

#### Capacity

Capacity measures volume, or how much something can hold. Measure capacity using **ounces, cups, pints, quarts**, and **gallons**.

> 8 ounces = 1 cup
> 2 cups = 1 pint
> 2 pints = 1 quart
> 4 quarts = 1 gallon

**Keep in Mind**

> Keep in mind that measurement conversions might not be listed on the test. That means you will need to memorize how many ounces in a cup, how many yards in a mile, and the other common conversions given in this section.

### Weight

Weight measures mass. The standard units used to measure weight are **ounces**, **pounds**, and **tons**.

16 ounces = 1 pound
2,000 pounds = 1 ton

### Time

The standard units of time are **seconds**, **minutes**, **hours**, **days**, **weeks**, **months**, and **years**.

60 seconds = 1 minute
60 minutes = 1 hour
24 hours = 1 day
7 days = 1 week
52 weeks = 1 year
12 months = 1 year
365 days = 1 year

## Converting Standard Units

Converting units means to change from one unit of measure to another. For example, to find out how many ounces are in 2 pounds, you would use conversion. To find how many feet are in 10 miles, you would use conversion.

To convert a large unit to a smaller unit, multiply by the number of small units in the larger unit.

Convert 6 feet into inches.

Since feet are larger than inches, multiply the number of inches in one foot by the number of feet.

6 feet = 6 × 12 inches
6 feet = 72 inches

To convert a smaller unit to a larger unit, divide by the number of small units in the larger unit.

Convert 56 ounces into cups.

Since ounces are smaller than cups, divide the number of ounces by the number of ounces in one cup.

56 ounces ÷ 8 ounces = 7 cups

## Operations with Measurement

At times, it is necessary to add, subtract, multiply, or divide measurements.

### Addition

To add measurements, first add the like units. Then convert the units to the simplest form.
Add 4 pounds 12 ounces and 5 pounds 9 ounces.

$$
\begin{array}{r}
4 \text{ pounds } 12 \text{ ounces} \\
+\,5 \text{ pounds } \phantom{0}9 \text{ ounces} \\
\hline
9 \text{ pounds } 23 \text{ ounces}
\end{array}
$$

Now convert 23 ounces to pounds.

$23 \div 16 = 1$ pound 7 ounces

Write the sum of the weights in the simplest form.

9 pounds 23 ounces = 9 pounds + 1 pound 7 ounces = 10 pounds 7 ounces

### Subtraction

To subtract measurements, subtract the like units, regrouping as needed. Then convert the units to the simplest form.
Subtract 3 feet 10 inches from 5 feet 7 inches.

$$
\begin{array}{r}
5 \text{ feet } \phantom{0}7 \text{ inches} \\
-\,3 \text{ feet } 10 \text{ inches}
\end{array}
$$

Since you cannot subtract 10 inches from 7 inches, regroup one foot into inches.

5 feet 7 inches = 4 feet 19 inches

Now subtract like units.

$$
\begin{array}{r}
4 \text{ feet } 19 \text{ inches} \\
-\,3 \text{ feet } 10 \text{ inches} \\
\hline
1 \text{ foot } \phantom{0}9 \text{ inches}
\end{array}
$$

### Multiplication

To multiply measurements, multiply each unit and then convert the units to the simplest form.
Multiply $4\frac{3}{4}$ cups by 5.

$$
\begin{array}{r}
4 \text{ cups } \phantom{0}6 \text{ ounces} \\
\times\,5 \\
\hline
20 \text{ cups } 30 \text{ ounces}
\end{array}
$$

Now convert 30 ounces to cups, since this would be the simplest form.

30 ounces $\div$ 8 ounces = 3 cups 6 ounces

Write the answer in the simplest form.

20 cups 30 ounces = 20 cups + 3 cups 6 ounces = 23 cups 6 ounces

## Division

To divide measurements, it is easiest to convert everything to the same unit of measure and then divide. For example, to divide 7 pounds 8 ounces by 6, you could either convert the measurement entirely to pounds or entirely to ounces. Remember, 1 pound is 16 ounces. That means in this case it would be pretty ease to convert to pounds, because 7 pounds 8 ounces could also be called 7.5 pounds. Usually it is easier to break everything down into the smallest common unit of measure. Since 16 ounces are in a pound, that means 7 pounds is 7 times 16, or 112. Then add 8 to 112. So 7 pounds 8 ounces converts to 120 ounces total.

Divide 7 pounds 8 ounces by 6.

$$7 \times 16 = 112$$
$$112 + 8 = 120$$

$$
\begin{array}{r}
20 \\
6\overline{)120} \text{ ounces} \\
-12 \\
\hline
00 \\
-0 \\
\hline
0
\end{array}
$$

The correct answer is 20 ounces.

## Metric Units

Metric units are a decimal-based measuring system that works in powers of 10; each unit of measure is 10 times larger than the next smaller unit of measure and 10 times smaller than the next larger unit of measure. Take a centimeter for example. A centimeter (which means one hundredth of a meter, by the way) is larger than a millimeter, the next smallest unit of measure for length. How much larger? Ten times larger. There are 10 millimeters in every centimeter. The next largest unit of measure of length after a centimeter is a decimeter (which means one-tenth of a meter). How much larger is a decimeter than a centimeter? Ten times larger. There are 10 centimeters in a decimeter. Here are the most common units of metric measurement.

## Length

**Meters** are used to measure length or distance with metric units. One meter is slightly longer than one yard.

1 meter = about 39 inches

## Capacity

**Liters** are used to measure liquid capacity. One liter is slightly larger than one quart.

1 liter = a little more than 1 quart

## Weight

**Grams** are very small units that are used to measure weight. A paper clip weighs approximately 1 gram.

28 grams = 1 ounce

## Meters, Liters, and Grams

Metric measurement is based on meters, liters, and grams. Prefixes attached to each of these units tell how many. Take a look at the list of prefixes.

**Kilo** (k) = 1,000 of the base unit
**Hecto** (h) = 100 of the base unit
**Deka** (dk) = 10 of the base unit

Base unit (meter, liter, gram)

**Deci** (d) = $\frac{1}{10}$ of the base unit

**Centi** (c) = $\frac{1}{100}$ of the base unit

**Milli** (m) = $\frac{1}{1,000}$ of the base unit

Take a look at the value associated with each prefix. Kilo, for example, is 1,000. That means, when this prefix is added to a unit, such as a meter, the unit is multiplied by 1,000. So a kilometer is the same as 1,000 meters. A centimeter is $\frac{1}{100}$ of a meter.

1 kilometer = 1,000 meters
1 meter = 100 centimeters
1 kilogram = 1,000 grams
1 liter = 1,000 milliliters

## Converting Metric Measurements

Converting metric measurements involves moving a decimal point. The key to converting metric measurements is knowing how many places—and in which direction—to move the decimal. Converting larger units to smaller units is the same as multiplying by 10; converting smaller units to larger units is the same as dividing by 10.

To change from a larger unit to a smaller one, move the decimal point to the right. To change from a smaller unit to a larger one, move the decimal point to the left.

Take a look at the following chart.

| kilo | hecto | deka | Unit (meter, liter, gram) | deci | centi | milli |
|------|-------|------|---------------------------|------|-------|-------|

Find the prefix of the original unit, then count how many places to move to get to the new unit. Move the decimal point that number of spaces in the same direction.

Convert 1,500 centimeters to meters.

Start at *centi* on the chart, since the original unit is centimeters. Count the number of spaces to the new unit, which is *meters*.

| kilo | hecto | deka | Unit (meter, liter, gram) | deci | **centi** | milli |
|------|-------|------|---------------------------|------|-----------|-------|

Since moving from centimeters to meters involves moving two spaces to the left, move the decimal point two places to the left.

1,500 cm = 15 meters

Another way to convert the base units to other metric units is to use multiplication. Take another look at the chart shown earlier.

**Kilo** (k) = 1,000 of the base unit
**Hecto** (h) = 100 of the base unit
**Deka** (dk) = 10 of the base unit

Base unit (meter, liter, gram)

**Deci** (d) $= \dfrac{1}{10}$ of the base unit

**Centi** (c) $= \dfrac{1}{100}$ of the base unit

**Milli** (m) $= \dfrac{1}{1000}$ of the base unit

Convert 5 liters to milliliters.

According to the chart, one milliliter is $\dfrac{1}{1,000}$ of a meter, so to change from the larger unit to the smaller one, multiply by 1,000.

$$5 \times 1,000 = 5,000$$
$$5 \text{ L} = 5,000 \text{ mL}$$

# Examples

Here are two sample measurement questions.

1.  **The entrance to the offices of WINK, Inc. is 660 feet from the mailbox at the corner post office. What fraction of a mile is the front door from the mailbox?**

    A  $\dfrac{1}{2}$

    B  $\dfrac{1}{4}$

    C  $\dfrac{1}{8}$

    D  $\dfrac{1}{12}$

    E  $\dfrac{3}{4}$

### Explanation

Read the problem and determine what is being asked. What fraction of a mile is 660 feet? Identify the pertinent information. Underline *660 feet* and *fraction of a mile*. Choose which operations to use. Divide 660 by the total number of feet in a mile. Then convert the answer to a fraction. Solve the problem:

$$660 \text{ feet} \div 5{,}280 = 0.125$$

$$0.125 = \frac{12.5}{100} = \frac{1}{8}$$

Check your work and select the correct answer. **The answer is C.**

2. **Mrs. Chen cooked a beef roast weighing 3.5 kilograms. Her family ate a total of 750 grams of the roast for dinner, and she used 300 grams of the roast to make sandwiches the next day. What is the weight of the remaining roast, in grams?**

   A   3,500
   B   3,350
   C   3,200
   D   2,750
   E   2,450

### Explanation

Read the problem and determine what is being asked. How many grams of roast are left? Identify the pertinent information. Underline *3.5 kilograms*, *750 grams*, and *300 grams*. Choose which operations to use. Convert 3.5 kilograms into grams. Subtract 750 grams and 300 grams. Solve the problem:

1 kilogram = 1,000 grams, so 3.5 kilograms = 3,500 grams.
3,500 − 750 − 300 = 2,450.

Check your work and select the correct answer. **The answer is E.**

# MEASUREMENT DRILLS

1. **There are 1,200 students at Woodland Hills Elementary. Approximately 600 of the students take the bus home. 50% of the students that do not take the bus ride their bicycles home. Approximately how many students ride their bicycles home?**

   A   100
   B   200
   C   300
   D   400
   E   500

2. The length of the sign in front of Dr. Decker's office is 75 inches. What is the length of the sign in feet?

   A   6.25

   B   6.5

   C   6.75

   D   7.25

   E   7.5

3. Omar bought apples weighing a total of 88 ounces. The cost of the apples was $1.90 per pound. How much did he pay for the apples?

   A   $9.28

   B   $10.45

   C   $13.93

   D   $16.72

   E   $20.90

4. A punch recipe calls for 750 milliliters of pineapple juice, 875 milliliters of cranberry juice, 625 milliliters of orange juice, and 3 liters of ginger ale. How many liters of punch will the recipe make?

   A   2.25

   B   2.55

   C   3.25

   D   5.25

   E   5.75

5. Wade spent 2 hours watching a movie on TV. During that time, there were 42 minutes of commercials. What percent of the time did Wade spend watching commercials?

   A   17.5 percent

   B   21 percent

   C   24 percent

   D   28.5 percent

   E   35 percent

6. To paint the interior of his house, William bought 3 gallons of yellow paint, 2 quarts of tan paint, and 3 quarts of white paint. He used a total of 7 quarts to paint the bedrooms. How much paint does he have left?

   A   1 gallon 1 quart

   B   1 gallon 3 quarts

   C   2 gallons 1 quart

   D   2 gallons 2 quarts

   E   2 gallons 3 quarts

7. The length of a map in Camille's geography book is 12 centimeters. What is the length of the map in millimeters?

A   0.12 mm

B   1.2 mm

C   120 mm

D   1,200 mm

E   12,000 mm

8. To make each costume for a play, a seamstress uses 3 yards 10 inches of fabric. How much fabric will she use to make 9 identical costumes?

A   27 yards 10 inches

B   27 yards 19 inches

C   28.75 yards

D   29.5 yards

E   30 yards

9. If 12 inches equals 1 foot, how many inches are there in 7.5 feet?

A   92

B   90

C   84

D   42

E   19

10. A painting on a wall is 36 inches tall. There are 42 inches below the bottom of the painting and 66 inches above the top of the painting? How many feet tall is the wall? (12 inches = 1 foot)

A   3

B   8

C   12

D   14.4

E   144

Answers are on page 725.

# 33 Measurement/ Geometry: Geometry

**G**eometry is the area of math that deals with lines, angles, and shapes. Not only will you need to recognize each of these, but you will also need to understand how they relate to one another and how to measure various aspects of them. This chapter will review the geometry skills you will need for the *HiSET*® Exam Mathematics test.

## What Is Tested?

### Lines

A **point** is a specific location in space and has no length or width. In geometry, points are labeled with letters. A **line** is a collection of points that continues forever in both directions. It is often labeled by naming two of the points through which it passes.

Notice that the ends of the lines contain arrows. This shows that the line continues in both directions. Since this line passes through point A and point B, it can be named line AB, or simply $\overleftrightarrow{AB}$. It can also be named line $k$, because of the label at the end of the line.

### Line Segments

**Line segments** have two definite endpoints. The ends of a line segment are indicated with a point.

J _____ K

This is line segment JK, or simply $\overline{JK}$.

## Rays

A **ray** has a specific beginning point and continues indefinitely in the opposite direction. The beginning is indicated by a point, and the other end has an arrow, showing that it continues forever in that direction, as shown in ray XY, or $\overrightarrow{XY}$.

## Parallel Lines

Lines that are **parallel** remain the same distance apart at all points. In other words, they never cross.

_____

_____

## Intersecting Lines

**Intersecting lines** cross at a common point.

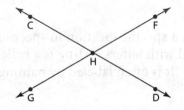

In the drawing, line CD and line FG intersect at point H.

## Perpendicular Lines

**Perpendicular lines** intersect to form a 90-degree angle, which is the shape of the letter L. In the following example, lines QR and ST are perpendicular.

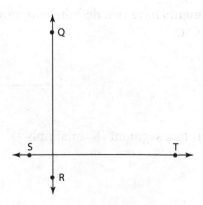

## Angles

An **angle** is formed when two lines, line segments, or rays intersect. The point of intersection is called the **vertex**. Take a look at the following angle.

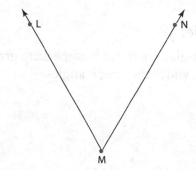

Rays ML and MN intersect at point M, so point M is the vertex. This can be labeled angle LMN or angle M. Using the symbol for angles, it would be ∠LMN or ∠M.

Angles are measured in degrees. A circle measures 360 degrees, and angles are measured according to which portion of a circle they represent. For example, a straight line is 180 degrees, since it would be half of a circle. A quarter of a circle is a 90-degree angle.

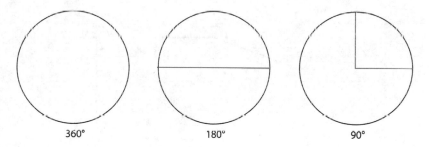

360°          180°          90°

## Right Angles

A 90-degree angle, which is the shape of the letter L, is called a **right angle**. The small square symbol indicates that the angle measures 90 degrees.

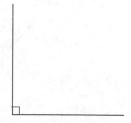

### Acute Angles

**Acute angles** are those that measure less than 90 degrees. Notice that an acute angle is narrower than a right angle.

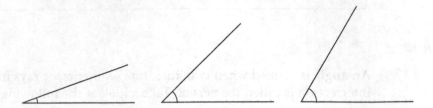

### Obtuse Angles

**Obtuse angles** are those that measure greater than 90 degrees. Notice that obtuse angles are wider than right angles.

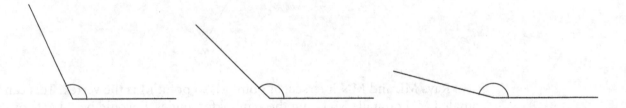

### Reflex Angles

**Reflex angles** are those whose measures are greater than 180 degrees. In other words, they are greater than a straight line.

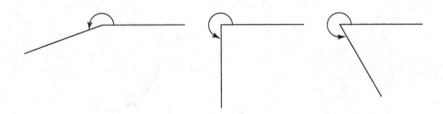

### Adjacent Angles

Angles that share a common side are **adjacent angles**. In the following figure, angles M and N are adjacent.

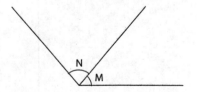

## Complementary Angles

Angles are **complementary** when their sum equals 90 degrees, meaning that when the two angles are put together, they create a right angle. Take a look at the following complementary angles. Angle A measures 20 degrees, and angle B measures 70 degrees. Since 20 + 70 = 90, these angles are complementary.

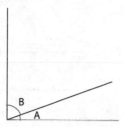

## Supplementary Angles

Angles are **supplementary** when their sum equals 180 degrees, meaning that when the two angles are put together, they create a straight line. Take a look at the following supplementary angles. Angle C measures 145 degrees and angle D measures 35 degrees. Since 145 + 35 = 180, these angles are supplementary.

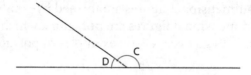

## Vertical Angles

When two lines intersect, they form angles. The angles that are opposite each other are **vertical angles**. They have equal measurements.

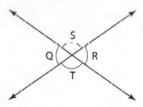

In this example, angle Q and angle R are vertical angles. Both of them measure 70 degrees. Likewise, angles S and T are vertical, because they both measure 110 degrees.

### Corresponding Angles

Two angles that are in the same relative position are called **corresponding angles** and have equal measurements. Suppose a pair of parallel lines is cut by a third line, known as a **transversal**. The angles that are in the same position relative to the transversal are corresponding.

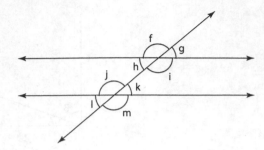

In this figure, angles f and i are corresponding, since they are in the same position relative to the transversal. Thus, they have equal measurements. Likewise, angles g and k are corresponding, as are angles h and j.

## Two-Dimensional Figures

Two-dimensional figures are formed by combining points, lines, and angles. Many two-dimensional figures are **polygons**, which are closed geometric figures with straight sides. Let's go over several examples of polygons.

### Triangles

**Triangles** are polygons with three sides and three angles. The sum of the interior angles of any triangle is 180 degrees.

An **equilateral triangle** has three equal sides and three angles measuring 60 degrees each. The little line across each side indicates that the lengths of the sides are equal.

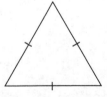

An **isosceles triangle** has two equal sides and two equal angles.

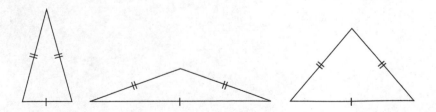

A **scalene triangle** has no equal sides and no equal angles.

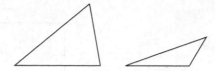

**Right triangles** have one right angle. The side opposite the right angle is called the **hypotenuse**. It is the longest side of the triangle.

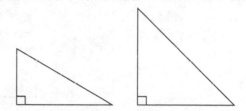

All angles of an **acute triangle** are less than 90 degrees. Equilateral triangles are acute since all of the angles measure 60 degrees.

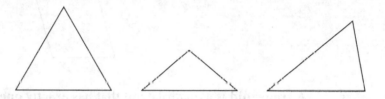

An **obtuse triangle** has one obtuse angle.

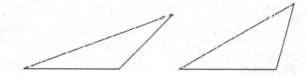

## Quadrilaterals

Polygons with four sides and four angles are **quadrilaterals**. The sum of the interior angles of any quadrilateral is 360 degrees. Let's review a few examples.

A **parallelogram** is a quadrilateral that has opposite parallel sides and opposite equal angles.

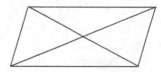

A **rectangle** is a quadrilateral with equal opposite sides and four right angles. Rectangles are a type of parallelogram.

A **square** is a quadrilateral with four equal sides and four right angles. Squares are examples of both rectangles and parallelograms.

A **rhombus** is a quadrilateral with four equal sides. Since a square also has four equal sides, it is an example of a rhombus.

A **trapezoid** is a quadrilateral that has exactly one pair of parallel sides.

## Other Polygons

Triangles and quadrilaterals are the most common types of polygons found on the HiSET Exam Mathematics test; however, there are a few others with which you should be familiar. Polygons with five sides and five angles are **pentagons**. Those with six sides and angles are **hexagons**, and those with eight are **octagons**.

Pentagon        Hexagon        Octagon

## Circles

**Circles** are also two-dimensional figures, but unlike triangles and quadrilaterals, they are not polygons because they have no straight sides. By definition, a circle is a plane figure with all points an equal distance from the center.

The distance from the center to any point on the circle is the **radius**. The **distance from one side of the circle to the other, passing through the center, is the **diameter**. Take a look at the following circles. Line segment AB is a radius; line segment CD is a diameter. The diameter is twice the length of the radius.

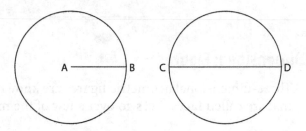

## Similarity and Congruence

Figures that are the same shape but different sizes are **similar**. Take a look at the following right triangles. The corresponding angles, or those in the same positions, have the same measurements. The second triangle is smaller than the first; however, the lengths of the sides are proportional. These are examples of similar figures.

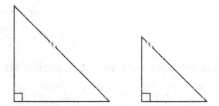

The corresponding sides of the figures can be written as a proportion to determine unknown measurements.

Figures that are the same shape and the same size are **congruent**. Since the following parallelograms have equal angle measurements and equal side lengths, they are congruent.

The figures may be turned in different directions and still be congruent.

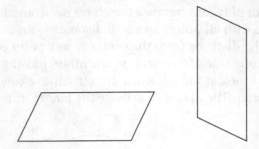

## Three-Dimensional Figures

Three-dimensional geometric figures are known as **solids**. Some solids have flat sides that are called **faces**. Let's go over a few of the most common geometric solids.

### Rectangular Solid

A **rectangular solid** has six faces, each in the shape of a rectangle. A shoe box is an example of a rectangular solid.

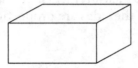

### Cube

A **cube** has six square faces, all of which are equal. A six-sided die is an example of this solid.

### Square Pyramid

A **square pyramid** has a base in the shape of a square and four triangle-shaped faces.

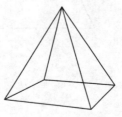

## Cylinder

A **cylinder** has two parallel bases, both of which are circles. The curved sides are perpendicular to the bases. A soup can is an example of a cylinder.

## Cone

A **cone** has one circular base; the sides are formed by a curved surface that connects to the vertex. As you can see, an ice cream cone and a pointed birthday hat are examples of cones.

# Examples

Here are two sample geometry questions.
Look at the diagram below.

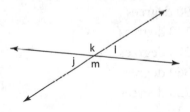

1. **The measure of angle _j_ is 37.5 degrees. What is the measure of angle _k_?**

   A  37.5 degrees

   B  52.5 degrees

   C  142.5 degrees

   D  152.5 degrees

   E  322.5 degrees

### Explanation

Read the problem and determine what is being asked. What is the measure of the supplementary angle? Identify the pertinent information. The measure of angle $j$ is 37.5 degrees. Since you need to know the location of angles $j$ and $k$ on the diagram, circle both of these. Choose which operations to use. To find supplementary angles, subtract the measure of angle $j$ from 180. Solve the problem:

$$180 - 37.5 = 142.5 \text{ degrees}$$

Check your work and select the correct answer. **The answer is C.**

2. **A right triangle has one angle that measures 63 degrees. What is the measure of the third angle?**

    A   27
    B   54
    C   63
    D   117
    E   207

### Explanation

Read the problem and determine what is being asked. What is the measure of the third angle? Identify the pertinent information. The measure of one angle is 63 degrees. Underline *right triangle*. Choose which operations to use. Angles of a right triangle must add up to 180 degrees, so subtract the measure of the right angle and the 63 degree angle from 180. Solve the problem:

$$180 - 90 - 63 = 27 \text{ degrees}$$

Check your work and select the correct answer. **The answer is A.**

# GEOMETRY DRILLS

1. **What is the sum of the interior angles of a hexagon?**

    A   90 degrees
    B   180 degrees
    C   270 degrees
    D   360 degrees
    E   720 degrees

2. **What is the complement of a 75-degree angle?**

    A   15 degrees
    B   75 degrees
    C   90 degrees
    D   165 degrees
    E   285 degrees

3. The measure of ∠Y is 60 degrees. If ∠Z and ∠Y are vertical angles, what is the measure of ∠Z?

A   30 degrees

B   60 degrees

C   90 degrees

D   120 degrees

E   180 degrees

4. Look at the illustration. The measure of ∠c is 65 degrees.

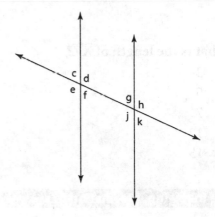

**Which is true?**

A   ∠d = 65 degrees

B   ∠h = 65 degrees

C   ∠j = 115 degrees

D   ∠k = 115 degrees

E   ∠e = 125 degrees

5. The design on Sean's business cards is a parallelogram.

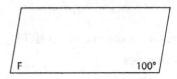

**What is the measure of angle F?**

A   40 degrees

B   80 degrees

C   90 degrees

D   100 degrees

E   260 degrees

6. The two sails on Michael's boat are similar triangles, as shown below.

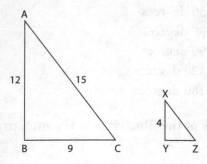

What is the length of $\overline{XZ}$?

A   3

B   5

C   7

D   12

E   15

**Use the following information to answer questions 7 and 8.**

In the figure shown, line segment ST is a diameter of the circle, and line segment QR is a radius. Line segment RU is also a radius. The measure of $\angle QRS$ is 62 degrees.

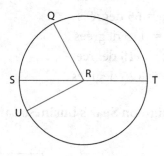

7. What is the measure of $\angle QRT$?

A   28 degrees

B   90 degrees

C   118 degrees

D   128 degrees

E   180 degrees

8. In the diagram, ∠QRU is a right angle. What is the measure of ∠SRU?

    A   118 degrees

    B   90 degrees

    C   31 degrees

    D   28 degrees

    E   18 degrees

9. New hardwood floors are to be laid in a rectangular closet that is 5 feet by 8 feet. The wood costs $3.40 per square foot. How much will the wood for the closet cost?

    A   $11.76

    B   $44.20

    C   $136.00

    D   $283.40

    E   $417.00

10. Which polygon has exactly eight sides?

    A   Hexagon

    B   Quadrilateral

    C   Octagon

    D   Pentagon

    E   Heptagon

Answers are on page 725.

# 34 Data Analysis/ Probability/ Statistics: Statistics

**Y**ou have probably read research involving facts and figures, such as the average wingspan of a bald eagle is between 80 and 90 inches, or the median income in Dover, Massachusetts, is more than $143,000 per year. Facts and figures such as these fall under the mathematical category of **statistics**, which deals with analyzing and interpreting numerical data based on samples and populations.

This chapter will review the definitions and skills you will need to know to answer the statistics and data analysis questions on the *HiSET*® Exam Mathematics test. As with other types of questions, you will need to apply some of the other mathematical skills you have learned in order to answer these questions. If necessary, review whole numbers, operations, estimation, and decimals. These topics are important to your understanding of statistics.

## What Is Tested?

### Population

A **population** is an entire group of people or objects about which data is considered. To generalize about a specific population, a sample is often collected or surveyed—for example, all trees in a particular forest, all male students attending a certain university, all employees of a given company, or all residents of the United States.

### Sample

A **sample** is a smaller group selected from the population. A sample is used when the population is too large to study every single element. For example, to determine the average age of the residents of a given city, *some* of the people's ages are recorded and analyzed. It would be difficult and time-consuming, if it were even possible, to record this information for every single resident. The portion of the population about which data are collected is the *sample*. The entire group, which would include every resident of the city, is the *population*. For a study to be accurate, the sample should be representative of the general population.

### Random Sample

A **random sample** is often the best way to ensure that a study represents the general population, although there are many problems with random sampling, especially if the sample is small. A random sample is a sample in which every individual or object from the general population has an equal chance of being selected.

### Biased

A sample is considered to be **biased** if some members of the populations are not represented or if certain members are more likely to be represented. Suppose you wanted to find out how the student population in a high school feels about increasing the budget for the music program. If only band members were surveyed, the sample would be biased, since it would not represent the entire school population.

### Unbiased

A sample is considered to be **unbiased** if every member of the population has been chosen on characteristics not based on their inherent characteristics. For example, a woman cannot be chosen simply because she is a woman or a child because he is a child. This may not seem much different from a random sample, but it is. Think of it this way: surveyors trying for an unbiased sample make an *effort* not to consider given qualities. In the example about the budget for the school music program, an unbiased sample would include some members of the band, some students who are involved in the sports program, and some students who are not involved in any after-school activities.

## Range

The **range** of a set of data is the difference between the highest and lowest values in the set. Suppose your math quiz scores this semester were 100 percent, 92 percent, 87 percent, and 98 percent. The highest score is 100 percent, and the lowest is 87 percent. The difference between these scores is 13, since $100 - 87 = 13$. The range of your quiz scores is 13.

## Outlier

An **outlier** is a data value that stands out from the rest of the set. Such values can affect measures of central tendency. For example, suppose you wanted to find the average test score of the students in your math class. Fifteen of the students scored between 85 percent and 95 percent on the test; one student scored a 37 percent. This score is an outlier. Including it in a report of the average test score would significantly lower the class average.

## Measures of Central Tendency

**Measures of central tendency** are at the heart of statistics. Basically, these are different ways to report the values at the center of a set of data. These measures include *mean*, *median*, and *mode*.

## Mean

When you think about the average of a set of data, you are generally referring to the arithmetic **mean**. To find the mean, add the values in a set of data and divide the sum by the number of addends.

Example: The ages of the people living in Jaqueline's house are 17, 12, 47, 50, and 14.

What is the mean age of the members of her household?
To find the mean, first find the sum of the numbers.

$$17 + 12 + 47 + 50 + 14 = 140$$

Next, divide the sum, 140, by the number of values in the set. Since there are five ages, divide the total by 5.

$$140 \div 5 = 28$$

The mean age in Jaqueline's household is 28. Notice that no one in her house is actually 28 years old. The mean may or may not be one of the values in the data set.

## Median

The **median** is the number in the middle of a set of data. To determine the median, first arrange the data in order from least to greatest. Then find the value in the middle of the list.

Pablo checked out five books from the public library for a research report. The numbers of pages in the books were 147, 653, 812, 92, and 281. What is the median number of pages in the books?

Begin by listing the values in order from least to greatest.

92, 147, 281, 653, 812

Find the number in the middle of the list.

92, 147, 281, 653, 812

There are five values, so the third value is in the middle. That means the median of the set is 281.

Finding the median value in a set containing an odd number of items is fairly simple. If the set contains an even number, arrange the items in order from least to greatest, identify the two values in the middle of the set, add them together, and divide by two.

Find the median of the following set of data.

73, 10, 82, 141, 155, 26

First, list the values in order from least to greatest.

10, 26, 73, 82, 141, 155

Now, since there is an even number of values, identify which two are in the middle of the list.

10, 26, 73, 82, 141, 155

Add these numbers together and divide the sum by 2.

$$73 + 82 = 155$$
$$155 \div 2 = 77.5$$

The median of the data set is 77.5. Notice that 77.5 is not one of the numbers in the set of data. When the set includes an odd number of items, the median will be one of the numbers in the set. However, when the set includes an even number of items, the median may not be included in the set.

## Mode

The **mode** is the value that appears most often in the data set. To determine the mode, look for any value that appears more than once. It may be easier to do this if you first arrange the numbers in order from least to greatest.

Over the past two weeks, Sheryl has traveled for work each day. The number of miles she drove daily is 72, 61, 25, 61, 43, 92, 84, 50, 71, 55.

What is the mode of the set of data?

First, arrange the data in order from least to greatest.

25, 43, 50, 55, 61, 61, 71, 72, 84, 92

Find any numbers that appear on the list more than once.

25, 43, 50, 55, 61, 61, 71, 72, 84, 92

Since 61 appears most frequently on the list, it is the mode of the data set.

If more than one number appears on the list more than once, the mode is the value that appears most often.

What is the mode of the following set of data?

68, 42, 30, 21, 42, 64, 21, 35, 30, 21, 40

First, arrange the numbers from least to greatest.

21, 21, 21, 30, 30, 35, 40, 42, 42, 64, 68

Identify any numbers appearing more than once in the set.

<u>21, 21, 21</u>, <u>30, 30</u>, 35, 40, <u>42, 42</u>, 64, 68

Three numbers are repeated in the set: 21, 30, and 42. Since 21 appears three times, and 30 and 42 each appear only twice, the mode of the data set is 21.

If two or more numbers appear an equal number of times, the set will have more than one mode.

What is the mode of the following set of data?

43, 80, 43, 91, 52, 43, 91, 75, 67, 91, 75

Arrange the data in order.

43, 43, 43, 52, 67, 75, 75, 80, 91, 91, 91

Now identify any numbers that are repeated.

<u>43, 43, 43</u>, 52, 67, <u>75, 75</u>, 80, <u>91, 91, 91</u>

Notice that 75 appears twice, but 43 and 91 each appear three times. Thus, this data set is bimodal, meaning it has two modes—43 and 91.

Unlike mean and median, the mode is always a number that appears in the set.

# Examples

Here are two sample questions involving statistics.

1. **Mark's power bills for the past six months have been approximately $174, $215, $183, $198, $225, and $192. What was his mean monthly payment during this time?**

   A   $195.00

   B   $197.83

   C   $199.00

   D   $201.71

   E   $202.60

## Explanation

Read the problem and determine what is being asked: What is the mean of the payment amounts listed? Identify pertinent information. You need to know the amounts of each bill: $174, $215, $183, $198, $225, and $192. You also need to understand the word *mean*. Choose which operations to use. To find the mean, add the amounts of the power bills. Then divide the sum by 6, since this is how many addends you have. Solve the problem:

$$174 + 215 + 183 + 198 + 225 + 192 = 1{,}187$$

$$1{,}187 \div 6 = \$197.83$$

Check your work and select the correct answer. **The answer is B**.

2. **Dawna runs a mile each afternoon after work. Her times for the past four days were 6 minutes 12 seconds, 5 minutes 34 seconds, 6 minutes 50 seconds, and 7 minutes 3 seconds. What is the median length of time she ran?**

   A   6 minutes 12 seconds

   B   6 minutes 19 seconds

   C   6 minutes 25 seconds

   D   6 minutes 31 seconds

   E   6 minutes 50 seconds

## Explanation

Read the problem and determine what is being asked: What is the median length of time she ran? Identify pertinent information. You need to know the times of each run. You also need to understand the word *median*. Choose which operations to use. To find the median, list the times in order. Since there are four times, add the middle two and divide by 2. Solve the problem:

5 minutes 34 seconds, 6 minutes 12 seconds, 6 minutes 50 seconds, 7 minutes 3 seconds.

The two middle times are: 6 minutes 12 seconds and 6 minutes 50 seconds. Since both are 6 minutes plus some seconds, just average the seconds.

$$12 + 50 = 62$$

62/2 = 31 seconds, so the median is 6 minutes 31 seconds.

Check your work and select the correct answer. **The answer is D**.

# STATISTICS DRILLS

**Use the following information to answer questions 1–3.**

The chart shows how many gallons of gasoline Elizabeth used each month.

| *Month* | *Gallons of Gasoline* |
|---|---|
| February | 53.5 |
| March | 48.7 |
| April | 61.9 |
| May | 54.8 |
| June | 82.3 |
| July | 45.6 |

1. **What is the mean number of gallons of gasoline Elizabeth used?**

   A 57.8
   B 54.8
   C 54.2
   D 53.5
   E 52.9

2. **What is the median of the data set?**

   A 53.5
   B 54.15
   C 54.8
   D 55
   E 61.9

3. **What is the range of the data set?**

   A 4.8
   B 7.9
   C 16.3
   D 36.7
   E 54.1

**Use the following information to answer questions 4–6.**

The winning bids at an art auction were $250, $170, $225, $185, $160, $250, $995, and $215.

4. **What was the median winning bid?**
   A  $215
   B  $220
   C  $250
   D  $172.50
   E  $306.25

5. **What is the mode of the data set?**
   A  $172.50
   B  $215
   C  $250
   D  $306.25
   E  $835

6. **What would be the result of eliminating the outlier from the data set?**
   A  The mode of the data would increase.
   B  The mean of the data would increase.
   C  The mean of the data would decrease.
   D  The median of the data would increase.
   E  The median of the data would decrease.

7. **Gary wants to conduct a survey to find out whether people feel that the restaurants in the mall's food court offer enough healthy options. Which would most likely be the best way for him to find an unbiased random sample to survey?**
   A  Ask every fifth person standing in line at the food court.
   B  Ask men shopping in the health food store in the mall.
   C  Talk with everyone currently eating in the food court.
   D  Talk with every tenth person who enters the mall.
   E  Ask women who are shopping in the mall.

8. **While shopping, Amy bought two blouses that were on sale for $18.95 each, a sweater for $25.70, and three T-shirts for $12.50 each. What is the mean price she paid for each item?**
   A  $12.50
   B  $13.20
   C  $15.73
   D  $16.85
   E  $19.05

| Number of Students | Test Score |
|---|---|
| 2 | 100 |
| 3 | 90 |
| 3 | 80 |
| 1 | 55 |

9. **What is the mean of the test scores?**

   A   85

   B   84.75

   C   83

   D   82

   E   81.25

10. **What would be the mean if the outlier were excluded?**

   A   90

   B   88.75

   C   87

   D   85

   E   81.25

**Answers are on page 725.**

# 35 Data Analysis/ Probability/ Statistics: Probability

Determining the likelihood of a given event occurring is the basis of probability. Whether you realize it or not, you likely use probability on a regular basis. When you flip a coin to see who picks up the check at dinner, buy a lottery ticket, or enter your name in a drawing for a prize, you are dealing with probability.

Some of the questions on the *HiSET*® Exam Mathematics test will address probability. This chapter will review definitions and strategies that you will need to succeed on the Mathematics test.

## What Is Tested?

**Probability** is the chance of something happening. An event that is guaranteed to take place is **certain**. For example, it is certain that the Earth will continue to revolve around the sun all day today. On the other hand, an event that has no chance of happening is **impossible**. For example, there is no way the sun will rotate around the Earth tomorrow. This event is impossible.

A few other definitions will also be helpful in understanding probability.

### Experiment

You probably did science experiments starting in grade school. Math involves experiments too. When dealing with probability, an **experiment** is a controlled, repeatable situation that involves probability or chance.

Rolling a die, flipping a coin, or drawing a name from a hat are examples of experiments. Each is a situation of chance. When rolling a die, there is a chance of rolling a 1. There is also an equal chance of rolling a 2, 3, 4, 5, or 6.

### Event

In probability, an **event** is the set of all possible outcomes for which a probability is assigned. Suppose you wanted to roll a 3 on a die. The event would be the die actually landing with 3 facing up. If you wanted to roll a number greater than 4, the event would be the die landing with either 5 or 6 facing up.

## Outcome

The **outcome** is one possible result of conducting a probability experiment a single time. As you know, the possible outcomes of rolling the die are 1, 2, 3, 4, 5, or 6. The possible outcomes of flipping a fair coin are heads or tails. The possible outcomes of drawing a name from a hat include each of the names entered.

When the result of rolling the die or flipping the coin is the outcome you were hoping for, we call it a **favorable outcome**. If you called "tails" while the quarter was in the air, and the coin landed with tails facing up, you experienced a favorable outcome.

## Sample Space

The set of all possible outcomes for an event is the **sample space**. The sample space for rolling a regular six-sided die is {1, 2, 3, 4, 5, 6}. Notice that all of the possible results of rolling the die are listed, and that the list is written within braces.

# Determining Probability

To determine the probability, or likelihood, of an event, use the following formula:

$$\text{Probability of an event} = \frac{\text{Number of favorable outcomes}}{\text{Total number of possible outcomes}}$$

The following is a shorthand version of this formula. Here, $p$ represents probability, and $A$ represents a particular event.

$$p(A) = \frac{\text{Number of favorable outcomes}}{\text{Total number of possible outcomes}}$$

Probability can be expressed as a ratio, a percent, or a fraction. A certain outcome, or one that is 100 percent likely to happen, has a probability of 1. An impossible outcome, or one that cannot occur, has a probability of 0. The probability of all other events range in value between 0 and 1.

Take a look at the following spinner.

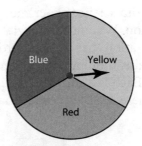

Notice that the sections of the spinner are equal. That means there is an equal chance of landing on any one of the colors. Find the probability of landing on yellow. Since landing on yellow is the only favorable outcome for this event, 1 is the number of favorable outcomes. Since it is possible to land on yellow, red, or blue, 3 is the number of possible outcomes.

$$p(yellow) = \frac{Number\ of\ favorable\ outcomes}{Total\ number\ of\ possible\ outcomes}$$

$$p(yellow) = \frac{1}{3}$$

The probability of landing on yellow is $\frac{1}{3}$.

What is the probability of landing on a primary color?

$$p(primary\ color) = \frac{Number\ of\ favorable\ outcomes}{Total\ number\ of\ possible\ outcomes}$$

$$p(primary\ color) = \frac{3}{3} = 1$$

The probability of landing on a primary color is 1. This event is certain, because there is a 100 percent chance of this outcome.

What is the probability of landing on green?

$$p(green) = \frac{Number\ of\ favorable\ outcomes}{Total\ number\ of\ possible\ outcomes}$$

$$p(green) = \frac{0}{3}$$

The probability of landing on green is 0 because this outcome is impossible.

When the probability of an event occurring is greater than 50 percent, the event is **likely**. In other words, there is a good chance that it will take place. When the weather forecast says there is a 75 percent chance of rain, you know that there is a good chance of this event taking place; it is likely to rain.

On the other hand, when the probability of an event is less than 50 percent, there is a small chance of it happening, and the event is considered **unlikely**. When you roll a die one time, it is unlikely that you will roll a 2. It is possible; however, the probability of this happening is only $\frac{1}{6}$, so it is unlikely.

When two events have the same probability of taking place, the events are **equally likely**. Take another look at the spinner. It is equally likely that the spinner will land on yellow or blue since the probability of each event is $\frac{1}{3}$.

## Independent Probability

So far, the events discussed have involved **independent probability**—in other words, the probability of one event does not depend on the outcome of a previous event.

Suppose you flipped a coin twice. The outcome of the first flip has absolutely nothing to do with the outcome of the second. The probability of the second event is not affected by the outcome of the first.

## Dependent Probability

Some events involve **dependent probability**, in which the outcome of one event depends on the outcome of a previous one. Suppose you have a standard deck of 52 playing cards and draw two cards, without returning the first to the deck. On the first draw, the probability of randomly drawing the ace of spades is $\frac{1}{52}$. However, on the second draw, there are no longer 52 cards in the deck; there are only 51. The probability of drawing the ace of spades on the second draw is now $\frac{1}{51}$. The probability of the second event is affected by the outcome of the first.

### Keep in Mind

Keep in mind that if a question states that an event occurred *with replacement*, the events are independent. The phrase *with replacement* means that whatever card was drawn, marble was pulled out of a bag, or name was removed from a hat, it was then replaced, or put back, following the experiment. If it was replaced, the outcome of the first event no longer affects the outcome of the second.

Take another look at the example involving the deck of playing cards. If, the first card was drawn and put back in the deck, the probability of drawing the ace of spades the second time is still $\frac{1}{52}$ because there are still 52 cards in the deck. The probability did not change from one event to the next.

## Mutually Exclusive Events

Events that cannot occur at the same time are considered to be **mutually exclusive**. Suppose you were to draw a single playing card from a standard deck. Drawing a heart and a queen would *not* be mutually exclusive because both events could occur at the same time. However, you could not draw a heart and a club at the same time; these events would be mutually exclusive.

Think about the spinner again. You could spin a primary color and red, so these events are not mutually exclusive; it is possible for them to happen at the same time. However, spinning blue and red would be mutually exclusive since these events cannot occur simultaneously.

# Examples

Here are two sample questions involving probability.

1. **Kenzie has 2 red mittens, 6 black mittens, and 8 gray mittens in her drawer. She reached into the drawer without looking and pulled out a black mitten. What is the probability that the second mitten she pulls from the drawer will be black?**

   A  $\dfrac{1}{3}$

   B  $\dfrac{5}{6}$

   C  $\dfrac{3}{8}$

   D  $\dfrac{1}{15}$

   E  $\dfrac{1}{16}$

## Explanation

Read the problem and determine what is being asked: What is the probability of the second mitten being black, without replacing the first mitten chosen? Identify pertinent information. There are 2 red mittens, 6 black mittens, and 8 gray mittens. She pulled out 1 black mitten. Choose which operations to use. Find the number of black mittens left in the drawer; then find the total number of mittens left. Divide the number of black mittens by the total number in the drawer. Solve the problem:

$$P(\text{black mitten}) = \frac{\text{Number of favorable outcome}}{\text{Total number of possible outcomes}}$$

$$P(\text{black mitten}) = \frac{5}{15}$$

$$\frac{5}{15} = \frac{1}{3}$$

Check your work and select the correct answer. **The answer is A.**

2. **A case of light bulbs contains 60 bulbs. During shipping, 18 of the bulbs broke. What is the probability of randomly selecting a bulb that is not broken?**

   A  $\dfrac{3}{7}$

   B  $\dfrac{3}{10}$

   C  $\dfrac{7}{10}$

   D  $\dfrac{1}{18}$

   E  $\dfrac{1}{60}$

### Explanation

Read the problem and determine what is being asked: What is probability of selecting an unbroken bulb? Identify pertinent information. You need to know the number of unbroken bulbs and the total number of bulbs. Choose which operations to use. Subtract the number of broken bulbs from the total to find the number of unbroken bulbs. Then divide the number of unbroken bulbs by the total number of bulbs. Solve the problem:

$$60 - 18 = 42$$

$$\frac{42}{60} = \frac{7}{10}$$

Check your work and select the correct answer. **The answer is C.**

# PROBABILITY DRILLS

For each question, choose the best answer.

1. **What is the probability of NOT getting a 3 when rolling a 6-sided die?**

    A  $\dfrac{1}{6}$

    B  $\dfrac{1}{4}$

    C  $\dfrac{1}{3}$

    D  $\dfrac{1}{2}$

    E  $\dfrac{5}{6}$

**Use the following information to answer questions 2–5.**

A bag contains 3 red marbles, 5 green marbles, 3 blue marbles, and 7 purple marbles.

2. **What is the probability of randomly selecting a purple marble from the bag?**

    A  $\dfrac{1}{7}$

    B  $\dfrac{1}{11}$

    C  $\dfrac{1}{18}$

    D  $\dfrac{7}{11}$

    E  $\dfrac{7}{18}$

3. Bailey pulled a purple marble from the bag and did not replace it. What is the probability that he will select a red marble next?

    A  $\dfrac{1}{6}$

    B  $\dfrac{1}{18}$

    C  $\dfrac{3}{17}$

    D  $\dfrac{6}{11}$

    E  $\dfrac{6}{17}$

4. What is the sample space of the experiment?

    A  {red, green, blue, purple}
    B  {green, blue, purple}
    C  {red, green, blue}
    D  {red, red, red}
    E  {purple}

5. Which two events are equally likely?

    A  selecting purple and selecting a primary color
    B  selecting red and selecting a primary color
    C  selecting purple and selecting green
    D  selecting blue or selecting green
    E  selecting red or selecting blue

6. Colin wrote his name on a piece of paper and cut the letters apart so that each was on a separate piece. He placed the pieces in a bag and selected one letter without looking. What is the probability that he chose the letter *n*?

    A  $\dfrac{1}{2}$

    B  $\dfrac{1}{5}$

    C  $\dfrac{1}{3}$

    D  $\dfrac{1}{6}$

    E  $\dfrac{1}{8}$

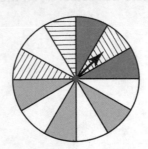

7. **Ian spun the spinner one time. Which of the following is true?**
   A    It is impossible that he landed on striped.
   B    It is unlikely that he landed on a solid color.
   C    It is certain that he landed on dark blue or light blue.
   D    It is likely that he either landed on light blue or white.
   E    It is equally likely that he landed on striped or dark blue.

8. **What is the probability that he landed on either striped or light blue?**
   A    $\dfrac{1}{4}$
   B    $\dfrac{1}{3}$
   C    $\dfrac{1}{2}$
   D    $\dfrac{2}{3}$
   E    $\dfrac{3}{2}$

9. **Fourteen men and six women entered a raffle. What is the probability that the third name drawn will be a woman, if the first two names were both men?**
   A    $\dfrac{1}{2}$
   B    $\dfrac{1}{3}$
   C    $\dfrac{1}{6}$
   D    $\dfrac{3}{7}$
   E    $\dfrac{3}{10}$

10. Charles rolled two identical six-sided die, with sides numbered 1 through 6. What is the probability that the total value of the numbers he rolled is less than or equal to 9?

    A   90%

    B   83%

    C   66%

    D   30%

    E   25%

Answers are on page 726.

# Data Analysis/ Probability/Statistics: Data Analysis

I f you ever looked at a chart that gives the weather forecast or looked at a graph in a textbook to find a piece of information, then you have used information from a data display. Some of the questions on the *HiSET®* Exam Mathematics test will require you to analyze and interpret data presented in various forms, such as graphs and tables. This chapter will review bar graphs, circle graphs, line graphs, and tables, and go over a few strategies for figuring out the meanings of the information in each type of display.

## What Is Tested?

Analyzing data often involves more than simply identifying information on a graph. To answer data analysis questions, you will use some of the skills already reviewed in this book, including whole numbers and operations, percents, and measures of central tendency.

Tables and graphs are types of data displays. They are often used to organize and display large amounts of data in a way that is easy to interpret, compare, or analyze. Each display is different and is used to report different types of data.

### Tables

A **table** displays information in rows and columns. One difference between a table and a graph is that tables present exact data, whereas data in a graph may be estimated or rounded for simplicity.

To interpret information in a table or chart effectively, pay close attention to headings and labels that indicate the type of information being displayed. Take a look at the following example.

According to the table, how much more precipitation falls during March in Garden City than in Denver during the same month?

| City | Average Precipitation for January | Average Precipitation for February | Average Precipitation for March |
|---|---|---|---|
| Denver, CO | 0.64 in. | 0.73 in. | 1.88 in. |
| Miami, FL | 2.09 in. | 2.42 in. | 3.0 in. |
| Garden City, NY | 3.62 in. | 3.17 in. | 4.35 in. |

First, look at each of the column headings and find the column that displays precipitation averages for March. Then find the rows that show these data for Garden City and Denver.

| City | Average Precipitation for January | Average Precipitation for February | Average Precipitation for March |
|------|-----------------------------------|------------------------------------|----------------------------------|
| Denver, CO | 0.64 in. | 0.73 in. | **1.88 in.** |
| Miami, FL | 2.09 in. | 2.42 in. | 3.0 in. |
| Garden City, NY | 3.62 in. | 3.17 in. | **4.35 in.** |

Next, determine what strategy to use to solve the problem. Since the question asks *how much more*, subtract to find the difference.

$$4.35 - 1.88 = 2.47$$

2.37 more inches of precipitation falls in Garden City than in Denver during March.

## Bar Graphs

**Bar graphs** organize information along a vertical axis and a horizontal axis. The bars on the graph may run either vertically or horizontally. Bar graphs are often used to compare amounts. One advantage of bar graphs, like other types of graphs, is that the information can quickly be interpreted visually.

As with tables, it is important to read the title of the bar graph and the labels on each axis and to notice the scale by which the data are listed. For example, are numerical data reported by ones, thousands, or millions?

Take a look at the following bar graph.

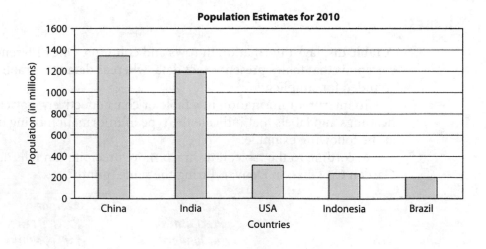

Notice that with a quick glance, you can easily compare the populations of the five countries. Take a look at the label on the *y*-axis, or vertical axis. It indicates that the data are reported in millions. As mentioned, the data displayed in graphs may be rounded and may require estimation to interpret. For example, the estimated population of the United States for the year 2010 was 309,975,000. By looking at the graph, you can estimate that the population was probably slightly more than 300 million, but the display did not intend for you to be able to determine an exact amount.

Use the bar graph to answer this example question.

Which country has a population that is approximately five times that of Indonesia?

First, find the population of Indonesia. Since the bar indicating the population of this country is slightly above the line for 200, you can estimate that the population is about 230 million. Now determine what number would be about five times that amount.

$$230 \text{ million} \times 5 = 1{,}150 \text{ million}$$

Find 1,150 million on the vertical axis of the graph. It will be slightly below the line indicating 1,200 million. Since the bar for India reaches to about that point, you can determine that the population of India is about five times that of Indonesia.

## Line Graphs

**Line graphs** are used to show trends, patterns, or changes over time. Each point on the line graph relates to a value on both the *x*-axis and the *y*-axis. As with other types of data displays, it is important to identify the title of the display, the labels on the axes, and the scale.

Take a look at this line graph.

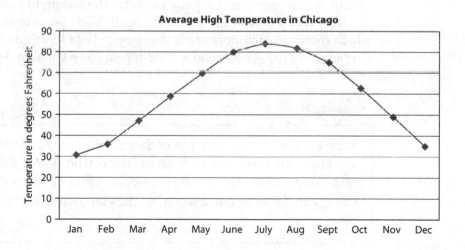

The graph clearly shows that the lowest temperatures in Chicago occur during January and the highest occur during July and August. It also shows more specific information, such as the fact that the average high temperatures in January are approximately 30°F and increase by about 5° the following month.

Some graphs will display more than one set of data at a time, as does the line graph below.

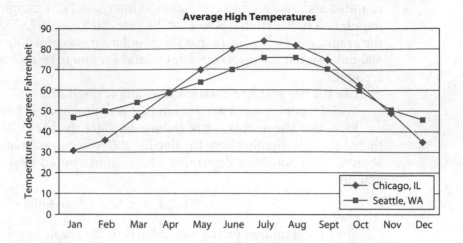

This includes the same data about the average high temperatures in Chicago; however, it also includes the average high temperatures for Seattle, Washington. A visual display such as this allows for a quick comparison of the temperatures in both cities. Use this graph to answer the following question.

During which month do the high temperatures in Chicago and Seattle appear to be equal?

First, look for any points where the lines cross. Next, determine if the symbols for each city appear to be in the same location on the graph. Take a look at the symbols positioned above October and November for each city. These appear to indicate similar temperatures; however, the temperature in Chicago seems to be slightly higher for the month of September and slightly lower for the month of November.

Now take a look at the points for April. These seem to indicate the same number, which means the temperature is the same in both locations for this month. The high temperatures in Chicago and Seattle appear to be equal in April.

### Keep in Mind

Keep in mind that some types of data displays may include additional information in a key, such as the one seen on the right-hand side of the double line graph. Make sure you read all of the information included. Without reading the key on this graph, for example, it would be difficult to determine which line represents which city.

# Circle Graph

A **circle graph**, sometimes called a *pie graph* or *pie chart*, represents a whole amount, and each section represents a percentage of that whole. The sum of the sections of the graph equal 100 percent. This type of visual display makes it easy to determine quickly what percent of the whole is represented by each group. Again, rather than giving exact numbers, the data are presented as percentages. Take a look at the following circle graph. Since the smallest section of the graph is labeled *seniors*, you know that this is the smallest class. Likewise, since the largest section is labeled *freshmen*, you know that this is the largest class.

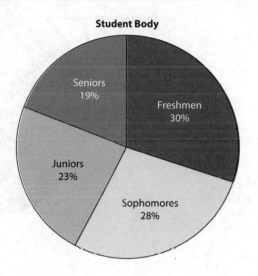

The circle graph represents the student body of Bellville High School. If the total number of students enrolled in the school is 960, how many students are in the freshman class?

According to the graph, 30% of the students are freshmen. Multiply the total number of students by 30% to find the number of freshmen in the school.

$$30\% \text{ of } 960 =$$

$$0.3 \times 960 = 288$$

288 students are in the freshman class.

# Examples

Here are two sample questions involving data analysis.

1.  **The graph shows Colleen's monthly expenses. According to the graph, what is the ratio of her rent and car expenses to her total budget?**

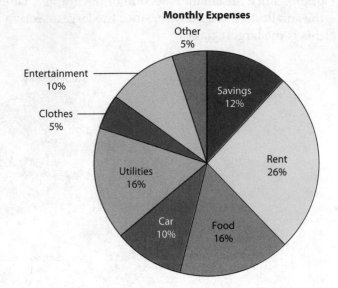

**Monthly Expenses**

A  $\dfrac{1}{10}$

B  $\dfrac{1}{26}$

C  $\dfrac{5}{13}$

D  $\dfrac{9}{25}$

E  $\dfrac{13}{50}$

## *Explanation*

Read the problem and determine what is being asked: What is the ratio of the sum of the car and rent expenses to the total? Identify pertinent information. Car = 10%, Rent = 26%, and Total = 100%. Choose which operations to use. Find the sum of the car and rent expenses. Form a ratio with this sum as the numerator and the total as the denominator. Simplify the ratio. Solve the problem:

$$\text{Car} + \text{Rent} = 10 + 26 = 36$$

$$\frac{36}{100}$$

$$\frac{9}{25}$$

Check your work and select the correct answer. **The answer is D.**

Use the same circle graph to answer the following question.

2.  **If Colleen makes $4,500 per month, what are her annual rent expenses?**

    A   $1,700

    B   $2,600

    C   $11,700

    D   $14,040

    E   $26,000

### Explanation

Read the problem and determine what is being asked: What are Colleen's annual rent expenses? Identify pertinent information. Rent is 26% of the total. Choose which operations to use. Multiply her monthly salary by 12 months. Then find 26% of the annual salary. Solve the problem:

$$4{,}500 \times 12 = 54{,}000 \text{ annual salary}$$

$$54{,}000 \times 0.26 = 14{,}040 \text{ rent expenses}$$

Check your work and select the correct answer. **The answer is D.**

# DATA ANALYSIS DRILLS

**Questions 1–3 refer to the following graph.**

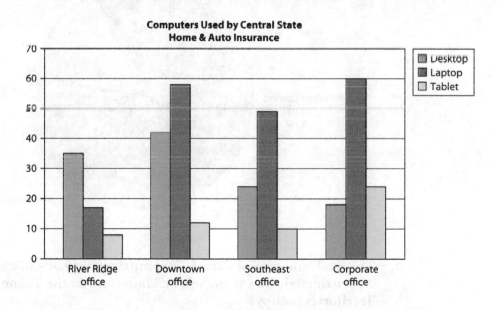

1.  **Approximately what percent of the computers in the River Ridge office are laptops?**

    A   8%

    B   17%

    C   30%

    D   40%

    E   60%

2. **About how many more tablets are in the corporate office than in the southeast office?**

   A   6

   B   10

   C   14

   D   20

   E   24

3. **Approximately how many desktop computers are in use throughout the company?**

   A   50

   B   120

   C   180

   D   300

   E   350

**Questions 4–6 refer to the following graph.**

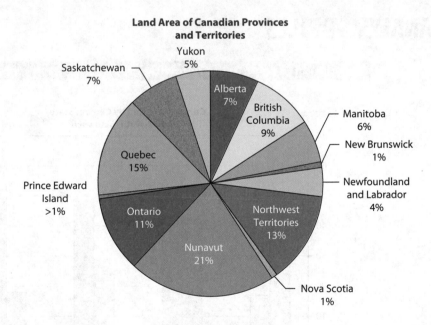

**Land Area of Canadian Provinces and Territories**

4. **The total land area of Canada is approximately 9,984,670 square kilometers. Approximately how many square kilometers do the Yukon and Northwest Territories occupy?**

   A   0.5 million

   B   1.3 million

   C   1.8 million

   D   2 million

   E   5 million

5. The total land area of Canada is approximately 9,984,670 square kilometers. How many square kilometers larger is the area of Nunavut than Quebec?

   A    0.6 million
   B    1.5 million
   C    2.1 million
   D    6 million
   E    15 million

6. Which provinces or territories combined equal approximately one-fourth of the land area of Canada?

   A    Newfoundland and Labrador
   B    Nunavut, Ontario, and Quebec
   C    Northwest Territories and Alberta
   D    Saskatchewan, Ontario, and Nunavut
   E    Nunavut, Newfoundland, and Labrador

**Questions 7 and 8 refer to the following information.**

During the first month in operation, a new car dealership recorded how each customer learned of the business.

|            | Week 1 | Week 2 | Week 3 | Week 4 |
|------------|--------|--------|--------|--------|
| Television | 20     | 22     | 18     | 34     |
| Internet   | 15     | 19     | 26     | 28     |
| Newspaper  | 12     | 35     | 32     | 29     |
| Mail       | 9      | 12     | 23     | 16     |
| Other      | 14     | 17     | 30     | 41     |

7. During the first month, how many customers learned of the car dealership from the Internet?

   A    15
   B    28
   C    70
   D    88
   E    94

8. What percent of the customers learned of the company from the newspaper during the third week of business?

   A    33.3%
   B    24.8%
   C    20.2%
   D    19.7%
   E    17.8%

Countryside Computer Services went into business during 2004. The graph shows the company's annual profits during its first few years in operation.

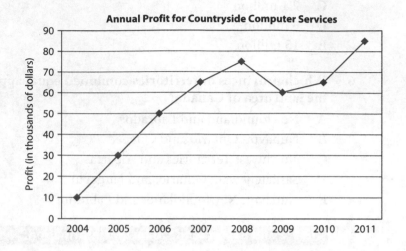

**Annual Profit for Countryside Computer Services**

9.  **By how much did the profits increase between 2005 and 2006?**

   A   $2,000

   B   $5,000

   C   $20,000

   D   $30,000

   E   $50,000

10.  **What was the company's mean annual profit during this period?**

   A   $55,000

   B   $65,000

   C   $70,000

   D   $75,000

   E   $85,000

**Answers are on page 726.**

# 37 Algebraic Concepts

**A**lgebra is the strand of math that involves unknown values, which are often represented by letters. When working to determine the values of these letters, you will use many of the skills you have reviewed in the previous chapters, including operations, fractions, exponents, and decimals.

First, you might want to review a few terms related to algebra.

## Variable

The letters or symbols that represent unknown values are called **variables**. In the equation $5 + x = 8$, the letter $x$ represents an unknown value. At times, more than one variable may be used in a given problem. In this case, each variable represents a different value.

$$4m - 3t + 7 = 16$$

In this example, $m$ and $t$ are variables, and each represents an unknown value.

## Constant

The numbers or values that are known are called **constants**. Constants and variables often appear together.

$$4m \quad 3t \mid 7 = 16$$

In this example, 7 and 16 are constants.

## Coefficients

When a number and a variable appear beside each other without an operating symbol between them, they are multiplied together. For example, $3t$ really means 3 *multiplied by t*. The number part of a term containing a number and a variable is the **coefficient**.

$$4m - 3t + 7 = 16$$

In this example, 4 and 3 are coefficients.

## Algebraic Terms

Any variable, constant, or multiplication or division of a number with a variable is known as an **algebraic term**.

$$8y$$
$$125z$$
$$9k^2$$

### Algebraic Expressions

An *expression* is a mathematical phrase that combines numbers and operations—and sometimes variables. An **algebraic expression** combines numbers, operations, and at least one variable.

$$5cd + 7 - \frac{a}{2}$$

In an algebraic expression, the terms are separated by plus or minus signs. This example has three terms. The first is $5cd$, the second is 7, and the third is $\frac{a}{2}$.

# What Is Tested?

## Evaluating Algebraic Expressions

Each variable in an algebraic expression represents an unknown value. To **evaluate algebraic expressions**, replace each variable with its numeric value and then evaluate the numerical expression. Basically, substitute the value for each variable and then find the value of the expression.

Evaluate $7s + 9t - 3a^2$ when $s$ is 5, $t$ is 4, and $a$ is 2.

$$7(5) + 9(4) - 3(2)^2 =$$
$$35 + 36 - 3(4) =$$
$$35 + 36 - 12 =$$
$$71 - 12 = 59$$
$$59$$

## Simplifying Algebraic Expressions

To **simplify** an expression means to combine like terms. That means, you combine terms that have the same variable and combine any constants.

Simplify $6a + 7 - a + 5$.

First, rearrange the terms so that like terms are together. Keep the term with the addition or subtraction sign that precedes it.

$$6a + 7 - a + 5$$
$$6a - a + 7 + 5$$
$$5a + 12$$

### Keep in Mind

Keep in mind that when a variable does not include the coefficient, it is the same as the coefficient being 1. So $x$ is the same as $1x$.

To combine terms, the variables must be exactly the same.

Simplify $5a + 3ab + 2a + 3$.

$$5a + 2a + 3ab + 3$$
$$7a + 3ab + 3$$

To simplify an expression that contains parentheses, use the distributive property first and then combine the terms.

$$4x + 7(x + 5)$$
$$4x + 7x + 35$$
$$11x + 35$$

## Solving Equations

An **equation** is different from an expression in that it includes an equal sign. Basically, an equation states that two amounts are equal to each other.

$$5y = 15$$
$$4 + 7b = 25$$
$$3x + 12 = 28 - x$$

The **solution** of the equation is the value for the variable that makes the equation true. Take a look at the first example here, $5y = 15$. You already know that $5y$ really means $5 \times y$. You also already know that $5 \times 3 = 15$. That tells you that the value of $y$ in the equation is 3. The solution is $y = 3$, since this makes the equation true.

$$5y = 15$$
$$5(3) = 15$$
$$y = 3$$

When you solve an equation, you find the solution, or value, of each variable. To do this, you must isolate the variable, which means getting the variable alone on one side of the equal sign.

Keep in mind that the expressions on either side of the equation are equal. Whenever you make any change to one side of the equation to isolate the variable, you must do exactly the same thing to the other side for the sides to remain equal.

To solve an equation that involves only one operation, use the inverse operation on both sides. Remember, inverse operations are opposites; addition and subtraction are inverse operations, as are multiplication and division.

$$t - 8 = 2$$

The example involves subtraction, so perform addition on both sides of the equation.

$$t - 8 = 2$$
$$t - 8 + 8 = 2 + 8$$
$$t = 10$$

The solution is $t = 10$.

Equations often involve more than one operation. In this case, perform any addition or subtraction first, then perform any multiplication or division. Take a look at the following example.

$$6x + 12 = 42$$

You need to isolate the $x$ in order to solve the equation. Notice that the first term involves multiplication, and the second term is added. To isolate the variable, use opposite operations. Remember, division is the opposite of multiplication, and subtraction is the opposite of addition. Start by subtracting the term that is added.

$$6x + 12 - 12 = 42 - 12$$
$$6x = 30$$

Since you subtracted 12 from both sides, both sides are still equal, and the equation remains true. Now use division to "undo" the multiplication.

$$6x \div 6 = 30 \div 6$$
$$x = 5$$

The solution of the equation is $x = 5$. To check your work, substitute the value of the variable in the original equation and make sure it is true.

$$6x + 12 = 42$$
$$6(5) + 12 = 42$$
$$30 + 12 = 42$$
$$42 = 42$$

When there are variables on both sides of the equation, first combine like terms by moving the variables to the same side. Then solve the equation as usual.

$$7 + 4s = s + 22$$

First, move the variable $s$ to the left side of the equation by subtracting it from both sides. Next, group the constants on the right side of the equation by subtracting 7 from both sides.

$$7 + 4s = s + 22$$
$$7 + 4s - s = s + 22 - s$$
$$7 + 3s = 22$$
$$7 - 7 + 3s = 22 - 7$$
$$3s = 15$$
$$\frac{3s}{3} = \frac{15}{3}$$
$$s = 5$$

**Keep in Mind**

Keep in mind that it may be easier to group variables on the side of the equation that contains the variable with the greatest coefficient. That way, you can avoid working with negative numbers.

## Solving Inequalities

**Inequalities** are statements that show that two amounts are not equal. They include one of the following symbols rather than an equal sign.

$>$ is greater than
$<$ is less than
$\geq$ is greater than or equal to
$\leq$ is less than or equal to

Inequalities are solved in the same way as equations, with one exception. When an inequality is divided by a negative number, the symbol is reversed. That means, if you have to divide both sides of an inequality by $-2$, for example, the *less than* sign becomes a *greater than* sign and vice versa.

$$4g - 6 > 14$$
$$4g - 6 + 6 > 14 + 6$$
$$4g > 20$$
$$\frac{4g}{4} > \frac{20}{4}$$
$$g > 5$$

The value of $g$ is greater than 5.

In the next example, notice that the sign is reversed when dividing by a negative number.

$$-3h - 8 \leq 16$$
$$-3h - 8 + 8 \leq 16 + 8$$
$$-3h \leq 16 + 8$$
$$-3h \leq 24$$
$$\frac{-3h}{-3} \leq \frac{24}{-3}$$
$$h \geq -8$$

## Solving Word Problems

To solve some word problems, it is necessary to translate the information into an algebraic expression. To do this, select a variable to represent the unknown value. Then look for key words that indicate the operation you need to use.

The square of a number decreased by 6 is greater than 4.

Use $x$ as the variable. The phrase *the square of a number* tells you to use $x^2$. *Decreased by 6* indicates subtraction. *Is greater than* indicates that this is an inequality.

$$x^2 - 6 > 4$$

Now solve the inequality.

$$x^2 - 6 > 4$$
$$x^2 - 6 + 6 > 4 + 6$$
$$x^2 > 10$$
$$\sqrt{x^2} > \sqrt{10}$$
$$x > \sqrt{10}$$

## Multiplying Algebraic Expressions

To multiply algebraic expressions, multiply the coefficients first and then multiply the variables.

$$5d \times 7e = 35de$$

When the expressions being multiplied contain exponents, add the exponents of like terms.

$$3a^2 \times 2ac = 12a^3c$$

As you know, some expressions contain more than one term. When multiplying a one-term expression by an expression with two or more terms, be sure to multiply the single term by each of the terms in the second expression.

$$4x(6x^2 + 3xy + 8) = 24x^3 + 12x^2y + 32x$$

When both expressions contain two terms, multiply both terms in the first expression by both terms in the second. To do this, use the FOIL method.

Multiply:

**F**   First $\times$ First
**O**   Outside $\times$ Outside
**I**   Inside $\times$ Inside
**L**   Last $\times$ Last

After multiplying, combine like terms.

$$(q + 3)\,(q - 6)$$
$$(q \times q)\,(q \times -6)\,(3 \times q)\,(3 \times -6) =$$
$$q^2 - 6q + 3q - 18 =$$
$$q^2 - 3q + 18$$

## Factoring

In multiplication, factors are the terms that are multiplied. To factor an expression, separate the numbers or terms that have been multiplied. Factoring is one way of solving some kinds of algebraic equations and expressions.

One way to factor is to find the greatest common factor among the terms in the expression. The first step is to look for any common factors. Next, separate those factors from the expression.

Factor $6m^3 - 21m$.

Since 3 is a factor of both coefficients, separate this from the expression. Since $m$ is a factor of both terms, separate this variable. Write the factors that have been separated outside of the parentheses and write the remaining values inside.

$$6m^3 - 21m = 3m(2m^2 - 7)$$

Take a look at the answer, $3m(2m^2 - 7)$. Notice that if you multiplied the terms together, the result would be the original expression, $6m^3 - 21m$.

Sometimes you will need to factor an expression that has four or more terms. To do this, you factor by grouping pairs of terms that contain common factors.

Then factor out the common factors from each of the pairs and place the common factor in front of the term in parentheses.

Factor $y^2 + 5y + 4y + 20$.

First, separate the terms into pairs.

$$y^2 + 5y + 4y + 20 = (y^2 + 5y) + (4y + 20)$$

Next, separate any common factors from both pairs.

$$(y^2 + 5y) + (4y + 20) = y(y + 5) + 4(y + 5)$$

Finally, write the common factor $(y + 5)$ first, followed by the terms that you factored out of each pair.

$$y(y + 5) + 4(y + 5) = (y + 5)(y + 4)$$

Another way to factor is to reverse the FOIL method used to multiply. This is used with expressions containing two or three terms that begin with a squared term and end with a constant, such as $x^2 + 6x - 2$.

Begin by determining which factors multiply together to result in the first term, or the term with the exponent. Then find two factors that are multiplied together to produce the final term and added together to produce the middle term. Pay close attention to the signs.

Factor $k^2 + 3k - 10$.

Since $k \times k = k^2$, this will be the first term in each set of parentheses.

$$(k)(k)$$

Now, determine what factors of $-10$ (the constant) can be added or subtracted to equal 3 (the coefficient of the middle term). Since $-2 \times 5 = -10$ and $-2 + 5 = 3$, write these values in the parentheses.

$$(k - 2)(k + 5)$$

# Examples

Here are two examples of algebra questions.

1.  **Which of the following is NOT a value of $x$ for the inequality $16x - 8 \geq 10x + 28$?**
    A   2
    B   6
    C   8
    D   14
    E   18

## Explanation

Read the problem and determine what is being asked: All but one of the answers is a possible solution. Which is not true in the inequality? Identify pertinent information. The word *NOT* and the greater than or equal to symbol are important. Choose which operations to use. First, subtract $10x$ from both sides to move the variables to the left of the inequality. Then add 8 to both sides. After that, divide both sides to isolate the variable. Solve the problem:

$$16x - 8 \geq 10x + 28$$
$$16x - 8 - 10x \geq 10x + 28 - 10x$$
$$6x - 8 \geq 28$$
$$6x - 8 + 8 \geq 28 + 8$$
$$6x \geq 36$$
$$\frac{6x}{6} \geq \frac{36}{6}$$
$$x \geq 6$$

Check your work and select the correct answer. **The answer is A.**

2.  **Which shows that 12 less than 9 times a number is the same as 28 more than 4 times the same number?**

    **A**   $9 - 12x = 28x + 4$

    **B**   $9x - 12 = 4x + 28$

    **C**   $9x - 12 = 28x + 4$

    **D**   $12 - 9x = 4x + 28$

    **E**   $12x - 9 = 28 + 4x$

## Explanation

Read the problem and determine what is being asked: Here you will need to write the equation. Identify pertinent information. All the numbers and their relationships are important. Choose which operations to use. *Less* means subtract, *more* means add, *is the same as* means equals, and *times* means multiply. Go slowly and carefully to translate the words into the equation you need. Remember the order of operations; multiply before adding or subtracting.

Solve the problem: $9x - 12 = 4x + 28$.

Check your work and select the correct answer. **The answer is B.**

# ALGEBRA DRILLS

1. Brittney is 5 years older than her brother Brandon. Three years from now, the sum of their ages will be 23. How old is Brandon now?

   A  13

   B  11

   C  9

   D  6

   E  5

2. Solve for $y$ in the equation $8y - 7 = 3y + 13$.

   A  $y = 4$

   B  $y = 5$

   C  $y = 6$

   D  $y = 16$

   E  $y = 20$

3. During a yard sale, Deb earned three times as much money as Andy. Anna made $10 more than twice what Deb made. Together, they made $150. How many dollars did Deb make?

   A  14

   B  15

   C  42

   D  84

   E  94

4. Factor $c^2 - 11 + 18$.

   A  $(c^2 - 2)(c - 9)$

   B  $(c + 9)(c + 2)$

   C  $(c^2 - 9)(c - 2)$

   D  $(c + 9)(c - 2)$

   E  $(c - 9)(c - 2)$

5. Jeff bought two adult tickets and three children's tickets to the zoo for a total of $66. Tiffany bought six adult tickets for $108. What is the cost of each children's ticket?

   A  $10

   B  $15

   C  $16

   D  $18

   E  $22

6. Evaluate $12y^2 - 4z + 7$ when $y = 3$ and $z = -2$.

   A   43

   B   51

   C   87

   D   107

   E   123

7. Simplify $7(r + 5) - 3(r - 8)$.

   A   $4r + 11$

   B   $4r + 27$

   C   $4r + 59$

   D   $10r + 11$

   E   $10r + 59$

8. Multiply $(v - 4)(v + 6)$.

   A   $v^2 + 2v - 2$

   B   $v^2 + 2v - 24$

   C   $v^2 - 2v - 24$

   D   $v^2 + 10v - 24$

   E   $v^2 - 10v - 2$

9. Two numbers have a sum of 14 and the larger number is 6 more than the smaller number. What is the value of the smaller number?

   A   14

   B   8

   C   10

   D   6

   E   4

10. For which of the following equations is $-2$ a solution?

   A   $-2x = 4$

   B   $2y = 4$

   C   $x + -3 = -1$

   D   $y - 4 = -2$

   E   $x^3 - 2 = 2$

**Answers are on page 726.**

# 38 Mathematical Formulas

A formula sheet is not provided for the *HiSET*® Exam Mathematics test. If a formula is required to solve a problem, it will be included in the test question itself. There is no need to memorize formulas, but you will need to understand when and how to use each of them.

This chapter will introduce and review the formulas that you may be required to use on test day. Using them will involve many of the math skills previously discussed, including whole numbers, operations, fractions, geometry, and statistics.

## Area

**Area** refers to the number of square units needed to cover a surface. Take a look at the following rectangle. If each square making up the rectangle is 1 unit, then the area of the figure is 12 square units, since there are 12 squares in the rectangle.

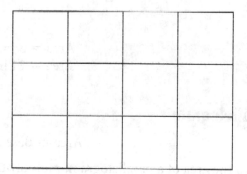

Here, you can easily count the number of squares to find the area, but this is not always possible. You will need formulas to find the areas of several common geometric shapes.

## Area of a Square

$$\text{Area} = \text{Side}^2$$

To find the area of a square, multiply the lengths of two sides. Since the sides are all equal, this is the same as finding the square of the length of any side.

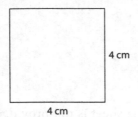

4 cm

$$\text{Area} = 4^2$$
$$\text{Area} = 16 \text{ cm}^2$$

The area of the square is 16 square centimeters, or 16 cm$^2$.

## Area of a Rectangle

$$\text{Area} = \text{Length} \times \text{Width}$$

To find the area of a rectangle, multiply the length and the width of the figure.

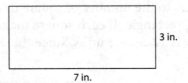

3 in.

7 in.

$$\text{Area} = 3 \text{ in.} \times 7 \text{ in.}$$
$$\text{Area} = 21 \text{ in.}^2$$

## Area of a Parallelogram

$$\text{Area} = \text{Base} \times \text{Height}$$

To find the area of a parallelogram, multiply the length of the base by the height of the figure. Notice the dotted line in the illustration. It shows the height of the figure, not the length of the side.

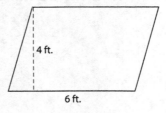

4 ft.

6 ft.

$$\text{Area} = 6 \text{ ft.} \times 4 \text{ ft.}$$
$$\text{Area} = 24 \text{ ft.}^2$$

Keep in mind that problems may give measurements you will not need to include in the formula to find area. For example, a diagram of a parallelogram may include measurements of the base, length, and height. Be careful to use the correct numbers in the formula and ignore any extra information.

## Area of a Triangle

$$\text{Area} = \frac{1}{2} \times \text{Base} \times \text{Height}$$

To find the area of a triangle, multiply $\frac{1}{2}$ by the base and the height of the figure. Notice the dotted line in the illustration. It shows the height of the triangle.

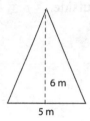

6 m

5 m

$$\text{Area} = \frac{1}{2} \times 5 \text{ m} \times 6 \text{ m}$$
$$\text{Area} = \frac{1}{2} (30) \text{ m}^2$$
$$\text{Area} = 15 \text{ m}^2$$

## Area of a Trapezoid

$$\text{Area} = \frac{1}{2} \times (\text{Base}_1 + \text{Base}_2) \times \text{Height}$$

A trapezoid has two bases. These are the sides of the figure that are parallel to one another. The formula for finding the area of a trapezoid calls one of these parallel sides $base_1$ and the other $base_2$. It does not matter which of the sides is called which.

To find the area of a trapezoid, multiply $\frac{1}{2}$ by the sum of $base_1$ and $base_2$; then multiply by the height of the figure.

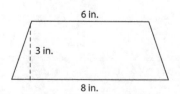

6 in.

3 in.

8 in.

$$\text{Area} = \frac{1}{2} \times (6 \text{ in.} + 8 \text{ in.}) \times 3 \text{ in.}$$

$$\text{Area} = \frac{1}{2} \times (14 \text{ in.}) \times 3 \text{ in.}$$

$$\text{Area} = 7 \text{ in.} \times 3 \text{ in.}^2$$

$$\text{Area} = 21 \text{ in.}^2$$

## Area of a Circle

$$\text{Area} = \pi \times \text{Radius}^2$$

Finding the area of a circle involves the symbol for **pi**. This symbol ($\pi$) represents the ratio of the circumference, or distance around, a circle, to its diameter. Pi is equal to approximately 3.14.

The formula for finding the area of a circle is Area = $\pi \times \text{Radius}^2$, although the shorthand version may sound more familiar: $\pi r^2$. To use the formula, multiply 3.14 by the square of the radius. As you know, the radius is the distance from the midpoint of the circle to the outside.

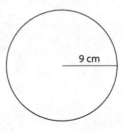

$$\text{Area} = \pi \times 9^2$$

$$\text{Area} = \pi \times 81$$

$$\text{Area} = 3.14 \times 81$$

$$\text{Area} = 254.34 \text{ cm}^2$$

# Perimeter

**Perimeter** is the distance around a figure. Basically, this measurement is the sum of the length of the sides of the figure. Here are the formulas that will help you determine this measurement.

## Perimeter of a Square

$$\text{Perimeter} = 4 \times \text{Side}$$

Since the sides of a square are equal in length, multiply the length of one side by 4 to find the perimeter, or distance around the square.

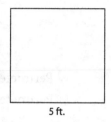

5 ft.

$$\text{Perimeter} = 4 \times 5 \text{ ft.}$$
$$\text{Perimeter} = 20 \text{ ft.}$$

## Perimeter of a Rectangle

$$\text{Perimeter} = 2 \times \text{Length} + 2 \times \text{Width}$$

To find the perimeter of a rectangle, multiply the length and width by 2, then add the products together. Remember that according to the order of operations, multiplication is performed before addition.

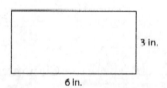

3 in.

6 in.

$$\text{Perimeter} = 2 \times 3 \text{ in.} + 2 \times 6 \text{ in.}$$
$$\text{Perimeter} = 6 \text{ in.} + 12 \text{ in.}$$
$$\text{Perimeter} = 18 \text{ in.}$$

A shortcut way to use the formula is to multiply the sum of the length and width by 2.

$$\text{Perimeter} = 2(\text{Length} + \text{Width})$$
$$\text{Perimeter} = 2(3 \text{ in.} + 6 \text{ in.})$$
$$\text{Perimeter} = 2(9 \text{ in.})$$
$$\text{Perimeter} = 18 \text{ in.}$$

## Perimeter of a Triangle

$$\text{Perimeter} = \text{Side}_1 + \text{Side}_2 + \text{Side}_3$$

To find the perimeter of a triangle, add the lengths of the sides.

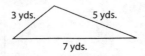

$$\text{Perimeter} = 7 \text{ yds.} + 3 \text{ yds.} + 5 \text{ yds.}$$
$$\text{Perimeter} = 15 \text{ yds.}$$

## Circumference of a Circle

$$\text{Circumference} = \pi \times \text{Diameter}$$

The distance around a circle is called the *circumference* rather than the perimeter. To find the circumference, you will again use $\pi$, which is approximately 3.14.

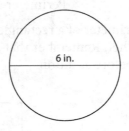

$$\text{Circumference} = \pi \times 6 \text{ in.}$$
$$\text{Circumference} = 3.14 \times 6 \text{ in.}$$
$$\text{Circumference} = 18.84 \text{ in.}$$

# Volume

Volume measures capacity; it tells how much a solid is able to hold and is measured in cubic units. Take a look at the following solid.

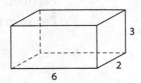

As you can see, the solid is 6 cubic units long, 2 cubic units wide, and 3 cubic units high. If you could count all of the cubic units, you would find that the solid has a capacity of 36. Since it is not possible to do this for most solids, you will need formulas to determine these measurements.

## Volume of a Cube

$$\text{Volume} = \text{Edge}^3$$

All of the sides of a cube are equal, so multiply this measurement by itself three times to find the volume.

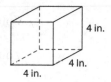

$$\text{Volume} = 4^3 \text{ in.}$$
$$\text{Volume} = 64 \text{ in.}^3$$

## Volume of a Rectangular Solid

$$\text{Volume} = \text{Length} \times \text{Width} \times \text{Height}$$

Multiplying length by width gives the area of the base. By multiplying the area of the base by the height, you can find the volume.

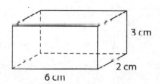

$$\text{Volume} = 6 \text{ cm} \times 2 \text{ cm} \times 3 \text{ cm}$$
$$\text{Volume} = 36 \text{ cm}^3$$

## Volume of a Square Pyramid

$$\text{Volume} = \frac{1}{3} \times (\text{Base edge})^2 \times \text{Height}$$

The base of a square pyramid is a square. Finding the square of the base edge is the same as finding the area of the base. This measurement is multiplied by $\frac{1}{3}$ and then by the height.

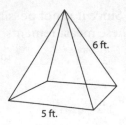

$$\text{Volume} = \frac{1}{3}(5\,\text{ft.})^2 \times 6\,\text{ft.}$$

$$\text{Volume} = \frac{1}{3} \times 25\,\text{ft.} \times 6\,\text{ft.}$$

$$\text{Volume} = 50\,\text{ft.}^3$$

## Volume of a Cylinder

$$\text{Volume} = \pi \times \text{Radius}^2 \times \text{Height}$$

Since the base of a cylinder is a circle, the formula for finding the volume of this solid includes $\pi \times \text{Radius}^2$, which gives the area of the circle. Then multiply the area of the base by the height.

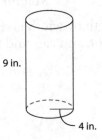

$$\text{Volume} = \pi \times 4^2\,\text{in.} \times 9\,\text{in.}$$
$$\text{Volume} = 3.14 \times 16\,\text{in.} \times 9\,\text{in.}$$
$$\text{Volume} = 452.16\,\text{in.}^3$$

## Volume of a Cone

$$\text{Volume} = \frac{1}{3} \times \pi \times \text{Radius}^2 \times \text{Height}$$

Notice that the only difference between this formula and the one for finding the area of a cylinder is that you multiply by $\frac{1}{3}$ when finding the volume of a cone.

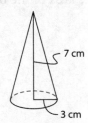

$$\text{Volume} = \frac{1}{3} \times \pi \times 3^2 \text{ cm} \times 7 \text{ cm}$$

$$\text{Volume} = \frac{1}{3} \times 3.14 \times 9 \text{ cm} \times 7 \text{ cm}$$

$$\text{Volume} = 65.94 \text{ cm}^3$$

# Coordinate Geometry

Coordinate geometry involves points that are plotted on a coordinate plane. The coordinates are the numbers that indicate the location of a point on the plane. The first coordinate, known as the $x$-coordinate, tells how many spaces to the left or right from 0 the point is along the horizontal axis. The second coordinate, known as the $y$-coordinate, tells how many spaces above or below 0 the point is along the vertical axis. The coordinates (3, 2) identify a point that is 3 spaces to the left of 0 and 2 spaces above it.

## Distance Between Points

$$\text{Distance between Points} = \sqrt{(x_2 - x_1)^2 + (y_2 - y_1)^2}$$

In this formula, $(x_1, y_1)$ and $(x_2, y_2)$ are points in a plane. Take a look at the coordinate plane shown.

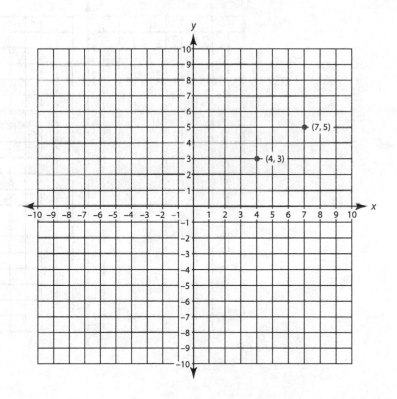

The first point marked is (4, 3) and the second is (7, 5). Use the formula to find the distance between these points. The ordered pair (4, 3) will be $(x_1, y_1)$ and (7, 5) will be $(x_2, y_2)$.

$$\text{Distance between points} = \sqrt{(x_2 - x_1)^2 + (y_2 - y_1)^2}$$

$$\text{Distance between points} = \sqrt{(7 - 4)^2 + (5 - 3)^2}$$

$$\text{Distance between points} = \sqrt{(3)^2 + (2)^2}$$

$$\text{Distance between points} = \sqrt{9 + 4}$$

$$\text{Distance between points} = \sqrt{13}$$

$$\text{Distance between points} = 3.6$$

## Slope of a Line

$$\text{Slope of a line} = \frac{y_2 - y_1}{x_2 - x_1}$$

In this formula, $(x_1, y_1)$ and $(x_2, y_2)$ are two points on the line. Take another look at the coordinate plane used previously and find the slope of the line that runs through the points (7, 5) and (4, 3).

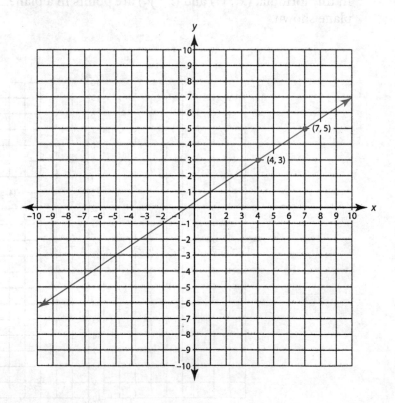

The first point marked is (4, 3) and the second is (7, 5). Again, the ordered pair (4, 3) will be $(x_1, y_1)$ and (7, 5) will be $(x_2, y_2)$. Use the formula to find the slope.

$$\text{Solope of a line} = \frac{y_2 - y_1}{x_2 - x_1}$$

$$\text{Solope of a line} = \frac{5 - 3}{7 - 4}$$

$$\text{Solope of a line} = \frac{2}{3}$$

# Pythagorean Relationship

$$a^2 + b^2 = c^2$$

In this formula, $a$ and $b$ are the legs of a right triangle. The legs are the sides that meet to form the right angle. The hypotenuse, which is the side opposite the right angle, is represented by $c$. The formula for the Pythagorean relationship, also known as the Pythagorean theorem, is used to find the length of one side of a right triangle when the other two sides are given.

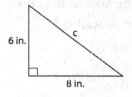

$$6^2 + 8^2 = c^2$$

$$36 + 64 = c^2$$

$$100 = c^2$$

$$\sqrt{100} = \sqrt{c^2}$$

$$10 = c$$

The length of the hypotenuse is 10 inches.

# Distance

$$\text{Distance} = \text{Rate} \times \text{Time}$$

To determine distance, multiply the rate, or speed, travelled by the length of time.
Jenna is training for a marathon. Today, she ran at an average speed of 4.2 miles per hour for 3 hours and 30 minutes. How far did she run?

$$\text{Distance} = 4.2 \times 3.5$$

$$\text{Distance} = 14.7 \text{ miles}$$

# Work

$$\text{Total amount of work} = \text{Rate} \times \text{Time}$$

The formula for finding the total amount of work performed is nearly the same as the distance formula.

If Carlos lays bricks at a rate of 20 bricks per hour, how many hours will it take him to complete a brick wall made up of 800 bricks?

$$800 = 20 \times x$$
$$x = \frac{800}{20}$$
$$x = 40 \text{ hours}$$

# Examples

Here are two example questions involving some of the formula in this chapter.

1.  **The round ice-skating rink in the center of town has a diameter of 140 feet. What is the area of the rink?**
    **(Area $= \pi \times$ Radius$^2$)**
    A  15,386 feet$^3$
    B  21,980 feet$^3$
    C  43,960 feet$^3$
    D  61,544 feet$^3$
    E  87,920 feet$^3$

### Explanation

Read the problem and determine what is being asked: What is the area of the rink? Identify pertinent information. The diameter is 140 feet. Choose which operations to use. First you will need to know that diameter is twice the radius. After finding the radius, use the area formula to find the total area. Solve the problem:

$$\text{Area} = \pi \times \text{Radius}^2$$
$$\text{Radius} = \text{Diameter} \div 2$$
$$\text{Radius} = 140 \text{ ft.} \div 2 = 70 \text{ ft.}$$
$$\text{Area} = 3.14 \times 70^2 = 3.14 \times 4,900 = 15,386 \text{ ft.}^2$$

Check your work and select the correct answer. **The answer is A.**

2. **Morgan wants to photograph an eagle sitting on the roof of her office building. She stands 64 feet from the building, and the distance between her and the bird is 80 feet. What is the height of the building?**

Pythagorean theorem: $(a^2 + b^2 = c^2)$

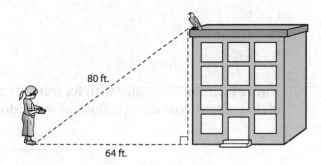

A  12 feet

B  32 feet

C  48 feet

D  64 feet

E  102.4 feet

## Explanation

Read the problem and determine what is being asked: What is the height of the building? Identify pertinent information. She is 64 feet away from the building and 80 feet from the bird. Choose which operations to use. The drawing shows a right triangle, so use the Pythagorean theorem to find the height of the building. Solve the problem:

$$a^2 + b^2 = c^2$$
$$64^2 + b^2 = 80^2$$
$$4096 + b^2 = 6400$$
$$b^2 = 2304$$
$$b - 48$$

Check your work and select the correct answer. **The answer is C.**

# FORMULA DRILLS

1. **What is the area of a circle with radius 4?**

$(\text{Area} = \pi \times \text{Radius}^2)$

A  $4\pi$

B  $8\pi$

C  $12\pi$

D  $16\pi$

E  $24\pi$

2. The rectangular flower bed in front of the public library is 35 feet long and 12 feet wide. What is the distance around the flower bed, in yards?

(Area of a rectangle = length × width)

A   37

B   47

C   94

D   188

E   420

3. Andre is filling his cooler with ice water. If 1 gallon is approximately 231 cubic inches, about how many gallons of water does the cooler hold?

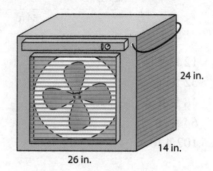

24 in.

26 in.

14 in.

A   12

B   19

C   38

D   76

E   87

4. The area of a square rug is 289 square feet. What is its perimeter?

(Perimeter = 4 × Side)

A   17 feet

B   34 feet

C   68 feet

D   72.25 feet

E   96.33 feet

5. Lakeisha has two storage containers. One is cylindrical, and the other is cubical. What is the difference in the capacity of the containers, in cubic centimeters?

(Volume of Cylinder = $\pi \times$ Radius$^2$ $\times$ Height)

(Volume of Cube = Edge$^3$)

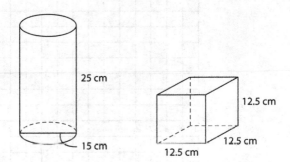

A    1,953.13

B    2,462.5

C    4,415.63

D   15,709.37

E   17,662.5

6. On a business trip, Colton traveled 218 miles before lunch and 184 miles after lunch. If his actual driving time was a total of 6 hours and 45 minutes, what was his average rate of speed to the nearest tenth of a mile per hour?

(Distance = Rate $\times$ Time)

A    40.1

B    57.4

C    58.1

D    59.6

E    62.3

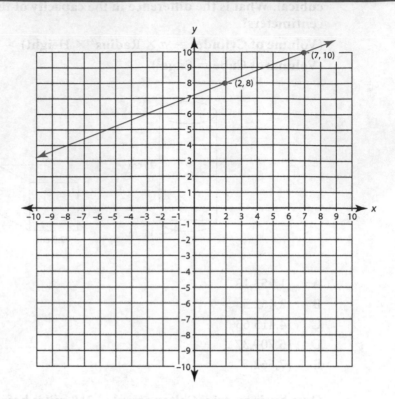

7. **What is the distance between the points on the coordinate plane, rounded to the nearest tenth?**

$$\left(\text{Distance between points} = \sqrt{(x_2 - x_1)^2 + (y_1 - y_3)^2}\right)$$

A  2.6

B  3.7

C  5.2

D  5.4

E  6.7

8. **What is the slope of the line?**

$$\left( \text{Slope of a line} = \frac{y_2 - y_1}{x_2 - x_1} \right)$$

A  $\dfrac{5}{2}$

B  $\dfrac{2}{5}$

C  $\dfrac{1}{2}$

D  $\dfrac{1}{4}$

E  $\dfrac{1}{8}$

9. **What is the surface area of a cube with sides of 2 feet?**

$(\text{Area} = \text{Side}^2)$

A  24 square feet
B  12 square feet
C  8 square feet
D  4 square feet
E  2 square feet

10. **Elba can paint a room in 4 hours. Jack can paint the same room in 3 hours. How long will it take them to paint the room if they work together?**

$(\text{Work} = \text{Rate} \times \text{Time})$

A  1.7 hours
B  2 hours
C  3 hours
D  4 hours
E  7 hours

**Answers are on page 727.**

Answers are on page 737.

# Part VIII
# Practice Tests

# 39

# HiSET® Exam
## Practice Test 1

# *HiSET*® Exam Practice Test 1
## Answer Sheet
## Language Arts—Writing, Part 1

| | A | B | C | D | | A | B | C | D |
|---|---|---|---|---|---|---|---|---|---|
| 1 | | | | | 26 | | | | |
| 2 | | | | | 27 | | | | |
| 3 | | | | | 28 | | | | |
| 4 | | | | | 29 | | | | |
| 5 | | | | | 30 | | | | |
| 6 | | | | | 31 | | | | |
| 7 | | | | | 32 | | | | |
| 8 | | | | | 33 | | | | |
| 9 | | | | | 34 | | | | |
| 10 | | | | | 35 | | | | |
| 11 | | | | | 36 | | | | |
| 12 | | | | | 37 | | | | |
| 13 | | | | | 38 | | | | |
| 14 | | | | | 39 | | | | |
| 15 | | | | | 40 | | | | |
| 16 | | | | | 41 | | | | |
| 17 | | | | | 42 | | | | |
| 18 | | | | | 43 | | | | |
| 19 | | | | | 44 | | | | |
| 20 | | | | | 45 | | | | |
| 21 | | | | | 46 | | | | |
| 22 | | | | | 47 | | | | |
| 23 | | | | | 48 | | | | |
| 24 | | | | | 49 | | | | |
| 25 | | | | | 50 | | | | |

# LANGUAGE ARTS—WRITING, PART 1

**50 Questions**

**75 Minutes**

## Directions

This is a test of some of the skills involved in revising written materials. There are selections similar to the reports, letters, and articles high-school students often need to write. Each selection is presented twice, first in a box in a conventional format and then in a spread-out format with certain parts underlined and numbered. Read quickly through the boxed text to get an idea of its purpose and style. Then go on to the spread-out format.

For each underlined part there are alternatives listed in the right-hand column. Choose the alternative that

- makes the statement grammatically correct
- expresses the idea in the clearest or most appropriate way
- is worded most consistently with the style and purpose of the writing
- organizes the ideas in the most effective way

In some cases, there may be more than one problem to correct or improve.

When you have decided which alternative is best, mark your choice on the answer sheet. If you think the original underlined version is best, choose *"No change."* In questions about organization, you will probably find it helpful to look at the boxed text. In the questions about spelling, you are to indicate which of three underlined words is misspelled, if any. If there are no errors in any of the words, mark *"None."*

Work as quickly as you can without becoming careless. Don't spend too much time on any question that is difficult for you to answer. Instead, skip it and return to it later if you have time. Try to answer every question even if you have to guess.

Mark all your answers on the answer sheet. Give only one answer to each question and make every mark heavy and dark. If you decide to change one of your answers, be sure to erase the first mark completely. Be sure that the number of the question you are answering matches the number of the row of answer choices you are marking on your answer sheet.

**GO ON TO THE NEXT PAGE ➡**

Read quickly through the draft article in the box below. Then go to the spread-out version and consider the suggestions for revision.

---

### Diggers Hotline

1. April is national safe digging month. With the approach of spring, the snow begins to disappear. Homeowners want to get started on outdoor projects and are hoping to get them done quickly. It's understandable.

2. Before starting on any project that require digging, all homeowners and contractors must call the Diggers Hotline at the toll-free number: (800) DIGGERS. According to state law, anyone digging must contact the hotline at least three business days before starting work. They must provide information on the type of work the location, and the type of equipment to be used. Diggers Hotline contacts the utility company. The utility company then sent out technicians. They mark the underground cables or pipes with spray paint and colored flags. After that, the digging can proceed safely.

3. Diggers Hotline helps avoid damaging homes. Basically ensures that neighborhoods will not be without gas or electricity for long periods of time. Nationally, every year there are more than 200,000 accidents that occur when excavating work is performed. These could be prevented but that's why it is important to call before you dig.

---

### Diggers Hotline

1. April is <u>national safe digging</u><br>        <sub>1</sub><br>   <u>month</u>. With the approach of<br>    <sub>1</sub><br>   spring, the snow begins to<br>   disappear. Homeowners want to get<br>   started on outdoor projects and<br>   <u>are hoping to get them done quickly</u>.<br>             <sub>2</sub><br>   It's understandable.

2. Before starting on any project that

   <u>require</u> digging, all homeowners<br>    <sub>3</sub><br>   and contractors must call the<br>   Diggers Hotline at the toll-free<br>   number: (800) DIGGERS.<br>   According to state law, anyone<br>   digging must contact the hotline at

**1**

A (*No change*)

B national Safe Digging Month

C National safe digging month

D National Safe Digging Month

**2**

A (*No change*)

B hoping to get it done quickly

C hoping, to get them done quickly

D hope to get them done quickly

**3**

A (*No change*)

B requires

C requiring

D required

least three business days before
starting work. They must provide
information on the type of work the
location, and the type of equipment
<sub>4</sub>
to be used. Diggers Hotline
contacts the utility company.

The utility company then sent out
<sub>5</sub>
technicians. They mark the
underground cables or pipes with
spray paint and colored flags. After
that, the digging can proceed safely.

3. Diggers Hotline helps avoid
damaging homes. Basically ensures
<sub>6</sub>
that neighborhoods will not be
without gas or electricity for long
periods of time. Nationally, every

year there are more than 200,000
<sub>7</sub>
accidents that occur when
excavating work is performed.

These could be prevented but that's
<sub>8</sub>
why it is important to call before
<sub>8</sub>
you dig.

**4**

A *(No change)*
B the type of work. The location, and
the type of equipment
C the type of work, the location, and
the type of equipment
D the type of work, the location and
the type of equipment

**5**

A *(No change)*
B utility company, then sent
C utility company then sends
D utility company then was sending

**6**

A *(No change)*
B Basically, it ensures
C Basically, they ensures
D Basically, one ensures

**7**

A *(No change)*
B there are more then
C their are more than
D they're are more than

**8**

A *(No change)*
B could be prevented, but that's why
C could be prevented but thats why
D would be prevented but that's why

## History of Video Gaming

1. In the 1950s and 1960s there were engineers that, in their spare time, designed games to be played on mainframe computers. They worked at universities and research facilities. The general public didn't have access. The father of video gaming was Ralph Baer. In 1972 he invented the Odyssey console. It was sold by magnavox and came with a cartridge that had 12 games.

2. During the 1970s and 1980s other console systems were introduced. The most notable was the Atari 2600. In 1981 Nintendo released Donkey Kong. It was the first game to have for levels of difficulty. More and more games was released, including classics like Flight Simulator, SimCity, and Street Fighter 2. Consoles became larger and graphics became more complex. In 1995 Sony introduced Playstation, featuring games on CDs with 3D graphics. Two million were sold the first year alone.

3. Today's consoles use motion control for the gamer to control the figures. Nintendo's Wii, the Sony Playstation 3, and Microsoft's Xbox 360 allow players access to long-running series hit games like Super Mario Brothers, Halo, Grand Theft, and Legend of Zelda. Cloud gaming, in which the game is stored on a server and streamed into a computer, is gaining in popularity. And video gaming isn't just for kids anymore. First-generation gamers had entered their thirties and forties.

## History of Video Gaming

1. In the 1950s and 1960s <u>there were engineers that,</u> in their spare time, designed games to be played on mainframe computers. They worked at universities and research facilities. <u>The general public didn't have access.</u> The father of video gaming was Ralph Baer. In 1972 he invented the Odyssey console. It

   <u>was sold by magnavox</u> and came with a cartridge that had 12 games.

2. During the 1970s and 1980s other console systems were introduced. The most notable was the Atari 2600. In 1981 Nintendo released

**9**
A (*No change*)
B there were engineers that
C there were engineers who,
D there was engineers that,

**10** **The most effective revision of this sentence would begin with which group of words?**
A (*No change*)
B As a result, the public
C Instead of this, the public
D No public access

**11**
A (*No change*)
B was sold by Magnavox
C is sold by magnavox
D was sold, by Magnavox

*Donkey Kong.* It was the first game

to have for levels of difficulty. More

and more games was released,

including classics like *Flight*

*Simulator*, *SimCity*, and *Street*

*Fighter 2*. Consoles became larger

and graphics became more

complex. In 1995 Sony introduced

Playstation, featuring games on

CDs with 3D graphics. Two million

were sold the first year alone.

3. Today's consoles use motion control

for the gamer to control the figures.

Nintendo's Wii, the Sony

Playstation 3, and Microsoft's Xbox

360 allow players access to long-

running series hit games like *Super*

*Mario Brothers*, *Halo*, *Grand Theft*

*Auto*, and *Legend of Zelda*. Cloud

**12** **Reread the following sentences:**
*During the 1970s and 1980s other console systems were introduced. The most notable was the Atari 2600.*

**The most effective combination of these sentences would include which group of words?**

A  (*No change*)

B  introduced and the most notable could be

C  introduced, however, the most notable

D  introduced, the most notable being

**13**

A  (*No change*)

B  was the first, game to have for levels

C  was the first game to have four levels

D  were the first game to have for levels

**14**

A  (*No change*)

B  is

C  are

D  were

gaming, in which the game is stored
<u>15</u>
on a server and streamed into a
<u>15</u>
computer, is gaining in popularity.
<u>15</u>
And video gaming isn't just for kids

anymore. First-generation gamers

**15**

**A** (*No change*)

**B** gaming, in which the game is stored on a server and streamed into a computer, are gaining

**C** gaming, where the game is stored on a server and streamed into a computer is gaining

**D** gaming, in which the game is stored on a server and streamed into a computer, was gaining

had entered their thirties and
<u>16</u>
forties.

**16**

**A** (*No change*)

**B** entered their thirties

**C** are entering their thirties

**D** had entered their thirties'

---

39 Lucas Ave.
Stillwater, AL 32100
dmays@gmail.org
July 6, 2011

Mr. Joe Menot
Pegasus Tool & Die Co.
3211 Hwy. 65 S
Stillwater, AL 32100

Dear Mr. Menot:

1. Please accept my application for the position of apprentice machinist, which was posted in Monday's *Post Star*. I would very much like to apply for that job. I graduated from Stillwater High School in June. While at the school, I took Shop my first year and I loved it. I went to elementary school in Stillwater too.

2. I learned more in Shop than I did in any other class. My project was to build a miniature steam engine. I completed it by the end of the school year with the help of Mr. Mylecrane. He is my teacher. I having always enjoyed working with my hands and I learn very quickly. I especially liked working on the lathe Mr. Mylecrane said he would write a letter of recommendation for me if it would help.

3. I am enclosing a resume. At the end of the week, will call you and see if I can arrange a visit. I would very much like to see how things are done at Pegasus and what kinds of things you manufacture. Thank you for your time. I look forward to hour meeting.

Sincerely yours,

David Mays

39 Lucas Ave.

Stillwater, AL 32100

dmays@gmail.org

July 6, 2011

Mr. Joe Menot

Pegasus Tool & Die Co.

3211 Hwy. 65 S

Stillwater, AL 32100

Dear Mr. Menot:

1. Please accept my <u>application</u> for the
   position of <u>apprentice machinist</u>,
   which was posted in Monday's Post
   Star. I would very much like to
   apply for that job. I graduated from
   Stillwater High School in June.
   While at the school, I took Shop my
   first year and I loved it. I went to
   elementary school in Stillwater too.

2. I learned more in Shop than I did in
   any other class. My project was to
   build a miniature steam engine. I
   completed it by the end of the
   school year with the help of Mr.
   Mylecrane. He is my teacher.

**17 Which, if any, of the three underlined words is misspelled?**

A None

B application

C apprentice

D machinist

**18 Which revision should be made to paragraph 1?**

A (*No change*)

B remove sentence 5

C begin a new paragraph after sentence 4

D move sentence 3 to the end of the paragraph

**19 Reread the following sentences:**
*I completed it by the end of the school year with the help of Mr. Mylecrane. He is my teacher.*

**The most effective combination of these sentences would include which group of words?**

A Mr. Mylecrane, my teacher.

B Mr. Mylecrane, which is my teacher.

C Mr. Mylecrane, and he is my teacher.

D Mr. Mylecrane, as he is my teacher.

GO ON TO THE NEXT PAGE ➡

I <u>having always enjoyed working</u>
<sub>20</sub>
with my hands and I learn very
quickly. I especially liked working

on the <u>lathe Mr. Mylecrane</u> said
<sub>21</sub>
he would write a letter of
recommendation for me if it
would help.

3. I am enclosing a resume. At the end
of <u>the week, will call you</u> and see if I
<sub>22</sub>
can arrange a visit. I would

very much like <u>to see how things</u>
<sub>23</sub>
<u>are done at Pegasus</u> and what kinds
<sub>23</sub>
of things you manufacture.

Thank you for your time. I look
forward to <u>hour</u> meeting.
<sub>24</sub>
Sincerely yours,

David Mays

**20**

A (*No change*)

B have always enjoyed working

C had always enjoyed

D was always enjoying working

**21**

A (*No change*)

B lathe, Mr. Mylecrane

C lathe, though Mr. Mylecrane

D lathe. Mr. Mylecrane

**22**

A (*No change*)

B the week, I will call you

C the week, will call them

D the week will call you

**23**

A (*No change*)

B to see, how things are done at Pegasus

C to see how things is done at Pegasus

D to see how things are done at pegasus

**24**

A (*No change*)

B your

C we

D our

## Jets: Then and Now

1. Jet aircraft are different from propeller planes, they use the exhaust from a gas turbine for propulsion. The first jet airplane, a Heinkel He 178, flew in 1939 in Germany. The Germans developed other jets during world war II, but they were never used extensively in the war or mass-produced. The first jet airliner was the de Havilland Comet. Its maiden flight was in 1952. The plane seated 78 passengers and had a top speed of 500 mph.

2. In 1958, Boeing introduced the 707. It had four wing-mounted jet engines and had a speed of 550 MPH. The aircraft was 128 feet long. With a wingspan of 130 feet and seating for 140 people. The early 707s had a range of 3,500 miles. Boeing also produced the Tri-jet in the 1960s. The plane having three jet engines mounted in the rear and was used extensively for shorter flights.

3. Today, both Boeing and Airbus are developing a new generation of wide body craft. Boeing has the 787 and Airbus the A-380. Seating up to 575 passengers, the planes will be 20 feet wide, will fly at 650 MPH. It will have a range of more than 8,000 miles. Jets truly have come a long way in a short time.

4. Another company, Airbus, rolled out its first of a new generation of jet aircraft, in 1972, called wide body jets. Called the A-300, the plane had too wing mounted engines, with a fuselage of 177 feet and a wing span of 147 feet. The plane seated 250, was cruising at 567 MPH, and had a range of 4,150 miles.

## Jets: Then and Now

1. Jet aircraft <u>are different from</u>
   <sub>25</sub>
   <u>propeller planes, they use</u> the
   <sub>25</sub>
   exhaust from a gas turbine for propulsion. The first jet airplane, a Heinkel He 178, flew in 1939 in Germany.

   The <u>Germans developed other jets</u>
   <sub>26</sub>
   <u>during world war II</u>, but they were
   <sub>26</sub>
   never used extensively in the war or mass-produced. The first jet airliner was the de Havilland Comet. Its maiden flight was in 1952. The plane seated 78 passengers and had a top speed of 500 mph.

**25**

A (*No change*)

B are different, from propeller planes, they use

C are different from propeller planes because they use

D are different from propeller planes they use

**26**

A (*No change*)

B Germans developed other jets during World War II,

C Germans' developed other jets during world war II,

D Germans developed other jets during world war II

GO ON TO THE NEXT PAGE ➡

2. In 1958, Boeing introduced the 707. It had four wing-mounted jet engines and had a speed of 550 MPH. The aircraft was 128 feet <u>long. With</u> a <sub>27</sub> wingspan of 130 feet and seating for 140 people. The early 707s had a range of 3,500 miles. Boeing also produced the Tri-jet in the 1960s.

The plane <u>having</u> three jet engines <sub>29</sub> mounted in the rear and was used extensively for shorter flights.

3. Today, both Boeing and Airbus are developing a new generation of wide body craft. Boeing has the 787 and Airbus the A-380. Seating up to 575 passengers, the planes will be 20 feet wide, will fly at 650 MPH. It will have a range of more than 8,000 miles. Jets truly have come a long way in a short time.

**27**

A (*No change*)

B long with

C long: with

D long; with

**28 Which sentence would be most effective if inserted at the beginning of paragraph 1?**

A The history of jet travel is as exciting as it is rich.

B Propeller planes are smaller than jet planes and cost less too.

C Traveling in a jet takes less time than traveling in a propeller plane.

D Traveling by plane is a lot nicer now that there are jets.

**29**

A (*No change*)

B had

C was having

D is having

**30 Reread the following sentences:**
*Seating up to 575 passengers, the planes will be 20 feet wide, will fly at 650 mph. It will have a range of more than 8,000 miles.*

**The most effective combination of these sentences would include which group of words?**

A and will have a range

B and having a range

C and had a range

D yet will have a range

4. <u>Another company, Airbus, rolled</u>
   <sup>31</sup>
   <u>out its first of a new generation of</u>
   <sup>31</sup>
   <u>jet aircraft, in 1972, called wide</u>
   <sup>31</sup>
   <u>body jets.</u> Called the A-300, the
   <sup>31</sup>
   plane had too wing mounted

   engines, with a fuselage of 177 feet

   and a wing span of 147 feet. The

   plane seated 250, <u>was cruising</u> at
   <sup>32</sup>
   567 MPH, and had a range of

   4,150 miles.

**31**

A (*No change*)

B Another company, Airbus, rolled out its first of a new generation of jet aircraft, called wide-body jets, in 1972.

C Another company, Airbus, rolled out it's first of a new generation of jet aircraft, in 1972, called wide-body jets.

D Another company, Airbus, rolled out its first of a new generation, of jet aircraft, in 1972, called wide-body jets.

**32**

A (*No change*)

B were cruising

C cruising

D cruised

**33 Which revision would improve the effectiveness of the article?**

A move paragraph 3 after paragraph 4

B join paragraphs 3 and 4

C begin a new paragraph after the second sentence of paragraph 3.

D join paragraphs 1 and 2

GO ON TO THE NEXT PAGE ➡

---

### Watch Out for Telemarketing Fraud

1. Every year hundreds of million dollars are losing by consumers due to telemarketing fraud. People are duped on the phone into sending money to someone. We end up getting nothing in return. Here are some warning signs of telephone fraud to watch out for.

2. If a person calls you and says that you have to act right away or the offer will expire that is a sign that something is wrong. Or, if he says you can't afford to miss out on a high profit opportunity, that is another sign of fraud. You should never give a credit card number or bank account number to anybody over the phone.

3. When someone calls you to sell you something, ask for a website address for the business so you can look to see if they is legitimate. Ask for references from other people who were called by the telemarketer. Whatever the situation, make sure you get something in writing before you agree to spend any money. A reputable telemarketer will have no problem agreeing to your requests. To summarize, be alert to the warning signs when a caller tries to sell you something over the phone. If the offer is for reel, then you can be confident in proceeding. If you feel that you have been a victim of fraud, make sure you call the authorities at once.

---

### Watch Out for Telemarketing Fraud

1. Every year hundreds of million dollars <u>are losing by consumers</u> due
   <sub>34</sub>
   to telemarketing fraud. People are duped on the phone into sending

   money to someone. <u>We</u> end up
   <sub>35</sub>
   getting nothing in return. Here are some warning signs of telephone fraud to watch out for.

**34**

A *(No change)*

B are losing by consumers

C are lost by consumers

D are losing to consumers

**35**

A *(No change)*

B She

C Them

D They

2. If a person calls you and says that you have to act right away or the offer will <u>expire that</u> is a sign that
   <sub>36</sub>
   something is wrong. Or, if he says you can't afford to miss out on a high profit opportunity, that is another sign of fraud.

**36**

A *(No change)*

B expire, that

C expiring, that

D expire; that

You <u>should never give</u> a credit card
<sub>37</sub>
number or bank account number to
anybody over the phone.

**37**
A  (*No change*)
B  would never giving
C  should never given
D  should never be giving

**38 Which sentence would be most effective if inserted at the beginning of paragraph 3?**

A  It is best to deal only with people who have been recommended by a friend.

B  Never give out personal information about yourself unless you are completely sure the person is legitimate.

C  Telephone fraud is one of the most devious crimes that exist in today's world.

D  There are other steps you can take to prevent yourself from being a victim of fraud as well.

3. When someone calls you to sell you something, ask for a website address for the business so you can look to see if <u>they is</u> legitimate. Ask
<sub>39</sub>
for references from other people who were called by the telemarketer. Whatever the situation, make sure you get something in writing before you agree to spend any money. A reputable telemarketer will have no problem agreeing to your requests. To summarize, be alert to the warning signs when a caller tries to sell you something over the phone.

**39**
A  (*No change*)
B  they are
C  he or she are
D  he or she is

If the offer is for <u>reel</u>, then you can
<sub>40</sub>
be <u>confident</u> in <u>proceeding</u>. If you
<sub>40</sub>          <sub>40</sub>
feel that you have been a victim of

fraud, make sure you call the

authorities at once.

**40** **Which, if any, of the underlined words is misspelled?**

A (*No change*)

B reel

C confident

D proceeding

**41** **Which revision would improve the effectiveness of paragraph 3?**

A Switch the order of the first and second sentences.

B Remove the sentence that begins with *To summarize,*

C Move the sentence that begins with *If the offer is for reel* to the beginning of the paragraph

D Begin a new paragraph with the sentence that begins with *To summarize,*

## E-mail

To: customerservice@bigboxappliance.com
Subject: Warranty Coverage
Dear Sir/Madam:

1. I bought a laptop computer at your store on February 12, 2009. It was a New World computer. At the same time I purchased a two-year extended warranty for $129. I took the computer back to the store about six months later because the DVD drive would not work properly. An associate sent the computer to your repair facility, and 10 days or so later, the laptop was returned in working order. There was no charge to me.
2. Then yesterday, the computer would not turn on. I brought the computer into the store. The computer was diagnosed as having a defective screen. I was told the cost to replace them would be $319 plus tax. I replied that I had purchased the extended warranty but the associate showed me on his computer that the warranty had expired six days ago.
3. Obviously I was outraged. Your circular last Sunday advertise a brand-new laptop for $399, which is practically what I would have to pay to fix my computer. I was never notified that my warranty would expire and was never offering the opportunity to extend it. I believe Big Box should take the responsibility and repair the computer at no charge. I have been a good customer and made many purchases at your store. I hope to hear from you soon. Luckily my friend let me use his computer so I could send this.

Andrea Fox
Cell: (654) 123-4567
foxyg@aol.net

## E-mail

To: customerservice@bigboxappliance.com

Subject: Warranty Coverage

Dear Sir/Madam:

1. I bought a laptop computer at your store on February 12, 2009. It was a New World computer.

**42 Reread the following sentences:**

*I bought a laptop computer at your store on February 12, 2009. It was a New World computer.*

**The most effective combination of these sentences would include which group of words?**

A  which was

B  which was just made

C  a New World laptop computer

D  a computer made by New World

At the same <u>time I</u> purchased a
<sub>43</sub>
two-year extended warranty for
$129. I took the computer back to
the store about six months later
because the DVD drive would not
work properly. An associate sent the
computer to your repair facility, and
10 days or so later, the laptop was
returned in working order. There
was no charge to me.

2. Then yesterday, the computer would
not turn on. I brought the computer
into the store. The computer was
diagnosed as having a defective
screen. I was told the cost <u>to replace</u>
<sub>44</sub>
<u>them would be $319</u> plus tax. I
<sub>44</sub>

replied that I <u>had purchased the</u>
<sub>45</sub>
<u>extended warranty</u> but the associate
<sub>45</sub>
showed me on his computer that the
warranty had expired six days ago.

3. Obviously I was outraged. Your
circular last Sunday <u>advertise</u> a
<sub>46</sub>
brand-new laptop for $399, which is
practically what I would have to pay
to fix my computer.

**43**

A  (*No change*)
B  time; I
C  time, I
D  time and I

**44**

A  (*No change*)
B  to be replacing them would be $319
C  to replace it would be $319
D  to replace them would be $319,

**45**

A  (*No change*)
B  had purchased the extend warranty
C  had purchased the extended
   warranty,
D  have purchased the extended
   warranty

**46**

A  (*No change*)
B  advertises
C  was advertising
D  advertised

I was never <u>notified that my</u>
<sub>47</sub>
<u>warranty would expire and was</u>
<sub>47</sub>
<u>never offering</u> the opportunity to
<sub>47</sub>

extend it. <u>I believe Big Box should</u>
<sub>48</sub>
<u>take the responsibility</u> and repair
<sub>48</sub>
the computer at no charge. I have

been a good customer and made

many purchases at your store.

I hope to hear from <u>you</u> soon.
<sub>49</sub>
Luckily my friend let me use his

computer so I could send this.

Andrea Fox

Cell: (654) 123-4567

foxyg@aol.net

**47**

A  (*No change*)

B  notifies that my warranty would expire and was never offering

C  notified that my warranty would expire; and was never offering

D  notified that my warranty would expire and was never offered

**48**

A  (*No change*)

B  I believe Big Box should be taking the responsibility

C  I believe Big Box should take the responsibility,

D  I believes Big Box should take the responsibility

**49**

A  (*No change*)

B  them

C  it

D  him

**50 Which revision would improve the effectiveness of paragraph 3?**

A  move the last sentence to after the first sentence

B  move the first sentence to before the last sentence

C  remove the last sentence

D  add this sentence to the end of the paragraph: *At least he does not let me down.*

**STOP. This is the end of Part 1 of the Language Arts—Writing test.**

# ANSWERS: LANGUAGE ARTS—WRITING, PART 1

1. **(D)** Option (D) is correct because it capitalizes all the words that make up the proper name.

2. **(D)** Option (D) is correct because the verb *hope* is parallel to the preceding verb, *want*.

3. **(B)** Option (B) is correct. The subject, *project*, is singular, so it needs a singular verb.

4. **(C)** Option (C) is correct because it places a comma between all the items in a series.

5. **(C)** Option (C) is correct because this sentence refers to the information in the previous sentence, which is in the present tense (*contacts*). To be parallel and remain in the same tense, the verb must be *sends*.

6. **(B)** Option (B) is correct because it adds the singular subject *it*, referring to the hotline and making it a complete sentence.

7. **(A)** Option (A) is correct because it has the correct possessive pronoun *there* and the correct idiom *more than*.

8. **(B)** Option (B) is the correct choice because it places a necessary comma between the two clauses in the compound sentence.

9. **(C)** Option (C) is correct because it replaces a pronoun that refers to a thing with a pronoun that refers to people—in this case, *engineers*. The correct pronoun to refer to people is *who*.

10. **(B)** Option (B) is correct; the transition phrase *as a result* indicates the cause-and-effect relationship that exists here. A comma should follow a transition phrase. Option (C) also uses a transition phrase with a comma, but expresses a contrasting relationship rather than a cause-and-effect one.

11. **(B)** Option (B) correctly capitalizes the name of the company, Magnavox. Option (D) does this as well, but includes an unnecessary comma.

12. **(D)** Option (D) combines the two sentences in the most succinct method, making the second one an appositive. Option (B) needs a comma to separate the two independent clauses, after the coordinating conjunction *and*. Option (C) combines the sentence inappropriately; the transition *however* needs a semicolon before it.

13. **(C)** Option (C) substitutes the correct homonym (the number) for the incorrect one (*for*).

14. **(D)** Option (D) is correct because it changes a verb in singular form to one in plural form so that it agrees with the subject, *games*.

15. **(A)** The sentence is correct as written. Option (B) is incorrect because it replaces a correct singular verb with a plural form. Option (C) would remove the necessary comma at the end of the modifying phrase and uses the incorrect modifier *where*. Option (D) is wrong because it changes the verb to past tense, but the action is in the present.

16. **(C)** Option (C) is correct because it changes a verb in the past tense to one in the active present tense, since the action is on going now.

17. **(A)** Option (A) is correct because none of the three words are misspelled.

18. **(B)** Option (B) correctly eliminates a sentence that does not support the main idea or serve any real function in the paragraph.

19. **(A)** Option (A) is correct because it uses a simple appositive to combine the two ideas in the sentences.

20. **(B)** Option (B) is correct because the verb is in the correct tense and form. Present perfect tense is appropriate for action that is ongoing.

21. **(D)** Option (D) correctly separates the run-on sentence, which consists of two complete ideas, with a period. Option (A) is a run-on sentence. Option (B) is a comma splice. Option (C) inserts a transition word that changes the meaning.

22. **(B)** Option (B) completes the fragment by inserting a subject, *I*.

23. **(A)** The sentence is correct as written. Option (B) inserts an unnecessary comma. Option (C) is wrong because the verb, *is*, does not agree with its subject, *things*. Option (D) uses lowercase for a proper name.

24. **(D)** Option (D) is correct because it uses the correct homonym (the possessive pronoun for the second person plural) instead of the word *hour* (a unit of time).

25. **(C)** Option (C) adds an appropriate and necessary subordinating conjunction to join the two sentences. Option (D) does not add the subordinating conjunction needed to separate the two clauses, making a run-on sentence.

26. **(B)** Option (B) is correct because a proper name—in this case, *World War II*—must be capitalized.

27. **(B)** Option (B) joins the fragment with the complete sentence before it. Options (C) and (D) incorrectly use a semicolon and a colon, respectively, to connect the fragment to the previous sentence.

28. **(A)** Option (A) is a topic sentence that introduces the historical information in paragraph 1.

29. **(B)** Option (B) corrects the verb by putting it in the past tense to agree with the verb in the previous sentence.

30. **(A)** Option (A) is correct because it combines the ideas using a conjunction and creates a parallel structure with the verb.

31. **(B)** Option (B) is correct because the phrase modifies *jet aircraft* and *in 1972*.

32. **(D)** Option (D) is correct because it creates parallel structure between the past tense verbs in the sentence.

**GO ON TO THE NEXT PAGE**

33. **(A)** Option (A) is correct because it moves the paragraph that talks about what is happening today to the end of the passage, which makes the passage flow logically.

34. **(C)** Option (C) is correct because it changes an improper verb form to a proper one.

35. **(D)** Option (D) is correct; *they* is the correct pronoun because it agrees with its antecedent in the previous sentence, *people*.

36. **(B)** Option (B) is correct because it inserts a comma after the opening clause of a compound sentence.

37. **(A)** The sentence is correct as written. Options (B), (C), and (D) have incorrect verb forms.

38. **(D)** Option (D) is a topic sentence that tells what the paragraph is about, so it is most effective at the beginning of the paragraph.

39. **(D)** Option (D) is correct because the antecedent *someone* is singular and must take a singular pronoun and verb.

40. **(B)** Option (B) is correct because the homonym *reel* (spool) is used rather than the correct *real* (genuine).

41. **(D)** Option (D) is correct because it splits the paragraph between two different topics: what to do when a person calls you and a summary.

42. **(C)** Option (C) is correct because the most effective combination. It puts the descriptors of the computer all together.

43. **(C)** Option (C) is correct because a comma is needed after an opening clause.

44. **(C)** Option (C) is correct because *it* agrees with its antecedent, *screen*.

45. **(C)** Option (C) is correct because a compound sentence needs a comma between its two clauses. The past perfect verb tense is correct.

46. **(D)** Option (D) is correct because it puts the verb in the past tense.

47. **(D)** Option (D) is correct because it changes the verb to agree with *notified* and creates parallel structure between them.

48. **(A)** The sentence is correct as written. The verbs *believe* and *take* are in the correct tense and are parallel.

49. **(A)** The sentence is correct as written. *It* refers to the company. None of the other options agree with the antecedent.

50. **(C)** Option (C) is correct because this sentence is the least related to the topic of the paragraph.

# *HiSET*® Exam Practice Test 1
## Answer Sheet
## Language Arts—Writing, Part 2

# LANGUAGE ARTS—WRITING, PART 2

## Essay Directions and Topic

In the box below is your assigned topic. You must write on the assigned topic ONLY.

You will have 45 minutes to write on your assigned essay topic. You may return to the multiple-choice section after you complete your essay if you have time remaining in this test period.

The essay will be evaluated based on the following features:

- Well-focused main points
- Clear organization
- Specific development of your ideas
- Control of sentence structure, punctuation, grammar, word choice, and spelling

REMEMBER, YOU MUST COMPLETE BOTH THE MULTIPLE-CHOICE QUESTIONS (PART 1) AND THE ESSAY (PART 2) TO RECEIVE A SCORE ON THE LANGUAGE ARTS—WRITING TEST. To avoid having to repeat both parts of the test, be sure to do the following:

- Do not leave the pages blank.
- Write legibly <u>in ink</u> so that the evaluators will be able to read your writing.
- Write on the assigned topic. If you write on a topic other than the one assigned, you will not receive a score for the Language Arts—Writing Test.
- Write your essay on the lined pages of the separate answer sheet booklet. Only the writing on these pages will be scored.

---

### TOPIC A

Many people today are able to work at home.

Write an essay that tells the advantages or disadvantages of working at home. Give your opinion and support your view from your own personal observations and experiences.

---

Part 2 is a test to determine how well you can use written language to explain your ideas. In preparing your essay, you should take the following steps:

- Read the DIRECTIONS and the TOPIC carefully.
- Plan your essay before you write. Use the scratch paper provided to make any notes. These notes will be collected but not scored.
- Before you turn in your essay, reread what you have written and make any changes that will improve your essay.

Your essay should be long enough to develop the topic adequately.

# ANSWERS: LANGUAGE ARTS—WRITING, PART 2

All essays should be scored according to the HiSET Exam essay rubric.

| Score Code | Description |
| --- | --- |
| 6 | **Proficient** |
| | Essays at this score point show proficient skill in responding to the task. The response demonstrates proficient skill in developing ideas. It maintains focus on a clear central idea throughout the response. The response provides several ideas with effective and thorough explanation, offering relevant and fully elaborated reasons, examples, and/or details to support ideas. The response demonstrates strong critical thinking and insight by discussing complications of the issue and/or successfully addressing counterarguments. The response demonstrates proficient skill in organization. It has an effective, well-developed introduction and conclusion, with an engaging introduction that clearly sets up the rest of the response. Clear and appropriate paragraphing is used, creating a coherent whole. Logical sequencing of ideas is demonstrated throughout the response. Effective transitions are used throughout the response to support coherence. The response demonstrates proficient skill in language. Word choice is precise, varied, and engaging. The response effectively varies sentence length and complexity. Voice is appropriate for audience and purpose, and enhances the effectiveness of the response. No errors or only a few superficial errors appear, and the response demonstrates sophisticated use of grammar, usage, and mechanics. |
| 5 | **Competent** |
| | Essays at this score point show competent skill in responding to the task. The response demonstrates competent skill in developing ideas. It maintains focus on a clear central idea throughout the response. The response provides several ideas with complete explanation, offering specific, relevant, and somewhat elaborated reasons, examples, and/or details to support ideas. The response demonstrates some critical thinking by introducing and addressing complications of the issue and/or addressing counterarguments. The response demonstrates competent skill in organization. The introduction and conclusion are clear and generally well-developed, and the introduction clearly sets up the rest of the response. Clear and appropriate paragraphing is used, with logical sequencing of ideas through most of the response. Varied transitions are used between and within paragraphs to support coherence. The response demonstrates competent skill in language. Word choice is usually precise and varied. The response uses well-controlled sentences that are varied in length and complexity. Voice is appropriate for audience and purpose. There are few grammar, usage, or mechanics errors and most are superficial. |

| Score Code | Description |
| --- | --- |
| 4 | **Adequate** |

Essays at this score point show adequate skill in responding to the task. The response demonstrates adequate skill in developing ideas. It maintains focus on a central idea, though there may be a few minor lapses. The response provides several ideas with adequate explanation, offering some specific and relevant examples and/or details to support ideas. The response demonstrates adequate skill in organization, with a clear introduction and conclusion that are somewhat developed. The response uses appropriate paragraphing and demonstrates some evidence of logical sequencing of ideas. Transitions are consistently used between and/or within paragraphs, though the transitions may be simple. Adequate skill in language use is demonstrated. Mostly specific and somewhat varied word choice is used. The response demonstrates control of sentences with some variety in length and structure. Voice is usually appropriate for audience and purpose. Some errors in sentence construction, pronoun use, verb forms, and/or spelling are present but do not interfere with understanding.

| | |
| --- | --- |
| 3 | **Limited** |

Essays at this score point show limited skill in responding to the task. The response demonstrates limited skill in developing ideas. It maintains focus on a central idea through some of the response. The response provides several ideas with limited or uneven explanation, offering few or only general examples and/or details to support ideas. Organization demonstrates some developing skill. The response has an introduction and conclusion, though one or both of these may be over- or under-developed. Ideas are grouped together in paragraphs, though the relationship among ideas may at times be unclear. The response uses a few transitions between and/or within paragraphs to support coherence. Some developing skill in language is demonstrated. Word choice is general and the response demonstrates a little variety in sentence structure, although a few long, uncontrolled sentences may be used. Errors in sentence construction, pronoun use, verb forms, and/or spelling are present and may occasionally interfere with understanding.

| | |
| --- | --- |
| 2 | **Weak** |

Essays at this score point show weak skill in responding to the task. The response demonstrates weak development. It provides a few ideas but explanation is minimal or superficial and parts of the explanation may be repetitions or lack relevance. Organization is weak. There is minimal evidence of an introduction and/or conclusion. Some related ideas are grouped together, though paragraphing may not be used. If transitions appear, their use is not controlled. Beginning skill in language is

*(Continued)*

| Score Code | Description |
| --- | --- |
| | demonstrated. Word choice is awkward and/or repetitive. The response has repetitive sentence structure and/or long, uncontrolled sentences. Numerous errors in sentence construction, pronoun use, verb forms, and/or spelling interrupt the flow of communication and some errors may interfere with understanding. |
| 1 | **Deficient**

Essays at this score point show little or no skill in responding to the task. The response has little or no development. It may provide a few ideas but lacks explanation of ideas, only repeats ideas, or the ideas lack relevance. Organization is minimal. The response lacks an introduction and conclusion and does not demonstrate any understanding of paragraphing. If transitions appear, their use is not controlled. Language control is minimal. Word choice and sentence structure are simple. Errors in sentence construction, pronoun use, verb forms, and/or spelling are frequent and may interfere with understanding. |

## Examples of Excellent Topic Sentences

*I think that working at home is a terrific convenience because you can have the best of both worlds.*

*I am totally against working at home because it means there is no separation between your private life and your career.*

## Examples of Using Varied Language and Details While Following the Rules of Edited American English (EAE)

*For instance, you will be able to manage your time more effectively since you won't have to commute to a job site. It also means you will work more effectively since you will not be interrupted by situations that may arise in an office setting.*

*For example, you may end up spending more time working than you would if you worked in an office, and this may have a negative effect on your family life. Also, there would be little or no communication between you and your fellow workers.*

- Organization should follow a clear, logical order.
- The essay should also have a closing that sums it up succinctly, such as:

*These are some of the reasons that I think it is much better to work at home than in an office setting.*

*To sum up my feelings, I think that it is not a good move to work from home because of the added pressures you would experience.*

# *HiSET*® Exam Practice Test 1
## Answer Sheet
## Social Studies

|    | A | B | C | D |    | A | B | C | D |
|----|---|---|---|---|----|---|---|---|---|
| 1  |   |   |   |   | 26 |   |   |   |   |
| 2  |   |   |   |   | 27 |   |   |   |   |
| 3  |   |   |   |   | 28 |   |   |   |   |
| 4  |   |   |   |   | 29 |   |   |   |   |
| 5  |   |   |   |   | 30 |   |   |   |   |
| 6  |   |   |   |   | 31 |   |   |   |   |
| 7  |   |   |   |   | 32 |   |   |   |   |
| 8  |   |   |   |   | 33 |   |   |   |   |
| 9  |   |   |   |   | 34 |   |   |   |   |
| 10 |   |   |   |   | 35 |   |   |   |   |
| 11 |   |   |   |   | 36 |   |   |   |   |
| 12 |   |   |   |   | 37 |   |   |   |   |
| 13 |   |   |   |   | 38 |   |   |   |   |
| 14 |   |   |   |   | 39 |   |   |   |   |
| 15 |   |   |   |   | 40 |   |   |   |   |
| 16 |   |   |   |   | 41 |   |   |   |   |
| 17 |   |   |   |   | 42 |   |   |   |   |
| 18 |   |   |   |   | 43 |   |   |   |   |
| 19 |   |   |   |   | 44 |   |   |   |   |
| 20 |   |   |   |   | 45 |   |   |   |   |
| 21 |   |   |   |   | 46 |   |   |   |   |
| 22 |   |   |   |   | 47 |   |   |   |   |
| 23 |   |   |   |   | 48 |   |   |   |   |
| 24 |   |   |   |   | 49 |   |   |   |   |
| 25 |   |   |   |   | 50 |   |   |   |   |

# SOCIAL STUDIES

## 50 Questions

## 70 Minutes

## Directions

This is a test of your skills in analyzing social studies information. Read each question and decide which of the four alternatives best answers the question. Then mark your choice on your answer sheet. Sometimes several questions are based on the same material. You should carefully read this material, then answer the questions.

Work as quickly as you can without becoming careless. Don't spend too much time on any question that is difficult for you to answer. Instead, skip it and return to it later if you have time. Try to answer every question even if you have to guess.

Mark all your answers on the answer sheet. Give only one answer to each question and make every mark heavy and dark. If you decide to change one of your answers, be sure to erase the first mark completely. Be sure that the number of the question you are answering matches the number of the row of answer choices you are marking on your answer sheet.

### Questions 1 and 2 are based on the following passage.

The Salem witch trials of 1692 in Massachusetts began when young girls from Salem village began to display strange behaviors such as screaming and twisting themselves into unnatural positions. The people of the town thought the girls were being harmed by witches.

More than 150 innocent people were arrested and imprisoned for witchcraft, and as a result of the subsequent trials, 19 people were hanged. In the years that followed, some of the accusers and jurors asked the community to pardon them for their actions. People who were convicted but not executed sent petitions demanding that their sentences be reversed. And centuries later, some descendants still seek to have the names of their ancestors cleared.

The events are an instance of mass hysteria, which occurs when one person exhibits symptoms, like nausea or headaches, and then others begin to show similar symptoms; the cause is psychological, not a contagion. The Salem witch trials are also frequently cited as an example of how things can go wrong in the legal system, such as when trials or interrogations occur based on false accusations. In fact, the term "witch hunt" is commonly used today to describe prosecutions fueled by panic and paranoia.

1. **Which of the following is an opinion, rather than a fact, about the Salem witch trials?**

   A   People in the seventeenth century were more scared of witches than people are today.

   B   The Salem witch trials took place during the colonial period.

   C   Mass hysteria is not caused by infection or disease.

   D   The trials are regularly referred to as an example of a legal system failure.

2. **Based on the passage, it can be assumed that**
   A the people of Salem forgave the accusers and jurors
   B the events of 1692 have reverberated through the ages
   C the young girls from Salem village did not know each other
   D the Salem witch trials were a dangerous time in U.S. history

## Question 3 is based on the following passage.

The Louisiana Purchase of 1803 was a contentious decision. On the one hand, the purchase was considered by some to be unconstitutional and an intrusion on states' rights. On the other hand, it would double the size of the United States. The territory that France offered to the United States stretched from the Gulf of Mexico in the south, north to Canada, west to the Rocky Mountains, and east to the Mississippi River. It would also provide crucial trade access for the United States through the port city of New Orleans. In the end, President Thomas Jefferson proceeded with the purchase, and it became a central moment in his presidency and for the United States.

3. **The title that best expresses the main idea of this passage is:**
   A The Louisiana Purchase: The Expansion of U.S. Territory in the Twentieth Century
   B The Louisiana Purchase: The Turning Point of the U.S.–French Alliance
   C The Louisiana Purchase: How California Became Part of the United States
   D The Louisiana Purchase: A Pivotal yet Controversial Event in U.S. History

## Question 4 is based on the following passage.

The Lewis and Clark Expedition, which took place from 1804 to 1806, was led by Meriwether Lewis and William Clark. The explorers were given two goals. The first was to examine and document the plants, animals, and landscape they found during their journey. The second was to uncover the economic possibilities of the region—specifically, a water-based "Northwest Passage" for sailing from the East Coast of the United States to Asia for trade.

The explorers started in St. Louis, Missouri; crossed the Rocky Mountains; and made it to the area that is present-day Oregon in 1805. They then returned to the East Coast of the United States.

Although the explorers never found the Northwest Passage, the expedition was highly successful. Lewis and Clark brought back essential information in their personal journals about the people, land, plants, and animals they encountered during their travels. The maps they created—the first precise maps of the U.S. Northwest Territory—led to great economic developments, further exploration, and the settlement of the land in the decades to come.

4. **Which of the following sentences summarizes the passage preceding?**

   A   After being unable to find the fabled Northwest Passage to Asia, the Lewis and Clark Expedition was deemed a failure and the group was ordered to return to Washington, DC.

   B   After crossing the Rocky Mountains, Lewis and Clark were surprised by an extremely harsh winter, so they settled in the region and lived among the indigenous people.

   C   Lewis and Clark effectively fulfilled the two goals of their expedition—to carefully document their journey and to open the West for economic development.

   D   The Lewis and Clark Expedition made it possible for the United States to take most territories in the West from Spain.

**Question 5 is based on the following cartoon.**

5. **This cartoon illustrates a foreign policy of the United States from the 1800s known as the Monroe Doctrine. The people in the far right corner of the cartoon represent**

   A   Asian countries

   B   U.S. congressmen

   C   European countries

   D   U.S. state governors

**Questions 6 and 7 are based on the following cartoon.**

LINCOLN'S LAST WARNING.
" Now, if you don't come down, I'll cut the Tree *from under you.*"

6.   **The person in the tree represents**

   A   settlers of the U.S. West

   B   Southern states

   C   Union soldiers

   D   General Ulysses Grant

7.   **What is the subject of this cartoon?**

   A   the execution of Army deserters during the Civil War

   B   the tenacity of the Confederate army as an opponent

   C   the Confederacy's refusal to voluntarily abolish slavery

   D   Lincoln's battles with the Southern states

**Question 8 is based on the following passage.**

Dust storms caused major damage to the American Great Plains in the 1930s. This was the result of severe drought as well as many years of farming where precautions, such as crop rotation or cover crops, were not taken to prevent wind erosion. The natural grasses that normally kept the soil in place and trapped moisture—even during periods of drought and high winds—were lost. This caused winds to blow the soil into huge clouds that traveled as far away as New York and Washington, DC.

Because this natural disaster took place during the Great Depression, many people could not find other work to support their families. Hundreds of thousands of people fled the now-useless farmlands of Texas and Oklahoma and parts of New Mexico, Colorado, and Kansas—or "the Dust Bowl" as the region was then called—to other states such as California, hoping to find employment there. However, many were not successful. They often moved from one area to another, picking fruit or other crops on other people's farms for very low wages.

8. **Which of these statements is accurate according to the information provided in the first paragraph?**

   A   The Great Depression of the 1930s had a devastating effect on the American Great Plains.

   B   Essential crops could not be shipped to the rest of the country because of the dust storms.

   C   People from New York or Washington, DC, fled the dust storms, settling in the American Great Plains.

   D   Proper farming techniques and natural vegetation are essential to maintaining healthy soil and renewable crops.

**Questions 9 and 10 are based on the following poster.**

9. **This poster was used by the U.S. government during which war?**
   A   World War I
   B   the Civil War
   C   World War II
   D   the Korean War

10. **What is the main idea represented by this poster?**
   A   Women must return to the home when men come back from the war.
   B   The homefront would be safer if there were fewer women in the workforce.
   C   The United States will single-handedly win the war.
   D   Women are capable of working the labor-intensive jobs that are crucial to the war effort.

**Question 11 is based on the following passage.**

The Montgomery Bus Boycott was a protest to oppose racial segregation on the public transit system in Montgomery, Alabama. At that time, African Americans were forced to sit at the back of the bus, and if the bus was full, they had to give up their seats to white people boarding the bus after them. The protest began in December 1955, after Rosa Parks, an African-American woman, was arrested for not giving up her seat. From that day forward, the city's African Americans stopped using the buses. People carpooled, took taxis, cycled, or simply walked. The protest was not short-lived, and since African Americans made up the majority of the system's customers, the city's bus system faced great financial hardship. This put pressure on city leaders to resolve the situation. In addition, the protest received a national audience after Martin Luther King's participation and subsequent arrest. The boycott finally ended in December 1956, after the U.S. Supreme Court upheld an earlier ruling in July by a U.S. district court that the bus system's segregation was unconstitutional.

11. **Which statement is supported by the information in the passage?**
   A   An important consequence of the protest was the considerable economic loss for the city transit system.
   B   People who could not walk or cycle were forced to hitchhike in order to get around the city.
   C   Many taxi drivers supported the protesters, even allowing them to pay less than the minimum fare.
   D   The protest was not supported by prominent civil rights leaders such as Martin Luther King

**Question 12 is based on the following passage.**

Although many languages were spoken throughout the lands conquered by the Romans, the official language of the Roman Empire was Latin. "Classical" Latin, as well as Greek, was used for literature and education. Classical Latin was both spoken and written, and it was taught in schools. It did not contain punctuation, lowercase letters, or even spacing between words. The "vulgar" Latin was commonly spoken in the western part of the empire but was rarely written down. In fact, it was written so infrequently that few examples of vulgar Latin exist today. However, vulgar Latin later evolved into the modern "romance" languages, such as Italian, French, Portuguese, and Spanish.

12. **According to the information in this passage, which of the following statements is true?**

    **A**   The eastern part of the Roman Empire spoke mostly Greek.

    **B**   All languages spoken today evolved from Latin.

    **C**   The use of punctuation became customary after the fall of the Roman Empire.

    **D**   Vulgar Latin was the preferred language of Roman soldiers.

**Question 13 is based on the following passage.**

In Western Europe during the Middle Ages, some peasants were known as serfs. The serfs lived on a piece of the land owned by a lord. On that land, the serfs could grow crops to provide for their families and sell the surplus produce for profit. In addition, the lord would protect the serfs' crops from robbers. In return, the serfs were expected to work the lord's fields. Serfs often had to pay the lord taxes or rent or give the lord produce from their parcel of land. Serfs also could not move away without the lord's permission. Serfdom began to decline in the fifteenth and sixteenth centuries. For some lords, it became more profitable to use all their land for their own crops and hire paid, temporary laborers instead.

13. **The overall effect of serfdom was that the peasants were**

    **A**   forced to grow crops instead of raising livestock

    **B**   legally and economically bound to a lord

    **C**   never able to provide surplus profits for the lord

    **D**   expected to hire temporary laborers to help them work the land

**Questions 14 and 15 are based on the following passage.**

In 1532, when Francisco Pizarro arrived in South America from Spain, he found an Incan empire that was torn apart by civil war. By the mid-sixteenth century, the Incan Empire had expanded from present-day Peru to much of Bolivia, Argentina, Chile, Ecuador, and Colombia. But just a few years before Pizarro's arrival, the Incan emperor Huayna Capac died from smallpox while on a military campaign in Colombia. His death sparked a war of succession between his sons, Atahualpa and Huascar.

Atahualpa was not a legitimate heir to the throne, as his mother was not an Inca, but at the time of his father's death, Atahualpa was in the north with most of the empire's army, which was loyal to him. Huascar, the legitimate heir, was in the empire's capital city of Cuzco and quickly declared himself emperor. A bloody civil war then took place. Huascar was eventually captured in Cuzco by Atahualpa's trusted generals.

As Atahualpa traveled south from the city of Quito to Cuzco to formally take over the Incan empire, he came across Pizarro in the city of Cajamarca on November 15. The next day, after a brief meeting with Pizarro, the Spaniard's forces of less than 200 men captured Atahualpa.

While he was under guard, Atahualpa ordered his men to have Huascar killed. He also offered his captors a room filled with gold and silver so that Pizarro would spare his life. Although the treasure was given to Pizarro, Atahualpa was eventually charged by the Spaniards with several crimes, including the death of Huascar, and Atahualpa was executed in August 1533.

14. **The author of this passage would believe which of the following statements about Pizarro?**

    A   Pizarro could not have defeated Atahualpa's army with just 200 men.

    B   Pizarro's conquest of the Incan empire was helped by the devastating civil war.

    C   Pizarro was responsible for the death of Huayna Capac.

    D   Pizarro ordered the death of Huascar to end the civil war.

15. **Which of the following is an opinion, rather than a fact, about the Incan Empire?**

    A   The Incan emperors were likely merciless conquerors of tribes they encountered.

    B   Atahualpa was not in Cuzco at the time of Pizarro's arrival in South America.

    C   Huascar would have been emperor if Atahualpa's generals had not captured him.

    D   Atahualpa was a prisoner under Pizarro for several months before he was executed.

**Question 16 is based on the following passage.**

On the evening of December 16, 1773, a group of men boarded the three ships in Boston Harbor and dumped more than 300 chests of tea into the water. The event was part of a resistance movement against both the East India Company, which controlled all the tea that was brought to the colonies, as well as the Tea Act, which was passed by Parliament in England in 1773. Some British citizens living in the colonies objected to the Tea Act mostly because they felt these taxes were being imposed upon them by people they didn't elect to power. Parliament reacted to the Tea Party by closing Boston commerce until the costs of the destroyed tea had been repaid, which, in turn, sparked more protests from the colonists. Eventually this led to a more formal, well-organized act of sedition, in the form of the First Continental Congress and the beginning of the American Revolutionary War.

16. **Based on the passage above, it can be assumed that**

    A   the East India Company was never repaid for the damaged tea

    B   the Boston Tea Party was a significant moment for the American Revolution

    C   the First Continental Congress was a failure

    D   Parliament was unsuccessful in its attempts to close down Boston commerce

**Questions 17 and 18 are based on the following cartoon.**

17. **What is the main idea of the cartoon?**

    A    Child labor is oppressive and harmful to children.

    B    All child labor employers are men.

    C    Girls did as much as work as boys in factories.

    D    Children should only do labor-intensive work before the age of 12.

18. **The ring on the hand implies that**

    A    child labor only occurs in developed nations

    B    these employers gain their wealth from the hard work of children

    C    these children work in diamond mines

    D    these children work in order to support their families

**Questions 19 and 20 are based on the following cartoon.**

THE GAP IN THE BRIDGE.

19. **In this cartoon, the "Keystone USA" that Uncle Sam is leaning on means that U.S. participation in the League of Nations is**

   A   negligible

   B   comical

   C   optional

   D   crucial

20. **Uncle Sam's posture in the cartoon suggests that he**

   A   does not care about the success of the League of Nations

   B   is enthusiastic about contributing in the League of Nations

   C   is concerned about the future of the League of Nations

   D   feels angry about the state of the League of Nations

**Question 21 is based on the following table.**

| Country | Population in 2011 | Population in 2001 | % Growth 2001–2011 |
|---|---|---|---|
| China | 1,336,720,000 | 1,265,830,000 | 6% |
| India | 1,210,200,000 | 1,008,730,000 | 20% |
| United States | 313,230,000 | 281,420,000 | 11% |
| Indonesia | 245,610,000 | 206,260,000 | 19% |
| Brazil | 203,430,000 | 172,300,000 | 18% |

21. According to the table, which of the following countries had the highest population growth rate for the 2001–2011 period?

    A   China
    B   India
    C   United States
    D   Indonesia

**Question 22 is based on the following table.**

| Density of the Six Most Populated U.S. Cities | |
| --- | --- |
| *City* | *Average # of People per Square Mile* |
| New York City | 27,000 |
| San Francisco | 18,000 |
| Chicago | 12,000 |
| Los Angeles | 6,500 |
| Dallas | 3,500 |
| Houston | 3,300 |

22. According to the table, the population density of Chicago is roughly double that of

    A   New York City
    B   Chicago
    C   Los Angeles
    D   Dallas

**Question 23 is based on the following graph.**

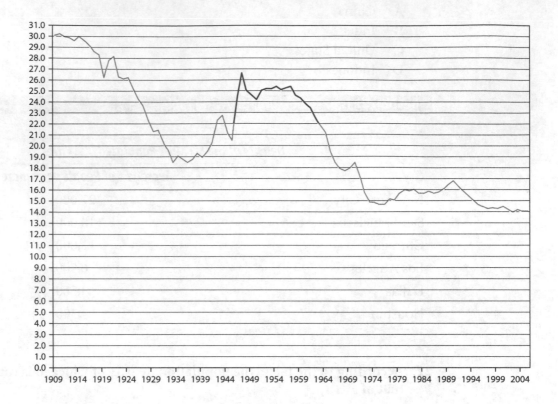

23. According to the graph, the U.S. population reached a stable rate of growth in the years from

    A   1940 to 1945

    B   1945 to 1950

    C   1950 to 1960

    D   1960 to 1965

    E   1960 to 1970

**Question 24 is based on the following passage.**

The Deepwater Horizon oil spill—also known as the BP oil spill—began in the Gulf of Mexico on April 20, 2010, and is the largest accidental marine oil spill in history. A geyser of seawater caused an explosion at an offshore drilling platform, killing 11 people. Two days later, the drilling unit sank to the sea floor, and oil was discovered to be leaking from the wellhead. The leak continued for 87 days.

BP executives and U.S. government officials scrambled to protect the U.S. Gulf coast from the damaging effects of the spill. Oil washed up on hundreds of miles of coastline in states such as Louisiana, Mississippi, Alabama, and Florida. Thousands of species and sensitive ecological habitats such as marshlands and mangroves were physically covered by the oil. In addition, other toxic chemicals were released by the spill that could be consumed by animals or could reduce the oxygen supply in the U.S. Gulf waters.

The terrible hidden and long-term effects of the oil spill are unknown. It is thought that it could take decades for the U.S. Gulf to fully recover.

24. **The author of the passage would likely agree with which of the following statements?**

    A   The demand for energy to fuel our modern world is more important than the potential damage to the environment.

    B   The U.S. government and BP company executives were not well prepared for the consequences of an offshore drilling platform accident of this magnitude.

    C   Most of the animals and habitats of the U.S. Gulf coast were unaffected by the oil spill.

    D   Other energy sources such as wind farms require the use of many acres of arable land and are dangerous to local birds.

**Question 25 is based on the following passage.**

Although coral reefs make up just a tiny portion of the surface of the world's oceans, they are one of the most diverse ecosystems on Earth. Reefs are created by corals—sea animals that secrete calcium carbonate, which forms the rigid structures of the reefs. The world's reefs provide a sanctuary for millions of creatures, from sharks and sea turtles to fish and crabs to clams, shrimp, and sponges. The world's reefs can be found in shallow, clear waters in warm climates, such as in the Caribbean and off the coasts of Hawaii and Australia.

Unfortunately, coral reefs are vulnerable to changes in the temperature of the ocean water. They are also in danger from overfishing and pollution, which often results in too much algae growing in and around the corals. Once destructive changes such as these occur, it is often impossible for the coral reefs to recover, and the reefs are permanently damaged.

25. **Which statement appears to be the best summary of the passage preceding?**

    A   Coral reefs are an important source of renewable energy.

    B   The world's coral reefs need to be protected from sea animals that secrete calcium carbonate.

    C   While coral reefs can be teeming with life, they are also delicate ecosystems in great danger of being permanently damaged or lost forever.

    D   The only way to save coral reefs is to put an end to overfishing.

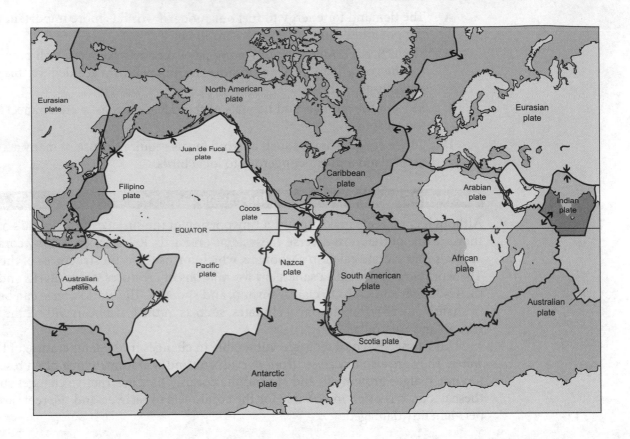

26. **Earthquakes in countries such as Chile and Ecuador are the result of friction between which two plates?**

    A   the Nazca and South American plates

    B   the Pacific and Australian plates

    C   the North America and Eurasian plates

    D   the African and South American plates

27. **According to the arrows on the map, the North American plate and Eurasian plate are**

    A   moving in the same direction

    B   sliding past each other

    C   moving toward each other

    D   moving away from each other

28. A continental collision occurs when the two plates moving toward each other both contain continental crust. Instead of creating a subduction zone, where the less-dense oceanic crust is pushed beneath the more-dense continental crust, a continental collision can result in dramatic land formations, such as the Himalayan Mountains. According to the map, a continental collision can be seen where the

    A   Indian plate meets the Eurasian plate

    B   Pacific plate meets the Nazca plate

    C   African plate meets the South American plate

    D   Pacific plate meets the Antarctic plate

**Questions 29 and 30 are based on the following graphic.**

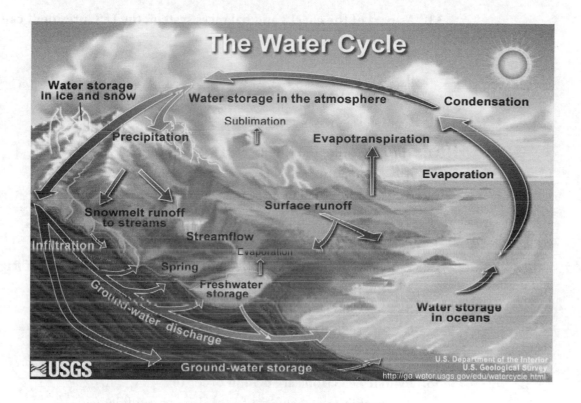

29. According to the map, water storage can occur

    A   in ice and snow

    B   in the ground

    C   in freshwater

    D   all of the above

30. Precipitation occurs when water moves from

    A   the ground to the atmosphere

    B   the groundwater storage to the ocean

    C   the ice and snow to the groundwater

    D   the atmosphere to the ground

31. **All of the following government officials are elected to power by the citizens of the United States except**
    A  the president
    B  a congressman
    C  a Supreme Court justice
    D  a senator

32. **As part of the federalist system, only the federal government can**
    A  levy taxes
    B  declare war
    C  establish schools
    D  elect state governors

33. **As part of the checks and balances system, the U.S. president can veto laws passed by**
    A  the Supreme Court
    B  Great Britain and Canada
    C  the United Nations
    D  the U.S. Congress

34. **The government of the United States is a**
    A  democratic republic
    B  constitutional monarchy
    C  dictatorship
    D  oligarchy

35. **Which of the following amendments is not part of the Bill of Rights?**
    A  the right to a speedy trial
    B  freedom from cruel or unusual punishment
    C  the right to vote for women
    D  freedom of speech

36. **Primary elections are held in order to**
    A  prohibit the viability of a third-party candidate
    B  allow political parties to select a candidate for the party's nomination
    C  remove a party from the political arena
    D  allow voters to choose the location of the party convention

37. **People who are in favor of maintaining the electoral college would disagree with which of the following statements?**

    A   The existence of the electoral college makes the national popular vote irrelevant.

    B   The electoral college encourages stability by maintaining the two-party system.

    C   If a candidate were unable serve, the electoral college could choose a suitable replacement.

    D   The electoral college neutralizes the effect of turnout disparities, which can be caused by inclement weather or when a highly contested issue is on the ballot.

38. **Foreigners are allowed to live in the United States with government permission. All of the following are people with legal residency except**

    A   a person born of or adopted by a U.S. citizen

    B   a person with an expired student visa

    C   a refugee fleeing warfare or prosecution

    D   a person with a valid residence card

39. **An authoritarian government is one in which political authority is concentrated in a small group of politicians. Power is maintained by the exclusion of potential political challengers through means such as violence and intimidation, as well as election rigging. Which of the following is the head of state of an authoritarian government?**

    A   a governor

    B   a queen

    C   a colonel

    D   a dictator

### Question 40 is based on the following passage.

According to the U.S. Census Bureau, about 131 million people reported voting in the 2008 U.S. presidential election, an increase of 5 million from the 2004 elections. This increase included about 2 million more African-American voters, 2 million more Hispanic voters, and about 600,000 more Asian voters. In addition, voter turnout in the 18-to-24 age group increased to 49 percent in 2008 compared with 47 percent in 2004. However, the higher voter turnout in these groups was offset by unchanged or reduced turnout among other groups, such as non-Hispanic white voters. This caused the overall 2008 voter turnout to remain statistically unchanged—at 64 percent—from 2004.

40. **Which statement is supported by information in the paragraph above?**

    A   African-American women had the highest voter turnout rate in the 2008 election.

    B   Most of the increased voter turnout was seen in Midwest states.

    C   About 95 percent of all African-American voters cast a ballot for Barack Obama.

    D   Voter participation of eligible voters among African Americans, Hispanics, and Asians all increased from 2004 to 2008.

41. All of the following are objects that can be a business's *capital* except

    A   monetary investments

    B   labor

    C   computers and printers

    D   farmland

42. A trade bloc is an agreement between governments where issues that could prohibit or impede trade or investments between nations are decreased or removed. Which of the following is an example of a trade bloc?

    A   NAFTA

    B   OPEC

    C   NATO

    D   the UN

43. When a new gaming console is released to the market, it often costs several hundreds of dollars and can be difficult to find in stores. This is also true of new video games, which can cost as much as $60. However, just a year or two after the release, these items can be found easily and often can be bought at half the price or less. This is an example of

    A   sellers competing aggressively for market share

    B   demand for a product outpacing supply

    C   poor management of inventory

    D   reduced prices due to increased supply and lower demand

## Questions 44–46 are based on the following passage.

In a capitalist economic system, all businesses are owned by individuals or groups of individuals (private), not by the government (public). Goods and services exist to generate profit, and prices are determined solely by supply and demand dynamics in the market. In a socialist economic system, goods and services exist for specific uses, not to generate revenue. Businesses are publicly owned, and price dynamics are centrally planned and controlled.

Many Western economies today combine elements of capitalism and socialism. While they are generally based on free-market capitalism, they also have socialist elements. These include industries that are owned and run by the government, such as transportation, infrastructure, education, and utilities. There are federal agencies in place to provide oversight on private businesses, which are also regulated by laws regarding the environment, labor, and product safety. Some industries are subsidized, meaning that the government sets prices for goods and services and disrupts the natural dynamics of price, supply, and demand in the free market. Many economies also include state-run, tax-funded programs such as welfare for the poor and social security for the aged.

44. **Which of the following sentences summarizes the above passage?**

   A   Most modern, Western economies can be described as "mixed" since they are not purely capitalist or socialist.

   B   Capitalism became the most prevalent economic system in the Western world in the nineteenth century.

   C   It is a mistake for Western countries to include state-run, tax-funded programs as part of their economic systems

   D   Federal agencies such as OSHA and the FDA are necessary to make sure citizens are healthy and safe.

45. **Which of the following is not an example of a subsidy?**

   A   Wheat farmers receive money from the government for exporting their product abroad.

   B   The price of gasoline is set at $2 per gallon at every gas station.

   C   Sugar is subject to sales tax at the supermarket.

   D   The minimum price of corn is guaranteed at $3.80 per bushel.

46. **What do capitalism and socialism have in common?**

   A   Prices are centrally planned and controlled.

   B   Both systems engage in producing goods and providing services.

   C   They are only found in modern Western countries.

   D   None of the revenue generated is taxed by the government.

**Question 47 is based on the following graphic.**

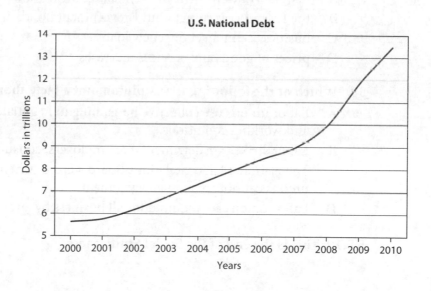

47. **In which year did the U.S. national debt reach at least $10 trillion?**

   A   2000

   B   2002

   C   2004

   D   2008

**Questions 48 and 49 are based on the following passage.**

The normal recession that occurred after the 1929 stock market crash turned into the Great Depression because of the actions—or lack of actions—by the Federal Reserve. After some large banks collapsed, people were afraid they would lose their savings. As a result, large groups descended on their local branches in panic, and there were runs on local banks, which subsequently collapsed. The supply of money in the U.S. marketplace therefore shrank from 1929 to 1933. This lack of liquidity meant that businesses were unable to secure new loans or renew loans, which slowed down market investments and worsened the economy. The Federal Reserve could have taken steps to reverse this trend, such as buying government securities or providing emergency funds to the large banks. Instead, unemployment soared, production declined, consumer spending plummeted, and the nation fell into a dramatic and prolonged economic depression.

48. **The author of this passage asserts that**
    A   the Federal Deposit Insurance Corporation, which guarantees the funds in personal accounts in case of bank failures, is a great achievement
    B   the Federal Reserve was not able to increase the supply of money because of regulation and the gold standard
    C   the Federal Reserve should have sold Treasury bonds to bring liquidity to the market
    D   if the Federal Reserve had acted more aggressively to increase the supply of money, the Great Depression could have been avoided

49. **Based on the information in the passage, a "run on the bank" occurs when**
    A   people withdraw their money, taking those funds out of circulation
    B   the federal government buys government bonds
    C   business cannot get or renew loans
    D   prices of goods and services increases

50. **Which of the following is an opinion, not a fact, about labor unions?**
    A   Labor unions use collective bargaining to negotiate for changes in wages and working conditions.
    B   Labor strikes are detrimental to employers, consumers, and the economy.
    C   The National Labor Relations Board steps in when companies and labor unions cannot come to an agreement.
    D   Labor unions are required for all business by law.

**STOP: This is the end of the Social Studies test.**

# ANSWERS: SOCIAL STUDIES

1. **(A)** All the other statements are facts based on the date of the trials, the definition of *mass hysteria*, and the use of the witch trials as an example of the misuse of authority. There is no evidence in the passage that people in the 1600s feared witches more than people do today.

2. **(B)** The last sentence of the second paragraph, as well as the last sentence of the passage, illustrate how people have been affected by the trials, even hundreds of years later. Although the other answer choices may be true, they cannot be deduced from the information provided in the text.

3. **(D)** This answer most accurately reflects the central theme of the passage, which is that the Louisiana Purchase was controversial ("a contentious decision") but also fundamental ("a central moment") for the United States. The other options do not capture this idea. In addition, options (A) and (C) are factually incorrect, and there is no indication in the passage about the effect of the Louisiana Purchase on U.S.–French relations.

4. **(C)** The passage describes what the goals of the expedition were and how Lewis and Clark fulfilled those goals. Options (A) and (B) are factually incorrect, and option (D) does not summarize the passage as a whole and is outside the scope of the passage.

5. **(C)** The Monroe Doctrine stated that if European nations tried to colonize land or interfere with countries in North or South America, it would be seen as an act of aggression, and the United States would have to intervene.

6. **(B)** The date on which the cartoon was published (October 11, 1862) and the actions and words of President Lincoln in the image indicate that the man in the tree represents the Southern states.

7. **(D)** The tree in which the man sits symbolizes the institution of slavery. The president had informed the rebellious Southern states that if they did not rejoin the Union, he would free their slaves by executive order on January 1, 1863. The president essentially "cut the tree out from under" the South when the Emancipation Proclamation took effect on that day.

8. **(D)** The topic of the first paragraph is the cause of the severe dust storms that occurred in the 1930s. Options (B) and (C) are not accurate statements. Options (A) is not based on the facts presented in the first paragraph, as the question states.

9. **(C)** This poster became the symbol of women laboring in manufacturing during World War II. The woman in the poster is commonly referred to as Rosie the Riveter.

10. **(D)** An able-bodied workforce was needed on the homefront to build planes and tanks and to work in munitions factories while millions of American men went to fight overseas in Europe and the Pacific region during World War II.

GO ON TO THE NEXT PAGE ➡

11. **(A)** Options (B) and (C) cannot be deduced from the text of the passage, and option (D) states the opposite of the information presented in the passage about Martin Luther King. Option (A) is supported by the statement in paragraph 2 that "the city's bus system faced great financial hardship" because of the boycott.

12. **(C)** Since classical Latin was the only kind that was written and punctuation was not used, the practice of adding periods, commas, and other symbols must have evolved at a later time. Option (B) is an inaccurate statement and options (A) and (D) cannot be deduced from the information in the passage.

13. **(B)** The question asks you to describe the general consequence of serfdom on the peasants. Only option (B) encompasses the overall effect, which was that the peasants' lives were decisively connected to that of the lord. Options (A) and (C) cannot be deduced from the information in the passage, and option (D) is untrue.

14. **(B)** Several statements in the passage describe the Incan civil war and indicates that it doomed the empire. In the first sentence, the author says Pizarro found an empire "torn apart" by civil war. And at the end of the second paragraph, he describes the civil war as bloody. Options (C) and (D) are factually incorrect, and option (A) cannot be deduced from the information provided by the author.

15. **(A)** The passage does not provide evidence or explanations of how the Incans came to rule over those areas of South America. Options (B) and (D) are facts, while option (C) cannot be deduced from the information provided by the author.

16. **(B)** More information is required to make the conclusions in options (A) and (D). While possibly true, they cannot be deduced from the information provided in the text. Option (C) is outside the scope of the passage.

17. **(A)** By portraying the children as being crushed by the weight of the hand of their employer, the artist of the cartoon is implying that the children are being mistreated. Option (D) expresses ideas that are the opposite of the main idea of the cartoon. Options (B) and (C) cannot be deduced from the information provided in the text.

18. **(B)** The ring on the hand of the employer suggests that the employer is financially successful and, at the same time, exploits the children. The artist is implying that the success is possible because of child labor. The ring on the hand does not give any indication of the country where this child labor is taking place (option A), where these children work (option C), or why these children work (option D).

19. **(D)** A keystone is a wedge-shaped stone that locks all the stones in an arch in place. Therefore, the artist of this cartoon is implying that the bridge, which represents the League of Nations, will collapse without the participation of the United States. This means that the United States plays an essential or "crucial" role. Options (A) and (C) suggest the opposite of what the artist is implying, and option (B) does not make sense in the context of the cartoon.

20. **(A)** Uncle Sam, as the personification of the United States, has a relaxed posture and therefore appears uninterested or indifferent about whether or not the League of Nations is successful. His posture does not imply that he is enthusiastic (option B), concerned (option C), or angry (option D).

21. **(B)** India showed a 20 percent growth in the years from 2001 to 2011, the highest among the five nations listed in the table.

22. **(C)** At 12,000, the average population density of Chicago is a little less than double the 6,500 average population density of Los Angeles.

23. **(C)** The graph shows a steady rate of growth, or plateau, that lasted from 1950 to 1955. During this time, the U.S. population did not drastically increase or decrease. Options (A) and (D) show steep declines in the U.S. population. It was particularly dramatic in option (A)—from 1940 to 1945—since this was during World War II. Option (B) shows a steep increase, commonly referred to as the baby boom, since this was when Americans returned home from the war.

24. **(B)** Only option (B) matches the content and tone of the author's passage. Options (A) and (C) express the opposite of the main idea of the passage and the author's point of view, while option (D) about wind farm energy is outside the scope of the passage.

25. **(C)** Option (A) is incorrect because the passage does not refer to coral reefs as a renewable energy source. Option (B) is factually inaccurate, as it is the corals themselves that secrete the calcium carbonate. Option (D) is too narrow in scope. Only option (C) accurately sums up the main ideas of the passage.

26. **(A)** Chile and Ecuador are on the west coast of the South American continent, which is found on the South American plate. According to the map, the Nazca plate pushes against the South American plate, which causes earthquakes in that part of the world.

27. **(D)** The arrows on the map show that the North American plate and Eurasian plate are moving away from each other.

28. **(A)** The map shows that where the Indian plate and the Eurasian plate collide, it is the convergence of continental crust. That is why the Himalayas, which contain the tallest mountain in the world, and the Tibetan plains are located there.

**GO ON TO THE NEXT PAGE** ➡

29. **(D)** Water can be stored as ice and snow, as water in the ground, and in rivers and lakes, as well as in clouds in the atmosphere.

30. **(D)** Option (A) is condensation, option (C) is infiltration, and option (B) is groundwater discharge.

31. **(C)** Supreme Court justices are nominated by the U.S. president and are appointed after having been confirmed by the U.S. Senate. The positions in the other options are all elected officials.

32. **(B)** Only the federal government can declare war. Both the state and federal governments can levy taxes (option A). Only state governments can establish schools (option C), and the people of each state elect their governors (option D).

33. **(D)** Legislation that is passed by both the House of Representatives and the Senate is presented to the U.S. president, who can then choose to veto the law. The president has no influence over laws passed by other nations (option B) or international bodies such as the United Nations (option C). The Supreme Court (option A) makes rulings; it does not pass laws.

34. **(A)** The United States is a democratic republic, which is a form of government in which the citizens of a nation choose the people who will run their government through elections of candidates from two or more political parties. In dictatorships (option C) and oligarchies (option D), a person or small group of people run the government but never step down or resign. In a constitutional monarchy (option B), a king or queen is the head of state, but he or she governs within the limits of a constitution and often works along with a parliament, which is similar to the U.S. Congress.

35. **(C)** It describes the Nineteenth Amendment. The Bill of Rights is the first 10 amendments to the Constitution. Option (A) is the Sixth Amendment, option (B) is the eighth, and option (D) is the first.

36. **(B)** Primary elections are run by political parties. Candidates within the party hold debates and compete against each other to secure the nomination as the party's official candidate in the presidential general election.

37. **(A)** Those who want to reform or eliminate the electoral college often cite the 2000 presidential election. In general, electors cast their votes based on the tally of popular vote for the state as a whole, despite differences within the state counties. In the case of Florida, the popular vote was split down the middle. The margin between Republican candidate George W. Bush and Democrat candidate Al Gore was just a few hundred votes. In the end, the Florida's 25 electoral votes went to Bush.

38. **(B)** Foreign visitors in the United States with student visas must renew their visas or return to their home country once the visa has expired.

39. **(D)** A dictator takes on exclusive and unlimited power without having inherited control through family connections the way option (B), a queen, might. A governor (option A) is a political official but not as high ranking as a head of state. A colonel (option C) is a high-ranking officer of the military, not of a government.

40. **(D)** More information is required to make the conclusions in options (A) and (C). While possibly true, they cannot be deduced from the information provided in the text. Option (B) is outside the scope of the passage

41. **(B)** Businesses use capital to produce earnings or profits. Money (option A) can be used in various ways to help a company earn revenue, such as making investments or purchasing equipment. Computers and printers (option C) are examples of a business's equipment. Land (option D) is an asset that can be rented or sold, also creating revenue for the business. Labor, however, is not capital. It is the actual work a person does. Through labor, a business can make goods or provide services, which in turn produce profits for the company.

42. **(A)** NAFTA stands for the North American Free Trade Agreement. It is a trade bloc between the United States, Mexico, and Canada. OPEC (option B) stands for Organization of Petroleum Exporting Countries and is an intergovernmental organization of 12 oil-producing countries. NATO (option C) stands for the North Atlantic Treaty Organization and is an intergovernmental military alliance. The UN (option D) stands for the United Nations, an international organization to foster cooperation and peace between nations.

43. **(D)** When the gaming console or video game is no longer brand-new to the market, demand for the item goes down and the item is no longer scarce. This increases sellers' supply. To move inventory out of their stores, they lower the price.

44. **(A)** It summarizes the main idea of the passage, which is that Western economies contain both capitalist and socialist elements. Option (B) cannot be deduced from the information provided in the text, and options (C) and (D) are too narrow in scope to provide a summary of the passage.

45. **(C)** Sales tax is not a government subsidy. It is a tax—collected by either the state or the federal government—that consumers pay at the point of purchase. The other options are examples of times when the government interferes with supply and demand dynamics.

46. **(B)** In both capitalism and socialism, goods are produced and services are provided. Price controls (option A) are characteristic of socialism only. Options (C) and (D) are factually incorrect.

47. **(D)** According to the graph, the U.S. national debt reached at least $10 trillion in 2008.

48. **(D)** The author of the passage places the blame for the Great Depression on the Federal Reserve, providing details of how it failed to stop the recession and even worsened it into a depression. Options (A) and (B) cannot be deduced from the information provided in the text. Option (C) states the opposite of what the author asserts about Treasury bonds and the efforts of the Federal Reserve.

**GO ON TO THE NEXT PAGE** ➡

49. **(A)** A run on a bank is when a large number of people withdraw their funds from a bank all at once. As the passage states, "After some large banks collapsed, people were afraid they would lose their savings. As a result, large groups descended on their local branches in panic, and there were runs on local banks, which subsequently collapsed. Therefore, the supply of money in the U.S. marketplace shrank from 1929 to 1933."

50. **(B)** It does not truthfully describe labor strikes but instead provides an opinion on the effect that strikes can have. Options (A) and (C) are accurate statements about labor unions, while option (D) is factually incorrect.

# *HiSET*® Exam Practice Test 1
## Answer Sheet
## Science

| | A | B | C | D | | A | B | C | D |
|---|---|---|---|---|---|---|---|---|---|
| 1 | | | | | 26 | | | | |
| 2 | | | | | 27 | | | | |
| 3 | | | | | 28 | | | | |
| 4 | | | | | 29 | | | | |
| 5 | | | | | 30 | | | | |
| 6 | | | | | 31 | | | | |
| 7 | | | | | 32 | | | | |
| 8 | | | | | 33 | | | | |
| 9 | | | | | 34 | | | | |
| 10 | | | | | 35 | | | | |
| 11 | | | | | 36 | | | | |
| 12 | | | | | 37 | | | | |
| 13 | | | | | 38 | | | | |
| 14 | | | | | 39 | | | | |
| 15 | | | | | 40 | | | | |
| 16 | | | | | 41 | | | | |
| 17 | | | | | 42 | | | | |
| 18 | | | | | 43 | | | | |
| 19 | | | | | 44 | | | | |
| 20 | | | | | 45 | | | | |
| 21 | | | | | 46 | | | | |
| 22 | | | | | 47 | | | | |
| 23 | | | | | 48 | | | | |
| 24 | | | | | 49 | | | | |
| 25 | | | | | 50 | | | | |

# SCIENCE

**50 Questions**

**80 Minutes**

## Directions

This is a test of your skills in analyzing science information. Read each question and decide which of the four alternatives best answers the question. Then mark your choice on your answer sheet. Sometimes several questions are based on the same material. You should carefully read this material, then answer the questions.

Work as quickly as you can without becoming careless. Don't spend too much time on any question that is difficult for you to answer. Instead, skip it and return to it later if you have time. Try to answer every question even if you have to guess.

Mark all your answers on the answer sheet. Give only one answer to each question and make every mark heavy and dark. If you decide to change one of your answers, be sure to erase the first mark completely. Be sure that the number of the question you are answering matches the number of the row of answer choices you are marking on your answer sheet.

1. **A dog is lying on a scale. The weight of the dog is 13 pounds (58 newtons). What is the force that the scale is exerting upward on the dog?**

   A  0 newtons

   B  13 newtons

   C  29 newtons

   D  58 newtons

2. **Which of the following statements provides evidence that visible light is made of electromagnetic waves rather than mechanical waves?**

   A  Sunlight can travel through window glass.

   B  Sunlight can travel through a vacuum.

   C  Sunlight can travel through clear plastic.

   D  Sunlight can travel through Earth's atmosphere.

3. **When a person touched a mug of tea, the person's hand felt warm. Which of the following statements gives the best explanation of this observation?**

   A  Thermal energy flowed from the person's hand to the mug.

   B  Thermal energy flowed from the mug to the person's hand.

   C  Thermal energy flowed in a continuous loop between the person's hand and the mug.

   D  The person's hand was originally at the same temperature as the mug.

**GO ON TO THE NEXT PAGE ➡**

4. Through which of the following materials does electricity travel most easily?
   A  glass
   B  plastic
   C  rubber
   D  metal

**Questions 5 and 6 refer to the following diagram of a light ray hitting a flat surface of a transparent object.**

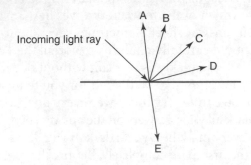

5. Which arrow shows the direction of the light ray that is reflected from the surface?
   A  arrow A
   B  arrow B
   C  arrow C
   D  arrow D

6. Which arrow shows the direction of the light ray that is refracted by the object?
   A  arrow A
   B  arrow B
   C  arrow C
   D  arrow E

7. A person is pushing a brick up a slanted wooden board. Which of the following statements gives the best comparison of the force required to cause the brick to begin moving and the force required to keep the brick moving?
   A  More force is required to cause the brick to begin moving because the roughness of the surface of the brick and the board increase the friction that must be overcome for movement to begin.
   B  More force is required to cause the brick to begin moving than to keep it moving because of the higher amount of potential energy in the board due to its greater mass.
   C  The same amount of force is required to cause the brick to move and to keep it in motion because the potential energy of the brick does not change.
   D  Less force is required to cause the brick to begin moving because there is less friction with the board than when the brick is already in motion.

8.  The graph below shows the relationship between distance an object traveled and time. Which of the following is the best conclusion that can be made about the movement of the object?

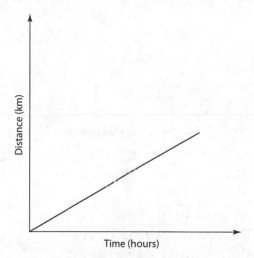

A   The object moved at a constant positive speed.
B   The object moved at a varying positive speed.
C   The object remained stationary during the time interval shown.
D   The object moved at a constant negative speed.

9.  In which of the following substances do the molecules have the highest average kinetic energy?
A   water boiling in a teakettle
B   water vapor in the air within a house
C   snowflakes falling to the ground
D   ice cubes in a freezer

GO ON TO THE NEXT PAGE ➡

10. The diagram below shows a model of the structure of a lithium atom. Which of the following describes a type of particle in the nucleus of the atom?

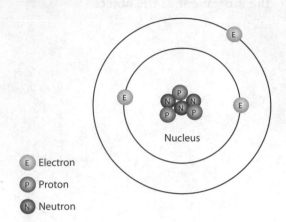

A   uncharged protons
B   positively charged protons
C   negatively charged neutrons
D   positively charged electrons

11. The diagram below shows models of neutral and electrically charged atoms. Which atom is a negative ion?

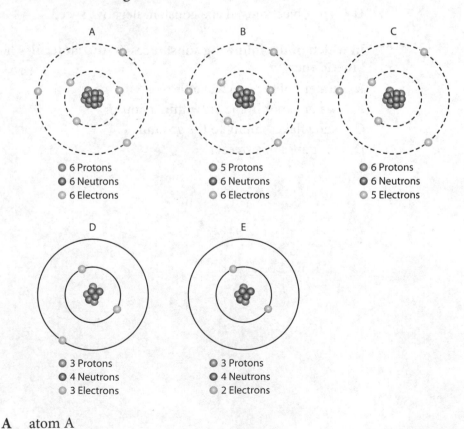

A   atom A
B   atom B
C   atom D
D   atom E

**Questions 12–14 refer to the chart below, showing functional groups in compounds of organic substances.**

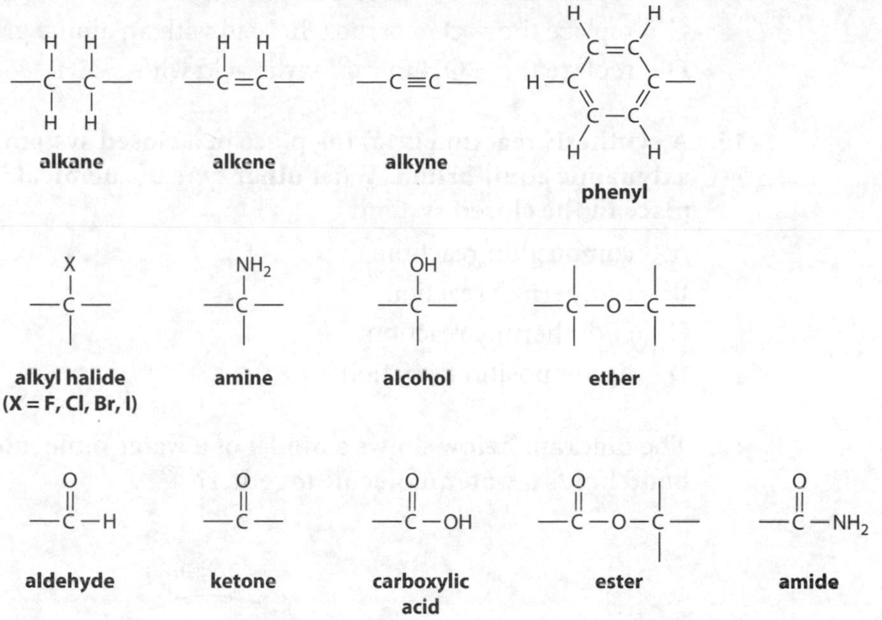

12. The diagram below shows a structural model of an organic compound. According to the chart of functional groups, what type of compound does the diagram show?

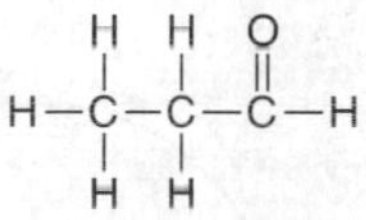

A  alkane
B  alcohol
C  aldehyde
D  carboxylic acid

13. In the chart of functional groups, a single line represents a single bond, a double line represents a double bond, and a triple line represents a triple bond. Which of the following compounds contain double bonds between carbon atoms?

A  alkene compounds
B  aldehyde compounds
C  alkane and alkyl halide compounds
D  ketone, carboxylic acid, and ester compounds

GO ON TO THE NEXT PAGE ➡

14. Which of the following processes describes how a carboxylic acid compound might be changed to an amide compound?

    A    replace the C=O in carboxylic acid with −NH₂

    B    replace the −C− in carboxylic acid with =O

    C    replace the =O in carboxylic acid with an amine group

    D    replace the −OH in carboxylic acid with −NH₂

15. A synthesis reaction is taking place in a closed system. The system has reached a dynamic equilibrium. What other type of chemical reaction must be taking place in the closed system?

    A    combustion reaction

    B    exothermic reaction

    C    endothermic reaction

    D    decomposition reaction

16. The diagram below shows a model of a water molecule. What type of chemical bond holds a water molecule together?

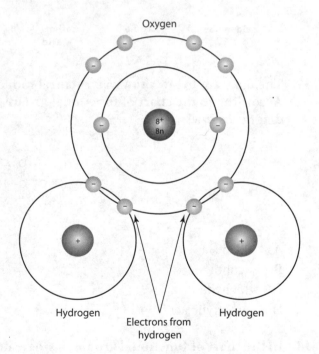

    A    covalent

    B    ionic

    C    metallic

    D    van der Waals

17. **Solid ammonium chloride, NH$_4$Cl(*s*), dissolves in water. Why does a solution of NH$_4$Cl(*aq*) have a pH that is less than 7.0?**

    A  (A) NH$_4^+$(*aq*) ions react with water to form hydronium ions (H$_3$O$^+$).

    B  (B) Ammonium chloride releases hydroxide ions (OH$^-$) into solution.

    C  (C) Chloride ions (Cl$^-$) remove hydroxide ions (OH$^-$) from solution.

    D  Ammonium chloride absorbs hydronium ions (H$_3$O$^+$) from solution.

18. **The chemical equation below shows that the reaction of nitrogen dioxide produces nitrogen gas and oxygen gas and releases energy.**

$$2NO_2(g) \rightarrow N_2(g) + 2O_2(g) + 66.4 \text{ kJ}$$

    **Which of the following statements best describes the reaction?**

    A  The reaction is endothermic, and the potential energy of the reactant is greater than that of the products.

    B  The reaction is endothermic, and the potential energy of the reactant is less than that of the products.

    C  The reaction is exothermic, and the potential energy of the reactant is greater than that of the products.

    D  The reaction is exothermic, and the potential energy of the reactant equals that of the products.

GO ON TO THE NEXT PAGE ➡

19. The diagram below shows characteristics of a woolly mammoth, African elephant, and Asian elephant.

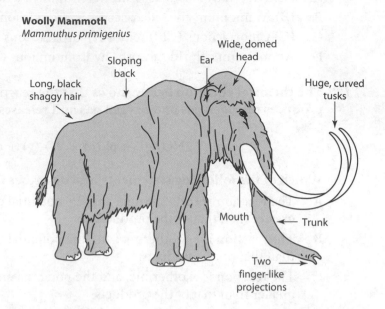

**Woolly Mammoth**
*Mammuthus primigenius*

Sloping back

Long, black shaggy hair

Ear

Wide, domed head

Huge, curved tusks

Mouth

Trunk

Two finger-like projections

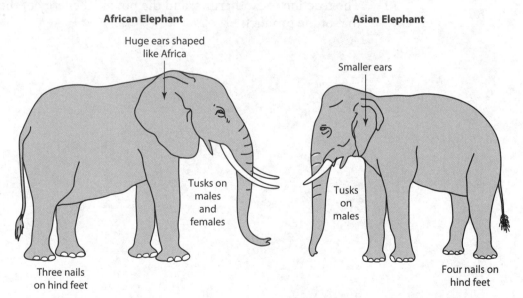

**African Elephant**

Huge ears shaped like Africa

Tusks on males and females

Three nails on hind feet

**Asian Elephant**

Smaller ears

Tusks on males

Four nails on hind feet

The frozen remains of woolly mammoths have been recovered from ice in Siberia. Analysis of DNA from the mammoths shows that they have many genetic similarities to modern elephants. The mammoth DNA is slightly more similar to that of Asian elephants than to that of African elephants. Which of the following conclusions is best supported by this DNA evidence?

A   Woolly mammoths lived only in Asia.

B   Woolly mammoths and modern elephants have a recent common ancestor.

C   Woolly mammoths and Asian elephants belong to the same species.

D   African elephants evolved from Asian elephants.

**Questions 20–22 refer to the following diagram of an ocean food web.**

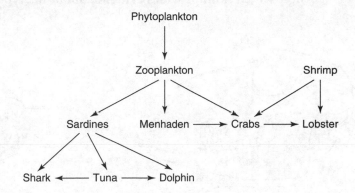

20. **In the food web diagram, the arrows point from an organism to another organism that eats it. Which of the following is most likely to occur first if the menhaden population decreases?**

    A   Sardines will have less competition for food.

    B   Crabs will not have a source of food.

    C   The population of shrimp will increase.

    D   Zooplankton will have more food available to them.

21. **According to the diagram, which of the following organisms consumes crabs?**

    A   zooplankton

    B   menhaden

    C   lobster

    D   sardines

22. **Which organism shown in the diagram obtains energy directly from the sun?**

    A   crabs

    B   shrimp

    C   phytoplankton

    D   zooplankton

GO ON TO THE NEXT PAGE ➡

23. The diagram below shows the skulls of two types of animals. One of the animals ate plants, and the other ate other animals. Which of the following best describes how which skull provides evidence about the type of animal it belonged to?

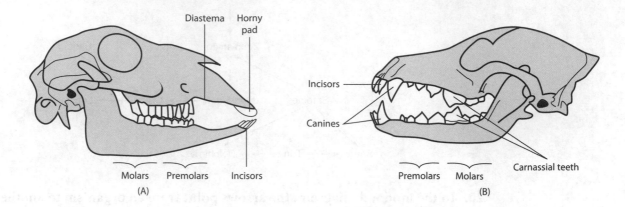

A  Skull A has flat molars suitable for crushing plants, so it belonged to a meat eater.

B  Skull A has incisors suitable for biting off plants, so it belonged to an herbivore.

C  Skull A has premolars suitable for cutting through flesh, so it belonged to a carnivore.

D  Skull B has canines suitable for stabbing and killing prey, so it belonged to a plant eater.

24. The figure shows a type of heron that lives in Africa and South Asia. Which characteristic of this bird supports the hypothesis that it spends a lot of time wading in bodies of water?

A  the shape of its neck

B  the size of its wings

C  the position of its eyes

D  the length of its legs

**25.** An organism's genes are made up of pairs of alleles that determine, among other characteristics, its physical appearance. An allele can be dominant or recessive. In pea plants, the allele (T) for a tall plant is dominant over the allele (t) for a short plant. A particular plant is tall. What conclusion can be made about its alleles for height?

   **A**   The allele pair could be Tt or TT.

   **B**   The allele pair must be TT.

   **C**   The allele pair could be Tt or tt.

   **D**   The allele pair must be tt.

**26.** Which pair of organisms has the same type of ecological relationship as the one between an owl and a mouse?

   **A**   wolf and rabbit

   **B**   squirrel and seeds

   **C**   honeybee and flower

   **D**   zebra and grass

**Questions 27 and 28 refer to the following diagram of the nitrogen cycle.**

**27.** According to the diagram, which form of nitrogen is most likely to be taken up by plants?

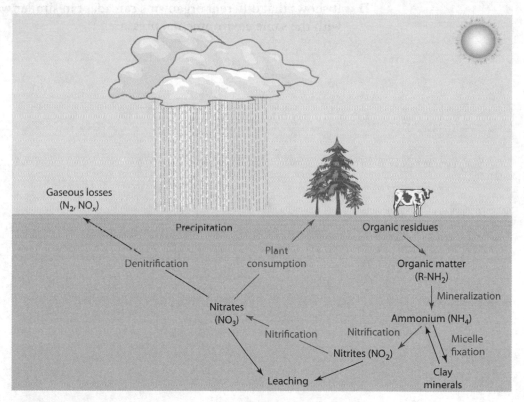

   **A**   $N_2$

   **B**   $R\text{-}NH_2$

   **C**   $NO_3$

   **D**   $NO_2$

GO ON TO THE NEXT PAGE ➡

28. Which of the following is directly involved in returning nitrogen ($N_2$) to the atmosphere?

A plant consumption

B leaching

C precipitation

D denitrification

29. The ocean around Antarctica, near the South Pole, is very cold. Fish die when their body fluids freeze. Some Antarctic fish have adapted by evolving compounds in their blood that lower the temperature at which their body fluids freeze. Some fish in the Arctic, near the North Pole, have evolved similar compounds that protect them from freezing. The genes that control the production of the compounds are very different in Arctic and Antarctic fish. These fish are not descended from a recent common ancestor. Which of the following best describes how this information about the fish provides evidence for evolution?

A It shows that different organisms can adapt to live in the same region.

B It shows that temperature is the strongest factor in natural selection.

C It shows that a variety of genes can function to protect organisms from cold temperatures.

D It shows that different organisms can adapt in similar ways when faced with the same environmental pressures.

30. The diagram below shows an example of recessive inheritance. The parents both carry a normal gene (*N*) that is dominant over the defective gene (*n*) they also carry that is recessive. Therefore, although the parents do not have the health disorder associated with the recessive gene, they are carriers for the disorder. The children of the parents can inherit two dominant *N* genes, a dominant *N* gene and a recessive *n* gene, or two recessive *n* genes. Which of the following statements always applies to the children of these parents?

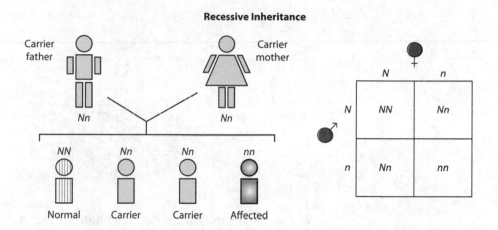

A    All of the children will inherit at least one of the defective genes.

B    Children who lack the dominant gene will have the genetically related health disorder.

C    A child with two copies of the dominant gene can, in turn, have children with the genetically related health disorder.

D    A child with two copies of the recessive gene cannot, in turn, have children.

31. Which of the following best describes how a producer in an ecosystem obtains energy?

A    by using sunlight to make sugars during photosynthesis

B    by breaking down organic matter to release nutrients

C    by consuming plants

D    by consuming other animals

32. In a type of small parrot called a budgerigar, the allele for green feathers (*G*) is dominant over the gene for blue feathers (*g*). A green bird with *Gg* alleles mates with another green bird with *Gg* alleles. What percentage of the baby birds would be expected to have green feathers?

A    0%

B    25%

C    50%

D    75%

GO ON TO THE NEXT PAGE ➡

33. A student made three terrariums like the one shown in the photograph below. The student put each terrarium in sunlight for a different amount of time for a month. One terrarium received a short period of sunlight each day, one received a medium period, and one received a long period. To determine which period of sunlight is best to maintain the health of the terrarium, which of the following variables should be held constant?

A  wavelengths of sunlight needed for photosynthesis
B  length of time sunlight is received
C  type of plants used
D  growth rate of the plants used

34. Genetic engineering is being used to make crops more resistant to pests. A caterpillar called a corn borer can cause extensive damage to corn plants. Genes are being transferred to corn plants to see if the genetically modified plants can produce proteins that kill the caterpillar. How can scientists assess whether the genes are helping the plants become more resistant to damage by corn borers?

A  by monitoring the reproductive cycle of the caterpillar in untreated corn
B  by determining whether the caterpillar can be controlled with the use of chemicals sprayed on the plants
C  by measuring the number of caterpillars affecting fields of untreated corn
D  by comparing the number of caterpillars affecting similar fields of untreated corn and genetically modified corn

35. Which of the following is required for aerobic cellular respiration?
A  chlorophyll
B  sunlight
C  oxygen
D  carbon dioxide

36. The diagram below shows a flatworm. Flatworms are nonparasitic worms that can be found in freshwater and saltwater, and sometimes in soil. They use hairlike projections called cilia to move. Some students wanted to test how being in freshwater affected the movement of flatworms. The students put 20 flatworms in freshwater and then recorded their observations in detail. What was the most significant flaw in the students' experimental design?

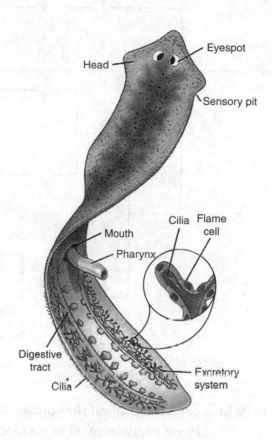

A   There was no control group of flatworms for comparison.

B   The number of flatworms used was too large.

C   The students did not first develop a hypothesis.

D   The experimental procedure had too many steps.

37. **Why can the introduction of non-native animal or plant species damage an ecosystem?**

A   Non-native species lack natural predators, parasites, or diseases to control their population size.

B   Non-native species provide excess food to native species.

C   Non-native species adapt more quickly to environmental changes than do native species.

D   Non-native species eat more food than native species.

**GO ON TO THE NEXT PAGE** ➡

**Questions 38 and 39 refer to the following diagram, which shows evolutionary relationships among several organisms.**

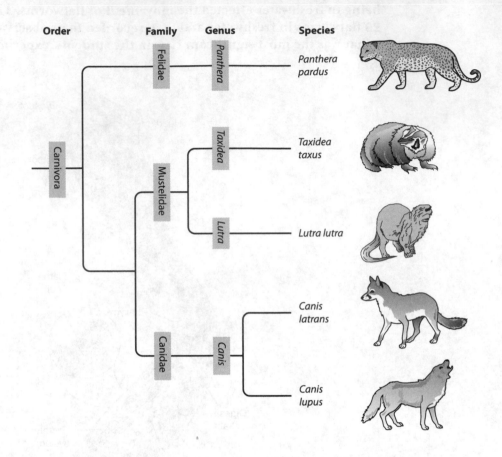

**38. Which conclusion about the animals is supported by the diagram?**

A   They are examples of the same species.

B   They are in the same family but are different species.

C   They are in the same genus and the same family.

D   They are in the same order but in different families.

**39. Which animal shown on the diagram is most closely related to *Lutra lutra*?**

A   *Panthera pardus*

B   *Taxidea taxus*

C   *Canis latrans*

D   *Canis lupus*

40. The diagram below shows stages of growth of a broad-bean plant. What is this process called?

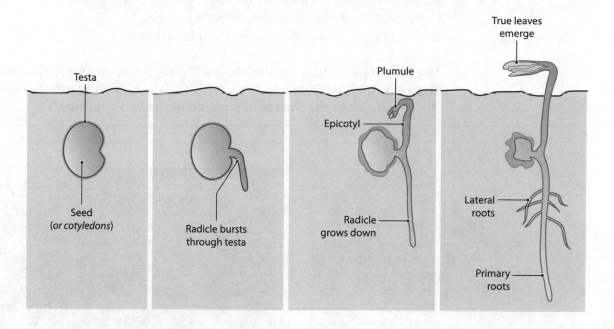

    A   photosynthesis
    B   germination
    C   dispersal
    D   reproduction

41. The chain-of-events chart below describes Earth's origin as part of the solar system. Which of the following statements belongs in the center oval of the chart?

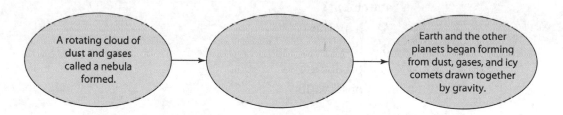

    A   A collision with another nebula provided energy for the solar system to begin to take form.
    B   The nebula moved from the center of the Milky Way galaxy to the Orion Arm.
    C   Gravity pulled most of the dust and gases into the center of the nebula, and the sun formed.
    D   Oceans formed as water vapor condensed and fell as rain throughout the nebular cloud.

GO ON TO THE NEXT PAGE ➡

42. **Which of the following best explains the magnitude of an earthquake?**

    A    depth at which the earthquake starts

    B    types of rocks that are affected by the earthquake

    C    extent of damage that the earthquake causes

    D    amount of energy that the earthquake releases

43. **The maps below show the positions of South America and Africa at two different times in Earth's history. Which of the following processes is most closely related to the change in position of the two continents?**

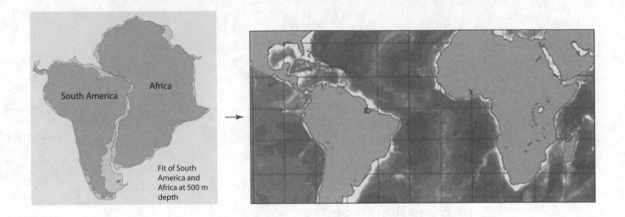

    A    reversals in the polarity of Earth's magnetic field

    B    flooding of continents caused by rising sea levels

    C    movements of Earth's tectonic plates

    D    volcanic eruptions along a deep-ocean trench

44. **A person states that a full moon and a new moon always occur 14.75 days apart. Which of the following could be used to test the accuracy of the person's statement?**

    A    hypothesis

    B    theory

    C    prediction

    D    observation

45. The map below shows part of the San Andreas fault system that marks the boundary between the Pacific plate and the North American plate. The arrows show how the plates are moving. Los Angeles is on the Pacific plate, and San Francisco is on the North American plate. Which of the following is most likely to happen at some time in the future if the movement of the plates remains the same?

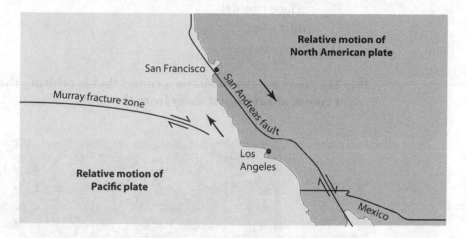

A   Los Angeles will move to the same latitude as San Francisco.
B   San Francisco will become an island in the Pacific Ocean.
C   San Francisco will be pulled down into a subduction zone.
D   Los Angeles will become part of the North American plate.

46. The diagram below shows Earth and the sun. What seasons do the Northern Hemisphere and Southern Hemisphere experience when Earth and the sun are in the positions shown?

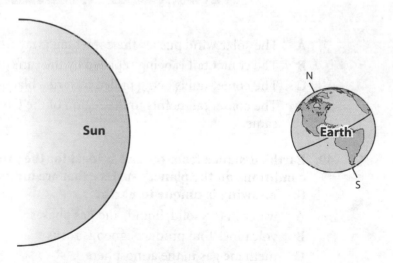

A   Northern Hemisphere: summer; Southern Hemisphere: summer
B   Northern Hemisphere: summer; Southern Hemisphere: winter
C   Northern Hemisphere: spring equinox; Southern Hemisphere: fall equinox
D   Northern Hemisphere: winter; Southern Hemisphere: winter

GO ON TO THE NEXT PAGE ➡

47. Water moves among Earth's surface, shallow subsurface, and atmosphere by a set of processes called the water cycle. Through which process in the water cycle does most of the water that falls as precipitation on land enter streams and lakes?

    A   flow of groundwater
    B   surface runoff
    C   infiltration
    D   transpiration

48. The diagram below shows a comet that is orbiting the sun. Why does the tail of a comet always point away from the sun?

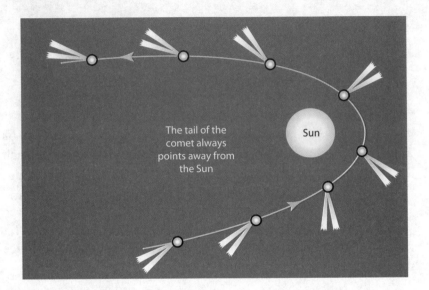

    A   The solar wind pushes the comet tail away from the sun.
    B   The comet tail is being repelled by the sun's gravity.
    C   The comet tail is being pulled toward a black hole in the Kuiper Belt.
    D   The comet tail points to the region of the Oort cloud from which the comet came.

49. Earth's distance from the sun is ideal for the presence of life because it sets up conditions on the planet's surface that are unique in the solar system. Which of the following is unique to Earth?

    A   water in the solid, liquid, and gas phases
    B   volcanoes that produce igneous rocks
    C   methane gas in the atmosphere
    D   a moon that causes ocean tides

50. The table below shows Mohs scale of hardness for 10 minerals. A mineral with a higher Mohs scale number can scratch a mineral with a lower number. The graph below compares the relative hardness of the 10 minerals. On the relative hardness scale, diamond is about 40 times harder than talc. Which of the following is NOT true based on the table and the chart?

**Mohs Scale**

| Hardness | 1 | 2 | 3 | 4 | 5 | 6 | 7 | 8 | 9 | 10 |
|----------|-----|--------|--------|----------|--------|-----------|--------|-------|----------|---------|
| Mineral | talc | gypsum | calcite | fluorite | apatite | orthoclase | quartz | topaz | corundum | diamond |

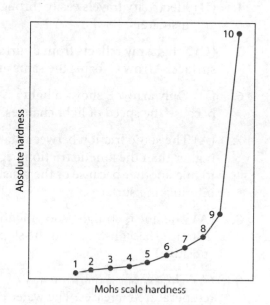

A   The absolute hardness of quartz is less than the absolute hardness of corundum but greater than the absolute hardness of gypsum

B   A mineral that can be scratched by orthoclase can scratch gypsum and calcite.

C   A mineral that can scratch apatite and be scratched by topaz is able to scratch corundum.

D   The intervals between the numbers on the Mohs scale represent varying amounts of change in absolute hardness.

**STOP. This is the end of the Science test.**

# ANSWERS: SCIENCE

1. **(D)** The surface supporting an object exerts an upward force on the object that is equal but opposite to the downward force of gravity on the object.

2. **(B)** Mechanical waves, such as sound waves, propagate through matter by actually causing an oscillation of the matter through which they are moving. Electromagnetic waves, such as visible light, can propagate through matter or through space that is devoid of matter.

3. **(B)** Thermal energy always flows from a warmer object to a cooler object.

4. **(D)** Electricity travels easily through a conductor; options (A), (B), and (C) are insulators.

5. **(C)** A light ray reflects from a surface at the same angle it struck the surface. Arrow C forms the same angle to the surface as the incident ray.

6. **(D)** Only arrow E shows a light ray that enters the object and bends because the speed of light changes.

7. **(A)** The static friction between stationary objects with irregular surfaces is higher than the kinetic friction between those same objects moving relative to one another because of the resistance to movement caused by the interlocking surfaces.

8. **(A)** The line is straight, showing that the relationship between time and distance was constant, and the slope of the line is upward toward the right (positive).

9. **(A)** The average kinetic energy of the molecules of a substance increases as temperature increases. The water in option (A) has the highest temperature.

10. **(B)** The nucleus shows two types of particles: neutrons, which are neutral, and protons, which have a positive charge.

11. **(B)** A negative ion has more electrons than protons. Options (A), (C), and (D) either have an equal number of electrons and protons or more protons than electrons.

12. **(C)** The compound contains a functional group made up of a carbon atom sharing a double bond with oxygen and a single bond with hydrogen, so the compound is an aldehyde.

13. **(A)** Alkenes contain a double bond between carbon atoms. (Phenyl compounds were not included in the answer choice because the bonds in a carbon ring are intermediate between single and double bonds.) The double bonds in options (B), (C), and (D) are between carbon and oxygen.

14. **(D)** A carboxylic acid compound can be converted to an amide compound by chemically transforming the identity of the functional group. The process involves detaching the $-OH$ group and replacing it with $-NH_2$.

15. **(D)** A synthesis reaction involves combining elements or simpler compounds into a single, more complex compound. Its opposite is a decomposition reaction in which a single reactant breaks apart into elements or simpler compounds. A synthesis reaction must be balanced by a decomposition reaction for a system to achieve a dynamic equilibrium.

16. **(A)** The model shows that the oxygen atom shares an electron with each of the hydrogen atoms. Covalent bonds are characterized by the sharing of electrons.

17. **(A)** The pH of a solution is determined by the concentration of hydronium ions relative to hydroxide ions. When there is an excess of hydronium ions, the solution is acidic (pH less than 7.0).

$$NH_4Cl\ (aq) \rightarrow NH_4^+\ (aq) + Cl^-\ (aq);\ NH_4^+ + H_2O \rightarrow H_3O^+ + NH_3$$

18. **(C)** The reaction produces energy, so it is exothermic. In an exothermic reaction, the potential energy of the reactant is higher than that of the products.

19. **(B)** The similarities in DNA show that all three species have a recent common ancestor. The evidence cannot be used to determine the range of woolly mammoths.

20. **(A)** Sardines, menhaden, and crabs all consume zooplankton. If the menhaden population decreases, sardines (and crabs) will have less competition for the zooplankton. With decreased availability of menhaden, crabs can still consume zooplankton and shrimp.

21. **(C)** An arrow points from crabs to lobsters, indicating that lobsters consume crabs.

22. **(C)** Phytoplankton are photosynthetic organisms, so they get energy to make food directly from the sun.

23. **(B)** The presence of incisors suitable for biting off plants indicates that skull A belonged to a plant-eating animal. Options (A), (C), and (D) all have a mismatch between evidence from the teeth and the conclusion about the type of food eaten.

24. **(D)** Wading birds have evolved long legs to allow them to spend a lot of time standing in shallow water.

25. **(A)** Because the allele that codes for tallness is dominant, a tall plant could be heterozygous (Tt) or homozygous (TT). A tt plant would be short.

26. **(A)** An owl is a predator that consumes mice. A wolf is a predator that consumes rabbits. The squirrel and zebra consume plants, and a honeybee pollinates a flower when seeking nectar.

27. **(C)** The arrow indicating the uptake of nitrogen by plants extends from nitrates.

**GO ON TO THE NEXT PAGE ➡**

28. **(D)** The arrow indicating denitrification points to losses of nitrogen from the ground in the form of a gas that enters the atmosphere.

29. **(D)** The ocean environment at the poles is similar, and fish in both locations must adapt to withstand cold. The two fish populations are at opposite poles, and they do not share a recent common ancestor, but they have similar biochemical adaptations.

30. **(B)** The lack of the dominant allele allows the recessive trait (the genetically related health disorder) to be expressed. It is not possible to draw any conclusions about the future offspring of the children without knowing the genotype of the other parent.

31. **(A)** A producer is at the base of a food web. A producer makes its own food via photosynthesis or, much more rarely, chemosynthesis.

32. **(D)** The Punnett square for the cross is:

|   | G | g |
|---|---|---|
| G | GG | Gg |
| g | Gg | Gg |

Therefore, 75 percent of the offspring would be expected to inherit at least one copy of the dominant allele from a parent. Because the dominant allele codes for green feathers, 75 percent of the offspring would be expected to be green.

33. **(C)** The terrariums should all have the same conditions except for the variable being tested. The same type of plants should be used in each terrarium, because different types of plants might have different growth requirements. The wavelengths of sunlight needed for photosynthesis (option A) is a property of a plant, not a variable to be manipulated. The length of time the terrariums receive sunlight (option B) is the variable being changed. Growth rate (option D) depends on the health of the plant.

34. **(D)** The caterpillar infestation rates for untreated corn and genetically modified corn must be compared to determine what effect, if any, the genetic modification has on the pest.

35. **(C)** Aerobic cellular respiration allows organisms to release energy stored in chemical bonds for use in metabolic processes. In the process, oxygen is combined with glucose to produce carbon dioxide, water, and energy.

36. **(A)** The lack of a control group gives no means of comparison as to how the flatworms might move differently in freshwater versus saltwater or soil.

37. **(A)** Non-native species, once established in an ecosystem, can outcompete native species because they have not coevolved with predators, parasites, or diseases that target them.

38. **(D)** The branches of the diagram show that all animals included belong to the order Carnivora but that they are in three different families.

39. **(B)** *Lutra lutra* and *Taxidea taxus* are the most closely related because they are in the same genus.

40. **(B)** The process by which a seed sprouts is called germination.

41. **(C)** Most of the mass of the nebula collected at the center and collapsed under the force of gravity until it became massive enough and hot enough for thermonuclear reactions to begin.

42. **(D)** The magnitude of an earthquake is a measure of the amount of energy released by the event.

43. **(C)** The continents were carried to different locations by the movement of the tectonic plates of which they are a part.

44. **(D)** The validity of a testable statement is determined by making observations that may support or contradict the statement.

45. **(A)** The map shows that the cities are on plates that meet along a transform boundary marked by the San Andreas fault. Relative plate motion is carrying Los Angeles north, so at some future time, the cities will be neighbors if the motion continues.

46. **(B)** The Northern Hemisphere is tilted toward the sun, so it is experiencing summer. The Southern Hemisphere is tilted away from the sun, so it is experiencing winter. At the equinox, neither hemisphere is tilted toward the sun.

47. **(B)** Most of the precipitation that falls on land runs over the surface of the ground before being channeled into rills and gullies that feed into streams, lakes, or other bodies of water.

48. **(A)** The charged particles of the solar wind sweep the ionized comet tail in the direction of the wind's movement (that is, away from the sun).

49. **(A)** Earth is the only planet in the solar system with a range of surface temperatures that allows large amounts of liquid water to be present.

50. **(C)** Choice (C) is not true because corundum is harder than topaz, so a mineral that can be scratched by topaz cannot scratch corundum. (A) and (B) are both true based on the position of the minerals in the chart. (D) is true because if the intervals between the numbers on the Mohs scale each represented the same amount of change in absolute hardness, then the graph would show a straight line rather than a curve.

# *HiSET*® Exam Practice Test 1
## Answer Sheet
## Language Arts—Reading

| | A | B | C | D | | A | B | C | D |
|---|---|---|---|---|---|---|---|---|---|
| 1 | | | | | 21 | | | | |
| 2 | | | | | 22 | | | | |
| 3 | | | | | 23 | | | | |
| 4 | | | | | 24 | | | | |
| 5 | | | | | 25 | | | | |
| 6 | | | | | 26 | | | | |
| 7 | | | | | 27 | | | | |
| 8 | | | | | 28 | | | | |
| 9 | | | | | 29 | | | | |
| 10 | | | | | 30 | | | | |
| 11 | | | | | 31 | | | | |
| 12 | | | | | 32 | | | | |
| 13 | | | | | 33 | | | | |
| 14 | | | | | 34 | | | | |
| 15 | | | | | 35 | | | | |
| 16 | | | | | 36 | | | | |
| 17 | | | | | 37 | | | | |
| 18 | | | | | 38 | | | | |
| 19 | | | | | 39 | | | | |
| 20 | | | | | 40 | | | | |

# LANGUAGE ARTS—READING

## 40 Questions

## 65 Minutes

## Directions

This is a test of some of the skills involved in understanding what you read. The passages in this test come from a variety of published works, both literary and informational. Each passage is followed by a number of questions. The passages begin with an introduction presenting information that may be helpful as you read the selection. After you have read a passage, go on to the questions that follow. For each question, choose the best answer, and mark your choice on the answer sheet. You may refer to a passage as often as necessary.

Work as quickly as you can without becoming careless. Don't spend too much time on any question that is difficult for you to answer. Instead, skip it and return to it later if you have time. Try to answer every question even if you have to guess.

Mark all your answers on the answer sheet. Give only one answer to each question and make every mark heavy and dark. If you decide to change one of your answers, be sure to erase the first mark completely. Be sure that the number of the question you are answering matches the number of the row of answer choices you are marking on your answer sheet.

---

**Questions 1–5 refer to the following excerpt adapted from the short story "To Build a Fire," by Jack London, 1910.**

The man flung a look back along the way he had come. The Yukon lay a mile wide and hidden under three feet of ice. On top of this ice were as many feet of snow. It was all pure white, rolling in gentle undulations where the ice-jams of the freeze-up had
*Line* formed. North and south, as far as his eye could see, it was unbroken white, save
5  for a dark hairline that curved and twisted from around the spruce-covered island to the south, and that curved and twisted away into the north, where it disappeared behind another spruce-covered island. This dark hairline was the trail—the main trail—that led south five hundred miles to the Chilcoot Pass, Dyea, and salt water; and that led north seventy miles to Dawson, and still on to the north a thousand miles
10  to Nulato, and finally to St. Michael on Bering Sea, a thousand miles and a half thousand more.

But all this—the mysterious, far-reaching hairline trail, the absence of sun from the sky, the tremendous cold, and the strangeness and weirdness of it all—made no impression on the man. It was not because he was long used to it. He was a newcomer
15  in the land, a cheechako, and this was his first winter. The trouble with him was that he was without imagination. He was quick and alert in the things of life, but only in things, not in the significances. Fifty degrees below zero meant eighty-odd degrees of frost. Such a fact impressed him as being cold and uncomfortable, and that was all. It did not lead him to meditate on his frailty as a creature of temperature, and upon man's
20  frailty in general, able only to live within certain narrow limits of heat and cold;

---

**GO ON TO THE NEXT PAGE ➡**

and from there on it did not lead him to the conjectural field of immortality and man's place in the universe. Fifty degrees below zero stood for a bite of frost that hurt and that must be guarded against by the use of mittens, ear flaps, warm moccasins, and thick socks. Fifty degrees below zero was to him just precisely fifty degrees below zero. 25 That there should be anything more to it than that was a thought that never entered his head.

1. **Which of the following phrases <u>best</u> describes what the man feels toward the cold?**
   A   hateful and bitter
   B   aware but indifferent
   C   oblivious and unconcerned
   D   frightened but reasonable

2. **What is the main effect of the author's description of the Yukon?**
   A   It impresses on the reader how vast, lonely, and cold it is.
   B   It allows the reader to understand how beautiful it is.
   C   It shows that the Yukon is an area like no other.
   D   It mirrors the feelings the man has as he walks through the Yukon.

3. **Which of the following <u>best</u> describes the mood created by this scene?**
   A   solemn
   B   serene
   C   sorrowful
   D   abandoned

4. **Which of the following <u>best</u> expresses the main idea of the excerpt?**
   A   Man may not be aware of his own limitations.
   B   Life takes many turns, and often they are sudden.
   C   Nature can be fickle at times.
   D   Life is a complicated path for most people.

5. **Which of the following can you infer about the author of the excerpt?**
   A   He has walked the entire length of the trail.
   B   He has experienced nearly dying from the cold.
   C   He is worried that the man does not know where the path is.
   D   He is very knowledgeable about the Yukon.

**Questions 6–9 refer to the following excerpt adapted from *Gorky Park* by Martin Cruz Smith, 1981.**

"Where do we go now?"

"You go."

"I came back for you," Irina said. "We can get away, we can stay in America."

"I don't want to stay." Arkady looked up. "I never wanted to stay. I only came because I knew Osborne would kill you if I didn't."

"Then we'll both go home."

"You are home. You're American now, Irina, you're what you always wanted to be." He smiled. "You're not Russian anymore. We always were different, and now I know what the difference was."

"You'll change, too."

"I'm Russian." He tapped his chest. "The longer I'm here, the more Russian I am."

"No." She shook her head angrily.

"Look at me." Arkady pulled himself to his feet. One leg was numb. "Don't cry. See what I am: Arkady Renko, former Party member and chief investigator. If you love me, tell me truthfully how American I could ever be. Tell me!" he shouted. "Tell me," he said more softly, "admit it, don't you see a Russian?"

"We came all this way. I won't let you go back alone, Arkasha—"

"You don't understand." He took Irina's face in his hands. "I'm not as brave as you are, not brave enough to stay. Please, let me go back. You will be what you already are, and I will be what I am. I will always love you."

6. **What is Arkady trying to do in this excerpt?**

   A  ask Irina to marry him

   B  persuade Irina to return to Russia with him

   C  find a way for him and Irina to stay in America

   D  convince Irina that he must go back to Russia

7. **From what type of work is this excerpt most likely taken?**

   A  a magazine article about the hardships Russian immigrants face

   B  a novel about two Russians in America

   C  a letter from an immigrant to his wife in Russia

   D  a newspaper editorial criticizing Soviet policies

8. **Based on the information given in the passage, what would Arkady have done if he had been a plantation owner in the Old South, after the Civil War?**

   A  considered suicide

   B  become a successful factory owner

   C  resisted adapting to a new way of life

   D  moved to the more prosperous North

9. **What does Arkady mean when he tells Irina, "You are home"?**

   A  She lives in America now.

   B  She has American beliefs and attitudes.

   C  Russia will always be with her.

   D  She must learn American ways if she wants to survive.

**Questions 10-12 refer to the following excerpt adapted from *The Red Badge of Courage* by Stephen Crane, 1895.**

The trees began softly to sing a hymn of twilight. The sun sank until slanted bronze rays struck the forest. There was a lull in the noises of insects as if they had bowed their beaks and were making a devotional pause. There was silence save for the chanted chorus of the trees.

Then, upon this stillness, there suddenly broke a tremendous clangor of sounds. A crimson roar came from the distance.

The youth stopped. He was transfixed by this terrific medley of all noises. It was as if worlds were being rended. There was the ripping sound of musketry and the breaking crash of artillery.

His mind flew in all directions. He conceived the two armies to be at each other panther fashion. He listened for a time. Then he began to run in the direction of the battle. He saw that it was an ironical thing for him to be running thus toward that which he had been at such pains to avoid. But he said, in substance, to himself that if the earth and the moon were about to clash, many persons would doubtless plan to get upon the roofs to witness the collision.

10. **What did the sudden noise of battle make the youth do?**
    A   rip apart his gun
    B   fly in all directions
    C   sing a hymn
    D   stop and stand still

11. **Why is it ironic that the youth ran toward the battle?**
    A   He wanted to see the battle from a roof.
    B   He had tried hard to escape the fighting.
    C   The earth and the moon were about to collide.
    D   He was in considerable pain.

12. **Which of the following <u>best</u> describes the mood created in this scene?**
    A   harmonious
    B   sorrowful
    C   lighthearted
    D   suspenseful

**Questions 13–17 refer to the following poem.**

### City Roofs

*Charles Hanson Towne*

Roof-tops, roof-tops, what do you cover?
Sad folk, bad folk, and many a glowing lover;
Wise people, simple people, children of despair—
Roof-tops, roof-tops, hiding pain and care.

*Line 5* Roof-tops, roof-tops, O what sin you're knowing,
While above you in the sky the white clouds are blowing;
While beneath you, agony and dolor and grim strife
Fight the olden battle, the olden war of Life.

Roof-tops, roof-tops, cover up their shame—
*10* Wretched souls, prisoned souls too piteous to name;
Man himself hath built you all to hide away the stars—
Roof-tops, roof-tops, you hide ten million scars.

Roof-tops, roof-tops, well I know you cover
Many solemn tragedies and many a lonely lover;
*15* But ah, you hide the good that lives in the throbbing city—
Patient wives, and tenderness, forgiveness, faith, and pity.

Roof-tops, roof-tops, this is what I wonder:
You are thick as poisonous plants, thick the people under;
Yet roofless, and homeless, and shelterless they roam,
*20* The driftwood of the town who have no roof-top and no home!

**13.** **Which of the following phrases <u>best</u> describes the overall mood of the poem?**
    **A** calm and tranquil
    **B** tender and hopeful
    **C** humorous and cheerful
    **D** angry and bitter

**14.** **Which of the following is the <u>most likely</u> explanation of why the poet says that the rooftops "hide ten million scars" (line 12)?**
    **A** The rooftops were built by man to keep people safe.
    **B** The rooftops keep the sadness in life from being seen.
    **C** The rooftops hurt the people who live under them.
    **D** The rooftops cannot keep everyone from hardship.

**15.** **Which is the <u>best</u> description of what the author thinks about the rooftops?**
    **A** They are helpful in cold weather.
    **B** They keep people from doing what they want.
    **C** They keep the good from being seen.
    **D** They protect the homeless.

**16.** **According to the poem, what effect do the rooftops have for the people under them?**
    **A** They show people how wonderful life is.
    **B** They give the homeless a place to rest.
    **C** They keep people dry in wet weather.
    **D** They keep people from seeing the stars.

**GO ON TO THE NEXT PAGE** ➡

17. **Based on the poem what does the author hope will happen?**

    A   that life will improve with more openness

    B   that the rooftops will be made stronger

    C   that people will stop building rooftops

    D   that people will move out of the city

**Questions 18–21 refer to the following memo.**

**Memo: To All Employees**

CHG Software is happy to announce that, after a six-month-long feasibility study, we have decided to offer an on-site day care facility for our employees. Realizing that our employees are our most valuable asset, and further realizing that employees appreciate being cared for, we decided to implement a day care center beginning in two months.

The center will be located in the former small business accounting module, which has consolidated its operations with personal accounting. It will be in Building 3, A-6 North Wing, on the ground floor. Construction workers have already started renovations.

HR has interviewed more than 75 applicants for day care employees. The center will be staffed with nine care providers. All workers will be certified in early childhood care and have an associate's degree in day care management. The day care center will have its own kitchen facilities, which will provide a daily lunch as well as morning and afternoon snacks.

The center will be equipped with state-of the-art activity and art tables; each child will have his or her own cubby. There will be an outside play area also with state-of-the-art playground equipment.

The center will be open Monday through Friday, from 8:00 A.M. to 6 P.M. Children from three months to age 12 are eligible. CHG Software has kept the cost to a minimum. Full-time day care will be provided for your children for only $580 per month, per child, with a 10 percent deduction for each additional child.

Enrollment applications are available at HR. All children will need to have proof of vaccinations. We look forward to a new era here at CHG. Let us know how we are doing.

*Line 5*

*10*

*15*

*20*

18. **Based on the excerpt, which of the following can be inferred about the directors of CHG?**

    A   They do not take the idea of day care seriously.

    B   They are charging too much for the day care service.

    C   They are not committed to the idea of having a day care facility.

    D   They are trying to make life easier for their employees.

19. **Which of the following best describes the style in which this memo is written?**

    A   detailed and technical

    B   tentative

    C   dry and clinical

    D   straightforward and orderly

20. **Which of the following best restates the phrase "Realizing that our employees are our most valuable asset" (lines 2–3)?**

   Realizing that

   A   our employees are important to us

   B   our employees are well paid by us

   C   our employees are fortunate

   D   our employees look for better treatment

21. **Which of the following best describes the way in which the memo is organized?**

   A   by listing information in order of importance

   B   by listing information in a sequential order

   C   in a cause-and-effect order

   D   in an order that follows logically

---

**Questions 22–28 refer to the following excerpt from the novel *Peace Corps* by Charles Houston.**

Cade settled into his seat on the plane. It was a long flight to Sierra Leone, where he served as a Peace Corps volunteer so long ago. He had wanted to return, but a civil war prevented it. As he landed, he thought of his first visit. He remembered the long truck
*Line*  ride to Joru where he was to teach English. When he arrived, covered with dust, the
5   children ran up to him, shouting, "*Pumoi, pumoi* (white man)."

He was going back to Joru, but first he was going to see Kandeh Massaquoi, his best student. He wanted to see the rice harvester which Kandeh had built with the help of groups in the United States and China. Kandeh had proudly written to Cade about it. It allowed the farmers to get their rice to market faster. Kandeh was always idealistic. He
10   cared about his people. He was Cade's favorite.

The next morning Cade hired a car and driver for the trip. It didn't take long to get there. When they arrived, Cade was surprised to see a large building. There was a Mercedes parked in front. Cade got out of the car and the front door opened. Kandeh approached quickly, holding out his arms. "Hello, my old friend," he said, grinning
15   broadly. His hair was graying, and there was a long scar on his right arm.

They went inside. The room was large and well furnished. Kandeh motioned for Cade to sit in a black leather chair, while he sat on an equally impressive sofa. Cade had expected something different. "Does the house belong to you?" he asked.

Kandeh sighed. "There is much you do not know. In 1993 I returned to my village,
20   Baiama. The rebels were in control. They were holding my family hostage. I had no choice but to join them. They armed me; we attacked neighboring villages, stole weapons and money. I did it to stay alive. When the U.N. troops came, I hid the money and fled to Liberia."

Incredulously, Cade asked him about the rice harvester. "It was destroyed years
25   ago," Kandeh said. "Now I am a businessman." Cade felt depressed. This wasn't what he imagined their reunion would be like.

Cade got up awkwardly. "I must go. I want to get to Joru before nightfall and it's a long trip," he said. They shook hands and then Cade walked out of the house to the waiting car.

**GO ON TO THE NEXT PAGE** ➡

22. Which of the following <u>best</u> describes the overall mood of the excerpt?

    A  expectant

    B  frightened

    C  confident

    D  humorous

23. Which of the following <u>best</u> describes Cade's feelings toward Kandeh at the end of the scene?

    A  compassion

    B  bitterness

    C  hatred

    D  confusion

24. Based on the excerpt, when does this scene <u>most likely</u> take place?

    A  late afternoon

    B  just after lunch

    C  middle of the night

    D  midmorning

25. Based on the excerpt, what will probably happen in the future?

    A  Cade will send Kandeh another rice harvester.

    B  Cade and Kandeh will stay good friends.

    C  Cade and Kandeh will go into business together.

    D  Cade will not contact Kandeh as much as before.

26. Which of the following phrases <u>best</u> describes Kandeh?

    A  cunning and sly

    B  realistic about what he has done

    C  afraid of the future

    D  proud of his accomplishments

27. Which of the following best describes why Cade "got up awkwardly" (line 27)?

    A  He felt hurt by Kandeh's lack of interest in his life.

    B  He realized that Kandeh did not want him to visit.

    C  He was taken aback by what Kandeh told him.

    D  He realized that Kandeh was a dangerous man.

28. Based on the information in this excerpt, Cade would most likely participate in which of the following activities?

    A  learn to fly

    B  work with a peace effort group

    C  take up painting as a hobby

    D  take classes in owning a business

**Questions 29–35 refer to the following excerpt from *The Garden Party and Other Stories* by Katherine Mansfield.**

"And so you go back to the office on Monday, do you, Jonathan?" asked Linda.

"On Monday the cage door opens and clangs to upon the victim for another eleven months and a week," answered Jonathan.

*Line*
5

Linda swung a little. "It must be awful," she said slowly.

"Would ye have me laugh, my fair sister? Would ye have me weep?"

Linda was so accustomed to Jonathan's way of talking that she paid no attention to it.

"I suppose," she said vaguely, "one gets used to it. One gets used to anything."

"Does one? Hum!" The "Hum" was so deep it seemed to boom from underneath the

10 ground. "I wonder how it's done," brooded Jonathan. "I've never managed it."

. . .

"It seems to me just as imbecile, just as awful, to have to go to the office on Monday," said Jonathan, "as it always has done and always will do. To spend all the best years of one's life sitting on a stool from nine to five, scratching in somebody's

15 ledger! It's a strange use to make of one's . . . one and only life, isn't it? Or do I fondly dream?" He rolled over on the grass and looked up at Linda. "Tell me, what is the difference between my life and that of an ordinary prisoner. The only difference I can see is that I put myself in jail and nobody's ever going to let me out. That's a more intolerable situation than the other. For if I'd been—pushed in, against my

20 will—kicking, even—once the door was locked, or at any rate in five years or so, I might have accepted the fact and begun to take an interest in the flight of flies or counting the warden's steps along the passage with particular attention to variations of tread and so on. But as it is, I'm like an insect that's flown into a room of its own accord. I dash against the walls, dash against the windows, flop against the ceiling, do

25 everything, in fact, except fly out again. And all the while I'm thinking, like that moth, or that butterfly, or whatever it is, 'The shortness of life! The shortness of life!' I've only one night or one day, and there's this vast dangerous garden, waiting out there, undiscovered, unexplored."

29. **Why is Jonathan upset?**

   A   He wants to get a raise.

   B   He cannot express himself.

   C   He does not enjoy his job.

   D   He does not have a job.

30. **Which of the following words <u>best</u> describes what Linda feels toward Jonathan?**

   A   She thinks he talks too much.

   B   She is worried he will quit his job.

   C   She cares about him.

   D   She wishes he were stronger.

**GO ON TO THE NEXT PAGE** ➡

31. **Based on the excerpt, which description <u>best</u> characterizes the relationship between Linda and Jonathan?**

    A   They put up with each other's complaints.

    B   They rarely talk to one another.

    C   They like to tell each other secrets.

    D   They can tell each other anything.

32. **Why does Jonathan liken his situation to being in jail?**

    A   He feels he should be punished.

    B   He spent time in jail when he was younger.

    C   He feels stuck in his situation.

    D   He thinks he has too many restrictions.

33. **Based on the excerpt, what is Jonathan <u>most likely</u> to do in the future?**

    A   insult Linda

    B   run away

    C   turn to another for help

    D   continue to work at his job

34. **Based on the excerpt, which of the following words would the narrator <u>most likely</u> use to describe Jonathan?**

    A   dramatic but ineffectual

    B   competitive but understanding

    C   lighthearted but practical

    D   indifferent but innocent

35. **Which of the following <u>best</u> describes the mood of the excerpt?**

    A   life-threatening

    B   ironic

    C   fanciful

    D   theatrical

**Questions 36–40 refer to the following movie review.**

Director Richard Moore has another blockbuster hit with *The Uranium Factor*. George Terry, played perfectly by Richard Burns, is a brilliant but somewhat eccentric (he sleeps in a Himalayan Dome Tent in his dorm room at MIT) college student. Bored with his courses, George designs and builds a time machine in the basement. On a cold, snowy January evening, he sets the time dial to 2150. With the push of a button, he is hurtled forward in time. Scenes rush by faster and faster until he passes out.

    George wakens in a crater. Predictably, the dormitory is gone. He covers the time machine with a camouflage net. As he walks through the streets of Cambridge, there are destroyed buildings everywhere; there also don't seem to be any people. Rounding a corner, he sees a huge spaceship, guarded by armed robots more than eight feet tall. One fires at him, and a laser beam blasts the paving beneath him. George falls, only to be whisked away by a rider on a motorcycle, which can also fly.

    They go far from town to a cabin in the woods. Over coffee in a bare room lit by a kerosene lamp, Anna (Violet Ritter) tells the story. They came in 2141. People fought back,

15 but they were no match for the robots. Their masters never come out of the spaceships, which are all over the planet. The robots call themselves Zorons. They have been rounding up humans, taking them to uranium mines in Russia, Australia, and Canada.

George learns the aliens came from the Centaurus Galaxy, nearly 12 light-years away. Their own planet ran out of uranium; they traveled to Earth, rich with the ore,
20 enslaving humans to work in the mines and load the space freighters. George and Anna are going to take on the Zorons.

I won't give the ending away, but the special effects are definitely Oscar winning. The camera work is stunning too, and the performances by Burns and Ritter are first-rate. It is the first role for both of them. The script, also by a newcomer, Alex
25 Brandeis, is taut and suspenseful; however, the plot does seem to be a bit familiar. It's a story that seems to occur in the movies from time to time. Even so, this movie will leave you clutching your seat the whole time.

**36. Which of the following is the main idea of the review?**

**The author**

    **A**   thinks the movie should not have been produced

    **B**   likes aspects of the film in spite of some faults

    **C**   feels the movie is too overwhelming

    **D**   believes the acting could have been crisper

**37. Which of the following best describes the tone of this review?**

    **A**   informative

    **B**   worried

    **C**   overwhelmed

    **D**   indifferent

**38. Why does the reviewer say, "Predictably, the dormitory is gone" (line 7)?**

    **A**   to show that the movie was terrible

    **B**   to suggest that this is what happens every day

    **C**   to show that the movie was funny

    **D**   to suggest that the story line has been used before

**39. Which of the following best expresses the reviewer's opinion of the special effects?**

    **A**   There were too many special effects.

    **B**   The special effects were first-rate.

    **C**   The special effects showed promise but were amateurish.

    **D**   They were exciting, but they interfered with the plot.

**40. Which of the following best describes the style in which this review is written?**

    **A**   breezy and humorous

    **B**   biased

    **C**   encouraging but critical

    **D**   methodical and clear

**STOP. This is the end of the Language Arts—Reading test.**

# ANSWERS: LANGUAGE ARTS—READING

1.  **(B)** The narrator makes it clear that the man is aware of the cold but does not respond to it in any way other than factually. There is no evidence for options (A) or (D). In option (C), while the man does not seem concerned, it is clear that he is not oblivious to the cold.

2.  **(A)** The description of the Yukon shows how large and cold and lonely it is. The author may think that the Yukon is beautiful, but that is not the primary effect of the description, so option (B) is incorrect. Option (C) may be true, but this is not the effect of the description of the Yukon. Option (D) is not correct.

3.  **(A)** The mood of the scene is very solemn; a man may be facing death because of the cold. The Yukon may seem serene, but that is not the mood of the scene, so option (B) is incorrect. Options (C) and (D) do not describe the mood.

4.  **(A)** The man does not realize that he is in danger of dying. Option (A) is the best expression of the main idea. Options (B) and (C) could be main ideas but not of this excerpt. Option (D) is likely true but, again, not the main idea of this excerpt.

5.  **(D)** Option (D) is something you can figure out about the author because of the way he writes about the Yukon. There is nothing to suggest that options (A) and (B) are true. Option (C) does not seem to be the author's concern.

6.  **(D)** Option (D) states what Arkady is trying to do, which is convince Irina that he must return to Russia. Throughout the excerpt, Arkady speaks of still being Russian. In the last paragraph, he says, "Please let me go back." He tells Irina that she belongs in America, so (B) is not the correct answer. (A) and (C) are also incorrect, as Arkady is not doing any of the things described in those answer choices.

7.  **(B)** The excerpt is a dialogue between two characters. This style of writing is often found in novels, as expressed in option (B). Nothing in the article is representative of a magazine article about the hardships of Russian immigrants, option (A). Option (C) is incorrect, as the excerpt is not in letter form. Option (D) is not correct because the text is not a newspaper editorial criticizing Soviet policies.

8.  **(C)** Option (C) is the best answer since it reflects the fact that there is no evidence in the excerpt that Arkady would convert to a new way of life. On the contrary, he is seeking to return to his old life in his former country. There is no basis for options (A) and (B). Option (D) cannot be verified either.

9.  **(B)** Arkady tells Irina, "You're American now…. You're not Russian anymore." She feels at home in America because she has the same beliefs and attitudes that Americans have. Therefore, option (B) is the best answer. It is not merely living in America that makes Arkady think Irina is at

home, which omits option (A). There is no evidence that Irina cares about her Russian heritage, so option (C) is not a good choice. Since she already knows American ways, option (D) is not correct.

10. **(D)** The youth stops because of the noise and becomes "transfixed," a word that means "stood still." If you didn't know the definition of that word, the context helps you out. The excerpt says he listens for a time and then begins running. You can infer that the youth stood still, option (D). Option (B) reflects the opposite of what the youth does. There is no evidence for options (A) and (C).

11. **(B)** Option (B) is the most reasonable answer. Initially, he had been running away trying to escape the battle, so it is ironic that he runs toward the fighting when it begins. Options (A) and (C) refer to a comment about human nature in the face of disaster. Option (D) is not supported by the text.

12. **(D)** Option (D) is the best description of the mood. What will happen to the youth in the face of battle is unknown. The mood is suspenseful. Options (A) and (C) are clearly incorrect. Although there is fighting going on, the overall mood is not sorrowful, so option (B) is wrong.

13. **(D)** The poet seems quite angry about the situation as it is. Option (A) does not describe the mood of the poem, nor do options (B) and (C).

14. **(B)** Option (B) best explains what the phrase means. Option (A) is not true. The poet does not say that the rooftops hurt the people who live under them, only that there is misery under them, so option (C) is incorrect. Option (D) does not explain the meaning of the phrase either.

15. **(C)** Option (C) is correct. This is what the author says about the rooftops. There is no mention of them in bad weather, nor does the poet say that they keep people from doing what they want, so options (A) and (B) are incorrect. The poet says that the homeless have no rooftops, so option (D) is wrong.

16. **(D)** Option (D) is what the poem says the rooftops do. They certainly don't show how wonderful life is, nor do they give the homeless a place to rest as options (A) and (B) say; in fact, they do the opposite. The poem says nothing about what happens when it rains, so option (C) is incorrect.

17. **(A)** Option (A) seems to be what the author most likely hopes will happen. Options (B) and (C) are not mentioned or hinted at, nor is option (D) suggested as likely.

18. **(D)** Option (D) is the correct answer; you can figure this out from the information in the memo. Option (A) is not plausible; they have studied having a day care center and are implementing it. They are taking the idea very seriously. Option (B) cannot be verified, so it cannot be the correct choice. Option (C) is contrary to what the memo says; they are instituting a day care facility, so they are committed to the idea.

GO ON TO THE NEXT PAGE ➡

19. **(D)** Option (D) is the best description of the style in which the memo is written. It is not technical or overly detailed, nor is it tentative; it is very direct. So options (A) and (B) are incorrect. The memo does not seem dry or clinical, so option (C) is also incorrect.

20. **(A)** Option (A) is a restatement of the phrase. Option (B) is incorrect because there is nothing said about how the employees are paid. Option (C) does not carry the same meaning; in fact, it is the opposite of the phrase. Option (D) does not restate the phrase correctly either.

21. **(D)** Option (D) best describes the way in which the memo is organized. The information it contains follows a logical order. Options (A) and (B) are incorrect; the information is not listed in the order of importance nor is it in a sequential order. While there might be a cause-and-effect issue about the day care, it doesn't exist in the memo, so option (C) is incorrect.

22. **(A)** Option A is correct. There is a feeling of expectancy throughout most of the excerpt. There is nothing to suggest that options (B) and (C) are correct. The excerpt is not humorous, so option (D) is wrong.

23. **(D)** Cade feels confused after meeting with Kandeh; the meeting was not what he expected, so option (D) is correct. Cade does not express compassion toward Kandeh nor is he bitter, so options (A) and (B) are incorrect. There is no hint that option (C) is correct.

24. **(D)** The excerpt says that Cade left to see Kandeh in the morning and that it didn't take long to get to his place, so it stands to reason that the meeting took place during midmorning. Option (A) is unlikely since he left in the morning and it was only a short trip to Kandeh's place. Option (B) is not the correct answer since it would mean it was a rather long trip to Kandeh's home. Option (C) does not make sense.

25. **(D)** Option (D) would most likely happen. Cade realizes that Kandeh is not the same person he knew; they probably would not be in contact as much as before when Cade was excited about the rice harvester. It is unlikely that Cade would send another rice harvester (option A). While Cade and Kandeh might stay good friends (B), the ending of the excerpt did not foretell this happening. Option (C) is definitely not likely to happen.

26. **(B)** Option (B) seems to be the best answer. Kandeh accepts what has happened to him in a realistic way. While hiding the money and running away might be considered cunning (option A), this is not the best description of Kandeh, who was forced to join the rebels. Option (C) certainly does not describe him. Option (D) does not seem to fit either. While he talks about what has happened, there is no sense that he was proud of what he did.

27. **(C)** Option (C) makes the most sense. Cade expected Kandeh to be the same as when he saw him last. What Kandeh told him upset him. There is no sign that option (A) is true. Kandeh was very friendly to Cade, so option (B) is wrong. Option (D) is very unlikely.

28. **(B)** Option (B) seems to be the most logical choice. Cade seems idealistic, so this activity would probably appeal the most. There doesn't seem to be any reason that he would want to learn to fly or take up painting, so options (A) and (C) are incorrect. There is nothing in the excerpt to suggest that he would want to own a business, so option (D) is incorrect as well.

29. **(C)** Option (C) is correct. Jonathan's words supply this information. There is no evidence in the excerpt for options (A), (B), and (D).

30. **(C)** The dialogue between Jonathan and Linda shows that Linda cares about Jonathan, so option (C) is correct. There is no support for option (A). She may worry that he will quit his job, but that is not indicated in the excerpt, so option (B) is wrong. Option (D) may be true, but there is nothing to indicate this.

31. **(D)** Option (D) is correct; the fact that Linda is "so accustomed to Jonathan's way of talking" shows they are completely open with each other. Option (A) might be true, but this is not the best characterization of their relationship. There is no evidence in the excerpt for options (B). Option (C) does not seem to be indicated.

32. **(C)** Option (C) is correct. His words indicate that he feels there is no solution to his situation. Options (A) and (B) are incorrect because there is no mention of punishment or spending time in jail. Option (D) could be something Jonathan is feeling, but it is not indicated in words.

33. **(D)** Option (D) is correct. He may be resigned ("another eleven months and a week"), but he will continue. Options (A), (B), and (C) have no support in the excerpt. There does not seem to be anyone else Jonathan would turn to, and he says himself that he cannot get out of his situation.

34. **(A)** Option (A) is correct. Jonathan certainly is dramatic, but at the same time he has no alternatives; he must return to work. He is not competitive, so option (B) is not correct. His attitude cannot be described as lighthearted or indifferent, so options (C) and (D) are incorrect.

35. **(D)** The references to prison and insects dashed against the wall give a theatrical tone to the excerpt; Jonathan doesn't really believe that. Option (A) is incorrect; brother and sister are lying on the grass, so there is nothing life threatening about the excerpt. Option (B) is incorrect; there is no irony in his words. Option (C) cannot be correct because he is portraying the reality of his job.

36. **(B)** Option (B) best sums up the main idea of the review. Option (A) is definitely not what the reviewer says or suggests. Neither option (C) nor (D) is suggested by the review.

37. **(A)** Option (A) describes the tone of the review the best. The tone is definitely not worried or overwhelmed, so options (B) and (C) are wrong. The reviewer does not seem indifferent; thus, option (D) is incorrect as well.

**GO ON TO THE NEXT PAGE** ➡

38. **(D)** This is the meaning of the reviewer's statement. The statement does not mean that the movie was terrible or that such a thing happens every day, so options (A) and (B) are incorrect. The meaning has nothing to do with the movie being funny, so option (C) is incorrect as well.

39. **(B)** The reviewer says that the special effects were Oscar quality, so option (B) is correct. The reviewer did not say that there were too many special effects or that they were amateurish, so options (A) and (C) are incorrect. The reviewer did say the special effects were exciting, but not that they interfered with the plot, making option (D) wrong as well.

40. **(C)** Option (C) seems to be the best description of the way in which the review is written. It does not seem breezy or humorous, so option (A) is incorrect. There is no sense that the review is biased, so option (B) is wrong. *Methodical* would not be a good word to describe the review, so option (D) is wrong also.

# *HiSET*® Exam Practice Test 1
## Answer Sheet
## Math

| | A | B | C | D | | | A | B | C | D |
|---|---|---|---|---|---|---|---|---|---|---|
| 1 | ☐ | ☐ | ☐ | ☐ | | 26 | ☐ | ☐ | ☐ | ☐ |
| 2 | ☐ | ☐ | ☐ | ☐ | | 27 | ☐ | ☐ | ☐ | ☐ |
| 3 | ☐ | ☐ | ☐ | ☐ | | 28 | ☐ | ☐ | ☐ | ☐ |
| 4 | ☐ | ☐ | ☐ | ☐ | | 29 | ☐ | ☐ | ☐ | ☐ |
| 5 | ☐ | ☐ | ☐ | ☐ | | 30 | ☐ | ☐ | ☐ | ☐ |
| 6 | ☐ | ☐ | ☐ | ☐ | | 31 | ☐ | ☐ | ☐ | ☐ |
| 7 | ☐ | ☐ | ☐ | ☐ | | 32 | ☐ | ☐ | ☐ | ☐ |
| 8 | ☐ | ☐ | ☐ | ☐ | | 33 | ☐ | ☐ | ☐ | ☐ |
| 9 | ☐ | ☐ | ☐ | ☐ | | 34 | ☐ | ☐ | ☐ | ☐ |
| 10 | ☐ | ☐ | ☐ | ☐ | | 35 | ☐ | ☐ | ☐ | ☐ |
| 11 | ☐ | ☐ | ☐ | ☐ | | 36 | ☐ | ☐ | ☐ | ☐ |
| 12 | ☐ | ☐ | ☐ | ☐ | | 37 | ☐ | ☐ | ☐ | ☐ |
| 13 | ☐ | ☐ | ☐ | ☐ | | 38 | ☐ | ☐ | ☐ | ☐ |
| 14 | ☐ | ☐ | ☐ | ☐ | | 39 | ☐ | ☐ | ☐ | ☐ |
| 15 | ☐ | ☐ | ☐ | ☐ | | 40 | ☐ | ☐ | ☐ | ☐ |
| 16 | ☐ | ☐ | ☐ | ☐ | | 41 | ☐ | ☐ | ☐ | ☐ |
| 17 | ☐ | ☐ | ☐ | ☐ | | 42 | ☐ | ☐ | ☐ | ☐ |
| 18 | ☐ | ☐ | ☐ | ☐ | | 43 | ☐ | ☐ | ☐ | ☐ |
| 19 | ☐ | ☐ | ☐ | ☐ | | 44 | ☐ | ☐ | ☐ | ☐ |
| 20 | ☐ | ☐ | ☐ | ☐ | | 45 | ☐ | ☐ | ☐ | ☐ |
| 21 | ☐ | ☐ | ☐ | ☐ | | 46 | ☐ | ☐ | ☐ | ☐ |
| 22 | ☐ | ☐ | ☐ | ☐ | | 47 | ☐ | ☐ | ☐ | ☐ |
| 23 | ☐ | ☐ | ☐ | ☐ | | 48 | ☐ | ☐ | ☐ | ☐ |
| 24 | ☐ | ☐ | ☐ | ☐ | | 49 | ☐ | ☐ | ☐ | ☐ |
| 25 | ☐ | ☐ | ☐ | ☐ | | 50 | ☐ | ☐ | ☐ | ☐ |

# MATH (Calculators Allowed)

## 50 Questions

## 90 Minutes

## Directions

This is a test of your skills in applying mathematical concepts and solving mathematical problems. Read each question carefully and decide which of the five alternatives best answers the question. Then mark your choice on your answer sheet. There are relatively easy problems scattered throughout the test. Thus, do not waste time on problems that are too difficult; go on, and return to them if you have time.

Work as quickly as you can without becoming careless. Don't spend too much time on any question that is difficult for you to answer. Instead, skip it and return to it later if you have time. Try to answer every question even if you have to guess.

Mark all your answers on the answer sheet. Give only one answer to each question and make every mark heavy and dark. If you decide to change one of your answers, be sure to erase the first mark completely. Be sure that the number of the question you are answering matches the number of the row of answer choices you are marking on your answer sheet.

1. If Bobby can run 8 miles in an hour, how many miles can he run in 15 minutes?
   A   1
   B   2
   C   4
   D   7
   E   120

2. If $5x + y = 27$, and $y = 2$, then $x =$
   A   $-5$
   B   $-2$
   C   2
   D   5
   E   7

3. Four people went to a restaurant and each paid separately. Their individual bills were $15, $17, $14, and $19. What was the average bill, in dollars?
   A   $14.50
   B   $15.65
   C   $16.25
   D   $17.00
   E   $19.10

GO ON TO THE NEXT PAGE ➡

4. A group contains 4 men and 20 women. If 1 person is selected, what is the probability the person is a man?

   A  $\dfrac{1}{4}$

   B  $\dfrac{1}{5}$

   C  $\dfrac{1}{6}$

   D  $\dfrac{4}{5}$

   E  $\dfrac{5}{6}$

5. A rectangular region has sides of 8 and 10. What is the perimeter of this region?

   A  2
   B  18
   C  26
   D  28
   E  36

6. A T-shirt costs *n* dollars to purchase, and a jacket costs *m* dollars to purchase. Before tax, which of the following represents the cost to purchase the T-shirt and the jacket?

   A  *nm*

   B  $\dfrac{n}{m}$

   C  $n + m$

   D  $\dfrac{m}{n}$

   E  $n - m$

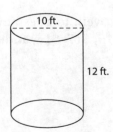

7. The diagram represents the dimensions of a cylindrical storage silo. If the silo already contains 100 cubic feet of grain, what is the maximum whole number of cubic feet of grain that can be added to the silo?

(Volume = $\pi \times$ Radius$^2 \times$ Height)

A  20

B  842

C  1,100

D  1,340

E  3,668

8. An office assistant can type 65 words per minute. If he spends 3 hours a day typing, how many words will he type in 5 days?

A  58,500

B  54,000

C  31,200

D  1,875

E  975

9. What percent of 650 is 78?

A  4%

B  8.33%

C  12%

D  31%

E  57.2%

10. The number of birds sighted by a bird watcher is directly proportional to the amount of time he spends in the park. If the bird-watcher sights 30 birds when he spends 2 hours in the park, how many birds will he sight if he spends 5 hours in the park?

A  60

B  75

C  80

D  90

E  150

11. If $\dfrac{2}{3}x = 6$ then $x =$

A  1

B  $1\dfrac{1}{2}$

C  4

D  $5\dfrac{1}{2}$

E  9

GO ON TO THE NEXT PAGE ➡

12. A box of pancake mix measures 11 inches tall, 5 inches long, and 3 inches wide. Shipments from the factory come in a single large box containing 20 boxes of pancake mix. In cubic inches, what is the smallest possible volume of the large box?

    (Volume = Length × Width × Height)

    A  3,300

    B  2,200

    C  1,100

    D  300

    E  165

13. Jacob purchased a $13,000 car with a 5 percent down payment. In dollars, how much was his down payment?

    A  600

    B  650

    C  800

    D  1,300

    E  2,600

14. Which of the following is a solution of $1 - 3x < 0$?

    A  3

    B  0

    C  −1

    D  −2

    E  −5

15. A portion of a kitchen floor measuring 60 inches long by 96 inches wide will be tiled. How many 6-inch-square tiles would be required to cover this portion of the floor?

    (Area = Length × Width)

    A  26

    B  52

    C  156

    D  160

    E  210

16. Two angles of a triangle have a sum of 150 degrees. What is the measure, in degrees, of the remaining angle?

    A  20

    B  30

    C  45

    D  60

    E  90

17. Sharice invested $500 in a CD (certificate of deposit) that earned 1.5 percent interest per year. After two years, how much interest had she earned?

    (Interest = Principle × Rate × Time)

    A   $51.50

    B   $15.00

    C   $5.50

    D   $7.50

    E   $1.50

18. The monthly cost of a cell phone plan is $35 plus 3 cents for every minute after a total of 500 minutes has been used. In dollars, what will Javonte's bill be if he uses 800 minutes in a single month?

    A   $24.00

    B   $44.00

    C   $59.03

    D   $70.00

    E   $130.15

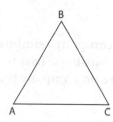

19. The triangle in the figure above is an equilateral triangle with a perimeter of 18. What is the length of side AB?

    A   18

    B   9

    C   6

    D   3

    E   1

20. A jar contains red and blue marbles. The probability that a randomly selected marble is red is $\frac{1}{4}$. If 27 of the marbles are blue, how many marbles are in the jar?

    A   6

    B   9

    C   24

    D   31

    E   36

GO ON TO THE NEXT PAGE ➡

21. At the beginning of the week, the balance of Paloma's bank account was $1,273. On Tuesday, she wrote a check for rent ($750) and a check for her electric bill ($60). On Wednesday, she wrote a check for groceries and other supplies ($81.96). Finally, on Friday, she used an ATM to take out $40 in cash. Assuming all of the checks went through on the same day they were written, what was her bank balance after these transactions?

    A  $188.20

    B  $217.97

    C  $341.04

    D  $412.13

    E  $931.96

22. Josh and Terry both collect coins. Together they have a total of 46 coins. If Josh has 12 more coins than Terry, how many coins does Josh have in his collection?

    A  15

    B  17

    C  29

    D  34

    E  40

23. Miguel's company reimburses him 52 cents for every mile he drives while on company business. Last week, he drove a total of 400 miles, and half of these miles were on company business. How much will Miguel be reimbursed?

    A  $52

    B  $104

    C  $152

    D  $208

    E  452

24. The average of four numbers is 8. If the sum of three of the numbers is 22, what is the value of the remaining number?

    $$\left(\text{Mean} = \frac{x_1 + x_2 + \cdots x_n}{n}\right)$$

    A  8

    B  10

    C  12

    D  22

    E  32

25. Which of the following is the sum of $3x$, $x$, $2y$, and $-5y$?

    A  $x$

    B  $-30xy$

    C  $4x - 3y$

    D  $3x - 10y$

    E  $4x + 7y$

**Questions 26–28 refer to the graph below.**

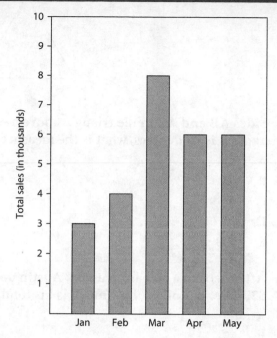

26. **What were the total sales in January?**
    A   3
    B   30
    C   3,000
    D   30,000
    E   3,000,000

27. **What were the total sales in January through May?**
    A   27,000
    B   21,000
    C   9,000
    D   6,000
    E   3,000

28. **Between which two months was there the biggest change in total sales?**
    A   January to February
    B   February to March
    C   March to April
    D   April to May
    E   this cannot be determined from the graph

GO ON TO THE NEXT PAGE ➡

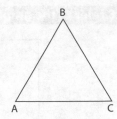

29. Sides AB and AC in the triangle above have the same length. If the measure of angle B is 80 degrees, what is the measure of angle A, in degrees?

    A   30

    B   40

    C   50

    D   80

    E   100

30. After getting a ride from a taxi, Austin decides to leave a 20 percent tip on a $30 fare. In dollars, how much is his total cost for the taxi ride?

    A   6

    B   25

    C   32

    D   36

    E   50

31. On the graph of $y = 3x - 5$, what is the $x$-coordinate of the point that has a $y$-coordinate of 22?

    A   6

    B   9

    C   20

    D   61

    E   71

32. In a small office, secretaries earn $14 an hour, while data entry specialists earn $12 an hour. If there are $a$ secretaries and $b$ data entry specialists in the office, which of the following represents their total hourly pay, in dollars?

    A   $a + b$

    B   $14a + 12b$

    C   $12a + 14b$

    D   $26ab$

    E   $26(a + b)$

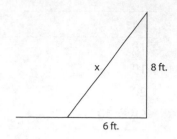

33. The diagram above shows a ladder of length $x$ leaning against a wall. Which of the following expressions represents the value of $x$, in feet?

A $\quad 6^2 + 8^2$

B $\quad \sqrt{6^2 + 8^2}$

C $\quad 6^2 - 8^2$

D $\quad 8^2 - 6^2$

E $\quad 6 + 8$

34. What is the slope of the line that passes through the points (2,2) and (5,6)?

$$\left( \text{Slope of a line } \frac{y_2 - y_1}{x_2 - x_1} \right)$$

A $\quad -\dfrac{4}{3}$

B $\quad -\dfrac{3}{4}$

C $\quad 1$

D $\quad \dfrac{3}{4}$

E $\quad \dfrac{4}{3}$

35. Which of the following is equivalent to $3x^4 - 6x^2$?

A $\quad 3x^2$

B $\quad 3x^2(x^2)$

C $\quad 3x^2(5x^2)$

D $\quad 3x^2(x^2 - 6)$

E $\quad 3x^2(x^2 - 2)$

GO ON TO THE NEXT PAGE ➡

| Age | Number of Students |
|-----|--------------------|
| 18 | 2 |
| 19 | 4 |
| 20 | 1 |
| Over 20 | 6 |

36. The table above shows the ages of students enrolled in a cooking class. What is the median age of the students?

    A   18

    B   19

    C   20

    D   24

    E   26

37. Rectangle A has a length of $\ell$ and a width of $w$. Rectangle B has a length of $\ell$ and a width of $2w$. Which of the following statements is true?

    A   The area of rectangle A is twice the area of rectangle B.

    B   The perimeter of rectangle A is 2 less than the perimeter of rectangle B.

    C   The area of rectangle A is half the area of rectangle B.

    D   The perimeter of rectangle A is 4 less than the perimeter of rectangle B.

    E   The area of rectangle A is a fourth of the area of rectangle B.

38. On a bookshelf, there are $x$ science books, $y$ math books, and $z$ history books. Which of the following expressions represents the percentage of history books on the shelf?

    A   $\dfrac{z}{100(x + y + z)}\%$

    B   $\dfrac{100z}{x + y}\%$

    C   $\dfrac{100z}{x + y + z}\%$

    D   $\dfrac{z}{100}\%$

    E   $100z\%$

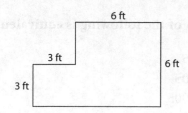

**39.** A vegetable garden is to be built by following the diagram above. How many feet of fencing will be needed to completely enclose the perimeter of the garden?

A   6

B   18

C   27

D   30

E   36

**40.** The square root of 38 is between which of the following pairs of numbers?

A   6 and 7

B   7 and 8

C   8 and 9

D   9 and 10

E   10 and 11

**41.** A 16-ounce box of cereal costs $3.75. Which of the following expressions represents the cost of a single ounce of this cereal, in dollars?

A   3.75(16)

B   16 − 3.75

C   3.75 ÷ 16

D   16 + 3.75

E   16 ÷ 3.75

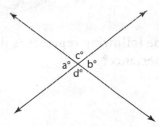

**42.** In the figure above $a = 80$. What is the value of $c + d$?

A   80

B   100

C   160

D   200

E   280

GO ON TO THE NEXT PAGE ➡

43. Which of the following is equivalent to $\dfrac{5}{1,000}$?

    A   0.5

    B   0.05

    C   0.005

    D   0.0005

    E   0.00005

44. If $x = 3$ and $y = -2$, what is the value of $x^2 - y^2$?

    A   2

    B   4

    C   5

    D   10

    E   13

**Questions 45 and 46 use the graph below.**

**Years of Experience for Employees at Company A**

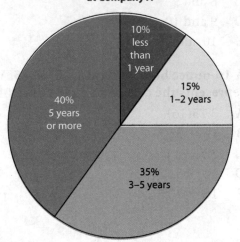

45. Which of the following represents the fraction of employees with 3 or more years of experience?

    A   $\dfrac{1}{10}$

    B   $\dfrac{1}{4}$

    C   $\dfrac{2}{5}$

    D   $\dfrac{3}{4}$

    E   $\dfrac{9}{10}$

46. If there are 500 employees at the company, how many have 5 or more years of experience?

    A   100
    B   200
    C   250
    D   300
    E   400

47. A custom piece of fabric can be made from a choice of 4 different colors, 3 different patterns, and 8 different types of stitching. How many combinations of colors, patterns, and stitching are possible?

    A   96
    B   72
    C   56
    D   20
    E   15

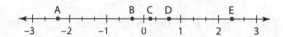

48. On the number line above, which of the following points represents $\frac{2}{3}$?

    A   A
    B   B
    C   C
    D   D
    E   E

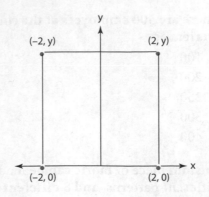

49. The area of the rectangle above is 24. What is the length?

   A  2

   B  4

   C  6

   D  12

   E  20

50. Joaquin is buying ground beef for his club's picnic. The club will make 76 hamburgers; each hamburger will contain 5 ounces of meat. Which of the following expressions can Joaquin use to find out how many pounds of beef he must buy?

   A  5 × 76

   B  5 + 76

   C  5 × 76 × 16

   D  (5 × 76) ÷ 16

   E  (76 ÷ 5) × 16

STOP. This is the end of the Math test.

# ANSWERS: MATH

1. **(B)** $\dfrac{8\text{ miles}}{1\text{ hour}} = \dfrac{8\text{ miles}}{60\text{ minutes}} = \dfrac{\frac{1}{4}(8)\text{ miles}}{\frac{1}{4}(60)\text{ minutes}} = \dfrac{2\text{ miles}}{15\text{ minutes}}.$

2. **(D)** $x = 5$ Plug the value of $y$ into the equation and solve for $x$:
$$5x + y = 27$$
$$5x + 5 = 27$$
$$5x = 25$$
$$x = 5$$

3. **(C)** In general, to find the average, you find the sum of all the values and then divide by the number of values. In this case, there are four values so the average is
$$\frac{15 + 17 + 14 + 19}{4} = 16.25.$$

4. **(C)** The probability that the person selected is a man can be found by dividing the total number of men by the total number of people in the group: $\dfrac{4}{24} = \dfrac{1}{6}.$

5. **(E)** The perimeter is the sum of the lengths of all the sides. The rectangle has two sides with lengths of 8 and two sides with lengths of 10. Therefore, the perimeter is $8 + 8 + 10 + 10 = 36$.

6. **(C)** The total cost would be the sum of the individual prices. In other words, the total cost is $n + m$.

7. **(B)** Essentially, this question is asking you to find the volume that remains if 100 cubic feet is already used. Before you can calculate this, you must find the total volume of the silo. Using the formula for the volume of a cylinder, the total available volume is $12 \times 3.14 \times 5^2 = 942$. Since 100 cubic feet is already being used, 842 cubic feet of space is still available.

8. **(A)** In a single day, the office assistant types for $3 \times 60 = 180$ minutes, and since he types 65 words a minute, he will type $65 \times 180 = 11,700$ words a day. Finally, he will type $5 \times 11,700 = 58,500$ words in 5 days.

9. **(C)** $\left(\dfrac{78}{650} \times 100\right)\% = 12\%.$

10. **(B)** If $y$ is directly proportional to $x$, $y = kx$ for some number $k$. If you let the number of birds sighted be represented by $n$ and the amount of time spent in the park be represented by $t$, you get the formula $n = kt$. Plugging in the initial information yields the equation $30 = 2k$, and solving this yields $k = 15$. Therefore, the formula is $n = 15t$. Finally, plugging in 5 for $t$ yields $n = 15 \times 5 = 75$.

GO ON TO THE NEXT PAGE ➡

11. **(E)** Multiply both sides by $\frac{3}{2}$: $x = \frac{3}{2}(6) = 9$.

12. **(A)** The large box must be large enough to accommodate all 20 of the smaller boxes, which each have a volume of $11 \times 5 \times 3 = 165$ cubic inches. Thus, it must have a volume of at least $20 \times 165 = 3,300$ cubic inches.

13. **(B)** $\frac{5}{100} \times 13,000 = 650$.

14. **(A)** The key here is to solve for $x$ while remembering that the direction of the inequality will switch when you divide or multiply by a negative number. The inequality $1 - 3x < 0$ is the same as $x > \frac{1}{3}$ and only option (1) is larger than $\frac{1}{3}$.

15. **(D)** The total area to be tiled is $60 \times 96 = 5,760$ square inches, and the tiles are $6 \times 6 = 36$ square inches each. Therefore, it will require $\frac{5,760}{36} = 160$ tiles to cover this portion of the floor.

16. **(B)** The sum of the measure of all the angles in a triangle is 180 degrees. Since you are given two angles, the remaining angle has a measure of $180 - 150 = 30$ degrees.

17. **(B)** $15 \quad 500 \times \frac{1.5}{100} \times 2 = 15$.

18. **(B)** $44 Javonte will be charged $35 plus 3 cents for every minute over 500. In this case, he used 300 minutes over 500, so his bill will be $35 + 0.03 \times 300 = 44$.

19. **(C)** All three sides of an equilateral triangle have the same length, and the perimeter is the sum of these lengths. If the perimeter is 18, then the length of any side is $18 \div 3 = 6$

20. **(E)** Let represent the number of red marbles. Since the probability that a marble is red is $\frac{1}{4}$, it must be that $\frac{x}{x + 27} = \frac{1}{4}$. When this is solved, you find that $x = 9$, and the total number of marbles is $27 + 9 = 36$.

21. **(C)** $1,273 - 750 - 60 - 81.96 - 40 = 341.04$.

22. **(C)** Let $x$ represent the number of coins in Josh's collection and $y$ represent the number of coins in Terry's collection. Since there is a total of 46 coins, $x + y = 46$. Also, since Josh has 12 more coins than Terry, $x = y + 12$. Substituting this value for $x$ in the original equation, $y + 12 + y = 46$, and $y = 17$. Since Josh has 12 more, the final answer is $12 + 17 = 29$.

23. **(B)** Half of the 400 miles were on company business, so he will be reimbursed $200 \times 0.52 = 104$.

24. **(B)** Let $x$ represent the unknown number. Since you know the average is 8, you know the sum of the numbers divided by 4 is 8. But you already know the sum of the first three numbers is 22. This gives you the equation $\dfrac{22+x}{4}=8$, which has a solution of $x=10$.

25. **(C)** $3x + x + 2y + (-5y) = (3+1)x + (2-5)y = 4x - 3y$.

26. **(C)** Total sales are in thousands, so multiply 3 by 1,000 to get 3,000.

27. **(A)** $3,000 + 4,000 + 8,000 + 6,000 + 6,000 = 27,000$.

28. **(B)** The biggest height difference between bars on the graph is between the second and third bars.

29. **(C)** Since sides AB and AC have the same length, angles A and C have the same measure. In total, there are 180 degrees in the triangle, and 80 are accounted for with angle 2. Therefore, angle A will have a measure of $\dfrac{180-80}{2}=50$ degrees.

30. **(D)** The tip was $\dfrac{20}{100}\times 30 = 6$ giving a total fare of $30 + 6 = \$36$.

31. **(B)** The $x$-coordinate can be found by replacing the value of $y$ in the equation given to get $22 = 3x - 5$ and solving for $y$. The solution to this equation is $x = 9$.

32. **(B)** Each of the secretaries earns \$14 an hour, and the total paid to the secretaries is $14a$. Each of the data entry specialists earns \$12, and the total paid to them is $12b$. Finally, the overall total paid to both is $14a + 12b$.

33. **(B)** By the Pythgorean theorem, $x^2 = 6^2 + 8^2$ and $x = \sqrt{6^2 + 8^2}$

34. **(E)** $m = \dfrac{6-2}{5-2} = \dfrac{4}{3}$.

35. **(E)** Factor $3x^2$ out from both terms.

36. **(C)** There is a total of 13 data values, and the median is the middle, or seventh value.

37. **(C)** The area of rectangle A is $\ell \times w$, while the area of rectangle B is $\ell \times 2w = 2lw$. Therefore, rectangle B has twice the area of A, or A has half the area of B.

38. **(C)** In general, you can think of finding a percentage as dividing the part you are interested in by the whole and then multiplying by 100. In this case, the part is the number of history books, $z$, and the whole is the total number of books, $z + x + y$.

GO ON TO THE NEXT PAGE ➡

39. **(D)** The perimeter is the sum of the lengths of all the sides. In this case, it is $3 + 3 + 3 + 6 + 6 + 9 = 30$.

40. **(A)** The square root of 36 is 6, and the square root of 49 is 7. Since 38 is between 36 and 49, the square root of 38 must be between 6 and 7.

41. **(C)** To find the unit price, divide the total price by the number of units (in this case, ounces).

42. **(D)** Since these lines meet at a single point, the sum $a + b + c + d = 360$. As opposite angles, $a = b = 80$ and $c + d = 360 - 2(80) = 200$.

43. **(C)** There are three zeros in 1,000, so starting with 5, move the decimal to the left three digits.

44. **(C)** $3^2 - (-2)^2 = 9 - 4 = 5$.

45. **(D)** Using the chart, $35\% + 40\% = 75\%$ of employees who have 3 or more years of experience. As a fraction, $75\% = \dfrac{75}{100} = \dfrac{3}{4}$.

46. **(B)** $200 \ \dfrac{40}{100} \times 500 = 200$.

47. **(A)** There are $4 \times 3 \times 8 = 96$ possible combinations.

48. **(D)** There are two tick marks between each whole number, each representing a third. Since D is on the second tick mark from zero, D represents the point $\dfrac{2}{3}$.

49. **(C)** The area of 24 is found by multiplying the length and the width of the rectangle. The width is the distance between $-2$ and 2, which is 4. The length will then be $24 \div 4 = 6$.

50. **(D)** The expression $(5 \times 76) \div 16$ will show how many ounces of meat he needs. 76 burgers times 5 ounces each gives you the total in ounces. There are 16 ounces in a pound, so to find the number of pounds, you must divide this amount by 16.

# 40 *HiSET*® Exam Practice Test 2

# *HiSET*® Exam Practice Test 2
## Answer Sheet
## Language Arts—Writing, Part 1

|  | A | B | C | D |  |  | A | B | C | D |
|---|---|---|---|---|---|---|---|---|---|---|
| 1 | | | | | | 26 | | | | |
| 2 | | | | | | 27 | | | | |
| 3 | | | | | | 28 | | | | |
| 4 | | | | | | 29 | | | | |
| 5 | | | | | | 30 | | | | |
| 6 | | | | | | 31 | | | | |
| 7 | | | | | | 32 | | | | |
| 8 | | | | | | 33 | | | | |
| 9 | | | | | | 34 | | | | |
| 10 | | | | | | 35 | | | | |
| 11 | | | | | | 36 | | | | |
| 12 | | | | | | 37 | | | | |
| 13 | | | | | | 38 | | | | |
| 14 | | | | | | 39 | | | | |
| 15 | | | | | | 40 | | | | |
| 16 | | | | | | 41 | | | | |
| 17 | | | | | | 42 | | | | |
| 18 | | | | | | 43 | | | | |
| 19 | | | | | | 44 | | | | |
| 20 | | | | | | 45 | | | | |
| 21 | | | | | | 46 | | | | |
| 22 | | | | | | 47 | | | | |
| 23 | | | | | | 48 | | | | |
| 24 | | | | | | 49 | | | | |
| 25 | | | | | | 50 | | | | |

# LANGUAGE ARTS—WRITING, PART 1

**50 Questions**

**75 Minutes**

## Directions

This is a test of some of the skills involved in revising written materials. There are selections similar to the reports, letters, and articles high-school students often need to write. Each selection is presented twice, first in a box in a conventional format and then in a spread-out format with certain parts underlined and numbered. Read quickly through the boxed text to get an idea of its purpose and style. Then go on to the spread-out format. For each underlined part there are alternatives listed in the right-hand column. Choose the alternative that

- makes the statement grammatically correct
- expresses the idea in the clearest or most appropriate way
- is worded most consistently with the style and purpose of the writing
- organizes the ideas in the most effective way

In some cases, there may be more than one problem to correct or improve.

When you have decided which alternative is best, mark your choice on the answer sheet. If you think the original underlined version is best, choose *"No change."* In questions about organization, you will probably find it helpful to look at the boxed text. In the questions about spelling, you are to indicate which of three underlined words is misspelled, if any. If there are no errors in any of the words, mark *"None."*

Work as quickly as you can without becoming careless. Don't spend too much time on any question that is difficult for you to answer. Instead, skip it and return to it later if you have time. Try to answer every question even if you have to guess.

Mark all your answers on the answer sheet. Give only one answer to each question and make every mark heavy and dark. If you decide to change one of your answers, be sure to erase the first mark completely. Be sure that the number of the question you are answering matches the number of the row of answer choices you are marking on your answer sheet.

**GO ON TO THE NEXT PAGE** ➡

Read quickly through the draft article in the box below. Then go to the spread-out version and consider the suggestions for revision.

**Questions 1–8 refer to the following letter.**

---

### Shining Star Insurance Company

318 North 26th Street
Wilson, OK 61007

Dear Ms. Cruz:

1. Thank you for choosing Shining Star to insure your home and it's possessions. We are pleased to be of service to you and want to introduce you to the information you will need about our company. We pride ourselves on our customer service who we believe is the most user-friendly in the industry. Our customer service experts will help you settle any claim that you need to make speedily, with the least amount of inconvenience.

2. We are enclosing a booklet that Shining Star sends to every new customer. It is being packed with information on how to protect your home from theft and burglary. There are blank pages at the back where you can make a record of your valuables. The booklet also contain important facts about making sure your home does not have any situations which could increase the possibility of a fire. It's a good idea to keep the booklet in a safe place.

3. In addition to providing fast, worry-free claim service, Shining Star can also help you choose a contractor to perform any repairs needed after damage occurs in your home, or finding a person to oversee the repairs. Just go to our website at www.shiningstarinsco.net, enter your zip code. A list of qualified, approved contractors will appear.

4. Our claims specialists are available seven days a week, from 7 A.M. to 9 P.M., central time. If you have any questions, please don't hesitate to call us. Every member of the team at Shining Star Insurance Company looks forward to serving your insurance needs for many years; we want to thank you again for choosing us.

Sincerely,
Shining Star Insurance Company

---

## Shining Star Insurance Company

318 North 26th Street
Wilson, OK 61007

Dear Ms. Cruz:

1. Thank you <u>for choosing Shining Star</u>
   <sub>1</sub>
   <u>to insure your home and it's</u>
   <sub>1</sub>
   possessions. We are pleased to be of
   service to you and want to introduce
   you to the information you will need
   about our company. We pride
   ourselves on <u>our customer service</u>
   <sub>2</sub>
   <u>who we believe is</u> the most user-
   <sub>2</sub>
   friendly in the industry. Our
   customer service experts will help
   you settle any claim that you need to
   make speedily, with the least amount
   of inconvenience.

2. We are enclosing a booklet that
   Shining Star sends to every new
   customer. It <u>is being packed with</u>
   <sub>3</sub>
   information on <u>how to protect</u> your
   <sub>3</sub>
   home from theft and burglary.
   There are blank pages at the back
   where you can make a record of

**1**

A (No change)

B for having chosen Shining Star to insure your home and it's

C for choosing Shining Star, to insure your home and it's

D for choosing Shining Star to insure your home and its

**2**

A (No change)

B our customer service, which we believe is

C our customer service. Who we believe is

D our customer service, who we are believing

**3**

A (No change)

B is packed with information on how to protect

C is being packed with information, on how to protect

D is being packed with information on how to protecting

GO ON TO THE NEXT PAGE ➡

your valuables. The booklet <u>also</u>
[4]
<u>contain important facts about</u>
[4]
<u>making sure your home does not</u>
[4]
<u>have any situations which could</u>
[4]
<u>increase</u> the possibility of a fire. It's
[4]
a good idea to keep the booklet in a

safe place.

3. In addition to providing fast,

worry-free claim service, Shining

Star can also help you choose a

contractor to <u>perform any repairs</u>
[5]
<u>needed after damage occurs in your</u>
[5]
<u>home, or finding</u> a person to
[5]
oversee the repairs. Just go to our

website at www.shiningstarinsco

.net, enter your zip code. A list of

qualified, approved contractors will

appear.

**4**

A (No change)

B also contain important facts about making sure your home does not have any situations which could increased

C also contains important facts about making sure your home does not have any situations which could increase

D also contain important facts about making sure your home does not having any situations which could increase

**5**

A (No change)

B performing any repairs needed after damage occurs in your home, or finding

C perform any repairs needed after damage occurs, in your home, or finding

D perform any repairs needed after damage occurs in your home, or find

**6 Reread the following sentences:**
*Just go to our website at www.shiningstarco.net, enter your zip code. A list of qualified, approved contractors will appear.*

**The most effective combination of these sentences would include which group of words?**

A code, however a list

B code, yet a list

C code and a list

D code, and a list

**4.** Our claims specialists are available <u>seven days a week, from 7 A.M. to 9 P.M., central time</u>. If you have any questions, please don't hesitate to call us. Every member of the team at Shining Star Insurance Company looks forward to serving your insurance <u>needs for many years; we want to thank you</u> again for choosing us.

$$_7$$

$$_8$$

Sincerely,
Shining Star Insurance Company

**7**

**A** (No change)

**B** seven days a week, from 7 A.M. to 9 P.M., Central Time

**C** seven days a week from 7 A.M. to 9 P.M. central time

**D** seven days, a week, from 7 A.M. to 9 P.M., Central Time

**8**

**A** (No change)

**B** needs for many years, we want to thank you

**C** needs, for many years; we want to thank you

**D** needs for many years, we will want to thank you

---

**Questions 9–16 refer to the following article.**

---

## Gray Whales

1. The gray whale is one of nature's most majestic creatures. Its size is notable, a gray whale can reach as long as 45 feet in length and weigh more than 30 tons. From April to November the gray whale lives in the Arctic waters of the Bering and Beaufort Seas. The whale then travels to the warm waters off the coast of Baja California, Mexico, where they mate. Their migration habits are unique as well.

2. The females birth and nurse their young in Baja. The baby whales, which are called calves, grew very quickly. The whales return to the North, after the young have become strong, in late winter. The round trip is more than 10,000 miles, making it the longest migration of any mammal on Earth.

3. The whales swim in groups called pods, each pod can contain as many as 16 whales. While migrating, the whales swimming 24 hours a day. Gray whales can swim underwater for up to an hour. Because they are mammals they must eventually come to the surface for air.

4. When the whales surface, they exhale a powerful stream of air, vapor, and water called a blow. The blow can reach as high as 15 feet. The gray whale is truly an awesome animal, and whale watchers enjoy every opportunity to see them.

---

**GO ON TO THE NEXT PAGE** ➡

# Gray Whales

1.  The gray whale is one of nature's most majestic creatures. Its size is <u>notable, a gray</u> whale can reach as
    <sub>10</sub>
    long as 45 feet in length and weigh more than 30 tons. From April to November the gray whale lives in the Arctic waters of the Bering and Beaufort Seas. The whale then travels to the warm waters off the coast of Baja California, Mexico, where they mate. Their migration habits are unique as well.

2.  The <u>females birth</u> and nurse
    <sub>11</sub>
    their young in Baja. The baby

    <u>whales, which are called calves,</u>
    <sub>12</sub>
    <u>grew</u> very quickly. The whales
    <sub>12</sub>

    <u>return to the North, after the</u>
    <sub>13</sub>
    <u>young have become strong, in late</u>
    <sub>13</sub>
    <u>winter.</u> The round trip is more
    <sub>13</sub>
    than 10,000 miles, making it the longest migration of any mammal on Earth.

**9** Which revision should be made to paragraph 1?

A move sentence 1 to the end of the paragraph

B remove sentence 2

C move the last sentence to after sentence 2

D move sentence 3 to the beginning of the paragraph

**10**

A (No change)

B notable a gray

C notable, however a gray

D notable because a gray

**11**

A (No change)

B females give birth

C female birth

D females birthed

**12**

A (No change)

B whales which are called calves, grew

C whales, which are called calves, grow

D whales, which are calling calves, grew

**13**

A (No change)

B returning to the North, after the young have become strong, in late winter

C return to the North in late winter, after the young have become strong

D return to the north, after the young have become strong, in late winter

3. The whales swim in groups called <u>pods, each pod</u> can contain as many
   <sub>14</sub>
   as 16 whales. While migrating, the whales <u>swimming</u> 24 hours a day.
   <sub>15</sub>
   Gray whales can swim underwater for up to an hour. Because they are mammals they must eventually come to the surface for air.

4. When the whales surface, they exhale a powerful stream of air, vapor, and water called a blow. The blow can reach as high as 15 feet. The gray whale is truly an awesome animal, and whale watchers enjoy every opportunity to see them.

**14**
A (No change)
B pods, every pod
C pod, each pod
D pods, and each pod

**15**
A (No change)
B swims
C having swam
D swim

**16 Which sentence would be most effective if inserted at the beginning of paragraph 4?**
A The baby whales are very affectionate, and many times will allow humans to come up very close to them.
B Every year, whale watchers up and down the California coast thrill to observe the gray whales on their long journey.
C Baleen whales don't have teeth, they have plates that filter tiny fish and shrimp when water passes over them.
D In addition to whales, dolphins and porpoises also belong to the order of cetaceans.

**GO ON TO THE NEXT PAGE** ➡

---

### How to Dress for a Job Interview

1. Dressing correctly for a job interview is very important. The first thing an interviewer will noticing is what you're wearing. If the interviewer does not like how you are dressed. Then you will already have a strike against you. Is an old saying, "Dress for success," and it's very true when dressing for a job interview.
2. Both men and women should dress conservatively. Wear a solid-colored dark blue or gray suit, with a white shirt or blouse, or a shirt/blouse coordinated with the suit. Make sure your shoes is polished. Men should wear dark socks, and women should have a neutral or light colored panty hose. Make sure you have a full tank of gasoline and a car that is working.
3. Avoid using to much aftershave, cologne, or perfume. Men shouldn't wear any jewelry, and women should go easy with the jewelry. Men should select a conservative tie, and women should have chosen a skirt that is not too short. Any tattoos should be covered. Finally, bringing a briefcase or portfolio will give you a professional touch. Check yourself in a mirror one last time before you goes in.

---

### How to Dress for a Job Interview

1. Dressing correctly for a job interview is very important. The first thing an <u>interviewer will noticing is what you're wearing</u>. If the interviewer does not like how you are dressed. Then you will already have a strike against you.
   <sub>17</sub>
   <sub>17</sub>

**17**

A (No change)

B interviewer will notice is what you're wearing

C interviewer will noticing is what your wearing

D interviewer will noticing is what you're worn

**18 Reread the following sentences:** *If the interviewer does not like how you are dressed. Then you will already have a strike against you.*

**Which is the most effective combination of these sentences?**

A Then, you will already have a strike against you, if the interviewer does not like how you are dressed.

B You will already have a strike against you, then; if the interviewer does not like how you are dressed.

C If the interviewer does not like how you are dressed, then you will already have a strike against you.

D You will already have a strike against you, if the interviewer does not like how you are dressed then.

Is an old saying, "Dress for success,"
    19
and it's very true when dressing for
    19
a job interview.

**19**

A (No change)

B Is an old saying, "dress for success," and it's very true

C Is an old saying, "Dress for success," and its very true

D There is an old saying, "Dress for success," and it's very true

2. Both men and women should dress conservatively. Wear a solid-colored
    20
dark blue or gray suit, with a white
    20
shirt or blouse, or a shirt/blouse
    20
coordinated with the suit.
    20

**20**

A (No change)

B Wear a solid-colored, dark blue or gray suit with a white shirt or blouse, or a shirt/blouse coordinated

C Wearing a solid-colored dark blue or gray suit with a white shirt or blouse, or a shirt/blouse coordinated

B Wear a solid-colored dark blue or gray suit with a white shirt or blouse, or a shirt/blouse coordinate

Make sure your shoes is polished.
    21
Men should wear dark socks, and women should have a neutral or light colored panty hose. Make sure you have a full tank of gasoline and a car that is working.

**21**

A (No change)

B Making sure your shoes is polished

C Make sure your shoes are polished

D Make sure, your shoes is polished

**22 Which revision would improve the effectiveness of paragraph 2?**

A remove the last sentence

B move the second sentence to the beginning of the paragraph

C move the third sentence to the end of the paragraph

D move the fourth sentence after the first sentence

**GO ON TO THE NEXT PAGE** ➡

3. Avoid <u>using to much aftershave,</u>
   <sub>23</sub>
   <u>cologne, or perfume</u>. Men shouldn't
   <sub>23</sub>
   wear any jewelry, and women
   should go easy with the jewelry.
   Men should select a conservative

   tie, and women <u>should have chosen</u>
   <sub>24</sub>
   a skirt that is not too short. Any
   tattoos should be covered. Finally,
   bringing a briefcase or portfolio
   will give you a professional touch.
   Check yourself in a mirror one last
   time <u>before you goes in</u>.
   <sub>25</sub>

**23**

A (No change)

B using too much aftershave, cologne, or perfume

C using to much aftershave cologne, or perfume

D using to much aftershave, cologne, or perfumes

**24**

A (No change)

B should be choosing

C choose

D should choose

**25**

A (No change)

B before you go in

C before you going in

D before you did go in

---

**Questions 26–33 refer to the following article.**

---

## Riding Toy Recalled

1. The Consumer Safety Bureau (CSB) announced today that it is recalling a children's riding toy called "Scurry n Go." "Scurry n Go" was intending for children at least two years of age. The manufacturer, kid fun, of Brooklyn, NY, said that it was taking back about 120,000 units that were sold. The company said that consumers will receive the full purchase price. Another 30,000 toys will be returned by department stores toy stores discount outlets and mail order firms.

2. The CSB has found that children riding the toy can tip forward. Children fall to the ground. The danger of falling has been confirmed by reports of 20 incidents nationwide over the past four months. There will be reports of four children receiving cuts on the chin severe enough to need stitches.

3. Parents who need more information are encouraged to call the CSB at its recall hotline toll free number: 888-123-4567, or go to the website at www.csb.net. "Scurry n Go" is made of yellow molded plastic with black wheels. The riding toy is 20 inches long, 10 inches wide and 12 inches in height. The toy's model number is 0318QS. The model number can be found on the underside of the toy. It is printed in black on a white Universal Product Code (UPC) sticker. An aid for the CSB said the recall is proceeding smoothly.

# Riding Toy Recalled

1. The Consumer Safety Bureau (CSB) announced today that it is recalling a children's riding toy called "Scurry n Go." "Scurry n Go" <u>was intending</u> for children at least
   26
   two years of age. The manufacturer,

   <u>kid fun, of Brooklyn, NY, said that</u>
   27
   <u>it was taking</u> back about 120,000
   27
   units that were sold. The company said that consumers will receive the full purchase price. Another 30,000 toys will be returned by

   <u>department stores toy stores discount</u>
   28
   <u>outlets and mail order firms</u>.
   28

2. The CSB has found that children riding the toy can tip forward. Children fall to the ground. The danger of falling has been confirmed by reports of 20 incidents nationwide over the past

**26**

A (No change)

B was intend

C were intending

D was intended

**27**

A (No change)

B kid fun, of Brooklyn, NY, said that it has been taken

C Kid Fun, of Brooklyn, NY, said that it was taking

D kid fun, of Brooklyn, NY, said that they were taking

**28**

A (No change)

B department stores, toy stores discount outlets, and mail order firms.

C department stores toy stores discount outlets, and mail order firms.

D department stores, toy stores, discount outlets, and mail order firms.

**29** **Reread the following sentences:**
*The CSB has found that children riding the toy can tip forward. Children fall to the ground.*

**The most effective combination of these sentences would include which group of words?**

A forward, and, as a result, they can fall

B forward, and, however, they can fall

four months. There <u>will be reports</u>
<sub>30</sub>
of four children receiving cuts on the chin severe enough to need stitches.

3. Parents who need more information are encouraged to call the CSB at its recall hotline toll free number: 888-123-4567, or go to the website at www.csb.net. "Scurry n Go" is made of yellow molded plastic with black wheels. The riding toy is 20 inches long, 10 inches wide and 12 inches in height. The toy's model number is 0318QS. The model number can be found on the underside of the toy. It is printed in black on a white Universal Product Code (UPC) sticker. <u>An aid for the CSB said the</u>
<sub>32</sub>
<u>recall is proceeding smoothly</u>.
<sub>32</sub>

C forward, and one falls

D forward, unless they fall

**30**

A (No change)

B have been reports

C will have been reports

D is reports

**31 Reread the following sentences:**
*The toy's model number is 0318QS. The model number can be found on the underside of the toy.*

**The most effective combination of these sentences would include which group of words?**

A and it can

B and them can

C and one there can

D and then their can

**32**

A (No change)

B An aide for the CSB said the recall is proceeding smoothly

C An aid below the CSB said the recall is proceeding smoothly

D An aid for the CSB said the recall are proceeding smoothly

**33 Which revision would improve the effectiveness of paragraph 3?**

A move the first sentence to the end of the paragraph

B remove the fourth sentence

C remove the last sentence

D move the second sentence to the end of the paragraph

---

## Date: 05/17/2012

To: All Employees
From: Paul Carson, CEO
Subject: ID Badges

1. Security has notified me that there has been a large increase in the number of ID badges that have been reported lost or missing. There have also been reports of employees loaning their badges to other employees when they go out to lunch. While some may think these acts is minor, I cannot say how important it is to make sure that our customers' data are secure at all times.

2. Beginning next Monday, the company will put in place a new security policy. This policy will ensure the confidentiality of our clients and is called Security Enforcement 5. The policy is also known as "Be On Guard." Any employee who reports a lost or misplaced ID badge will be issued a warning. A second violation has resulted in the employee having the cost of the ID badge taken out of his or her paycheck. A third violation will mean that the person will lose her or his rite to a pay raise for one year.

3. This new policy will be strictly followed. Any questions or comments can be directed to Mrs. May Head of Human Resources. I thank all of you for your hard work and understanding but I know you understand the importance of this safeguard.

4. Swiping your ID when you enter, and leave the building allows security to know who is and who isn't in the building at all times. Without that information, it is impossible to know whether strangers are accessing our database with illegal goals. Our first and foremost mission is to protect the information in our files from those who would use them for deceitful purposes.

---

**GO ON TO THE NEXT PAGE** ➡

**Date: 05/17/2012**

To: All Employees
From: Paul Carson, CEO
Subject: ID Badges

1. Security has notified me that there has been a large increase in the number of ID badges that have been reported lost or missing. There have also been reports of employees loaning their badges to other employees when they go out to lunch. While some may think these acts is minor, I cannot say
   34
   how important it is to make sure that our customers' data are secure at all times.

2. Beginning next Monday, the company will put in place a new security policy. This policy will ensure the confidentiality of our clients and is called Security Enforcement 5. The policy is also known as "Be On Guard." Any employee who reports a lost or misplaced ID badge will be issued a warning. A second violation

**34**

A (No change)

B are

C has been

D were

**35 Reread the following sentence:**
*Beginning next Monday, the company will put in place a new security policy.*

**The most effective revision of this sentence would begin with which words?**

A As a consequence, beginning

B For instance, beginning

C Even though, next

D However, next

**36 Reread the following sentences:**
*This policy will ensure the confidentiality of our clients and is called Security Enforcement 5. The policy is also known as "Be on Guard."*

**The most effective combination of these sentences would include which group of words?**

A Security Enforcement 5, "Be on Guard"

B that is also called

C a confidential policy

D ("Be on Guard")

has <u>resulted</u> in the employee having
<sub>37</sub>
the cost of the ID badge taken out

of his or her paycheck. A third

<u>violation will mean that the person</u>
<sub>38</sub>
<u>will lose her or his rite</u> to a pay raise
<sub>38</sub>
for one year.

3. This new policy will be strictly

followed. Any questions or

comments can be directed to

<u>Mrs. May Head of Human</u>
<sub>39</sub>
<u>Resources</u>. I thank all of you for
<sub>39</sub>
your hard work and understanding

but I know you understand the

importance of this safeguard.

4 Swiping your ID when you

<u>enter, and leave</u> the building allows
<sub>40</sub>
security to know who is and who

isn't in the building at all times.

Without that information, it is

impossible to know whether

strangers are accessing our database

with illegal goals. Our first and

**37**

A (No change)

B resulted

C results

D will result

**38**

A (No change)

B violation will means that the person
will lose her or his rite

C violation will mean which the
person will lose her or his rite

D violation will mean that the person
will lose her or his right

**39**

A (No change)

B Mrs May, Head of Human
Resources

C Mrs. May, Head of Human
Resources

D Mrs. May head of human resources

**40**

A (No change)

B enter and leave

C enter and can leave

D enter, but leave

foremost <u>mission is to protect the</u><br>
41<br>
<u>information in our files from those</u><br>
41<br>
<u>who would use them</u> for deceitful<br>
41<br>
purposes.

**41**

A (No change)

B mission is to protect the information in your files from those who would use them

C mission is to protect the information in our files from those who would use it

D mission is protect the information in our files from those who would be using them

**42 Which revision would improve the effectiveness of the memo?**

A Join paragraphs 1 and 2.

B Join paragraphs 2 and 3.

C Move paragraph 4 after paragraph 1.

D Begin a new paragraph before the sentence in paragraph 2 that begins *Any employee who reports a lost or misplaced ID.*

**Questions 43–50 refer to the following passage.**

## Quaker Cola Co. Annual Report

1. Quaker Cola Company announced its annual report for 2011 on Friday. Its annual sales increased 11 percent over 2011. After taxes, its profits rose 14 percent, which is in large part the result of cost-cutting measures put in place by ceo Arthur Fletcher. The company also announced plans to create an employee profit sharing plan. Details will be on the company website within three months.

2. You can hear about packaging and new fruit drinks. New packaging for the cola products has been put in place. The new design conveys a feeling of youthfulness and making our product more attractive to young people. Quaker also introduced a new line of cranberry fruit juice drinks. That represented 3 percent of sales for the year. A new energy drink, with promising results, was test-marketed in California. This year the test marketing will be done, and in eight additional western states.

3. After several years of planning and research, Quaker launched your marketing plan in 2011 to establish a presence in the booming Southeast Asian market. Forecasts predict that by 2015 the Asian market will grow. To 15 percent of total revenue. The company had planned to open a regional office in Ho Chi Minh City, Vietnam, in early 2013.

# Quaker Cola Co. Annual Report

1. Quaker Cola Company announced its annual report for 2011 on Friday. Its annual sales increased 11 percent over 2011. After taxes, its profits <u>rose 14 percent, which is in large</u>[43] <u>part the result of cost-cutting</u>[43] <u>measures put in place by ceo</u>[43] Arthur Fletcher. The company also announced plans to create an employee profit sharing plan. Details will be on the company website within three months.

2. You can hear about packaging and new fruit drinks. New packaging for the cola products has been put in place. The new design conveys a feeling of youthfulness and <u>making our product</u>[45] more attractive to young people. Quaker also introduced a new line of cranberry fruit juice drinks. That represented 3 percent of sales for the year. A new energy <u>drink, with promising</u>[46] <u>results, was test-marketed in</u>[46] <u>California</u>. This year the test[46]

**43**

A (No change)

B rise 14 percent, which is in large part the result of cost-cutting measures put in place by ceo

C rose 14 percent, which is in larger part the result of cost-cutting measures put in place by ceo

D rose 14 percent, which is in large part the result of cost-cutting measures put in place by CEO

**44 Reread the following sentence:**
*You can hear about packaging and new fruit drinks.*

**Which revision would improve the effectiveness of this sentence?**

A Quaker has done a great deal to expand its marketing.

B Packaging and new fruit drinks were added.

C Packaging was something that was changed.

D The new kind of drinks proved very successful.

**45**

A (No change)

B are making our product

C makes our product

D were making our product

**46**

A (No change)

B drink, with promised results, was test-marketed in California

marketing will be <u>done, and analyzed</u>
<sub>47</sub>
and in eight additional western

states.

3. After several years of planning and

<u>research, Quaker launched your</u>
<sub>48</sub>
<u>marketing plan in 2011 to establish</u>
<sub>48</sub>
<u>a presence in the booming</u>
<sub>48</sub>
Southeast Asian market. Forecasts

predict that by 2015 the Asian

market <u>will grow. To 15 percent</u> of
<sub>49</sub>
total revenue. The company

<u>had planned</u> to open a regional
<sub>50</sub>
office in Ho Chi Minh City,

Vietnam, in early 2013.

---

**C** drink was test-marketed in
California, with promising results

**D** drink with promising results, was
test-marketed in California

**47**

**A** (No change)

**B** done and analyzed

**C** done, yet analyzed

**D** done, and also analyzed

**48**

**A** (No change)

**B** research, Quaker launching your
marketing plan in 2011 to establish
a presence in the booming

**C** research, Quaker launched its
marketing plan in 2011 to establish
a presence in the booming

**D** research, Quaker launched your
marketing plan in 2011 to establish
a booming presence in the

**49**

**A** (No change)

**B** will grow, to 15 percent

**C** will grow to 15 percent

**D** will grow: to 15 percent

**50**

**A** (No change)

**B** was planning

**C** will plan

**D** plans

# ANSWERS: LANGUAGE ARTS—WRITING, PART 1

1. **(D)** Option (D) is correct because it changes the contraction that means *it is* to the possession form of *it, its*. Option (B) is not correct because the verb form *having chosen* is incorrect grammatically and does not make sense in the sentence. Option (C) inserts an unnecessary comma and does not fix the original error.

2. **(B)** Option (B) is correct because it exchanges the relative pronoun *which* for *who* since it refers to *customer service*, which is not a human but a thing. Option (C) makes an incomplete sentence from the clause. Option (D) uses an incorrect verb form.

3. **(B)** Option (B) is correct because it changes the incorrect verb form to a correct verb form. Option (C) is incorrect because it has an incorrect verb form and because it inserts a comma where none is needed. Option (D) is incorrect because it has an incorrect verb form.

4. **(C)** Option (C) is correct because this verb form agrees with the subject. Options (B) and (D) have incorrect verb forms.

5. **(D)** Option (D) is correct because the verb *find* agrees with the verb *choose*; they are parallel. Option (B) replaces a correct verb form with an incorrect one. Option (C) inserts a comma where none is needed.

6. **(D)** Option (D) is correct because it combines the ideas of the two sentences clearly, and it correctly uses a comma to join them. Option (A) is incorrect because the conjunction *however* does not make sense. Option (B) is incorrect because *yet* doesn't make sense. Option (C) has the correct conjunction but incorrectly omits the comma.

7. **(B)** Option (B) is correct because it capitalizes the proper name *Central Time* and has correct comma usage. Option (C) removes necessary commas. Although option (D) does capitalize *Central Time* correctly, it inserts an unnecessary comma after *days*.

8. **(A)** Option (A) is correct because it uses a semicolon to join two complete ideas. Option (B) is incorrect because a comma is not used to join two complete ideas. Option (D) uses a verb in the future tense rather than the present tense. While option (C) uses a semicolon correctly, it incorrectly inserts a comma that is not needed.

9. **(C)** Option (C) correctly rearranges the paragraph so that it has a cohesive train of thought. Option (A) moves the topic sentence to the end, which is incorrect. Option (B) would leave out a key idea of the paragraph. Option (D) would break up the coherence of the paragraph.

10. **(D)** Option (D) is correct because it adds an appropriate and necessary subordinating conjunction to join the two sentences. Option (B) creates a run-on sentence. Option (C) incorrectly uses the conjunction *however*, which does not make sense in the sentence.

GO ON TO THE NEXT PAGE ➡

11. **(B)** Option (B) is correct because the verb *give* is necessary to complete the thought. The present tense is used to agree with *nurse*. Option (C) is wrong because the writer is talking about more than one whale, and *birth* is not a verb. Option (D) is incorrect because *birthed* is not standard usage; in any case, the tense does not agree with the second verb.

12. **(C)** Option (C) is correct because the present tense, *grow*, should follow the present tense of the preceding verb, *are*. Option (B) removes a necessary comma. Option (D) changes the verb to an incorrect form.

13. **(C)** Option (C) is correct because the adverbial phrase modifies the verb phrase *return to the North*. Option (B) is an incorrect verb form. Option (D) is incorrect because when a direction is used as a locality and not a direction, it is capitalized.

14. **(D)** Option (D) is correct because the conjunction *and* makes the comma splice a compound sentence. Option (B) is incorrect since *each* indicates individuality. Option (C) is wrong because *pods* refers to *groups* and should be plural.

15. **(D)** Option (D) is correct because the present tense agrees with the present participle, *migrating*. Option (B) incorrectly uses the singular verb with the plural noun *whales*. Option (C) puts the idea in the past.

16. **(B)** Option (B) is correct because it best introduces the information given in the rest of the paragraph. Option (A) belongs with paragraph (B). Options (C) and (D) don't have anything to do with the information in paragraph (D).

17. **(B)** Option (B) is correct because the verb form is correct. Option (C) incorrectly uses a possessive pronoun rather than the contraction for *you are*. Option (D) uses an incorrect verb form.

18. **(C)** Option (C) is correct because it combines sentences 3 and 4 in a logical compound sentence. Options (A) and (D) do not make sense. Option (B) incorrectly uses a semicolon to join a dependent and independent clause.

19. **(D)** Option (D) is correct as it creates a complete sentence with a subject. Option (B) is incorrect because the first word in a quote is always capitalized. Option (C) incorrectly changes the contraction *it's* to the possessive *its*.

20. **(B)** Option (B) is correct because multiple adjectives are separated by commas. Option (C) makes no sense because it uses the present participle *wearing*. Option (D) incorrectly changes an adjective verb form to a present tense verb.

21. **(C)** Option (C) is correct because the plural verb *are* agrees with the plural subject *shoes*. Option (B) does not make sense. There is no grammatical reason to install a comma after *sure* as in option (D).

22. **(A)** Option (A) is correct because sentence 10 does not relate to the subject of the paragraph. Option (B) would put a sentence that is not a topic sentence at the start of the paragraph. Option (C) is incorrect because this sentence belongs with the following sentence. Option (D) is wrong because logically the sentence does not belong there.

23. **(B)** Option (B) is correct; *too*, meaning *excessively*, is needed in the context of the sentence. Option (C) incorrectly removes a necessary comma. Option (D) creates a plural noun where a singular is preferred.

24. **(D)** Option (D) is correct because *should choose* agrees with the previous verb *should select* and is parallel. Options (B), and (C) are incorrect because, in each case, the second verb is not parallel with the first verb.

25. **(B)** Option (B) is correct because the singular verb *go* agrees with the singular subject *you*. Options (C) and (D) have a different tense than the first verb *check*.

26. **(D)** Option (D) is correct because it uses a correct verb form. Option (B) has a grammatically incorrect verb. Option (C) is plural when it should be singular and is also an incorrect verb form.

27. **(C)** Option (C) is correct because *Kid Fun* is the name of a specific company and should be capitalized. Option (B) is incorrect because the verb tense does not make sense. Option (D) is wrong because *manufacturer* is singular, so a pronoun referring to it should be singular as well.

28. **(D)** Option (D) is correct because it places commas between all the words in a series. Option (B) does not have a comma after *toy stores*. Option (C) is wrong because there should be commas after *department stores* and *toy stores*.

29. **(A)** Option (A) is correct because it combines the two sentences using a conjunction that makes sense in the context of the sentence and has the correct pronoun. Option (B) uses an incorrect conjunction; it does not make sense. Option (C) uses an incorrect pronoun for the antecedent *children*. Option (D) uses an incorrect conjunction.

30. **(B)** Option (B) is correct because the action took place in the past not in the future. Option (C) is incorrect because the future tense *will have been* does not follow the tense of the previous sentence. Option (D) is wrong because the verb is singular and the subject *reports* is plural.

31. **(A)** Option (A) is correct because *The toy's model number is 0318QS, and it can be found on the underside of the toy* is the most straightforward. Options (B), (C), and (D) use an incorrect pronoun as well as unnecessary words.

32. **(B)** Option (B) is correct because it replaces the homonym *aid* (to help) with *aide* (assistant). Option (C) would not make sense. Option (D) is not correct because it does not fix the original misspelling and it uses an incorrect verb.

33. **(A)** Option (A) is correct because it makes an effective closing statement. Options (B) and (C) are incorrect because they present supporting details. Option (D) creates an illogical sequence of ideas.

34. **(B)** Option (B) is correct because *are* agrees with the plural subject, *acts*. Option (C) is a singular verb. Option (D) is plural but the wrong tense.

35. **(A)** Option (A) is correct because it shows a causality relationship between what has happened and what will happen. Option (B) is incorrect because it suggests an example where none exists. Options (C) and (D) suggest relationships that do not exist in the sentence.

36. **(A)** Option (A) is correct because it uses an appositive to combine the ideas in the two sentences. Option (B) repeats words unnecessarily. Option (C) changes the idea of the original sentences. Option (D) is incorrect because the parentheses are unnecessary.

37. **(D)** Option (D) is correct because the future is implied in the context of the sentence. Options (B) and (C) have verb tenses that are inconsistent with the idea of the sentence.

GO ON TO THE NEXT PAGE ➡

38. **(D)** Option (D) is correct because it correctly changes *rite* to *right*. Option (B) is wrong because the future tense does not require an *s* added to the verb. Option (C) makes no sense.

39. **(C)** Option (C) is correct because it uses a comma to set off an appositive phrase. Option (B) has the comma, but it omits the period after *Mrs.* Option (D) has no comma, and the title is lowercase.

40. **(B)** Option (B) is correct because the subject of the sentence, *you*, has two verbs, *enter* and *leave*. Options (C) and (D) do not make sense.

41. **(C)** Option (C) is correct because the pronoun *it* agrees with its antecedent *information*. Option (B) is incorrect because the sentence would make no sense. Option (D) would result in an incorrect verb form.

42. **(C)** Option (C) is correct because paragraph (D) continues the discussion of missing ID badges. Options (A) and (B) are incorrect because the paragraphs discuss different subjects. Option (D) is wrong because sentence 7 does not begin a new subject.

43. **(D)** Option (D) is correct because it capitalizes the title CEO. Option (B) changes the proper verb form to an incorrect one. Option (C) incorrectly changes a correct adjective to a comparative form.

44. **(A)** Option (A) is the best choice because it is a topic sentence that covers the entire paragraph. While option (B) talks about what was done, it is not broad enough to be a topic sentence. Option (C) just repeats the information in the following sentence. Option (D) talks about only one of the changes, so it is not a good topic sentence.

45. **(C)** Option (C) is correct since it creates a parallel structure between the verbs *conveys* and *makes*. Option (B) is an incorrect verb form and not parallel. Option (D) is incorrect since it is not a correct verb form (it is in the past), and it is not parallel with *conveys*.

46. **(C)** Option (C) is correct because it moves the phrase *with promising results* after the phrase that it modifies, *was test-marketed in California*. Option (B) substitutes an incorrect form of the adjective *promising*. Option (D) removes a necessary comma.

47. **(B)** Option (B) is correct because the subject of the sentence, *test marketing*, has two verbs—*will be done* and *analyzed*—and no comma is needed between them. Option (C) keeps the unnecessary comma and adds a conjunction, *yet*, which does not make sense in the sentence. Option (D) is wrong because *also* repeats the same idea as *and* and is not needed.

48. **(C)** Option (C) is correct because it replaces an incorrect possessive pronoun with the correct form. Option (B) replaces the correct verb with an incorrect verb form. Option (D) changes the meaning of the sentence.

49. **(C)** Option (C) is correct because it correctly joins the fragment *to 15 percent of total revenue* to the main clause of the sentence. Option (B) is wrong because no comma is needed between the prepositional phrase and the main clause of the sentence. Option (D) is similarly incorrect since a colon is not required between the phrase and the main clause of the sentence.

50. **(D)** Option (D) is correct because present tense is the correct verb form. Option (B) is in the past tense and makes no sense in the sentence. The plan is already in place, so option (C) is incorrect.

# *HiSET*® Exam Practice Test 2
## Answer Sheet
## Language Arts—Writing, Part 2

# LANGUAGE ARTS—WRITING, PART 2

## Essay Directions and Topic

In the box below is your assigned topic. You must write on the assigned topic ONLY.

You will have 45 minutes to write on your assigned essay topic. You may return to the multiple-choice section after you complete your essay if you have time remaining in this test period.

The essay will be evaluated based on the following features:

- Well-focused main points
- Clear organization
- Specific development of your ideas
- Control of sentence structure, punctuation, grammar, word choice, and spelling

REMEMBER, YOU MUST COMPLETE BOTH THE MULTIPLE-CHOICE QUESTIONS (PART 1) AND THE ESSAY (PART 2) TO RECEIVE A SCORE ON THE LANGUAGE ARTS—WRITING TEST. To avoid having to repeat both parts of the test, be sure to do the following:

- Do not leave the pages blank.
- Write legibly so that the evaluators will be able to read your writing.
- Write on the assigned topic. If you write on a topic other than the one assigned, you will not receive a score for the Language Arts—Writing Test.
- Write your essay on the lined pages of the separate answer sheet booklet. Only the writing on these pages will be scored.

---

### TOPIC A

Many schools are adopting a uniform code.

Write an essay that tells whether you think required uniforms are a good idea or a bad idea. Give your opinion and support your view from your own personal observations and experiences.

---

Part 2 is a test to determine how well you can use written language to explain your ideas. In preparing your essay, you should take the following steps:

- Read the DIRECTIONS and the TOPIC carefully.
- Plan your essay before you write. Use the scratch paper provided to make any notes. These notes will be collected but not scored.
- Before you turn in your essay, reread what you have written and make any changes that will improve your essay.
- Your essay should be long enough to develop the topic adequately.

# ANSWERS: LANGUAGE ARTS—WRITING, PART 2

All essays will be scored according to the HiSET Exam essay rubric.

| Score Code | Description |
| --- | --- |

**6**    **Proficient**

Essays at this score point show proficient skill in responding to the task. The response demonstrates proficient skill in developing ideas. It maintains focus on a clear central idea throughout the response. The response provides several ideas with effective and thorough explanation, offering relevant and fully elaborated reasons, examples, and/or details to support ideas. The response demonstrates strong critical thinking and insight by discussing complications of the issue and/or successfully addressing counterarguments. The response demonstrates proficient skill in organization. It has an effective, well-developed introduction and conclusion, with an engaging introduction that clearly sets up the rest of the response. Clear and appropriate paragraphing is used, creating a coherent whole. Logical sequencing of ideas is demonstrated throughout the response. Effective transitions are used throughout the response to support coherence. The response demonstrates proficient skill in language. Word choice is precise, varied, and engaging. The response effectively varies sentence length and complexity. Voice is appropriate for audience and purpose, and enhances the effectiveness of the response. No errors or only a few superficial errors appear, and the response demonstrates sophisticated use of grammar, usage, and mechanics.

**5**    **Competent**

Essays at this score point show competent skill in responding to the task. The response demonstrates competent skill in developing ideas. It maintains focus on a clear central idea throughout the response. The response provides several ideas with complete explanation, offering specific, relevant, and somewhat elaborated reasons, examples, and/or details to support ideas. The response demonstrates some critical thinking by introducing and addressing complications of the issue and/or addressing counterarguments. The response demonstrates competent skill in organization. The introduction and conclusion are clear and generally well-developed, and the introduction clearly sets up the rest of the response. Clear and appropriate paragraphing is used, with logical sequencing of ideas through most of the response. Varied transitions are used between and within paragraphs to support coherence. The response demonstrates competent skill in language. Word choice is usually precise and varied. The response uses well-controlled sentences that are varied in length and complexity. Voice is appropriate for audience and purpose. There are few grammar, usage, or mechanics errors and most are superficial.

| Score Code | Description |
| --- | --- |

**4**   **Adequate**

Essays at this score point show adequate skill in responding to the task. The response demonstrates adequate skill in developing ideas. It maintains focus on a central idea, though there may be a few minor lapses. The response provides several ideas with adequate explanation, offering some specific and relevant examples and/or details to support ideas. The response demonstrates adequate skill in organization, with a clear introduction and conclusion that are somewhat developed. The response uses appropriate paragraphing and demonstrates some evidence of logical sequencing of ideas. Transitions are consistently used between and/or within paragraphs, though the transitions may be simple. Adequate skill in language use is demonstrated. Mostly specific and somewhat varied word choice is used. The response demonstrates control of sentences with some variety in length and structure. Voice is usually appropriate for audience and purpose. Some errors in sentence construction, pronoun use, verb forms, and/or spelling are present but do not interfere with understanding.

**3**   **Limited**

Essays at this score point show limited skill in responding to the task. The response demonstrates limited skill in developing ideas. It maintains focus on a central idea through some of the response. The response provides several ideas with limited or uneven explanation, offering few or only general examples and/or details to support ideas. Organization demonstrates some developing skill. The response has an introduction and conclusion, though one or both of these may be over- or under-developed. Ideas are grouped together in paragraphs, though the relationship among ideas may at times be unclear. The response uses a few transitions between and/or within paragraphs to support coherence. Some developing skill in language is demonstrated. Word choice is general and the response demonstrates a little variety in sentence structure, although a few long, uncontrolled sentences may be used. Errors in sentence construction, pronoun use, verb forms, and/or spelling are present and may occasionally interfere with understanding.

**2**   **Minimal**

Essays at this score point show minimal skill in responding to the task. The response demonstrates minimal development. It provides a few ideas but explanation is minimal or superficial and parts of the explanation may be repetitions or lack relevance. Organization is weak. There is minimal evidence of an introduction and/or conclusion. Some related ideas are grouped together, though paragraphing may not be used. If transitions appear, their use is not controlled. Beginning skill in language is demonstrated. Word choice is awkward and/or repetitive. The response has repetitive sentence structure and/or long, uncontrolled sentences. Numerous errors in sentence construction, pronoun use, verb forms, and/or spelling interrupt the flow of communication and some errors may interfere with understanding.

*(Continued)*

| Score Code | Description |
| --- | --- |
| 1 | **Deficient** |

Essays at this score point show little or no skill in responding to the task. The response has little or no development. It may provide a few ideas but lacks explanation of ideas, only repeats ideas, or the ideas lack relevance. Organization is minimal. The response lacks an introduction and conclusion and does not demonstrate any understanding of paragraphing. If transitions appear, their use is not controlled. Language control is minimal. Word choice and sentence structure are simple. Errors in sentence construction, pronoun use, verb forms, and/or spelling are frequent and may interfere with understanding.

**Example of Excellent Topic Sentences**

*I believe that requiring uniforms in school is a good idea because it makes every student look the same rather than having clothing that announces who a student thinks he or she is.*

*I am totally against having students wear uniforms because it invades the private choices of students, and there are very few choices left in schools.*

**Examples of Paragraphs Using Varied Language and Details While Following the Rules of Edited American English (EAE)**

*For instance, I have seen students with very strange outfits that really made me nervous. I know that people who dress dramatically are trying to draw attention to themselves, but when they do so, I think it takes away from an atmosphere where people can be serious and learn.*

*For example, requiring uniforms means that everyone will look the same, which means no one will be able to be creative in his or her choice of clothing. I don't mean that clothes that are too revealing or weird should be allowed. There can be some kind of dress code, but uniforms are too restrictive.*

- Organization should follow a clear, logical order.
- The essay should also have a closing that sums up it up succinctly, such as:

*These are some of the reasons that I believe that uniforms should be required in schools so that the school can have a better atmosphere that helps students learn.*

*To sum up my feelings, I think that it goes too far to require students to dress in uniforms because it steals their right to express themselves.*

# *HiSET*® Exam Practice Test 2
## Answer Sheet
## Social Studies

|    | A | B | C | D |    |    | A | B | C | D |
|----|---|---|---|---|----|----|---|---|---|---|
| 1  | ☐ | ☐ | ☐ | ☐ |    | 26 | ☐ | ☐ | ☐ | ☐ |
| 2  | ☐ | ☐ | ☐ | ☐ |    | 27 | ☐ | ☐ | ☐ | ☐ |
| 3  | ☐ | ☐ | ☐ | ☐ |    | 28 | ☐ | ☐ | ☐ | ☐ |
| 4  | ☐ | ☐ | ☐ | ☐ |    | 29 | ☐ | ☐ | ☐ | ☐ |
| 5  | ☐ | ☐ | ☐ | ☐ |    | 30 | ☐ | ☐ | ☐ | ☐ |
| 6  | ☐ | ☐ | ☐ | ☐ |    | 31 | ☐ | ☐ | ☐ | ☐ |
| 7  | ☐ | ☐ | ☐ | ☐ |    | 32 | ☐ | ☐ | ☐ | ☐ |
| 8  | ☐ | ☐ | ☐ | ☐ |    | 33 | ☐ | ☐ | ☐ | ☐ |
| 9  | ☐ | ☐ | ☐ | ☐ |    | 34 | ☐ | ☐ | ☐ | ☐ |
| 10 | ☐ | ☐ | ☐ | ☐ |    | 35 | ☐ | ☐ | ☐ | ☐ |
| 11 | ☐ | ☐ | ☐ | ☐ |    | 36 | ☐ | ☐ | ☐ | ☐ |
| 12 | ☐ | ☐ | ☐ | ☐ |    | 37 | ☐ | ☐ | ☐ | ☐ |
| 13 | ☐ | ☐ | ☐ | ☐ |    | 38 | ☐ | ☐ | ☐ | ☐ |
| 14 | ☐ | ☐ | ☐ | ☐ |    | 39 | ☐ | ☐ | ☐ | ☐ |
| 15 | ☐ | ☐ | ☐ | ☐ |    | 40 | ☐ | ☐ | ☐ | ☐ |
| 16 | ☐ | ☐ | ☐ | ☐ |    | 41 | ☐ | ☐ | ☐ | ☐ |
| 17 | ☐ | ☐ | ☐ | ☐ |    | 42 | ☐ | ☐ | ☐ | ☐ |
| 18 | ☐ | ☐ | ☐ | ☐ |    | 43 | ☐ | ☐ | ☐ | ☐ |
| 19 | ☐ | ☐ | ☐ | ☐ |    | 44 | ☐ | ☐ | ☐ | ☐ |
| 20 | ☐ | ☐ | ☐ | ☐ |    | 45 | ☐ | ☐ | ☐ | ☐ |
| 21 | ☐ | ☐ | ☐ | ☐ |    | 46 | ☐ | ☐ | ☐ | ☐ |
| 22 | ☐ | ☐ | ☐ | ☐ |    | 47 | ☐ | ☐ | ☐ | ☐ |
| 23 | ☐ | ☐ | ☐ | ☐ |    | 48 | ☐ | ☐ | ☐ | ☐ |
| 24 | ☐ | ☐ | ☐ | ☐ |    | 49 | ☐ | ☐ | ☐ | ☐ |
| 25 | ☐ | ☐ | ☐ | ☐ |    | 50 | ☐ | ☐ | ☐ | ☐ |

# SOCIAL STUDIES

### 50 Questions

### 70 Minutes

### Directions

This is a test of your skills in analyzing social studies information. Read each question and decide which of the four alternatives best answers the question. Then mark your choice on your answer sheet. Sometimes several questions are based on the same material. You should carefully read this material, then answer the questions.

Work as quickly as you can without becoming careless. Don't spend too much time on any question that is difficult for you to answer. Instead, skip it and return to it later if you have time. Try to answer every question even if you have to guess.

Mark all your answers on the answer sheet. Give only one answer to each question and make every mark heavy and dark. If you decide to change one of your answers, be sure to erase the first mark completely. Be sure that the number of the question you are answering matches the number of the row of answer choices you are marking on your answer sheet.

**Questions 1–3 refer to the quotation below.**

We hold these truths to be self-evident: that all men and women are created equal; that they are endowed by their Creator with certain inalienable rights; that among these are life, liberty, and the pursuit of happiness; that to secure these rights governments are instituted, deriving their just powers from the consent of the governed. . . . The history of mankind is a history of repeated injuries and usurpations on the part of man toward woman, having in direct object the establishment of an absolute tyranny over her.

1. **The document from which this quotation is taken is modeled after which of the following founding documents of the United States?**
   A   The Mayflower Compact (1620)
   B   The Fundamental Orders of Connecticut (1639)
   C   The Declaration of Independence (1776)
   D   The Virginia Statute for Religious Freedom (1786)

2. **The authors of this quotation were early advocates of**
   A   religious freedom and toleration
   B   women's rights
   C   separation of church and state
   D   states' rights

GO ON TO THE NEXT PAGE ➡

3.  The concept that governments derive "their just powers from the consent of the governed" is known in American political thought as

    A   popular sovereignty

    B   checks and balances

    C   civil rights

    D   the Establishment Clause

**Questions 4 and 5 refer to the quotation below.**

. . . we may hear without surprise or scandal that the introduction, or at least the abuse of Christianity, had some influence on the decline and fall of the Roman empire . . . the active virtues of society were discouraged; and the last remains of military spirit were buried . . . a large portion of public and private wealth was consecrated to the . . . demands of charity and devotion.

—*The History of the Decline and Fall of the Roman Empire* (1776), ch. 39

4.  In this excerpt, historian Edward Gibbon discusses the influence of which of the following on the decline of the Roman Empire?

    A   the Protestant Reformation

    B   the overextension of the Roman military

    C   burdensome taxation policies

    D   the early Catholic church

5.  Gibbon's contention that "a large portion of public and private wealth was consecrated to the . . . demands of charity and devotion" most likely refers to

    A   the cost of public games, like chariot races, in the Roman Empire

    B   the large sums of money spent by early Christians to support the Church

    C   the rising cost of the imperial military establishment

    D   the growing cost of providing social services to Roman citizens

**Questions 6–8 refer to the chart below.**

| *Persons Obtaining Legal Permanent Resident Status in the United States* | | | | | |
|---|---|---|---|---|---|
| *Year* | | *Year* | | *Year* | |
| 1950 | 249,187 | 1987 | 601,516 | 2008 | 1,107,126 |
| 1967 | 361,972 | 1997 | 797,847 | 2009 | 1,130,818 |
| 1977 | 462,315 | 2007 | 1,052,415 | 2010 | 1,042,625 |

*Source: U.S. Department of Homeland Security, Persons Obtaining Legal Permanent Resident Status: Fiscal Years 1820 to 2010.*

6.  Which of the following might account for the steady rise in immigrants gaining legal permanent resident status over the period covered in the chart?

    A   the rapid growth of illegal immigration over the last 75 years

    B   the increase in available unskilled factory jobs in the United States since 1967

    C   the abolition of restrictive immigration quotas with the passage of the Immigration and Nationality Act of 1965

    D   new immigration policies implemented in the United States following the September 11 attacks

7.  **Which of the following two areas represent the most common places of origin of the immigrants to the United States referenced in the chart?**

    A   northern and western Europe

    B   the former Soviet Union and the Balkans

    C   Latin America and Asia

    D   Africa and the Middle East

8.  **Which of the following was a major pull factor for immigration to the United States in the period covered in the chart?**

    A   wars in Europe and Asia

    B   economic opportunity in the growing U.S. economy

    C   religious persecution

    D   oppressive totalitarian regimes in various parts of the world

**Questions 9–11 refer to the graph below.**

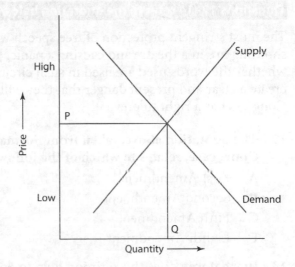

9.  **According to this graph, which of the following is a likely outcome if the quantity of a good available to the public, represented by the horizontal axis of the graph, is INCREASED?**

    A   Nothing will happen, as the graph demonstrates that quantity and price are not related.

    B   Supply of the good will decrease.

    C   Demand for the product will decrease.

    D   The price of the good will decrease.

**GO ON TO THE NEXT PAGE** ➡

10. **According to this graph, which of the following would likely happen to the price of a good if demand remains unchanged and supply DECREASES?**

    A  The price of the good will increase.

    B  Only inflation can raise prices in any appreciable way.

    C  Because demand remains constant, the effect on price cannot be determined.

    D  The graph does not provide enough information to determine the effect on price given these conditions.

11. **According to this graph, if supply of a good increased dramatically and demand for that good fell sharply, what would be the effect on the price of the good?**

    A  The price would increase sharply.

    B  The price would increase but only slightly.

    C  The price would decrease sharply.

    D  The price would decrease but only slightly.

---

**Questions 12–14 refer to the quotation below.**

The most stringent protection of free speech would not protect a man in falsely shouting fire in a theatre and causing a panic. [. . .] The question in every case is whether the words used are used in such circumstances and are of such a nature as to create a clear and present danger that they will bring about the substantive evils that Congress has a right to prevent.

12. **The quotation above, taken from the majority opinion in a 1919 Supreme Court case, relates to which of the following constitutional amendments?**

    A  First Amendment

    B  Second Amendment

    C  Fifth Amendment

    D  Eighth Amendment

13. **In what way does this opinion help to define a right guaranteed to the American people under the Constitution?**

    A  It affirms the right of Americans to protect themselves by carrying weapons in public.

    B  It further strengthens protections against cruel and unusual punishment.

    C  It articulates a "right to privacy" by reinforcing Americans' right to see whatever films they choose in a theater.

    D  It places limits on free speech by defining a category of speech that is not protected.

14. **The law that gave rise to this Supreme Court case, the Sedition Act of 1918, was passed due to American involvement in which war?**

    A  the American Revolution

    B  the War of 1812

    C  the Spanish-American War

    D  World War I

NO Freeman shall be taken or imprisoned, or be disseized of his Freehold, or Liberties, or free Customs, or be outlawed, or exiled, or any other wise destroyed; nor will We not pass upon him, nor condemn him, but by lawful judgment of his Peers, or by the Law of the land. We will sell to no man, we will not deny or defer to any man either Justice or Right.

15. **This excerpt, from the Magna Carta of 1297 and still a statute today, helped to establish one of the fundamental principles of**

    **A**   international trade and finance

    **B**   English Common Law

    **C**   the French Revolution

    **D**   Spanish control of its North American colonies

16. **The principle outlined in this provision of the Magna Carta is associated with which of the following freedoms or rights?**

    **A**   freedom of religion

    **B**   freedom of speech

    **C**   right to due process of law

    **D**   protection from cruel and unusual punishment

17. **According to Thomas Jefferson, violations of the right established in clause 29 of the Magna Carta of 1297 were responsible in part for causing what war between the United States and Great Britain?**

    **A**   Queen Anne's War

    **B**   King George's War

    **C**   the French and Indian War

    **D**   the American Revolution

GO ON TO THE NEXT PAGE ➡

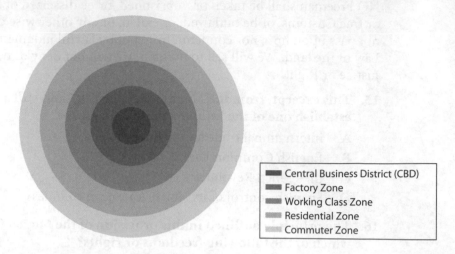

Central Business District (CBD)
Factory Zone
Working Class Zone
Residential Zone
Commuter Zone

18. The illustration above, called the Concentric Zone Model, is used by geographers as one possible explanation for

   A   the distribution of social groups within urban areas

   B   the placement of urban centers near natural resources

   C   the existence of zones of gentrification in inner-city areas

   D   the reliance of major American cities on extensive public transportation systems

19. In the Concentric Zone Model, poor urban dwellers and factory workers would be most likely to live in the zone labeled

   A   Central Business District

   B   Factory Zone

   C   Working Class Zone

   D   Residential Zone

20. Under this model, why would the wealthiest residents of cities most likely move to the outermost rings of the city?

   A   to be nearer to entertainment and cultural options, which would also be located on the outskirts of the city

   B   to escape the pollution and poverty of some of the inner rings of the city

   C   to be closer to their places of employment, which would be located near the outside of the Residential Zone

   D   because only the outer rings of the city have housing units, and none exist in the inner rings of the city

21. Some criticisms of the Concentric Zone Model might include

   A   its inability to account for physical features that might impede or change growth patterns in a city

   B   its inability to account for gentrification and urban renewal in inner cities

   C   that most cities that fit this model are located in the United States, where inner-city areas tend to be poorer, unlike many European or Asian cities

   D   all of the above are legitimate criticisms of the Concentric Zone Model

**Questions 22–25 refer to the graph below.**

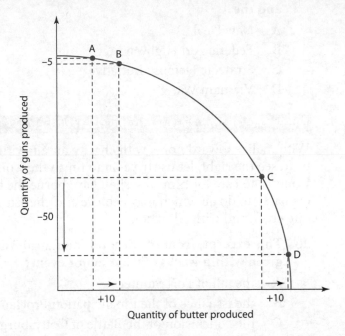

22. **The production possibilities curve illustrates which of the following concepts in economics?**
    A   that certain commodities can never be produced at the same time in a given economy
    B   the combination of two commodities that can be produced simultaneously in a given period of time and their effect on each other
    C   that goods are generally produced independently from each other in a given economy
    D   that the resources needed to produce guns are in chronically short supply

23. **In economics, the sacrifice in production of one good to increase production of another good is referred to as**
    A   means of production
    B   human capital
    C   opportunity cost
    D   purchasing power parity

24. **One of the assumptions made by this graph is that**
    A   the factors of production needed to produce the two goods are roughly equivalent
    B   the raw materials needed to produce the two goods must be the same
    C   the two goods are made side by side in the same factory
    D   both goods are equally significant to the overall national economy
    E   production of one good has no effect on the production of the other

**GO ON TO THE NEXT PAGE** ➡

25. The "guns or butter" argument was used by Lyndon Johnson during his second term to illustrate the difficulties of spending money on both social programs and the

   A   New Deal
   B   Federal Aid Highway Act
   C   Strategic Defense Initiative
   D   Vietnam War

**Questions 26 and 27 refer to the passage below**

With malice toward none; with charity for all; with firmness in the right, as God gives us to see the right, let us strive on to finish the work we are in; to bind up the nation's wounds; to care for him who shall have borne the battle, and for his widow, and his orphan—to do all which may achieve and cherish a just and lasting peace among ourselves, and with all nations.

26. This excerpt, from the Second Inaugural Address of Abraham Lincoln, was given within weeks of what major event?

   A   the fall of Fort Sumter
   B   the issuance of the Emancipation Proclamation
   C   the conclusion of the Battle of Gettysburg
   D   the surrender of Robert E. Lee's army to Ulysses Grant

27. Which of the following statements most accurately summarizes Lincoln's views toward the South as stated in the passage?

   A   The Union should surrender to the South so the war can come to a quick end.
   B   Although the Union has won the war, the government intends to treat the South with respect and to bring the nation back together.
   C   The Union, with God's help, has defeated the South, and the South should be harshly punished.
   D   The South should pay heavy war reparations to care for orphans and widows from the Union army.

**Questions 28–30 refer to the quotation below.**

A good person will resist an evil system with his whole soul. Disobedience of the laws of an evil state is therefore a duty.

28. The quotation above, from Mohandas K. Gandhi, relates to the efforts of

   A   Gandhi to end segregation in South Africa, where he was employed as an attorney
   B   African Americans to gain civil rights in 1950s and 1960s America
   C   India to gain its independence from Great Britain
   D   people across the world to resist the spread of Soviet Communism

29. Mohandas Gandhi was an advocate of which of the following philosophies?

   A   anarchism
   B   nonviolent resistance
   C   accommodationism
   D   apartheid

30. **The quotation above, written by Gandhi in the 1930s, was heavily influenced by the writings and philosophies of which of the following?**
    A   American transcendentalist author Henry David Thoreau
    B   American civil rights leader Martin Luther King, Jr.
    C   German leader Adolf Hitler
    D   Soviet leader Vladimir Lenin

**Questions 31–34 refer to the quotation below.**

The interpretation of the laws is the proper and peculiar province of the courts. A constitution is, in fact, and must be regarded by the judges, as a fundamental law. It therefore belongs to them to ascertain its meaning, as well as the meaning of any particular act proceeding from the legislative body. If there should happen to be an irreconcilable variance between the two, that which has the superior obligation and validity ought, of course, to be preferred; or, in other words, the Constitution ought to be preferred to the statute, the intention of the people to the intention of their agents. . . .

31. **The quotation above, from Federalist No. 78, lays the groundwork for which of the following powers that the Supreme Court would gain in the 1803 case of *Marbury v. Madison*?**
    A   the ability to suspend the writ of habeas corpus
    B   impeachment
    C   judicial review
    D   regulation of interstate commerce

32. **According to the passage, "interpretation of the laws is the peculiar province of the courts." This statement is an example of what doctrine essential to the American constitutional system?**
    A   direct democracy
    B   proportional representation
    C   separation of powers
    D   term limits

33. **The statement that "the Constitution ought to be preferred to the statute," advocates the position that the Constitution is**
    A   the supreme law of the land
    B   unable to be amended
    C   able to be changed or affected by state laws
    D   not subject to interpretation

34. **Federalist No. 78, along with the other Federalist Papers, were published between 1787 and 1788 in support of**
    A   protests against the Stamp Act
    B   the start of the American Revolution
    C   the ratification of the Treaty of Paris
    D   the ratification of the Constitution

GO ON TO THE NEXT PAGE ➡

| | Line | GDP Components–United States($ Billions) | 2009 I | 2009 II | 2009 III | 2009 IV | 2010 I |
|---|---|---|---|---|---|---|---|
| | 1 | Gross domestic product | 14,178.0 | 14,151.2 | 14,242.1 | 14,453.8 | 14,601.4 |
| | 2 | Personal consumption expenditures | 9,987.7 | 9,999.3 | 10,132.9 | 10,236.4 | 10,362.3 |
| | 3 | Goods | 3,197.7 | 3,193.8 | 3,292.3 | 3,337.1 | 3,406.6 |
| | | Durable goods | 1,025.2 | 1,011.5 | 1,051.3 | 1,052.0 | 1,072.8 |
| | 5 | Nondurable goods | 2,172.4 | 2,182.2 | 2,241.0 | 2,285.1 | 2,333.8 |
| | 6 | Services | 6,790.0 | 6,805.6 | 6,840.6 | 6,899.3 | 6,955.8 |
| I | 7 | Gross private domestic investment | 1,689.9 | 1,561.5 | 1,556.1 | 1,707.8 | 1,763.8 |
| | 8 | Fixed investment | 1,817.2 | 1,737.7 | 1,712.6 | 1,731.4 | 1,726.9 |
| | 9 | Nonresidential | 1,442.6 | 1,391.8 | 1,353.9 | 1,366.9 | 1,371.3 |
| | 10 | Structures | 533.1 | 494.8 | 457.9 | 434.1 | 417.5 |
| | 11 | Equipment and software | 909.5 | 897.0 | 895.9 | 932.8 | 953.9 |
| | 12 | Residential | 374.6 | 345.9 | 358.8 | 364.5 | 355.5 |
| | 13 | Change in private inventories | −127.4 | −176.2 | −156.5 | −23.6 | 36.9 |
| X-4 | 14 | Net exports of goods and services | −378.5 | −339.1 | −402.2 | −449.5 | −499.4 |
| | 15 | Exports | 1,509.3 | 1,493.7 | 1,573.8 | 1,680.1 | 1,729.3 |
| | 16 | Goods | 989.5 | 978.1 | 1,045.2 | 1,140.6 | 1,180.0 |
| | 17 | Services | 519.8 | 515.6 | 528.5 | 539.6 | 549.3 |
| | 18 | Imports | 1,887.9 | 1,832.8 | 1,976.0 | 2,129.7 | 2,228.7 |
| | 19 | Goods | 1,508.2 | 1,461.1 | 1,592.8 | 1,739.4 | 1,827.8 |
| | 20 | Services | 379.6 | 371.7 | 383.1 | 390.3 | 400.9 |
| G | 21 | Government consumption expenditures and gross investment | 2,879.0 | 2,929.4 | 2,955.4 | 2,959.2 | 2,974.7 |
| | 22 | Federal | 1,106.7 | 1,138.3 | 1,164.3 | 1,170.1 | 1,186.4 |
| | 23 | National defense | 750.7 | 776.2 | 795.8 | 793.5 | 805.6 |
| | 24 | Nondefense | 356.0 | 362.1 | 368.5 | 376.7 | 380.7 |
| | 25 | State and local | 1,772.3 | 1,791.2 | 1,791.1 | 1,789.0 | 1,788.3 |

*Source:* U.S. Bureau of Economic Analysis

35. Gross domestic product, an important measure of a country's economic well-being and standard of living, encompasses which of the following?

    A   the potential number of goods and services a country can produce within a given time period

    B   the final market value of all goods and services produced within a country in a given time period

    C   the amount of goods and services people of a country can buy under the right conditions

    D   only a comparison of net imports and exports

36. The chart above, listing the components of the gross domestic product of the United States, shows which of the following?

    A   that investment in nonresidential structures, like office buildings, has fallen from the first quarter of 2009 to the first quarter of 2010

    B   that the country is importing less each quarter than it exports

    C   that government investment in the American economy fell in one quarter

    D   that the GDP of the United States expanded in the second quarter of 2009

37. Federal government expenditures, listed as one of the components of GDP, were used by the federal government to combat the Great Depression. Advocacy of using federal government expenditures to alleviate economic downturns is most closely associated with which of the following economists?

    A   Adam Smith

    B   Milton Friedman

    C   John Maynard Keynes

    D   Karl Marx

38. The Human Development Index (HDI), which until 2010 used gross domestic product as one component of its measure of quality of life, is an important tool used by geographers and economists to track human development. Given this information, which of the following is likely true of the Human Development Index?

    A   African countries, due to their generally high GDP figures, would likely rank high in the HDI.

    B   The countries with the highest HDI scores in North America are all likely to be Latin American countries.

    C   Of the 45 countries in the Low Human Development category of the HDI, nearly all of them are from South America.

    D   Countries in the European Union are likely to score very high on the HDI scale.

GO ON TO THE NEXT PAGE ➡

Article I, Section 8, Clause 1. The Congress shall have Power to lay and collect Taxes, Duties, Imposts and Excises, to pay the Debts and provide for the common Defense and general Welfare of the United States; but all Duties, Imposts and Excises shall be uniform throughout the United States.

Amendment XVI. The Congress shall have power to lay and collect taxes on incomes, from whatever source derived, without apportionment among the several States, and without regard to any census or enumeration.

39. The quotations above, from the *U.S. Constitution* and the Sixteenth Amendment to the Constitution, define in part the federal government's power of taxation. In what way does the Sixteenth Amendment change the original language of Article I, Section 8?

   A   It allows the federal government to impose taxes that do not provide for the common defense or general welfare.

   B   It allows the federal government to levy taxes, like income taxes, that are not equally imposed on all states.

   C   It mandates that the federal government take a census and enumerate the people of a given state before imposing an income tax.

   D   It places the power of taxation with the president, while Article I, Section 8, gives that power to Congress.

40. Article I, Section 8, allows for the collection of "Taxes, Duties, Imposts and Excises" by the federal government. Given that an impost is a type of tax levied on imports, which of the following most likely defines an excise tax?

   A   a tax levied on property owned by an individual

   B   a tax on inheritances or gifts from deceased relatives

   C   a tax levied on goods manufactured within the United States

   D   a tax on profits made from investments

41. The Sixteenth Amendment, ratified in 1913, was one of four amendments, including those dealing with women's suffrage and Prohibition, that are associated with which political movement in America?

   A   Reconstruction

   B   the Great Society

   C   civil rights

   D   Progressivism

42. The above cartoon, which appeared in Benjamin Franklin's *Philadelphia Gazette* in 1754, most likely originally called for the American colonists to do which of the following?

    A become members of a mutual defense pact against the French in the upcoming French and Indian War

    B protest against the Intolerable Acts

    C join with the British to defend Georgia against an invasion from Spanish Florida

    D draft the Articles of Confederation

43. What is the most likely reason for this cartoon becoming such an important symbol during the American Revolution?

    A Patriots were drawn to the biblical connotations of the snake as a force in opposition to power.

    B Benjamin Franklin was the leading political figure in the American colonies and demanded his cartoon be used.

    C Colonists intended to exclude colonies like Georgia and Delaware, not pictured in the cartoon, from the new American nation.

    D Only united could the colonies hope to defeat the British Empire, which was much stronger, wealthier, and better equipped.

GO ON TO THE NEXT PAGE ➡

**Questions 44–46 refer to the cartoon below.**

44. **The above cartoon, from a French newspaper in 1898, depicts which of the following?**

    A economic competition between the European powers and Japan in China at the turn of the century

    B European rivalries during the height of imperialism

    C Chinese indignation at the interference of Europe and Japan in its affairs

    D all of the above are correct interpretations

45. **The British monarch depicted in this cartoon, seated on the far left, is a representation of**

    A Queen Elizabeth I

    B Queen Mary

    C Queen Victoria

    D Queen Anne

46. **The competition over China, Africa, and other areas of the world in the late nineteenth century was one of the major causes of**

    A the Great Depression

    B the rise of Soviet Communism

    C the Crimean War

    D World War I

**Questions 47–50 refer to the quotation below.**

That they will view this as seizing the rights of the states, and consolidating them in the hands of the general government, with a power assumed to bind the states, not merely in cases made federal, but in all cases whatsoever, by laws made, not with their consent, but by others against their consent; that this would be to surrender the form of government we have chosen, and live under one deriving its powers from its own will, and not from our authority; and that the co-states, recurring to their natural rights not made federal, will concur in declaring these void and of no force, and will each unite with this commonwealth in requesting their repeal at the next session of Congress.

—The Kentucky Resolution of 1798

47. **The quotation above, from a document written by Thomas Jefferson in 1798, advocates what position with regard to the *U.S. Constitution*?**

    **A**   a position of federal government sovereignty

    **B**   a position of states' rights over national authority

    **C**   a position of minority rule over the majority

    **D**   a position that the legislative power of the Congress should be paramount

48. **This resolution, along with a companion resolution in Virginia, was written in response to which of the following acts of the federal government under John Adams?**

    **A**   the "undeclared war" with France

    **B**   the "Citizen Genet" affair

    **C**   Jay's Treaty

    **D**   the Alien and Sedition Acts

49. **The Virginia and Kentucky Resolutions became the basis for what constitutional theory, that would allow states to strike down acts of the federal government they found unconstitutional and would be revived again by the South in the 1820s and 1830s?**

    **A**   judicial review

    **B**   nullification

    **C**   majority rule

    **D**   popular sovereignty

50. **In the *Declaration of Independence*, Thomas Jefferson articulated his vision of the "natural rights" mentioned in the passage. Which of the following was the phrase Jefferson used to define these natural rights?**

    **A**   self-evident truths

    **B**   life, liberty, and the pursuit of happiness

    **C**   all men are created equal

    **D**   deriving their just powers from the consent of the governed

# ANSWERS: SOCIAL STUDIES

1. **(C)** This excerpt—from the Declaration of Sentiments, drafted at the Women's Rights Convention in Seneca Falls, New York, in 1848—is very closely modeled on the Declaration of Independence. The Declaration of Sentiments replaces key sections of Jefferson's original document with references to women and women's rights.

2. **(B)** This analysis question requires that you notice key portions of the text, including "all men and women are created equal," and "on the part of man toward woman." These portions of the excerpt reveal the advocacy of women's rights intended by the authors of the document.

3. **(A)** This question tests your knowledge of significant principles of American constitutional government. The concept of popular sovereignty is one of the founding governmental principles of the United States and has been articulated on numerous occasions, including in the Declaration of Independence.

4. **(D)** This passage discusses the profound effect of the early Catholic Church on the Roman Empire and is one of the main contentions of Gibbon's seminal work.

5. **(B)** This question requires you to interpret Gibbon's argument and determine which of the options best applies to that argument. In this case, the economic impact of the early church and its effect on the empire is the crux of the argument.

6. **(C)** The passage of the Immigration and Nationality Act of 1965, which ended the immigration quota system established in the early 1920s, is the main reason for the upsurge.

7. **(C)** The majority of the immigrants coming into the United States since 1965 have been from Latin America and Asia. The majority came from countries such as Mexico, China, the Philippines, and India.

8. **(B)** Pull factors are those positive factors that attract immigrants to their new area. Of the options, only option (B) is a pull factor. All the others, including wars and persecution, are push factors, which are negative factors that cause immigrants to leave their old area to seek better living conditions.

9. **(D)** According to the graph, and the law of supply and demand, increasing the supply of a good will result in a decrease in price.

10. **(A)** The law of supply and demand states that if supply deceases while demand remains unchanged, prices in the market will increase. Only option (A) correctly accounts for these forces.

11. **(C)** As both an increase in supply and a decrease in demand will serve to lower prices, the combination of the two would lower the price of the good significantly.

12. **(A)** This question asks you to interpret a passage from the majority opinion in *Schenck v. United States* and to connect its limitations on freedom of speech with the rights granted under the First Amendment to the U.S. Constitution. The "clear and present danger" test was one of the standards for free speech protections in the United States until the 1960s.

13. **(D)** For this question, you need to determine the intent of the justices in the majority opinion in the case and to connect that opinion to a fundamental constitutional right guaranteed to Americans.

14. **(D)** This question asks about the chronology of major American military engagements and the relation of the stated opinion to those engagements. Information provided in the question gives you some reference point to help answer this question.

15. **(B)** The year 1297 predates the French Revolution and the Spanish colonial period, and it is far too late to relate to the Roman Empire. This eliminates options (A), (C), and (D).

16. **(C)** This question asks you to interpret the meaning of the passage and connect that meaning to the rights and freedoms fundamental to both Great Britain and the United States.

17. **(D)** In the Declaration of Independence, Jefferson claims that King George III of Great Britain has "obstructed the Administration of Justice," a reference to the violation of due process in the colonies. Jefferson's connection to the American Revolution and authorship of the Declaration of Independence leads you to option (D).

18. **(A)** Reading the key to the chart should provide enough information to eliminate option (B) which deals with physical features. The chart does not provide information about options (C) or (D), leaving option (A).

19. **(C)** This question requires you to interpret the information on the chart to determine where poor workers would live in the Concentric Zone Model.

20. **(B)** Since the Concentric Zone Model places industry and lower-class housing toward the middle of the city, it is most likely under this model that wealthier residents would move away from the city center to escape the pollution of the factories and the poverty of the lower-class neighborhoods.

21. **(D)** The Concentric Zone Model does not account for factors like physical geography, municipal politics, gentrification, or the inapplicablity of the model to many major cities, especially those outside the United States. Thus, option (D) is the correct answer.

22. **(B)** The graph illustrates the interconnection of two seemingly unrelated items being produced over a period of time and how the production of one good necessarily affects the other.

23. **(C)** In economics, the opportunity cost is the sacrifice in production of one good for increased production of another. The production possibilities curve helps to illustrate the opportunity cost for production of the goods depicted on the graph.

24. **(A)** The factors of production—the materials, labor, and resources needed to produce a given good—must be roughly equivalent for the principles illustrated by the graph to hold true.

**GO ON TO THE NEXT PAGE** ➡

25. **(D)** Lyndon Johnson used the "guns or butter" example to illustrate the difficulty of maintaining spending on the social programs of his Great Society and on the rapidly escalating Vietnam War.

26. **(D)** Lincoln's Second Inaugural Address, given in March 1865, gave a brief summary of his views on the end of the Civil War, which was rapidly drawing to a close. The speech took place about two weeks before Robert E. Lee surrendered his forces to Ulysses S. Grant at Appomattox Court House, Virginia, and less than a month before Lincoln's assassination.

27. **(B)** Lincoln famously and eloquently outlines his views on the coming period of Reconstruction, namely that the South should be welcomed back to the Union without the retribution and punishment demanded by many in the North.

28. **(C)** Mohandas Gandhi, the most significant leader of the Indian independence movement, wrote this quotation during his country's struggle to gain its independence from the British Empire. Gandhi wrote and spoke extensively on the subject of Indian independence during the early twentieth century.

29. **(B)** The quotation advocates nonviolent civil disobedience, which was the core philosophy of Gandhi's Indian independence movement.

30. **(A)** Gandhi was heavily influenced, as was Martin Luther King, Jr., by the writings of American Transcendentalist author Henry David Thoreau. Thoreau's treatise *On the Duty of Civil Disobedience* helped form much of Gandhi's own philosophy of satyagraha.

31. **(C)** This quotation, examining the powers of the federal courts in relation to the legislative branch, lays the groundwork for the majority opinion in *Marbury v. Madison* by articulating the responsibility of the courts to resolve conflicts between acts of the legislature and the Constitution. This power, known as judicial review, allows the Supreme Court to determine the constitutionality of federal laws.

32. **(C)** The fundamental principle of the separation of powers is the division of the various mechanisms and functions of government among the three branches to ensure that no one branch will become too powerful.

33. **(A)** This question requires a close reading of the text and a knowledge of American federalism to eliminate options (B), (C), and (D).

34. **(D)** Given the years 1787–1788, the first three options can be eliminated, as they all happened before that period. Given the quotation and the time period, option (D), the ratification of the Constitution, makes the most sense.

35. **(B)** In economics, one definition of gross domestic product is the final market value of all goods and services produced within a country in a given time period.

36. **(A)** The information in the chart shows that only choice (A) is true.

37. **(C)** John Maynard Keynes, whose work on employment and monetary policy was one of the theoretical underpinnings of the New Deal, advocated government spending to alleviate bad economic conditions within a given country.

38. **(D)** Africa, due to its high number of poor and underdeveloped nations, has the largest concentration of "low human development" countries, eliminating options (A) and (C). The United States and Canada (option B) are the highest-ranked HDI countries in North America, leaving only option (D).

39. **(B)** The Sixteenth Amendment allows the federal government to legally levy an income tax on American citizens.

40. **(C)** Excise taxes, which were a very important source of revenue for the U.S. government before the Sixteenth Amendment, are taxes on goods manufactured within the country in which they are levied.

41. **(D)** The Sixteenth, Seventeenth (direct election of U.S. Senators), Eighteenth (Prohibition), and Nineteenth (women's suffrage) Amendments are known collectively as the Progressive Amendments due to their close ties to that political movement of the early twentieth century.

42. **(A)** The "Join, or Die" cartoon, published at the beginning of what would become the French and Indian War, called for the American colonists to join a mutual defense pact against the French and their Native American allies.

43. **(D)** The colonies used the "Join, or Die" cartoon in various forms, including one labeled "Unite, or Die" as a symbol to encourage colonial unity during the Revolution against the much more powerful British.

44. **(D)** This cartoon represents the European powers (Britain, France, Germany, and Russia) and Japan competing for economic gains and territory in China near the end of the Chinese imperial period. China, whose imperial government was increasingly weak near the end of the nineteenth century, was powerless to stop the growing "spheres of influence" of these powers.

45. **(C)** This is a depiction of Queen Victoria, who reigned over the height of the British Empire at the end of the nineteenth century.

46. **(D)** The competition among the European powers over territory in several parts of the world, including China, is often cited by historians as one of the major causes of World War I, in which the competing European alliances of the day drew most of the world into a protracted and bloody conflict between 1914 and 1918.

47. **(B)** The Kentucky Resolution was one of the strongest statements of states' rights in the early republic. It was the basis for many of the states' rights arguments used by the South in the antebellum period.

48. **(D)** The Virginia and Kentucky Resolutions were written as a direct response to the Alien and Sedition Acts, which Jefferson's Democratic Republicans felt were unconstitutional. As there was no mechanism in 1798 for laws to be declared unconstitutional, Jefferson advanced this theory to dispose of the laws.

49. **(B)** The theory of nullification was the name given to the proposed ability of the states to declare laws unconstitutional. This theory was revived by South Carolina during the so-called Nullification Crisis in the late 1820s and 1830s.

50. **(B)** Jefferson used the phrase *life, liberty and the pursuit of happiness* to articulate his vision of the natural rights to which all men were entitled.

# *HiSET*® Exam Practice Test 2
## Answer Sheet
## Science

|  | A | B | C | D |  | A | B | C | D |
|---|---|---|---|---|---|---|---|---|---|
| 1 | ☐ | ☐ | ☐ | ☐ | 26 | ☐ | ☐ | ☐ | ☐ |
| 2 | ☐ | ☐ | ☐ | ☐ | 27 | ☐ | ☐ | ☐ | ☐ |
| 3 | ☐ | ☐ | ☐ | ☐ | 28 | ☐ | ☐ | ☐ | ☐ |
| 4 | ☐ | ☐ | ☐ | ☐ | 29 | ☐ | ☐ | ☐ | ☐ |
| 5 | ☐ | ☐ | ☐ | ☐ | 30 | ☐ | ☐ | ☐ | ☐ |
| 6 | ☐ | ☐ | ☐ | ☐ | 31 | ☐ | ☐ | ☐ | ☐ |
| 7 | ☐ | ☐ | ☐ | ☐ | 32 | ☐ | ☐ | ☐ | ☐ |
| 8 | ☐ | ☐ | ☐ | ☐ | 33 | ☐ | ☐ | ☐ | ☐ |
| 9 | ☐ | ☐ | ☐ | ☐ | 34 | ☐ | ☐ | ☐ | ☐ |
| 10 | ☐ | ☐ | ☐ | ☐ | 35 | ☐ | ☐ | ☐ | ☐ |
| 11 | ☐ | ☐ | ☐ | ☐ | 36 | ☐ | ☐ | ☐ | ☐ |
| 12 | ☐ | ☐ | ☐ | ☐ | 37 | ☐ | ☐ | ☐ | ☐ |
| 13 | ☐ | ☐ | ☐ | ☐ | 38 | ☐ | ☐ | ☐ | ☐ |
| 14 | ☐ | ☐ | ☐ | ☐ | 39 | ☐ | ☐ | ☐ | ☐ |
| 15 | ☐ | ☐ | ☐ | ☐ | 40 | ☐ | ☐ | ☐ | ☐ |
| 16 | ☐ | ☐ | ☐ | ☐ | 41 | ☐ | ☐ | ☐ | ☐ |
| 17 | ☐ | ☐ | ☐ | ☐ | 42 | ☐ | ☐ | ☐ | ☐ |
| 18 | ☐ | ☐ | ☐ | ☐ | 43 | ☐ | ☐ | ☐ | ☐ |
| 19 | ☐ | ☐ | ☐ | ☐ | 44 | ☐ | ☐ | ☐ | ☐ |
| 20 | ☐ | ☐ | ☐ | ☐ | 45 | ☐ | ☐ | ☐ | ☐ |
| 21 | ☐ | ☐ | ☐ | ☐ | 46 | ☐ | ☐ | ☐ | ☐ |
| 22 | ☐ | ☐ | ☐ | ☐ | 47 | ☐ | ☐ | ☐ | ☐ |
| 23 | ☐ | ☐ | ☐ | ☐ | 48 | ☐ | ☐ | ☐ | ☐ |
| 24 | ☐ | ☐ | ☐ | ☐ | 49 | ☐ | ☐ | ☐ | ☐ |
| 25 | ☐ | ☐ | ☐ | ☐ | 50 | ☐ | ☐ | ☐ | ☐ |

# SCIENCE

### 50 Questions

### 80 Minutes

## Directions

This is a test of your skills in analyzing science information. Read each question and decide which of the four alternatives best answers the question. Then mark your choice on your answer sheet. Sometimes several questions are based on the same material. You should carefully read this material, then answer the questions.

Work as quickly as you can without becoming careless. Don't spend too much time on any question that is difficult for you to answer. Instead, skip it and return to it later if you have time. Try to answer every question even if you have to guess.

Mark all your answers on the answer sheet. Give only one answer to each question and make every mark heavy and dark. If you decide to change one of your answers, be sure to erase the first mark completely. Be sure that the number of the question you are answering matches the number of the row of answer choices you are marking on your answer sheet.

1. **Which of the following statements describes the transfer of heat mainly by convection?**

    A   Ceramic floor tiles feel cold to a barefoot person.

    B   Air in contact with the warm ground rises higher into the atmosphere.

    C   When one end of an iron nail is put into a candle flame, the other end becomes warm.

    D   The handle of a metal spoon resting in a bowl of ice cubes becomes cold.

2. **The diagram below shows the forces acting on a rock resting motionless on the ground.**

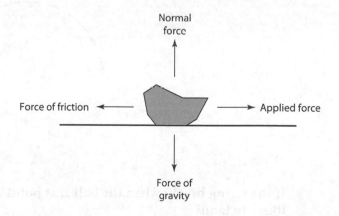

**Why is the rock not moving in response to the applied force acting on it?**

A    The applied force is less than or equal to the force of friction.

B    The force of gravity is less than the normal force.

C    The normal force is greater than the force of friction.

D    The force of gravity is greater than the applied force.

3.    **A sample of nitrogen gas has a temperature of 25°C and a pressure of 0.1 MPa.**

**Which of the following would cause the temperature of the gas to increase?**

A    decreasing the mass of the gas while keeping the pressure constant

B    increasing the rate of diffusion of the gas

C    increasing the pressure of the gas by decreasing its volume

D    insulating the gas from its surroundings

4.    **The diagram below shows a wave.**

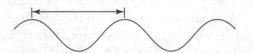

**What does the arrow indicate?**

A    amplitude

B    frequency

C    wavelength

D    period

5.    **The diagram below shows a ball on a string traveling in a circle. The arrow shows the direction the ball is moving in.**

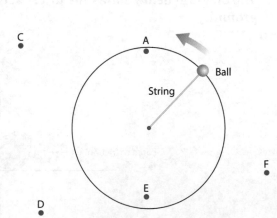

**If the string breaks when the ball is at point A, at which point is the ball most likely to land?**

A    point B

B    point C

C    point D

D    point E

6. **A recreational boat traveled at an average speed of 14 meters per second for 200 seconds.**

   **Which of the following can be determined using this information?**

   A   distance traveled

   B   acceleration

   C   inertia

   D   instantaneous speed

7. **A flash of lightning can be seen before the thunder associated with it can be heard.**

   **Which of the following statements best explains this observation?**

   A   A thunderstorm produces electromagnetic waves more quickly than mechanical waves.

   B   Electromagnetic waves are diffracted more than mechanical waves when traveling through air.

   C   The amplitude of electromagnetic waves is lower than that of mechanical waves.

   D   The speed of electromagnetic waves traveling through air is faster than that of mechanical waves.

8. **The graph below shows the relationship between the distance an object traveled and time.**

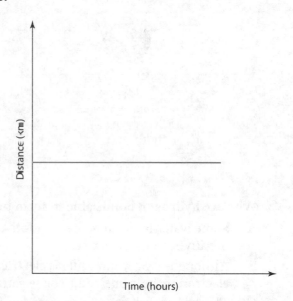

   **Which of the following is the best conclusion that can be made about the movement of the object?**

   A   The object moved at a constant positive speed.

   B   The object moved at a varying positive speed.

   C   The object remained stationary during the time interval shown.

   D   The object moved at a constant negative speed.

**GO ON TO THE NEXT PAGE** ➡

9. Electrical forces are able to act between electrically charged particles that are not in contact. The strength of the electrical force is greatly affected by the distance between the particles. The electrical force can be attractive, causing the particles to move together, or repulsive, causing the particles to move apart.

   Which of the following statements is the best description of the electrical force between two oppositely charged particles?

   A  The strength of the electrical force decreases as the particles move closer together.

   B  The repulsive force and the attractive force balance one another when the particles touch.

   C  The repulsive force changes to an attractive force as the particles move farther apart.

   D  The attractive force increases as the distance between the particles decreases.

10. The diagram below shows a model of a single water molecule and a group of water molecules connected by hydrogen bonds.

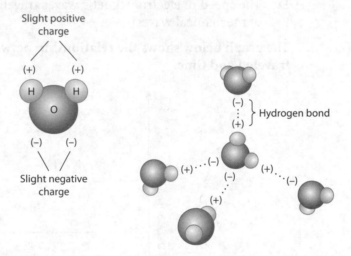

   Why are hydrogen bonds able to form between water molecules?

   A  Some water molecules have a positive electrical charge, and some have a negative electrical charge.

   B  Although a water molecule is electrically neutral, the distribution of electrons causes one end to be negative and the other to be positive.

   C  The negative charge of one water molecule attracts the negative charges of other water molecules.

   D  The electrical charges between water molecules are stronger than the covalent bonds within the molecules.

Questions 11–13 refer to the following skeleton equation for a chemical reaction:

$$C_6H_{14}(l) + O_2(g) \rightarrow CO_2(g) + CO(g) + C(s) + H_2O(g)$$

11. Which of the following shows the correctly balanced equation?

A $C_6H_{14}(l) + 5O_2(g) \rightarrow CO_2(g) + CO(g) + 4C(s) + 7H_2O(g)$

B $2C_6H_{14}(l) + 4O_2(g) \rightarrow CO_2(g) + 4CO(g) + C(s) + 14H_2O(g)$

C $C_6H_{14}(l) + 6O_2(g) \rightarrow 2CO_2(g) + 2CO(g) + 2C(s) + 6H_2O(g)$

D $2C_6H_{14}(l) + 3O_2(g) \rightarrow 5CO_2(g) + 3CO(g) + 4C(s) + H_2O(g)$

12. Which of the following reactants or products is in either the liquid or the solid state?

A $CO_2$, $H_2O$

B C, $O_2$

C $C_6H_{14}$, C

D $O_2$, $CO_2$

13. What type of chemical reaction does the equation represent?

A combustion

B synthesis

C decomposition

D single replacement (single displacement)

14. The diagram below shows a model of an atom.

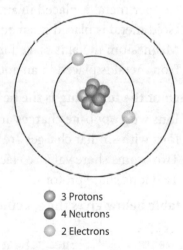

🔵 3 Protons
🔵 4 Neutrons
⚪ 2 Electrons

Which of the following is the best description of the atom?

A negative ion

B positive ion

C radioactive ion

D catalyst atom

GO ON TO THE NEXT PAGE ➡

15. The chart below shows the reactivity series of metals.

The Reactivity Series of Metals

| Potassium | Most reactive |
| Sodium | |
| Calcium | |
| Magnesium | |
| Aluminium | |
| Zinc | |
| Iron | |
| Tin | |
| Lead | |
| Copper | |
| Silver | |
| Gold | |
| Platinum | Least reactive |

According to the chart, which of the following results in a chemical reaction taking place?

A   Copper metal is placed in an aqueous solution of a silver compound.

B   Gold metal is placed in an aqueous solution of a zinc compound.

C   Magnesium metal is placed in an aqueous solution of a sodium compound.

D   Iron metal is placed in an aqueous solution of a calcium compound.

16. Which of the following is the best description of an ionic bond?

A   Ions with opposite charges are attracted to one another.

B   Ions with similar charges are attracted to one another.

C   Two atoms share valence electrons.

D   Two ions share protons.

17. The table below gives the specific heat capacity of various substances.

| Substance | Specific Heat Capacity J/(kg · K) |
| --- | --- |
| Aluminum | 900 |
| Glass | 670 |
| Granite | 840 |
| Platinum | 130 |
| Silver | 230 |
| Water | 4,186 |
| Wood | 1,700 |

If the same amount of heat is transferred to 1 kilogram of each of the following substances, which substance will have the greatest increase in temperature?

A    water

B    aluminum

C    silver

D    wood

18. The element iron (Fe) has 26 protons.

What is a conclusion that can be made using this information?

A    Iron contains no neutrons.

B    Iron contains 26 electrons.

C    Iron contains 13 neutrons and 13 electrons.

D    Iron contains a total of 56 neutrons and electrons.

19. The diagram below shows the components of an animal cell and a plant cell.

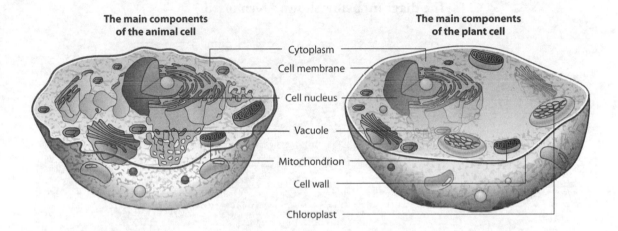

A person is using a microscope to examine some cells.

The presence of which features would indicate that the cells are from a plant?

A    vacuoles and mitochondria

B    nuclei and cytoplasm

C    cell membrane and vacuoles

D    cell walls and chloroplasts

GO ON TO THE NEXT PAGE ➡

20. Before Europeans settled in Illinois, the dominant species of trees in the forests were oaks that were fire-tolerant. Large fires were common, and many were set by Native Americans when they were hunting. When the Europeans arrived, they suppressed fires, so fires became much less common. Oak trees need high levels of light for growth. Fires cleared out shrubs that would otherwise shade young oak trees. After the fires were suppressed, the number of shade-tolerant trees such as sugar maples increased dramatically, and the number of oaks greatly decreased.

Why has the balance shifted between oak trees and sugar maple trees?

A   The suppression of fire affected the thickness of soil in the forests.

B   The suppression of fire decreased the amount of light needed by the sugar maple trees.

C   The suppression of fire changed the pattern of succession in the forests.

D   The suppression of fire increased the rate of leaf production by sugar maple trees.

21. The diagram below shows a fern fossil.

In what type of environment did this fossil most likely form?

A   desert

B   coral reef

C   deep ocean

D   forest

**Questions 22–24 refer to the following food web diagram.**

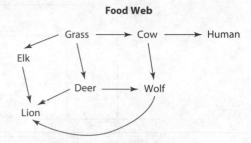

**Food Web**

22. In the food web diagram, the arrows point from an organism to another organism that eats it.

    **Which two organisms compete for prey?**

    A   lion and wolf
    B   deer and lion
    C   wolf and cow
    D   grass and human

23. According to the diagram, which of the following organisms is a carnivore?

    A   elk
    B   lion
    C   deer
    D   cow

24. According to the diagram, if the wolf population increases, the population of which of the following organisms would be most likely to decrease first?

    A   elk and human
    B   cow and lion
    C   deer and cow
    D   grass and elk

25. The diagram below shows a representation of the carbon cycle.

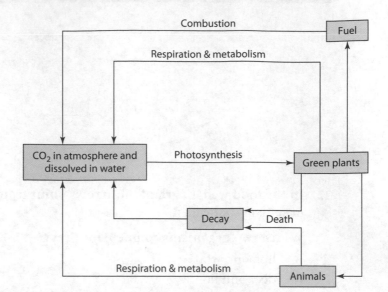

The carbon cycle describes how carbon moves among the atmosphere, Earth's surface, and living organisms.

Which process in the carbon cycle is likely to be affected the most by human activity?

A   photosynthesis by green plants

B   respiration and metabolism of animals

C   combustion of fuel

D   respiration and metabolism of green plants

26. Why do bacteria adapt more quickly to environmental changes than whales do?

A   Bacteria are much smaller than whales.

B   Bacteria live in many more types of ecosystems than whales do.

C   There are many more bacteria than there are whales.

D   Bacteria reproduce much more rapidly than whales do.

27. Genes are made up of pairs of alleles. An allele can be dominant or recessive. In humans, the allele for dimples is dominant, and the allele for no dimples is recessive. If a person has one dominant allele and one recessive allele for dimples, which of the following would be true for this person's child?

A   The child will inherit the dominant allele for dimples.

B   The child will inherit the recessive allele for dimples.

C   The child has an equal chance of inheriting the dominant allele or the recessive allele for dimples.

D   The child has a greater chance of inheriting the dominant allele for dimples.

28. **Which pair of organisms has the same type of ecological relationship as the one between a panda and bamboo?**

    A   giraffe and tree leaves

    B   mouse and owl

    C   alligator and fish

    D   bison and sheep

29. **Which of the following is required for photosynthesis by green plants?**

    A   glucose

    B   chlorophyll

    C   hydrogen sulfide

    D   bacteria

30. **Which of the following is a characteristic shared by all mammals?**

    A   producing milk for their young

    B   having sharp claws

    C   having large, sensitive eyes

    D   being able to hibernate

31. **The diagram below shows an example of dominant inheritance.**

The father carries a defective gene (*D*) that is dominant over the recessive gene (*d*) he carries that is normal. Therefore, the father has the health disorder associated with the dominant gene. The mother has two copies of the normal recessive gene. The children of the parents can inherit a dominant *D* gene and a recessive *d* gene, or two recessive *d* genes.

**Which of the following statements always apply to the children of these parents?**

A   All of the children will inherit the defective gene from the father.

B   Children without the dominant gene will have the genetically related health disorder.

C   A child with two copies of the recessive gene cannot in turn have children with the genetically related health disorder.

D   A child with two copies of the recessive gene is not at risk of having the genetically related health disorder.

GO ON TO THE NEXT PAGE ➡

32. Which of the following best describes how a carnivore in an ecosystem obtains energy?

    A   by consuming plants

    B   by consuming other animals

    C   by living as a parasite on other organisms

    D   by breaking down organic matter to release nutrients

33. In a type of squirrel called the Eastern gray squirrel, the allele for gray fur (*G*) is dominant over the gene for brown fur (*g*). A squirrel with *GG* alleles mates with a squirrel with *gg* alleles.

    What percentage of the baby squirrels would be expected to have gray fur?

    A   100 percent

    B   75 percent

    C   50 percent

    D   25 percent

34. The diagram below shows the spectrum of visible light. Each color of visible light has a particular wavelength in nanometers. For example, green light has wavelengths around 550 nanometers.

| 400 (ultra) Violet | 450 Blue | 500 Cyan | 550 Green | 600 Yellow | 650 Orange | 700 Red | 750 (Infra) |

A student is conducting an experiment on the growth rate of algae in response to wavelengths of light. The student's hypothesis is that red algae will grow fastest when exposed to red light.

Which variable should be manipulated to test the hypothesis?

A   rate of cellular respiration in the algae

B   color of light to which the algae are exposed

C   time of day that the algae are exposed to light

D   color of the algae used

35. Which of the following is most likely to lead to ecological succession?

    A   Leaves drop from trees as the seasons change from fall to winter.

    B   A developer builds a road through a forest.

    C   Two wolves fight to establish which one is dominant.

    D   Existing organisms are disturbed or removed by a powerful flood affecting a large area.

36. The table below shows when some forms of life first appeared in the geologic record or when they became extinct.

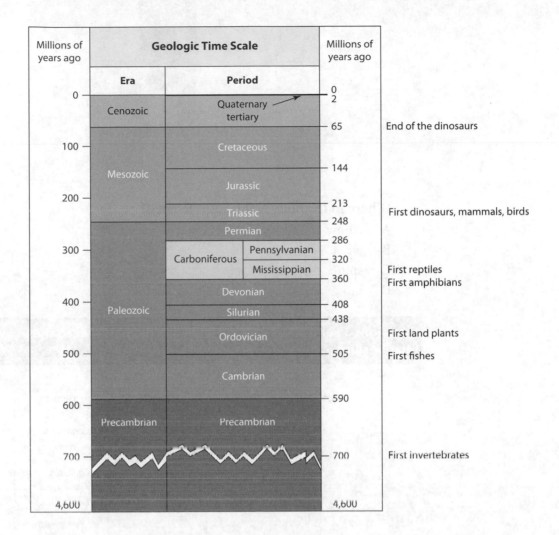

| Millions of years ago | Geologic Time Scale | | Millions of years ago | |
|---|---|---|---|---|
| | Era | Period | | |
| 0 | Cenozoic | Quaternary tertiary | 0<br>2<br>65 | End of the dinosaurs |
| 100 | Mesozoic | Cretaceous | 144 | |
| 200 | | Jurassic | 213 | |
| | | Triassic | 248 | First dinosaurs, mammals, birds |
| | Paleozoic | Permian | 286 | |
| 300 | | Carboniferous — Pennsylvanian | 320 | First reptiles |
| | | Carboniferous — Mississippian | 360 | First amphibians |
| 400 | | Devonian | 408 | |
| | | Silurian | 438 | First land plants |
| | | Ordovician | 505 | First fishes |
| 500 | | Cambrian | | |
| 600 | | | 590 | |
| 700 | Precambrian | Precambrian | 700 | First invertebrates |
| 4,600 | | | 4,600 | |

Which of the following gives the correct order of evolution of organisms, from oldest to youngest?

A  dinosaurs, reptiles, land plants, invertebrates

B  fishes, land plants, amphibians, birds

C  invertebrates, amphibians, mammals, reptiles

D  land plants, reptiles, fishes, dinosaurs

**GO ON TO THE NEXT PAGE ➡**

37. The diagram below shows a joint in the human body.

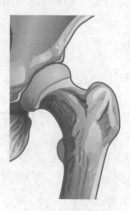

Where in the body is this joint located?

A   elbow

B   wrist

C   spine

D   hip

**Questions 38 and 39 refer to the following diagram, which shows evolutionary relationships among several types of birds.**

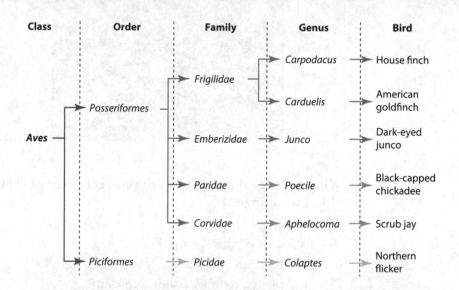

38. **What conclusion can be made regarding the dark-eyed junco and the scrub jay?**

A   They are in the same class and in the same family.

B   They are in the same family and in the same genus.

C   They are in the same order but in different families.

D   They are in the same genus but in different classes.

39. **Which bird shown on the diagram is least closely related to the American goldfinch?**
    A   house finch
    B   dark-eyed junco
    C   northern flicker
    D   scrub jay

40. **The diagram below shows the structure of a plant leaf.**

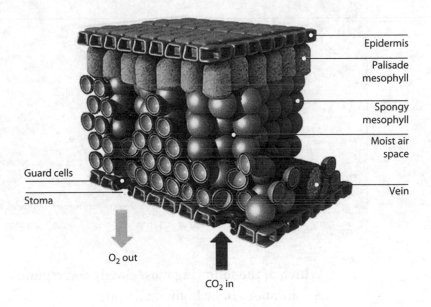

**Which of the following is a function of the stoma?**
    A   They allow gas exchange between the plant and the surrounding air.
    B   They provide support that helps keep the plant upright.
    C   They contain chloroplasts where photosynthesis takes place.
    D   They transport water and dissolved food throughout the plant.

41. **Which of the following factors is most important in causing Earth's seasons?**
    A   tilt of Earth's axis
    B   speed of Earth's rotation
    C   convection cells in the atmosphere
    D   distance from the sun during the year

GO ON TO THE NEXT PAGE ➡

42. The map below shows the locations of earthquakes that occurred over a 15-year period.

**World Seismicity 1977–1992**

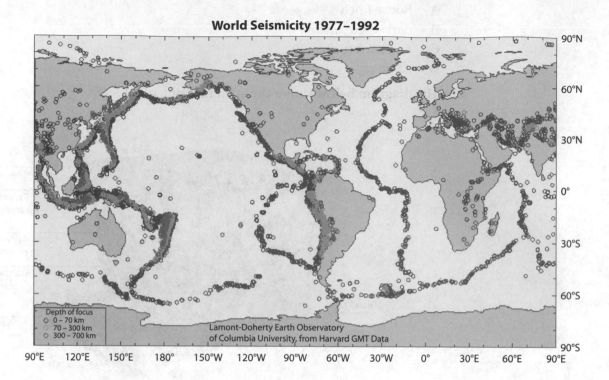

Which of the following most closely corresponds to the earthquake locations?

A   locations of hydrothermal vents

B   locations of oceanic spreading centers

C   locations of tectonic plate boundaries

D   locations of mantle plumes and hotspots

43. **Hurricanes are powerful tropical cyclones.**

**What is the source of energy that powers hurricanes?**

A   heavy rainfall caused by changes in land elevation

B   the collision of a warm air mass and a cold air mass along a frontal boundary

C   differences in climate due to seasonal changes that occur in the tropics and subtropics

D   the release of stored heat into the atmosphere as water vapor condensing in rising air

44. **Which of the following is mainly caused by the gravitational attraction between Earth and the moon?**

A   eclipses of the moon

B   mountains and valleys on the moon's surface

C   ocean tides on Earth

D   aurora displays (Northern and Southern Lights) in Earth's atmosphere

**Distribution of Earth's Water**

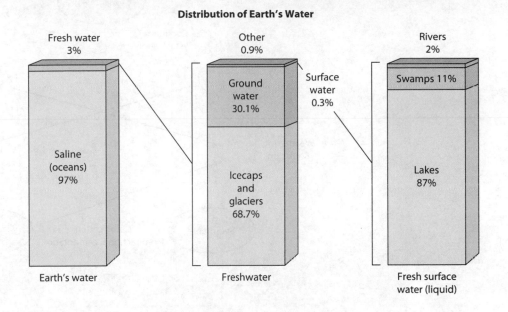

45. **About how much of Earth's total water is contained in rivers?**
    A   less than 0.3 percent
    B   2 percent
    C   between 11 percent and 38.6 percent
    D   17 percent

46. **Where is most of Earth's freshwater located?**
    A   groundwater
    B   icecaps and glaciers
    C   rivers
    D   swamps

47. **Geologists study sedimentary rock layers to determine what conditions were like on Earth's surface long ago.**

    **Which of the following ideas are the geologists' conclusions based on?**
    A   The rate at which rocks change is constant over time.
    B   The processes operating at Earth's surface today are the same as the ones in the past.
    C   Chemical reactions affecting rocks were slower in the past than they are today.
    D   The types of minerals making up Earth's crust have changed steadily over time.

**GO ON TO THE NEXT PAGE ➡**

48. The diagram below shows processes in the rock cycle.

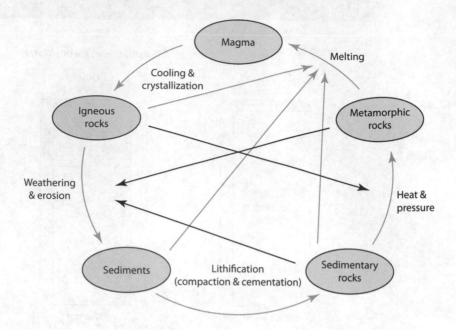

**According to the diagram, what is a major source of the sediments that make up sedimentary rocks?**

A   minerals that form as magma cools and crystallizes into solid rock

B   evaporation of water that leaves behind minerals that had been dissolved in it

C   compaction and cementation of particles into new rocks

D   particles derived from metamorphic rocks as they break apart

**Questions 49 and 50 refer to the following table of characteristics of planets in the solar system.**

| Characteristic | Mercury | Venus | Earth | Mars | Jupiter | Saturn | Uranus | Neptune |
|---|---|---|---|---|---|---|---|---|
| Diameter (km) | 4,878 | 12,104 | 12,756 | 6,787 | 142,800 | 120,000 | 51,118 | 49,528 |
| Orbital period (Earth years) | 0.24 | 0.62 | 1 | 1.88 | 11.86 | 29.46 | 84.01 | 164.8 |
| Rotation period (in Earth days) | 58.65 | −243* | 1 | 1.03 | 0.41 | 0.44 | −0.72* | 0.72 |
| Inclination of axis (degrees) | 0.0 | 177.4 | 23.45 | 23.98 | 3.08 | 26.73 | 97.92 | 28.8 |

*A negative value for the rotation period shows that the direction of rotation of the planet is opposite to the direction in which it orbits the sun.

49. **Which of the following planets takes the shortest time to complete one rotation on its axis?**

   A   Mercury

   B   Saturn

   C   Earth

   D   Mars

50. **Which of the following planets completes an orbit around the sun in less time than Earth does?**

   A   Venus

   B   Jupiter

   C   Saturn

   D   Uranus

# ANSWERS: SCIENCE

1. **(B)** Convection is heat transfer by the movement of matter; it takes place in liquids and gases. Conduction is heat transfer between objects that are in direct contact. Radiation is energy transfer by electromagnetic waves.

2. **(A)** An applied force must be greater than the force of friction for an object to move across a surface with which it is in contact.

3. **(C)** The temperature and pressure of a gas are directly proportional to each other. If one increases, the other increases.

4. **(C)** Wavelength is the distance between identical points on neighboring cycles of a waveform.

5. **(B)** When the string breaks, the centripetal force that was pulling the ball inward is removed. The ball continues in its direction of movement in a straight line.

6. **(A)** Distance can be determined when the average speed and elapsed time are known. Distance equals speed multiplied by time.

7. **(D)** Mechanical waves are produced by vibrations of particles in a medium. They have a much slower speed than electromagnetic waves, which can travel through a vacuum.

8. **(C)** The line is straight, showing that the relationship between time and distance was constant, but the line has no slope, indicating that distance did not change over time.

9. **(D)** Electrical forces are extremely sensitive to distance. Decreasing the separation distance between particles with opposite charges greatly increases the force of attraction between them.

10. **(B)** Water is a polar molecule, so one end is slightly positive and the other is slightly negative, even though the overall charge of the molecule is neutral. Hydrogen bonds form as the negative end of one molecule is attracted to the positive end of another molecule.

11. **(A)** When properly balanced, the equation shows an equal number of each element on both sides—6 carbon atoms, 14 hydrogen atoms, and 10 oxygen atoms.

12. **(C)** The states of matter of the reactants and products are shown in the equation as being liquid ($l$), solid ($s$), or gas ($g$). The compound $C_6H_{14}$ is in the liquid state, and the element C is in the solid state. In this reaction, $H_2O$ is in the gas state.

13. **(A)** The reaction is a combustion reaction because oxygen reacts with another compound to form carbon dioxide and water. In this case, the combustion is incomplete (insufficient oxygen is available) because elemental carbon and carbon monoxide are also produced.

14. **(B)** A positive ion has more protons than electrons.

15. **(A)** An element that is higher in the activity series (more reactive) will displace an element that is lower in the activity series (less reactive). Copper is higher than silver in the series. Options (B), (C), and (D) give metals that are lower in the series than the metal that might be displaced.

16. **(A)** Ionic bonds form because of the attractive electrostatic force between oppositely charged ions.

17. **(C)** Of the substances, silver has the lowest specific heat capacity. Therefore, the temperature of silver will rise fastest with the addition of thermal energy.

18. **(B)** An atom of an element has the same number of protons and electrons.

19. **(D)** A plant cell has a cell wall and chloroplasts, but an animal cell does not.

20. **(C)** The change in the environment (less frequent fires) made it possible for different types of trees to become dominant, thus changing the pattern of succession.

21. **(D)** Ferns thrive in moist, shady, warm conditions. They are likely to be found in a temperate or tropical forest.

22. **(A)** The diagram shows arrows pointing from deer to both lions and wolves. Both lions and wolves eat deer, so they are in competition for a food resource.

23. **(B)** Of the organisms given, only a lion eats meat.

24. **(C)** Wolves eat deer and cows, so an increase in the wolf population would put downward pressure on the populations of deer and cows first.

25. **(C)** The combustion of fuel, especially oil and coal, by humans greatly affects the concentration of carbon dioxide in the atmosphere. Although humans also affect the growth of plants and animals, these activities do not have as strong an impact on the carbon cycle as the burning of fuel.

26. **(D)** Generations of bacteria can be produced very rapidly, so their populations can adapt to environmental pressures in a fairly short time. Whales take years to reach maturity and produce only one calf at a time, so their reproduction rate is slow.

27. **(C)** The child will inherit one allele that codes for dimples from each parent. There is an equal chance for either the dominant or the recessive allele to be passed to the child.

28. **(A)** A panda is an herbivore (an animal that gets its food from plants) that eats bamboo. A giraffe is an herbivore that eats tree leaves.

29. **(B)** Chlorophyll is a green pigment that uses energy from sunlight to synthesize simple carbohydrates from carbon dioxide and water. Oxygen is a by-product.

30. **(A)** All mammals produce milk for their young. Not all mammals have claws or have the ability to hibernate. Many marine and freshwater mammals have poor eyesight.

31. **(D)** The lack of the dominant allele allows the recessive trait (absence of the genetically related health disorder) to be expressed. It is not possible to draw any conclusions about the future offspring of the children without knowing the genotype of the other parent.

**GO ON TO THE NEXT PAGE ➡**

32. **(B)** A carnivore is an animal that gets its food by eating other animals.

33. **(A)** The Punnett square for the cross is

|   | $g$ | $g$ |
|---|-----|-----|
| $G$ | $Gg$ | $Gg$ |
| $G$ | $Gg$ | $Gg$ |

Therefore, all of the offspring would inherit a dominant allele from the $GG$ parent. Because the dominant allele codes for gray fur, 100 percent of the offspring would be gray.

34. **(B)** The color of light to which the algae are exposed must be varied among all the colors to test whether a particular color enhances the growth rate.

35. **(D)** Ecological succession is the natural change in the species structure of an ecosystem following a disturbance to the ecosystem (or in the initial colonization of a new habitat).

36. **(B)** The table shows that only option (B) lists organisms in order of their first appearance.

37. **(D)** A hip joint (option D) is a ball-and-socket joint. An elbow (option A) is a hinge joint. A wrist (option B) and spine (option C) have gliding joints. A skull has fibrous (unmoving) joints.

38. **(C)** The diagram shows that both birds are in the order *Passeriformes* but in different families.

39. **(C)** The northern flicker is least closely related to any of the other birds on the diagram because it is in a separate order from the others.

40. **(A)** The diagram shows carbon dioxide entering the leaf and oxygen exiting. Therefore, stoma allow gases to enter and leave the plant.

41. **(A)** The tilt of Earth's axis causes seasons because it allows for the uneven distribution of solar energy hitting the surface over the course of a year.

42. **(C)** Most earthquakes occur along tectonic plate boundaries.

43. **(D)** The release of latent heat by the condensation of water vapor provides fuel for further intensification of a tropical cyclone. The heated air expands and rises, causing surface air pressure to decrease further.

44. **(C)** Ocean tides are caused mainly by the gravitational attraction between Earth and the moon, with a smaller component being caused by the gravitational attraction between Earth and the sun. Eclipses (option A) are caused by the relative positions of Earth, the moon, and the sun.

45. **(A)** The diagram shows that about 3 percent of Earth's total water is freshwater. Of that, about 0.3 percent is surface water. Rivers account for only a small portion of surface water.

46. **(B)** Only 3 percent of Earth's total water is freshwater. Icecaps and glaciers contain 68.7 percent of the planet's freshwater.

**47. (B)** The principle of uniformitarianism is a basic underpinning of geology. It states that the processes shaping Earth are uniform through time. Therefore, processes that affect the formation of sedimentary rocks today can be used as models for processes that operated in the past.

**48. (D)** Weathering and erosion break down rocks. Sediments derived from existing rocks (sedimentary, igneous, or metamorphic) can be compacted and cemented to form new sedimentary rocks.

**49. (B)** The rotation period of a planet is the length of time required for one complete rotation about its axis. Of the planets listed, Saturn has the shortest rotation period.

**50. (A)** Earth requires one year to complete an orbit around the sun. Venus completes an orbit in about a quarter of the time (0.24 Earth year).

# *HiSET*® Exam Practice Test 2
## Answer Sheet
## Language Arts—Reading

|    | A | B | C | D |    | A | B | C | D |
|----|---|---|---|---|----|---|---|---|---|
| 1  |   |   |   |   | 21 |   |   |   |   |
| 2  |   |   |   |   | 22 |   |   |   |   |
| 3  |   |   |   |   | 23 |   |   |   |   |
| 4  |   |   |   |   | 24 |   |   |   |   |
| 5  |   |   |   |   | 25 |   |   |   |   |
| 6  |   |   |   |   | 26 |   |   |   |   |
| 7  |   |   |   |   | 27 |   |   |   |   |
| 8  |   |   |   |   | 28 |   |   |   |   |
| 9  |   |   |   |   | 29 |   |   |   |   |
| 10 |   |   |   |   | 30 |   |   |   |   |
| 11 |   |   |   |   | 31 |   |   |   |   |
| 12 |   |   |   |   | 32 |   |   |   |   |
| 13 |   |   |   |   | 33 |   |   |   |   |
| 14 |   |   |   |   | 34 |   |   |   |   |
| 15 |   |   |   |   | 35 |   |   |   |   |
| 16 |   |   |   |   | 36 |   |   |   |   |
| 17 |   |   |   |   | 37 |   |   |   |   |
| 18 |   |   |   |   | 38 |   |   |   |   |
| 19 |   |   |   |   | 39 |   |   |   |   |
| 20 |   |   |   |   | 40 |   |   |   |   |

# LANGUAGE ARTS—READING

## 40 Questions

## 65 Minutes

## Directions

This is a test of some of the skills involved in understanding what you read. The passages in this test come from a variety of published works, both literary and informational. Each passage is followed by a number of questions. The passages begin with an introduction presenting information that may be helpful as you read the selection. After you have read a passage, go on to the questions that follow. For each question, choose the best answer, and mark your choice on the answer sheet. You may refer to a passage as often as necessary.

Work as quickly as you can without becoming careless. Don't spend too much time on any question that is difficult for you to answer. Instead, skip it and return to it later if you have time. Try to answer every question even if you have to guess.

Mark all your answers on the answer sheet. Give only one answer to each question and make every mark heavy and dark. If you decide to change one of your answers, be sure to erase the first mark completely. Be sure that the number of the question you are answering matches the number of the row of answer choices you are marking on your answer sheet.

---

**Questions 1–6 refer to the following excerpt from the novel *Winesburg, Ohio* by Sherwood Anderson.**

George came down the little incline from the New Willard House at seven o'clock. Tom Willard carried his bag. The son had become taller than the father.

On the station platform, everyone shook the young man's hand. More than a
*Line*  dozen people waited about. George was embarrassed. Gertrude Wilmot, a tall thin
5  woman of fifty who worked in the Winesburg post office, came along the station platform. She had never before paid any attention to George. Now she stopped and put out her hand. In two words she voiced what everyone felt. "Good luck," she said sharply and then, turning, went on her way. When the train came into the station, George felt relieved. He scampered hurriedly aboard. George glanced up and down the
10  car to be sure no one was looking, then took out his pocket-book and counted his money. His mind was occupied with a desire not to appear green. Almost the last words his father had said to him concerned the matter of his behavior when he got to the city. "Be a sharp one," Tom Willard had said. "Keep your eyes on your money. Be awake. That's the ticket. Don't let anyone think you're a greenhorn." After George
15  counted his money, he looked out of the window and was surprised to see that the train was still in Winesburg. The young man, going out of his town to meet the adventure of life, began to think but he did not think of anything very big or dramatic. He thought of little things—Turk Smollet wheeling boards through the main street of his town in the morning, Butch Wheeler the lamp lighter of Winesburg hurrying

---

**GO ON TO THE NEXT PAGE** ➡

20 through the streets on a summer evening and holding a torch in his hand, Helen White standing by a window in the Winesburg post office and putting a stamp on an envelope.

The young man's mind was carried away by his growing passion for dreams. One looking at him would not have thought him particularly sharp. With the recollection of 25 little things occupying his mind, he closed his eyes and leaned back in the car seat. He stayed that way for a long time, and when he aroused himself and again looked out of the car window, the town of Winesburg had disappeared and his life there had become but a background on which to paint the dreams of his manhood.

1. **Which of the following words *best* describes what George feels about leaving his hometown?**

   A   indifferent

   B   frightened

   C   eager

   D   sad

2. **Why does George feel relieved when the train arrives at the station?**

   A   He can look out and remember what his town looks like.

   B   He was worried the train would be cancelled.

   C   He is able to finally get away from his father.

   D   He can get away from the people who have come to say good-bye.

3. **Which of the following *best* describes what Tom Willard means when he tells George, "Be a sharp one" (line 13)?**

   A   Have a nasty tongue.

   B   Watch out for your things.

   C   Improve your mind.

   D   Do not hurt anyone.

4. **Based on the excerpt, what description *best* characterizes the relationship between George and his father?**

   A   They have a strong bond.

   B   They are both opinionated.

   C   They have different views of society.

   D   They both want to escape from their lives.

5. **Based on the excerpt, what is George *most likely* to do in the future?**

   A   return home on the next train

   B   fail to find himself

   C   seek out adventure

   B   call home immediately

6. **Which of the following *best* describes the mood created in the excerpt?**

   A   anxious

   B   dreamy

   C   humorous

   D   fanciful

**Questions 7–12 refer to the following excerpt from the short story "The Gift of the Magi" by O. Henry, 1906.**

For there lay The Combs—the set of combs, side and back, that Della had worshiped for long in a Broadway window. Beautiful combs, pure tortoise shell, with jeweled rims—just the shade to wear in the beautiful vanished hair. They were expensive combs, she knew, and her heart had simply craved and yearned over them without the least hope of possession. And now they were hers, but the tresses that should have adorned the coveted adornments were gone.

But she hugged them to her bosom, and at length she was able to look up with dim eyes and a smile and say, "My hair grows so fast, Jim!"

And then Della leaped up like a little singed cat and cried, "Oh, oh!"

Jim had not yet seen his beautiful present. She held it out to him eagerly upon her open palm. The dull precious metal seemed to flash with a reflection of her bright and ardent spirit.

"Isn't it a dandy, Jim? I hunted all over town to find it. You'll have to look at the time a hundred times a day now. Give me your watch. I want to see how it looks on it."

Instead of obeying, Jim tumbled down on the couch and put his hands under the back of his head and smiled.

"Della," said he, "let's put our Christmas presents away and keep 'em awhile. They're too nice to use just at present. I sold the watch to get the money to buy your combs. And now suppose you put the chops on."

7. **Where does the action in this excerpt take place?**

   A   a jewelry store

   B   the couple's home

   C   Jim's office

   D   Della's office

8. **Why does Jim suggest they put their Christmas presents away?**

   A   They cannot use their gifts.

   B   Neither of them likes the presents.

   C   It is not Christmas yet.

   D   The presents are too nice to use.

9. **How do Jim and Della feel about each other?**

   A   Jim loves Della, but his love is not returned.

   B   They dislike each other.

   C   Della loves Jim, but her love is not returned.

   D   They love each other.

10. **Which of the following *best* describes the mood of the excerpt?**

    A   lighthearted

    B   tense

    C   suspenseful

    D   tender

GO ON TO THE NEXT PAGE ➡

11. **Why can't Della use the combs?**

   A   Her hair is too short for combs.

   B   She has to sell them so that Jim can buy a new watch.

   C   Jim will not let her wear them.

   D   They are too expensive and must be returned to the store.

12. **What is the best definition of the word *dandy* as used in the story?**

   A   a fashionable, refined man

   B   a fine Christmas gift

   C   something of exceptional quality

   D   a beautiful woman

**Questions 13–17 refer to the following poem.**

My mother's hands are cool and fair,

They can do anything.

Delicate mercies hide them there

Like flowers in the spring.

*Line*
5   When I was small and could not sleep,

She used to come to me,

And with my cheek upon her hand

How sure my rest would be.

For everything she ever touched

10   Of beautiful or fine,

Their memories living in her hands

Would warm that sleep of mine.

Her hands remember how they played

One time in meadow streams, —

15   And all the flickering song and shade

Of water took my dreams.

Swift through her haunted fingers pass

Memories of garden things; —

I dipped my face in flowers and grass

20   And sounds of hidden wings.

One time she touched the cloud that kissed

Brown pastures bleak and far; —

I leaned my cheek into a mist

And thought I was a star.

<sup>25</sup> All this was very long ago

And I am grown; but yet

The hand that lured my slumber so

I never can forget.

For still when drowsiness comes on

<sup>30</sup> It seems so soft and cool,

Shaped happily beneath my cheek,

Hollow and beautiful.

—"Her Hands" from *Songs for My Mother*, by Anna Hempstead Branch, 1917

**13. When does the first part of the poem *most likely* take place?**

    **A**   during the spring

    **B**   when the child was in a pasture

    **C**   when the child was in a meadow

    **D**   when the child was going to sleep

**14. Which of the following phrases *best* describes the overall mood of the poem?**

    **A**   lighthearted

    **B**   nostalgic

    **C**   confused

    **D**   contrary

**15. Which of the following is the most likely explanation of why the poet uses phrases such as "memories living in her hands" and "haunted fingers" (lines 11 and 17)?**

    **A**   to suggest that her mother had many experiences

    **B**   to show that her mother's hands were unattractive

    **C**   to suggest that her mother's hands were old

    **D**   to show that her mother was unwell

**16. What can you infer about the poet's mother?**

    **A**   She had little understanding of nature.

    **B**   She was a practical woman.

    **C**   She was always very formal.

    **D**   She enjoyed comforting her child.

**17. If the poet could give advice to a friend about how to help her child go to sleep, which of the following would she be *most likely* to say?**

    **A**   Sing to her.

    **B**   Tell her a story.

    **C**   Caress her.

    **D**   Leave her alone.

GO ON TO THE NEXT PAGE ➡

**Questions 18–22 refer to the following memo.**

Memo: To All Employees

Because the company has grown so fast over the last 12 months, it has become evident that there is often not enough parking for everyone. Many times employees are forced to park on the grass, which, besides being unattractive, does damage to the ground.
*Line*
5    Adding new parking spaces is expensive and environmentally unfriendly.

Management here at Solarama has therefore decided to take a proactive position regarding carpooling. There are many advantages to carpooling. It helps the environment; you will use less gas and cause fewer emissions. You will save money; by ride sharing, you will end up purchasing less gasoline. It will resolve the company's parking problem. And carpooling will enhance the image of Solarama with our
10    customers and with our community. Let's set an example and make the concept of driving alone a thing of the past!

To that end, we are setting up a system of incentives to reward those who carpool, take a bus, bicycle, or walk to the office. Employees who carpool will be given preferred parking spaces. Those who ride the bus or subways will be given rebates
15    toward the cost of the ticket. Bike racks will be installed in the front. We will start construction next week on locker room and shower facilities and should be completed in two weeks.

In addition, all employees who participate and use alternate means to driving alone to commute to and from the office will receive a reward equal to 1 percent of their net
20    biweekly income on each paycheck for as long as they continue to participate.

Sign-up sheets are now available. A database will be set up so you can easily find those who live near you, and routes will be mapped. Existing bus routes and bike trails will also be mapped. We are very excited here at Solarama with our new carpooling program.

18.  **Which of the following *best* restates the phrase "To that end" (line 12)?**

   **A**   Since we have noticed

   **B**   In order to solve the problem

   **C**   Getting to the end

   **D**   Because we want to change

19.  **Based on the memo, what does Solarama *most likely* make?**

   **A**   children's toys

   **B**   ski equipment

   **C**   gasoline engines

   **D**   photovoltaic panels

20.  **Which of the following *best* describes the style in which this memo is written?**

   **A**   technical and dry

   **B**   straightforward and detailed

   **C**   amusing and humorous

   **D**   scholarly and involved

21. **Based on the memo, who would most likely benefit from the locker and shower facilities?**

    **A**   employees who ride buses to work

    **B**   employees who carpool to work

    **C**   employees who bike to work

    **D**   employees who ride alone to work

22. **Which of the following best describes the way in which the memo is organized?**

    **A**   by comparing and contrasting information

    **B**   by presenting a problem and suggesting a solution

    **C**   by discussing familiar terms first, then going on to unfamiliar terms

    **D**   by giving a sequence of events

**Questions 23–28 refer to the following excerpt from a short story.**

Josh woke up early. Today was the big game with Rosentown High, their arch rival. Valley needed this win. The winner would go on to the division semi-finals. And Coach Murphy said Josh would be the closer. He had to pitch his best. He dressed quickly and did his morning workout routine. Driving to the field, Josh thought how remarkable it was that he would be graduating in just a few more weeks. He crossed his fingers and hoped that there would be some scouts in the bleachers.

As game time approached, Josh headed out to the bullpen. He was nervous; Rosentown had beaten them last year 5–1. Andy, the starting pitcher, was already warming up. Soon the game started. The first five innings were a pitcher's duel and the game remained scoreless. During the sixth inning Valley's second baseman, Willie, drove in two runs with a solid home run. When Valley took the field at the bottom of the seventh inning it was clear that Andy was tiring. Coach Murphy motioned to the bullpen, and Josh began to warm up.

All of a sudden, the bases were loaded. There were no outs. Coach signaled, and Josh headed for the mound. "Throw with confidence," he said as he gave Josh the ball. "Focus on the potential positive of each pitch. Keep your wrist loose, and remember to follow through." Then he patted him on the back.

Josh fingered the ball in his glove, lining up the seams. He threw; the batter hit an infield pop fly. The next batter quickly took two called strikes. "I can do this," Josh told himself, but inside he was not so sure. The next pitch he threw was in the dirt. Then two more balls, and the count was full. He wiped the sweat from his forehead. His mouth was dry. His vision seemed blurred. He took a long, deep breath and focused. Coach's words echoed in his mind. "Throw with confidence," he heard his coach say. It was almost hypnotic.

Josh positioned his middle finger and index finger on the ball, wound up, and threw as hard as he could. The batter swung wildly. "Strike three," called the umpire. Josh had thrown a magnificent slider. One out to go, he thought. Again, he heard Coach's voice. And he threw three strikes, all perfect sliders. Valley won 2–0!

**GO ON TO THE NEXT PAGE ➡**

23. **Which of the following *best* describes the relationship between Josh and Coach Murphy?**

    A   easygoing but distant

    B   cordial and pleasant

    C   friendly but disciplined

    D   indifferent and cool

24. **Which of the following *best* expresses the main idea of the excerpt?**

    A   A young pitcher could not overcome his nervousness about a big baseball game even though he won it.

    B   A young pitcher performed well in front of baseball scouts.

    C   A young pitcher was able to overcome his fears and throw the strikes he needed to win an important game.

    D   A young pitcher doubted his ability to win an important game.

25. **Which of the following is the *most likely* reason that the author says, "It was almost hypnotic" (line 24)?**

    A   to suggest that Coach's words were unclear

    B   to suggest that Coach was not telling Josh the right advice

    C   to suggest that Josh was feeling sleepy

    D   to suggest that Coach's words had a deep effect on Josh

26. **Based on the information in this excerpt, how would Josh *most likely* behave during a chess competition?**

    **He would**

    A   focus completely on each play

    B   start to get more nervous with every play

    C   forget the rules of the game

    D   tell his opponent that he did not stand a chance

27. **Which of the following *best* describes Josh?**

    A   a brilliant pitcher who is self-trained

    B   someone who will succeed in college

    C   a hard worker who is able to concentrate

    D   someone who is ambitious and driven

28. **Which of the following can you infer about Coach Murphy?**

    A   He thinks that coaching is not challenging.

    B   He gets angry at players very easily.

    C   He is a helpful and effective coach.

    D   He does not enjoy coaching.

**Questions 29–35 refer to the following excerpt from the novel Babbitt by Sinclair Lewis.**

"Ted! Will you kindly not interrupt us when we're talking about serious matters!"

"Aw, punk," said Ted. "Ever since somebody slipped up and let you out of college, you've been pulling these nut conversations about what-nots and so-ons. Are you going to—I want to use the car tonight." Babbitt, his father, wailed, "Oh, you do! I may want it myself!" Verona protested, "Oh, you do, Mr. Smarty! I'm going to take it myself!" Tinka cried, "Oh, papa, you said maybe you'd drive us down to Rosedale!" and Mrs. Babbitt, "Careful, Tinka, your sleeve is in the butter." They glared, and Verona said, "Ted, you're a perfect pig about the car!"

"Course you're not! Not a-tall! You just want to grab it off, right after dinner, and leave it in front of some girl's house all evening while you sit and chat about the men you're going to marry—if only they'd propose!"

"Well, Dad oughtn't to NEVER let you have it! You and those beastly Jones boys drive like maniacs!"

"Aw, where do you get that stuff! You're so darn scared of the car that you drive uphill with the emergency brake on!"

"I do not! And you—Always talking about how much you know about motors, and Eunice Littlefield told me you said the battery fed the generator!"

"You—why, my good woman, you don't know a generator from a battery." Not unreasonably was Ted lofty with her. He was a natural mechanic, a maker and tinkerer of machines.

"That'll do now!" Babbitt flung in mechanically.

Ted negotiated: "Gee, honest, Rone, I don't want to take the old boat, but I promised a couple of girls in my class I'd drive them down to chorus rehearsal, and, gee, I don't want to, but a gentleman's got to keep his social engagements."

"Well, upon my word! You and your social engagements! In high school!"

"Oh, aren't we select since we went to college! Let me tell you there isn't a private school in the state that's got as swell a bunch as we have."

Somewhat later as it was getting dark, after diplomacies, Ted persuaded Verona to admit that she was merely going to the Armory that evening to see the dog and cat show. She was then, Ted planned, to park the car in front of the candy store across from the Armory and he would pick it up.

29. **What is the overall mood of the excerpt?**

   A   congenial

   B   depressed

   C   argumentative

   D   exciting

30. **Why is Verona upset?**

   A   She wants to visit her friends, and Ted wants to visit his too.

   B   Ted thinks her friends are silly.

   C   She thinks her father favors Ted over her.

   D   She wants to use the car, and Ted wants to use it too.

**GO ON TO THE NEXT PAGE ➡**

31. Based on the excerpt, what does Ted *most likely* think about his sister?

    **A**   He thinks she should have more friends.

    **B**   He thinks that college ruined her.

    **C**   He believes that she is too ambitious.

    **D**   He likes to tease her, but he cares about her.

32. When does the scene in this excerpt take place?

    **A**   during dinner

    **B**   late at night

    **C**   in the morning

    **D**   before lunch

33. Which phrase *best* describes Ted?

    **A**   emotionless and sad

    **B**   humorous but argumentative

    **C**   anxious and shy

    **D**   confused but forgiving

34. What is the most likely meaning of line 26, "Oh, aren't we select since we went to college!"?

    **A**   You chose to go to college, so you should be happier.

    **B**   You think you are perfect because you went to college.

    **C**   You became an outstanding student while at college.

    **D**   You think that college is more important than a social life.

35. In which of the following ways are Ted and Verona alike?

    **A**   They are both stubborn and want their own way.

    **B**   They are both worried about their future.

    **C**   They are both worried about each other.

    **D**   They are both helpful and watch over each other.

**Questions 36–40 refer to the following theatrical review.**

With the opening of his first play, *Eighth Street*, last night at the Orpheum, Hector Clemente promises to be a rising new star on the theatrical scene. Set in Miami's Little Havana along Calle Ocho, or Eighth Street, the center of the bustling area that is home *Line* to many Cuban Americans, the play breaks down stereotypes about class strictures 5 and love.

    Isabella, played by the beautiful Emily Garcia, is a student at the university majoring in art. There she meets Santiago (Jack Bernardo), a young attorney who also teaches an introductory course on constitutional law. Bernardo's magnetism radiates on stage, so much so that young Emily at times blurts out her lines confusedly.

10     Santiago, the only son of a wealthy bond trader on Wall Street, is immediately attracted to Isabella, and soon, it is evident they are falling in love. Much of their dialogue is clichéd and certainly could be reworked in this reviewer's opinion, as they talk in a trendy night club in South Beach, but his presence is undeniable.

    Act Two opens in Isabella's home, a modest one-story bungalow off Eighth Street. 15 Her mother, Pilar (Natalie Rivera), has worked hard her whole life as a hotel maid, raising her daughter by herself. They argue; Isabella wants to bring Santiago to dinner, but her mother refuses. "Wasn't Raul good enough for you?" Pilar screams, referring to Isabella's boyfriend before she went to college. Isabella runs crying from the house.

20     The final act takes place in Domino Park. Amid the seated men playing chess, checkers, and dominoes, Pilar sits apprehensively. Isabella and Santiago enter. The tension is thick, and the three heatedly exchange accusations at each other, playing their Latin temperaments to the hilt. Then Santiago goes down on his knees and proposes to Isabella. Pilar softens and tears run down her cheeks. She realizes they are 25 one family now.

    Although flawed in some aspects, the play certainly kept the audience's attention, and there were cheers at the end. I look forward to Clemente's next play.

**36.** **Which of the following *best* describes the tone of the review?**

    **A**   fresh and thoughtful

    **B**   sarcastic and critical

    **C**   humorous and lighthearted

    **D**   clever but breezy

**37.** **Which of the following *best* expresses the author's opinion of *Eighth Street*?**

    **A**   He liked the dialogue but not the plot.

    **B**   He thought that Bernardo could have been better.

    **C**   He wanted the playwright to make Pilar's role larger.

    **D**   He thought it was absorbing.

**38.** **Which of the following *best* describes the style in which the review is written?**

    **A**   methodical and trying

    **B**   ornate and flowery

    **C**   economical and brief

    **D**   detailed and professional

**39.** **Based on the information in the review, what can you infer about what the author thinks of Jack Bernardo?**

    **A**   He thinks he overacts.

    **B**   He thinks he has a future in acting.

    **C**   He thinks he has great looks.

    **D**   He thinks he has excellent communication skills.

**40.** **Why does the author include the audience's response to the play?**

    **A**   to show that most people really liked the play

    **B**   to show that the audience had mixed feelings about the play

    **C**   to suggest that the audience was filled with friends of the actors

    **D**   to suggest that the audience was new to theater

# ANSWERS: LANGUAGE ARTS—READING

1. **(C)** Option (C) is the best choice; George is relieved to get on the train and dreams of adulthood. Options (A) and (B) are incorrect; there is nothing in the passage that indicates indifference or fear. Option (D) is incorrect; he does not seem sad to be leaving.

2. **(D)** Option (D) is correct. The excerpt clearly states the he "was embarrassed" by all the people who had come to say good-bye. There is no indication that option (A) is true. Options (B) and (C) cannot be correct because there is no mention of the train being cancelled or that he wants to get away from his father.

3. **(B)** Option (B) is correct. In this context, *sharp* connotes being observant. Option (A) is incorrect because, although the word *sharp* can have this meaning, it makes no sense here. Option (C) could be a possible connotation of *sharp*, but there is no evidence that this is what his father meant. Option (D) could be a possibility, but it is not the best answer in the context of the excerpt.

4. **(A)** Option (A) is correct. The father and son are clearly close to each other; the father offers advice and the son accepts without question. Father and son may be opinionated, but there is nothing in the passage to indicate that, so option (B) is incorrect. There is no mention of either's views of society (option C). While George may feel he is escaping from his life, option (D) is incorrect because there is no mention of his father's desire to do the same.

5. **(C)** Option (C) is correct. George is setting out "to paint the dreams of his manhood." Option (A) cannot be correct as there is little likelihood that he will return anytime soon. Perhaps in the end he will fail to find himself, but there is nothing in the excerpt to support that conclusion (option B). Option (D) is wrong because there is no suggestion that he will call home immediately.

6. **(B)** Option (B) is correct. The final paragraph confirms a dreamy mood. Option (A) is incorrect because George does not seem anxious, even though he is nervous about his money. The passage might be considered slightly humorous, but this is not its mood, so option (C) is also incorrect. Option (D) is wrong because there is no suggestion of anything fanciful.

7. **(B)** You can infer that the action occurs in their home because Jim sits on the couch and suggests that Della start the chops for dinner.

8. **(A)** Although Jim says that the presents are too nice to use, that is an excuse, so option (D) is not correct. The real reason is option (A), that they cannot use their gifts because he sold his watch to buy Della hair combs that she cannot use because she has cut her hair. Option (B) is incorrect, as both Jim and Della like the gifts they receive. There is no evidence from the excerpt to support option (C).

9. **(D)** The interaction and dialogue between Jim and Della shows that they both love each other. None of the other answer choices reflect their feelings for one another.

10. **(D)** Option (D), tender, best describes the mood depicted by the loving scene in the excerpt. Although Della is excited about her gift, that is not the overall mood of the excerpt, which eliminates option (B) and (C).

11. **(A)** Option (A) is correct because the excerpt mentions Della's "vanished hair" and says that "the tresses that should have adorned the coveted adornments were gone." Della sold her hair to buy Jim's gift; she does not have to sell her combs. For this reason, option (B) is incorrect. Option (C) is not correct because Jim bought Della the combs with the intention of her wearing them. Jim suggests putting their gifts away until they can use them; he does not expect her to return the combs to the store, as indicated in option (D).

12. **(C)** You can use context clues to determine that option (C) is the best definition of the word *dandy*. Della says, "Isn't it a dandy, Jim? I hunted all over town to find it." The watch chain is described as "beautiful" and made of "precious metal." Another definition of *dandy* is option (A), a fashionable, refined man, but this definition does not fit the context of Della's statement. Options (B) and (D) are not supported by the context of the excerpt.

13. **(D)** Option (D) is correct; the poet is remembering when she was "small and could not sleep." Option (A) is incorrect; the poet only compares the touch of her mother's hand to flowers in the spring. Options (B) and (C) are incorrect; meadows and pastures are used as metaphors to describe the child's dreams.

14. **(B)** Option (B) is correct because the poet talks of "Memories of garden things," which strongly suggests that she is nostalgic. Option (A) is wrong because there are no lines that suggest lightheartedness. Likewise, nothing in the poem indicates confusion (option C). Option (D) is incorrect because the poet is not contrary in tone.

15. **(A)** The phrases in option (A) serve to reinforce the image that the poet's mother had experienced life to the fullest. The poet never describes her mother's hands as either unattractive or old (options B and C). Option (D) is obviously wrong; if anything, the poem suggests that her mother was healthy and vibrant.

16. **(D)** Option (D) is correct; the entire poem describes the many ways the mother comforted her child. Contrary to option (A), it is evident that the mother had a great understanding of nature. Option (B) is incorrect because, although the poet's mother may have been practical, there is nothing in the poem that says this. Option (C) is incorrect because nothing in the poem shows the mother as formal.

17. **(C)** Option (C) is correct because the entire poem is about the mother's hands and how comforting they were. The poet's mother may also have sung to her, but it is not mentioned in the poem (option A). Similarly, the poem does not talk of her telling a story (option B). Option (D) is incorrect because the mother is with her child in each stanza.

18. **(B)** Option (B) is correct; the phrase is a continuation of the company's decision from the previous paragraph: "to take a proactive position regarding carpooling." Option (A) doesn't logically follow the idea of the previous paragraph. Option (C) is incorrect; it does not make any sense in the context of the sentence. Option (D) is incorrect, because the idea is *to solve* and not *to change*.

**GO ON TO THE NEXT PAGE** ➡

19. **(D)** Option (D) is correct; because the company's name has *solar* in it, it follows that it would make solar photovoltaic panels. The name Solarama does not suggest either toys (option A) or ski equipment (option B). Option (C) is incorrect because it is illogical that a company that manufactures gasoline engines would be interested in saving gasoline through carpooling.

20. **(B)** Option (B) is correct; the main idea is presented clearly, with detailed information. Option (A) is incorrect because no technical details are included. Option (C) is incorrect because the memo is not humorous but factual. Option (D) is wrong since nothing scholarly is presented, just easy-to-understand facts.

21. **(C)** Option (C) is correct; those who bike to work would need to freshen up and change clothes, especially in the warmer months. Employees who ride buses (option A) or carpool (option B) to work would not need to change clothes. Option (D) is incorrect; the main idea of the memo is to encourage carpooling, not to drive alone.

22. **(B)** Option (B) is correct; the problem is lack of parking, and the solution is carpooling, public transportation, biking, or walking. None of the other options correctly describe the organization of the excerpt.

23. **(C)** Option (C) is correct; the coach is friendly but keeps a professional attitude with Josh, and Josh takes his words to heart. Option (A) is incorrect; the relationship seems easygoing, but there is no distance between them. Option (B) could be a possible choice, but it misses the professional advice Coach gives Josh, so it is incorrect. Option (D) is wrong because there is no evidence of indifference in their relationship.

24. **(C)** Option (C) is correct; the pitcher was able to overcome his nervousness and come through with some big pitches. This is the main idea of the excerpt. Option (A) is incorrect because Josh overcame his nervousness and did not give in to it. Although scouts are mentioned, it is not clear whether there actually were scouts at the game (option B), and this is not the main idea. Although the pitcher did doubt if he could win (option D), this is not the main idea.

25. **(D)** Option (D) is correct. The author uses the adjective *hypnotic* to reinforce the idea that Josh completely and unconsciously accepted Coach's words to throw confidently. Option (A) is incorrect because *hypnotic* is not synonymous with *unclear*. Option (B) is incorrect because it does not make sense. It is not logical that a pitcher would feel sleepy while pitching (option C).

26. **(A)** Option (A) is correct since Josh is portrayed as someone who concentrates deeply on what he is doing. Option (B) is incorrect because he did overcome his nervousness on the mound and would do the same if he were playing chess. There is no evidence in the excerpt that Josh would forget the rules of the game, so option (C) is incorrect. Josh does not challenge his opponent when he plays baseball (option D).

27. **(C)** Option (C) is correct; Josh is portrayed as someone who works hard at pitching and can concentrate on getting the job done. While he may be a brilliant pitcher, there is no evidence in the passage that he is self-trained, so option (A) is incorrect. The reader has no way of knowing if he will succeed in college (option B). Josh may be ambitious, but he is not described as driven (option D) in the excerpt.

28. **(C)** Option (C) is correct because the coach says the right things to Josh to calm him down. There is no evidence that he thinks coaching is not challenging (option A), and he does not display any anger in the excerpt (option B). Option (D) is incorrect because he is portrayed as a good and understanding coach.

29. **(C)** Option (C) is correct; the overall mood is combative as Ted and Verona argue over who will get the car that night. Option (A) is incorrect because, while they may be congenial most of the time, there is no evidence that the family is congenial in the excerpt. The mood is not depressed because their words do not evoke depression (option B). Although Ted seems somewhat excitable, the mood of the excerpt is not exciting (option D).

30. **(D)** Option (D) is correct because they both have plans to go out for the evening. Option (A) is incorrect because this is not the issue; who is going to get the car is the issue. Option (B) is wrong because, while Ted does somewhat insult her friends, he does it after they have started fighting, so this is not the reason she is upset. Option (C) is wrong; there is no evidence to suggest that Verona thinks her father favors Ted.

31. **(D)** Option (D) is correct. Ted is definitely teasing his sister, with phrases like "you drive uphill with the emergency brake on!" Yet he obviously cares about her as well. Option (A) is incorrect; there is nothing in the passage to indicate he thinks she should have more friends. Option (B) is wrong; if anything, he is a little jealous of her going off to college. Option (C) is incorrect because there is no evidence that indicates he thinks she is too ambitious.

32. **(A)** Option (A) is correct; Mrs. Babbitt says to Verona's sister Trinka, "Your sleeve is in the butter." Later, the excerpt states that it was getting dark, which makes option (B) incorrect; they are talking about later that evening, not late at night. Options (C) and (D) are illogical; the time frame is right after dinner.

33. **(B)** Option (B) is correct; Ted is portrayed as having a sense of humor but also as being quarrelsome. He is certainly emotional, which negates option (A). Option (C) is incorrect because there is nothing shy about him. He does not seem confused (option D).

34. **(B)** Option (B) is correct because the way in which *select* is used indicates superiority or perfection. Option (A) is incorrect; there nothing in the passage to indicate that Verona went to college to be happier. Although she may be an outstanding student (option C), there is nothing in the excerpt about that. There is also no evidence that Verona thinks college is more important than a social life (option D).

35. **(A)** Option (A) is correct because they fight over who will get to use the car and refuse to give up. Options (B) and (C) are wrong because no worry is expressed in the passage about either's future or that one is worried about the other. Perhaps they do watch over each other, but that is not indicated; they don't seem particularly helpful either, so option (D) is incorrect.

**GO ON TO THE NEXT PAGE** ➡

36. **(A)** This is the best description of the review. The reviewer seems very thoughtful about the play and the characters in it. The writing is not trite or used. Option (B) is not correct because, while the reviewer does criticize some aspects of the play, that is not the overall tone of his review, and the review is definitely not sarcastic. Option (C) does not seem correct; the tone is not lighthearted but rather serious. Option (D) is not correct either; the review is not breezy.

37. **(D)** Option (D) is correct; the playwright says the play kept the audience's attention. Option (A) is wrong; the reviewer thought some of the dialogue was clichéd. He thought the opposite of option (B). He did not say anything about making Pilar's role larger, so option (C) is wrong.

38. **(D)** The reviewer seems to know a lot about theater and is detailed in his review, so option (D) is correct. The review does not seem methodical or trying, and it is certainly not ornate or flowery, so options (A) and (B) are wrong. The review also does not seem brief, so option (C) is incorrect.

39. **(B)** The reviewer talks about Bernardo's magnetism. He certainly likes him as an actor, so option (B) is the most likely choice. While Bernardo has a strong magnetism, the reviewer does not think he overacts, so option (A) cannot be true. Option (C) might be true, but there is nothing in the review to suggest this. Option (D) is not indicated by the review.

40. **(A)** Option (A) is the best answer. Option (B) is definitely incorrect; the audience liked the play. There is no suggestion that the audience was filled with friends of the actors, so option (C) is wrong. Option (D) is not indicated by the review.

# *HiSET*® Exam Practice Test 2
## Answer Sheet
## Math

|   | A | B | C | D | E |   | A | B | C | D | E |
|---|---|---|---|---|---|---|---|---|---|---|---|
| 1 |   |   |   |   |   | 26 |   |   |   |   |   |
| 2 |   |   |   |   |   | 27 |   |   |   |   |   |
| 3 |   |   |   |   |   | 28 |   |   |   |   |   |
| 4 |   |   |   |   |   | 29 |   |   |   |   |   |
| 5 |   |   |   |   |   | 30 |   |   |   |   |   |
| 6 |   |   |   |   |   | 31 |   |   |   |   |   |
| 7 |   |   |   |   |   | 32 |   |   |   |   |   |
| 8 |   |   |   |   |   | 33 |   |   |   |   |   |
| 9 |   |   |   |   |   | 34 |   |   |   |   |   |
| 10 |   |   |   |   |   | 35 |   |   |   |   |   |
| 11 |   |   |   |   |   | 36 |   |   |   |   |   |
| 12 |   |   |   |   |   | 37 |   |   |   |   |   |
| 13 |   |   |   |   |   | 38 |   |   |   |   |   |
| 14 |   |   |   |   |   | 39 |   |   |   |   |   |
| 15 |   |   |   |   |   | 40 |   |   |   |   |   |
| 16 |   |   |   |   |   | 41 |   |   |   |   |   |
| 17 |   |   |   |   |   | 42 |   |   |   |   |   |
| 18 |   |   |   |   |   | 43 |   |   |   |   |   |
| 19 |   |   |   |   |   | 44 |   |   |   |   |   |
| 20 |   |   |   |   |   | 45 |   |   |   |   |   |
| 21 |   |   |   |   |   | 46 |   |   |   |   |   |
| 22 |   |   |   |   |   | 47 |   |   |   |   |   |
| 23 |   |   |   |   |   | 48 |   |   |   |   |   |
| 24 |   |   |   |   |   | 49 |   |   |   |   |   |
| 25 |   |   |   |   |   | 50 |   |   |   |   |   |

# MATH (calculators allowed)

## 50 Questions

## 90 Minutes

## Directions

This is a test of your skills in applying mathematical concepts and solving mathematical problems. Read each question carefully and decide which of the five alternatives best answers the question. Then mark your choice on your answer sheet. There are relatively easy problems scattered throughout the test. Thus, do not waste time on problems that are too difficult; go on, and return to them if you have time.

Work as quickly as you can without becoming careless. Don't spend too much time on any question that is difficult for you to answer. Instead, skip it and return to it later if you have time. Try to answer every question even if you have to guess.

Mark all your answers on the answer sheet. Give only one answer to each question and make every mark heavy and dark. If you decide to change one of your answers, be sure to erase the first mark completely. Be sure that the number of the question you are answering matches the number of the row of answer choices you are marking on your answer sheet.

1. **A rectangular storage bin is 3 feet wide, 6 feet long, and 3 feet tall. If ⅔ of the bin is filled with animal feed, how many cubic feet of animal feed are stored in the container?**

    **(Volume = Length × Width × Height)**

    A  9
    B  12
    C  18
    D  36
    E  54

2. **A company charges a late fee as a percentage of the bill. If a customer's bill is $125 and the late fee is $3.75, what percentage does the company charge?**

    A  3.00%
    B  3.75%
    C  4.00%
    D  7.50%
    E  35.75%

GO ON TO THE NEXT PAGE ➡

3. To rent a car, Cesar must pay $15 a day plus 5 cents for every mile he drives. In dollars, what is his final bill if he rents a car for 3 days and drives a total of 50 miles?

   A  $45.00

   B  $45.25

   C  $47.50

   D  $50.05

   E  $95.00

| Age (in years) | Frequency of Attendance |
| --- | --- |
| Younger than 10 | 12 |
| 10 to 14 | 8 |
| 15 to 20 | 1 |
| Older than 20 | 18 |

4. The table above represents the ages of people attending a child's birthday party. If a person is randomly selected from the group, what is the probability that the person is younger than 10 years old?

   A  0.1832

   B  0.3077

   C  0.496

   D  0.85

   E  0.967

5. If $2x + 2y = 10$, then $x + y =$

   A  2

   B  5

   C  6

   D  8

   E  12

6.  Which of the following is a solution of $7 - 5x \leq 42$?
    A   $-12$
    B   $-10$
    C   $-9$
    D   $-8$
    E   $-6$

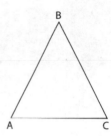

7.  In the diagram above, the measures of angle A and angle C are 60 degrees. If the length of AB is 12, what is the length of AC?
    A   12
    B   6
    C   4
    D   3
    E   1

8.  A teacher has determined that, at most, only two students should share a computer at a time. If she has 21 students, what is the smallest number of computers she should have available to students?
    A   8
    B   9
    C   10
    D   11
    E   12

GO ON TO THE NEXT PAGE ➡

9. A backyard pool measures 6 feet wide and 10 feet long. How many feet of safety fencing are required to surround the entire perimeter of the pool?

(Perimeter = 2 × Length + 2 × Width)

A   16

B   22

C   26

D   32

E   60

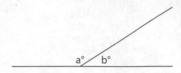

10. In the diagram above, angles a and b are along a straight line. If the measure of angle a is 130 degrees, what is the measure of angle b?

A   30

B   40

C   50

D   60

E   80

11. At a company picnic, 25 percent of the people attending are managers. If there are 300 people at the picnic, how many are managers?

A   25

B   75

C   100

D   120

E   750

12. A train can travel 125 kilometers in 2½ hours. If the train maintains the same speed, how many hours will it take to travel 400 kilometers?

A   20

B   16

C   8

D   4

E   2

13. Which of the following is equivalent to $9x^2 - 5x + 3x$?

A   $9x^2 - 2x$

B   $9x^2 - 8x$

C   $17x^2 - x$

D   $7x^2$

E   $17x^2$

14. Gary purchased 3 shirts that cost $9.99 each, 2 pairs of pants that cost $14.99 each, and 1 hat that cost $12.99. Assuming a 3 percent sales tax is charged on all items, what was the total cost of Gary's purchases?

    A   $37.97
    B   $57.95
    C   $72.94
    D   $75.13
    E   $75.94

15. Jacob plays chess regularly with his friends. On each of 5 days last week, he played 14, 15, 19, 20, and 25 games. What was the average number of games he played per day?

$$\left( \text{Mean} = \frac{x_1 + x_2 + \cdots x_n}{n} \right)$$

    A   17
    B   18.6
    C   23.3
    D   31
    E   93

16. The interest on a simple interest loan was $45. If the loan term was 6 months at 8%, how much, in dollars, was borrowed?

    (Interest = Principal × Rate × Time)

    A   2,160
    B   1,125
    C   1,080
    D   563
    E   360

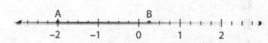

17. Using the number line above, what is the value of A − B?

    A   −2½
    B   −2¼
    C   −1¼
    D   1¼
    E   2¼

18. The average of 5 and $x$ is 10. What is the value of $x$?

    A   5
    B   10
    C   15
    D   20
    E   25

GO ON TO THE NEXT PAGE ➡

19. Amy is planning a wedding and has decided that she will provide each of her 38 guests with 2 small gift bags. If the gift bags are $10.50 each, how many dollars in total will she spend on the gift bags?

    A  398

    B  420

    C  475

    D  798

    E  855

20. Hank has a total of 58 sports cards in his collection. His collection consists of only football and baseball cards, and he has 14 more baseball cards than football cards. How many football cards are in Hank's collection?

    A  22

    B  36

    C  40

    D  44

    E  72

21. Last year, a newspaper reached 35,000 households a day. If circulation is down 20 percent, how many households a day does the newspaper currently reach?

    A  7,000

    B  17,500

    C  16,560

    D  28,000

    E  34,980

22. If $\frac{1}{4}x + 1 = 8$, then $x =$

    A  36

    B  32

    C  28

    D  18

    E  12

23. The value of $a$ is directly proportional to the value of $b$. If $a = 21$ when $b = 3$, what is the value of $a$ when $b = 5$?

    A  18

    B  23

    C  24

    D  29

    E  35

24. A business owner pays a graphic designer a flat fee of $x$ dollars plus $y$ dollars per hour to design her logo. If the designer takes $t$ hours to complete the logo, which of the following represents the business owner's cost?

    A  $t(x + y)$

    B  $tx + y$

    C  $x + ty$

    D  $x + y$

    E  $x + y + t$

25. While he is at work, Jackson receives 4 e-mails an hour from an automated monitoring service. If he works 8 hours a day, how many e-mails will he receive from this service in 6 work days?

    A   18
    B   24
    C   32
    D   192
    E   208

26. If $n = -5$, then $n^2 - 1 =$

    A   $-26$
    B   $-11$
    C   9
    D   10
    E   24

**Questions 27 and 28 refer to the graph below, which represents the number of customers per week for the first five weeks a hardware store was open.**

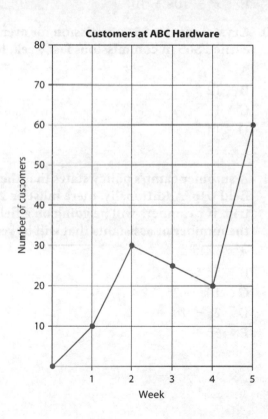

27. In total, how many customers did the store have in its first five weeks?

    A   80

    B   95

    C   140

    D   145

    E   310

28. In which week were there the fewest customers?

    A   Week 1

    B   Week 2

    C   Week 3

    D   Week 4

    E   Week 5

29. Which of the following is equivalent to $(x + 5)(x - 5)$?

    A   $x^2 - 25$

    B   $x^2 - 10$

    C   $x^2 + 10x - 25$

    D   $x^2 + 10x - 10$

    E   $x^2 - 10x - 10$

30. Crystal earns a $5 commission for every customer she refers to her bank. If she earned $65 in commissions last week, how many customers did she refer?

    A   11

    B   12

    C   13

    D   14

    E   15

31. A summer camp's policy states that there must be 3 camp counselors for every field trip. Additionally, there must be 2 assistants for every 10 campers on the trip. If $c$ campers will be going on a field trip, which of the following represents the number of assistants that will be required?

    A   $c/5$

    B   $5c$

    C   $10c + 2$

    D   $2c + 10$

    E   $5c + 2$

| Total Entertainment Center Orders in the First Quarter | | | |
|---|---|---|---|
| | **Model A** | **Model B** | **Total** |
| Design 1 | 150 | 120 | 270 |
| Design 2 | 200 | 30 | 230 |
| Total | 350 | 150 | 500 |

32. The table above represents the different types of entertainment centers ordered from a furniture company in the first quarter of the year. What fraction of orders was for Model A?

   A   3/10
   B   2/5
   C   3/5
   D   7/10
   E   4/5

33. What are the coordinates for the point on the line $2x + 5y = 10$ where $x = 10$?

   A   (20, 10)
   B   (10, −2)
   C   (2, −5)
   D   (0, 0)
   E   (5, −2)

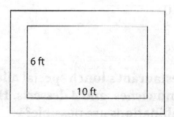

34. A concrete walkway will be installed around a garden with the measurements shown in the figure above. If the walkway will be $m$ feet wide, which of the following expressions represents its area?

   A   $60 + 16m + m^2$
   B   $60 + 32m + 4m^2$
   C   $16m + m^2$
   D   $20m + m^2$
   E   $32m + 4m^2$

GO ON TO THE NEXT PAGE ➡

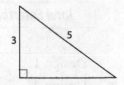

35. What is the area of the triangle pictured above?

(Area = ¼ × Base × Height)

   A   6
   B   12
   C   15
   D   20
   E   22

36. The median of 4, 7, 10, 12, and *x* is 7. What is the largest possible value of *x*?

   A   0
   B   4
   C   7
   D   10
   E   12

37. What is the *x*-coordinate of the point where $y = 3x - 9$ crosses the *x*-axis?

   A   −9
   B   −3
   C   0
   D   3
   E   9

38. A restaurant's lunch special allows customers to pick from 3 soups, 6 sandwiches, and 4 desserts. How many soup, sandwich, and dessert combinations are possible?

   A   13
   B   22
   C   25
   D   68
   E   72

39. **What is the value of (⅔)³?**

    A  $\dfrac{8}{27}$

    B  $\dfrac{4}{9}$

    C  $\dfrac{1}{2}$

    D  $\dfrac{2}{3}$

    E  2

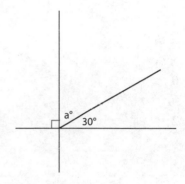

40. **In the figure above, what is the value of *a*?**

    A  30

    B  40

    C  15

    D  60

    E  90

41. **Which of the following is equivalent to $5.1 \times 10^{-3}$?**

    A  0.00051

    B  0.0051

    C  0.051

    D  5,100

    E  51,000

42. **A 64-ounce bottle of soda costs $1.59. Which of the following represents the cost of a single ounce of this soda, in dollars?**

    A  64(1.59)

    B  64 − 1.59

    C  1.59 ÷ 64

    D  64 + 1.59

    E  64 ÷ 1.59

GO ON TO THE NEXT PAGE ➡

43. The area of triangle A is 4. The height of triangle B is twice that of triangle A, and the length of the base of triangle B is the same as that of triangle A. What is the area of triangle B?

A   2

B   4

C   8

D   16

E   32

44. What is the slope of the line that passes through the points (0, 0) and (2, 5)?

$$\left(\text{Slope of a line} = \frac{y_2 - y_1}{x_2 - x_1}\right)$$

A   $-{}^5/_2$

B   $-{}^2/_5$

C   0

D   ${}^5/_2$

E   2

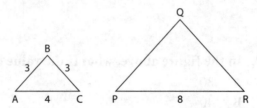

45. The triangles in the figure above are similar. What is the perimeter of triangle PQR?

A   10

B   14

C   16

D   20

E   48

46. Carey's washing machine required repair, and the bill was $150 plus an 8 percent restocking fee for parts the repairman had to use. What was the total repair bill, in dollars?

A   142

B   158

C   162

D   166

E   178

47. An exercise set comes with 10-pound and 25-pound weights. Which of the following represents the total weight of $x$ 10-pound weights and $y$ 25-pound weights?

    A   $35xy$

    B   $35(x + y)$

    C   $35x + y$

    D   $10x + 25y$

    E   $x + y + 35$

48. The longest side of a triangle is 10 units long and the shortest side is 6 units long. If the largest angle in the triangle is 90 degrees, what is the length of the remaining side of the triangle?

$$(a^2 + b^2 = c^2)$$

    A   8

    B   7

    C   6

    D   5

    E   4

49. What is the product of $4x^2$ and $5x^4$?

    A   $9x^8$

    B   $20x^8$

    C   $9x^6$

    D   $20x^6$

    E   $9x^2$

50. If $\dfrac{x}{6} = \frac{1}{2}$, what is the value of $x$?

    A   2

    B   3

    C   12

    D   20

    E   24

# ANSWERS: MATH

1. **(D)** The volume of the entire bin is $3 \times 6 \times 3 = 54$ cubic feet. The two-thirds that are filled accounts for $\frac{2}{3} \times 54 = 36$ cubic feet of the storage.

2. **(A)** Let $x$ represent the percentage the company charges. Translating the given information into an equation yields $125x = 3.75$. The solution is found by dividing both sides by 125.

3. **(C)** The charge for the 3 days is $15 \times 3 = 45$, while the charge for the 50 miles is $0.05 \times 50 \times 2.5$. Finally, the total is $45 + 2.5 = 47.5$.

4. **(B)** The probability is found by dividing the frequency by the total. In this case, $\dfrac{12}{12 + 8 + 1 + 18} = 0.3077$.

5. **(B)** Both of the terms $2x$ and $2y$ share a factor of 2. When this is factored out, the equation becomes $2(x + y) = 10$. Dividing both sides by 2 yields the equation $x + y = 5$.

6. **(E)** When solving the inequality, remember that the direction will change if you divide or multiply by a negative number. The inequality $7 - 5x \leq 42$ is equivalent to the inequality $x \geq -6$. Only option (E) satisfies the resulting inequality.

7. **(A)** Since the measures of angles A and C are 60 degrees, the measure of angle B must be $180 - 60 - 60 = 60$. When all three angles in a triangle are equal, the lengths of all of the sides are also equal.

8. **(D)** $21 \div 2 = 10.5$, but it isn't possible to have half a computer. To make sure there are enough, round up to 11.

9. **(D)** The perimeter is the sum of the lengths of all the sides: $6 + 10 + 6 + 10 = 32$.

10. **(C)** Two angles along a straight line must have a sum of 180 degrees. The measure of angle b is $180 - 130 = 50$.

11. **(B)** $300 \times {}^{25}/_{100} = 75$.

12. **(C)** The train is traveling at a speed of $125 \div 2\frac{1}{2} = 125 \div 2.5 = 50$ kilometers per hour, and it will take the train $400 \div 50 = 8$ hours to travel 400 kilometers.

13. **(A)** Only terms with the same exponent and same variable can be combined. Thus, $9x^2 - 5x + 3x = 9x^2 + (-5 + 3)x = 9x^2 - 2x$.

14. **(D)** Before tax, Gary's total was $3(9.99) + 2(14.99) + 12.99 = 72.94$. To find the value after tax, multiply 72.94 by 1.03 to get the final answer.

15. **(B)** The average is found by adding all of the values and dividing by the number of values: $\dfrac{14 + 15 + 19 + 20 + 25}{5} = 18.6$.

16. **(B)** The formula for the interest on a simple interest loan is $I = Prt$ where $t$ is in years. In this case, $45 = P(0.08)({}^6/_{12})$ where $P$ represents the principal, or amount borrowed. Solving for $P$ yields the final answer of 1,125.

17. **(B)** The space between 0 and 1 has 3 tick marks representing $\frac{1}{4}$, $\frac{1}{2}$, $\frac{3}{4}$, and the point B is on the tick mark representing $\frac{1}{4}$. The value of $A - B$ is $-2 - \frac{1}{4} = -2\frac{1}{4}$.

18. **(C)** If the average of 5 and $x$ is 10, then $\frac{x+5}{2} = 10$. This equation has a solution of $x = 15$.

19. **(D)** Amy will need to buy a total of $38 \times 2 = 76$ gift bags for a total cost of $76 \times 10.5 = \$798$.

20. **(A)** Let $f$ represent the number of football cards and $b$ the number of baseball cards in Hank's collection. Since there is a total of 58 cards, $f + b = 58$. Also, since there are 14 more baseball cards than football cards, $b = 14 + f$. Substituting the second equation into the first yields the equation $f + 14 + f = 58$. In other words, $2f = 44$ and $f = 22$.

21. **(D)** The total reduction in circulation is $^{20}/_{100} \times 35,000 = 7,000$. Therefore, the current circulation is $35,000 - 7,000 = 28,000$.

22. **(C)** Subtract 1 from both sides of the equation to get $\frac{1}{4}x = 7$ and then multiply both sides of the equation by 4 to get $x = 28$.

23. **(E)** If $a$ is directly proportional to $b$, there is a number $k$ such that $a = bk$. You know that $a$ is 21 when $b$ is 3 and plugging this into the statement above will give you the value of $k$, which is 7. Therefore, $a = 7b$, and when $b$ is 5, $a$ is $5 \times 7 = 35$.

24. **(C)** Only $y$ depends on the number of hours ($t$). The total hourly pay will be $yt$, and the total pay will include the flat fee of $x$ dollars, giving a total fee of $x + yt$.

25. **(D)** Jackson receives $4 \times 8 = 32$ e-mails a day. Therefore, over 6 days, he will receive $6 \times 32 = 192$ e-mails.

26. **(E)** $(-5)^2 - 1 = 25 - 1 = 24$.

27. **(D)** $10 + 30 + 25 + 20 + 60 = 145$.

28. **(A)** Week 1 had only 10 customers.

29. **(A)** Use FOIL to multiply the two binomials: $(x + 5)(x - 5) = x^2 - 5x + 5x - 25 = x^2 - 25$.

30. **(C)** The total commission Crystal will earn is \$5 for each customer, or 5 times the number of customers. Since you know her commission is \$65, you can divide by 5 to find that the number of customers is 13.

31. **(A)** If $x$ represents the number of assistants, the equation $^2/_{10} = {}^x/_c$ can represent the information we are given. Cross multiplying and solving for $x$ yields:

$$2c = 10x$$
$$x = {}^{2c}/_{10} = {}^c/_5$$

32. **(D)** 350 of the 500 orders were for model A. As a fraction, this is $^{350}/_{500} = {}^{35}/_{50} = {}^7/_{10}$.

33. **(B)** When $x = 10$, $2(10) + 5y = 10$ and $y = -2$. The point plotted should therefore be $(10, -2)$.

34. **(E)** The area of the larger rectangle is $(6 + m)(10 + m)$ and the area of the garden is $6 \times 10 = 60$ square feet. The area of the walkway is the area left over when the garden area is subtracted from the larger rectangular area: $(6 + 2m)(10 + 2m) - 60 = 60 + 12m + 20m + 4m^2 - 60 = 32m + 4m^2$.

GO ON TO THE NEXT PAGE ➡

35. **(A)** The area of any triangle is ½$bh$ where $b$ represents the length of the base and $h$ represents the height. Here, you have the height but not the base. However, since the triangle is a right triangle, you can find the length of the base with the Pythagorean theorem: $3^2 + b^2 = 5^2$. Solving this, $b = 4$, and the area is ½ × 4 × 3 = 6.

36. **(C)** The median is the middle value when all of the values are put in order from least to greatest. Ignoring $x$ and placing these numbers in order, you get the list: 4, 7, 10, 12. For 7 to be the median when $x$ is placed in the list, 7 must be in the middle. This means the $x$ must be to the left of 7 in the list. The largest possible value that will allow this to occur is if $x = 7$.

37. **(D)** When the line crosses the $x$-axis, the value of $y$ is 0. Using this in the equation, you will find $0 = 3x - 9$ or $x = 3$.

38. **(E)** There are a total of 3 × 6 × 4 combinations possible.

39. **(A)** $\left(\dfrac{2}{3}\right)^3 = \dfrac{2^3}{3^3} = \dfrac{2 \times 2 \times 2}{3 \times 3 \times 3} = \dfrac{8}{27}$.

40. **(D)** The sum of $a + 30 = 90$ since the two combined are opposite a 90-degree angle. Therefore, $a = 90 - 30 = 60$.

41. **(B)** The $-3$ exponent on the 10 tells you to move the decimal to the left 3 digits to get 0.0051.

42. **(C)** To find the unit cost, divide the total cost by the number of ounces, 64.

43. **(C)** The area of triangle A is 4, so if you call the height of triangle A $h$ and the base $b$, ½$bh$ = 4. Since the height of triangle B is twice the height of triangle A, and the length of the base is the same, the area of triangle B is ½$b(2h) = bh = 8$.

44. **(D)** $m = \dfrac{5 - 0}{2 - 0}$.

45. **(D)** Since triangle ABC is similar to triangle PQR, there is a single number you can multiply each side of ABC by to get the length of the corresponding side in PQR. If you notice that AB has a length of 4 while PR has a length of 8, you can see that multiplier is 2. This means that the length of PQ and QR are both 3 × 2 = 6, and the perimeter is 6 + 6 + 8 = 20.

46. **(C)** $150 + {}^8/_{100}(150) = 162$.

47. **(D)** If there are $x$ 10-pound weights, they will weigh a total of $10x$ pounds. Similarly, if there are $y$ 25-pound weights, they will weigh a total of $25y$ pounds. Therefore, the set will weigh a total of $10x + 25y$ pounds.

48. **(A)** A triangle with a 90-degree angle is called a right triangle, and the Pythagorean theorem will apply. The Pythagorean theorem states that $a^2 + b^2 = c^2$ where $c$ is the longest side (the hypotenuse). Applying that to this problem: $6^2 + b^2 = 10^2$ and $b = 8$.

49. **(D)** The word *product* involves multiplication, and when you multiply two terms that have the same base, you add exponents. Therefore, $(4x^2)(5x^4) = 20x^{2+4} = 20x^6$.

50. **(B)** Cross multiply to get the equation $2x = 6$. Dividing both sides by 2 yields $x = 3$.

## ANSWER KEYS

### CHAPTER 5: Basic English Usage Drills

1. **D**
2. **C**
3. **C**
4. **B**
5. **D**
6. **C**
7. **B**
8. **A**
9. **D**
10. **B**
11. **A**
12. **B**
13. **C**
14. **D**
15. **A**

### CHAPTER 6: Mechanics Drills

1. **A**
2. **D**
3. **B**
4. **C**
5. **C**
6. **A**
7. **D**
8. **B**
9. **B**
10. **D**
11. **C**
12. **D**
13. **D**
14. **A**
15. **B**

### CHAPTER 7: Sentence Structure Drills

1. **A**
2. **D**
3. **C**
4. **B**
5. **C**

6. C
7. B
8. D
9. A
10. C
11. B
12. D
13. C
14. B
15. A

# CHAPTER 8: Organization Drills

1. B
2. A
3. D
4. A
5. B
6. D
7. C
8. B
9. C
10. C
11. B
12. D
13. A
14. B
15. A

# CHAPTER 11: World History Drills

1. D
2. B
3. A
4. C
5. C
6. B
7. D
8. A
9. B
10. A
11. D
12. C
13. D
14. A
15. B

## CHAPTER 12: US History Drills

1. C
2. A
3. D
4. B
5. C
6. B
7. A
8. C
9. B
10. D
11. C
12. A
13. D
14. B
15. A

## CHAPTER 13: Civics and Government Drills

1. C
2. A
3. C
4. D
5. A
6. B
7. D
8. C
9. A
10. B
11. D
12. C
13. D
14. A
15. B

## CHAPTER 14: Economics Drills

1. A
2. D
3. B
4. C
5. A
6. D
7. D

8. **B**
9. **C**
10. **B**
11. **C**
12. **D**
13. **A**
14. **B**
15. **A**

# CHAPTER 15: Geography Drills

1. **C**
2. **A**
3. **B**
4. **C**
5. **D**
6. **A**
7. **D**
8. **B**
9. **D**
10. **B**
11. **A**
12. **C**
13. **B**
14. **C**
15. **A**

# CHAPTER 17: Life Science Drills

1. **A**
2. **C**
3. **B**
4. **D**
5. **D**
6. **A**
7. **B**
8. **A**
9. **C**
10. **B**
11. **B**
12. **C**
13. **C**
14. **C**
15. **B**

## CHAPTER 18: Earth and Space Science Drills

1. C
2. D
3. A
4. B
5. D
6. D
7. A
8. C
9. B
10. D
11. A
12. C
13. D
14. B
15. A

## CHAPTER 19: Physical Science: Chemistry Drills

1. C
2. C
3. B
4. D
5. B
6. A
7. C
8. B
9. D
10. B
11. B
12. A
13. C
14. D
15. C

## CHAPTER 20: Physical Science: Physics Drills

1. C
2. C
3. D
4. B
5. A
6. D
7. C

8. **C**
9. **C**
10. **A**
11. **D**
12. **A**
13. **C**
14. **D**
15. **B**

# CHAPTER 22: Prose Fiction Reading Comprehension Drills

1. **A**
2. **A**
3. **B**
4. **D**
5. **D**
6. **B**
7. **A**
8. **C**
9. **A**
10. **D**
11. **A**
12. **B**
13. **C**
14. **C**
15. **B**

# CHAPTER 23: Poetry Reading Comprehension Drills

1. **A**
2. **B**
3. **D**
4. **C**
5. **A**
6. **C**
7. **A**
8. **C**
9. **D**
10. **D**
11. **C**
12. **A**
13. **A**
14. **B**
15. **D**

## CHAPTER 24: Informational Texts Reading Comprehension Drills

1. D
2. A
3. D
4. B
5. D
6. D
7. B
8. C
9. C
10. A
11. B
12. A
13. C
14. D
15. C

## CHAPTER 26: Whole Number and Operations Drills

1. C
2. A
3. B
4. D
5. D
6. A
7. C
8. C
9. B
10. A

## CHAPTER 27: Number Sense Drills

1. B
2. D
3. C
4. D
5. B
6. A
7. A
8. C
9. B
10. D

## CHAPTER 28: Decimal Drills

1. **B**
2. **C**
3. **C**
4. **D**
5. **B**
6. **C**
7. **B**
8. **A**
9. **D**
10. **B**

## CHAPTER 29: Fractions Drills

1. **A**
2. **B**
3. **C**
4. **C**
5. **D**
6. **B**
7. **D**
8. **A**
9. **C**
10. **B**

## CHAPTER 30: Percent Drills

1. **B**
2. **C**
3. **D**
4. **E**
5. **B**
6. **C**
7. **C**
8. **D**
9. **A**
10. **B**

## CHAPTER 31: Number Relationship Drills

1. **A**
2. **D**
3. **C**
4. **A**

5. **B**
6. **C**
7. **B**
8. **C**
9. **A**
10. **E**

# CHAPTER 32: Measurement Drills

1. **C**
2. **A**
3. **B**
4. **D**
5. **E**
6. **D**
7. **C**
8. **D**
9. **B**
10. **C**

# CHAPTER 33: Geometry Drills

1. **E**
2. **A**
3. **B**
4. **C**
5. **B**
6. **B**
7. **C**
8. **D**
9. **C**
10. **C**

# CHAPTER 34: Statistics Drills

1. **A**
2. **B**
3. **D**
4. **B**
5. **C**
6. **C**
7. **D**
8. **D**
9. **A**
10. **B**

## CHAPTER 35: Probability Drills

1. E
2. E
3. C
4. A
5. E
6. B
7. D
8. C
9. B
10. B

## CHAPTER 36: Data Analysis Drills

1. C
2. C
3. B
4. C
5. A
6. E
7. D
8. B
9. C
10. A

## CHAPTER 37: Algebra Drills

1. D
2. A
3. C
4. E
5. A
6. E
7. C
8. B
9. E
10. A

## CHAPTER 38: Formulas Drills

1. **B**
2. **C**
3. **C**
4. **C**
5. **B**
6. **D**
7. **D**
8. **B**
9. **A**
10. **A**